D0276795

HISTORY OF THE FIRST WORLD WAR

B. H. LIDDELL HART

HISTORY OF THE
FIRST WORLD WAR

BOOK CLUB ASSOCIATES · LONDON

Copyright 1930, 1934, © 1970 Lady Liddell Hart
Maps in this edition © Cassell & Co. Ltd. 1970
All rights reserved. No part of this publication
may be reproduced, stored in a retrieval system,
or transmitted, in any form or by any means,
electronic, mechanical, photocopying, recording
or otherwise, without the prior permission of
Cassell and Company Ltd.

First published as *The Real War 1914–1918*,
1930. Enlarged edition, published as *A History
of the World War 1914–1918*, 1934 and pub-
lished in larger format as *History of the First
World War* in 1970.
Second impression May 1971.
This edition published 1973 by
Book Club Associates
by arrangement with
Cassell and Company Ltd.

Reprinted 1977
Reprinted 1979,

Printed in Great Britain by
Redwood Burn Limited
Trowbridge & Esher

TO
JOHN BROWN
AND
THE LEGION

ACKNOWLEDGMENT

I WISH to acknowledge the kindness of those who read various parts of this book in proof, and their helpfulness in contributing criticisms and suggestions. They include Lieut.-Colonel H. G. de Watteville, Mr. E. G. Hawke, and one unnamed whose knowledge of sources was as boundless as the trouble he took to aid me.

ORIGINAL PREFACE TO 'THE REAL WAR'

ON finishing this book I am conscious of its imperfections
—some consolation comes from the reflection that every
book worth reading is imperfect. This book may at least claim
one merit, and one contrast to most war 'histories'. I have as
little desire to hide its imperfections as to hide the imperfections of any who are portrayed in its pages. Hence in writing
it my pursuit of the truth has not been interrupted by recourse
to the pot of hypocritical varnish that is miscalled 'good
taste'. In my judgment of values it is more important to
provide material for a true verdict than to gloss over disturbing facts so that individual reputations may be preserved
at the price of another holocaust of lives. Taking a long view
of history, I cannot regard the repute of a few embodied
handfuls of dust as worth more than the fate of a nation and
a generation.

On the other hand, I have equally little desire to exaggerate
the imperfections of individuals for the sake of a popular
effect, or to shift on to them the weight of folly and error
which should be borne by the people as a whole.

The historian's rightful task is to distil experience as a
medicinal warning for future generations, not to distil a drug.
Having fulfilled this task to the best of his ability, and
honesty, he has fulfilled his purpose. He would be a rash
optimist if he believed that the next generation would trouble
to absorb the warning. History at least teaches the historian
a lesson.

The title of this book, which has a duality of meaning, re-
quires a brief explanation. Some may say that the war
depicted here is not 'the real war'—that this is to be discovered in the torn bodies and minds of individuals. It is far
from my purpose to ignore or deny this aspect of the truth.
But for anyone who seeks, as I seek here, to view the war as

9

an episode in human history, it is a secondary aspect. Because the war affected individual lives so greatly, because these individuals were numbered by millions, because the roots of their fate lay so deep in the past, it is all the more necessary to see the war in perspective, and to disentangle its main threads from the accidents of human misery. Perhaps this attempt is all the more desirable by reason of the trend of recent war literature, which is not merely individualistic but focusses attention on the thoughts and feelings of some of the pawns of war. The war was, it is true, waged and decided in the minds of individuals more than in the physical clash of forces. But these decisive impressions were received and made in the cabinets and in the military headquarters, not in the ranks of the infantry or in the solitude of stricken homes.

The other—and more intentional—meaning of the title is that the time has come when a 'real' history of the war is possible. Governments have opened their archives, statesmen and generals their hearts with an unparalleled philanthropy. It is safe to say that most of the possible documentary evidence on the war has now been published or is available for the student. But it has not yet been collated for the information of the public.

The flood of documents, diaries and memoirs has one outstanding advantage. They have come when they can still be tested by the personal witness of those who took part in the crises and critical discussions of the war. A few years hence would be too late. Yet in the application of this test lies the only chance that history may approximate to truth. The more that any writer of history has himself been at hand when history is being made, or in contact with the makers, the more does he come to see that a history based solely on formal documents is essentially superficial. Too often, also, it is the unwitting handmaiden of 'mythology'.

ORIGINAL PREFACE TO
'A HISTORY OF THE WORLD WAR'

IT is more than four years since *The Real War* was published. That title was chosen for reasons explained above. It fulfilled a purpose, but with the passage of time the need for it has passed. As a summary of the significant facts of the war it has met no serious challenge, and even its interpretation of them has been endorsed by the innermost observers of events, in the various countries, to an extent which has come as a pleasant surprise to the author. Now, twenty years have passed since the war came, and a generation has grown up that has no personal memory of it. The war is history. Hence the time has come, as well as the justification, for adopting a title that has no longer a contemporary note. An enlargement of the contents is a further reason. However much it still falls short of completeness, and my own ideal, it may at least be termed 'A history' of the World War. Also it may contribute to the growth of *the* history of the World War.

It is itself a growth from *The Real War*, just as the original volume evolved from a series of monographs on particular aspects and episodes. Personal experience makes me doubt whether it would be possible to compile a satisfactory history of 1914-1918 by a less gradual method. Confronted suddenly by the whole mass of evidence now at hand, it would be difficult to maintain a clear view, and so easy for the pattern to be distorted by the very weight of the records. For my own part, I have found the practical value of a method which has allowed me, over a period of years, to fit each fresh bit of evidence into an expanding frame.

In evolving the present volume from *The Real War* there has been some revision, but more enlargement. 'The Opposing Forces and Plans' are now described in separate chapters, each augmented by new material. Two new 'scenes' have been added to make the story of 1914 more complete: one deals with the opening clash of the Austrian and Russian armies; and the other with the autumn struggle at Ypres and on the Yser which determined the possession of the Channel Ports. An outline of the war in the air is given under the title 'Panorama'. But the greater part of the enlargement is due to the expansion of the existing chapters and 'scenes' through the incorporation of fresh evidence that has come to light in the past four years. Thus, in the chapter outlines, there is somewhat fuller treatment of the German advance into France in 1914; the Austro-German offensive against Russia and the Balkan situation in 1915; the Palestine situation in 1916; the spring campaign of 1917 on the Western Front; and the Allied discussions which preceded the German offensives of 1918. The main expansion, however, and most of the new material, will be found in the 'scenes', especially those which deal with Verdun, the Somme, Passchendaele, the 'First Break-Through' and the 'Break-Through in Flanders'. To a lesser extent, there is an infusion of fresh facts about the Brusilov, the Arras, the Messines, and the Cambrai offensives, and the Second Battle of the Marne.

The revision needed has been comparatively slight. But new evidence that has come out in the past four years has led me to modify my view of such questions as the German strategy at Verdun, the projected move against Austria, the cause of Nivelle's failure in 1917, the Versailles committee and the preparations to meet the German offensive in 1918. On a number of points, fuller knowledge has amplified the earlier view, and while it has tended to illuminate the mistakes that were committed, it has also helped to elucidate their cause. I have also modified or omitted my original comments on certain episodes, and in their place have quoted from the evidence of those who were responsible, leaving the facts to form the conclusion.

CONTENTS

CONTENTS

Chapter VI
THE 'DOG-FALL'
(1916)
page 269

Chapter VII
THE STRAIN
(1917)
page 383

Chapter VIII
THE BREAK
(1918)
page 465

EPILOGUE
page 586

BIBLIOGRAPHY
page 594

INDEX
page 621

MAPS

DRAWN FOR THIS EDITION BY
PETER McCLURE

CHAPTER I

THE ORIGINS OF THE WAR

FIFTY years were spent in the process of making Europe explosive. Five days were enough to detonate it. To study the manufacture of the explosive materials—which form the fundamental causes of the conflict—is within neither the scope nor the space of a short history of the World War. On the one side we should have to trace the influence of Prussia on the creation of the Reich, the political conceptions of Bismarck, the philosophical tendencies in Germany, and the economic situation—a medley of factors which transmuted Germany's natural desire for commercial outlets, unhappily difficult to obtain, into a vision of world power. We should have to analyse that heterogeneous relic of the Middle Ages known as Austria-Hungary, appreciate her complex racial problems, the artificiality of her governing institutions, the superficial ambitions which overlay a haunting fear of internal disruption and frantically sought to postpone the inevitable end.

On the other side we should have to examine the strange mixture of ambition and idealism which swayed Russia's policy, and the fear it generated beyond her frontiers, especially among her German neighbours—perhaps the deadliest of all the ingredients in the final detonation. We should have to understand the constant alarms of fresh aggression which France had suffered since 1870, study the regrowth of confidence which fortified her to resist further threats, and bear in mind the wounds left in her side by Germany's surgical excision of Alsace-Lorraine. Finally, we should have to trace Britain's gradual movement from a policy of isolation into membership of the European system and her slow awakening to the reality of German feeling towards her.

In such a study of European history during half a century, a generalization can for once be closer to exactness than the most detailed history. The fundamental causes of the conflict can be epitomized in three words—fear, hunger, pride. Beside them, the international 'incidents' that occurred between 1871 and 1914 are but symptoms.

All that is possible, and sensible, here is to trace the most significant turning points in the trail of causation which led to combustion. This trail runs through the structure of alliances which Bismarck built after 1871. Ironically, Bismarck intended it as a shelter for the peaceful growth of his creation, the German Empire, and not as a magazine for explosives. For although his philosophy was epitomized in his 1868 phrase—'The weak were made to be devoured by the strong'—his own hunger was satiated, after three meals, by the war of 1870-71. It cannot be charged against him that his eyes were larger than his stomach; feeling that Germany now was, as he said, a 'saturated' state, his governing idea henceforth was not expansion but consolidation. And to secure time and peace for this consolidation of the new Germany he aimed to keep France in a state of permanent powerlessness to wage a war of revenge. But the result was to prove that two wrongs do not make a Reich.

Apart from frequent direct menaces to France, he sought to counteract her annoyingly rapid recovery by the indirect method of depriving her of friends or supporters. To this end his first effort was to bring Austria and Russia together by forging a common link with Germany, while he strove to ensure peace in the Balkans as a means to avoid any dangerous strain on the link. For some years his policy was that of acting as the 'honest broker' in the diplomatic exchange of Europe without committing himself to any party. But friction with the Russian chancellor, Gortchakov, and the complications caused by the Russo-Turkish war of 1877, led him to make a defensive alliance with Austria in 1879, despite the objections of the old Emperor William I, who regarded it as 'treachery' to Russia and even threatened to abdicate. This definite commitment was to have infinite consequences. Nevertheless, Bismarck temporarily regained his central position by his diplomatic masterstroke of 1881, the famous 'three emperors' alliance', whereby Russia, Austria and Germany undertook to act together in all Balkan affairs. And although it lapsed in 1887, Germany's connection with Russia was strengthened in compensation by the secret 'Reinsurance Treaty', by which the two powers agreed to maintain benevolent neutrality towards each other in case of war with a third. It was not, however, to apply if Germany attacked France or Russia attacked Austria. By this second masterstroke, executed with great duplicity, Bismarck averted the risk, then imminent, of an alliance between Russia and France.

Meantime, the alliance between Germany and Austria had been enlarged by the inclusion of Italy in 1882. The object was to safeguard Austria against a stab in the back if at war with Russia, and in return Italy's new allies would come to her assistance if attacked by France. But as a safeguard to her old friendship with Britain and to her own coasts, Italy had a special protocol appended to the treaty stating that it was in no case to be directed against Britain. In 1883, Rumania, through her King's personal and secret act, was attached to the new Triple Alliance. Even Serbia was temporarily linked on by a separate treaty with Austria, and Spain by an agreement with Italy.

In regard to Britain, Bismarck's aim seems to have been to keep her in friendly isolation from Germany and unfriendly isolation from France. His feelings towards Britain oscillated between friendship and contempt, and the political party system formed the pivot. For the 'old Jew', Disraeli, he had genuine respect, but he could not understand the point of view of the Gladstonian Liberals, and their wavering actions he despised. While Disraeli was in power Bismarck toyed with the idea of linking Britain to his chain of alliances, but although Queen Victoria was plaintively 'sure that Germany would be the safest ally in every way', she was less sure of Bismarck's safety as a repository of trust, and Disraeli shared her doubts. Hence Bismarck continued, with equal satisfaction, his policy of playing off Britain against Russia and France in turn. And with shrewd calculation he favoured Britain's occupation of Egypt because it embroiled her with France, and resisted the growing clamour in Germany for colonial expansion—'our colonial jingos' greed is greater than we need or can satisfy'—because it threatened future trouble with Britain, yet made his support to Britain in Egypt a means of extracting oversea concessions as morsels with which he could assuage the colonial hunger of a body of German interests too powerful even for him to ignore. The Conservatives' return to power in Britain, and the intensified friction with France, led to a fresh tightening of the links with Germany, and Bismarck's offer of a formal alliance was eagerly welcomed by Lord Salisbury's Cabinet who seem only to have held back from fear of Parliamentary objection to foreign entanglements. Bismarck, however, profited from the informal entente to secure the cession of Heligoland—so vital to German naval operations a generation later—at a paltry price.

Thus at the end of the 'eighties Bismarck's great structure seemed complete. Germany was buttressed by the Triple Alliance while the attached yet semi-detached position of Russia and Britain gave her advantages without encumbrances. From this secure base she was ready to develop her commercial expansion. And Bismarck had placed France in the combined solitude and circumscription of a political isolation ward.

But with the beginning of the 'nineties the first crack appeared in the structure, close upon the dismissal of the builder. The accession in 1888 of the young Emperor William II was disagreeable to the Tsar, Alexander III, who disliked his 'aggressive amiability' and distrusted his intentions. Yet the breach came not from Alexander, but from William. Bismarck's control irked him just as it irked the General Staff, and in the soldiers, among whom he had been brought up, he so naturally found allies that in linking himself with them he did not realize that he was forging fresh fetters for himself.

The first effect, after the dismissal of the 'pro-Russian' Chancellor, was his successor's refusal to renew the 'Reinsurance Treaty' with Russia. The second effect, a natural sequel to the first, was that the Tsar swallowed his aversion to republicanism and, in 1891, made an agreement with France which, a year later, was developed into a military convention for mutual assistance in case of attack. In this convention a significant point was that if any member of the Triple Alliance mobilized its forces, both France and Russia were instantly to mobilize. The Tsar at least could not complain that he did not understand the meaning, for the French negotiator, General Boisdeffre, took pains to explain that 'mobilization means declaration of war'.

In the Tsar's case, the draught was swallowed under the fear that Britain was about to ally herself with Germany; it lay heavy on his stomach, so that it was long in producing any diplomatic value for France.

Nevertheless, France had left 'quarantine'. Henceforth there was not one political group, but two, in Europe. Although one was loose, the other compact, the two groups formed a balance of power, if their power was not yet balanced evenly.

A doubly significant sidelight upon Germany's renunciation of the Russian secret treaty is that the council in Berlin which reviewed the matter decided against the treaty on the ground that it was disloyal not only to Austria but to Britain. Whatever the Kaiser's failings, he was more sincere than Bismarck, and the insincerity apparent in his contradictory utterances seems to have been due to his combination of excessive frankness with a quick-changing mind. An essential difference between the two men was that the one sought security through consistent dishonesty, and the other gained insecurity through spasmodic honesty. The consideration shown for Britain was in accord with the Kaiser's views.

For, although he had reversed Bismarck's attitude towards Russia, he maintained Bismarck's policy of friendship towards Britain, perhaps owing to more sincere, and less political motives. The one personal source of cleavage lay in the mutual antipathy of the Kaiser and his uncle, the Prince of Wales—later King Edward VII. And, curiously, it was the Bismarck family who worked to widen this personal breach.

But this could not have developed into a national cleavage without greater causes being at work. More truly, it was one cause with sundry accretions. Its origin and its foundation lay in Germany's change of policy from internal to external expansion. The growth of her commerce and influence to a world-wide scale inevitably brought her interests and those of Britain into contact at many points. Under tactful or even Bismarckian guileful handling this contact might not have caused such friction as to strike sparks, for British statesmanship was peculiarly insensitive. The party most conscious of Britain's imperial estate happened to be the party most sympathetic to imperial Germany. But Bismarck had gone and tact did not fill his place. As so commonly happens with great men, his disciples forgot his principles and remembered only his method—the mailed fist. Yet the Kaiser himself could also exert charm, and through it succeeded not only in maintaining his popularity in England despite repeated irritation, but in gaining a strong hold on the new and weakly amiable Tsar Nicholas II. For a time he thereby acquired influence without obligation.

The first friction with Britain came over Turkey—a shadow cast on the future. A Liberal government was in power again in 1892, when, as Grey relates, 'suddenly there came a sort of ultimatum from Berlin, requiring us to cease competition' with Germans 'for railway concessions in Turkey'. And in the years that followed the Kaiser lost no opportunity to emphasize that the spreading web of German commerce had a sharp-fanged spider at its centre. In 1895 his intervention made it possible for Russia to deprive Japan of her spoils in the war with China. In 1896 came the next, and more serious, friction with Britain. Ironically, its source was an Englishman's too ardent admiration for Bismarckian imperialism. The Kaiser, unsoothed by Rhodes's equal admiration for himself, became more and more irritated by Rhodes's schemes of British expansion in South Africa, frustrating his own. After several sour complaints, and sweet encouragement of the Transvaal Boers, he found a tempting pretext in the Jameson raid into the Transvaal. At a council on January 3rd, 1896, he suggested that Germany should proclaim a protectorate over the Transvaal and send troops thither. When the Chancellor, Hohenlohe, objected 'that would be war with England', the Kaiser ingenuously replied, 'Yes, but only on land.' As a less drastic alternative the Kaiser was encouraged to send a congratulatory telegram to President Kruger, so worded as not only to be highly offensive to Britain, but to deny her suzerainty over the Transvaal.

Popular feeling boiled over in both countries, due in the one case to ill-suppressed jealousy and in the other to pained surprise at discovering a fresh rival in a traditional friend. Germans felt a natural chagrin that Britain, with already so many colonies, should be gaining more in the one part of the world where a late-comer might hope to stake a claim. Englishmen had made such a habit of colonization that they blandly assumed it could only fit John Bull's figure, and could not understand that anyone, save the traditional rivals, France and Russia, might be anxious. However unconsciously provoking in ordinary intercourse, this calm assurance was a sedative in a crisis, and it largely saved this one. Warlike measures were actually ordered by Germany, and she suggested to France and Russia a combination against Britain. But lack of response from these countries, the calmness of Lord Salisbury's government, and a sense of her own naval weakness, restrained Germany and averted the immediate danger to peace.

But a danger put off by lack of power is not a danger removed. From this moment dates the real growth of German

naval ambition, expressed in the Kaiser's words of 1897—
'the trident must be in our fist'—and in the Kaiser's action
of summoning Admiral Tirpitz to manufacture the trident.
The next year saw the first large naval programme. It also
heard the Kaiser proclaim himself, during his visit to Damascus, the protector of all Mahommedans throughout the world
—a direct provocation to Britain and France. And not only to
them. For the Kaiser's undisguised assumption of the rôle of
patron saint of Turkey was fatal to his accord with Russia.
His shadow now obscured Russia's view of Constantinople,
the goal of her dreams. Like the opponents whom Napoleon
derided, the Kaiser failed in policy because he 'saw too
many things at once', and forced the other powers, whom
Bismarck had played off against each other, to see only one
thing—the fist of Germany—wherever they looked. Nevertheless, the affront to Britain in South Africa was followed, in
1898, by the offer from Chamberlain of that very alliance
which Bismarck had sought in vain. But it was now the turn
of Germany to be suspicious of the offer. On the British side
the offer was impelled by a new and uncomfortable consciousness of isolation and weakness, while based on the old
consciousness of natural affinity with Germany. But it
looked, as it was in part, a confession of weakness, and weakness was not a quality to appeal to the new Germany.
And one of Bismarck's few legacies to his successors was
the habit of underrating Britain's strength and overrating
Russia's.

In Germany's repeated rejections of Chamberlain's proposals between 1898 and 1901, the dominant factor was a
personal factor—the concealed figure of Holstein. This
crabbed, suspicious and miserly official of the Foreign Office,
who loved obscurity because its dimness enhanced his real
power in the pursuit of 'real policy', who would not buy himself a new suit although he did not shrink from using his
official knowledge for private speculation, who had intrigued
for his master's dismissal while posing as his pupil, was now
viewed with awe as the spiritual heir of Bismarck when he

had only inherited his immoral methods. Above all, he lacked Bismarck's confidence.

In consequence, although he would have liked to accept the British offers he shrank back from fear that Germany would become Britain's catspaw, and be converted into her shock-absorber against Russia. On the other hand he felt that Britain's weakness might now be exploited for Germany's benefit by holding Britain at arm's length and wringing concessions from her, while still keeping her hopeful of closer ties. In this view at least he was supported by the Chancellor, Bülow, and the Kaiser, whose outlook was well summed up in his words to Bülow—'I have now got the British, despite their twisting and wriggling, where I want them.' And the German navy, expanded afresh in 1900, was the means of putting the screw on harder.

During the next few years, and especially during the South African crisis and war, the British Government had to pay heavily, not for German support, but merely for the privilege that German threats and insults should not be pressed to action. Over the Portuguese colonies, over Samoa, over China, Lord Salisbury's Government showed such contemptible weakness as almost to justify the Kaiser's description of them as 'unmitigated noodles'; the revelations from the diplomatic archives of these years are sorry reading. To them, indeed, can be traced an indirect responsibility for the eventual conflict, for it was natural that the Kaiser and his advisers should be confirmed in their good opinion of the mailed fist method. He can be acquitted of a desire to press his method as far as actual war, not only because of the evidence of his distaste for it, but because of his tendency to superficial judgment. The limited menace was so obviously yielding the profits of war without the hazards, that the too obvious deduction was just the one to appeal to his mentality.

His responsibility for the war lies in these years. And it is a large responsibility, indeed, the largest. By the distrust and alarm which his bellicose utterances and attitude created everywhere he filled Europe with gunpowder. It is as irra-

tional to fix the chief blame on those who eventually struck
the sparks as it is to concentrate investigation of the war's
origins on the brief month when the sparks were struck.

In reaction from the unhistorical propaganda which pictured the Kaiser as seeking, or even planning the war, the
pendulum has swung too far the other way. To recognize
his erratic good intentions should not lead us to underestimate his bad effects. And they came essentially from the
fact that he was too well pleased with the reflection of his
acts and himself. He saw himself arrayed in 'shining armour'
when actually he was wearing the garb of Puck. He proved
that making mischief makes war.

In delaying any acceptance of British overtures the Kaiser
and Bülow felt secure. They underrated the effect of a common uneasiness in making easy bedfellows. With undue
assurance they argued that there could be no real union
'between the whale and the bear', and by their acts they
compelled this union. In retrospect, the most extraordinary
feature is the number of kicks required to drive Britain away
from Germany and into the awkward embrace of the Dual
Alliance. Germany had at least full warning, for Chamberlain
warned her in 1898 and again in 1901 that 'the period of
England's splendid isolation is past . . . we should prefer adherence to Germany and the Triple Alliance. But if this
proves impossible then we, too, contemplate a *rapprochement*
with France and Russia.'

The German belief in its impossibility proved a fallacy.
That belief was summed up in Holstein's words—'the
threatened understanding with Russia and France is purely
an English swindle. . . . A reasonable agreement with England can, in my opinion, only be attained when the feeling
of compulsion over there has become more general.' He was
too clever. By his 'reasonable agreement' he meant not an
alliance between equals but the relation of master and servant. Weakly as the British government had behaved, and
weaker still as it appeared to one imbued with the 'blood and
iron' philosophy, this weakness is not sufficient to explain

Holstein's amazing presumption. This is, indeed, an illustration that the real trouble in Germany, and the cause of her troubles, was not any true Machiavellian design, but merely the complaint summed up in the schoolboy phrase 'swelled head'.

Britain's first attempt to strengthen her position in other directions was her alliance with Japan in 1902. Its European significance is that it did not carry Britain away from Germany, but tended to raise a fresh barrier between Britain and the Dual Alliance. It sprang from Chamberlain's original proposal of a treaty between Britain, Germany, and Japan, in close touch with the United States. Germany held back and so almost did Japan. For the Japanese statesman, Marquis Ito, preferred to seek an alliance with Russia, and was only turned from his purpose because his arrival in St. Petersburg was outstripped by the progress of the negotiations in London between Baron Hayashi, the Japanese ambassador, and Lord Lansdowne, the Foreign Secretary. Even then, the Japanese Council of Elder statesmen wavered, under Ito's pressure, before accepting the British alliance—whose indirect result was thus to precipitate the Russo-Japanese war, a result neither desired by nor palatable to Britain.

For by 1904 a dramatic change had occurred in the European situation. Only five years before, France had been so bitter against Britain over Fashoda that she had almost forgotten Alsace-Lorraine. But fear of Germany, more deep-seated, made her statesmen open to approach when, in 1901, Chamberlain fulfilled his warning to Germany. The first step in the eventual negotiations between Lansdowne and Paul Cambon, the French Ambassador, was to remove causes of friction at the most sensitive point—overseas. The greatest obstacle was Egypt, still a cherished object of French ambition, and it was no mean diplomatic feat that recognition of Britain's actual occupation was exchanged for recognition of French right to occupy Morocco if she could. The agreement was signed in April, 1904. Although the popular idea of King Edward VII's responsibility for the agreement is purely legendary—still more so the popular German idea of him as spinning a Machiavellian web around Germany—his visit to Paris created the atmosphere in which agreement was possible. At first his reception was frigid, but his tact and understanding of the French combined with their truly republican love of royalty to hasten a thaw, and succeeding visits uncovered common ground. Thus if it is not true that he made the new *entente*, he undoubtedly made it *cordiale*.

But the Kaiser also helped. Deeply chagrined that the lover whose advances Germany had spurned had dared to woo another, his mischief-making was now redoubled. His efforts were directed to break up the Franco-British entente. And the coincident Russo-Japanese war provided the opportunity. His first move was a failure, for the peace-loving Tsar rejected his advice to send the Black Sea Fleet through the Dardanelles in defiance of Britain. But when the Baltic Fleet, Russia's last naval trump, sailed for the Far East it received false information—the Russians later alleged that it came from German sources—that Japanese torpedo craft were lying in wait in the North Sea. Through a panic mistake they fired on British trawlers, and made no effort to redeem their error, which brought Russia and Britain momentarily to the brink of war. For some days the British Channel Fleet shadowed the Russians, until the tension was eased by a message of regret from the Tsar, against the wishes of the war party in Russia. The Tsar, bitter at his humiliation, now, to the Kaiser's delight, proposed a combination of Russia, Germany and France 'to abolish English and Japanese arrogance and insolence'. The Kaiser promptly despatched a draft treaty between Russia and Germany, but urged the Tsar not to divulge it to the French, arguing that the 'Treaty once a *fact*, our combined powers will exert a strong attraction on France', and adding that 'an excellent expedient to cool British insolence and overbearing would be to make some military demonstration on the Perso-Afghan frontier . . . .' But it was the Tsar who cooled, on reflection.

The next German move was singularly inapt, and for it

28

the Kaiser was not responsible. Now, too late, he wanted to woo France instead of trying to separate her from Britain by threat. But he was sent off by Bülow and Holstein to Tangiers, there to 'throw down the glove to France' by a speech which challenged French claims in Morocco. Bülow followed it up by calling for a conference to review the future of Morocco. The challenge came at an awkward moment. The French army was suffering one of its periodical crises, Russia was entangled with Japan, and the French Prime Minister, Rouvier, doubted both the assurance and value of British support. Thus the foreign minister, Delcassé, was sacrificed and France accepted the demand. The mailed fist had scored afresh, but the alarm had driven Britain and France closer together.

The third move was the Kaiser's own. In July, 1905, when on board the Tsar's yacht at Bjorko, he suddenly produced the draft treaty, and in his hybrid 'Willy-Nicky' English, asked—'Should you like to sign it? It would be a very nice souvenir of our *entrevue*.' The Kaiser relates that, when Nicholas answered 'Yes, I will', 'tears of joy filled my eyes— a thrill ran down my spine', and he felt that all his ancestors including 'Grandpapa' and the 'old Prussian God' were giving him their benediction. This phase of royal diplomacy, however serious its implication, was not without its humorous relief. There is a delightful commercial touch in one of his letters to 'Dearest Nicky'—'Now that the programme for the renewal of your fleet has been published, I hope you won't forget to remind your authorities to remember our great firms at Stettin, Kiel, etc. They will, I am sure, furnish fine specimens of line of battleships.' Melodrama marks his aggrieved letter to Bülow who, as the treaty ran counter to his own anti-French aims in Morocco, threatened resignation— 'The morning after your resignation reaches him, the Kaiser will no longer be in this world! Think of my poor wife and children.'

But when the Tsar's ministers saw the treaty, they objected that it could not be reconciled with the French alliance, and sufficient hint of it leaked out to cause strong protests from France. Thus the 'masterpiece' was quietly dropped into the diplomatic waste-paper basket.

In justice to the Kaiser it must be mentioned that at the time he had some cause for personal grievance against Britain, even though it was largely the reaction to his long-standing habit of seeking his end by threats. His forceful impulsiveness had a counterpart in Sir John Fisher, just become First Sea Lord, who constantly talked of a preventive war and freely aired suggestions that if Germany would not limit her naval expansion her fleet should be 'Copenhagened' —on the Nelson model. Such wild suggestions naturally made more impression in Berlin than in London. King Edward VII's share as a cause of irritation was social and personal rather than political. A little more tolerance towards his nephew's *gaucherie* might have helped to make relations smoother. Lord Lansdowne records that 'the King talks and writes about his royal brother in terms which make one's flesh creep'. These personal antipathies and pinpricks, of little account on the British side, where the King was a constitutional ruler and also had a sense of humour, had a deeper reaction on the German side of the North Sea, where the ruler could influence policy decisively and had no sense of humour. And by inciting the Kaiser to further mischief-making intrigues and menaces they had an ultimate reaction in Britain, where even the new Liberal government of Campbell-Bannerman could not ignore them, and was unwillingly forced closer into the arms of France.

While the government refused to commit Britain to a formal alliance with France, it held out the hope that British public opinion might favour intervention if France was attacked. And when the French logically argued that emergency aid would be no use unless its method of application had been thought out, Campbell-Bannerman authorized discussions between the two general staffs. While these had no effect upon the eventual decision for war, they were to have a great influence on the conduct of the war. It is significant

also that in 1905 the new German war plan made allowance
for a British expeditionary force of 100,000 men—the very
figure the French asked for—being present on the French side.

Baulked of his idea of drawing France, with Russia, into a
combination against Britain, the Kaiser now reverted to the
idea of action against France over Morocco. He decided,
however, that 'from a technico-military standpoint' conditions were not suitable, and that an alliance with Turkey,
'which would place the forces of Mahommedanism to the
furthest extent—under Prussian leadership—at my disposal',
and a secure internal position were necessary preliminaries.
This illuminating example of his unbalanced mind is contained in a letter of December 31st, 1905, to Bülow, which
concludes—'First shoot the Socialists down, behead them,
render them impotent—if necessary per Blood bath—and
then war abroad! But not before, and not *à tempo*.'

Yet the next change in the European situation was not to
strengthen his foundations, but to weaken them, by weakening his influence over Russia in the person of the Tsar. With
supreme irony the change came in the most unlikely way—by
the drawing together of the new British government and its
antipathy, despotic Russia. Impelled partly by its general
pacifism and partly by its natural reaction to German
menaces, the Liberal government continued the effort begun
by Lansdowne to remove the traditional sources of friction
with Russia. And in 1907 the points of difference at the
points of contact were settled by an arrangement. While
there was no definite agreement, the natural effect was to
smoothe the way to co-operation in Europe. Although
Britain was not tied either to France or Russia by any formal
agreement she was tied to their side by the bonds of loyalty,
and so could no longer impose a check upon them without
suspicion of disloyalty. Thus her old independent influence
in a crisis had slipped away.

The dilemma was realized and well summed up by the
Foreign Secretary, Sir Edward Grey, in a memorandum of
February 20th, 1906:

'There would, I think, be a general feeling in every country that we had behaved meanly and left France in the lurch. The United States would despise us, Russia would not think it worth while to make a friendly arrangement with us about Asia, Japan would prepare to reinsure herself elsewhere, we should be left without a friend and without the power of making a friend and Germany would take some pleasure in exploiting the whole situation to our disadvantage. . . . On the other hand the prospect of a European War and of our being involved in it is horrible.'

Henceforth the great powers were in fact, if not in name, divided into two rival groups. During the next few years Germany, whose aggressive and impolitic policy had created the counter group, so curiously assorted, was also to help and be helped by Austria in hardening it, as a snowball is hardened when squeezed. But she was also to suffer from her own creation. Britain's adhesion to the new group weakened the old, by making Italy a doubtful partner. Hence Germany was compelled to cling more closely to her other partner, Austria, whom formerly she had led. If Germany wished for war, this bondage was an advantage, but if she wished for peace she would be hampered even as Britain was hampered.

The new grouping of Europe was not the old balance of power but merely a barrier between powers. That barrier, moreover, was charged with explosives—the armaments which the several countries, now driven more by fear than by ambition, hurriedly augmented. Another ill consequence was that fear of a sudden detonation led the autocratic powers at least to give the military custodians of these armaments a dangerously free hand in disposing them. Fear had taken charge of reason long before July 1914.

The first spark came from the Balkans in 1908. The Revolution in Turkey was seized upon by Bulgaria to throw off Turkish suzerainty and by Austria to annex the provinces of Bosnia and Herzegovina, which she had administered since 1879. This annexation had been discussed between the Austrian and Russian foreign ministers, Ahrenthal and

Isvolsky, and Isvolsky had been willing to assent to it in return for Austrian support in securing the opening of the Dardanelles. But before Isvolsky could sound France and Britain, the annexation was declared. In Italy it was justly felt to be an affront, and in Serbia to be a menace. But in Russia the effect was made worse by the German ambassador's peremptory demand that Russia should recognize it under pain of a combined Austrian and German attack.

Russia, caught when she had been acting single-handed, and threatened by a two-handed combination, gave way from fear, and was left with resentment, aggravated by the sense of having forfeited her standing in the Balkans. Isvolsky felt that he had been not only browbeaten but duped, and resigning soon after, went to the Paris embassy as an embittered foe of the Germanic powers. Another personal factor. And Austria, flattered by this first success in imitating Germany's mailed fist method of diplomacy, was encouraged to continue it.

This Bosnian deceit of Ahrenthal's stands out predominantly among the immediate origins of the war. Its intervention was the more unfortunate because the years 1906-1914 saw an improvement in Germany's official relations, at least, with France and Britain. It would have been more marked but for the continued ominous increase in the German navy. It is easy to appreciate now that the Kaiser's encouragement to Tirpitz's anti-British naval ambitions was due largely to vanity, but then it looked more naturally a consistently designed challenge. And even when he tried to repair the damage the Kaiser was unhappy in his method. His way of conciliating British feeling was to declare, in the famous *Daily Telegraph* interview of 1908, that the British were 'mad as March hares' not to recognize his friendship, and that he was in a minority in a land 'not friendly to England'. Without soothing British fears, it caused an outcry in Germany, a public repudiation by Bülow. And it thus weakened the Kaiser's own power to check the war party in Germany.

But it at least led to the Kaiser's replacement of Bülow as Chancellor by the well-meaning Bethmann-Hollweg, who was more desirous of peace if less capable of preserving it. He promptly opened negotiations for an Anglo-German agreement, and met with an eager response from the Liberal government, now renewed in power by the elections of 1910. But practical results were barred, first, by Tirpitz's opposition to any naval adjustment and, second, by the German demand that any agreement must be so worded as to bar Britain from coming to the aid of France.

This was too obviously a strategic move. Sir Edward Grey made the only possible reply—'one does not make new friendships worth having by deserting old ones'.

Nevertheless the tension was eased. The German public, press and Kaiser—as shown by his documentary comments —still suffered from Anglophobia, owing largely to the feeling of thwarted aims and the much-propagated idea that King Edward VII had planned a vast hostile encirclement of Germany. Perhaps the most illuminating reaction was the belief that the King's 1908 visit to the Emperor Francis Joseph was a move to detach Austria from Germany, whereas we now know from the Austrian archives that the King actually asked Francis Joseph's assistance towards reducing the friction between Britain and Germany, and valued the alliance as a common link. But the discussions helped the relations between the British and German foreign ministries and led them to co-operate in settling several points of dispute. Relations were also helped by the settlement between France and Germany over Morocco.

Characteristically, this settlement followed a new crisis. The crisis, curiously enough, was provoked by the otherwise pacific Foreign Minister, Kiderlen-Wächter, and opposed by the Kaiser, another instance of that incalculable double-headedness which was so dangerous a feature of German policy. As a means of encouraging France to grant concessions in Africa, in June, 1911, Kiderlen-Wächter despatched a gunboat to Agadir. In reply, Lloyd George, the former opponent of the Boer War and the leading pacifist in the British Cabinet, warned Germany in a public speech against such threats to peace. The effect, in conjunction with firm indication of a readiness to support France, was to damp the war spark. But resentment made public opinion in Germany more combustible than ever, and it enthusiastically approved yet another increase in the German Navy. Nevertheless, the subsequent settlement over Morocco removed a serious source of friction between France and Germany, and thus indirectly contributed to the better official atmosphere in which Haldane's 1912 mission to Germany took place. Yet even Haldane had to confess that his 'spiritual home' had become a 'powder magazine', although he communicated his fears only to his colleagues in the Cabinet. The growth of the war party in Germany, however, was accompanied by a consolidation of the peace elements, most marked among the Socialists, and the presence of a pacifically minded Chancellor kept open a possible avenue for further negotiations.

But at this very time a fresh powder trail was laid—in the Balkans. The weakness of Turkey, and the example of Italy in occupying Tripoli, encouraged Bulgaria, Serbia, and Greece to claim autonomy for Macedonia as a step to ejecting the Turks from Europe. The Turks were quickly defeated. Serbia's share of the spoils was to be Northern Albania. But Austria, already fearful of Serb ambitions, had no intention of allowing a Slav state to gain access to the Adriatic. She mobilized her troops and her threat to Serbia was naturally answered by Russia's similar preparations. Fortunately, Germany joined with Britain and France to forestall the danger. Less fortunately, their settlement was the cause of a fresh crisis. For, by setting up Albania as an independent state, they upset the division of the spoil. Serbia now claimed part of Macedonia; Bulgaria refused not only by word but by blow, only to be overcome by the combined weight of Serbia and Greece, while Rumania joined in, and Turkey slipped back to recover her lost property under cover of the dust raised by the 'dog-fight'.

As a result Serbia was the chief gainer and Bulgaria the chief loser. This was much to Austria's distaste and in the summer of 1913 she proposed an immediate attack on Serbia. Germany restrained her, counselling moderation, but herself gave Russia a fresh cause of offence by extending German control of the Turkish Army. Russia saw her dream of the Dardanelles fading, and her ministers came to the conclusion that it could only be revived if a general European war occurred—a dangerful attitude of mind. Their immediate aim was now to recover their shaken influence in the Balkans, and they sought to win over Rumania as a first step towards building a new Balkan alliance. The prospect created fresh alarm in Austria, already distracted by the internal strain of her diverse racial parts.

Force was her method to suppress the dissatisfaction of her Serb and Croat subjects in the annexed provinces and of her Rumanian subjects in Transylvania. And her desire was to apply the same remedy in time to the external state—Serbia —which formed a natural rallying point for all the dissatisfied elements within. Her leaders felt that war beyond her frontiers would be the best way to silence discord within. In this feeling they were not alone. The popular unrest in Russia, only half stifled by the use of knout and exile, and the clamour for universal suffrage in Germany, made the war-parties in both countries look to war as a safety-valve.

During the last year incitements multiplied on all sides— bellicose speeches, articles, rumours, frontier incidents. President Wilson's confidant, Colonel House, left Berlin with the conviction that the military party was determined on war, at the earliest opportunity, and would force the Kaiser to abdicate if he opposed their desire. Their excitement was certainly aggravated by the three years' service act which France had passed as a remedy for her inferior man power in face of recent developments in the German Army. But the German ambassador reported to Bethmann-Hollweg that: 'In spite of the chauvinistic attitude of many circles and the general dream of a recovery of the lost provinces, the French

nation as a whole could be described as desirous of peace.'
The most that could be said, even of Poincaré, the President,
was what Poincaré himself expressed, 'that France did not
want war, but did not fear it'. Elsewhere, however, the surface of the continent was now strewn with powder. And
everywhere the air was heavy with fatalism.

The fatal spark was struck at Serajevo, the Bosnian capital,
on June 28th, 1914. Its first victim marked the irony of destiny. The fiery Slav nationalists who sought to advance their
cause by murdering the Archduke Franz Ferdinand, the heir
to Francis Joseph, singled out the one man of influence in
Austria who was their friend. For Franz Ferdinand also had
dreams—of a reconstructed empire in which the several
nationalities were held together not in bondage but in
federation. But to most of the Bosnian Slavs he was merely
the symbol of the oppressor, and to the extreme nationalists
who plotted his death he was the more to be hated because
his dream of reconciliation within the empire might thwart
theirs of breaking away from the empire, to join with Serbia
in creating a wider Yugo-Slav state.

The handful of youthful conspirators sought and received
help from the Serbian secret society known as the 'Black
Hand'. This was largely composed of army officers, who
formed a group hostile to the existing civil government in
Serbia. Rumours of the conspiracy seem to have reached the
ears of ministers, and orders were sent to the frontier to intercept the conspirators, but as the frontier guards were members of the 'Black Hand' the precautions naturally failed. It
seems also, but is not certain, that a vague warning was sent
to Vienna. What is certain is the amazing carelessness of the
Austrian authorities in guarding the Archduke, and their
cynical indifference to the fate that befell this highly unpopular heir to the throne. Potiorek, the military governor
of Bosnia and future commander of the offensive against
Serbia, could not have done more to facilitate the task of the
assassins if he had connived at it. Hence there must always
be a suspicion that he did.

After a first attempt, on the Archduke's passage to the city hall, had failed, Potiorek so clumsily directed the return journey that the Archduke's car had to pull up, and two shots rang out, mortally wounding the Archduke and his court-despised morganatic consort. He died at 11 a.m.—a prophetic hour.

The news of the crime caused horror and indignation in all countries save two—Austria and Serbia. The Serbian press made little effort to conceal its pleasure, and the Serbian public still less, while the government which, exhausted by the Balkan wars, had every incentive for peace in order to consolidate its gains, was foolishly remiss in making or offering an investigation into the complicity of its subjects.

Austrian police investigation was also leisurely, and after a fortnight Wiesner, who was deputed to conduct it, reported that while Serbian societies and officials were implicated there were 'no proofs of the complicity of the Serbian government. . . . On the contrary there are grounds for believing it quite out of the question.'

But Austrian decision was prompt, although any outward appearance of action was long delayed. Count Berchtold, the Foreign Minister—who had added an air of elegance to the tradition of deceit bequeathed by Ahrenthal—gracefully and gratefully seized the opportunity to retrieve Austria's and his own lost prestige. The day after the crime he declared to the Chief of the General Staff that the time had come to settle with Serbia once for all—words that seemed to Conrad von Hötzendorf the echo of his own repeated promptings to war. But Berchtold met an unexpected obstacle in Count Tisza, who objected strongly, on the score of expediency, not of morality—'There can be no difficulty in finding a suitable *casus belli* whenever it is needed.' Conrad also considered expediency and remarked to Berchtold—'We must above all ask Germany whether she is willing to safeguard us against Russia.' Berchtold, too, had no wish to meet a rebuff from Germany such as so damaged his prestige two years before. Hence the aged Emperor was induced to sign a memorandum for the Kaiser, accompanied by a personal letter.

But the Kaiser needed no appeal. For when the German ambassador, Tschirschky, had sent off a report of his conversation with Berchtold on June 30th, saying that he had given a warning against hasty steps, the Kaiser scribbled in the margin—'Who authorised him to do this? It is idiotic. It is none of his business. . . . Tschirschky must be good enough to stop this lunacy. We must clear the Serbians out of the way, and that too forthwith.' Poor Tschirschky, he was not equal to his master's somersaults. Formerly energetic in incitement, he presumably remembered his master's voice, urging restraint two years before, and now thought that he was fulfilling the Kaiser's wish by changing his own tune—only to find that the Kaiser had also changed. How shall we explain it? Most probably by the Kaiser's fear of being again reproached with weakness and by his characteristic indignation that royal blood had been shed, if also by the more creditable motive of his friendship with the murdered man.

Thus to Count Hoyos, the Austrian letter-bearer, he gave the assurance, on July 5th, that Austria 'could depend on the complete support of Germany'. 'In the Kaiser's opinion there must be no delay . . . if it was to come to a war between Austria-Hungary and Russia she could be assured that Germany would stand at her side', although he added that Russia 'was in no way ready for war'. Germany was—so he was assured. In a series of hasty consultations with his military and naval advisers, various precautionary measures were ordered. Meantime, the Kaiser left, as arranged, to visit Norway. A few days later, on the 17th, Waldersee, the Assistant Chief of the General Staff, reported to the Foreign Minister—'I shall remain here ready to jump. We are all prepared.'

This blank cheque, endorsed by the Chancellor and given with full recognition of the consequences, stands out predominant among the immediate causes of the war. Austria hurried to cash it, and Tschirschky was only too eager to repair his blunder in urging caution. Unlike later decisions this was taken in a calm if not a cool atmosphere, a fact which gives it special significance in assessing the will to war. Significant also is the care taken by Germany and Austria to lull suspicion of any impending move—in Conrad's words, 'peaceful intentions should be simulated'. While giving no advice to Austria to keep her demands within moderation, the German government showed its anxiety that the support of Italy, Bulgaria, Rumania and Turkey should be ensured for a war. Italy was to be given no hint of the action intended, but Austria was urged to be ready with a price for her support when war came.

Now assured of Germany's backing, Berchtold's next problem is so to draft the ultimatum to Serbia that it will be unacceptable. This takes some thought and on July 10th Berchtold confesses to Tschirschky that he is still considering 'what demands could be put that it would be wholly impossible for Serbia to accept'. The only dissenting voice is that of Tisza, but he is told—'A diplomatic success would be valueless.' He threatens to withhold his support, but suddenly veers round—after Berchtold has warned him of 'the military difficulties which would be caused by a delay', and has impressed the fact that 'Germany would not understand any neglect on our part to use this opportunity for striking a blow'. Austria might forfeit her partnership with Germany if she showed weakness.

The ultimatum is drawn up, and after reading it the old Emperor says—'Russia cannot accept this . . . this means a general war.' But its delivery is delayed until various war preparations are complete—and Poincaré has sailed from St. Petersburg, where he has been visiting the Tsar. The Russian ambassador in Vienna is also induced by peaceful assurances to go on leave. But the German steamship lines are warned of the date on which the Austrian note would be delivered, and that they must be ready for swift 'developments'.

At 6 p.m. on July 23rd the ultimatum is presented to the Serbian government—when the Prime Minister is away. Its terms not only demand the repression of all propaganda against Austria, but Austria's right to order the dismissal of any Serbian officials that she cares to name and to post her own officials in Serbia. This directly violates Serbia's status as an independent country. Only forty-eight hours are allowed for acceptance. Next day the German government delivers notes in St. Petersburg, Paris and London, which state that the Austrian demands are 'moderate and proper' —the German government had not even seen the ultimatum when it light-heartedly wrote this—and add the threat that 'any interference . . . would be followed by incalculable consequences'. In London the note caused stupefaction, in Russia fierce indignation.

But, two minutes before the ultimatum expired the Serbian reply was handed to the Austrian ambassador. Without waiting to read it, he broke off relations and caught the train from Belgrade, in accordance with his instructions. Formal orders were issued three hours later for Austria's partial mobilization—on the Serbian front. Simultaneously preparatory measures for mobilization took place in Germany and Russia.

Yet the Serbian Note had accepted all the Austrian demands except the two which definitely violated her independence. When the Kaiser read it, on July 28th, after his return, he wrote the comment—'A brilliant performance for a time limit of only forty-eight hours. . . . A great moral victory for Vienna; but with it every reason for war drops away.' And in reference to Austria's partial mobilization he adds—'on the strength of this I should never have ordered mobilization.' Once more the mailed fist has triumphed and the Kaiser, having shown the doubters that he is a strong man, is eager to rest on his laurels. Royal honour is satisfied. But he unwisely suggests that Austria might well occupy part of Serbia until her demands are fulfilled—an act that Russia could never be expected to permit. Bethmann-Hollweg agreed with the Kaiser's view, and on the morning of the 28th the advice was sent to Vienna, adding that, 'If Austria continues her refusal to all proposals for mediation or arbitration, the odium of being responsible for a world war will in the eyes of the German people fall on the German Government.'

But the changed tone was fatally belated. Germany had herself blocked these proposals during the most auspicious period. When the German note was delivered, on July 24th, Russia was at once assured of France's support, and Grey was pressed by his allies to declare Britain's solidarity with them. But his parliamentary responsibility and the divided views of the Cabinet, as well as the uncertainty of public support, hindered any such declaration. He feared, too, that any such action might strengthen the war parties in Russia and Germany. Instead, he tried to open a path to mediation. His first move, on the 24th, was to urge through Berlin an extension of the Austrian time limit. It received no support in Berlin and was tardily passed on to Vienna where it arrived two hours before the expiration, when it was at once rejected. On the 25th and 26th he made further proposals for joint mediation by Germany, Britain, France and Italy, while Austria, Russia, and Serbia were to abstain from military operations. Prompt acceptance came at once from Paris and Rome. Sazonov in St. Petersburg, who had originally mooted the idea, now agreed in principle but preferred first to try direct discussions with Vienna. Berlin refused. The Kaiser scribbled his usual incendiary comments on the reports that came to him—'That is a tremendous piece of British insolence. I am not called upon to prescribe à la Grey to H.M. the Emperor [of Austria] how to preserve his honour.' There is much evidence that German opinion was encouraged by Britain's attitude to count on her neutrality in case of war. But in the newspapers of July 27th the British government published the news that the fleet, assembled for manœuvres, had been ordered not to disperse. This hint in combination with the nature of Serbia's reply caused a change of official tone in Berlin—where, the day before, the General Staff had sent to the Foreign Office the ultimatum they had drafted in readiness for delivery to Belgium.

Thus, later on July 27th, the German government decided to pass Grey's proposals on to Vienna. They sent Grey word that this action implied that they 'associate themselves to a certain extent with your hope'. But after seeing the German Foreign Minister, the Austrian Ambassador telegraphed to Vienna—'The German government offers the most unqualified assurances that it in no way identifies itself with them, but on the contrary is decidedly opposed to their consideration, and only communicates them in order to satisfy the English. . . . The German government is so acting because its point of view is that it is of the utmost importance that England, at the present moment, should not make common cause with Russia and France.' On the 28th, after the Kaiser had seen Serbia's reply, there was a further cooling of tone as we have seen. But Bethmann-Hollweg's cautionary message, his first, to Vienna that day was too late and too tepid.

For at 11 a.m.—again!—on July 28th, Austria's telegraphed declaration of war was delivered to Serbia. And the same day Berchtold refused Sazonov's proposal for direct conversations, giving as his reason the fact that war was now declared! A grim humour underlies both the cause and method of Austria's precipitate decision. Militarily there was every reason for delay in the actual declaration, as the army could not be ready to move until August 12th. But messages from Germany had been inciting Austria to haste; Berchtold and Conrad feared to lose her support and the chance of war if they dallied. Berchtold cynically summed up the position to the Emperor on July 27th—'I think that a further attempt by the Entente Powers to bring about a peaceful solution remains possible only so long as a new situation has not been created by the declaration of war.' And in obtaining the Emperor's signature to the declaration of war, he quenched any doubts by incorporating the justification that Serbian had attacked Austrian troops. Having achieved his end, he then deleted the sentence referring to this imaginary attack!

The rush to the abyss now gathered unbrakable speed—driven by the motor of 'military necessity'. In constructing their huge and cumbrous machines the general staffs of Europe had forgotten the first principle of war—elasticity. Alike in mobilization and in use the conscript armies of the Continent were almost unmanageable. Events were soon to show that they could be set in motion, but could not be effectively guided; their steering lock was inadequate. In this deficiency, now a danger to peace, they afforded a contrast both to the fleets of the time and to the small professional armies of the past.

The one thought of the Generals during these critical days was to start their machines. Desire, for war, and fear, of being caught at a disadvantage, reacted on each other. Thus in Germany and Russia, as already in Austria, any desire among the statesmen for peace suffered the counter pull of the Generals' entreaties to action, and predictions of dire consequences if their technical advice was disregarded. Already in Austria, the Generals shared with Berchtold the sombre distinction of having initiated the war.

Their next success was in Russia—also a land of military mediocrity. There, the news of the Austrian declaration of war wrought a decisive change. Hitherto Sazonov had kept the Generals in hand. Now he begins to succumb to inevitability, and suggests that partial mobilization shall be carried out—of the troops on the Austrian front only. The General Staff argue that for 'technical reasons' this is impracticable, and urge that only a general mobilization can avoid upsetting the machine. Unwilling to yield to their arguments, yet unwilling to override them, Sazonov makes a compromise. Two *ukases* are prepared for the Tsar's signature, one for partial and one for general mobilization, and a decision between them is put off.

But the General Staff are working on the second. Next morning, the chief of the mobilization branch receives the order for general mobilization signed provisionally by the Tsar, and goes round to obtain the necessary signature of the Ministers. One of them cannot be found until the evening. Meantime the German ambassador calls on Sazonov, about 6 p.m., and gives him a message from Bethmann-Hollweg, that—'If Russia continues her mobilization measures Germany will mobilize, and mobilization means war.' The message is delivered with the assurance that it is 'not a threat, but a friendly opinion'; to Sazonov it sounds more like a threat, and it seems to prohibit even partial mobilization on the Austrian frontier. His opposition to his own clamorous General Staff weakens, and after a conference with its chief, Yanushkevich, he apparently consents to general mobilization and obtains the Tsar's approval.

Let us shift our gaze for a moment to Berlin. There the same nervous tension exists and the same tug of wills is in progress. But the Kaiser and his political advisers are now seriously alarmed that Austria's action will make them appear the guilty party, and so cost them the support of Italy while ensuring the entry of Britain against them. Thus a demand of the General Staff for immediate mobilization is refused, and late in the evening Bethmann-Hollweg sees the British ambassador. He tries to bargain for Britain's neutrality and suggests that in return Germany would not annex any part of France—but he 'cannot give him such an assurance' as regards the French colonies. The ambassador tells him that acceptance of the offer is highly improbable, wherein he proves a true prophet. Lichnowsky's warnings from London, that British opinion is hardening, send the Kaiser into a paroxysm of frightened rage. He scrawls abusive epithets about 'English pharisaism', calling Grey 'a mean deceiver', and, rather oddly in view of Bethmann-Hollweg's offer, terms the British a 'pack of base hucksters'. But Lichnowsky's report of Grey's renewed proposals for mediation at least induces Bethmann-Hollweg to send a string of telegrams to Vienna exhorting the Austrians not to continue their open refusal, lest they drag Germany into war at a disadvantage.

The Kaiser, also, telegraphs to the Tsar saying that he is trying to persuade Vienna to agree to 'frank negotiations'. It crosses a similar conciliatory telegram from the Tsar, and is answered by a second, suggesting that—'It would be right to give over the Austro-Serbian problem to the Hague Conference. I trust in your wisdom and friendship.' The fact that the Kaiser's marginal comment is 'Rubbish' casts a doubt upon his sincerity. But the Kaiser has also sent a second telegram of appeal to check military measures which 'would precipitate a calamity. . . .' This produces an actual effect.

The Tsar, about 10 p.m., rings up the Chief of Staff, and despite Yanushkevich's horrified protests that the orders have now gone out, directs him to cancel them and substitute a partial mobilization.

But the General Staff, though discomfited, are not defeated. Next morning, in order to retrieve the position, they bring fresh arguments and all their weight to bear. First they try to approach the Tsar, but he takes refuge from their pressure by refusing to see the Minister of War. Yanushkevich then seeks out Sazonov, and insists that any further delay in general mobilization will 'dislocate' the army organization and endanger Russia's safety. He further contends that partial mobilization will give the French the impression that, when war came, Russia will be unable to help her in resisting Germany's onslaught. Sazonov, now resigned to the certainty of war, agrees to visit the Tsar that afternoon. The Tsar, pale and worried, gives way and gives the order —after Sazonov has soothingly assured him that whatever happens his conscience will be clear. Sazonov telephones the order to Yanushkevich, and advises him to 'disappear for the rest of the day', as a safeguard against the Tsar's vacillation. Sazonov first thinks of trying to keep the general mobilization as secret as possible, without issuing any proclamation, but finds it technically impossible, and the *ukase* is posted up next morning, July 31st. That same day, but a few hours later, the Austrian order for general mobilization is given. Henceforth the 'statesmen' may continue to send telegrams, but they are merely waste paper. The military machine has completely taken charge.

Indeed, it had done so on the 30th—not only in Russia. At 2 p.m. Moltke, the Chief of the German General Staff, had sent a message to the Austrian General Staff through their attaché that Russia's military measure 'will develop into a *casus foederis* for Germany. . . . Decline the renewed advances of Great Britain in the interest of peace. A European war is the last chance of saving Austria-Hungary. Germany is ready to back Austria unreservedly'. Subsequently he sent a telegram direct to Conrad—'Mobilize at once against Russia. Germany will mobilize. Persuade Italy, by offering compensation, to do her duty as an ally.' Thus Moltke counteracted the irresolute telegrams of Bethmann-Hollweg. The Austrian military and civil leaders needed no urging, merely the assurance of Germany's support, and had no intention of acceding to any proposals for mediation unless Germany threatened to withdraw that support. And 'Germany' now meant the General Staff.

As soon as news reached Berlin of the Russian order, a 'state of danger of war' was proclaimed, which comprised the first step of mobilization—a neat military device to gain a lead without giving away a trick. At the same time ultimatums were despatched both to St. Petersburg and Paris. The ultimatum to Russia demanded that she 'must suspend every war measure against Austria and ourselves within twelve hours', and 'definitely notify us of this'. Sazonov, in reply, said that it was technically impossible to stop the mobilization but that, so long as negotiations continued, Russia would not attack. The Tsar reinforced this statement with another telegram to the Kaiser—'Understand that you are obliged to mobilize, but wish to have the same guarantee from you as I gave you that these measures do not mean war, and that we shall continue negotiating. . . .' But, without waiting to hear the reply to their ultimatum, the German government despatched a formally worded declaration of war to their ambassador in St. Petersburg, who duly delivered it, after the expiry of the time limit, in the early evening of August 1st. Almost coincidently German mobilization began.

Yet General von Chelius had shrewdly reported from St. Petersburg—'people have mobilized here through fear of coming events with no aggressive purpose, and are already terrified at the result.' And the Kaiser had made the note—'Right; that is the truth.' But the Kaiser, now equally frightened, and willing, could not stop his own military machine. For Moltke was insistent that 'the unusually favourable situation should be used to strike', pointing out that 'France's military situation is nothing less than embarrassed, that Russia is anything but confident; moreover, the time of year is favourable'. The rashness of the Russian General Staff might at least be excused by 'nerves', but hardly Moltke's. If three men can be singled out as the main personal causes of the war, at this time, they are Berchtold, Conrad and Moltke. But Moltke was really a limited company—the Great General Staff.

Yet, if their action was deliberate, fear was the background of their thought, not merely militaristic ambition. Fear, among the Austrian General Staff, of the doubling of the Serbian Army in consequence of Serbia's gain of territory in the Balkan war. Fear, among the German General Staff, of the Russian Army's unexpectedly rapid recovery, from its 1905 sickness under the ministrations of Sukhomlinov. Like a hard-pressed hero of the towpath, Moltke now pushed Austria into war so that he could jump in to her rescue, and then be sure of her help in return.

The German ultimatum to France demanded to know whether France would remain neutral 'in a Russo-German War', gave her eighteen hours for a reply, and added the menace, 'Mobilization will inevitably mean war'. In case she offered to remain neutral, the German ambassador was instructed to make the impossible demand that France must hand over the fortresses of Verdun and Toul as a pledge. For Moltke's plans were made for a two-front war, and his aim would be upset if only one target appeared! Could military folly go further?

The German ambassador called for his answer on August 1st, and was simply told that France 'would act as her interests required'. That afternoon the French mobilization was ordered, but in Republican France the civil government was still superior to the General Staff, and since July 30th the frontier forces had been withdrawn to a line ten kilometres inside the frontier as a pacific gesture and a safeguard against the danger that a frontier skirmish might provide an excuse for war. If a military handicap, the political wisdom of this withdrawal was seen in the fact that German patrols crossed the actual frontier on the 30th and again, by German official admission, on the 31st. Thus when, on August 3rd, Germany declared war on France, she could only allege the one concrete excuse that a French aviator had 'thrown bombs on the railway near Karlsruhe and Nuremberg'—a rumour already contradicted in Germany before the declaration was delivered.

Why was the actual declaration delayed two days in delivery? First, because of the fresh suggestion from Grey that so long as there was any chance of agreement between Russia and Austria, Germany and France should refrain from any attack. The suggestion was vaguely worded and Lichnowsky, in his eager desire for peace, enlarged it in telegraphing to Berlin that 'this would appear to mean that in case we did not attack France, England would remain neutral and would guarantee France's neutrality'. The Kaiser and his Chancellor clutched at the straw. The former said to Moltke—'We march, then, with all our forces, only toward the East.' Moltke, as his memoirs relate, replied, 'that this was impossible. The advance of armies formed of millions of men . . . was the result of years of painstaking work. Once planned, it could not possibly be changed'. The Kaiser bitterly retorted—'Your uncle would have given me a different reply.' Moltke gained his way as regards the continued concentration against France, but a twenty-four hour brake was ordered to be put on the actual crossing of the frontier of France and Luxembourg. Moltke pathetically records—'It was a great shock to me, as though something had struck at my heart.' However his heart attack was soon relieved, for late that evening further telegrams from London showed that Britain was not promising neutrality. The brake was released. And if it had caused some check on Moltke's arrangements, some of his advanced troops had actually entered Luxembourg that day in advance of timetable!

Nevertheless the British Cabinet was still wavering. A majority of its members were so anxious for peace and uncertain of the public attitude that they had failed to give a clear warning which might have strengthened Bethmann-Hollweg in his feeble efforts to withstand his own war party. Now it was too late and the military machine was in control. Nothing could have averted war after July 31st. Thus the British Cabinet's continued uncertainty, however natural and creditable, merely increased the anxiety of France, fearful of desertion.

Germany came to the rescue. Her long-prepared ultimatum to Belgium, demanding a free passage for her troops as required by her still longer-prepared war plan, was delivered on the evening of August 2nd. The Belgian government sturdily refused to allow its neutrality to be violated. On the morning of August 4th, the German troops began their invasion. The threat, even before the act was known, was decisive in hardening British opinion to the point of intervention, even though that intervention was already inevitable, as the German Staff had correctly calculated. An ultimatum was delivered that Germany should respect Belgian neutrality, and was received by Bethmann-Hollweg with the pitiful complaint that Britain was going to war 'just for a scrap of paper'. At 11 p.m.—by German time—the ultimatum expired. Britain also was in the war—and Italy was out of it, having already decided for neutrality on July 31st.

Thus in the final act, as in the earlier acts, 'technical

military arguments' were decisive. The German army *must* go through Belgium, even though with the certainty that Britain would thereby be drawn in against Germany. Military technique—how competent in peace to gain war; how impotent in war to gain victory, so it was soon to prove!

CHAPTER II

THE OPPOSING FORCES

THE nations entered upon the conflict with the conventional outlook and system of the eighteenth century merely modified by the events of the nineteenth century. Politically, they conceived it to be a struggle between rival coalitions based on the traditional system of diplomatic alliances, and militarily a contest between professional armies—swollen, it is true, by the continental system of conscription, yet essentially fought out by soldiers while the mass of the people watched, from seats in the amphitheatre, the efforts of their champions. The Germans had a glimpse of the truth, but —one or two prophetic minds apart—the 'Nation in Arms' theory, evolved by them during the nineteenth century, visualized the nation as a reservoir to pour its reinforcements into the army, rather than as a mighty river in which are merged many tributary forces of which the army is but one. Their conception was the 'Nation in Arms', hardly the 'Nation at War'. Even to-day this fundamental truth has yet to be grasped in its entirety and its full implications understood. Progressively throughout the years 1914-1918 the warring nations enlisted the research of the scientist, the inventive power and technical skill of the engineer, the manual labour of industry, and the pen of the propagandist. For long this fusion of many forces tended to a chaotic maelstrom of forces; the old order had broken down, the new had not yet evolved. Only gradually did a working co-operation emerge, and it is a moot point whether even in the last phase co-operation of forces had attained to the higher level of co-ordination—direction by unity of diversity.

The German army of 1914 was born in the Napoleonic wars, nursed in infancy by Gneisenau and Scharnhorst, and guided in adolescence by the elder Moltke and Roon. It reached maturity in the war of 1870, when it emerged triumphantly from a trial against the ill-equipped and badly led long-service army of France. Every physically able citizen was liable to service; the State took the number it desired, trained them to arms for a short period of full-time service, and then returned them to civil life. The feature, as also the object, of the system, was the production of a huge reserve by which to expand the active army in war. A man served two or three years full-time, according to his branch of the service, followed by five or four years in the regular reserves. He then served in the Landwehr for twelve years, and finally passed into the Landsturm from the age of thirty-nine till forty-five. Further, an Ersatz reserve was formed of those who were not called on for service with the colours.

In this organization and in the thoroughness of the training lay the secret of the first great surprise of the war, one which almost proved decisive. For instead of regarding their reservists as troops of doubtful quality, fit only for an auxiliary rôle or garrison duty, the Germans during mobilization were able to duplicate almost every first-line army corps with a reserve corps—and had the courage, justified by events, to use them in the opening clash. This surprise upset the French calculations and thereby dislocated their entire plan of campaign.

The Germans have been reproached for many miscalculations; less than justice has been done to the correctness of many of their intuitions. They alone realized what is to-day an axiom—that, given a highly trained cadre of leaders, a military machine can be rapidly manufactured from short-time levies, like molten liquid poured into a mould. The German mould was a long-service body of officers and N.C.O.'s who in their standard of technical knowledge and skill had no equal on the Continent. But if the machine was manufactured by training it gained solidity from another process. The psychological element plays an even greater part in a 'national' than in a professional army. Esprit de corps is not enough; the stimulus of a great moral impulse to action is

necessary, a deep-rooted belief in the policy for which citizens
are called on to fight. The leaders of Germany had worked
for generations to inspire their people with a patriotic conviction of the grandeur of their country's destiny. And if their
opponents went forth to battle in 1914 with as intense a belief
in their country's cause, this flaming patriotism had not the
time to consolidate such a disciplined combination as years of
steady heat had produced in Germany. The German people
had an intimacy with and a pride in their army, notwithstanding the severity of its discipline, that was unknown
elsewhere.

This unique instrument was handled by a general staff
which, by rigour of selection and training, was unmatched
for professional knowledge and skill, if subject to the mental
'grooves' which characterize all professions. Executive skill is
the fruit of practice; and constant practice, or repetition, tends
inevitably to deaden originality and elasticity of mind. In a
professional body, also, promotion by seniority is a rule difficult to avoid. The Germans, it is true, tended towards a
system of staff control, which in practice usually left the real
power in the hands of youthful general staff officers. As war
memoirs and documents reveal, the chiefs of staff of the various
armies and corps often took momentous decisions with hardly
a pretence of consulting their commanders. But such a system
had grave objections, and from it came the grit in the wheels
which not infrequently marred the otherwise well-oiled working of the German war machine.

Tactically the Germans began with two important material
advantages. They alone had gauged the potentialities of the
heavy howitzer, and had provided adequate numbers of this
weapon. And if no army had fully realized that machine-guns
were 'concentrated essence of infantry', nor fully developed
this preponderant source of fire power, the Germans had
studied it more than other armies, and were able to exploit
its inherent power of dominating a battlefield sooner than
other armies. In this anticipation of the value of heavy
artillery and machine-guns the German General Staff seems

54

to have been largely influenced by the acute diagnosis of Captain Hoffmann, its youthful attaché with the Japanese Army in Manchuria. Strategically, also, the Germans had brought the study and development of railway communications to a higher pitch than any of their rivals.

The Austro-Hungarian army, if patterned on the German model, was a vastly inferior instrument. Not only had it a tradition of defeat rather than of victory, but its racial mixture prevented the moral homogeneity that distinguished its ally. This being so, the replacement of the old professional army by one based on universal service lowered rather than raised its standard of effectiveness. The troops within the borders of the empire were often racially akin to those beyond, and this compelled Austria to a politically instead of a militarily based distribution of forces, so that kinsmen should not fight each other. And her human handicap was increased by a geographical one, namely, the vast extent of frontier to be defended.

Nor were her leaders, with rare exceptions, the professional equals of the Germans. Moreover, if common action was better understood than among the Entente Powers, Austria did not accept German direction gladly.

Yet despite all its evident weaknesses the loosely knit conglomeration of races withstood the shock and strain of war for four years, in a way that surprised and dismayed her opponents. The explanation is that the complex racial fabric was woven on a stout Germanic and Magyar framework.

From the Central we turn to the Entente Powers. France possessed but sixty per cent of the potential man power of Germany (5,940,000 against 9,750,000), and this debit balance had forced her to call on the services of practically every able-bodied male. A man was called up at twenty, did three years' full-time service, then eleven in the reserve and finally two periods of seven years each in the Territorial Army and Territorial Reserve. This system gave France an initial war strength of nearly four million trained men, compared with Germany's five; but she placed little reliance on the fighting value of reservists. The French command counted only on the semi-professional troops of the first line, about 1,000,000 men, for the short and decisive campaign which they expected and prepared for. Moreover, they assumed a similar attitude on the part of their enemy—with dire result. But this initial surprise apart, a more profound handicap was the lesser capacity of France for expansion, in case of a long war, due to her smaller population—under 40,000,000 compared with Germany's 65,000,000. Colonel Mangin, later to become famous, had advocated tapping the resources in Africa, the raising of a huge native army, but the Government had considered the dangers to outweigh the advantages of such a policy, and war experience was to show that it had military as well as political risks.

The French General Staff, if less technically perfect than the German, had produced some of the most renowned military thinkers in Europe, and its level of intelligence could well bear comparison. But the French military mind tended to lose in originality and elasticity what it gained in logic. In the years preceding the war, too, a sharp division of thought had arisen which did not make for combined action. Worse still, the new French philosophy of war, by its preoccupation with the moral element, had become more and more separated from the inseparable material factors. Abundance of will cannot compensate a definite inferiority of weapons, and the second factor, once realized, inevitably reacts on the first. In material, the French had one great asset in their quick-firing 75mm. field gun, the best in the world, but its very value had led them to undue confidence in a war of movement and a consequent neglect of equipment and training for the type of warfare which came to pass.

Russia's assets were in the physical sphere, her defects in the mental and moral. If her initial strength was no greater than that of Germany, her man-power resources were immense. Moreover the courage and endurance of her troops were famous. But corruption and incompetence permeated her leadership, her rank and file lacked the intelligence and initiative for scientific warfare—they formed an instrument of great solidity but little flexibility—while her manufacturing resources for equipment and munitions were far below those of the great industrial powers. This handicap was made worse by her geographical situation, for she was cut off from her allies by ice- or enemy-bound seas, and she had to cover immense land frontiers. Another radical defect was the poverty of her rail communications, which were the more essential as she relied for success on bringing into play the weight of her numbers. In the moral sphere Russia's condition was less clear. Her internal troubles were notorious and must be a brake on her efforts unless the cause was such as to make a crusade-like appeal to her primitive and incoherent masses.

Between the military systems of Germany, Austria, France and Russia there was a close relation; the differences were of detail rather than fundamental; and this similarity threw into greater contrast the system of the other great European Power —Britain. Throughout modern times she had been essentially a sea power, intervening on land through a traditional policy of diplomatic and financial support to Allies, whose military efforts she reinforced with a leaven from her own professional army. This regular army was primarily maintained for the protection and control of the overseas dependencies—India in particular—and had always been kept down to the minimum strength for this purpose. The reason for the curious contrast between Britain's determination to maintain a supreme navy and her consistent neglect, indeed starvation, of the army lay partly in her insular position, which caused her to regard the sea as her essential life-line and main defence, and partly in a constitutional distrust of the army, an illogical prejudice, which had its almost forgotten source in the military government of Cromwell. Small as to size, it enjoyed a practical and varied experience of war without parallel among the continental armies. Compared with them, its obvious professional handicap was that the leaders, however apt in handling small columns in colonial expeditions, had never been prepared to direct large formations in *la grande guerre*.

But the value of such practice, and the British handicap, are easily overrated by the layman. For experience has tended to show that the larger the force, the smaller the scope for generalship, and the less the call upon it. Compared with the manifold personal initiative of a Marlborough or a Napoleon before and during battle, the decisions of an army commander in 1914-1918 were necessarily few and broad—his rôle was more akin to that of managing director of a vast department store. And in a war where all the leaders were soon out of their depth, and slow to recover, practical acumen counted for more than the theoretical technique acquired in peacetime exercises. These, especially in the French Army, too often bred the delusion that the issue of an order at a distance was equivalent to its fulfilment on the spot.

In the little British Army which originally took the field, personality had for a time more scope. And much was to depend upon it. Unfortunately, the issue was to suggest that the process of selection had not succeeded in bringing to the fore the officers best fitted for leadership. It is significant that, on the way out to France, Haig spoke to Charteris (his military secretary and future chief intelligence officer) of his qualms concerning the Commander-in-Chief, Sir John French, whose right hand he had been in South Africa: 'D.H. unburdened himself to-day. He is greatly concerned about the composition of British G.H.Q. He thinks French quite unfit for high command in time of crisis. . . . He says French's military ideas are not sound; that he has never studied war; that he is obstinate, and will not keep with him men who point out even obvious errors. He gives him credit for good tactical powers, great courage and determination. He does not think Murray will dare to do anything but agree with everything French suggests. In any case he thinks French would not listen to Murray but rely on Wilson, which is far worse. D.H. thinks Wilson is a politician, and not a soldier, and "politician" with Douglas Haig is synonymous with crooked dealing and wrong sense of values.' This judgment is similar to that of another general, eminent as a military historian: 'There could hardly have been worse selected G.H.Q's than those with which we began the South African War and 1914.'

But apart from errors in selection, there is the question whether officers were miscast for their actual rôles. In 1912 French himself had expressed the opinion that certainly Haig and perhaps Grierson would 'always shine more and show to greater advantage as superior Staff Officers than as Commanders'. Because of his unrivalled knowledge of the German Army and cordial relations with the French, as well as his gift for putting juniors at their ease, Grierson would have been a peculiarly good Chief of Staff for French. Yet 'when Grierson—his Chief Staff Officer at manœuvres—had pointed out to French the impracticability of some of his proposals, he had at once been replaced by Sir Archibald Murray'. Grierson, instead, went to France as commander of an army corps. A man of full figure and sedentary habits, fifty-five years old, the combination of good living and hard work had undermined his constitution; he collapsed and died on his way to the front. If this was a great loss to the Army, it was a less immediate danger than Murray's subsequent collapse on August 26th, the critical day of Le Cateau. Worse still, Murray would recover sufficiently to think that he was functioning when actually he was still unfit. These were but two of the most prominent instances of the trouble caused by a system which brought officers to high position at an age when their energy was declining, and their susceptibility to the strain of war increasing. As a fortunate offset the enemy suffered at least as heavily from this handicap: indeed, the directing head of the German armies, Moltke, who had recently been undergoing treatment, caused alarm among his entourage in the very first days of war by his state of semi-collapse.

The other British corps commander, Haig, had taken too

good care of his health to cause any such anxiety. Physically, his fitness at fifty-three was exceptional. In the South African War, his thoroughness and methodicity had made him an ideal staff officer to French; but later, when given command of a mobile column, those qualities had not proved all-sufficing. It is worth recalling that when Colonel Woolls-Sampson, 'the incomparable Intelligence Officer and fighting scout', was told of Haig's appointment as column commander, he remarked: 'He's quite all right, but he's too —— cautious: he will be so fixed on not giving the Boers a chance, he'll never give himself one.' Thirteen years later Woolls-Sampson's point was borne out. For the revised Official History of 1914, published after a generation has passed, has revealed that at Haig's first serious test as a corps commander he was temporarily thrown off his balance by a trifling encounter in the dark, so that he reported 'situation very critical', and repeatedly called for help—from a neighbour who was really hard pressed. It has also revealed that Haig's excessive caution on reaching the Aisne allowed the day of opportunity to slip away, and the enemy to establish their four years' tenure of the position beyond. Yet if command was not Haig's natural rôle, he had developed qualities which others lacked, and once the battlefront became static the conditions of warfare tended to change the rôle of a commander into that of a super-staff officer.

Errors of conception were to cost more than any errors of execution. Lessons of the South African War that went wider than the selection of leaders had been overlooked. Read in the light of 1914-1918, the "Evidence taken before the Royal Commission on the War in South Africa" offers astonishing proof of how professional vision may miss the wood for the trees. There is little hint, among those who were to be the leaders in the next war, that they had recognized the root problem of the future—the dominating power of fire defence and the supreme difficulty of crossing the bullet-swept zone. Sir Ian Hamilton alone gave it due emphasis, and even he was too sanguine as to the possibility of overcoming it. His proposed solution, however, was in the right direction. For he urged not only the value of exploiting surprise and infiltration tactics to nullify the advantages of the defence, but the need of heavy field artillery to support the infantry. Still more prophetically, he suggested that the infantry might be provided with 'steel shields on wheels' to enable them to cross no-man's-land and make a lodgment in the enemy's position.

Mr. Amery, author of *The Times* history of the War, probed a weak spot in the prevailing European theory by arguing that superior skill now counted more than superior numbers, and that its proportionate value would increase with material progress. The same note was struck by General Baden-Powell, who urged that the way to develop it was to give officers responsibility when young—he was left to find his channel for proving this in the Boy Scout movement, and not in the Army.

Two generals, Paget and Hunter, had a vision of the value and future use of motor vehicles in war, while Haig said that, rather than mounted infantry, he would prefer infantry 'on motors'. In view of the development of the motor between 1903 and 1914 it is strange how little use of it was made at the outset of the next war—or even at the end!

But the most remarkable feature of this Royal Commission was the way that French and Haig discoursed on the paramount value of the *arme blanche*, implying that so long as the cavalry charge was maintained all would be well with the conduct of war. An equally striking underestimate of fire power was contained in Haig's forecast that 'artillery seems only likely to be really effective against raw troops'. His confident opening declaration was that 'cavalry will have a larger sphere of action in future wars'. And he went on to say: 'Besides being used before, during, and after a battle as hitherto, we must expect to see it employed strategically on much larger scale than formerly.' What a contrast there was to be between this expectation and the event! French, Germans, Russians, and Austrians certainly had unexampled masses of cavalry ready at the outbreak of war. But in the opening phase they caused more trouble to their own sides than to the enemy. From 1915 on, their effect was trivial, except as a strain on their own country's supplies: despite the relatively small number of British cavalry, forage was the largest item of supplies sent overseas, exceeding even ammunition, and thus the most dangerous factor in aggravating the submarine menace; while, by authoritative verdict, the transport trouble caused in feeding the immense number of cavalry horses was an important factor in producing Russia's collapse.

In the British Army, also, one unfortunate result of this delusion was that when the cavalry school came to the top in the years just before the War, there was the usual human tendency to penalize the careers of officers who propounded more realistic ideas, while a still larger circle were thereby induced to maintain silence. This was the greater pity because the cavalry sense of mobility was as vital a necessity as the cavalry means of mobility was decadent; and by undue emphasis on the old means the chance of re-creating the means was hindered.

But in other ways the bitter lessons of the South African War brought profit, exerting an influence which to some extent counteracted that inelasticity of mind and ritualism of method which have increased with the increasing professionalization of armies. For the progress in organization in the years before 1914, the British Army owed much to Lord Haldane,* and to him also was due the creation of a second line of partially trained citizens—the Territorial Force. Lord Roberts had pleaded for compulsory military training, but the voluntary principle was too deeply embedded in the national mind for this course to be adopted, and Haldane wisely sought to develop Britain's military effectiveness within the bounds set by traditional policy. As a result, 1914 found England with an expeditionary force of some 160,000 men, the most highly

* He found an ardent assistant in Haig, whose appointment to the War Office had been strongly urged by King Edward.

trained striking force of any country—a rapier among scythes. To maintain this at strength the old militia had been turned into a special reserve for drafting. Behind this first line stood the Territorial Force, which if only enlisted for home defence had a permanent fighting organization, unlike the amorphous volunteer force which it superseded. The British Army had no outstanding asset in war armament, but it had developed a standard of rifle-shooting unique among the world's armies.

The reforms by which the army had been brought into line with continental models had one defect, accentuated by the close relations established between the British and French General Staffs since the Entente. It induced a 'continental' habit of thought among the General Staff, and predisposed them to the rôle, for which their slender strength was unsuited, of fighting alongside an Allied Army. This obscured the British Army's traditional employment in amphibious operations through which the mobility given by command of the sea could be exploited. A small but highly trained force striking 'out of the blue' at a vital spot can produce a strategic effect out of all proportion to its slight numbers.

The last argument brings us to a comparison of the naval situation, which turned on the balance between the fleets of Britain and Germany. Britain's sea supremacy, for long unquestioned, had in recent years been challenged by a Germany which had deduced that a powerful fleet was the key to that colonial empire which she desired as an outlet for her commerce and increasing population. This ambition was fostered, as its instrument was created, by the dangerous genius of Admiral von Tirpitz. To the spur of naval competition the British people eventually responded, determined at any cost to maintain their 'two-power' standard. If this reaction was instinctive rather than reasoned, its subconscious wisdom had a better foundation than the catchwords with which it was justified, or even than the need of defence against invasion. The industrial development of the British Isles had left them dependent on overseas supplies for food, and on the secure flow of sea-borne imports and exports for industrial existence. For the navy itself this competition was a refining agency, leading to a concentration on essentials. Gunnery was developed and less value attached to polished brasswork. Warship design and armament were transformed; the 'Dreadnought' ushered in the new era of the all big-gun battleship. By 1914 Britain had twenty-nine such capital ships and thirteen building, to the eighteen built and nine building, of Germany. Further, Britain's naval strength had been soundly distributed, the main concentration being in the North Sea.

More open to criticism in view of the forecasts of several naval authorities, was her comparative neglect of the potential menace of the submarine. Here German opinion was shown rather by the number building than those already in commission. It is to Germany's credit that though lacking a sea tradition, her fleet an artificial rather than a natural product, the technical skill of the German Navy made it a formidable rival to the British ship for ship, and perhaps its superior in scientific gunnery.

But in the first stage of the struggle the balance of the naval forces was to affect the issue far less than the balance on land. For a fleet suffers one inherent limitation—it is tied to the sea, and hence cannot strike direct at the hostile nation. The fundamental purpose of a navy is therefore to protect a nation's sea communications and sever those of the enemy; although victory in battle may be a necessary prelude, blockade is its ultimate purpose. And as blockade is a weapon slow to take effect, its influence could only be decisive if the armies failed to secure the speedy decision on land, upon which all counted.

In this idea of a short war lay also the reason for the comparative disregard of economic forces. Few believed that a modern nation could endure for many months the strain of a large-scale conflict. The supply of food and of funds, the supply and manufacture of munitions, these were problems that had been only studied on brief estimates. Of the belligerents, all could feed themselves save Britain and Germany, and Germany's deficit of home-grown supplies could only be serious in the event of a struggle of years. But Britain would starve in three months if her outside supplies were cut off.

In munitions and other war material Britain's industrial power was greatest of all, though conversion to war production was a necessary preliminary, and all, again, depended on the security of her sea communications. France was weak, and Russia weaker still, but the former unlike the latter could count on outside supplies so long as Britain held the seas. As Britain was the industrial pivot of the one alliance, so was Germany of the other. A great manufacturing nation, she had also a wealth of raw material, especially since the annexation of the Lorraine ironfields after the 1870 war. But the stoppage of outside supplies must be a handicap in a long war, increasing with its duration, and serious from the outset in such tropical products as rubber. Moreover, Germany's main coal and ironfields lay dangerously close to her frontier, in Silesia on the east and in Westphalia and Lorraine on the west. Thus for the Central Alliance a quick decision and an offensive war were more essential than for the Entente.

Similarly, financial resources had been calculated on a short war basis, and all the Continental Powers relied mainly on large gold reserves accumulated specially for war purposes. Britain alone had no such war chest, but she was to prove that the strength of her banking system and the wealth distributed among a great commercial people furnished the 'sinews of war' in a way that few pre-war economists had realized.

If the economic forces were neglected in the war calculations of the Powers, the psychological forces were an unexplored region, except in their purely military aspect. And even here little study had been devoted to the moral element compared with the physical element. Ardant du Picq, a soldier-philosopher who fell in the 1870 war, had stripped battle of its aura of heroic fictions, portraying the reaction of normal men in the presence of danger. Several German critics had described from experience the reality of battle morale as shown in 1870, and had deduced how tactics should be based on the ever-present and balancing elements of fear and courage. At the close of the century a French military thinker, Colonel Foch, had demonstrated how great was the influence of the moral element in the higher sphere of command, although his teaching was concerned rather with fortifying the will of the commander than with unhinging the will of the opponent. But only the surface of the subject had been penetrated. Its civil aspects were untouched, and in the opening weeks of the conflict the general misunderstanding of national psychology was to be shown in the muzzling of the press—in Britain due mainly to Kitchener, followed by the equally stupid practice of issuing *communiqués* which so veiled the truth that public opinion became distrustful of all official news and rumour was loosed on its infinitely more damaging course. The true value of wisely calculated publicity and the application of the propaganda weapon were only to be learnt after many blunders.

CHAPTER III

THE RIVAL WAR PLANS

In an historical survey the German plan must justly take priority, for not only was it the mainspring which set in motion the hands of the war clock in 1914, but it may even be said to have governed the course of the war thereafter. It is true that, from the autumn of 1914 onwards, this course outwardly seemed to be of the nature of a stupendous 'siege' of the Central Powers, an idea incompatible with the terms we have used. But the conception of the Germanic Alliance as a besieged party, although true of the economic sphere, suggests a loss of initiative which their strategy contradicts. Although the initial German plan miscarried, even in its failure it dictated the general trend of operations thereafter. Tactically, most of the fighting resembled siege operations, but the actual strategy on land long erred rather by its disregard of these tactical conditions than by its conformity with them.

The Germans were faced with the problem that the combined forces of themselves and Austria were decidedly inferior to those of France and Russia. To offset this adverse balance, however, they had a central position and the anticipation that Russia's mobilization would be too slow to allow her to exert serious pressure in the opening weeks. While this assumption might suggest a decisive blow at Russia before she was ready, it was equally probable that she would concentrate her main forces too far back for such a German blow to reach—and the experience of Napoleon was not an example to encourage an advance deep into the interior of Russia, with its vast distances and poor communications. The plan long since adopted by Germany was, therefore, to deliver a rapid offensive against France while holding the Russian advanced forces at bay; and later, when France was crushed, to deal with the Russian army. But this plan, in turn, was complicated by the great natural and artificial barriers which the French frontier offered to an invader. It was narrow, only some 150 miles across, and so afforded little room to manœuvre or even to deploy the masses that Germany planned to launch against her foe. At the south-eastern end it abutted on Switzerland, and after a short stretch of flat country known as the Gap of Belfort the frontier ran for 70 miles along the Vosges mountains. Behind and prolonging this natural rampart ran an almost continuous fortress system, based on Epinal, Toul, Verdun, and twenty miles beyond the last-named lay not only the frontiers of Luxembourg and Belgium but the difficult Ardennes country. Apart from the strongly defended avenues of advance by Belfort and Verdun, the only feasible gap in this barrier was the Trouée de Charmes between Epinal and Toul, left open originally as a strategic trap in which the Germans could be first caught and then crushed by a French counterstroke.

Faced with such a mental and physical blank wall, the logical *military* course was to go round it—by a wide manœuvre through Belgium. Graf Schlieffen, Chief of the German General Staff from 1890 to 1905, conceived and developed the plan, by which the French Armies were to be enveloped and a rapid decision gained; and as finally formulated it came into force in 1905. To attain its object Schlieffen's plan concentrated the mass of the German forces on the right wing for a gigantic wheel and designedly took risks by reducing the left wing, facing the French frontier, to the slenderest possible size. The swinging mass, pivoting on the fortified area Metz-Thionville, was to consist of fifty-three divisions, backed up as rapidly as possible by Landwehr and Erşatz formations, while the secondary army on the left wing comprised only eight divisions. Its very weakness promised to aid the main blow in a further way, for if a French offensive pressed the left wing back towards the Rhine, the attack through Belgium on the French flank would be all the more difficult to parry. It would be like a revolving door—if a man pressed heavily on one side the other side would swing round and strike him in the back. Here lay the real subtlety of the plan, not in the mere geographical detour.

The German enveloping mass was to sweep round through Belgium and northern France and, continuing to traverse a vast arc, would wheel gradually east. With its extreme right passing south of Paris and crossing the Seine near Rouen it would then press the French back towards the Moselle, where they would be hammered in rear on the anvil formed by the Lorraine fortresses and the Swiss frontier.

Schlieffen's plan allowed ten divisions to hold the Russians in check while the French were being crushed. It is proof of his clear sight, if not of his long sight, that he counted on the intervention of Britain, and allowed for an expeditionary force of 100,000 'operating in conjunction with the French'. To him also was due the scheme for using the Landwehr and Ersatz troops in active operations and fusing the resources of the nation into the army. His dying words are reported to have been: 'It must come to a fight. Only make the right wing strong.'

Unhappily for Germany, his successor, Moltke 'the younger', lacked his moral courage while sharing his disregard of international morality. Moltke retained Schlieffen's plan, but he whittled away the essential idea. Of the nine new divisions which became available between 1905 and 1914 Moltke allotted eight to the left wing and only one to the right. True, he added another from the Russian front, but this trivial increase was purchased at a heavy price, for the Russian Army of 1914 was a more formidable menace than when Schlieffen's plan came into force. In the outcome two army corps were taken from the French theatre at the crisis of the August campaign, in order to reinforce the Eastern front. Schlieffen's deathbed entreaty was lost on his successor.

Moltke also made a change of great political significance in the plan. Schlieffen had intended that the right wing should deploy along not only the Belgian but also the Dutch frontier, as far north as Crefeld. By crossing the strip of Dutch territory known as the 'Maastricht Appendix' it would be able to turn the flank of the Liége forts, which barred the way through the narrow Belgian gateway north of the Ardennes. He hoped that German diplomacy might secure permission for this passage through Holland, and he did not wish to violate the territory of either Belgium or Holland if he could avoid the moral reproach. For it was his calculation that the undisguised deployment there of part of his force would so alarm the French as to induce them to cross the southern frontier of Belgium and occupy the natural defensive position in the Meuse valley, south of Namur. Thereby they would provide a pretext for his own advance into neutral territory. Even should this subtle trap fail, Schlieffen calculated that he would be able to capture Liége in time to avoid any check on his main advance. And he was willing to cut his margin of time so close as to afford German statecraft the fullest chance to escape the charge of rape.

Such imaginative craft was beyond Moltke's capacity, and he decided that Liége must be taken by a *coup de main* immediately after the outbreak of war. Thus for a fancied addition to military security he deliberately invited the condemnation of neutrals, provoked Belgium to resistance, and drew the weight of Britain into the scales against his own forces. Moltke's method of 'drawing' the enemy was certainly the antithesis of Schlieffen's. And it is a glaring example of the dangers, even the military dangers, which may ensue if strategy is allowed to dominate policy.

If the fault of the final German plan was a lack of courage, that of the French plan was due to an excess. In their case, also, a miasma of confused thought seemed to creep over the leadership in the years just before the war. Since the disasters of 1870 the French Command had planned an initial defensive, based on the frontier fortresses, followed by a decisive counterstroke. To this end the great fortress system had been created and gaps like the Trouée de Charmes left to 'canalize' the invasion ready for the counter. But in the decade before 1914 a new school of thought had risen, who argued that the offensive was more in tune with French character and tradition, that the possession of the '75'—a field gun unique in mobility and rapidity of fire—made it tactically possible, and that the alliance with Russia and Britain made it strategically possible. Forgetful of the lessons of 1870 they imagined that *élan* was proof against bullets. Napoleon's much-quoted saying that 'the moral is to the physical as three to one' has much to answer for; it has led soldiers to think that a division exists between the two, whereas each is dependent on the other. Weapons without courage are ineffective, but so also are the bravest troops without sufficient weapons to protect them and their morale. Courage soon oozes when soldiers lose confidence in their weapons.

The outcome was disastrous. The new school, who found their prophet in Colonel de Grandmaison, found in General Joffre, appointed Chief of the General Staff in 1912, a lever for their designs. Under the cloak of his authority, the advocates of the *offensive à outrance* gained control of the French military machine, and, throwing aside the old doctrine, formulated the now famous, or notorious, Plan XVII. It was based on a negation of historical experience, indeed, of common sense, and on a double miscalculation—of force and place, the latter more serious than the former. Accepting the possibility that the Germans might employ their reserve formations at the outset, the strength of the German army in the west was estimated at a possible maximum of sixty-eight infantry divisions. The Germans actually deployed the equivalent of eighty-three, counting Landwehr and Ersatz troops. But French opinion was, and continued to be, doubtful of this contingency, so much so that during the crucial days when the rival armies were concentrating and moving forward the French Intelligence counted only the forty-five active divisions in its estimates of the enemy strength—a miscalculation by half. If the plan had been framed on a miscalculation less extreme, this recognition does not condone but rather increases its fundamental falsity: for history affords no vestige of justification for a plan by which a frontal offensive was to be launched with bare equality of force against an enemy who would have the support of his fortified frontier zone, while the attackers forswore any advantage from their own.

The second miscalculation—of place—was that although the possibility of a German move through Belgium was recognized, the wideness of its sweep was utterly misjudged. The Germans were expected complaisantly to take the difficult route through the Ardennes in order that the French might conveniently smite their communications! Based on the idea of an immediate and general offensive, the plan ordained a thrust by the First and Second Armies towards the Saar into Lorraine. On their left were the Third Army opposite Metz and the Fifth Army facing the Ardennes, which were either to take up the offensive between Metz and Thionville, or, if the Germans came through Luxembourg and Belgium, to strike north-east at their flank. The Fourth Army was held in strategic reserve near the centre and two groups of reserve divisions were disposed in rear of either flank—relegation to such a passive rôle expressing French opinion on the capacity of reserve formations.

Britain's contingent share in this plan was settled less by calculation than by the 'Europeanization' of her military organization during the previous decade. This continental influence drew her insensibly into a tacit acceptance of the rôle of acting as an appendix to the French left wing, and away from her historic exploitation of the mobility given by sea power. At a council of war on August 5th, Sir John French, who was to command the expeditionary force, expressed a doubt of 'the prearranged plan', and, as an alternative, suggested its despatch to Belgium—where it would have stiffened the Belgian resistance and threatened the flank of the wheeling German mass. Haig seems to have had a similar view. But the plan did not provide for variation, and in any case the General Staff, through Henry Wilson, had virtually pledged themselves to act in direct co-operation with the French. When the General Staffs of the two countries conducted their informal negotiations between 1905 and

1914, they were paving the way for a reversal of England's centuries-old policy, for a war effort such as no Englishman had ever conceived.

Lord Kitchener, who had just been made War Minister in the emergency, had a remarkably accurate intuition of the German plan and tried to avert the danger by advocating that the expeditionary force should concentrate near Amiens, where it would be less exposed. But French was now in accord with Wilson, and his vehement support of the French plan induced Kitchener to give way—later he lamented his consent as a mistaken weakness. Kitchener, however, gave French instructions which, designed to reduce the risks, were in the issue to complicate and even to increase them. For while French's assigned purpose was 'to support, and co-operate with, the French Army', it was qualified by the somewhat contradictory statement 'that the gravest consideration will devolve upon you as to participation . . . where your force may be unduly exposed. . . .' Further, 'you will in no case come in any sense under the orders of any Allied General.'

The smoothness and secrecy with which the expeditionary force moved to France (the main part between August 12th and 17th) was a testimony to the transport arrangements and counter-espionage measures, if still more to the shortsightedness of the Germans. Not merely did their intelligence service fail to gain news of the British expeditionary force until it was actually encountered, but the supreme Command showed little concern with its whereabouts. When Moltke was asked if he desired the Navy to interfere with the passage of the British troops, he showed no enthusiasm for the idea, saying that 'it would be indeed splendid if the Army in the West could settle with the 160,000 English at the same time as with the other enemies'. In their pedantic adherence to the principle of concentration both the General Staff and the Naval Staff ignored the importance of distraction. And each remained in its own narrow compartment, with little interest in what the other was doing and less desire to communicate its own intentions.

The General Staff's mind was fixed on the aim of a decisive battle, without a thought for the Channel ports; the detachments it made, so fateful in their effect, were for the negative purpose of protecting its own march, and not to embarrass the enemy. The Naval Staff's dominant idea was to keep the Fleet concentrated in the North Sea, ready for eventualities but with little concern to influence events. Its positive action was limited to sending out a few submarines in a half-hearted manner. The idea of a landing on the English coast, or even a feint, does not seem to have been considered—although the mere possibility sufficed to detain a considerable part of Britain's military strength. Nor had the General Staff made plans for embarrassing Britain at long range by encouraging native risings. A swift victory over the main armies in the main theatre of war was the German General Staff's solution for all outside difficulties, and absolved them from thinking of war in its wider aspects.

On the Russian front, the plans of campaign were more fluid, less elaborately worked out and formulated, although they were to be as kaleidoscopic in their changes of fortune as in the Western theatre. The calculable condition was geographical; the main incalculable, Russia's rate of concentration. Russian Poland was a vast tongue of country projecting from Russia proper, and flanked on three sides by German or Austrian territory. On its northern flank lay East Prussia with the Baltic Sea beyond. On its southern flank lay the Austrian province of Galicia with the Carpathian mountains to the south, guarding the approach to the plain of Hungary. On the west lay Silesia. As the Germanic border provinces were provided with a network of strategic railways whilst Poland, as well as Russia itself, had only a sparse system of communications, the Germanic Alliance enjoyed a great advantage, in power of concentration, for countering a Russian advance. But if its armies took the offensive, the further they progressed into Poland or Russia proper the more would they lose this advantage. Hence their most profitable strategy was to lure the Russians into a position favourable for a counterstroke rather than to inaugurate an offensive themselves. The one drawback was that such a Punic strategy gave the Russians time to concentrate and set in motion their cumbrous and rusty machine.

From this arose an initial cleavage between German and Austrian opinion. Both agreed that the problem was to hold the Russians in check during the six weeks which must elapse before the Germans should have crushed France, and so could switch their forces eastwards to join the Austrians in a decisive blow against the Russians. The difference of opinion turned on the method. The Germans, intent on a decision against France, wished to leave a minimum force in the East, and only a political dislike of exposing national territory to invasion prevented them from evacuating East Prussia and standing on the Vistula line. But the Austrians, under the influence of Conrad von Hötzendorf, chief of their General Staff, were anxious to throw the Russian machine out of gear by an immediate offensive, and, as this promised to keep the Russians fully occupied while the campaign in France was being decided, Moltke fell in with this strategy.

Conrad's plan was that of an offensive northwards into Poland by two armies, protected by two more on their right, further east. The two attacking armies would then wheel eastwards, and all four would join hands in driving the Russians back towards the Black Sea. Complementary to this plan, as originally designed, the Germans in East Prussia were to strike south-east, the two forces converging to cut off the Russian advanced forces in the Polish 'tongue'. But Moltke failed to provide sufficient German troops for this offensive thrust.

Conrad's own offensive was to be impaired by the combination of a variable state of mind with an inelastic basis of movement. The Austrian forces had been divided into three parts: 'Echelon A' (28 divisions) for deployment on the Russian front; '*Minimum Balkan*' (8 divisions) for deployment on the Serbian front; 'Echelon B' (12 divisions) for use according to circumstances. The plan thus had more adaptability, on paper, than those of other armies; unfortunately, the instrument was not equal to the intention. Conrad's desire to settle with Serbia led him to begin moving 'Echelon B' thither, despite the likelihood of Russia's intervention. Then, on July 31st, he changed his mind and decided to stop it. But 'the Chief of the Field Railways informed him that if utter confusion was to be avoided he must allow "B" to go to its original destination on the Danube frontier, and from there it could be transported to Galicia'. As a result, its withdrawal from the Danube impaired the offensive against Serbia without helping that against Russia, for which it arrived too late. Thus a conflict of purpose in the Austrian Command accentuated the ill effects of a conflict of interests between Austria and her Ally.

On the opposing side also, the desires of one Ally vitally affected the strategy of the other. The Russian command, both for military and for racial motives, wished to concentrate first against Austria, while the latter was unsupported, and leave Germany alone until later, when the full strength of the Russian Army would be mobilized. But the French, anxious to relieve the German pressure against themselves, urged the Russians to deliver a simultaneous attack against Germany, and persuaded the Russians to consent to an extra offensive for which they were ready neither in numbers nor in organization. On the south-western front two pairs of two armies each were to converge on the Austrian forces in Galicia; on the north-western front two armies were to converge on the German forces in East Prussia. Russia, whose proverbial slowness and crude organization dictated a cautious strategy, was about to break with tradition and launch out on a gamble that only an army of high mobility and organization could have hoped to bring off.

When put to the test, the plans of all the military commanders would quickly collapse. At a superficial examination, the fault would seem due to divided purposes in the minds of the leaders—to their failure to maintain the principle of 'concentration' with which they had been indoctrinated. It is easy to point out how they failed in this way—

many books by military experts have done so. But such a judgment is too academic. The fact that the fault was common to all sides suggests a deeper explanation. Not one of the leaders was anything but a devout upholder of the principle of concentration in theory: the trouble came when they tried to apply it to reality—to the political and tactical conditions in which strategy operates. Their failure to adapt their plans to the actual situation may be traced to the habit of mind formed in peace training; especially in war games and exercises, where battle was the ruling idea, the conventions too exclusively military, and the values too purely numerical. By treating concentration as a matter of assembling superior numbers, its dependence on the enemy's distraction and on freedom from external interference was too commonly obscured.

Peace training tended towards solutions that were idealistic rather than realistic. For war, like politics, is a series of compromises. Hence the need of adaptation should be foreseen, the power of adjustment developed, in the pre-war preparation. This was rare among the staff-trained leaders of 1914. They had been brought up on a diet of theory, supplemented by scraps of history cooked to suit the prevailing taste: not on the experience contained in real history. For this to be attainable a critical mind is the first requirement; but such a faculty was frowned on by the military tradition of the nineteenth century—although marked in many great leaders of the eighteenth century.

WESTERN FRONT

- - - Approximate line at end of 1914
-o-o-o- Line at end of Hindenburg Retreat, February 1917
——— Line on 11th. Nov. 1918

ALSACE

VOSGES

LORRAINE

Saarburg
R. Saar
R. Moselle
Thionville
Metz
Morhange
Nancy
R. Meurthe
R. Moselle
Charmes
Epinal
Belfort

Luxembourg

Virton
Longuyon
Briey
FEB. 1916
St. Mihiel
Toul
FEB. 1916
FEB. 1916
Verdun
R. Meuse
Bar le Duc
R. Ornain
R. Marne

FOREST OF ARGONNE

Châlons

CHAMPAGNE

APRIL 1917
Reims
R. Marne
Epernay
MARSHES OF ST. GOND
Pt. Morin
Gd. Morin

R. Aisne
APRIL 1917
Laon
La Fère
APRIL 1917
Soissons
R. Ourcq
Château Thierry

PICARDY
Ham
Montdidier
Lassigny
Noyon
Compiègne
R. Oise
Senlis
Chantilly

Paris

R. Seine

0   50
Miles

© Cassell & Co. Ltd. 1970

CHAPTER IV

1914—THE CLINCH

THE German invasion of France was designed as a methodical sweep, in which unexpected checks should not upset the timetable. The railway system in Germany had been developed under military guidance and supervision—so strict that not even a narrow-gauge line or road rail could be laid without the approval of the Chief of the General Staff. As a result the number of double lines running to the western frontier had been increased from nine to thirteen between 1870 and 1914. On August 6th the great deployment began; 550 trains a day crossed the Rhine bridges, and by the 12th the seven German armies (1,500,000 men) were ready to advance. Over the Hohenzollern bridge at Cologne a train passed about every ten minutes during the first fortnight of war. This vast railway movement was a masterpiece of organization, but when the deployment, completed on August 17th, merged into the forward march, the friction of war soon revealed weaknesses in the German military machine and its control.

To meet the case of Belgian resistance the German plan, as revised by Moltke, provided an instantly available detachment, under General von Emmich, to clear a passage through the Meuse gateway into the Belgian plain north of the Ardennes, ready for the ordered advance of the main armies concentrating behind the German frontier. The ring fortress of Liége commanded this channel of advance, but, after an initial check on August 5th, a German brigade penetrated between the forts and occupied the town. The interest of this feat is that it was due to the initiative of an attached staff officer, Ludendorff, whose name ere long was to be world famous. The forts themselves offered a stubborn resistance

78

and forced the Germans to await the arrival of their heavy howitzers, whose destructive power was to be the first tactical surprise of the World War.

The very success of the Belgians' early resistance cloaked the weight of the main German columns and misled the Allies' Intelligence. The Belgian field army lay behind the Gette covering Brussels and, even before the Liége forts fell, the advanced guards of the German First and Second Armies were pressing against this line. The Belgians, deprived of support owing to the mistaken French plan and British conformity with it, decided to preserve their army by falling back on the entrenched camp of Antwerp—where its location would at least make it a latent menace to the German communications. The Germans, their immediate passage now clear, entered Brussels on August 20th, and on the same day appeared before Namur, the last fortress barring the Meuse route into France. Despite the Belgian resistance the German advance was abreast of its timetable; but it might have been four or five days ahead. And if the Belgian withdrawal to a flank momentarily expedited, it ultimately hindered the German progress, far more than any sacrifice in battle could have done.

Meanwhile, away on the other flank, the French offensive had opened on August 7th with the advance of a detached army corps into Upper Alsace, a move intended partly as a military distraction and partly for its political effect. Its actual goal was the destruction of the German station at Basle and the Rhine bridges below. Soon brought to a halt, it was renewed on the 19th by a larger force under General Pau, which actually reached the Rhine. But the pressure of disasters elsewhere compelled the abandonment of the enterprise and the dissolution of the force—its units being despatched westward as reinforcements. Meantime the main thrust into Lorraine by the French First (Dubail) and Second (de Castelnau) Armies, totalling nineteen divisions, had begun on August 14th and been shattered in the battle of Morhange-Sarrebourg, August 20th, where the French discovered that the material could subdue the moral, and that in their enthusiasm for the offensive they had blinded themselves to the defensive power of modern weapons, a condition which was to throw out of balance the whole mechanism of orthodox warfare. Yet it is fair to add that this abortive French offensive had an indirect effect on the German plan, although this would hardly have occurred if a Schlieffen or a Ludendorff had been in charge at German Headquarters instead of the vacillating opportunist Moltke.

The fact that Moltke had almost doubled the strength of his left, compared with Schlieffen's plan, meant that it was unnecessarily strong for a yielding and 'enticing' defensive such as Schlieffen had conceived, while lacking the superiority necessary for a crushing counter-offensive. But when the French attack in Lorraine developed and Moltke appreciated that the French were leaving their fortified barrier behind he was tempted momentarily to postpone the right-wing sweep, and instead seek a decision in Lorraine. This impulse led him to divert thither the six newly formed Ersatz divisions that should have been used to increase the weight of his right wing. He had hardly conceived this new plan before he abandoned it and, on August 16th, reverted to Schlieffen's 'swing-door' design.

But he also told his left-wing commanders somewhat ambiguously that they must detain as many French troops as possible, and when the Crown Prince Rupprecht of Bavaria argued that he could only do this by attacking, Moltke left the decision to him. We may suspect that Rupprecht was loth to forfeit the opportunity of glory by retiring while the German Crown Prince was advancing. But nothing could have been more foolishly ambiguous than the Supreme Command's attitude. For when Rupprecht refused to refrain unless given a clear order, Moltke's deputy, Stein, said on the telephone to Krafft von Delmensingen, Rupprecht's Chief of Staff—'No, we won't oblige you by forbidding an attack. You must take the responsibility. Make your own decision as your conscience tells you.' Conscience seems a curious basis for strategy. And when Krafft retorted, 'It is already made. We attack', Stein fatuously exclaimed, 'Not really! Then strike and God be with you.'

Thus, instead of continuing to fall back and draw the French on, Rupprecht halted his Sixth Army on the 17th, ready to accept battle. Finding the French attack slow to develop, he planned to anticipate it by one of his own. He struck on August 20th in conjunction with the Seventh Army (Heeringen) on his left, but although the French were taken by surprise and rolled back from the line Morhange-Sarrebourg, the German counterstroke had not the superiority of strength (the two armies now totalled twenty-five divisions) or of strategic position to make it decisive. Further, the attempt to envelop the French right flank by a movement through the Vosges was begun too late and failed. Thus the strategic result was merely to throw back the French on to a fortified barrier which both restored and augmented their power of resistance. And thereby they were enabled to despatch troops to reinforce their western flank—a redistribution of strength which was to have far-reaching results in the decisive battle, on the Marne.

With similar disregard of superior authority, the German Crown Prince, commanding the pivotal Fifth Army between Metz and Thionville, attacked when he had been ordered to stand on the defensive. The lack of what Colonel Foch had termed 'intellectual discipline' was to be a grave factor in Germany's failure, and for this the ambitions and jealousies of generals were to be largely responsible.

While this 'seesaw' campaign in Lorraine was in progress more decisive events were occurring to the north-west. The attack on Liége awakened Joffre to the reality of a German advance through Belgium, but not to the wideness of its sweep. And the sturdy resistance of Liége confirmed him in the opinion that the German right would pass south of it, between the Meuse and the Ardennes. Plan XVII had visualized such a move, and prepared a counter. Grasping once more at phantoms, the French Command embraced this idea so fervently that they transformed the counter into an imaginary *coup de grâce*. Their Third Army (Ruffey) and the reserve Fourth Army (de Langle de Cary) were to strike north-east through the Ardennes against the rear flank of the Germans advancing through Belgium, and thus dislocate their enveloping manœuvre. The left wing (Fifth) Army, under Lanrezac, was moved further to the north-west into the angle formed by the Sambre and Meuse between Givet and Charleroi. With the British Expeditionary Force coming up on its left, it was to deal with the enemy's forces north of the Meuse and to converge on the supposed German main forces in conjunction with the attack through the Ardennes. Here was a pretty picture—of the Allied pincers closing on the unconscious Germans! Curiously, the Germans had the same idea of a pincer-like manœuvre, with rôles reversed, and with better reason.

The fundamental flaw in the French plan was that the Germans had deployed twice as many troops as the French Intelligence estimated, and for a vaster enveloping movement. For information the French relied mainly on their cavalry, of which they had 100,000, but 'this enormous mass of cavalry discovered nothing of the enemy's advance . . . and the French armies were everywhere surprised'. The French Third and Fourth Armies (twenty divisions), pushing blindly into the Ardennes against a German centre supposedly denuded of troops, blundered against the German Fourth and Fifth Armies (twenty-one divisions) in a fog on August 22nd, and were heavily thrown back in encounter-battles around Virton-Neufchâteau. The troops attacked blindly with the bayonet and were mown down by machine-guns. Fortunately the Germans were also too vague as to the situation to exploit their opportunity.

But to the north-west the French Fifth Army (ten divisions) and the British (four divisions) had, under Joffre's orders, put their head almost into the German noose. The German masses of the First and Second Armies were closing on them from the north, and the Third Army from the east—a total of thirty-four divisions. Lanrezac alone had an inkling of the hidden menace. All along he had suspected the wideness of the German manœuvre, and it was through his insistence that his army had been permitted to move so far north-west. It was due to his caution in hesitating to advance across the Sambre, to the arrival of the British on his left unknown to the German Intelligence, and to the premature attack of the German Second Army, that the Allied forces fell back in time and escaped from the trap.

The Retreat to the Marne. The first four British divisions, after concentrating near Maubeuge, had moved up to Mons on August 22nd, ready to advance further into Belgium as part of the offensive of the Allied left wing. On arrival, however, Sir John French heard that Lanrezac had been attacked on the 21st and deprived of the crossings of the Sambre. Although thus placed in an exposed forward position, he agreed to stand at Mons to cover Lanrezac's left. But next day, the 23rd, Lanrezac had word of the imminent fall of Namur and of the appearance of the German Third Army (Hausen) on his exposed right flank near Dinant, on the Meuse. In consequence, he gave orders for a retreat that night. The British, after resisting the attacks of six German divisions during the day, fell back on the 24th in conformity with their Allies. Not a moment too soon in view of the fact that the rest of the German First Army was marching still further westward to envelop their open left flank.*

* Happily, the task of reducing Namur absorbed six German divisions and five hundred guns from August 20th to 25th—when the last forts succumbed. This detachment, added to that already left to stand guard over Antwerp, seriously weakened the German right wing during the critical days when it fell upon and sought to overwhelm the Allied left wing in the battles of Charleroi and Mons. The delay, apparently so slight, imposed by the obsolete and neglected defences of Namur, contributed in turn to the resistance of the equally neglected French fortress of Maubeuge which did not capitulate until September 7th and detained two and a half divisions from the battlefield of the Marne. Less happily, this detachment was set free just in time to reach the Chemin des Dames ridge north of the Aisne—filling part of the gap between Kluck and Bülow (see page 130)—a few hours before the British advanced guards came up on September 12th.

But if the British had begun to retreat later than their Allies, they continued faster and further. This less happy effect was mainly due to Sir John French's sudden revulsion of mind and emotion. He had gone forward almost too eager to fulfil the task given in Kitchener's instructions. He came back with his mind concentrated on the qualifying clause. And the change was due more to the French than to the Germans. The trouble began when Lanrezac, irritated by Joffre's blindness to the close-looming danger, vented on his newly arrived neighbour the indignation he could not show to his superior. This feeling was illustrated in the greeting which Lanrezac's Chief of Staff gave to Huguet, who came with French to visit Lanrezac—'At last you're here; it's not a moment too soon. If we are beaten we shall owe it all to you!' And when French, on being excitedly told that the Germans had reached the Meuse at Huy, inquired what they were likely to do, Lanrezac irascibly replied—'Why have they come there? Oh, to fish in the river.' The sarcasm was modified in translation. But even French's ignorance of the French language could not prevent him understanding the impatience and rudeness which Lanrezac showed in their discussion. Quick to resent this, his resentment changed to alarmed disgust when he found that the French had retired and left him isolated. Henceforward his mind was obsessed with the idea that they had left him in the lurch, and he thought of leaving them. The experience of the next few days hardened his thought of retiring independently to Havre, there to fortify himself in the peninsula with a modern version of the 'Lines of Torres Vedras'. From this disastrous intention he was dissuaded by Wilson's playful cajolery as well as by Kitchener's urgent and less tactful intervention, but still more by the turn of events.

The hurried recoil of the French left wing had at last awakened Joffre to the true situation and to the utter collapse of Plan XVII. From the wreckage he now tried to piece together a new plan. He decided to swing back his centre and left, with Verdun as the pivot, while drawing troops from the right in Alsace and forming a fresh Sixth Army on his left to enable the retiring armies to return to the offensive.

His optimism, soon to wane, might have been again misplaced but for German mistakes. The first was Moltke's folly in detaching seven divisions to invest Maubeuge and Givet and watch Antwerp, instead of using Landwehr and Ersatz troops as Schlieffen had intended. More ominous still was his decision on August 25th to send four divisions to check the Russian advance in East Prussia. These also were taken from the right wing (actually from the force besieging Namur), and the excuse afterwards given was that the German Command thought that the decisive victory had already been won! Further, the German Command lost touch with the advancing armies* and the movements of these became disjointed.

The British II Corps stand at Le Cateau, made by Smith-Dorrien against his superior's wish, and Lanrezac's riposte at Guise, in which French forbade his I Corps to help, were also factors in checking the German enveloping wing, and each had still greater indirect effects. For Le Cateau apparently convinced the German First Army Commander, Kluck, that the British Army could be wiped from the slate, and Guise led Bülow (Second Army) to call on Kluck for support, whereupon Kluck wheeled inwards, thinking to roll up the French left. The idea of a Sedan was an obsession with the Germans, and led them to pluck the fruit before it was ripe. This premature wheel before Paris had been reached was an abandonment of the Schlieffen plan, and exposed the German right to a counter-envelopment.

* This vital breakdown was essentially due to the failure of the German higher command to grasp the importance of good communication. The Chief of the Field Telegraphs was not even consulted as to the location of the Supreme Command. And no attempt was made to utilize the many trained operators available in the German civil telegraph and telephone service. The German Official History says that, as the advance proceeded 'Practically nothing was done to extend without delay the inadequate communications between Luxembourg and the right wing of the Armies, or to improve them by making use of the various supplementary technical means of communication: wireless, cable, motors, aeroplanes.' Moreover, the cavalry leading the advance had shown no discrimination, and had 'recklessly destroyed both lines and instruments'.

This rash movement was in progress when Moltke also sacrificed the conception of Schlieffen to the dream of Sedan —in a different sector. His centre and left were ordered to close like pincers round either side of Verdun, while the right wing was to turn outwards and face Paris as a shield to these pincers. This sudden reversal of direction and inversion of rôle was akin to the folly of a driver who jams on his brakes and slews his front wheels hard round on a greasy road. One further factor must be mentioned, perhaps the most significant of all: the Germans had advanced so rapidly, outrunning their timetable, that their supplies failed to keep pace, so that the fatigue of the troops was increased by hunger.* Indeed, when the chance of battle came, their fighting power was practically numbed by physical exhaustion—a condition much aggravated by the thorough demolitions which the French had carried out as they fell back. Thus, in sum, so much grit had worked into the German machine that a slight jar would suffice to cause its breakdown. This was delivered in the battle of the Marne.

The Tide Turns. The opportunity was perceived, not by Joffre, who had ordered a continuance of the retreat, but by Galliéni, the Military Governor of Paris, where the newly formed Sixth Army had assembled in shelter. On September 3rd Galliéni realized the meaning of Kluck's wheel inwards, directed the Sixth Army (Maunoury) to be ready to strike at the exposed German right flank, and the next day with difficulty won Joffre's sanction. Once convinced, Joffre acted with decision. The whole left wing was ordered to turn about and return to a general offensive beginning on September 6th. Maunoury was already off the mark on the 5th and, as his pressure developed on the German's sensitive flank, Kluck was

* In one typical regimental history it is mentioned that, in order to march fast, the field kitchens had been left behind, and that there was no issue of bread for four days. The troops had to forage for what could be found in a country exhausted of supplies. And it is not surprising that on reaching the Marne the men were dead-beat, when a man went forty-eight hours on 'one piece of bread—one cup of soup—one cup of coffee—unripe fruit and a raw turnip'.

constrained to draw off first one part and then the remaining part of his army to support his threatened flank guard. Thereby a thirty-mile gap was created between Kluck's and Bülow's armies, a gap covered only by a screen of cavalry. Kluck was emboldened to take the risk because of the rapid retreat of the British opposite, and still with their backs to, this gaping sector. Even on the 5th, when the French on either flank were turning about, the British continued a further day's march to the south. But in this 'disappearance' lay the unintentional cause of victory. For when the British retraced their steps, it was the report of their columns advancing into the gap which, on September 9th, led Bülow to order the retreat of his army. The superficial advantage which Kluck's First Army, already isolated by its own act, had gained over Maunoury was thereby nullified, and it fell back the same day. By the 11th the retreat had extended, independently or under orders from Moltke, to all the German armies.

The attempt at a partial envelopment, pivoting on Verdun, had already failed, the jaw formed by the Sixth and Seventh Armies merely breaking its teeth on the defences of the French eastern frontier. The attack by Rupprecht's Sixth Army on the Grand Couronné, covering Nancy, was a particularly costly failure. It is difficult to see how the German Command could have reasonably pinned their faith on achieving as an improvised expedient the very task which, in cool calculation before the war, had appeared so hopeless as to lead them to take the momentous decision to advance through Belgium as the only feasible alternative.

Thus, in sum, the battle of the Marne was decided by a jar and a crack. The jar administered by Maunoury's attack on the German right flank causing a crack in a weak joint of the German line, and the penetration of this physical crack in turn producing a moral crack in the German Command.

The result was a strategic but not a tactical defeat and the German right wing was able to reknit and stand firmly on the line of the Aisne. That the Allies were not able to draw greater advantage from their victory was due in part to the

comparative weakness of Maunoury's flank attack, and in
part to the failure of the British and the French Fifth Army
(now under Franchet d'Esperey) to drive rapidly through the
gap while it was open. Their direction of advance was across
a region intersected by frequent rivers and this handicap was
intensified by a want of impulsion on the part of their chiefs
—each politely looking to his neighbour and, timorously, to
his own flanks. Their feelings can best be described by the
apt verse:

> 'Lord Chatham with his sword undrawn
> Kept waiting for Sir Richard Strachan:
> Sir Richard, longing to be at 'em,
> Kept waiting too—for whom? Lord Chatham.'

It seems, too, that greater results might have come if more
effort had been made, as Galliéni urged, to strike at the German rear flank instead of the front, and to direct reinforcements to the north-west of Paris for this purpose. This view
is strengthened by the sensitiveness shown by the German
Command to reports of landings on the Belgian coast, which
might threaten their communications. The alarm caused by
these reports had even led the German Command to contemplate a withdrawal of their right wing before the battle of the
Marne was launched. When the moral effect of these phantom forces is weighed with the material effect—the detention
of German forces in Belgium—caused by fears of a Belgian
sortie from Antwerp, the balance of judgment would seem to
turn heavily in favour of the alternative which French had
tentatively suggested. By it the British Expeditionary Force
might have had not merely an indirect but a direct influence
on the struggle, and might have made the issue not merely
negatively but positively decisive.

But, considering the battle of the Marne as it shaped, the
fact that twenty-seven Allied divisions were pitted against
thirteen German divisions on the decisive flank is evidence,
first, of how completely Moltke had lapsed from Schlieffen's
intention; second, of how well Joffre had reshuffled his forces

under severe pressure; third, of how such a large balance afforded scope for a wider envelopment than was actually attempted.

The frontal pursuit was checked on the Aisne before Joffre, on September 17th, seeing that Maunoury's attempts to overlap the German flank were ineffectual, decided to form a fresh army under de Castelnau for a manœuvre *round and behind* the German flank. By then the German armies had recovered cohesion, and the German Command was expecting and ready to meet such a manœuvre, now the obvious course. The Allied chiefs, however, if cautious in action were incautious in speculation. Critics may complain that they were not sufficiently ingenious, but they were certainly ingenuous. Wilson and Berthelot, the guiding brains of French and Joffre, were discussing on September 12th the probable date when they would cross the German frontier. Wilson modestly estimated it at four weeks hence; Berthelot thought that he was pessimistic and reckoned on reaching the frontier a week earlier.

Flux and Stagnation. Unhappily for their calculations, on the Aisne was re-emphasized the preponderant power of defence over attack, primitive as were the trench lines compared with those of later years. Then followed, as the only alternative, the successive attempts of either side to overlap and envelop the other's western flank, a phase known popularly, but inaccurately, as the 'race to the sea'. This common design brought out what was to be a new and dominating strategical feature—the lateral switching of reserves by railway from one part of the front to another. Before it could reach its logical and lateral conclusion, a new factor intervened. Antwerp, with the Belgian Field Army, was still a thorn in the German side, and Falkenhayn, who had succeeded Moltke on September 14th, determined to reduce it while a German cavalry force swept across to the Belgian coast as an extension of the enveloping wing in France. One of the most amazing features, and blunders, of the war on the German side is that while the Allied armies were in full retreat, Moltke had made no attempt to secure the Channel ports, which lay at his mercy. The British had evacuated Calais, Boulogne and the whole coast as far as Havre; even transferred their base to St. Nazaire on the Bay of Biscay, a step which not only revealed the measure of their pessimism but delayed the arrival of the reinforcing 6th Division until the German front had hardened on the Aisne. And, during the Allied retreat, German Uhlans had roamed at will over the north-west of France, settled down in Amiens as if they were permanent lodgers, yet left the essential ports in tranquil isolation. The Supreme Command was so mesmerized by its Clausewitzian dogma—'We have only one means in war: the battle'—that it could see no purpose in securing the spoils before it had won the 'decisive battle'. A month later the Germans were to sacrifice tens of thousands of their men in the abortive effort to gain what they could have secured initially without cost.

We must pause here to pick up the thread of operations in Belgium from the moment when the Belgian Field Army fell back to Antwerp, divergently from the main line of operations. On August 24th the Belgians began a sortie against the rear of the German right wing to ease the pressure on the British and French left wing, then engaged in the opening battle at Mons and along the Sambre. The sortie was broken off on the 25th when news came of the Franco-British retreat into France, but the pressure of the Belgian Army (six divisions) led the Germans to detach four reserve divisions, besides three Landwehr brigades, to hold it in check. On September 7th the Belgian Command learnt that the Germans were despatching part of this force to the front in France; in consequence King Albert launched a fresh sortie on September 9th—the crucial day of the battle on the Marne. The action was taken unsolicited by Joffre, who seems to have shown curiously little interest in possibilities outside his immediate battle zone. The sortie led the Germans to cancel the despatch of one division and to delay that of two others to France, but the Belgians were soon thrown back. Nevertheless the news of it seems to have had a distinct moral effect on the German Command, coinciding as it did with the initiation of the retreat of their First and Second Armies from the Marne. And the unpleasant reminder that Antwerp lay menacingly close to their communications induced the Germans to undertake, preliminary to any fresh attempt at a decisive battle, the reduction of the fortress and the seizure of potential English landing places along the Belgian coast.

The menace to Britain, if the Channel ports fell into German hands, was obvious. It is a strange reflection that, inverting the German mistake, the British command should hitherto have neglected to guard against the danger, although the First Lord of the Admiralty, Winston Churchill, had urged the necessity even before the battle of the Marne. When the German guns began the bombardment of Antwerp on September 28th England awakened, and gave belated recognition to Churchill's strategic insight. He was allowed to send a brigade of marines and two newly formed brigades of naval volunteers to reinforce the defenders, while the Regular 7th Division and 3rd Cavalry Division, under Rawlinson, were landed at Ostend and Zeebrugge for an overland move to raise the siege. Eleven Territorial divisions were available in England, but, in contrast to the German attitude, Kitchener considered them still unfitted for an active rôle. The meagre reinforcement delayed, but could not prevent, the capitulation of Antwerp, October 10th, and Rawlinson's relieving force was too late to do more than cover the escape of the Belgian Field Army down the Flanders coast.

Yet, viewed in the perspective of history, this first and last effort in the west to make use of Britain's amphibious power applied a brake to the German advance down the coast which just stopped their second attempt to gain a decision in the west. It gained time for the arrival of the main British force, transferred from the Aisne to the new left of the Allied line, and if their heroic defence at Ypres, aided by the French and Belgians along the Yser to the sea, was the human barrier to the Germans, it succeeded by so narrow a margin that the Antwerp expedition must be adjudged the saving factor.

How had the main battleground come to be shifted from France to Flanders? The month following the battle of the Marne had been marked by an extremely obvious series of attempts by each side to turn the opponent's western flank. On the German side this pursuit of an opening was soon replaced by a subtler plan, but the French persevered with a straightforward obstinacy curiously akin to that of their original plan. By September 24th, de Castlenau's outflanking attempt had come to a stop on the Somme. Next, a newly formed Tenth Army, under de Maudhuy, tried a little further north, beginning on October 2nd, but instead of being able to pass round the German flank soon found itself struggling desperately to hold Arras. The British Expeditionary Force was then in course of transfer northwards from the Aisne, in order to shorten its communications with England, and Joffre determined to use it as part of a third effort to turn the German flank. To co-ordinate this new manœuvre he appointed General Foch as his deputy in the north.

Foch continued Joffre's efforts to induce the Belgians to join this wheeling mass, but King Albert with more caution, or more realism, declined to abandon the coastal district for an advance inland that he considered rash. It was. For on October 14th, four days after the fall of Antwerp, Falkenhayn planned a strategic trap for the next Allied outflanking manœuvre which he foresaw would follow. One army, composed of troops transferred from Lorraine, was to hold the expected Allied offensive in check while another, composed of troops released by the fall of Antwerp and of four newly raised corps, was to sweep down the Belgian coast and crush in the flank of the attacking Allies. He even held back the troops pursuing the Belgians in order not to alarm the Allied Command prematurely.

Meanwhile the new Allied advance was developing piecemeal, as corps detrained from the south and swung eastwards to form a progressively extended 'scythe'. The British Expeditionary Force, now three corps* strong, deployed in turn

* At this time a corps consisted of two divisions, although later of three or even four divisions.

between La Bassée and Ypres—where it effected a junction with Rawlinson's force. Beyond it the embryo of a new French Eighth Army was taking shape, and the Belgian continued the line along the Yser to the sea. Although the British right and centre corps had already been held up, Sir John French, discounting even the underestimate of the German strength furnished by his Intelligence, ordered his left corps (Haig) to begin the offensive from Ypres towards Bruges. The effort was still-born, for it coincided with the opening of the German offensive, on October 20th, but for a day or two Sir John French persisted in the belief that he was attacking while his troops were barely holding their ground.* When enlightenment came he swung to the other extreme and anxiously urged the construction of a huge entrenched camp near Boulogne 'to take the whole Expeditionary Force'. But his recurrent desire to retreat was overborne by the greater will-power, and perhaps the more consistent self-delusion of Foch, who by flattering deference, as well as forceful personality, had now gained a strong influence over French. And French's regard was increased when Foch let him know privately that Kitchener had proposed—in imagined privacy—

* One cause of French's susceptibility to delusions is suggested in General Gough's record of a conversation with him shortly after the battle—when further experience should have opened his eyes—'he thought the war would be over in three months, and that Germany could not bear the strain longer. . . . This seems to show that with French the wish is father to the thought, and that the thought is not the child of the careful consideration of the facts, however unpleasant, as it should be in all great men. It seems to me also to show, to some extent, his failing energy. He does not want to do any more, he does not want to be called on to make further exertions of either intellect or will-power. He hopes it is going to be ended by Russia while we remain passive here. And so his hopes become his thoughts'. Another cause lay in his physical unfitness. French, who was sixty-two, had just suffered from a severe heart attack, and was under doctor's orders to go carefully. Murray, his chief of staff, had collapsed on the critical day of Le Cateau early in the retreat from Mons. Grierson, the original commander of the II Corps, had died suddenly on the way out to France. Such facts suggest the dangers of a system of promotion which brought men to the top at a comparatively advanced age.

to replace him by Sir Ian Hamilton. Too often in this war did the leaders fight each other while the troops fought the foe.

The failure of the higher commanders to grasp the situation left the real handling of the battle to Haig and his divisional commanders. And they for want of reserves could do little more than cement the crumbling parts of the front, by scraping reserves from other parts, and encourage the exhausted but indomitable troops to hold on. Thus Ypres was essentially, like Inkerman, a 'soldiers' battle'. Already, since the 18th, the Belgians on the Yser had suffered growing pressure which threatened a disaster that was ultimately averted, by the end of the month, through the opening of the sluices and the flooding of the coastal area. At Ypres the crisis came later and was repeated, October 31st and November 11th marking the turning points of the struggle. That the Allied line, though battered and terribly strained, was in the end unbroken was due to the dogged resistance of the British and the timely arrival of French reinforcements.

This defence of Ypres is in a dual sense the supreme memorial to the British Regular Army, for here its officers and men showed the inestimable value of the disciplined morale and unique standard of musketry which were the fruit of long training, and here was their tombstone. 'From failing hands they threw the torch' to the 'New Armies' rising in England to the call of country. With the Continental Powers the merging of normal into national armies was the natural product of their system of universal service. But with Britain it was revolution, not evolution. With a supreme flash of vision Kitchener had grasped, in contrast to Governments and General Staffs alike, the probable duration of the struggle. More questionably, he decided that it meant the abandonment of Britain's traditional strategy of semi-detachment, and, donning the continental habit of thought, took the view that Britain could only exercise a decisive influence through the creation of mass armies. The people of Britain responded to his call to arms, and poured into the recruiting stations.

By the end of the year nearly 1,000,000 men had enlisted, and the British Empire had altogether some 2,000,000 under arms.

Having decided on this vast expansion, Kitchener chose to build a new framework rather than to use the existing Territorial foundation. It is fair to point out that the Territorial Force was enlisted for home defence and that, initially, its members' acceptance of a wider rôle was voluntary. But the duplication of forces and of organization was undoubtedly a source of delay and waste of effort. Kitchener has also been reproached for his reluctance to replace the voluntary system by conscription, but this criticism overlooks how deeply rooted was the voluntary system in British institutions, and the slowness with which lasting changes can be effected in them. If Kitchener's method was characteristic of the man, it was characteristic of England. If it was unmethodical, it was calculated to impress most vividly on the British people the gulf between their 'gladiatorial' wars of the past and the national war to which they were committed. It took even longer to impress the British military mind, as represented by General Headquarters in France. Henry Wilson wrote that Kitchener's 'ridiculous and preposterous army of twenty-five corps is the laughing stock of every soldier in Europe . . . under no circumstances could these mobs take the field for two years. Then what is the use of them?' For by his calculation the British Army was almost due to arrive in Berlin.

While a psychological landmark, the battle of Ypres is also a military landmark. For, with the repulse of the German attempt to break through, the trench barrier was consolidated from the Swiss frontier to the sea. The power of modern defence had triumphed over attack, and stalemate ensued. The military history of the Franco-British Alliance during the next four years is a story of the attempts to upset this deadlock, either by forcing the barrier or by haphazardly finding a way round.

On the Eastern Front, however, the greater distances and the greater differences between the equipment of the armies

Line at outset of German Offensive, May 1915
Line at outset of 2nd. Phase, July, 1915
Line at close of main offensive, early in
Sept. 1915 (before Ludendorf's Vilna manoeuvre)
Direction of main German thrusts
Railways

Miles
0   50   100

RUSSIA

Minsk

Lake Narocz

R. Dvina

Dvinsk

Riga

Gulf of
Riga

Vilna

Kovno

R. Niemen

Bialystock

Libau

R. Niemen

Gumbinnen

Augustova

MASURIAN LAKES

Königsberg

EAST
PRUSSIA

Lautern

Allenstein

Hohenstein

Tannenberg

Marienburg

R. Vistula

R. Narew

R. Bug

Warsaw

R. Bzura

R. Bzura

Pinsk

Danzig

Baltic Sea

Thorn

Posen

N

R. Dniester

R. Prut

R. Siret

RUMANIA

R. Stokhod

Tarnopol

R. Strypa

BUKOVINA

Luck

Brody

Czernowitz

Kovel

R. Dniester

Stanislau

R. Bug

Lemberg

GALICIA

Lublin

Przemysl

Jaroslav

R. San

EASTERN FRONT

R. Vistula

R.

Wisloka

R. Nida

Tarnow

Gorlice

R. Dunajec

Cracow

R. Wesel

CARPATHIANS

SILESIA

AUSTRIA-
HUNGARY

Breslau

Budapest

POLAND

© Cassell & Co. Ltd. 1970

ensured a fluidity which was lacking in the West. Trench lines might form, but they were no more than a hard crust covering a liquid expanse. To break the crust was not difficult, and, once it was broken, mobile operations of the old style became possible. This freedom of action was denied to the Western Powers, but Germany, because of her central position, had an alternative choice, and from November, 1914, onwards, Falkenhayn adopted, although for his own part unwillingly, a defensive in France while seeking to cripple the power of Russia.

The Russian Front. The opening encounters in the East had been marked by rapid changes of fortune rather than by any decisive advantage. The Austrian Command had detached part of their strength in an abortive attempt to crush Serbia. And their plan for an initial offensive to cut off the Polish 'tongue' was further crippled by the fact that the German part of the pincers did not operate. It was indeed being menaced by a Russian pair of pincers instead, for the Russian Commander-in-Chief, the Grand Duke Nicholas, had urged his First and Second Armies to invade East Prussia without waiting to complete their concentration, in order to ease the pressure on his French Allies. As the Russians had more than a two-to-one superiority, a combined attack had every chance of crushing the Germans between the two armies. On August 17th, Rennenkampf's First Army (six and a half divisions and five cavalry divisions) crossed the East Prussian frontier, and on August 19th–20th met and threw back the bulk (seven divisions and one cavalry division) of Prittwitz's Eighth Army at Gumbinnen. On August 21st Prittwitz heard that the Russian Second Army (ten divisions and three cavalry divisions) under Samsonov had crossed the southern frontier of East Prussia, in his rear, which was guarded by only three divisions. In panic Prittwitz momentarily spoke on the telephone of falling back behind the Vistula, whereupon Moltke superseded him by a retired general, Hindenburg, to whom was appointed, as Chief of Staff, Ludendorff, the hero of the Liége attack.

Developing a plan which, with the necessary movements, had been already initiated by Colonel Hoffmann of the Eighth Army Staff, Ludendorff concentrated some six divisions against Samsonov's left wing. This force, inferior in strength to the Russians, could not have been decisive, but finding that Rennenkampf was still near Gumbinnen, Ludendorff took the calculated risk of withdrawing the rest of the German troops, except the cavalry screen, from that front, and bringing them back against Samsonov's right wing. This daring move was aided by the folly of the Russian commanders in sending out unciphered wireless orders, to which the Germans listened in.

Under the converging pressure Samsonov's flanks collapsed, his centre was surrounded, and his army almost destroyed. If the opportunity was presented rather than created, this brief campaign and its sequel, afterwards christened the battle of Tannenberg, is a significant example of the use of what are technically called 'interior lines'—more simply, a central position.

Then, receiving his two fresh army corps from the French front, the German Commander turned on the slow advancing Rennenkampf, and drove him out of East Prussia. As a result of these battles Russia had lost a quarter of a million men and, what she could afford still less, much war material. But the invasion of East Prussia had at least, by causing the despatch of two corps from the West, helped to make possible the French recovery on the Marne. And, with peculiar irony, these corps had arrived too late to be of service at Tannenberg.

But the effect of Tannenberg was diminished because, away on the southern front, in Galicia, the scales had tilted against the Central Powers. The offensive of the Austrian First and Fourth Armies into Poland had at first made progress, but this was nullified by the onslaught of the Russian Third and Eighth Armies upon the weaker Second and Third Armies which were guarding the Austrian right flank. These armies were heavily defeated (August 26th–30th), and driven back through Lemberg. The advance of the Russian left wing thus threatened the rear of the victorious Austrian left wing. Conrad tried to swing part of his left round, in turn, against the Russian flank, but this blow was parried. And then, caught, with his forces disorganized, by the renewed advance of the Russian right wing, he was forced on September 11th to extricate himself by a general retreat, falling back almost to Cracow by the end of September. Austria's plight compelled the Germans to send aid, and the bulk of the force in East Prussia was formed into a new Ninth Army and switched south to the south-west corner of Poland, whence it advanced on Warsaw in combination with a renewed Austrian offensive. But the Russians were now approaching the full tide of their mobilized strength; regrouping their forces and counter-attacking, they drove back the advance and followed it up by a powerful effort to invade Silesia.

The Grand Duke Nicholas formed a huge phalanx of seven armies—three in the van and two protecting either flank. A further army, the Tenth, had invaded the eastern corner of East Prussia and was engaging the weak German forces there. Allied hopes rose high as the much-heralded Russian 'steam-roller', of sixty massed divisions, began its ponderous advance. To counter it the German eastern front was placed under Hindenburg, for whom Ludendorff and Hoffmann devised a masterstroke, based on the system of lateral railways inside the German frontier, and also on a means of knowledge which to a large extent dispersed the fog of war on their side. For the continued interception of the wireless messages sent out by the Russian General Staff gave the German leaders 'a clear picture of how the enemy viewed the situation and what he intended to do'. Superior knowledge proved a compensation for inferior strength, as well as an invaluable insurance on behalf of audacity.

The Ninth Army, retreating before the advancing Russians, slowed them down by a systematic destruction of the scanty communications in Poland. On reaching its own frontier unpressed, it was first switched northwards to the Posen-Thorn area, and then thrust south-east, on November 11th—

with its left flank on the Vistula—against the joint between the two armies guarding the Russian right flank.

The wedge, driven in by Ludendorff's mallet, sundered the two armies, forced the First back on Warsaw and almost effected another Tannenberg against the Second, which was nearly surrounded at Lodz, when the Fifth Army from the van turned back to its rescue. As a result, part of the German enveloping force almost suffered the fate planned for the Russians, but managed to cut its way through to the main body. If the Germans were baulked of decisive tactical success this manœuvre had been a classic example of how a relatively small force, by using its mobility to strike at a vital point, can paralyse the advance of an enemy several times its strength. The Russian 'steamroller' was thrown out of gear, and never again did it threaten German soil.

Within a week, four new German army corps arrived from the Western front, where the Ypres attack had now ended in failure, and although too late to clinch the missed chance of a decisive victory, Ludendorff was able to use them in pressing the Russians back by December 15th to the Bzura-Ravka river line in front of Warsaw. This setback and the drying up of his munition supplies decided the Grand Duke Nicholas to break off the seesaw fighting still in progress near Cracow, and fall back on winter trench lines along the Nida and Dunajec rivers, leaving the end of the Polish 'tongue' in the hands of the enemy. Thus, on the east as on the west, the trench stalemate had settled in, but the crust was less firm, and the Russians had drained their stock of munitions to an extent that their poorly industrialized country could not make good.

The Grip on the Seas. We deal thirdly with the operations at sea, which actually occurred first in chronological order. The reason is that sea power only came to exert a dominant, eventually the dominant, influence on the war after the initial plans on land had miscarried. If the quick decision expected by the military leaders had been reached, it is questionable whether sea power could have affected the issue. How narrowly Germany missed decisive victory, and by what a combination of hardly conceivable blunders, is in the light of history now clear. While it is possible that Britain could, and would, have carried on the war unaided, we need to remember that in August, 1914, the condition was still that of a professional war with popular backing rather than a truly national war; that British intervention was still regarded as a chivalrous effort to succour violated Belgium and challenged France rather than as a life and death struggle for Britain's existence. And when a friend lies prone in a tiger's claws it is mistaken friendship to engage in a tug-of-war for the fragments if there is any chance of enticing the tiger from his prey.

But fortunately, in 1914, the tiger was held at bay and, with this breathing space gained, Britain had the opportunity to exert her traditional weapon—sea power. Its effect on the war was akin not to a lightning flash, striking down an opponent suddenly, but to a steady radiation of heat, invigorating to those it was used in aid of, and drying up the resources of the enemy.

But if its effect was extended and cumulative, its application was instantaneous, comparable almost to turning on an electric switch. This simple act, yet perhaps the most decisive of the war, took place before the actual outbreak—on July 29th when at seven o'clock in the morning that greater Armada, the British Grand Fleet, sailed from Portland for its war station at Scapa Flow. Few eyes saw its passage, fewer minds knew its destination in those northerly Orkney Isles controlling the passage between North Britain and Norway, but from that moment Germany's arteries were subjected to an invisible pressure which never relaxed until on November 21st, 1918, the German Fleet arrived in those same northern waters to hand itself into the custody of a force of whom it had seen no more than a few fleeting glimpses during four and a half years of intangible struggle.

The fundamental cause of this unprecedented type of conflict lay in the recent development of new weapons, the mine and the submarine, which reproduced in naval warfare that s me predominance of defensive over offensive power which was the key factor on land. The immediate cause, however, was the strategy adopted by Germany's Naval Command, partly through a miscalculation of Britain's probable strategy. Appreciating their own inferiority to the British Fleet as well as the impossibility of a surprise blow in face of its preparedness, and believing that their enemy was obsessed with the Nelsonian tradition of seeking battle, the German Command adopted a Fabian strategy. They aimed to refuse conflict until their minelayers and submarines had weakened the strength of the British Navy, until the strain of a close blockade had begun to tell on the superior fleet, and perhaps provided the chance of a surprise stroke, and until the conquest of Britain's Allies on land had made her position more difficult.

The plan had at least a sound geographical basis, for the nature and configuration of the German coast lent itself to this strategy. The short North Sea coastline was heavily indented, the estuaries a maze of difficult channels, and screened by a fringe of islands—of which Heligoland formed a strongly fortified shield to the naval bases at Wilhelmshaven, Bremerhaven and Cuxhaven. Best of all, from the estuary of the Elbe there was a back door into the Baltic Sea, the Kiel Canal. By this the naval forces in the Baltic could be rapidly reinforced, while an enemy advance into that land-locked sea was not only hampered by the neutral possession of its approaches but could be imperilled by submarine and destroyer attack while passing through the narrow channels between the Danish islands. The natural defensive power of Germany's sea frontiers made attack almost impossible, and conversely gave her an excellent base for raiding operations —save for the geographical handicap that the coastline of Great Britain, like a vast breakwater, narrowed the exit for operations on the outer seas.

The one obvious defect of this Fabian strategy was that it involved the immediate abandonment of Germany's foreign trade and reduced the possibility of her interference with the sea-borne supplies of Britain and her Allies. Moreover, the

German plan of progressive attrition was vitiated by the strategy adopted by the British Admiralty, which abandoned the direct doctrine of seeking out the enemy for the indirect doctrine of 'the fleet in being'. Realizing how the mine and submarine, combined with Germany's natural advantages, had made a close blockade hazardous, the Admiralty adopted a strategy of distant surveillance, keeping the battle fleet in a position which commanded the North Sea and in instant readiness for action if the enemy appeared, and using the light craft for closer, but not close observation. This strategy was not as passive as it seemed to a critical public, eagerly expecting a new Trafalgar. It appreciated that Britain's general command of the sea was the pivot of the Allied cause, and that to hazard it by exposure to uncompensated losses was the negation of this supreme requirement. Therefore, while desiring battle and being ready for it, the Admiralty quietly set about its primary duties of maintaining the security of the ocean routes, dealing with the sporadic threats to those routes, and, thirdly, ensuring the safe passage to France of the British Expeditionary Force.

The idea of economic pressure exercised by sea power was still in embryo. Not until a later phase did it crystallize into a formal doctrine, and the term 'blockade' assume a new and wider definition. The attack on sea-borne commerce was deep rooted in the traditions of the British Navy, and thus the transition to an indirect attack on the life of the enemy nation —her supplies of food and raw material—was an almost imperceptible progress. When this pressure was exercised against herself in a novel form and by a new weapon—the submarine —it was human, if illogical, that she should decry it as an atrocity. It was not easy for a conservative mind to realize that with the transition from a war of government policies into a war of peoples, intoxicated with Clausewitzian catch-phrases about a 'fight to the finish', the indefinite code of military chivalry must be submerged by the primitive instincts let loose. But in 1914 this 'absolute' war was still only a theory, and had little influence on the opening operations.

The history of the naval struggle must be dated from July 26th, 1914, when the Admiralty, in view of the clouded international situation, sent orders to the fleet assembled for review at Portland not to disperse. If the review was a happy chance the use made of it was one of the decisive acts and wisest judgments of the war, for while free from any of the provocation of an army mobilization, it placed Britain in automatic control of the situation at sea. It was followed, on July 29th, by the unnoticed sailing of the fleet for its war stations in the North Sea, and warning telegrams to all squadrons abroad. To students of war and politics the lesson should not be lost for, whatever its other limitations, a professional force has this power of unprovocative readiness which a national force inevitably lacks. 'Mobilization' is a threat, creating an atmosphere in which peaceful argument withers and dies. Between negotiations and mobilization there is a gulf, between mobilization and war an imperceptible seam, and the act of any irresponsible man can draw a nation across it.

Admiral Jellicoe, the new commander of the Grand Fleet, had one initial weakness to contend with; his base at Scapa was without defences against torpedo attack, and the fortified base being prepared at Rosyth was still incomplete. The historic concentration of British sea power had been on the Channel coast, where lay the best-prepared and defended harbours, and the Government had been slow to provide funds for bases on the North Sea to accompany the change in the concentration areas.

The danger compelled him to take his fleet west of the Orkneys, although it came down as far as the Forth during the transport to France of the Expeditionary Force—which was directly protected by the older battleships of the Channel Fleet, and by a layered system of patrols in the southern waters of the North Sea. The safe passage of the Expeditionary Force was the first direct achievement of the Navy. The next followed on August 29th when Beatty's battle-cruiser squadron and Tyrwhitt's destroyer flotillas made a swoop into the Bight of Heligoland, sank several German light cruisers, and achieved the much greater indirect effect of confirming the Germans in their strictly defensive strategy—not an unmixed blessing, for it led them to concentrate on the development of submarine attack. Apart from this engagement the story of 1914 in the North Sea is a record of unceasing vigilance on the one side; of minor submarine and minelaying successes and losses, on the other.

The war in the Mediterranean opened with a mistake that was to have far-reaching political consequences. Two of Germany's fastest ships were there, the battle cruiser *Goeben* and the light cruiser *Breslau*, and received orders from Berlin to steer for Constantinople. They evaded the British efforts made to cut them off, partly owing to inelasticity in applying the Admiralty instructions.

On the high seas the chase was more prolonged. Germany had not been allowed time to send out commerce-destroyers from home waters, but for some months her few cruisers on foreign service were a thorn in the side of the British Navy. It was not easy to reconcile the needs of the North Sea concentration with the duty of patrolling and protecting the tremendous length of sea routes along which supplies as well as troops were flowing from India and the Dominions to the support of the Mother Country. By the destruction of the *Emden* on November 9th, the Indian Ocean was finally cleared, but this success was offset by disaster in the Pacific, where Admiral Cradock's cruiser squadron was crushed by the heavier metal of Admiral von Spee's armoured cruisers, *Scharnhorst* and *Gneisenau*. This setback was, however, promptly redeemed by the Admiralty, who despatched Admiral Sturdee with two battle cruisers, *Inflexible* and *Invincible*, on a lightning dash to the south Atlantic, while another battle cruiser, *Australia*, swept down from Fiji on Admiral von Spee's rear. Trapped on December 8th at the Falkland Isles, by this finely conceived surprise, Spee was sunk, and with him the last instrument of German naval power upon the oceans.

From this time onwards, the ocean communications of

Britain and her Allies were secured for trade, for supplies and for the conveyance of troops. But as to all ocean routes there must be a land terminus, the development of the submarine made this security gradually less effective than it seemed on the morrow of Sturdee's victory.

The nature of the war at sea began to undergo definite changes early in 1915. During the first phase Britain had been too busy in clearing the seas and maintaining the security of the sea routes to devote much attention to the use of her sea command as an economic weapon against Germany. In any case her naval power was fettered by the artificial restrictions on blockade embodied in the Declaration of London of 1909, which the British Government with singular blindness announced on the outbreak of war that it would accept as the basis of maritime practice. Their release from these self-imposed fetters was aided by Germany's action.

On November 2nd, 1914, a German battle-cruiser squadron made a raid on the Norfolk coast, as a reconnaissance to test the scope of Britain's naval defence. Another followed on December 16th against the Yorkshire coast, Scarborough, Whitby and the Hartlepools being bombarded. Each time the Germans slipped away safely, but when they attempted a third, on January 24th, the English battle-cruiser squadron, under Beatty, trapped them off the Dogger Bank, sank the *Blücher* and badly damaged the *Derrfflinger* and *Seydlitz*. Although the stroke missed full success, it convinced the Germans of the futility of their attrition strategy, and Ingenohl, the Commander of their High Seas Fleet, was replaced by Pohl, who proposed to Falkenhayn an offensive submarine campaign, which for success must be unlimited.

As a result, on February 18th, Germany proclaimed the waters round the British Isles a war zone where all ships, enemy or neutral, would be sunk at sight. This gave Britain a lever to loosen the Declaration of London, and she replied by claiming the right to intercept all ships suspected of carrying goods to Germany, and bring them into British ports for search. This tightening of the blockade caused serious difficulties with neutrals, America especially, but Germany eased the friction by torpedoing the great liner *Lusitania*, May 7th, 1915. The drowning of 1100 people, including some Americans, was a spectacular brutality which shocked the conscience of the world, and appealed more forcibly to American opinion than even the desolation of Belgium. This act, succeeded by others, paved the way for the entry of the United States into the war, though it was to be later than seemed likely on the morrow of the tragedy.

One result of Britain's early established command of the sea was that it gave her the opportunity to sweep up Germany's oversea colonies with little hindrance or expenditure of force. Their seizure was valuable in that it gave the Allies important assets to bargain with in case of an unfavourable or negative issue to the war. At the end of August a New Zealand expedition captured Samoa, and in September an Australian expedition took possession of New Guinea; the Australian Navy also cleared several important German wireless stations in the Pacific Isles. Japan, entering the war on Britain's side, sent a division with a naval squadron, to besiege the German fortress of Tsing-tao on the coast of China. The first landing took place on September 2nd, and a tiny British contingent arrived on the 23rd, but the defences were modern, the land approach narrow, and the actual siege was not begun until October 31st. Seven days' bombardment was followed by an assault, which led to the capitulation of the garrison, after a rather feeble resistance.

In Africa, Togoland was occupied in August; the equatorial forest of the Cameroons was a sterner obstacle, and not until the beginning of 1916 were the German forces conquered by joint British and French forces after a prolonged but economically conducted campaign. General Botha, the South African Premier, once in arms against England, now for her, organized a force which conquered German South West Africa. Almost concurrently Botha rendered a still greater service to the British cause by putting down the rebellion of a section of disaffected Boers, which, save for the Irish rising of Easter,

1916, was the only revolt within the borders of the Empire during these four trying years.

Only German East Africa, the largest and richest of Germany's colonies, remained, and that, owing to the difficulties of the country and the skill of General von Lettow-Vorbeck, the German Commander, was not to be completely subdued until the end of 1917. An Expeditionary Force was sent thither in November to support the local British East African forces, and was repulsed at Tanga. To compensate his lack of troops, the German commander, Lettow-Vorbeck, found allies in the local bees, and his skilful tactics produced panic among the Indian battalions. Not until late in 1915 could the British Government, occupied with greater problems, spare either the time or the force to deal with this hornet's nest.

The year 1915 witnessed the dawn of another new form of war which helped to drive home the new reality that the war of armies had become the war of peoples. From January onwards, Zeppelin raids began on the English coast and reached their peak in the late summer of 1916, to be succeeded by aeroplane raids. The difficulty of distinguishing from the air between military and civil objectives smoothed the path for a development which, beginning with excuses, ended in a frank avowal that in a war for existence the will of the enemy nation, not merely the bodies of their soldiers, is the inevitable target. Although the Zeppelin raids in 1915 and 1916, through misdirection, did little material damage and caused less than two thousand casualties, it has been estimated that, by their disorganizing effect, about 'one sixth of the total normal output of munitions was entirely lost'.

The first psychological symptom of the World War, as it seemed to many, was an immeasurable sigh of relief. Had the peoples of Europe sat on the safety-valve too long? The war-weary mind of to-day cannot reconstruct the tension and anxiety, the strain and stress of hope and fear of the long years of the peace that was no peace and yet was not war. It may be read as a revolt of the spirit against the monotony and triviality of the everyday round, the completion of a psychological cycle when the memories of past wars have faded, and paved the way for the emergence and revival of the primordial 'hunting' instinct in man.

This first phase of enthusiasm was succeeded by one of passion, the natural ferocity of war accentuated by a form of mob spirit which is developed by a 'nation in arms'. The British Army was relatively immune because of its professional character, whereas in the German Army, the most essentially 'citizen', it gained scope because of the cold-blooded logic of the general staff theory of war. With the coming of the autumn a third phase became manifest, more particularly among the combatants. This was a momentary growth of a spirit of tolerance, symbolized by the fraternization which took place on Christmas Day, but this in turn was to wane as the strain of the war became felt and the reality of the struggle for existence came home to the warring sides.

CHAPTER IV

SCENE I

THE BATTLE THAT WAS NOT, YET TURNED THE TIDE—THE MARNE

No battle has caused more controversy, produced so large a literature in so short a time, or given rise to more popular interest and legend than that of the Marne. But then this crisis of September, 1914, wrought the downfall of the German war plan and thereby changed the course of history. For if it be true, as it certainly is in part, that Germany lost the war when she lost this battle, it is natural that claimants to the distinction of having won it should be many.

The first legend to arise was that Foch had won it by driving the German centre into the marshes of St. Gond, and even to-day, in total disregard of the facts and times of the battle, this is still given currency by reputable historians outside France.

But while, like a pebble dropped in water, the ripples of this story were still spreading, knowledgeable opinion in France was violently arguing whether the credit was due to Joffre, the Commander-in-Chief, or Galliéni, his quondam superior and then subordinate, who had delivered from Paris the blow at the German flank, exposed by Kluck's wheel inwards before Paris. One school contended that Joffre had conceived the idea of the counter-offensive, and at most admitted under pressure of facts that Galliéni's initiative in seeing the opportunity had given an impulse to Joffre's decision to seize it. The other school argued that Joffre, after the failure of his first attempt to stage a counter-offensive on the line of the Somme, had given up all idea of a fresh attempt at an early date, and that but for Galliéni's fiery determination and persuasion the retreat would have continued. A dispassionate judgment is now possible, and if we recognize that on Joffre fell the grave responsibility of taking the decision, the weight

THE MARNE, 1914

Allied Armies
German Armies

5th Sept. ▬▬▬   ▭▭▭
9th Sept. ▬ ▬ ▬   ▫▫▫▫

Miles
0   10   20   30   40   50

N

Amiens

Le Câteau

Péronne

R. Oise

Senlis

R. Aisne

Soissons

R. Ourcq

I ARMY (Kluck)

FR. 6th. ARMY

PARIS

Lagny

B.E.F.

Gd. Morin

Pt. Morin

Mélun

R. Seine

Reims

R. Marne

II ARMY (Bülow)

III ARMY

MARSHES OF ST. GONDE

FR. 9th. ARMY

FR. 5th. ARMY

Châlons-sur-Marne

IV ARMY

V ARMY

FR. 3rd. ARMY

Verdun

R. Ornain

FR. 4th. ARMY

R. Marne

R. Aube

R. Seine

VI ARMY

GD. COURONNE DE NANCY

Nancy

Toul

FR. 2nd. ARMY

Morhange

Saarebourg

VII ARMY

GAP OF CHARMES

FR. 1st. ARMY

Epinal

© Cassell & Co. Ltd. 1970

of evidence shows that Galliéni's inspiration dictated both the site and promptness of the thrust. Furthermore, it rebuts the alternative case of Joffre's advocates that Galliéni marred the prospect by precipitating the blow, for we know that twenty-four hours' delay would have enabled the Germans to complete the protective redistribution which Galliéni interrupted.

On the German side a similar controversy has raged as to whether the order to retreat was a mistake, and whether Kluck of the First Army, Bülow of the Second, or the envoy of the Supreme Command, Colonel Hentsch, was responsible for the fatal decision.

The multiple controversy has at least served to show that the Marne was a psychological rather than a physical victory. So, also, have been most of the immortal victories of history, with the actual fighting a secondary influence. For the profoundest truth of war is that the issue of battles is usually decided in the minds of the opposing commanders, not in the bodies of their men. The best history would be a register of their thoughts and emotions, with a mere background of events to throw them into relief. But the delusion to the contrary has been fostered by the typical military history, filled with details of the fighting and assessing the cause of a victory by statistical computations of the number engaged.

The Marne was so clearly a psychological issue that the minds of the commanders have received due analysis. But even so, the 'combat complex' has tended to narrow the analysis of minds to the area where the clash of bodies took place. Thereby certain suggestive evidence has escaped comment. This evidence may be expressed in a startling question. Was the victory primarily due to the heated imagination of an English railway porter and to a party of temporary visitors to Ostend? Or, at the least, did these humble worthies constitute with Galliéni the mainspring of victory?

The suggestion is not so fantastic as it seems when we study the mental atmosphere of the German commanders. Before and during the crisis they were constantly looking backward apprehensively over their right shoulders, fearful of an Allied stroke against their ever-lengthening communications in Belgium and Northern France. Unfortunately for the Allies, there was small warrant for this nervousness. The belated plea for landing the B.E.F. on the Belgian coast had been overruled by the Wilsonian pledge and policy of tying it as an appendix to the French left wing. Yet the Belgian Field Army, if under German guard at Antwerp, had at least caused a serious detachment of German strength to this guard —and more, was a chronic irritation to German nerves.

The fertile brain of Mr. Churchill was also at work. Resources were scanty, but he despatched a brigade of marines under Brig.-General Aston to Ostend, with orders to give their presence the fullest publicity. They landed on August 27th, and stayed ashore until the 31st.

Now to turn to the 'other side of the hill'. On September 5th, the day when the French troops were moving forward to strike at Kluck, Colonel Hentsch, the representative of the Supreme Command, came to the threatened army with this ominous and despairing warning—'The news is bad. The VI and VII Armies are blocked. The IV and V are meeting with strong resistance. . . . The English are disembarking fresh troops continuously on the Belgian coast. There are reports of a Russian expeditionary force in the same parts. A withdrawal is becoming inevitable.' We know from other sources that the 3000 marines had grown in the German Command's imagination to 40,000, and that the Russians were said to be 80,000.

Thus the German flank army was left to face its ordeal with the belief that its rear was seriously menaced, and that in any case the Supreme Command was contemplating a withdrawal. At the least such knowledge must have been insidiously enervating during a period of strain. If the Supreme Command came to have doubts of the Belgian news, it also became imbued with the idea of a retirement, and when Hentsch came again on September 9th with full powers to coordinate it, 'should rearward movements have begun', not only had these begun, but they also coincided with fresh disturbing news from Belgium. For if the Belgian sortie from Antwerp that day was shortlived, it had all the incalculable psychological effect of menacing news at a moment of crisis. The German retreat gathered momentum and spread. With it turned the tide of the war.

History should do justice to Mr. Churchill's happy inspiration and General Aston's handful of 'Marine promenaders'. But equally helpful was that amazing 'Russian' myth which originated and spread so mysteriously. Mr. Churchill, we know, had actually proposed to bring a Russian expeditionary force in such a way. Did the proposal perhaps leak out and become exaggerated into realization in the process? General opinion, however, has long ascribed the legend to the heated imagination of a railway porter working on the simple fact of the night passage of troop trains with Gaelic-speaking occupants. If so, a statue in Whitehall 'to the Unknown Porter' is overdue.

Keeping this external factor on the circumference of our thought, let us turn to trace the sequence of events in the actual battle zone. The immediate chain of causation begins with the escape by retreat of the French and British armies from the frontier trap into which Joffre's plan had led them. The first, highly coloured, reports from the army commands in the battles of the frontiers had given the German Supreme Command the impression of a decisive victory. It was under this hallucination that Moltke, on August 25th, cheerfully and needlessly despatched four divisions to the Russian front—to the detriment of his right-wing punch, already weakened by seven divisions left for the investment of derelict fortresses—truly a bad investment. Then the comparatively small totals of prisoners raised doubts in Moltke's mind and led him to a more sober estimate of the situation. The Kaiser's easy optimism now irritated him—'He has already a shout-hurrah mood that I hate like death.' The new pessimism of Moltke combined with the renewed optimism of his army commanders to produce a fresh change of plan, which contained the seeds of disaster.

While Kluck's army, on the German extreme right or outer flank, was pressing on the heels of the British—so close that the 'outside' British corps (Smith-Dorrien) was forced to halt and give battle—Kluck's neighbour on the inside, Bülow, was following up Lanrezac's French Fifth Army. When on August 26th the British left wing fell back southwards badly mauled from Le Cateau, Kluck had turned south-westwards again. If this direction was partly due to misconception of the line of retreat taken by the British—the idea that they were retreating to the Channel ports—it was also in accordance with his original rôle of a wide circling sweep. And by carrying him into the Amiens-Péronne area, where the first parts of the newly formed French Sixth Army were just detraining after their 'switch' from Alsace, it had the effect of dislocating Joffre's design for an early return to the offensive—by compelling the Sixth Army to fall back hurriedly towards the shelter of the Paris defences.

But Kluck had hardly swung out to the south-west before he was induced to swing in again. For in order to ease the pressure on the British, Joffre had ordered Lanrezac to halt and strike back against the pursuing Germans, and Bülow, shaken by the threat, called on Kluck for aid. Lanrezac's attack, on August 29th, was stopped before Bülow needed this help, but he asked Kluck to wheel in nevertheless, in order to cut off Lanrezac's retreat. Before acceding, Kluck referred to Moltke. The request came at a moment when Moltke was becoming perturbed in general over the way the French were slipping away from his embrace and, in particular, over a gap which had opened between his Second (Bülow) and Third (Hausen) Armies through the latter having already turned south, from south-west, to help the Fourth Army, its neighbour on the other flank. Hence Moltke approved Kluck's change of direction—which meant the inevitable abandonment of the original wide sweep round the far side of Paris. Now the flank of the wheeling German line would pass the near side of Paris and across the face of the Paris defences. By this contraction of his frontage for the sake of security Moltke sacrificed the wider prospects inherent in the wide circling sweep of the original plan. And, as it proved, instead of contracting the risk he exposed himself to a fatal counterstroke.

On the night of September 2nd Moltke sent a message to the right-wing commanders which confirmed the change of plan and foreshadowed a new one. 'The French are to be forced away from Paris in a south-easterly direction. The First Army will follow in echelon behind the Second Army, and will be responsible henceforward for the flank protection of the force.' But the First Army was a full day's march ahead of the second: if Kluck tried to carry out the second part of the message he would be neglecting the first part. Hence he decided to march on, while detailing an incomplete Reserve Corps and a depleted cavalry division to serve as a flank guard. How lightly he regarded any danger from Paris is also shown in the facts that no aircraft were allotted to the flank guard, and no air reconnaissance ordered to the westward.

Meantime Moltke was growing depressed and his decision to abandon the original plan was definitely taken on September 4th. In place of it, Moltke substituted a narrower envelopment, of the French centre and right. His own centre (Fourth and Fifth Armies) was to press south-east while his left (Sixth and Seventh Armies), striking southwestwards, sought to break through the fortified barrier between Toul and Epinal, the jaws thus closing inwards on either side of Verdun. Meantime his right (First and Second Armies) was to turn outwards and, facing west, hold off any countermove which the French might attempt from the neighbourhood of Paris. Moltke's order continued to ignore that Kluck was ahead of Bülow in the race southward and had already crossed the Marne. For it not only told Kluck to 'remain facing the east side of Paris' (i.e. facing west), but to remain north of the Marne while Bülow wheeled into line, facing west, between the Marne and the Seine. Thus to fulfil the order Kluck had not merely to halt, while Bülow caught up and passed him, but to perform a sort of backward somersault.

Such gymnastics are somewhat upsetting to the equilibrium of a large army; and in this case the French countermove which Moltke wished to guard against had already begun before his new plan could take effect. Moreover Kluck, reluctant to be thus deprived of the chance of being the agent of decisive victory, continued his advance south towards the Seine on the 5th, saying that 'the movement to face west might be made at leisure'. For the moment he still left the weak detachment of three brigades and a few cavalry to guard his flank. Next morning it was struck by the French Sixth Army moving out from Paris.

During these days the Franco-British retreat had continued. On August 30th, Joffre—yielding to the pressure of a Government alarmed at seeing him abandon the capital by his direction of retreat—detached Maunoury's Sixth Army to reinforce the Paris garrison. Parting with it signified his abandonment of the flank counterstroke, for this was the force he had assembled for its execution. Moreover, a memorandum drawn up that same day shows that he had transferred his faith to a counter-offensive against the German centre 'in the hope of accomplishing . . . the rupture which we formerly attempted facing north-east and debouching from the Meuse'. On September 1st, Joffre issued orders for the retreat of the allied armies to be continued to a line south of the Seine, Aube and Ornain rivers. Not only was the effect to take the armies away from and far to the south-east of Paris, but a commander who is contemplating an early counter-offensive does not place the obstacle of a river barrier between himself and the enemy. And a further note to the several army commanders next day added that it was Joffre's intention to 'organize and fortify' this line, whence he planned to deliver not an immediate but an eventual counter-offensive. That same day he replied to a suggestion of a stand on the Marne, made by Sir John French and communicated through the Minister of War:

'I do not believe it possible to envisage a general action on the Marne with the whole of our forces. But I consider that the co-operation of the English army in the defence of Paris is the only course that can give an advantageous result.'

To the Minister of War and to Galliéni he repeated the same verdict. When zealous apologists say that the idea of a counter-offensive was at the *back* of Joffre's mind, the historian can agree. This array of evidence is more than sufficient to dispel the legend that Joffre had any intention of giving battle on the Marne or that he planned the counterstroke which tilted the balance so dramatically.

The definite nature of his reply was the more significant because, on September 1st, a staff officer with Lanrezac's army had found the German order for a change of direction in the wallet of a dead officer, and this was sent to Joffre's headquarters early next day. And on the morning of the 3rd, the changed direction, to the south-east, of Kluck's marching columns had been noticed and reported by British aviators. In the afternoon they added that these columns were crossing the Marne and in the evening Maunoury reported that there were no German troops left in the area west of the line Paris-Senlis. All this was reported to Joffre without making any impression on his plans—save that on the night of the 2nd he altered the limit of his retirement to a line still further south!

But from Galliéni, the new military governor of Paris, even a fragment of information gained on the 3rd had drawn an instant response. He ordered Maunoury to carry out further air and cavalry reconnaissances as soon as it was light on the 4th. Quickly convinced by these early reports that the Germans were moving obliquely past the front of the Paris defences, exposing their own flank, Galliéni was equally quick to act. At 9 a.m. he ordered Maunoury's army to get ready for a move eastward to strike the Germans in flank. He then informed Joffre by telephone of his preparatory moves, and urged him to sanction a counter-offensive. (This consent was necessary not only to ensure a combined effort but because

Joffre had persuaded the new Minister of War to subordinate Galliéni to himself.)

Galliéni's fiery and inspired arguments made an impression, but no more, on the slow-thinking Commander-in-Chief of the field armies. To save time while Joffre was still cogitating Galliéni rushed off by motor to Melun to explain the new situation to the British, and if possible gain their co-operation. Unfortunately, Sir John French was absent from his headquarters, and at first Galliéni could not even find Archibald Murray, his chief of the general staff. It was a curious scene. Galliéni, for his part, found the British staff unsettled and depressed, not hesitating to say that if England had known the condition of the French army she would not have entered the war. They were hardly in the mood to discern the underlying qualities of this most unmilitary-looking military genius, bespectacled and untidy, with shaggy moustache, black buttoned boots and yellow leggings. Little wonder perhaps that one eminent soldier with a pungent gift of humour remarked that 'no British officer would be seen speaking to such a —— comedian'.

Galliéni pointed out to Murray that it was vital to seize the opportunity which the Germans had given by offering their right flank, told him that the 'Army of Paris' was already in motion against the German flank, and begged that the British should cease to retreat and join with his forces in an offensive next day. Murray, however, showed 'une grande repugnance... à entrer dans nos vues', and declared that he could do nothing in the absence of his Commander. After waiting three hours in vain for Sir John French's return, Galliéni had to leave at 5 p.m. with the mere promise of a telephone message later. This brought no satisfaction, for its purport was that the British would continue their retreat next day. Their decision had been confirmed by receiving a letter, written that morning, from Joffre who said: 'My intention, in the present situation, is to pursue the execution of the plan that I have had the honour to communicate to you—that of retiring behind the Seine—and only to engage on the selected line with all

forces united.' The meagre influence which the news of
Kluck's change of direction had achieved was shown by a
subsequent paragraph which said: 'In the case of the German
armies continuing their movement towards the S.S.E. . . .
perhaps you will agree that your action can be most effectively
applied on the right bank of this river, between the Marne
and Seine.' This casual qualification to the definite opening
statement gave the British little encouragement to fall in with
Galliéni's audacious suggestion. There is a dramatic contrast
between the sluggish working of Joffre's mind, gradually but
all too slowly veering round, and Galliéni's swift *coup d'œil*
and instantaneous reaction.

After Galliéni's morning message, Joffre had been moved
so far as to send a telegram, timed 12.45 p.m., to Franchet
d'Esperey (who had superseded Lanrezac in command of the
Fifth Army), saying—'Please inform me if you consider that
your army is in a state to make it [an attack] with any chance
of success'—an inquiry which hardly suggests a sense of vital
opportunity or an urge to action. This reached Franchet d'
Esperey while Henry Wilson, of French's staff, was with him,
and, after discussion, a reply was drafted, saying 'the battle
cannot take place before the day after to-morrow', and that
the Fifth Army would continue its retreat on the morrow,
attacking on the 6th. To this message he added, in his own
hand, a qualifying note even less encouraging: 'In order that
the operation may be successful the necessary conditions are:
(1) The close and absolute co-operation of the Sixth Army
debouching on the left bank of the Ourcq on the morning of
the 6th. It must reach the Ourcq to-morrow . . . or the
British won't budge. (2) My army can fight on the 6th,
but its situation is not brilliant. No reliance can be placed on
the Reserve divisions.'

What was likely to be the effect on a Joffre of such a discouraging reply to his tentative enquiry? To harden his
hesitation.

That hesitation was the more natural because Berthelot,
his chief adviser, was vehemently in favour of continuing the

retreat and maintaining the original plan. Then early in the afternoon came an ominous report of German progress across the Marne. As Joffre's own memoirs relate: 'This was all that was needed to cause Berthelot to return to the charge.' The memoirs, it is true, argue that Joffre merely continued to put off a decision, but they admit that he issued new instructions that were designed to accord with Berthelot's plan. Still more significantly, the decision was taken to move the headquarters over thirty miles further south. Then, while Joffre was having an early dinner, Franchet d'Esperey's message arrived.

The next link in the chain of causation fits in with a click—the click of a telephone switch putting a call through. For if Galliéni's *coup d'œil* gained the opportunity it was, as he himself said, '*coups de téléphone* which gained the Battle of the Marne'. On returning to his headquarters in Paris he had found a belated message from Joffre which was favourable to his proposal for a counterstroke, but preferred it to be delivered south of the Marne—where it would have lost the greater effect given by a blow against the enemy's flanks and rear.

Galliéni seized the telephone, got through to Joffre, and by the fervour and force of his arguments at last won his sanction for the 'Army of Paris' to strike north of the Marne as part of a general counter-offensive by the left-wing armies. Joffre promised to obtain the co-operation of the British. Galliéni promptly issued orders (8.30 p.m.) to Maunoury's army, which he reinforced. After several hours' delay Joffre's orders were sent out for the offensive on September 6th—it was too late now for the 5th, and too late to be generally effective even for the 6th. The delay had far-reaching consequences—not all ill.

On the 5th while Maunoury's troops were moving east towards the enemy, both the British and Franchet d'Esperey's were marching south in accord with their original orders—away from the enemy, and even away from each other. But for Galliéni, the gap they thus opened might have proved perilous. When they turned about next day, they had much ground to recover, and were not as quick in retracing their steps as the situation demanded. This 'disappearance' of the British not only enabled but encouraged Kluck—who had been taken completely unawares—to pull back half his main body (II and IV Corps) from the sector where the British had been, to reinforce the hard-pressed flank guard which was trying to hold off Maunoury's menacing advance against the German rear. The arrival of these fresh forces began to check Maunoury's advance on the 7th, and Galliéni pushed forward every possible reserve he could scrape up in order to strengthen Maunoury.

Here occurred the famous if legend-crusted episode of the Paris taxicabs. A fresh division had just detrained near Paris, but it was forty miles from the battlefront. If it marched thither it would be too late, and there was only sufficient rail transport to take half the division. That afternoon, the police held up taxicabs in the streets, bundling the passengers out in some cases, and, after collecting 600 cabs, sent them to the suburb of Gagny where they filled up with soldiers. Galliéni came to see the performance and, with mingled gratification and amusement, exclaimed: 'Well, at least it's not commonplace!' During the night this forerunner of the future motorized column swept, as only Paris taxicabs can sweep, through the outlying villages and past their amazed inhabitants, making two journeys, with 3000 soldiers at a time. Unfortunately these taxicabs maintained their traditional preference for speed over reliability and, passing and repassing, became so mixed that on the morning of the 8th several hours were spent in sorting out their passengers before the division could attack.

The pressure on the Germans gained extra force from the fact that it was directed against their rear flank. If Galliéni had received the two further Army Corps for which he had asked days before and which were only just arriving piecemeal, the German forces south of the Marne might have been cut off and the battle been as decisive tactically as it was strategically. Even in the actual situation, the menace was such that at 10 p.m. on the 6th Kluck called back his two remaining army corps, so creating a thirty-mile-wide gap between himself and the neighbouring army of Bülow. Only two weak cavalry corps, with a few Jäger battalions, were left to fill it and Kluck failed to arrange that this thin screen should be put under a single command. The consequences were fatal. Although he was able to hold and even press back Maunoury's troops, the gap he had left in the southern front uncovered Bülow's flank. Although still untouched by Franchet d'Esperey's slow advance on the 7th, Bülow, sensitive to his raw side, drew back his right to the north bank of the Petit Morin. And when news came that the British were advancing into the centre of the gap, it proved the signal for the German retreat, which began on September 9th. If the continuance of the British withdrawal on September 5th had marred the chance of a crushing victory, it was a pleasant irony of fate that their very withdrawal made possible the 'victory' as actually achieved.

It is necessary, however, to take account of the situation on other parts of the battlefront for, unless the German intentions elsewhere had been frustrated, Joffre's victory would have been impossible and defeat probable. To the frustration of their left wing attack in the east, or Lorraine sector, the Germans themselves were the chief contributors; for by pressing the French back on their own fortress line they had already made their task of breaking through it almost impossible. And yet another of the many 'accidents of the Marne' made their repulse certain; for when Dubail's and de Castelnau's armies, after their defeat in the battle of Morhange-Sarrebourg, ended their hasty retreat, their line sagged inwards; and into this re-entrant, formed quite unintentionally, the main German attack was launched, pushing towards that very 'gap of Charmes' which the French in earlier years had prepared for their reception.

Thus the French were given an opportunity to strike back effectively at the German flanks, and thereby they temporarily paralysed the original German advance, which came to a halt on August 27th. This not only gave the French breathing space to strengthen their position, but enabled Joffre, with safety, to transfer part of the force from the right wing to the more critical left wing. News of this transfer inspired Moltke to frame his new plan of September 5th, and lured him into another vain attack on the French fortified barrier, despite protest from the Crown Prince Rupprecht of Bavaria, commanding the Sixth Army. The new attack was launched frontally against the Grand Couronné de Nancy, the ridge which formed a flank buttress for the gap of Charmes. And the Kaiser arrived with his white cuirassiers, like an actor waiting his call, to make a triumphal entry into Nancy. But successive assaults, inadequately prepared, collapsed under the well-knit and superior fire of the French artillery, and on September 8th Moltke ordered Rupprecht to stop the offensive and the vain loss of life. Rupprecht had been urged into it against his own judgment by the excessive confidence of the artillery expert, Major Bauer, that his super-heavy howitzers would have the same effect as on the obsolete Belgian fortresses. Yet, curiously, he now only gave up the attack under protest—so Micawberish was the judgment of the military leaders of 1914–1918.

The German centre (Fifth and Fourth Armies), west of Verdun, was no better able to fulfil its rôle as the right arm of the pincer-like squeeze ordained in Moltke's modified plan. In the Verdun area Sarrail had replaced Ruffey as commander of the French Third Army, and the first instructions he received indicated not only a continued retreat but the abandonment of Verdun. Sarrail thought differently, however, and determined to cling on to the Verdun pivot as long as possible, without losing touch with the Fourth Army to the west. It was a happy piece of initiative, and the brake thus placed on the south-eastward advance of the enemy's Fifth Army (under the German Crown Prince) was an essential factor in upsetting Moltke's plan. The stout resistance of Sarrail's troops, and still more the deadly fire of their artillery, not only held up but paralysed the Crown Prince's advance. And a belated attempt on the 9th to break the deadlock by a night attack, ended in a suicidal fiasco, with the Germans firing on each other. Sarrail, however, asked in vain for reinforcements which might have enabled him to convert his resistance into a dangerous counterstroke from Verdun westwards against the German flank—for by holding on to Verdun he had formed one side of a sack into which the German armies between him and Maunoury, on the other side, had pushed.

The German Third Army (Hausen) formed a link between the German centre and right wing, and was assigned the indefinite rôle of being ready to support either. This rôle was perhaps in part the reflection of the fact that, being composed of Saxons, the Prussians tended to discount its value. In the event it was virtually divided. Its left was used to help the Fourth Army in the abortive attack on the French Fourth Army (de Langle de Cary); an attack which, after perhaps the severest fighting of the whole battle, was driven to ground by the French artillery. Its right joined with Bülow's left in an attack on Foch, who had taken over command of a new Ninth Army, in the French centre, formed by simple subtraction from de Langle de Cary's army.

Among all the legends of the Marne that which has grown up round Foch's part is the most comprehensive and has the least substance. The first claim, still widely believed, is that Foch decided the issue of the whole battle by a counterstroke which threw the Prussian Guard 'into the marshes of St. Gond'. In fact, however, the Germans took their leave without interference—after the issue had been decided further west. The second, and more modest claim, is that Foch made the victory possible by preventing a German break-through in the French centre. Even this is inaccurate—because the Germans were not trying to break through here. Bülow was merely carrying out his new protective task of wheeling his line to face west. And, in the course of this wheel, his left wing naturally bumped against Foch's front.

A further paradox is that although Foch issued repeated orders for attacks, his troops in reality were on the defensive, a defence needlessly desperate owing to his own disobedience of orders.

At 1.30 a.m. on September 6th, Foch had received Joffre's famous order for the general 'about turn'. Unlike the other armies, he received it in time to act on his share of it, which was to cover the flank of Franchet d'Esperey's attack by holding the southern exits of the marshes of St. Gond. Instead, he concentrated the bulk of his forces for an offensive north of the marshes, leaving the weak XI corps to hold the wide and vulnerable sector east of the marshes. His troops were tired and much reduced by the hard retreat, and their offensive quickly died away; in their reflux they failed to hold firmly the southern exits of the marshes. Thus Foch continued to keep his main strength on that flank. But the Germans could only cross by the narrow causeways, and in consequence made a side-step—as they might have done earlier. On the 7th, their attack east of the marshes broke down under the fire of the French artillery. As the only way of evading it, a bayonet attack in the half light before dawn was arranged. This caught Foch's right by surprise and it gave way rapidly. Fortunately the Germans did not follow up as rapidly and so captured few of the tormenting guns. Even so, the situation was serious and Foch called for help; Franchet d'Esperey lent a corps to support his left and Joffre sent another to fill the gap now yawning on his right. On the 9th the continued German attack against Foch's right made fresh progress and met little resistance—until, shortly before 2 p.m., it was stopped by receiving Bülow's now notorious order for a general retirement. The Germans drew off undisturbed and even unobserved. To meet the earlier emergency Foch had taken the 42nd Division from his intact left wing and switched it across to his right; but it only arrived in time to fire its guns in the twilight after the vanished foe—contrary to the popular legend of its decisive counterstroke against the flank of the German break-through. And one has to add that although Bülow had exposed his flank in making the wheel, Foch thought only of making a frontal counterattack. On the battle as a whole his main, and most serious, effect was that he detracted from the main offensive instead of helping to cover it.

In our survey of the battlefront we have now travelled back to the decisive western flank. Let us focus our eyes on the various headquarters behind the German front and examine the wavering gusts of opinion which culminated in the German retirement. The Supreme Command was back at Luxembourg, whither it had moved from Coblenz, on August 30th, and depended for communication with the armies on wireless, supplemented by occasional visits by staff officers in motor cars. No regular motor or motorcycle despatch service had been organized, and wireless communication suffered not only from the time lost in enciphering and deciphering but from interference from the Eiffel Tower in Paris. As the Army commanders, faithful to the tradition of 1870, were jealous of control, information was as sparse as it was slow except when they had successes to report—and exaggerate. Throughout the crisis of the battle, from September 7th–9th, no single report of any value came back from the front and, as late as the 12th, Moltke had no knowledge of what had happened to Kluck's army, or where it was. Perhaps this ignorance made little difference, for on the 5th, Falkenhayn, then at Luxembourg in his capacity of Minister of War, noted in his diary: 'Only one thing is certain: our General Staff has completely lost its head. Schlieffen's notes do not help any further, and so Moltke's wits come to an end.'

Moreover, Moltke had already reconciled himself to defeat. For the gloom at Luxembourg is well shown by the fact that when, on September 8th, Lieut.-Colonel Hentsch left, as his emissary, to visit in turn the five armies west of Verdun, he was given full powers to co-ordinate the retreat, 'should rearward movements have been initiated'. He found none had occurred, if he found little confidence, at the headquarters of the Fifth, Fourth, and Third Armies. Passing on he spent the night of the 8th with Bülow, and there found such an intensification of gloom that when he left in the morning he could at least feel confidence on one point—that orders for a retreat would soon be given. And about 9 a.m. on the 9th air reports told Bülow that six enemy columns (five British and one of French cavalry) were approaching the Marne—and so entering the mouth of the gap. By 11 a.m. he had issued orders for the retreat of his army to begin at 1 p.m., sending word to Kluck of his action.

Hentsch, delayed by blocks and panics on the road, did not reach Kluck's headquarters till almost noon. There, according to his evidence, he found that orders for a retirement had already gone out, and in confirming them merely added the direction of the retreat—north-eastward. But Kluck's Chief of Staff, Kuhl, asserts that these orders were only the mistake of a subordinate and that he had merely ordered a swing-back of his left in view of the fact that the British were almost behind it. He further says that Hentsch, in view of Bülow's situation, gave him orders to retreat. And Hentsch is not alive to contradict him. But the facts that the withdrawal began at 2 p.m., that the roads behind had been cleared, and that neither Kuhl nor Kluck troubled to ask for a written order, go far to support Hentsch—by showing their eagerness to be off. Kuhl, indeed, has admitted that the imminent break-through of the British and Franchet d'Esperey made the retreat inevitable. And, owing to the British penetration, Kluck's army had to retreat northward, thus leaving the gap still open.

The most curious of all the many accidents of the Marne is its accidental reproduction of the perfect pattern Napoleonic battle—the pattern which Napoleon several times fulfilled and which General Camon and other students believe was normally in his mind. Its characteristics were that while the enemy was gripped in front, a manœuvre was directed against one of his flanks, a manœuvre which was intended not to be decisive in itself but to create the opportunity for a decisive stroke. For the threat of envelopment caused a stretching of the enemy's line to ward it off and so created a weak joint on which the decisive stroke then fell. On the Marne Galliéni caused this stretching and the British pierced the joint. The pattern was executed perfectly, yet quite unconsciously.

Hence we see clearly that the continued retreat of the British on the 5th and their slow advance on the 6th and 7th were strategically invaluable, holding back unintentionally as Napoleon would have done purposely. If their 'decisive' thrust had been disclosed earlier, the joint would hardly have been weakened by the removal of Kluck's last two corps—the departure of which, even as it was, Bülow delayed until early on the 8th. And the fact that Maunoury's stroke was definitely checked while these two corps were still on the march towards him is sufficient evidence that his stroke in itself could not have caused a decision.

But the continued slowness of the advance on the 8th, 9th and 10th was the negation of the Napoleonic pattern. And it proved fatal to the chance of converting the German retreat into a disaster. Thereby it paved the way for the four long years of trench warfare. In part it was due to the obstacle provided by successive rivers. But in still greater part it was due to want of impulsion, and misguided direction. Sir John French seems to have had little faith in the prospect, and still less in his Allies' efforts. In consequence he trod on the brake rather than the accelerator, besides keeping most of his cavalry on his right flank, and even in rear of it, as a link with his French neighbour instead of a spearhead of the pursuit.*

---

* The average advance on the 6th was eleven miles; on the 7th, less than eight miles; on the 8th, ten miles; on the 9th, seven miles. The Official History argues that, under the conditions, 'little more could be expected'. This view does not agree with the evidence of numerous officers who took part. Thus General Charteris has a diary note, referring to the 7th—'Actually, our own troops, though the men were very keen, moved absurdly slowly. . . . The cavalry were the worst of all, for they were right behind the infantry.' He also says that Haig went 'from one Divisional H.Q. to another trying to urge them forward', but the divisional diaries imply the opposite; it is certain that on the 9th Haig imposed a halt of several hours after crossing the Marne until his aircraft reported 'all clear'. He was then stopped again by French. The slowness of the advance is ascribed by General Gough to the fact that 'no attempt

Indeed, not until the 11th was the cavalry really launched in pursuit. Franchet d'Esperey's advance was even more cautious: his right was tied back to Foch; his centre slowly followed up, but did not catch up, Bülow's retiring wing; his left neglected to push along a completely open path.

A further cause of delay, however, was the tactical method employed in the advance. The old idea of keeping an even alignment still ruled, as it did until 1918, so that if one corps or division was checked its neighbours tended to halt. Thus frequent opportunities were missed for pushing on past the flanks of a temporary resistance and maintaining the momentum of the advance. And because the British and French missed this opportunity it was to be left for 1918 to see and the Germans to apply the method of Nature—for thus does any current or stream take the line of least resistance, finding a way past an obstacle and then flowing on, while the back eddies wash away the now isolated obstacle.

Perchance also the victory might have been more decisive —to the shortening of the war—if its creator had not been removed from control at the beginning of it. Having already limited the power of Galliéni's blow, Joffre seized the first chance to deprive him of his powers of directing it. Would that he had been as quick in exploiting the weakness of the rival army! For on September 11th Joffre informed Galliéni that he would resume direct control of Maunoury's army, leaving Galliéni to fret his soul within the confines of Paris while watching the fruits of victory slipping from the grasp of his slow-thinking superior. Throughout the battle Galliéni's governing idea had been to direct all reserves to the north— towards the enemy's rear—although several times frustrated by Joffre. With Galliéni's disappearance the advance became purely frontal, giving the Germans the breathing space to reorganize and stand firm on the line of the Aisne. Not until then, September 17th, did Joffre's mind awake to the idea of

was made by G.H.Q. to explain to the Corps and Divisional Commanders the extraordinary opportunity now available for a decisive blow at the enemy'.

concentrating by rail a fresh mass of manœuvre behind the German flank. As a result, in the so-called 'Race to the Sea', the French were always 'an army corps too few and twenty-four hours too late', until the trench front stretched to the sea.

But his was not the sole failure to take advantage of the temporary state of disorder and indecision behind the German line. It is the sober verdict of General Edmonds, the British official historian, that—'Had some of the 14 British Territorial Force Divisions and 14 mounted brigades, with the 6th Division still in England, been landed at the Channel coast ports to fall on the German communications and rear, a decisive tactical result might have been obtained and the war finished.'

Even as it was, on reaching the Aisne an opportunity had remained, only to be missed. Indeed, the Official History states that 'The prospects of a break-through never were brighter' than on the morning of the 13th. Thanks to German carelessness and the initiative of various junior commanders, the passage of the river had been achieved on both flanks. And 'from all the information furnished to General Haig the gap had not been closed which had existed between the German First and Second Armies ever since the Battle of the Marne. . . .' But the race was lost owing to 'a failure of the High Command to appreciate the situation'. On the 13th 'the divisions made a rather cautious and leisurely advance', and 'in the G.H.Q. orders there was no hint whatever of the importance of time'.

'By the evening of the 13th September the situation had completely changed. German reinforcements were known to have arrived, and serious resistance was to be expected on the 14th; yet the G.H.Q. orders merely repeated the formula that "the Army will continue the pursuit".' 'There was no plan, no objective, no arrangements for co-operation, and the divisions blundered into battle.' With their failure, the flux crystallized and deadlock ensued.

A still greater opportunity was thrown away by the French to the eastward; for, on reaching the Aisne, Conneau's cavalry corps and a group of reserve divisions were opposite a ten-mile gap in the German front. After crossing the river the cavalry rode on thirteen miles northward to Sissonne—but then, 'seeing the danger' of being cut off, 'the order was given to retire to the bridges'. This inglorious sense of precaution forfeited an opening such as cavalry would never again enjoy on the Western Front. For, at Sissonne, Conneau's cavalry corps was fifteen miles north of the thrown-back flank of the German Second Army, and forty miles behind the line of the Third Army. 'It had only to move eastwards across the enemy lines of communication to cause at least alarm and confusion.'

The question has often been posed whether the trench stalemate would have come to pass if France had possessed a Napoleon. Although the unappreciated defensive power of modern weapons and the unwieldy masses of 1914 weighted the scales against the mobility and decisiveness of warfare, the Galliéni interlude raises a doubt. For not only did Galliéni afford the one instance of 'Napoleonic *coup d'œil*' witnessed on the Western Front in 1914-1918, but his intuition, his boldness of manœuvre and his swift decision were so vivid a contrast to that of the other leaders, French, British and German, as to suggest that it was possible to snatch a decision by manœuvre from the jaws of trench warfare—before the artisan swallowed the artist.

The hypothesis is strengthened by the fact that Galliéni's influence was exercised under the most shackling conditions. The command of a fortress was governed by rules and limitations which ordained a strictly defensive rôle, even gave the governor power to refuse assistance to the field armies, and discouraged him from any wider horizon than that of his immediate responsibility for the defence of the fortress. It was the irony of fortune that the Commander-in-Chief in the field should have led the way to universal siege warfare; that the commander of a fortress should have conceived and launched the most decisive manœuvre of the war. Yet war is a game where the 'joker' counts, and when Joffre withheld the trump Galliéni played the 'joker'. As he remarked later, half humorously, half bitterly, 'There has not been a Battle of the Marne. Joffre's instructions ordained a retreat on the Seine and the evacuation of Verdun and of Nancy. Sarrail did not obey: he saved Verdun; Castlenau held on to the Grand Couronné: he saved Nancy. I have taken the offensive. As for asserting now that it is the Commander-in-Chief—who had gone back far to the rear while I advanced—who conducted, foresaw, and arranged it all . . . it is hard to believe!'

The truest phrase of all was his first—'There has not been a Battle of the Marne.' Nor had there been a 'battle' of Sedan in 1870. The folly of MacMahon in face of the first Moltke was paralleled, and even excelled, by the folly of the second Moltke in face of shadows.

CHAPTER IV

SCENE 2

THE FIELD OF LEGEND—TANNENBERG

Like that of the Marne, the popular story of the great German victory of Tannenberg is a monument of monumental error. For it consists, actually, of a figure of wood, on a pedestal of clay, varnished with legend.

The first and most popular of these legends provided a romantic picture of an old general who, as the hobby of his years of retirement, spent his time in devising a gigantic trap for a future Russian invasion, exploring paths through and sounding the bottom of the marshes in which the Russian hordes were to be engulfed—and then, when war came, carrying his dream to fulfilment. The next legend, which rose as the shadow of Ludendorff rose behind the figure of Hindenburg, was of a masterly plan for a second Cannae conceived and dictated in the train that was carrying Ludendorff to pick up his nominal master *en route* to East Prussia. History, alas, must dissipate both.

For the Germans, essentially a people of combination, found their Galliéni in a conjunction between the brain of a young staff officer and the drive of an old corps commander. And they, in turn, were much helped because Russian leadership was able to combine the faults of a Moltke and a Joffre. Indeed, the military history of modern Russia is epitomized in the brief record of the invasion of East Prussia.

The man who was, in large measure, responsible for the blundering execution was also responsible for that disastrous invasion being made, and being made before the Russian forces were ready. This was General Jilinsky, who had been Chief of the General Staff until 1913. For he had made the military convention with France whereby Russia was pledged to put 800,000 men in the field on the fifteenth day of mobi-

TANNENBERG
1914

Baltic
Sea

N

Königsberg

Situation on Aug. 27 th.
VI ⇦ Russian Corps
XX ⇐ German Corps
- - → Subsequent
     German movements
+++ Railway

XX Insterburg
Gumbinnen

III

IV

FIRST ARMY
(Rennenkampf)

East Prussia

Mulhausen

½ II   ½ II
                Lötzen

Lautern

Bossau

MASURIAN
LAKES

Allenstein

Osterode

IR XVII

VI

Deutsch Eylau

XIII

Hohenstein

Ortelsburg

XV

Tannenberg

½ XXIII

Frogenau   XX

Lahna

I

Neidenburg   Willenburg

Usdau

RUSSIA

Soldau

SECOND ARMY
(Samsonov)

Frontier

Mlawa

Ostrolenka

0 10 20 30 40
Miles

© Cassell & Co. Ltd. 1970

lization. This arrangement put a strain on the cumbrous Russian war machine which caused numerous cracks and local failures when it began moving. And it also put a strain on the Russian Headquarter Staff which led them to make decisions in a state of nervous flurry. But the arrangement did not end with this promise, for the new plan envisaged an offensive against the Germans simultaneously with the main thrust against the Austrians.

To increase the drawbacks the plan was to be carried out by a man who had not worked it out; who had even been deprived deliberately of any influence upon it by General Sukhomlinov, the Minister of War. Sukhomlinov, indeed, was scheming to get command himself. But he was not the only one who had a belief in his own divine fitness for command. And his rival claimed divine right. For when the war came the Tsar proposed to take command himself—to the alarm of his Ministers. Under pressure from them the Tsar regretfully appointed the Grand Duke Nicholas, who was at least a trained soldier, but handicapped him by nominating his two principal assistants. One of these, Yanushkevich, was a courtier general, unpopular with the working army. The second, Danilov, was an able but orthodox soldier, and really directed the Russian strategy.

From the earliest days of August the Grand Duke was incessantly pressed by the French, through the Russian Foreign Office, to do something to relieve the German pressure on the French, and to do it quickly. Thereby, although the Russian invasion of East Prussia did not begin before the promised time it began before it was ready.

East Prussia formed a long tongue of land pointing across the Niemen river, to the heart of Russia, and flanked on the north by the Baltic and on the south by Russian Poland. Along the land frontier two armies had been assembled, the First or Vilna Army under Rennenkampf and the Second or Warsaw Army under Samsonov. The two formed a group under the higher control of Jilinsky. His plan was that Rennenkampf should advance against the eastern tip of East

Prussia, drawing upon himself the German defending forces; then, two days later, Samsonov was to cross the southern frontier and bestride the Germans' rear, cutting them off from the Vistula. The fault of this plan lay not in the conception but in the execution. Its potential value was well proved by the alarm—indeed, the dislocation of mind—caused in the German headquarters when the menace was disclosed. But it suffered two natural handicaps, apart from faulty leadership and military unreadiness. The first was that the two armies were separated by the fifty-mile chain of the Masurian Lakes; these also, in conjunction with the fortified Königsberg area on the west, narrowed Rennenkampf's line of advance to a gap only about forty miles wide. Secondly, the Russians' own invasion from the south was now to be handicapped by the fact that they had left the border country a desert, with poor railways and worse roads, as a barrier against a German invasion.

On August 17th, Rennenkampf crossed the eastern frontier with six and a half divisions and five cavalry divisions. The problem of meeting such a double thrust had long been studied, and Schlieffen's solution had been that of utilizing the obstacles of the country, especially the Masurian Lakes, to strike hard and with full strength at whichever Russian army first came within reach, and then to turn against the other. But Prittwitz, the commander in East Prussia, was akin to his superior, Moltke, in his fear of taking calculated risks. Unwilling to rely on Landwehr and garrison troops to supplement natural obstacles in delaying Samsonov, he also left the two divisions of the XX Corps (Scholtz) on the southern front. The remainder of his Eighth Army, seven divisions and one cavalry division, concentrated to oppose Rennenkampf. And, to handicap himself further in gaining quick and decisive results, he launched a frontal attack on the invaders—owing to a mistaken idea of their position.

This attack was delivered near Gumbinnen on August 20th. The German centre corps, the XVII (Mackensen), had to deliver the most straightforward attack and suffered a heavy repulse, which offset—at least psychologically—the success of the corps on either wing. Even so, Rennenkampf was on the point of ordering a retreat to save his own centre from encirclement when, next morning, he found that the Germans were retreating instead.

For on the day of Gumbinnen Samsonov had reached the frontier, so hurried on by Jilinsky, that his troops were tired and hungry, their transport incomplete and the supply services in chaos. He had with him eight divisions and three cavalry divisions, while two more divisions were following on.

His appearance was reported by the XX Corps to Prittwitz, and his force was rather under than over estimated. Prittwitz was unnerved by the news, although the XX Corps was not. That evening two of his staff, General Grünert and Lieut.-Colonel Max Hoffmann were talking outside their office in the headquarters at Neidenburg—uncomfortably close to the southern frontier—when Prittwitz appeared and called them into his office. There also was his Chief of Staff, Count Waldersee, another wavering bearer of a famous name. With anxiety writ on his face, Prittwitz said—'I suppose, gentlemen, you also have received this fresh news from the southern front? The army is breaking off the battle and retiring behind the Vistula.'

Both the junior staff officers protested, urging that the Gumbinnen thrust should first be driven home, that there was adequate time, and that, in any case, a precipitate retreat without fighting would give Samsonov, who was much nearer the Vistula, the chance to cut off the main German forces. Prittwitz, however, curtly told them that the decision rested with him and not with them. He then left the office, leaving them to continue the argument with Waldersee—and, eventually, to persuade him to take bolder measures. It was decided that, to gain time, and room, an attack should be launched against Samsonov's left or western flank. And for this purpose three divisions should be railed back from the Gumbinnen area to reinforce the XX Corps, while the remainder of the force there (I Reserve and XVII Corps) were to retreat westwards by road. Here was the foundation of the Tannenberg manœuvre.

On returning to the office Prittwitz agreed to their moves, and spoke no more of retiring behind the Vistula. Next day he grew quite cheerful when word came that his forces had been disengaged safely from Rennenkampf's front, and that Samsonov had almost come to a standstill. But on the 22nd, when the headquarters had been moved north to Mühl-hausen, a bombshell was exploded by a telegram which announced that a special train was on its way with a new Commander-in-Chief and a new Chief of Staff on board—the first being General von Hindenburg and the second, General Ludendorff. Half an hour after came the delayed telegram which told Prittwitz and Waldersee that they had been superseded.

Not until later did the astonished staff discover the clue to this dramatic upset. It lay in the fact that while Prittwitz was out of the office, during the discussion on the 20th, he had not only telephoned to Mackensen and to the Lines of Communication authorities, to tell them that he was going to retire behind the Vistula, but had telephoned also to the Supreme Command—then at Coblenz on the Rhine. He had even told Moltke that he could only hold the Vistula line if he received reinforcements. To crown his nerve-broken folly, he forgot to tell his staff of this telephone talk when he came back, and so prevented them informing Moltke of his change of plan. And Moltke, whose own loss of nerve and lapse into pessimism were still to come, though imminent, was remarkably quick to penalize it in a subordinate.

He looked round at once for a man of decision and found him in Ludendorff, who had just wrenched victory from defeat at Liége. Then as an afterthought, he chose a nominal superior for Ludendorff, who was summoned to Coblenz. Arriving there on the 22nd, he had the situation in East Prussia explained to him, despatched his initial orders direct to the unfortunate Prittwitz's corps commanders, caught the train for his new 'command', and picked up his 'commander', Hindenburg, at Hanover.

Let us pause to contemplate this delightful and amusing picture of the German system of command. The staff officer chosen first and alone consulted, while the figurehead waits unclaimed in the 'lost property office' at Hanover; the staff officer telegraphing *his* orders, and then collecting his 'baggage' on the way; but the supreme jest was that the plan had already been framed and the necessary movements made by a still more junior staff officer, Hoffmann, who was to remain under Ludendorff in his post as head of the Operations branch.

The calculated daring of the plan, moreover, owed much to an earlier experience of Hoffmann's. For Schlieffen, with discerning insight, had picked this impishly brilliant young captain, whom many deemed merely a witty flaneur, to go as observer with the Japanese forces in the war against Russia. There he learnt much about the Russian army, and not least a story that two Generals, Rennenkampf and Samsonov, had boxed each other's ears on the railway platform at Mukden. Thus, in his judgment, Rennenkampf would be in no hurry to aid Samsonov by pressing on from Gumbinnen. He had also learnt in Manchuria the incredible carelessness of Russian methods and this knowledge led him in August, 1914, to accept the intercepted Russian wireless orders, sent out 'in clear', as authentic, whereas his seniors were distrustfully inclined to regard them as an artful deception.

Paradoxically, the fulfilment of Hoffmann's plan and its development by Ludendorff—the plan on which Ludendorff was to rise to world fame—were hindered by Ludendorff's initial orders. For, in order to amputate Prittwitz's control, Ludendorff had telephoned from Coblenz to the several army corps, telling them to act independently until he arrived. The I Reserve and XVII Corps on Rennenkampf's front utilized this order to take a day's rest in their retreat westwards. Another check on rapidity was that the whole of the Eighth Army headquarters had to move back to Marienburg to meet the new commanders.

On arrival there on the 23rd, Ludendorff was pleasantly surprised to find that the movements already in progress fitted in with his own half-formed plan, and he confirmed Hoffmann's arrangements. Next day it became clear that Rennenkampf was not moving forward in pursuit, and Ludendorff enlarged the plan by accelerating the retirement of the I Reserve Corps (Below), so that it could strike Samsonov's right flank. Then, on the 25th, intercepted wireless messages showed him the slowness of Rennenkampf's movements, and he began to think that he could use the XVII Corps (Mackensen) also, leaving only the cavalry to watch and hoodwink Rennenkampf. Thereby he might strike hard at not one but both of Samsonov's flanks, and bring off a decisive double envelopment. Unfortunately for his now matured plan, even forced marches could not overtake the lost day of rest.

Samsonov meantime had been staggering forward, driven on by telegraphic lashes from Jilinsky who had jumped to the conclusion that the Germans were doing what Prittwitz had contemplated—retreating to the Vistula. And in driving Samsonov on to cut them off, Jilinsky not only neglected to hasten Rennenkampf, but even diverted his energy by orders to invest Königsberg. Meantime Samsonov's army was spread out over a front of nearly sixty miles, and his right, centre and left were widely separated. If they had been linked by mobility, this width might have been an advantage, but with sluggish troops and bad roads it became a danger. And an attempt to sidestep further west as he advanced led through self-dislocation to self-destruction.

Scholtz's XX Corps had been slowly giving way, and wheeling back westwards, before the advance of the Russian centre (XIII and XV Corps) towards the line Allenstein—Osterode. Fearing both the strain and the effect of a further retirement, Ludendorff ordered François's I Corps to attack on the 26th and break through the Russian left wing (I

Corps and two cavalry divisions) near Usdau. François protested that part of his troops, three-quarters of his field guns,
all his heavy guns, and his ammunition columns had not yet
arrived; he also urged that instead of making a frontal attack
he should get round the Russian flank. Ludendorff summarily
overrode these objections. His sense of time was perhaps
greater than his sense of tactical reality. But François, who
had no wish to repeat Mackensen's experience at Gumbinnen,
avoided the Russians' active resistance by passive resistance
to Ludendorff's orders, and contented himself with the capture of an outlying ridge. And any danger to Scholtz's XX
Corps was avoided by the inactivity of Samsonov's exhausted
troops—one corps, for example, had marched more than
150 miles in twelve days over roads that were merely deep
sand.

But the 26th did not pass without hard fighting. For away
on the other flank the Russian right wing (VI Corps and
cavalry division), separated by two days' march distance
from the rest of the army, had encountered near Lautern the
two German corps that were marching back from the east
front. The Russian right wing was thrown back in confusion,
but the attacks of Below and Mackensen were badly co-
ordinated, their troops were tired by the forced marches, and
they did not press the pursuit. Thus the Russian right wing,
although disorganized, was able to retire safely. Part of one
division, however, had been hemmed in with their backs to
the Bössau Lake, and in the panic a number were drowned.
From this small incident arose the legend that Hindenburg
had driven Samsonov's army into the lakes and marshes,
drowning thousands.

The real crisis of the battle, as a whole, came on the
27th. For that morning François, now amply supplied with
shells, opened a fierce bombardment on the position of the
Russian left wing near Usdau. The Russian troops could not
stand high explosive on top of an empty stomach, and they
broke in flight without waiting for the German infantry.
François ordered the pursuit to be made towards Neiden-

burg, to get across the rear of the Russian centre, but a Russian counterattack against his outer flank caused him to wheel south towards Soldau. At daybreak on the 28th, however, he discovered that the beaten Russian left wing had retired precipitately from Soldau across the frontier, and he once more turned his forces eastwards to Neidenburg.

The time that he had lost on the 27th was compensated for by the fact that the Russians had engulfed themselves still further—to their doom. For although Samsonov knew the night before that his right had been beaten and his left was menaced, he had ordered his centre to strike northward again. As he can be acquitted of undue optimism, there are two possible explanations—that he was too rigidly loyal to his orders in trying to carry out his mission, or that he was unwilling to retreat when Rennenkampf, his old enemy, was advancing. His attack probably saved the Germans a repulse, for Scholtz had been ordered by Ludendorff to chime in after François's attack. As it was, the Russian centre made several cracks in Scholtz's front, although at the price of further exhaustion to itself. These cracks seem to have momentarily cracked Ludendorff's nerve, for he ordered François both to send back assistance and, with the rest of his corps, to march north-east towards Lahna, against the immediate rear of the Russian centre. This direction, which traversed thick forest country, would have given François less time and chance to bar the Russian line of retreat. Fortunately, he again disregarded his orders, and continued towards Neidenburg. Soon after midday Ludendorff discovered that the Russians were not attempting to deepen the cracks, but, rather, were showing signs of retreat. So he sent François fresh orders not only to move on Neidenburg but, through it, eastward on Willenburg. And by the night of the 29th, François's troops held the road from Neidenburg to Willenburg, with a chain of entrenched posts between, forming a barricade across the line of retreat of the Russians who were now flowing back, and becoming inextricably mixed in the forest maze which François had avoided. With its rear closed and its roads congested, the Russian centre (XIII, XV and half the XXIII Corps) dissolved into a mob of hungry and exhausted men, who beat feebly against the ring of fire and then let themselves be rounded up in thousands.

The crowning scene of the tragedy was enacted by Samsonov himself, who had moved up from Neidenburg on the 27th to control the battle, only to find himself caught up in the swirling eddies of the retreat. Unable to do anything he turned and rode south again on the 28th, only to get lost in the depths of the forest. In the darkness he turned aside, and his absence was unnoticed by his staff until a solitary shot rang out—he had taken his own life rather than survive the disaster.

But when he died the disaster was not so complete as his despair, nor so certain. If the Russian centre had only been able to reorganize itself for an aimed attempt to break out, it might well have succeeded. For François's barricade was thin and was itself menaced from the outside. The source of the menace was Artamanov's I Corps which, after its defeat at Usdau and retreat over the frontier, had been reinforced, and now returned to the rescue. Air reports warned François of the danger on the 29th, but he stoutly refused to give up his 'blockade', although he despatched such force as he could possibly spare to check the advancing Russians at Neidenburg. Even so, the town was lost on the 30th, but Ludendorff was already sending reinforcements, and Artamanov, having made little attempt to press his advantage, retreated south once more on the 31st.

The cause of François's weakness, however, and the escape of part of Samsonov's army, was due to the failure of Mackensen and Below from the east to join up with François. Thus the barricade was neither as firm nor as complete as it might have been. Owing to faulty co-operation between Mackensen and Below, and lack of clear guidance from above, their corps abandoned the pursuit of the Russian right wing and turned northwards towards Allenstein—marching, in good German style, 'to the sound of the guns' instead of weaving a net round the enemy's rear in Hannibalic style. Ludendorff, divided between fear of Rennenkampf's advance and his desire to annihilate Samsonov, issued a contradictory series of orders which did not help to sort out the tangle into which Mackensen and Below had got their forces. In the outcome, he thereby risked more and gained less. For he took longer to close up his battle accounts and left a gap in the southeast through which part of the Russian XIII Corps actually escaped, and most of it might have escaped—if Mackensen, on his own initiative, had not turned southward again in an effort to close the gap, and the Russians had not been blinded by panic.

Nevertheless, 92,000 prisoners were taken, two and a half army corps annihilated, and the other half of Samsonov's army severely shaken, especially in morale. The Germans were certainly favoured by the enemy's folly—above all, in dispersing the fog of war at intervals by unciphered wireless messages. Yet if we make due allowance for these flashes of light, we should take due account of the 'blindness' and the difficulties of this wild region. The victory of Tannenberg remains a great achievement, as it was a unique one in the history of the war. But Ludendorff was not the designer of victory, and still less Hindenburg. To Hoffmann is due the chief credit of the design, if Prittwitz and Ludendorff have some share for accepting it in turn, and Ludendorff also for certain additions of detail. Nor was Ludendorff even the agent of victory, for François's share was the most essential. And against Ludendorff's share must be offset the fact that his original telegram from Coblenz was the original and echoing cause of the failure to complete Samsonov's encirclement. For the battle of Tannenberg was not a second Cannae, deliberately planned, as it has so often been acclaimed. The aim was to break the force of the Russian invasion, and not to surround the Russian army, and the idea of the double envelopment only an afterthought, which became possible of fulfilment when Rennenkampf continued to remain passive. As much an afterthought as the very name given to the victory. For Ludendorff's order for the pursuit on the 28th had been headed 'Frögenau', when Hoffmann suggested that he might aptly wipe out a stain on German annals by using instead the name of the town in front of them, Tannenberg, where in 1410 the Teutonic knights had suffered an historic rout.

THE LEMBERG CAMPAIGN
Aug.–Sept. 1914

RUSSIA

POLAND

● Lodz

N

R. Dniester

R. Prut

EIGHTH ARMY

Tarnopol

THIRD ARMY

R. Seret

● Dubno

● Luck

Brody ●

Sokal ●

Krylow ●

R. Bub

Cholm ●

Lublin
FIFTH ARMY

Krasnik ●

Komarow

TANEV FOREST

R. Tanev

DIRECTION OF ARRIVAL

NINTH ARMY
FOURTH ARMY

FIRST ARMY

Jaroslaw ●

Rawa Ruska

R. Wereszyka

Lemberg
THIRD ARMY

Zlota Lipa

Gnila Lipa

KÖVESS ARMY GROUP

Halicz ●

Stanislau ●

BUKOVINA

Cernowitz ●

Przemysl ●

Sambor ●

R. San

G A L I C I A

East Carpathians

SECOND ARMY
(from SERBIA)

FOURTH ARMY

Tarnow ●

R. Wisloka

Gorlice ●

R. Dunajec

Cracow

R. Vistula

West Carpathians

Miles

0   50   100

■■■ Russian   ▭ Austrian

© Cassell & Co. Ltd. 1970

CHAPTER IV

SCENE 3

THE MAN WHO JUGGLED WITH ARMIES, AND BROKE THEM—AT LEMBERG

No man in Europe had worked harder for war than Conrad von Hötzendorf, the directing head of the Austro-Hungarian armies. None surpassed him in eagerness. Fate determined that he, of all the military chiefs, should come to grief most utterly in the first clash of the armies. Yet he was, perhaps, the ablest strategist among them. Moltke, Joffre, and the Grand Duke Nicholas were conscientious pedestrian soldiers, with marked differences of temperament but not of *tempo*. They were slow-moving and slow-thinking, whereas Conrad had a sense of mobility and an aptitude for bold manœuvre. His strategy blended the spirit of an artist with the suppleness of an acrobat. If his ideas were bounded by the walls of the nineteenth-century school of war, they represented its best fruits. Also its worst defect—a failure to appreciate the growing part that material factors play in modern war. Lacking a sense of tactical reality, he would attempt feats of strategic virtuosity for which his instrument was inherently unfitted. When it bent under the strain, he merely pressed on it the harder—until it broke in his hands.

The Austrian Army was the most obsolete in equipment among those of the Great Powers; its field guns were fewer in proportion and shorter in range; some two-thirds of the rifles were of old pattern, a quarter of a century old, and its reserve was so inadequate that, even in September, the troops holding the Carpathian passes had to be issued with single-loaders; its transport was so scanty that it had to be supplemented by a cumbersome collection of assorted farm-carts, which congested the roads. Yet with all these hindrances to vigorous action the training of the Austro-

Hungarian army had been devoted purely to the offensive. This infatuation with a tactical impossibility seems to have been due to the influence of Conrad von Hötzendorf, who had himself compiled the manuals on which the army had been trained.

If the tactical instrument of his plan was brittle, its strategic foundation was hollow. The Polish salient, deep thrust between the jaws of Austrian and German territory, was on the map a morsel so inviting that any amateur strategist would have jumped at the idea of biting it off. It excited Conrad beyond discretion. He pictured to himself a strategic super-Sedan, with his own armies thrusting up from Galicia and the Germans driving down from East Prussia, to cut off the Russian masses in the wide plains of Poland. But this project was not easy to adjust to the practical problem of a double-fronted war conducted by a double-headed alliance.

Germany had long decided to concentrate her initial efforts against France. At a meeting in 1909, Moltke had told Conrad that he hoped to settle with France within six weeks, and then to switch his forces to the Russian front in support of Austria. In view of the German decision, Conrad might wisely have decided to stand on the defensive until the reinforcement came. If he had done so, geography and Russian lethargy would have worked in his favour, to gain time. The rivers and streams that run north from the Carpathians would have provided a series of delaying obstacles; and the Russian armies' slow rate of concentration would have withheld early danger. But, even to gain time, Conrad could only conceive one form of action—the offensive. And, with this obsession, Russia's lengthy process of mobilization served him as a justification. The sooner he struck the less force he would have to meet. It was calculated that the Russians would have thirty-one divisions on the Austrian front by the twentieth day of mobilization (August 18th) rising to fifty-two by the thirtieth day. Conrad counted on having available a force equal to the Russians by the first date, whereas he would be in an inferiority of 3 to 4 by the second. To him this was an incentive to prompt action, although to anybody save a military optimist of the 1914 kind bare equality of strength, and strength of such a dubious quality, might have seemed inadequate odds in launching a would-be decisive offensive.

But Conrad also counted on the strength of a vague promise from Moltke, in 1909, that the German forces in East Prussia would take the offensive. Although no direction was mentioned, and even the intention lapsed, Conrad continued to assume that such an offensive would take place.

If the German General Staff bears the responsibility of having failed to undeceive him—instead, Moltke indulged in schoolboyish exhortations to 'thrust the knout-carriers into the marches of the Pripet and drown them there'—Conrad was certainly eager to deceive himself, rather than forgo the opportunity of displaying his art. His two strongest armies, the First and the Fourth, were assembled on the left of his line in Galicia for a northward thrust, while the Third covered their eastern flank; it was to be joined by the Second when this eventually arrived from its 'circular tour' on the Serbian front. Conrad had admitted the possibility that the Russians, instead of assembling to be cut off in the Polish salient, might concentrate for an offensive against his eastern flank; in that case he proposed to swing his armies round to face them, on a line through Lemberg; but, as such a possibility did not accord with his desires, he was more than ready to discount it. This did not prove difficult, thanks to the defective means of information on which he relied. He had over a hundred thousand cavalry, but a mere forty-two aircraft, and of these only a few were serviceable.

The Austrian advance 'was preceded by a great mass of cavalry' sent forward on August 15th on a hundred-mile excursion to search a front 250 miles wide. Within a few days 'so many of the horses had sore backs that several entire divisions were put out of action'. Only a small proportion came within reach of the enemy, who did not use a cavalry screen; thus these Austrian cavalry bumped into the Russian infantry, who took heavy toll of them. The Austrian Official History candidly remarks that 'the results of the distant cavalry reconnaissance were not worth the cost of casualties'.

But the slight indications that he gleaned sufficed to satisfy Conrad that the Russians were assembling according to plan —his plan. So, on the 20th, he gave the fateful order for the northward offensive into the depths of Poland. Groping in the dark, the Austrian infantry pushed on towards Lublin, while Conrad, in false confidence, expressed his belief that 'there is no sign of any Russian movement from the east against the right flank'.

His delusion was soon to be rudely dispersed, for two whole Russian armies were marching against this flank. In contrast to the Germans, Conrad seems to have discovered too late the possibility of intercepting the enemy's wireless orders, although he learnt the trick in time to escape the closing of the net into which he had blindly walked.

By comparison, the Russian plan was of shrewd and simple design. It offered two essentially different alternatives, but the initial dispositions were made to suit either. In any event, all the Polish salient west of Warsaw and the Vistula was to be evacuated. The Russian forces were divided into two groups, one assembling on the north-western front facing East Prussia, and the other on the south-western front facing East Galicia. Each group comprised three armies, with a fourth guarding its outer flank. If the Germans concentrated for an offensive against Russia, the alternative that would be adopted was Plan G ('Germania') by which the Russian forces would fall back to a north-and-south line through Brest-Litovsk, retiring further if and when necessary, until the arrival of the troops from Siberia and Turkestan enabled them to take the counter-offensive in strength. If the Germans made their main effort against France, and remained inactive in the east, Plan A ('Austria') came into operation. In this, the south-western group of armies, reinforced by one from the north-western, would take the offensive against the

Austrians: the remainder of the north-western group would invade East Prussia.

In the light of orthodox theory, this plan of delivering a double attack on two widely separated points and in divergent directions, may seem unwise—and be too hastily condemned. Its justification lay in the weakness of the German forces in East Prussia and in the importance of a distraction to their effort against France—as the event proved. Also it would shield the flank of the main offensive, and shorten the front if it succeeded, while paving the way for the ultimate advance of the main armies into Silesia. Here were strong arguments. Moreover, it would have been difficult, because of poor communications, for more troops to be used effectively on the Galician side. The defects of the plan were less in the general design than in the conduct of the northern offensive and the crudeness of the instrument. Unfortunately, these defects were aggravated by the pressure which the French applied to the Russian command to accelerate its action.

The Grand Duke Nicholas resisted their suggestion that he should advance direct against Silesia, ignoring the enemy on his flanks; but in loyalty to his allies he began to assemble two fresh armies on the centre with a view to such a move, as soon as possible. Also, he tried to hasten the execution of his present moves, and thereby put a greater strain on the Russian organization than it could safely bear. If the consequences were most harmful on the East Prussian side, where they led to 'Tannenberg', their effects were felt earlier on the Galician side.

Here the Russians, like the Austrians, had a picture of their enemy's plan that was exactly the reverse of the reality. And no more than the Austrians did they have the means of information to correct it. Ivanov, commanding the south-western group of armies, imagined the enemy moving east: they would be met by his strong Third and Eighth Armies, advancing west: and then his Fourth and Fifth Armies would descend from the north across their rear. A delightful picture; and, although it was incorrectly conceived, it came near to being fulfilled—the other way round.

The opening, however, was unpropitious. Under pressure from the Grand Duke Nicholas, and contrary to Ivanov's wish, the Fourth Army on the extreme west began moving down before its mobilization was complete. In this unready state it collided on the 23rd with the Austrian First Army pushing northward. Both were surprised. But in this battle of Krasnik, superiority of force was on the Austrian side, and it enabled General Dankl to turn the flank of the Russians and drive them back.

The news of this reverse was an unpleasant shock to the Grand Duke and Ivanov; but, with eyes still glued on their original picture, they too easily slipped into the deduction that the Austrian stroke came merely from an offensive flank guard. And to punish the audacious intruder Plehve's Fifth Army was ordered to wheel westward against his flank and rear, so as to cut him off. Another picture.

Unfortunately for the Russians, this wheel presented their own flank to the northward-advancing Austrian Fourth Army (Auffenberg). The clash took place on the 26th. In this battle of Komarov, the Russians suffered the worse because their own commander was continuing to urge the westward wheel while the enemy was forcing them to face round to the south. Under this double pressure the Russian Fifth Army became badly bent, especially on the flanks, and by the evening of the 28th it was in grave danger of being encircled by Auffenberg's. It might have crumpled sooner if the Austrian cavalry had not fallen a prey to a panic, due to their own carelessness, which temporarily unhinged Auffenberg's advance. That hitch in drawing close the net had fateful consequences.

For the grey waves of the main Russian advance were now rolling on towards Lemberg, perilously close to Auffenberg's line of supply and retreat. The caution and cumbrousness of the Russian armies, by acting as a brake on their advance, had helped to keep Conrad in ignorance of the impending menace. And his own temperament had contributed to make this worse. Enthused by the opening success of his north-ward advance, he had drawn three divisions from the weak Third Army near Lemberg to increase Auffenberg's strength. And at the same time he approved a suggestion that what remained should advance east from Lemberg to strike at the supposedly small Russian forces now reported in that direction. His Second Army from the Danube was only just beginning to arrive on the scene—at Stanislau in the south.

The Third Army's rash advance to the Zlota Lipa on the 26th was followed by still rasher attacks, unprepared and disjointed, on the heads of the Russian columns, which had a five-to-two advantage in numbers. The Austrians recoiled in disorder to the Gnila Lipa. Lemberg itself, twenty-five miles behind the battlefield, was filled with panicstricken fugitives that night. Next morning Conrad ordered the battered Third Army to fall back on Lemberg, and sent word to Auffenberg to return the three divisions loaned to him. Conrad, indeed, was about to halt his two north-bound armies when news came that the Russians were not pursuing their progress. Thereupon he changed his mind, and also his previous orders.

Ivanov, still believing that he was faced by the mass of the Austrian forces, had decided to pause for forty-eight hours, so that his columns might close up and deploy for battle on the Gnila Lipa. Had he pushed on at once it is likely that he would have crashed through the shaken Austrians as through a paper screen. The Grand Duke, when he heard of the halt, sent orders that the advance on Lemberg was to be resumed immediately.

A remote Commander-in-Chief may propose, but his executive subordinates dispose—the troops under their con-trol. The Russian attack did not develop until the 30th, and even then its decisive impulse came, not from Ruzski's army facing Lemberg, but from Brusilov, who had made a side-step northward with the bulk of his army (the Eighth) by night, and then delivered a smashing blow with his right corps against one sector of the Austrian front. Its collapse produced a general reflux. The roads to the rear were congested with fugitives, intermingled with guns and transport. The Austrian Official History candidly relates that a mere cry of 'the Cossacks are coming' often sufficed to cause another panic surge. They were not coming, however, anything like as fast as in the Austrians' fears. Once more the Russians gave their enemy time to recover. They took nearly three days to advance the eighteen miles which their fugitive opponents had covered in less than one. Then, their belated approach produced fresh panics, which opened such gaps on the enemy front that Conrad was constrained to abandon Lemberg, late on September 2nd. But his enemy had given him time that he could not have gained.

He used it, not to hedge, but to plunge more heavily, staking everything on the completion of his success in the north. Here, by the 30th, Auffenberg's wings were well round Plehve's flanks, while Dankl's right was driving a wedge between the two Russian armies. Confident of an early decision, Auffenberg begged for two days' grace to achieve it. It was far easier for the local commander to ask than for Conrad to concede such an interval; he bore the responsibility for the whole, and had to face the alarming fact that only thirty miles and a panicky mob separated Ruzski and Brusilov from the communications of his own northern armies. Notwithstanding this grim situation, Conrad accepted Auffenberg's plea and allowed him to retain the extra divisions.

Like a left-handed swordsman beset by two adversaries, Conrad would guard his right side with a frail wicker shield while thrusting full out at the man in front of him. His will-power commands admiration: it would command unreserved admiration if one was sure that it was not fostered by self-delusion.

Moreover, in the modern war of masses, the will of the commander-in-chief, however strong, cannot dominate those of the men upon whom he depends; his will will not work unless his mind is attuned to theirs. In the events that now followed, the gulf between Conrad's ideas and the capacity of his instrument became manifest.

On the night of the 30th, the commander of the menaced Russian Fifth Army sought to extricate himself by an order for withdrawal. That order might not have availed to save him if fortune had not on this occasion favoured the discreet. Next morning the jaws of the trap, instead of closing, were drawn back. Two Archdukes controlled the jaws, Joseph on the right and Peter on the left. A solitary Austrian aeroplane, reconnoitring, magnified a handful of Russian cavalry into a division marching against Joseph's rear; he pulled back a large part of his force to guard it. On the other wing, the Austrian cavalry reported a similar threat, equally mythical, whereupon Peter drew back his whole force, to cover his rear. Thus the Russians safely withdrew, leaving an empty battle-field. Too late, Auffenberg the next morning ordered a rapid pursuit. Counter-orders came from Conrad.

These new orders were born of hope rather than of anxiety. It was unfortunate that Plehve's army had not been surrounded, but to Conrad's eyes it was routed. It is fair to point out that he could only see the enemy's condition through the magnifying glass provided by subordinates eager to flatter his hopes and enlarge their own achievements.

Encouraged by this view of a Plehve definitely removed from the board, Conrad conceived the picture of a new and greater encirclement. Auffenberg should turn about and descend from the north upon the slowly advancing armies of Ruzski and Brusilov, while the newly arrived Austrian Second Army should strike from the south against their other flank, and lap round their rear. It was a masterly conception, which in breath-taking boldness was worthy of Napoleon. Unfortunately, Conrad's picture did not coincide with the reality of his opponents' situation, and was affected by a change in their plans. Ivanov had ordered Ruzski to incline northward, with Brusilov conforming, so that he might take in flank and rear the forces that were pursuing

Plehve. The effect on Conrad's plan was that this movement brought Ruzski round to face the south-bound Austrians instead of presenting them his flank; also, it contracted the space in which Auffenberg could manœuvre between his late and his new opponent. Even this might not have mattered if Conrad's instrument, the Austrian army, had been fitted for bold and swift manœuvre. Its palpable unfitness formed Conrad's worst breach with reality.

Moreover, a new danger was arising. There were now two armies instead of one facing his own extreme left. For the newly formed Russian Ninth Army had been brought down the Vistula to support the Fourth. While the latter pinned Dankl's army, the former was to push past his flank and round the Austrian rear. Then the whole of the Austrian armies might be cut off from their natural line of retreat. Thus while Conrad was trying to catch part of Ivanov's forces in a deadly embrace, Ivanov was sidestepping to get round his left and take him in the rear.

The clash of these two plans produced a series of acrobatics such as huge armies have not attempted before or since, and to which these particular armies were most unsuited.

Auffenberg duly turned about and marched south, leaving the Archduke Joseph's divisions as a rearguard; the supposedly beaten Plehve also turned about and followed. On September 6th Auffenberg, expecting to strike Ruzski's flank, found Ruzski knocking against his own at Rava Russka. Fortunately for him, Ruzski was equally surprised, and this gave Auffenberg a chance to face round. Away to the far south, Conrad's other pincer had been no more effective; the Austrian Second Army came fresh, too fresh, to the fighting, but was travel-worn. Its advance soon petered out in a series of disjointed attacks, unsupported by artillery, which culminated in a rippling wave of panic during the night.

When the tangle was straightened out, the Austrian Second, Third and Fourth Armies stood in a line facing east. The one clear fact that emerged was that the Russian armies were inclining northward. This inspired Conrad to the conception of yet another offensive design, regardless of the state of his troops. On the evening of September 8th, Auffenberg was given the task of holding the Russians who faced him, while the other two armies left their prepared defensive positions and wheeled northwards to roll up the Russian line. But the day of the 9th brought disillusionment. Brusilov was also intent on taking the offensive, and the two sides met head on. The condition of the Austrian forces discounted their superiority of numbers, and the battle ended in stalemate, leaving each side with an exaggerated impression of the other's power.

With faith unquenched, Conrad that night sent a fresh order to his armies for a 'concentric attack against the enemy on the Lemberg front'. Next morning he went forward himself with the idea that his presence might be an encouragement. Not unnaturally, his presence at—or rather behind—one point of a fifty-mile line made no appreciable difference. He sent an urgent message to the commander of the Second Army to 'attack without halting, vigorously and regardless of loss'. The commander of the Second Army did not think the order worth passing on to the troops. Such orders were to be repeated so many thousand times on all sides during the World War that it would seem as if to those who uttered them they had the virtue of a magic incantation. An economy of the phrase might have endowed it with more potency. It is rare to trace any effect on those to whom it was addressed—still less on the enemy.

By his persistent pursuit of the tactically impossible, Conrad had engulfed his armies in a pit whence escape was hopeless unless fortune threw them a line. Fortune relented and did so—by a telegram that did not travel along a line.

While Conrad's disordered forces were throwing themselves against the Russians near Lemberg, in fulfilment of his plan, and becoming more entangled in the process, dark masses of the enemy were looming across their rear. Away to the north-west, Dankl's isolated army was struggling to hold up the Russian Fourth and Ninth Armies, double its strength, who were pushing down from the north. On the 9th Dankl warned Conrad that he could hold them no longer, but must fall back behind the San. Worse still there was a thirty-mile gap between Dankl's inner flank and Ruzski's. Into this gap Plehve's army and a whole cavalry corps were marching, unseen and unforeseen by Conrad.

But the ingenuous Russian command came to his rescue in the nick of time. Early on the 11th the Austrians intercepted a wireless order which the Russians, according to their habit, had sent out unciphered. The order showed that Plehve's left wing was expected to reach points well behind Rava Russka by that evening. Still clutching at straws Conrad delayed a few hours in the hope of a miracle on his other flank, and meantime sent an order for the remnant of the Archduke Joseph's divisions to drive back the intruding mass. Auffenberg did not think such an order fit to pass on. So, in the afternoon, as no news of a miracle came, Conrad at last gave the order to disengage the armies and fall back behind the San, as fast as possible.

By one of history's strangest coincidences, it was at almost the same hour that Moltke accepted the inevitable and gave the order that converted the enforced withdrawal of his right wing into a general retreat of the German armies in France.

The Austrian retreat, however, if less final, was far longer and harder. To quote the moving words of the Austrian Official History—'Day and night behind a huge train of transport vehicles marched the infantry, with bowed heads, yet undiscouraged (sic); the artillery, sinking in up to their axles in the morass that the roads became . . . the cavalry regiments, like horsemen of the Apocalypse, in molten confusion, made their way on, their presence palpable from afar by the penetrating smell of the festering galls of hundreds of led horses.'

The deep-churned mud of the roads luckily served as a brake on the inherently sluggish Russians. And frequent flickers of light from their wireless orders helped to guide the Austrians in evading interception. But Auffenberg's troops could only do so by turning so far south that they became intermingled with the retreating tide of the Third Army. Less than two-thirds of the Austrian troops whom Conrad had confidently pushed forward in August reached the shelter of the San. Even there they did not tarry. They were so obviously unfit to fight that on September 16th, when the first Russians approached, Conrad ordered a fresh retreat to the Dunajec, a further eighty miles west, leaving behind the great fortress of Przemysl and its garrison as an obstacle to the pursuers. Conrad would, almost surely, have saved himself and his country this additional draught of gall if he had abstained from his last futile assaults near Lemberg. But his rosy imagination had prevented him.

This had certainly revived when, after the War, he wrote in his memoirs: 'The Austro-Hungarian Armies were not beaten. They had to be withdrawn to escape a situation that might well have led to a defeat if the battle had continued. From this they were saved!' He saved them from annihilation but not from ruin. He had lost some 350,000 men out of 900,000, and the survivors had retreated over 150 miles, abandoning the province of Galicia. But the ultimate effects were worse than the immediate results. Conrad had juggled with armies—and broken them. If he was able to collect the pieces and stick them together with German glue, they never again had a sound ring.

CHAPTER IV

SCENE 4

'FIRST YPRES'—THE REAL AND THE SHADOW BATTLE

WITHIN nine months of its beginning, the War produced two Battles of Ypres. And of these 'First Ypres' was itself a twin battle. In its inception and its course it was closely related to the struggle simultaneously in progress along the Yser between Ypres and the sea. But it had also a dual nature. There was the battle fought by the Allied troops who held the shallow trenches in front of Ypres. There was a different battle being fought, in imagination, by the two chief commanders on the Allied side—at their headquarters behind Ypres. The latter were attacking shadows while the former were defending themselves against the sternest realities. Rarely, if ever, have the view at the front and the view behind the front been so widely apart.

The clash at Ypres followed, yet was not truly a continuation of, the outflanking attempts that followed the deadlock on the Aisne. For while Joffre and Foch continued to concentrate their gaze on the immediate western flank of the German line in France, and their thoughts on the next overlapping move, Falkenhayn had shifted his attention to Flanders and was planning a wider manœuvre—as wide, in fact, as the coastline would allow. A new Sixth Army, composed of troops switched from the eastern flank in Lorraine, was to counter Joffre's next narrow swing. Meantime another fresh army would sweep down the Belgian coast behind the Allies' flank. That army, the Fourth, was made up of the troops set free by the fall of Antwerp together with four newly raised army corps; in these an enthusiastic crowd of young volunteers was blended with a 25 per cent nucleus of trained reservists.

The abandonment of Antwerp, and its possible consequences, did not obtrude into Foch's horizon. On October 10th he sketched out his picture of the future—'I propose to advance our left (Tenth Army) by Lille to the Scheldt at Tournai or Orchies, the British army . . . forming line from Tournai through Courtrai. . . . In this way all the French, British and Belgian detachments would be united on the left banks of either the Scheldt or the Lys. After that we can see.'

Had this intention been fulfilled the Allied forces would have been moving eastward while the new German forces were marching southward behind their backs.

On the 13th Foch wrote to Joffre concerning Sir John French's intentions: 'The marshal wishes at all costs to go to Brussels. I shall not hold him back.' Fortunately for the Allied troops, King Albert held them both back by his sagacious reluctance to let go of the coast and embark on an inland excursion. And the Germans soon supplemented his restraining check, besides confirming his wisdom.

When the British II Corps began moving forward to fulfil its part of the wheeling sweep, it found that the French left was falling back. By the 18th it had been brought to a halt itself, before Lille even was reached. The III Corps, and Allenby's Cavalry Corps, coming up on its left, were likewise held up, and on the 20th found themselves resisting an enemy offensive. The day previously the German onslaught on the Yser line, near the sea, had begun.

Until now the six weak Belgian divisions, stiffened by Admiral Ronarc'h's brigade of French marines, had been occupying the line from the sea almost to Ypres. But, just in time, two French Territorial Divisions, covered by Mitry's Cavalry Corps, took over the right half of the line, as far as Dixmude, reinforcing Ronarc'h's brigade and linking up with Rawlinson's force at Ypres.

The attack on the Belgian sector was made by Beseler's three divisions from Antwerp. Screened by these until the last moment, a greater force was converging against the Dixmude-Ypres sector.

At this moment of approaching crisis Foch was still intent

on carrying out his eastward offensive, and his chief concern seems to have been with the uncertain spirit of the British Commander-in-Chief. Sir John French had moved his forces to Flanders only after prolonged hesitation, anxious lest by taking position on the left flank of the French he might again be exposed as at Mons in August. Once committed to the move, he had quickly become optimistic, with the help of Foch's tactful handling and assiduous flattery. Then, however, he was disquieted by the resistance his II Corps met in the initial advance towards Lille: he spoke of constructing a huge entrenched Camp at Boulogne to shelter the whole Expeditionary Force.

Sensitive as a weathercock, his mind had swung round again by the 19th, under Foch's gusts of optimistic encouragement. Although Rawlinson's attempt that day to advance eastward on Menin had been abortive, French ordered Haig's Corps to advance north-eastward 'with the object of capturing Bruges', saying that 'the enemy's strength on the front Menin-Ostend is estimated at about a corps and no more'. Yet his own intelligence officers estimated, and underestimated, the enemy's strength as being three and a half corps. As one of the officers later explained: 'The old man only believed what he wished to believe.' Foch's power of 'suggestion' for the moment dominated French's mind. For two more days French persisted in the belief that he was attacking, while, in reality, his troops were barely holding their ground.

The imagined offensive remained imaginary, because it clashed with the opening of the German offensive against Ypres and a simultaneous renewal of the German offensive against the southern part of the British line. Everywhere the British were thrown on the defensive, and in several places lost ground. But French that evening renewed his attack orders to Haig, apparently with the idea that his left wing would still find the enemy's open flank. So on the 21st Haig's Corps duly tried to advance past Rawlinson's flank, only to be first held up and then menaced on its left. The troops dug in where they stood, and, as their left had been swung back, the Ypres salient of now immortal memory was formed.

That same day, Joffre, visiting Flanders, had come to see French and, as an encouragement to fresh offensive efforts, had told him that the French detachment was being increased by the despatch of the IX Corps. The weathercock, however, was now veering—back to a former direction. Until the French reinforcements arrived, the British Commander was unwilling to give any more far-reaching order than that 'Action against enemy will be continued to-morrow on general line now held.' It was a euphemistic way of recognizing the defensive!

Foch still persisted in the offensive idea. Although the enemy's strength was now unmistakable, he ordered his own troops—now forming the embryo of d'Urbal's Eighth Army —to make a general offensive on the 23rd in the three widely spread directions of Roulers, Thourout, and Ghistelles. At the same time he asked the Belgians and British to take part, the latter again to swing east. If they had done so they would have laid open their flank. Happily the enemy gave them no chance of trying.

Foch's request did not reach British General Headquarters until a few hours before the French attack was supposed to start. It was also complicated by the receipt of a request from d'Urbal that the British would attack in a different direction, and by d'Urbal's instructions to his own right wing to advance on a line which would take it through the British front. The official history remarks, with moderation, that such proposals 'could not be taken seriously'. On hearing of them Haig telegraphed to G.H.Q. that 'there must be some misapprehension of the situation, that there was no time for concerted action, and every chance of confusion'. But his anxiety was needless. The leading French troops did not appear until the afternoon, and the enemy's fire at once stopped their attempt to advance. But they were a welcome reinforcement to the line of defence. Their arrival made the two sides approximately equal in strength, numerically, from Ypres to the sea.

Next day, the 24th, the French IX Corps was ordered 'to continue to advance'. Foch telegraphed direct to the corps commander, Dubois, 'all the units of the IX Corps are de-trained'—which was anticipation, not fact. 'Make your dispositions that all these units are employed to-day, and that the action receives a new impulse. There must be decision and activity.' The result at least gave an air of vindication to Foch's theory, for Dubois's men advanced over half a mile before they were finally held up, while the British, fighting defensively, lost some ground. But the German records suggest that in the proportion of loss inflicted the defensive was the more profitable, and that by the night of the 24th the new German corps had blunted their fighting edge.

Realizing that their effort was spent, the German Fourth Army Commander pinned his hopes to a continued effort against the Yser sector, 'where a decision seemed imminent'. This, if achieved, would open the path to Dunkirk and Calais. Under cover of darkness the Germans had gained a footing across the Yser near Tervaete on the night of the 22nd. Counter-attacks failed to dislodge them, all the Belgian reserves were used up, and the French 42nd Division, which would have been invaluable for the purpose, had unfortunately been committed to a vain offensive in the coastal corridor near Nieuport. By the 24th the Germans had brought the infantry of two and a half divisions across the Yser to expand this foothold, and the Belgian centre gave way under the strain. Fortunately it managed to rally on the embankment of the Dixmude-Nieuport railway, whither the 42nd Division was switched in time to stiffen the resistance. And Ronarc'h's marines splendidly withstood a succession of assaults on the key point of Dixmude.

But the situation was still critical, and next day King Albert sanctioned the attempt to create a water barrier by opening the locks at Nieuport so as to flood all the country between the Yser and the railway embankment. These arrangements took time. But, happily, the line of the railway embankment was held, without suffering much pressure, until at high tide on the evening of the 28th the Belgian engineers succeeded in opening one of the locks at Nieuport and letting in the sea. If it crept in slowly, each day brought a fresh reinforcement to the flood, until 'it seemed to the Germans as if the whole country had sunk with them and behind them'. With the impetus of desperation they renewed their attack and breached the embankment line of defence at Rams-capelle. But the rising flood came to the rescue, and during the night the Germans began to retire across the Yser to escape being cut off.

The crisis on the Yser was the prelude to a greater crisis at Ypres. This, again, followed on a fresh attempt by the Allies to take the offensive, which weakened them for the subsequent defensive struggle.

No sooner had the first crisis at Ypres passed than Foch resumed the offensive—in his own mind he had never discontinued it. That he had again infused French with his own assurance is clear from the telegram which French had sent to Kitchener: 'The enemy are vigorously playing their last card.' In the night of the 24th French wired again, suggesting that the battle was 'practically won'.

But on the 25th the Allied offensive made practically no progress against newly wired German defences. On the 26th Dubois and Haig continued the attack, but only advanced a few hundred yards. In contrast, the sharp southern corner of the salient, where Rawlinson's men (the 7th Division) stood, was smashed in by a German attack, and for a time converted into an equally sharp re-entrant. Luckily the assailants did not follow up their success. They were preparing and screening a greater stroke.

A new German army under Fabeck was being brought up, to be inserted like a wedge on the south side of the Ypres salient, between the Fourth and Sixth Armies. This wedge was made up of six divisions, heavily buttressed with artillery. Its entry into the battle on the 29th would give the Germans a two-to-one superiority of numbers. With unforeseeing irony, French had just wired to Kitchener that they were 'quite incapable of making any strong and sustained attack'.

For two days more the Allied offensive was continued without effect, although Dubois had been reinforced by a third division. Faced with a strong line, and themselves provided with little ammunition, the fighting commanders were wise enough to water down the orders received from behind. And although on the night of the 28th these orders again prescribed the offensive, the troops in front suspected the coming storm. It broke, over the British front, at half past five next morning. It was now the Germans' turn to leave the shelter of their trenches and offer themselves as targets. An infantry trained to fire 'fifteen rounds rapid' in the minute with the rifle was thus enabled to prove its hitting power, and to produce a leaden counterstorm that obscured its lack of machine-guns so well that its German assailants thought it had 'quantities'; they declared that 'over every bush, hedge and fragment of wall floated a thin film of smoke, betraying a machine-gun rattling out bullets'. Thus at the end of the day the British front was intact, save at one point—Gheluvelt crossroads. But Haig, under whom all three divisions had now been placed, had no reserve left intact.

During the day French had been to Cassel for another injection of Fochian serum. Foch told French that he was satisfied with 'the advance' of his own troops between Ypres and the sea, but admitted that he was 'far from well informed as to their doings'. French on his return ordered the British advance to be continued! He also wired to Kitchener that 'if the success can be followed up, it will lead to a decisive result'. Haig, with the greater realism that came from a closer view, told his troops to entrench, and added that he would postpone 'orders as to the resumption of the offensive' until he saw what the situation was in the morning.

The enemy command at the same time were issuing an Order of the Day which said: 'The break-through will be of decisive importance. We must and therefore will conquer, settle for ever the centuries-long struggle, end the war, and strike the decisive blow against our most detested enemy. We will finish with the British, Indians, Canadians, Moroccans, and other trash, feeble adversaries who surrender in mass if they are attacked with vigour.'

The attack was aimed at the Zandvoorde and Messines Ridges—to break through the southern hinge of the salient with the object of reaching the Kemmel heights. Thus the main weight fell on the 7th Division and on the thin chain of three dismounted cavalry divisions which linked Haig's force with the III Corps. A bad break was made in the cavalry line. But the war-experienced assailants did not show the reckless courage of the volunteers who had been repulsed earlier, and their caution in following up their success enabled Haig and Allenby to 'putty up' the gaps. Haig also made an appeal to Dubois, who generously sent his own small reserve to strengthen the line south of Ypres, where it certainly did more good than in supporting an imaginary offensive on the north side.

Foch, back on the hill of Cassel, had little idea of what had happened. 'Towards the end of the afternoon a first report of these events' was brought to him, but, as he says: 'It was impossible for me to estimate their full significance.' About 10 p.m. one of his staff came back with word that 'There was certainly a gap in the British cavalry front, which they could not fill for want of men. If this breach was not quickly closed, the road to Ypres would be open.' Foch at once telephoned to the British G.H.Q. at Saint-Omer to ask for fuller news, but was told that 'nothing more definite was known'. So, just before midnight, Foch himself set off for St. Omer. To counteract French's depression, and to fill the physical gap, he promised that if French would hold on he would send him eight battalions of the 32nd Division, which was just arriving in the French sector. Foch did not get back to Cassel until about 2 a.m. Summarizing his action up to this moment, he said, pointing to the map: 'I've stuck a wafer there and there;

then, at Hollebeke, the English broken through, the Boches passing through—a wafer here.'

A few hours later, after daybreak, the worst crisis of the whole struggle arose. The main German attack was once more aimed, with odds of five to one, at the sagging line of Allenby's cavalry. But this line, now reinforced by a few battalions of British infantry and Dubois's timely contribution, stood firm until the attacks died away at nightfall. Half, a bare half, of Foch's promised contribution arrived in time to relieve part of the line in the evening.

The crisis of the battle occurred further north—at Gheluvelt on the Ypres-Menin road. Lying on a forward spur of the low ridge that covers Ypres, Gheluvelt was the last point retained in British hands from which the eyes of ground observers could overlook the enemy's line. Under increasing pressure the front of the 1st Division caved in, and shortly before noon Gheluvelt was lost. The divisional commander, Lomax, on hearing the news, rode back to the headquarters he shared with Monro of the 2nd Division, and laconically remarked: 'My line is broken.' Half an hour later a shell burst into the room where they were holding a conference with their staffs. Lomax and several others were fatally injured. Only one of those present was unhurt. Control was temporarily disorganized.

Haig meantime had left his headquarters at the White Château and ridden forward up the Menin road 'at a slow trot with part of his staff behind him as at an inspection'. If the sight of him brought reassurance to the stragglers and wounded who were trickling down the road, the sight of them and the nearer fall of the enemy shells told its significant tale to him. On his return he heard definite news of the break in the line. It moved him to issue orders for his troops to fall back to a rearward line just covering Ypres, and to hold it to the last, if they could not hold on where they were. But, unknown to him, the immediate danger had already been averted.

Soon after the Germans captured Gheluvelt, a counter-

attack by a remnant of the 1st South Wales Borderers had
retrieved the position on the flank. But, clearly, it could
only be maintained if an adequate reinforcement arrived.
So Brigadier - General FitzClarence, commanding the 1st
(Guards) Brigade, sent up the few oddments he still had at
hand, and then raced back to find the divisional commander.
Lomax's resources were exhausted, but he had arranged with
Monro that in case of any break the 2nd Division reserves
should aid him by coming down on the enemy's flank from
the north. And earlier in the morning, one battalion (the
2nd Worcestershires) had been placed at his disposal. Thus
Lomax, barely half an hour before being himself mortally
wounded, was able to give FitzClarence the means of saving
the situation. Swiftly, FitzClarence studied the map and the
ground and gave his orders to Major Hankey, commanding
the 2nd Worcestershires; his staff officer, Captain Thorne,
went with them as guide. The counterstroke caught the
Germans relaxing after their own success, and, coming unexpectedly, tumbled them out of Gheluvelt before they could
rally. If the German artillery was quick to exact a toll, the
German infantry had shown a remarkable incapacity to exploit their opportunities. The disciplined cohesion of their
superior numbers enabled them to break into the thin Allied
defences; once inside, and themselves disordered, they failed
to produce the initiative that might have guided them
through, and became the victims of their own too machine-
like discipline. It was a serious reflection on the system and
spirit of their pre-war training.

But the enemy's initial success, naturally, made a strong
impression behind the defender's front, where impressions
perforce operate sooner than facts, and often more decisively.
Sir John French himself came up to the White Château about
2 p.m. No better news had yet come to relieve the gloom, and
French had scarcely need to be told of the critical situation,
for he could feel it in the atmosphere. Haig himself was in a
mood that recalled the night of Landrecies during the
retreat from Mons. Every reserve had been used, and

French had none to offer. White with anxiety, he hurried off on foot to regain his car and go in search of aid from Foch. But he had barely departed when, just as Haig was preparing to ride forward himself, Brigadier-General Rice 'came galloping back, as red as a turkeycock and sweating like a pig, with the news that Gheluvelt had been retaken and the line re-established'. Charteris adds: 'It was just as if we had all been under sentence of death and most suddenly received a free pardon.' Haig alone showed no sign of the reaction; pulling at his moustache, he remarked: 'I hope that it's not another false report.' Despite Rice's assurances, he seemed still doubtful, although he sent an aide-de-camp to tell French.

The aide-de-camp caught up French just as he had reached his car. How far the news was convincingly communicated, and how far French understood its significance, is uncertain. He drove off at breakneck pace on the way to Cassel. But as his car slowed down in passing through Vlamertinghe a French staff officer recognized him and told him that Foch was there, conferring with d'Urbal and Dubois in the town hall. French went thither to catch Foch. In making his appeal for aid he painted a black picture of the situation and the state of Haig's corps. The reality was certainly dark, but perhaps the picture seemed blacker because Foch and French had so long persisted in seeing it brightly coloured. French naturally told Foch of Haig's orders for a withdrawal, and it was equally natural for Foch to regard any limited withdrawal as tantamount to disaster. He protested vehemently against any withdrawal, crying: 'If you retreat voluntarily you will be swept up like straws in the gale'—he could not picture the palsy that afflicted the Germans in following up their attacks.

According to Foch, French replied that if his exhausted troops were asked to continue the battle, 'there is nothing left for me to do save to go up and be killed with the I Corps'. It is possible that the dramatic note was heightened in interpretation. Whether or not Foch replied: 'You must not talk of dying, but of winning', he certainly proposed to apply his usual remedy. 'I'll attack to right and left.' He promised that at daybreak six battalions of the 32nd division—actually two less than he had promised at midnight—should counter-attack on the right flank of the I Corps, while part of Du-bois's corps counterattacked on its left.

He then sat down and drafted a note: 'It is absolutely essential that *no retirement is made*, and to that end to dig in wherever you happen to be. This does not prevent you from organizing a rear position which should join up, at Zonne-beke, with our IX Corps. But any movement made to the rear by a considerable body of troops will lead to an enemy push and to certain disorder among the retiring troops. This must absolutely be prevented. . . .' He handed this epistle to French with the words: 'There, if I were in your shoes, those are the orders I'd send to Haig.'

Of Foch's influence on French there is little question. It is reflected in the note which French now despatched to Haig along with Foch's memorandum. 'It is of the *utmost impor-tance* to hold the ground you are on now. It is useless for me to say this, because I know you will do it if it is humanly possible. I will see if it is possible to send you any more sup-port myself when I reach headquarters. I will then finally arrange with Foch *what* our future role is to be.'

But of Foch's practical influence on the battle situation at the time there is no evidence. The Worcestershires' counter-attack had saved it before Foch and French had their talk. And before their notes reached Haig he had settled his new line of resistance. For tactical security he had decided to straighten the front of the 1st Division by withdrawing to a line just behind Gheluvelt, while the 2nd Division was to stand on its existing line. And as the enemy pressure had ceased, what Foch said merely confirmed what had already happened. We may admire the spirit that inspired it, but we cannot regard this celebrated note as materially and historic-ally decisive.

For the next ten days Haig's line remained without change

and unshaken, save for a minor withdrawal of his right on the 5th to conform to a recoil of the French troops on his right.

On November 1st the main German effort was again made on the flank of the salient, against its southern hinge. This time they tried an assault under cover of darkness, as early as 1 a.m., and the experiment was repaid by the capture of the Messines Ridge. The inward bulge of Allenby's line was deepened by over a mile. But the arrival of the French 32nd Division soon after daybreak relieved the strain, although its counterattack could not redeem the lost ground. If the other French 'attack' on Haig's left also made no measurable progress, its appearance likewise tended to discourage the enemy from pressing his own attack.

Foch wrote: 'The battle continues. It seems to me calmer. More troops are constantly arriving. In a few days we shall be able to renew the attack in full force.'

On the 2nd the French attack to reduce the Messines bulge was forestalled by a German attack, causing a French recoil, during which Wytschaete was lost and the bulge somewhat deepened. But most of the French 39th Division and half of Conneau's Cavalry Corps arrived from the south to relieve the strain; and the 43rd Division was just detraining. The French now took over the larger part of Allenby's line. Thus they held henceforth two-thirds of the battle line formed by the Ypres salient and the Messines re-entrant, leaving the weary and intermixed units under Haig's command to maintain the central sector. Worst hit of all was the 7th Division, whose infantry were reduced from 12,300 men to 2400—a bare fifth of their original strength.

During the next few days Foch pursued his attacks—without progress. While those of November 1st and 2nd by their boldness damped the enemy's will to advance, these later attacks had no such moral effect to compensate their lack of visible progress. For the German command was marking time until, by combing their line elsewhere, they could bring up six more divisions for a renewed effort. In this, the points of their attack were to be successively closed inwards like a pair of calipers. Initially, abandoning the attempt to deepen the Messines bulge, they would place the points against the two hinges of the salient.

Meantime, Foch and d'Urbal were playing into the enemy's hands by a reckless persistence in abortive local attacks. The sequel to this self-exhausting impulse is to be traced in the dangerous recoil which came on November 6th at the southern hinge in face of the Germans' new pressure—itself a preliminary to their final stroke. At St. Eloi the grey tide came within two miles of Ypres, lapping round the rear of the British, who were holding the nose of the salient. Haig warned his chief that, to avoid being cut off, he would have to fall back to a line through Ypres itself. Foch, however, sent to assure Haig that he would regain the lost ground by an attack next day. At 9-30 a.m. on the 7th he sent a message that the French line had been re-established. But in fact nothing had been done. His men were too dead-beat to respond to orders. And when eventually they were spurred to an offensive effort, it naturally failed, thus failing to remove the menacing wedge that lay embedded in the flank of the salient.

On the 8th Haig went with French to see Foch at Cassel, and found him as exuberantly confident as ever. But it was his indefiniteness rather than his assurance that kept them from fulfilling their intention to fall back to a straighter and safer line. So, unable to obtain any satisfaction, and unwilling to leave his allies in the lurch, Haig was fain to hold on as best he could, scraping the human putty off one crack to cement another. Happily, if deceptively, the next two days were comparatively quiet along the British sector. Not so for the French.

For on November 10th the enemy struck heavily against the northern hinge of the salient, and as far as Dixmude. The blow was parried, the French profiting by the natural line of the Yser canal, across which their left retired. Its more significant result was to convince the French command that their own line north of Ypres was the spot selected for the enemy's final effort. And thither were diverted such few reserves as they could spare, at the expense of the already weakened southern hinge.

But this blow against the northern hinge had been intended by the Germans as simultaneous with one against Gheluvelt and the southern hinge (as far south as the Comines canal): a blow for which a new corps under Plettenberg had been brought up—it comprised a division of the Prussian Guard and another picked division. As Plettenberg was not ready, the left-hand blow had been postponed.

On the 11th the attack was launched, in a grey November mist, and prepared by the heaviest bombardment yet experienced. But at all save two points it was repulsed. One was at the actual hinge, where the wedge was driven in as far as the later famous Hill 60. The French detachment there appealed for help to the French and British Corps on either side, but neither could spare any reserves. The 'ever-willing' Dubois, however, once more sent his only reserve, and with its help the line was restored. The other and deeper penetration was made in the British line just north of the Menin road. Here the German 1st Guard Brigade broke through the weak front of the British 1st (Guards) Brigade—a strange coincidence of history, even though only the remnants of one Guards' battalion were left in the latter brigade. But the Prussian Guardsmen, bewildered by the woods, failed to exploit their success and were driven back by a flank counterattack. In this the 52nd Light Infantry played the leading part, as they had done in repelling the final assault of the Imperial Guard at Waterloo.

Although the blow had been heavier than on October 31st, the situation had never been so critical, perhaps largely because it had made less impression on the minds of the commanders in rear. And with the failure of this blow on November 11th—date of prophetic symbolism—the crisis at Ypres finally passed. It is true that the German Higher Command would, in its own mind, still deliver several powerful attacks before it admitted defeat. But the men who were called on to execute its orders were no longer capable of vigorous effort, or inclined to pursue such an unhopeful prospect. Thus the spasmodic attacks that continued during the following week, chiefly against Dubois's front, were but the fading flickers of a storm that is travelling away. The relief of the I Corps, so long demanded by Haig and refused by Foch with the word 'Impossible', was now carried out, and the French took over for a time the whole salient.

'First Ypres' had been essentially a 'soldier's battle'—a greater Inkerman. In a memorable sentence General Edmonds has epitomized the situation: 'The line that stood between the British Empire and ruin was composed of tired, haggard, and unshaven men, unwashed, plastered with mud, many in little more than rags.' Its only divergency from accuracy lies in its one deviation from stark simplicity. The British Empire has shown a capacity for survival, even when its military expeditions have actually been driven back to their ships, and when its enemy has been in possession of the Channel ports. And it is by no means sure that, if the expeditionary force had been defeated at Ypres, the Germans were capable of following so closely on its heels as to bring disaster. In the light of the succeeding years there is, indeed, reason for regret that Haig did not fulfil his idea of withdrawing to the straighter and stronger line along the canal through Ypres. It would have saved cost and simplified defence. And its hindrance to the later attempts at the offensive in Flanders, an impossible country for the offensive, might have been an additional advantage.

The danger at 'First Ypres' was certainly aggravated by the failure of Foch, French, and d'Urbal to realize this impossibility. Herein lay their most material influence on the battle. For the real handling of the battle was left in the hands of Haig and Dubois. Even they, for want of reserves, could do little more than cement the crumbling parts of the defence by judicious thinning of other parts of an ominously thin front. Perhaps to Dubois, for the way he took, not once alone, the calculated risk of parting with his own reserves, is due the highest credit of command earned in the defensive battle.

Foch undoubtedly had a moral influence on the battle, no less by his obstinate refusal to listen to reason than by the unconquerable strength of his will. This never wilted. Detach it from the actual ebb and flow of the battle line, and we can admire it unreservedly. It made an impression on all who came in contact with it. But one is not able to detect any point at which it touched the men in the battle line. And where it touched the fighting commanders the effect seems to have become a source more of exasperation than exaltation. The one sure point where Foch's will fortified another will was at the back of the front—at the allied general headquarters. While some of the claims made for its influence on the Belgian command may be discounted, especially in regard to King Albert, they cannot be disregarded. On Sir John French the influence is more measurable, but here the measure of its effect is inevitably as infinitesimal as Sir John French's influence on the battle.

The German design was foiled, and Ypres saved, in spite of the delusions of the Higher Command—by the troops in the front line. The men who defended Ypres against the German onslaughts were front-line troops in the strictest sense—their defence had length without depth. Its shallowness was the measure of their numerical weakness, but also the supreme tribute to their moral strength. The 'thin red line' of the past was never so thin as the line at Ypres—and never so hardly tried. The 'thin khaki line' withstood a strain that lasted for weeks compared with the hours of the past.

By a patriotic falsification of history, into which military chroniclers easily lapse, too many accounts of 'First Ypres' have represented it as a nearly all-British battle. Ungenerously, and untruly, they have obscured the great part played by our Allies, just as a century earlier they distorted the outline of Waterloo, and the vital share of the Prussians. To correct the proportions does not diminish the credit of the

British troops. It is in quality, not in quantity, that military virtue lies. And no battle in Britain's annals has given clearer proof of fighting quality, and of its value, than 'First Ypres'. It was a battle in the natural line of British tradition—a defensive attitude combined with timely ripostes. Thus it suited the nature of the troops who conducted it. If it did not directly fit their pre-war tactical training, predominantly offensive in imitation of the continental fashion, it appealed to their native instincts, which count for more than a fashionable dogma under the test of battle. And because of the extent of their training, compared with the conscript armies of the Continent, they had acquired elements of skill that were of value in any form of action. Above all was this true of their shooting skill—with the rifle. In defence it had greater scope and effect than in attack. Such was the ability of the British infantry to produce 'fifteen rounds rapid' a minute that the Germans credited them with 'quantities of machine-guns' whereas, in fact, each battalion had come to France equipped only with two, and in many cases had lost these by the time Ypres was reached. The delusion in the minds of the enemy, which such weapon-skill created, redressed the delusions of the Allied Higher Command, and was a decisive factor in the issue. Indeed, it was the decisive factor when coupled with the morale of the men who handled the weapons.

No praise can be too high for the indomitable spirit which inspired their collective endurance. This was, in a sense, a special product. The enemy had no lack of courage. Their discipline was equally strong—and perhaps too strong for their own tactical effectiveness. But the little British Army had a corporate sense that was unique. To this its very smallness, as well as its conditions of service and traditions, contributed. 'First Ypres', on the British side, was not merely a soldiers' battle but a 'family battle'—against outsiders. The family spirit was its keynote, and the key to the apparent miracle by which, when formations were broken up and regiments reduced to remnants, those remnants still held together. They attained their end—in both senses. Ypres saw the supreme vindication and the final sacrifice of the old Regular Army. After the battle was over, little survived, save the memory of its spirit.

CHAPTER V

1915—THE DEADLOCK

BEFORE the end of 1914 the state of deadlock on the Western Front was realized, if in varying degree, by the Governments and General Staffs of the warring countries, and each was seeking a solution. The reaction varied in form and in nature, according to the mental power and predisposition of the different authorities. With the Germanic Powers the opinion of Falkenhayn was the decisive factor, and the impression derived not merely from his critics, but from his own account, is that neither the opinion nor the direction was really clear as to its object.

On his appointment after the Marne reverse, he still adhered to the Schlieffen plan of seeking a decision in the west, but he did not follow the Schlieffen method of weakening his left wing in order to mass on the vital right wing. The autumn attack at Ypres was made largely with raw formations, while war-experienced troops lay almost idle between the Aisne and the Vosges. Colonel Gröner, Chief of the Field Railways, even went so far as to submit a detailed plan to Falkenhayn for transferring six army corps to the right wing, but it was rejected. When we remember how close to breaking point the British front came at Ypres, it can only be said that for a second time the German Supreme Command saved the Allies. At this juncture, too, Ludendorff was pleading for reinforcements to make his wedge-blow at the Russian flank near Lodz decisive, but Falkenhayn missed the chance by delaying until the Ypres failure had passed from assurance to fact.

Reluctantly dissuaded from a fresh attempt to break the trench barrier in the west, Falkenhayn seems to have been vague as to any alternative object. His feeling that the War must ultimately be decided in France led him to distrust the value, as he doubted the possibility, of a decision against Russia. Hence while he realized that the Eastern Front was the only practicable theatre for operations in the near future, he withheld the necessary reinforcements until his hands were forced by the threatening situation of the Austro-Hungarian front. And even then he doled out reserves reluctantly and meagrely; enough to secure success, but never in sufficient quantity or in time for decisive victory.

It is to his credit, however, that he realized a long war was now inevitable, and consequently set to work to develop Germany's resources for such a warfare of attrition. The technique of field entrenchment was carried to a higher pitch than with any other army; the military railways were expanded for the lateral movement of reserves; the supply of munitions and of the raw material for their manufacture was tackled so energetically and comprehensively that an ample flow was ensured from the spring of 1915 onwards—a time when the British were only awakening to the problem. Here was laid the foundation of that economic organization and utilization of resources which were to be the secret of Germany's resisting power to the pressure of the British blockade. For the scientific grasp of the economic sphere in war Germany owed much to Dr. Walter Rathenau, a great captain of industry. She was also a pioneer in the psychological sphere for, as early as the autumn of 1914, German agents launched a scheme of propaganda in Asia to undermine British prestige and the loyalty of Britain's Mahommedan subjects. The defect of German propaganda, its crudeness, was less apparent when concerned with primitive peoples than when applied to the civilized peoples of Europe and America.

The same period witnessed also the one great success for German diplomacy, the entry of Turkey into the war, although this was fundamentally due to a combination of pre-war causes with military events. Since 1909 the country had been under the control of the Young Turk party, to whom traditions, including that of friendship with Britain, were abhorrent. Germany, filled with her own dream of a Germanic Middle East—of which the Baghdad railway was the symbol—had skilfully exploited the opportunity to gain a dominating influence over the new rulers of Turkey. Their leader, Enver Pasha, had been military attaché in Berlin; German instructors permeated the Turkish army; and a definite understanding existed between Germany and the Young Turk leaders as to common military action—urged by the common bond of necessary safeguard against danger from Russia. The arrival of the *Goeben* and *Breslau* reinforced the moral pressure of Wangenheim, the German Ambassador, and eventually on October 29th the Turks committed definite acts of war—at Odessa against Russia, and in Sinai against Britain.

Falkenhayn has shown 'the decisive importance of Turkey joining in the struggle'—first as a barrier across the channel of munition supply to Russia, and secondly as a distraction to the military strength of Britain and Russia. Under German dictation, Turkey struck as early as mid December against the Russians in the Caucasus, but Enver's over-ambitious plan ended in disaster at the battle Sarikamish. Turkey was no more fortunate in her next venture—to cut Britain's Suez Canal artery with the East. The Sinai Desert was a check on an invasion in strength, and the two small detachments which got across were easily repulsed, at Ismailia and Tussum, although allowed to make good their retreat. But if both these offensives were tactical failures, they were of great strategic value to Germany by pinning down large Russian and British forces.

As an offset to Turkey joining the Central Powers, Italy definitely threw over the artificial ties of the Old Triple Alliance and joined the Entente. On May 24th she declared war on Austria—her hereditary enemy—although avoiding an open breach with Germany. If her main object was to seize the chance of redeeming her kinsmen in Trieste and the Trentino from Austrian rule, there was also a spiritual desire to reassert her historic traditions. Militarily, however, her aid could not have an early or far-reaching effect on the situation, for her army was unready to deliver a prompt blow, and the Austrian frontier was a mountainous obstacle of great natural strength.

On the Entente side the reality of the trench deadlock produced different and diverse reactions. If the desire to hold on to territorial gains swayed German strategy, the desire to recover their lost territory dominated the strategy of the French. It is true that their mental and material concentration on the Western Front, where lay the main armed force of the enemy, was justified by military tenets, but without any key to unlock the barrier they were merely knocking themselves to pieces. Winter attacks in Artois, on the Aisne, in Champagne and the Woevre afforded costly proof that against the Germans' skill in trench fighting, Joffre's 'nibbling' was usually attrition on the wrong side of the balance sheet. As for any new key, the French were singularly lacking in fertility of idea.

Britain's trouble was rather an excess of fertility, or rather an absence of decision in choosing and bringing to fruition these mental seeds. Yet in great measure this failing was due to the obscurantism of professional opinion, whose attitude was that of blank opposition rather than expert guidance.

British-inspired solutions to the deadlock crystallized into two main groups, one tactical, the other strategical. The first was to unlock the trench barrier by producing a machine invulnerable to machine-guns and capable of crossing trenches, which would restore the tactical balance upset by the new preponderance of defensive over offensive power. The idea of a machine for this definite purpose was conceived by Colonel Swinton in October, 1914, was nourished and tended in infancy by Mr. Winston Churchill, then First Lord of the Admiralty, and ultimately, after months of experiment hampered by official opposition, came to maturity in the tank of 1916.

The strategical solution was to go round the trench barrier. Its advocates—who became known as the 'Eastern' in contrast to the 'Western' school—argued that the enemy alliance should be viewed as a whole, and that modern developments had so changed conceptions of distance and powers of mobility, that a blow in some other theatre of war would correspond to the historic attack on an enemy's strategic flank. Further, such an operation would be in accordance with the traditional amphibious strategy of Britain, and would enable it to exploit the advantage of sea power which had hitherto been neglected. In October, 1914, Lord Fisher, recalled to the office of First Sea Lord, had urged a plan for landing on the German coast. In January 1915, Lord Kitchener suggested another, for severing Turkey's main line of eastward communication by a landing in the Gulf of Alexandretta. The post-war comments of Hindenburg and Enver show how this would have paralysed Turkey. It could hardly, however, have exercised a wider influence, and it was anticipated by another project—partly the result of Churchill's strategic insight and partly due to the pressure of circumstances.

This was the Dardanelles Expedition, about which controversy has raged so hotly that the term just applied to Churchill may be disputed by some critics. This is answered by the verdict of Falkenhayn himself—'If the straits between the Mediterranean and the Black Sea were not permanently closed to Entente traffic, all hopes of a successful course of the war would be very considerably diminished. Russia would have been freed from her significant isolation . . . which offered a safer guarantee than military successes . . . that sooner or later a crippling of the forces of this Titan must take place . . . automatically.' The fault was not in the conception, but in the execution. If the British had used at the outset even a fair proportion of the forces they ultimately expended in driblets, it is clear from Turkish accounts that victory would have crowned their undertaking.

The cause of this piecemeal application of force, and dissipation of opportunity, lay in the opposition of Joffre and the French General Staff, supported by Sir John French. Despite the evidence of the sequel to the Marne, of the German

failure at Ypres, and of his own ambitious yet utterly ineffectual offensive in December, Joffre remained confident
of his power to achieve an early and decisive victory in
France. His plan was that of converging blows from Artois
and Champagne upon the great salient formed by the entrenched German front, to be followed by an offensive in
Lorraine against the rear of the enemy armies. The idea was
similar to that of Foch in 1918, but the vital difference lay in
the conditions existing and the methods employed. A study
of the documents conveys the impression that there has rarely
been such a trinity of optimists in whom faith was divorced
from reason as Joffre, Foch, his deputy in Flanders, and
French—albeit the latter's outlook oscillated violently. In
contrast, the British Government considered that the trench-
front in France was impregnable to frontal attacks, had
strong objection to wasting the man-power of the new armies
in a vain effort, and at the same time felt increasing concern
over the danger of a Russian collapse. These views were
common alike to Churchill, Lloyd George and Kitchener,
who on January 2nd, 1915, wrote to Sir John French—'The
German lines in France may be looked upon as a fortress that
cannot be carried by assault and also that cannot be completely invested, with the result that the lines may be held
by an investing force while operations proceed elsewhere.'

Lloyd George advocated the transfer of the bulk of the
British forces to the Balkans, both to succour Serbia and to
develop an attack on the rear of the hostile alliance. In a
memorandum on January 1st he suggested Salonika or the
Dalmatian coast as bases of operation. That same day,
curiously, Galliéni proposed to the French Government a
landing at Salonika, as a starting point for a march on Constantinople with an army strong enough to encourage Greece
and Bulgaria to combine with the Entente. The capture of
Constantinople was to be followed by an advance up the
Danube into Austria-Hungary in conjunction with the
Rumanians. Franchet d'Esperey expressed similar views.
But the commanders on the Western Front, buoyantly con-

fident of an early break-through, argued vehemently against any alternative strategy, stressing the difficulties of transport and supply and insisting on the ease with which Germany could switch troops to meet the threat.* If there was force in their contention, it tended to ignore the experience of military history, that 'the longest way round is often the shortest way there', and that the acceptance of topographical difficulties has constantly proved preferable to that of a direct attack on an opponent firmly posted and prepared to meet it.

The weight of 'Western' opinion prevailed and the Balkan projects were stifled. But misgivings were not silenced, and at this juncture a situation arose which revived the Near Eastern scheme in a new if attenuated form.

The Dardanelles. On January 2nd, 1915, Kitchener received an appeal from the Grand Duke Nicholas for a diversion which would relieve the Turkish pressure on Russia's army in the Caucasus. Kitchener felt unable to provide troops and suggested a naval demonstration against the Dardanelles, which Churchill, appreciating the wider strategic and economic issues, proposed to convert into an attempt to force the passage. His naval advisers, if not enthusiastic, did not oppose the proposal and, in response to a telegram, the Admiral on the spot, Carden, submitted a plan for a methodical reduction of the forts and clearance of the minefields. A naval force, mainly of obsolete vessels, was got together with French aid and, after a preliminary bombardment, entered the straits on March 18th. Drift mines, however, caused the sinking of several ships, and the attempt was abandoned.

---

* The Germans, in contrast, pointed out in their staff calculations that it was far easier for the Allies to move troops by sea to the Balkans than for them to move troops by rail! The facts show that troop shipments from France to Salonika averaged a week, and from England about twelve days; whereas the Germans took nine days to move an army corps even from the French to the Russian frontier. To move any considerable force to the Balkans would have taken over a month. If sufficient shipping had been made available, the Allies could have sent a force far quicker by sea.

It is a moot point whether a prompt renewal of the advance would not have succeeded, for ammunition in the Turkish forts was exhausted, and in such conditions the mine obstacle might have been overcome. But the new Naval commander, Admiral de Robeck, decided against it, unless military aid was forthcoming. Already, a month before, the War Council had determined on a joint attack, and began the despatch of a military force under Sir Ian Hamilton. But as the authorities had drifted into the new scheme, so were they tardy in releasing the necessary troops, and even when sent, in inadequate numbers, several more weeks' delay had to be incurred—at Alexandria—in order to redistribute the force in its transports suitably for tactical action. Worst of all, this fumbling policy had thrown away the chance of surprise, which was vital for a landing on an almost impregnable shore. When the preliminary bombardment took place in February, only two Turkish divisions were at the straits, this was increased by four by the date of the naval attack, to six when Ian Hamilton was at last able to attempt his landing. For this he had only four British divisions and one French division—actually inferior in strength to the enemy in a situation where the inherent preponderance of defensive over offensive power was multiplied by the natural difficulties of the terrain. His weakness of numbers and his mission of aiding the passage of the fleet compelled him to choose a landing on the Gallipoli peninsula in preference to one on the mainland or on the Asiatic shore; and the rocky coastline limited his possible landing places.

On April 25th he made his spring, at the southern tip of the peninsula near Cape Helles, and—with Australian and New Zealand troops—near Gaba Tepe, some fifteen miles up the Aegean coast; the French, as a diversion, made a temporary landing at Kum Kale on the Asiatic shore. Owing to the Turks' uncertainty the British were able to gain a lodgment on several beaches, strewn with barbed wire and swept by machine-guns. But the momentary asset of tactical surprise was forfeited, and the difficulties of supply were immense, while the Turks held the commanding heights and were able to bring up their reserves. The invaders managed to hold on to their two precarious footholds, but they could not expand them appreciably, and the stagnation of trench warfare set in. They could not go on, and national prestige forbade them to go back.

Ultimately, in July, the British Government decided to send a further five divisions to reinforce the seven now on the peninsula. By the time they arrived the Turkish strength in the region had also risen, to fifteen divisions. Ian Hamilton decided on a double stroke—a reinforced blow from Gaba Tepe and a new landing at Suvla Bay, a few miles north—to sever the middle of the peninsula and secure the heights commanding the Narrows. He deceived the Turkish Command and achieved surprise on August 6th, but the first blow failed and the second lost a splendid chance by the inexperience of the troops, and still more by the inertia and fumbling of the local commanders. For over thirty-six hours, before reserves arrived, only one and a half Turkish battalions barred the path. Energetic new commanders, for whom Ian Hamilton had previously asked, were sent out when the opportunity had passed. The British were once more condemned to hang on to tenuous footholds, and, with the autumn rains setting in, their trials were increased. The Government had lost faith and were anxious to withdraw, but fear of the moral effect delayed their decision. Ian Hamilton was asked for his opinion, however, and when he pronounced in favour of continuing—in which course he still had confidence—he was replaced by Sir Charles Monro, who immediately declared for evacuation.

It was a remarkable example of prompt decision. While Monro visited Anzac, Suvla, and Helles during a single morning, without going further than the beach, his Chief of Staff sat on board ship drafting the recommendation for evacuation. Well may Churchill say—'He came, he saw, he capitulated.' Kitchener at first refused to sanction the withdrawal and himself hurried out to investigate. The Government was most relieved to see him go because they hoped to utilize his absence to relieve him of his post. Most of the Coalition Cabinet were united in dissatisfaction with his secretiveness and his administration, although disunited over the question of evacuating Gallipoli. Mr. Bonar Law, the leader of the Conservative Party, took a strong line on both questions. The Prime Minister, however, feared a public outcry over Kitchener's removal only less than he feared Mr. Bonar Law's resignation, and so temporized by giving way to Bonar Law's demand for evacuation, and by excluding Churchill from the War Committee of the Cabinet. Evacuation, therefore, was virtually decided upon before Kitchener reached Gallipoli. The fresh wave of opinion at home undoubtedly had an effect on his mind, and after his revived proposal for a fresh landing near Alexandretta had been vetoed by the War Committee, he reluctantly veered round and consented to evacuation.

Curiously, in the last phase it was the navy that tried to avert this. For de Robeck, who had passively resisted since March all promptings to a further naval attack, was now relieved by Admiral Wemyss, who not only opposed evacuation but, basing himself on a plan devised by Commodore Keyes, offered 'to force the straits and control them for an indefinite period'. The proposal came too late. The forces of opposition at home were now too strong, and in obedience to orders a withdrawal of the troops was carried out from Suvla and Anzac on the night of December 18th, and from Helles on that of January 8th. If the bloodless evacuation was an example of masterly organization and co-operation, it was also a proof of the greater ease of such operations in modern warfare. And as a final touch of irony Monro and his Chief of Staff, who had nothing to do with its skilful execution, received high decorations in reward. Thus the curtain rang down on a sound and far-sighted conception, marred by a chain of errors in execution almost unrivalled even in British history.

The German Campaign. While the British were striving to

unlock the back door to Russia, the Germanic Powers were hammering the Russians, whose resistance was collapsing in large measure from a lack of munitions which could only be made good by foreign supplies through that locked entrance, the Dardanelles. This fact and its effect was acutely appreciated by Russia's most formidable opponent. In the autumn of 1915, Hoffmann emphatically declared that the success of Germany's efforts against Russia depended on keeping 'the Dardanelles firmly closed'. For if 'the Russians saw that there was no means of exporting their wheat, or importing war material, there would be a gradual collapse in that country.'

On the Eastern Front, the campaign of 1914 had shown that a German force could count on defeating any larger Russian force, but that when Russians and Austrians met on an equality victory rested with the Russians. Falkenhayn was forced, reluctantly, to despatch German reinforcements as a stiffening to the Austrians, and thus was dragged into an offensive in the East, rather than adopting it as a clearly defined plan. Ludendorff, in contrast, had his eyes firmly fixed on a particular object, and from now on advocated unceasingly a wholehearted effort to break Russia. Ludendorff's was a rigid strategy of decision, Falkenhayn's an opportunistic strategy of attrition. The one took too little account of political factors, the other too much.

In the conflict of wills between these two men, lies the clue to the resultant strategy of Germany—highly effective, yet not decisive. This tug of wills was marked by the 'offensive' use of the telegraph and by the unceasing pull of wires, with the Kaiser as the chief puppet. While Falkenhayn was constantly trying to nullify a potential supplanter by denuding Hindenburg of the power to strike the enemy effectively, Ludendorff countered by screwing Hindenburg up to threats of resignation. Well might Hoffmann watching the intrigues, note in his diary—'When one gets a close view of influential people—their bad relations with each other, their conflicting ambitions, one must always bear in mind that it is certainly much worse on the other side among the French, English and Russians, or one might well be nervous'. His intuition was correct. 'The race for power and personal position seems to destroy all men's characters. I believe that the only creature who can keep his honour is a man living on his own estate; he has no need to intrigue and struggle—for it is no use intriguing for fine weather.'

The Russian plan for 1915 embodied some of the lessons of experience and was soundly conceived, but the means were lacking and the instrument defective. The Grand Duke Nicholas aimed to secure both his flanks solidly before attempting a fresh blow towards Silesia. From January until April, under bitter winter conditions, the Russian forces on the southern flank of the Polish salient strove to gain possession of the Carpathians and the gateways into the Hungarian plain. The Austrians, with a German infusion, parried their efforts, and the loss was disproportionate to the small gains. But the long-besieged fortress of Przemysl, with 120,000 men, at last fell into Russian hands on March 22nd. In Northern Poland the Russians were preparing to strike upwards at East Prussia, when they were forestalled by a fresh Ludendorff stroke eastwards towards the frontier of Russia proper. The blow was launched on February 7th, over snow-buried roads and frozen swamps, and was distinguished by the envelopment and capture of four Russian divisions in the Augustovo forests—near the Masurian Lakes. Moreover, it extracted the sting from the Russian attack further west.

These moves were, however, merely a 'curtain-raiser' to the real drama of 1915. But before turning to this it is necessary to glance at events on the Western Front, the importance of which is partly as a signpost to the future and partly because of their reaction on the Eastern Front.

While a way round the trench barrier was being sought in Gallipoli and experiments with a novel key were being carried out in England, the Allied Commands in France were trying more orthodox solutions. In February and March the French lost 50,000 men in nibbling their way 500 yards into the Ger-

man defences in Champagne; in his report Joffre claimed
that the offensive 'was none the less fecund in results'. In
April the French sacrificed 64,000 men in an attack against
the St. Mihiel salient which proved a complete fiasco.
Smaller, yet more significant, was the British attack at Neuve
Chapelle on March 10th. Save as a pure experiment the
attempt stood self-condemned. For it was an isolated attempt on a small front with inadequate resources. The
arrival in France of several new regular divisions—made
up from foreign garrisons, of the Indian Corps, and of the
1st Canadian Division, had brought the British strength up
to thirteen divisions and five cavalry divisions, besides a
number of selected territorial battalions. This increase
enabled French to divide his forces into two armies, and
gradually to extend his share of the front. But Joffre was
insistent that French should relieve the French of the Ypres
salient, which they had taken over in November, and he made
the intended French attack contingent on this relief. Sir John
French considered that he had not sufficient troops for both
purposes, and so decided to carry out the attack single-
handed. An additional motive was his resentment of the
constant French criticisms that the British were not 'pulling
their weight'.

In design, however, the attack, entrusted to Haig's First
Army, was both original and well thought out. After an
intense bombardment of thirty-five minutes' duration on a
two thousand yards' frontage, the artillery lengthened their
range and dropped a curtain of fire to prevent reinforcements
reaching the enemy's battered trenches, which were rapidly
overrun by the British infantry.

Complete surprise was attained, and most of the first
positions captured; but when, in the second phase, the frontage was extended, the artillery support proved inadequate.
Further, owing to scanty information and to the two Corps
commanders waiting upon each other, a long pause occurred
which gave the Germans five clear hours to organize fresh
resistance. Then, too late and mistakenly, Haig ordered the

attack to be pressed 'regardless of loss'. And loss proved the only result. An underlying factor was that the narrowness of the attack sector made the breach more easy for the defenders to close, although this defect was unavoidable owing to the general shortage of munitions, especially heavy guns and high explosive shell for them.

The British had been slower than the Germans to awaken to the scale of munition supply required for this new warfare. Even so, deliveries fell far behind contract, owing largely to the handicap imposed by trade-union rules on the dilution of skilled labour. These could only be modified after long negotiation, and the shortage of shells became so obvious in the spring of 1915 as to lead to a public outcry initiated by Colonel Repington, the military correspondent of *The Times*, after consultation with Sir John French. Lord Northcliffe, with fearless disregard of the odium, threw the full weight of his newspaper into the campaign which culminated in the establishment of a Ministry of Munitions, under Lloyd George, to co-ordinate and develop both the supply and the manufacture of raw materials. Although this press campaign failed to recognize some of the major causes of the shortage, as well as the fact that the need was for more heavy guns and not merely for more shells, its general effect was of incalculable value. Nothing else could have so roused the people or cleared away obstructions. Apart from shells, the crudeness and inferiority of all the British trench-warfare weapons, compared with the German, made such a radical reorganization overdue, and its urgency was emphasized by the near approach of the time when Britain's new national armies would take the field. If the task was undertaken late, it was carried out with energy and thoroughness, although improvisation was long in overtaking the evil consequences of earlier neglect. Apart from labour difficulties the immediate fault lay largely with military shortsightedness, which manifested itself in a constant tendency to underestimate needs and underrate novelties.

It is significant that as far back as 1908 the Financial

Secretary of the War Office, impressed by an official observer's report of the growing use of machine-guns in the
German Army, wrote to the Master-General of the Ordnance
that 'if the military members of the Council would like to
have more machine-guns for the Army that at any rate the
Finance Department of the War Office would make no
objection'. He received the reply that two machine-guns per
battalion were enough. And to that scale the War Office
authorities stubbornly adhered, although in 1909 the School
of Musketry urged an increase to six.

Even when the machine-gun had obviously gained a dominance of the battlefield, General Headquarters in France
resisted its growth from the puny pre-war scale of two in each
battalion. One Army commander, Haig, declared that it
was 'a much overrated weapon' and that this scale was 'more
than sufficient'. Even Kitchener laid down that four were a
maximum and any in excess a luxury—until the Ministry of
Munitions came to the rescue of the machine-gun advocates
and boldly multiplied the scale of provision by sixteen. It
was due also to Mr. Lloyd George that the Stokes Gun, a
quick-firing light mortar, had the chance to surmount the
official barrier and develop into the outstanding and ubiqui-
tous trench weapon of the war. And later, the Ministry of
Munitions succoured the tank when it was repeatedly threatened by the suffocating embrace of the War Office.

Nevertheless the ultimate responsibility for the munition
failure lay with the British people, and their representatives
in Parliament. Although, before the war came, the new Committee of Imperial Defence had done much preparatory spade
work, a strict limit was set to its efforts by the passivity as well
as parsimony of Parliament and people in face of the growing
danger of war. Preparedness crawled forward to meet the
onrushing menace. Most fundamental of all faults was the
neglect to organize the industrial resources of the country for
conversion and expansion in case of war. While an increase
in the fighting forces may, by its air of threat, accelerate the
danger of war, readiness for industrial mobilization is unpro-

vocative and, if war comes, a more essential foundation for the power to wage it.

This pre-war neglect is a far graver charge against the Government which declared war on August 4th, 1914, than any failure to increase the army estimates or to introduce conscription. Yet in making that declaration the Government, however conscious of the political and moral issues, appears to have been unconscious that it was dooming the manhood of the nation to a terrible drain of life through want of weapons. It is a moral question how far, in such circumstances, any Government is justified in taking the decision for war and in retaining office. The only excuse lies in the sanction of public indifference to such needs. And unhappily, experience has shown the practical difficulties suffered by a democratic Government which tries to outstrip public opinion. Thus the ultimate responsibility falls on the British people. Even the military conservatism which obstructed improvements and reorganization during the war may be charged to lack of public concern with the training and selection of officers in peace. In the light of 1914-1918 the whole people bear the stigma of infanticide.

No belated wartime spurt could overtake the consequences of pre-war neglect until many thousands of lives had been wasted vainly. Even the Somme offensive was to be hampered by a limited supply of ammunition, while of this much was wasted because of the failure of hastily produced fuses. Not until the end of 1916 did the flow of munitions reach a volume, still expanding, which finally removed any material handicap on the strategy of the British leaders.

The tactical sequel of Neuve Chapelle was less fortunate. It was clear that the small-scale experiment had only missed success by a narrow margin, and that there was scope for its development. But the Entente commands missed the true lesson, which was the surprise attainable by a short bombardment that compensated its brevity by its intensity. And only partially did they appreciate the fact that the sector attacked must be sufficiently wide to prevent the defender's artillery commanding, or his reserves closing, the breach. Instead, they drew the superficial deduction that mere volume of shell-fire was the key to success. Not until 1917 did they revert to the Neuve Chapelle method. It was left to the Germans to profit by the experience against the Russians in May.

But before that occurred, the Western Front was destined to increase the tally of military blunders. In the first, it was the Germans' turn to find and misuse a new key to the trench deadlock. This was the introduction of gas, and, unlike the British introduction of tanks later, the chance, once forfeited, did not return, owing to the relative ease of providing an antidote. On October 27th, 1914, in the Neuve Chapelle sector, the Germans fired three thousand shrapnel shells containing a nose and eye irritant as well as bullets. This was the first battlefield experiment, but the effect was so weak that the fact was not even known until revealed by the Germans after the war. Then, in a local attack in Poland on January 31st, 1915, the Germans tried the use of improved lachrymatory gas shell, but the experiment was a failure owing to the nullifying effect of the intense cold. At the next attempt the gas was lethal and was discharged from cylinders owing to the failure of the authorities to provide the inventor, Haber, with adequate facilities for the manufacture of shells. Further, the initial disappointment led the German Command to place little trust in its value. In consequence, when gas was discharged against the French trenches at Ypres on April 22nd, there were no reserves at hand to pour through the wide breach it created. A strange green vapour, a surging mass of agonized fugitives, a four-mile gap without a living defender —such was the sequence of events. But the resistance of the Canadians on the flank of the breach and the prompt arrival of English and Indian reinforcements saved the situation in the absence of German reserves.

The chlorine gas originally used was undeniably cruel, but no worse than the frequent effect of shell or bayonet, and when it was succeeded by improved forms of gas both experience and statistics proved it the least inhumane of modern weapons. But it was novel and therefore labelled an atrocity by a world which condones abuses but detests innovations. Thus Germany incurred the moral odium which inevitably accompanies the use of a novel weapon without any compensating advantage.

On the Entente side, wisdom would have counselled a period of waiting until their munition supply had grown and the new British armies were ready, but the desire to regain lost territory and the duty of relieving the pressure on Russia, combined with ill-founded optimism to spur Joffre to premature offensives. The German losses were exaggerated, their skill and power in defence underrated, and a series of diffused and unconnected attacks were made. The chief was by the French between Lens and Arras, under Foch's direction, when the earlier experience of failure to make an effective breach in the trench barrier was repeated. The attack was launched on May 9th by d'Urbal's Army (of eighteen divisions) on a four-mile frontage. It was quickly checked with murderous losses except on the front of Pétain's corps which, thanks to meticulous preparation, broke through to a depth of two miles. But the penetration was too narrow, reserves were late and inadequate and the gap closed. Foch, however, persevered with vain attacks which gained a few acres of ground at excessive loss. Meantime Haig's First Army had attacked towards Aubers Ridge simultaneously with the larger French attempt. The plan was to penetrate at two points north and south of Neuve Chapelle, four miles apart—the total frontage of the two being two and a quarter miles—and then to converge in exploiting the double penetration. But the Germans, profiting also from the experimental value of Neuve Chapelle, had developed their defences. Thus the attack died away quickly from a surfeit of German machine-guns and an insufficiency of British shells. Under pressure from Joffre the attack was renewed on May 15th on the Festubert sector south of Neuve Chapelle, and continued by small bites until May 27th. The larger French offensive between Lens and Arras was not abandoned until June 18th, when the French had lost 102,500 men—nearly double the defenders' loss.

The effect of these attacks was, moreover, to convince even the dubious Falkenhayn of the strength of his Western line, and of the remoteness of any real menace from the Franco-British forces. His offensive on the Eastern Front had already opened. Tactically unlimited, its strategic object was at first only the limited one of relieving the pressure on the Austrian front, and, concurrently, of reducing Russia's offensive power. Conrad proposed and Falkenhayn accepted a plan to break through the Russian centre as the best means to this end. In this plan the Gorlice-Tarnow sector between the upper Vistula and the Carpathians was selected as offering the fewest obstacles to an advance and best protection to the flanks of a penetration.

The break-through was entrusted to Mackensen, whose Chief of Staff and guiding brain was Seeckt, the man who was to rebuild the German army after the war. Mackensen's force comprised the newly formed German Eleventh Army—made up with eight divisions from the west, and the Fourth Austro-Hungarian Army. The Ypres gas attack and a large cavalry raid from East Prussia were initiated to cloak the concentration on the Dunajec of fourteen divisions and one thousand guns against a front held by only six Russian divisions. This front was composed of several lines of trenches but not highly fortified. Between the opposing sides there was a wide no-man's-land, as much as two miles across, in which 'the inhabitants were still living in their farms, the cattle pasturing undisturbed'—until the Germans removed these people as a precaution against any leakage of news.

Mackensen's army arrived on the scene and took over its allotted sector during the last week in April, being inserted between two Austrian armies. For his 18-mile front of attack Mackensen had one field gun to every 45 yards, and one heavy gun to every 132 yards. If this was not large by later standards it was ample to solve the problem of breaking *into* a position such as the Russians had organized. The greater problem was that of maintaining the momentum of the advance so as to break *through* the rearward positions before the Russian reserves could arrive and man them. To meet this need Seeckt issued instructions that 'all staffs must strive to keep the advance continuously moving'. No definite daily objectives were to be assigned to corps and divisions 'lest by fixing them the possibility of further progress might be stopped'. 'The quick advance of one part of the front will ease the situation at other parts where there is more resistance . . . disposition in depth should enable the success at one place to be extended to a neighbouring front.' This conception of a varying progress coupled with a flexible use of reserves foreshadowed the famous 'infiltration' method of 1918, with its keynote of backing up success instead of trying to redeem local failure. To the further benefit of the Germans Ivanov (the Russian Army Group Commander) would not believe reports of the impending attack and was thus caught with his reserves badly placed.

During the night of May 1st the storm troops moved forward across no-man's-land and dug in close to the enemy front line. At 10 a.m. on the 2nd, after a four hours' intense bombardment had flattened the Russian trenches, the attack was launched and the infantry swept forward through the dust and smoke. 'Here and there loam-grey figures jumped up and ran back, weaponless, in grey fur caps and fluttering, unbuttoned greatcoats. Soon there was not one of them remaining. Like a flock of sheep they fled in wild confusion.' The surprise was complete, the exploitation rapid, and despite a gallant stand on the Wisloka river, the whole Russian line along the Carpathians was rolled up, until on May 14th the Austro-German advance reached the San, eighty miles from its starting point. Russian defeat almost turned into disaster when the San was forced at Jaroslav, but the impetus of the advance had momentarily spent itself and reserves were lacking. A new factor was introduced by Italy's declaration of war against Austria, but Falkenhayn persuaded the Austrian

Command, with some difficulty, not to move troops from the Russian front, and to maintain a strict defensive on their Italian frontier, which was secured by the mountain barrier. He realized that he had committed himself too far in Galicia to draw back, and that only by bringing more troops from France could he hope to fulfil his object of transferring troops back there. For this could only be possible when Russia's offensive power was crippled and her menace to Austria removed. Strengthened by these reinforcements, Mackensen attacked again in co-operation with the Austrians, retook Przemysl on June 3rd and captured Lemberg on June 22nd, cutting the Russian front into two separated portions.

But neither Falkenhayn nor Conrad had foreseen such results, and in consequence no arrangements had been made to maintain supplies during so long an advance. Hurried improvisation could not atone for lack of preparation, and the consequent delays allowed the enemy to retire without dissolving, though he left copious drippings.

The Russians, from their vast man-power resources, had almost made good the loss of 400,000 prisoners, so that Falkenhayn's anxiety about the stability of his Austrian Allies led him to yield to Seeckt's insistence and to continue the offensive, although still with limited objects and with one eye on the situation in France. Mackensen's direction was changed, however, from eastwards to northwards, up the wide corridor between the Bug and Vistula, where lay the main Russian forces. In conjunction, Hindenburg was ordered to strike south-east from East Prussia, across the Narew and towards the Bug. Ludendorff disliked the plan as being too much of a frontal attack; the Russians might be squeezed by the closing in of the two wings, but their retreat would not be cut off. He urged once more his spring scheme for a wide enveloping manœuvre through Kovno on Vilna and Minsk. Conrad took the same view. Falkenhayn opposed this plan, fearing that it would mean more troops and a deeper commitment. And on July 2nd the Kaiser decided in favour of his plan. But the result justified Ludendorff's expectation—

the Grand Duke extricated his troops from the Warsaw salient before the German shears could close on him. Falkenhayn, on the other hand, considered that Ludendorff had not put his full weight into the attack. The controversy became bitter. Hindenburg wrote not only to Falkenhayn but to the chief of the Kaiser's Military Cabinet, declaring that his title of Commander-in-Chief on the Eastern Front had become a 'cutting irony'. Falkenhayn unkindly took him at his word, by taking away one of his armies, and forming a fresh group of Armies, thus reducing his status.

By the middle of August, 750,000 prisoners had been taken, Poland had been occupied, and Falkenhayn decided to break off large-scale operations on the Eastern Front. Bulgaria's entry into the war was now arranged and he wished to support the combined attack of Austria and Bulgaria against Serbia, as well as to transfer troops back to meet the French offensive expected in September. Yet, in hope of redeeming the lost opportunity and placating his personal opponents, he was led to sanction one more effort to break the Russians. Ludendorff was given belated permission to carry out his Vilna scheme, with such resources as he had, while Conrad planned to strike eastward from Luck in an attempt to repeat 'Gorlice' and cut off the Russian forces south of the Pripet marshes.

Ludendorff's move began on September 9th, Below's Army of the Niemen and Eichhorn's Tenth Army forming two great horns which gored their way into the Russian front, the one east towards Dvinsk and the other south-east towards Vilna. The Russians were driven back in divergent directions and the German cavalry, advancing between the horns, far overlapped Vilna and drew near the Minsk railway. But the German strength was slender, and the Russians free to concentrate against this isolated menace. In face of stiffening resistance and shrinking supplies Ludendorff was driven to suspend operations. The crux of the situation was that the Russian armies had been allowed to draw back almost out of the net before the long-delayed Vilna manœuvre was attempted.

The Austrian offensive did not develop until September 26th, and then failed dismally. Conrad unwisely persisted in renewing it, and, by the middle of October, the Austrians had sacrificed 230,000 men without affecting the general issue. Russia had been badly lamed, but not destroyed, and, although never again a direct menace to Germany, she was able to delay the full concentration of German strength in the west for two years, until 1918. Falkenhayn's cautious strategy was to prove the most hazardous in the long run, and indeed to pave the way for Germany's bankruptcy.

By October, the Russian retreat, after a nerve-racking series of escapes from the salients which the Germans systematically created and then sought to cut off, came to a definite halt on a straightened line, stretching from Riga on the Baltic to Czernowitz on the Rumanian frontier. The Russian armies, however, had gained this respite at a ruinous price, and their Western Allies had effected little in repayment of Russia's sacrifice on their behalf in 1914.

For the Franco-British relief offensive of September 25th had been no more fruitful than its predecessors. The main blow was launched by the French in Champagne, in conjunction with a Franco-British attack in Artois, on either side of Lens. One fault was that the sectors were too far apart to have a reaction on each other, but a worse was that the Command tried to reconcile two irreconcilable factors—they aimed at a break-through, but preceded it with a prolonged bombardment which gave away any chance of surprise. Joffre's plan was that the break-through in these two sectors was to be followed by a general offensive on the whole Franco-British front which would 'compel the Germans to retreat beyond the Meuse and possibly end the war'. The unquenchable optimist! Both in Champagne and Artois the attacks penetrated the German forward positions without difficulty, but subsequent delay in bringing reserves forward allowed the German reserves to close the gaps, a task simplified by the narrowness of the frontage of attack. The slight gains of ground in no way compensated for the heavy price paid for them—the Allied loss was approximately 242,000 against 141,000 Germans. And if the Allied Commands had gained more experience, so had the Germans, in the art of defence. The British share in this offensive is, however, notable as marking the appearance in strength of the New Armies; at Loos they were 'blooded', and if inexperience detracted from their effectiveness, their courage and driving force were an omen of Britain's power to improvise a national effort comparable with the long-created military machines of the Continent.

The direction of this effort inspired less confidence, and Sir John French gave place to Sir Douglas Haig as Commander-in-Chief, just as already in September the Russian Command had been transferred from the Grand Duke Nicholas, nominally to the Tsar, as a moral symbol, but actually to General Alexeiev, the new Chief of Staff.* Simultaneously, French's Chief of Staff, William Robertson, who had been long slighted by him owing to Henry Wilson's stronger influence, went home to become Chief of the Imperial General Staff, in order to give a stronger direction to the general strategy of Britain—if also to give it a Western Front bias. Somewhat curiously, Haig chose as his own Chief of Staff an old friend, Kiggell, who had not hitherto seen any service in France.

Italy's First Campaign. Italy's military contribution to the Allied balance sheet of 1915 was handicapped not only by her unreadiness, but by the awkward strategic position of her frontier, difficult for initiating an offensive and hardly more favourable for a secure defensive. The Italian frontier province of Venezia formed a salient pointing to Austria and

* General Brusilov, Russia's most successful commander, has described him as 'a fine strategist. His chief fault was indecision and want of moral courage'. 'I consider that had he been the Chief of Staff of a real Commander-in-Chief, he would have been beyond criticism. But with a Commander [the Tsar] whose mind he had to make up for him, and whose feeble will he had to strengthen, Alexeiev was not the right man.' Trotsky, more contemptuously, depicts him as a 'grey mediocrity, the oldest military clerk of the Army, worn out through mere perseverance'.

flanked on the north by the Austrian Trentino, on the south by the Adriatic. Bordering on the Adriatic was a stretch of relatively low ground on the Isonzo sector, but the frontier then followed the Julian and Carnic Alps in a wide sweep round to the north-west. Any advance eastwards inevitably suffered the potential menace of an Austrian descent from the Trentino upon its rear.

Nevertheless the easterly sector, though difficult enough, seemed to offer more prospect of success—besides threatening a vital part of Austria—than an advance northward into the Alps. When Italy was preparing to enter the war, General Cadorna, who assumed command, drew up his plan on this basis of an offensive eastwards and a defensive attitude in the north. The overhanging menace of the Trentino was mitigated by the expectation of simultaneous pressure upon Austria from Russia and Serbia. But on the eve of Italy's declaration of war this hope faded, the Russian armies falling back under Mackensen's blows, while the Serbs, despite requests from the Allies, failed to make even a demonstration. This lack of pressure enabled the Austrians to despatch five divisions to the Isonzo from the Serbian front, these being relieved by three newly formed German divisions. Three more divisions were sent from Galicia. Even so there were only some thirteen divisions in all available to oppose the Italians, who had a numerical superiority of more than two to one.

In order to secure good covering positions on the north a limited advance was made into the Trentino, with success, but another into the north-east corner of the frontier salient —towards Tarvis in the Carnic Alps—was forestalled. This local failure was to have unfortunate results later—in 1917, for it left the Austrians with a good strategic sally port into the Tagliamento valley.

Meantime the main Italian advance, by the Second and Third Armies, had begun at the end of May, but out of their total of twenty-four divisions only seven were ready. Bad weather increased the handicap, the Isonzo coming down in flood, and the initial advance soon came to a standstill. The

Isonzo front crystallized, like the others, into trench warfare. The Italian mobilization, however, was now complete and Cadorna mounted a deliberate attack, which opened on June 23rd. This first battle of the Isonzo continued until July 7th with little gain to show. A fresh series of efforts after a ten days' pause were hardly more effective, and the front then relapsed into the spasmodic bickering characteristic of trench warfare, while Cadorna made preparations for a new and larger effort in the autumn. When it was launched in October he had a two-to-one superiority in numbers, but was weak in artillery. This defect, coupled with the superior experience of the defender, rendered the new offensive as barren as its predecessors. It was sustained too obstinately and, when finally broken off in December, the Italian loss in the six months' campaign totalled some 280,000—nearly twice that of the defenders, who had shown on this front a fierce resolution which was often lacking when they faced the Russians.

The Conquest of Serbia. While stalemate, although with marked changes beneath the surface, had once more settled in on both the Russian and French fronts, the later months of 1915 witnessed fluid operations elsewhere which were to have an unforeseen influence on the war.

One of the most remarkable 'blind spots' in the strategy of the Allies was the failure to perceive the importance of Serbia as an irritation, and consequent distraction, to the Austro-German alliance in a most sensitive region. Such a menace to uneasy Austria's rear flank was an invaluable distraction to the forces and plans of the enemy alliance as a whole. It was, indeed, a necessary distraction if Serbia's allies were to concentrate with effective results in the main theatres. Geography made Serbia a potential 'Austrian ulcer', at a politically and militarily tender spot. To maintain the irritation, quality rather than quantity of aid was needed. Not the despatch of large allied forces, which could scarcely be supplied until communications were improved; but the provision of technical troops and material. The Serbs themselves were magnificent fighting troops, and naturally suited to the terrain: what they required were the means of fighting effectively. To provide these was a far more urgent, and more economic, step than to equip the newly raised armies of Britain. By neglecting it the Allies allowed their Austro-German opponents to operate on and excise the ulcer: this blindness was the source of wider, and widening, trouble to themselves.

Austria had proved capable of holding the Italians on the Isonzo, and once the Russian danger began to fade under the pressure of the summer offensive, her Command was anxious to deal conclusively with Serbia. Austria's attempted invasions in August and September, and again in November, 1914, had been brusquely repulsed by Serbian counterstrokes, and it was not pleasant for a great Power, especially one with so many Slav subjects, to swallow such military rebuffs. Her impatience coincided with Falkenhayn's desire to gain direct railway communication with Turkey, hard pressed at the Dardanelles. Throughout the summer the rival coalitions had been bidding for Bulgaria's support, and in this bargaining the Entente suffered the moral handicap of military failure, and the material handicap caused by Serbia's unwillingness to give up any part of Macedonia—of which she had despoiled Bulgaria in 1913. As Austria had no objection to offering territory that belonged to her enemy, Bulgaria accepted her bid. This accession of strength enhanced the chance of a decision against Serbia, and in August Falkenhayn decided to reinforce the Austrian Third Army with Gallwitz's Army from the Russian front. In addition two Bulgarian armies were available. Mackensen and Seeckt were sent to direct the operations. To meet this new threat Serbia, apart from her own relatively small forces, had only a treaty guarantee of Greek aid and promises from the Entente Powers. The first disappeared with the fall of Venizelos, the pro-Ally Greek Premier, and the second, as usual, were too late.

On October 6th, 1915, the Austro-German armies attacked

southwards across the Danube, with a flanking movement across the Drina on the right. The sturdy resistance of the Serbs in delaying actions and the natural difficulty of the mountainous country checked the advance, but before Franco-British reinforcements could arrive the Bulgarian armies struck westwards into southern Serbia, across the rear of the main Serbian armies. This drove a deep wedge between the Serbs and their Allies, moving up from Salonika, and automatically loosened the resistance in the north. With their line bent at both ends until it resembled a vast bow, threatened with a double envelopment, and with their retreat to the south cut off, the Serbian armies decided to retire west through the Albanian mountains. Those who survived the hardships of this mid-winter retreat were conveyed to the island of Corfu, and after being re-equipped and reorganized, joined the Entente force at Salonika in the spring of 1916. The conquest of Serbia—though not, as it proved, of Serbian military power—relieved Austria of danger on her southern frontier, and gave Germany free communication and control over a huge central belt from the North Sea to the Tigris. For the Entente this campaign dug a military sump-pit which for three years was to drain their military resources, there to lie idle and ineffective. Yet ultimately that sump-pit was to overflow and wash away one of the props of the Central Alliance.

The Salonika Expedition. When at the beginning of October the Entente Governments had awakened to Serbia's danger, British and French divisions had been despatched hurriedly from Gallipoli to Salonika, which was the only channel of aid to Serbia—by the railway to Uskub. The advanced guard of this relieving force—which was under the command of General Sarrail—pressed up the Vardar and over the Serbian frontier, only to find that the Bulgarian wedge had cut it off from the Serbians, and it was forced to fall back on Salonika, pursued by the Bulgarians. On military grounds an evacuation of Salonika was vigorously urged by the British General Staff, but political reasons induced the Allies to remain. The Dardanelles failure had already diminished their prestige, and by convincing the Balkan States of German invincibility had induced Bulgaria to enter the war and Greece to break her treaty with Serbia. To evacuate Salonika would be a further loss of prestige, whereas by holding on the Allies could check German influence over Greece, and maintain a base of operations from which to aid Rumania, if, as expected, she entered the war on their side. To this end the Salonika force was augmented with fresh British and French divisions, as well as contingents from Italy and Russia, and there also the rebuilt Serbian army was brought. But apart from the capture of Monastir in November, 1916, and an abortive attack in April, 1917, the Entente forces made no serious offensive until the autumn of 1918. Its feeble effect was partly due to the natural difficulties of the country in the form of mountain ridges guarding the approach to the Balkans, partly to the feeling of the Allied Governments that it was a bad debt, and partly to the personality of Sarrail, whose conduct and reputation for political intrigues failed to command the confidence and co-operation essential if such a mixed force was to 'pull its weight'. On their side the Germans were content to leave it in passivity, under guard of the Bulgarians, while they steadily withdrew their own forces for use elsewhere. With gentle sarcasm they termed Salonika their 'largest internment camp', and with half a million Allied troops locked up their gibe had some justification—until 1918.

Mesopotamia. Nor was Salonika the only 'drain' opened in 1915. Mesopotamia was the site of a fresh diversion of force from the centre of military gravity, and one which could only be excused on purely political grounds. It was not, like the Dardanelles and Salonika, undertaken to relieve a hard-pressed ally, nor had it the justification of the Dardanelles expedition of being directed at the vital point of one of the enemy States. The occupation of Mesopotamia might raise British prestige, and it might annoy Turkey, but it could not endanger her power of resistance. Although its origin was sound its development was another example of 'drift' due to the inherent faultiness of Britain's machinery for the conduct of war.

The oilfields near the Persian Gulf were of essential importance to Britain's oil supply, and thus, when war with Turkey was imminent, a small Indian force of one division was despatched to safeguard them. To fulfil this mission effectively it was necessary to occupy the Basra vilayet at the head of the Persian Gulf, in order to command the possible lines of approach.

On November 21st, 1914, Basra was captured, but the rising stream of Turkish reinforcements compelled the Indian Government to add a second division. The Turkish attacks in the spring of 1915 were repulsed, and the British commander, General Nixon, judged it wise to expand his footing, for greater security. Townshend's division was pushed up the Tigris to Amara, gaining a brilliant little victory, and the other division up the Euphrates to Nasiriya. Southern Mesopotamia was a vast alluvial plain, roadless and railless, in which these two great rivers formed the only channels of communication. Thus a hold on Amara and Nasiriya covered the oilfields; but Nixon and the Indian Government, inspired by these successes, decided to push forward to Kut-el-Amara. This move led the British a hundred and eighty miles further into the interior, but had a partial military justification in the fact that at Kut the Shatt-el-Hai, issuing from the Tigris, formed a link with the Euphrates by which Turkish reserves might be transferred from one river line to the other.

Townshend was sent forward in August; he defeated the Turks near Kut, and his cavalry carried the pursuit to Aziziya, halfway to Baghdad. Enthusiasm spread to the Home Government, anxious for a moral counterpoise to their other failures, and Nixon received permission for Townshend to press on to Baghdad. But after an indecisive battle at Ctesiphon, the growing superiority of the Turkish strength compelled Townshend to retreat to Kut. Here, isolated far from help, he was urged to remain, as several fresh divisions were being sent to Mesopotamia. Kut was invested by the Turks on December 8th, 1915, and the relieving forces battered in vain against the Turkish lines covering the approach on either bank of the Tigris. The conditions were bad, the communications worse, the generalship faulty, and at last on April 29th, 1916, Kut was forced to surrender. However unsound the strategy which despatched Townshend on this adventure, it is just to emphasize the actual achievements of his small force in face of superior numbers. With inadequate equipment and primitive communications, and utterly isolated in the heart of an enemy country, it wrote a glorious page of military history. When these handicaps are compared with the four-to-one superiority in number, and highly organized supply system of the force which ultimately took Baghdad, the comparison explains the awe in which Townshend and his men were held by the Turks.

The Home Front, 1915. Perhaps one of the most significant landmarks in the transition of the struggle from a 'military' to a 'national' war was the formation of a National Ministry in Britain, which occurred in May, 1915. For the prototype of Parliaments to abandon the deep-rooted party system and pool the direction of the war was proof of the psychological upheaval of traditions. The Liberal Prime Minister, Asquith, remained, but the Conservative element acquired a preponderant voice in the Cabinet, although the dynamic personality of Lloyd George began to gain such a hold on public opinion that the real leadership slipped into his hands. Churchill, whose vision had saved the menace to the Channel ports and made possible the future key to the deadlock, was shelved, as already had been Haldane, the creator of the Expeditionary Force.

Political changes were general in all countries, and were symptomatic of a readjustment of popular outlook. The early fervour had disappeared, and been repulsed by a dogged determination which, if natural to the British, was in strange contradiction to popular, if superficial, conceptions of the French temperament.

Economically, the strain had yet to be felt severely by any country. Finance had shown an unexpected power of accommodation, and neither the blockade nor the submarine campaign had seriously affected food supply. If Germany was beginning to suffer some shortage, her people had more tangible omens of success to fortify their resolution than had their enemies. In 1916, however, the strain on them was to be intensified by the failure of the 1915 harvest—the worst for forty years. Fortunately for Germany's powers of endurance the danger was to be relieved, and the British blockade partly nullified, by the inexpensive capture of a wheat-growing country on the Eastern Front. Ironically, the enemy were to throw Germany this lifebuoy, by encouraging Rumania to enter the war, after Falkenhayn had almost drowned the war-will of the German people in a bath of blood and tears by his renewed offensive on the Western Front.

CHAPTER V

SCENE I

THE BIRTH OF A 'PLAN'—
THE DARDANELLES

A GIANT, three ships, and the fear of a rape were the main factors in bringing Turkey into the war against her traditional ally, Britain. The giant was Baron Marschall von Bieberstein, who for fifteen years, until 1912, was German Ambassador at Constantinople. To a race whose sole criterion of conduct and admiration was might, whose 'chivalry' was only extended to the mighty, Marschall von Bieberstein's huge frame, scarred face and trampling manner formed a living picture of the growing power of Germany. Perhaps one man alone could have counteracted the impression with that of Britain's more mature and quieter strength. This man was Kitchener, who, curiously, seems to have felt an ungratified desire for the post. Instead, the British Ambassador during the critical years was one from whose personality the requisite prestige and strength were absent—and who, during the critical weeks, was even absent on leave.

The ships were the new German battle cruiser *Goeben*, and the British-built battleships *Sultan Osman* and *Reschadieh*. A shrewd step to enhance German prestige and weaken the one remaining foothold of British influence—that of the naval mission—the *Goeben* was sent out early in 1914 to Constantinople and for long lay anchored near the entrance to the Golden Horn. Then, in the war-charged atmosphere of late July, the ever-present Turkish fear of Russian lust for the Dardanelles developed almost to panic point. It was none the less powerful because mingled with Turkish lust for wider dominion. Certain of war between Germany and Russia, uncertain of Britain's entry, and egged on by the Germanophil Enver Pasha, the Turkish Grand Vizier responded to previous German overtures by asking the German

ambassador, on July 27th, for a secret alliance against
Russia. Next day the proposal was accepted, and on August
2nd the treaty was signed—unknown to most of the Turkish
Cabinet. On the morrow the first mines were laid in the
Dardanelles; and Enver had already mobilized the Turkish
forces on his own initiative. But the news of Britain's entry
into the war was a shock which nearly burst the new treaty
like a paper balloon. Indeed, so much 'hot air' was generated
during the next few days that it even sufficed to blow out
another *ballon d'essai*—the astonishing offer to Russia of a
Turkish Alliance. But this offer did not suit Russia's ambition, even though it promised her the one chance of having
a channel through which she could receive munitions from
her Western allies. She preferred isolation to the sacrifice of
her dream of annexation, and did not even report the offer
to her allies.

But Turkey's sudden reversal of attitude, and the predominance of her fear of British power over the fear of
Russian ambition, were short-lived. And the revival of confidence was greatly helped by annoyance. Turkey, smarting
under her wounds of the Balkan War, had been awaiting the
delivery of her first two modern battleships with an eagerness
and pride all the more general because the money had been
raised by collections among the people. On August 3rd,
however, the British government informed Turkey that it
was taking over the ships—and the announcement caused an
explosion of indignation. Every man who had contributed
his mite felt an injury akin to a personal betrayal. This
popular outcry was at its height when, on August 10th, the
Goeben, accompanied by the cruiser *Breslau*, appeared at the
entrance to the Dardanelles, having slipped past the British
Fleet near Sicily.

An officer of the German Military Mission, Lieut.-Colonel
von Kress, brought the news to the War Minister, Enver
Pasha, and told him that the forts were asking instructions as
to whether they should allow the warships to enter. Then a
vital interchange took place. Enver—'I can't decide that

now. I must first consult the Grand Vizier.' Kress—'But we must wire immediately.' A moment of inward turmoil. Then —'They are to allow them to enter.' A further and guileful question from Kress—'If the English warships follow the Germans, are they to be fired on if they also attempt an entrance?' 'The matter must be left to the decision of the Cabinet.' 'Excellency, we cannot leave our subordinates in such a position without issuing immediately clear and definite instructions. Are the English to be fired on or not?' Another pause. 'Yes.' As General Kannengiesser, a German witness of this eventful discussion, says—'We heard the clanking of the portcullis descending before the Dardanelles.'

International law was evaded, British objections frustrated, Turkish pride satisfied, and Enver's dubious colleagues calmed by arranging the fictitious sale to Turkey of these warships. Turkey was not yet ready for nor agreed upon war, and Britain had every motive to avoid it.

Thus, during the weeks that followed, the Turks were successively enabled and emboldened to advance along the path to war by the passivity of Britain in face of growing provocation. The German crews were kept, the German Admiral appointed to command the Turkish Navy, the British naval Mission removed from control, and then forced to withdraw; British ships were detained, their wireless dismantled; German soldiers and sailors filtered into Constantinople, and the straits were closed. Meantime Turkish Ministers, ever ready with glib assurances, congratulated themselves on the gullibility of the British, whose restraint was rather due to an acute sense of vulnerability, as a power with millions of Moslem subjects. Conciliation was pressed to the point of folly, however, when the British Admiralty's intention to appoint Admiral Limpus, ex-chief of the Naval Mission to Turkey, to command the British Dardanelles Squadron was abandoned for fear of giving offence to the Turks! And when the need for conciliation had passed, a misplaced chivalry seems to have taken its place in preventing the use of the one man who knew the Turks and the Dardanelles intimately.

Even the Germans began to be worried when a series of raids on the Egyptian frontier could not goad Britain to war. So the German Admiral, with Enver's connivance, led the Turkish Fleet on a raid into the Black Sea against Britain's more sensitive ally, shelling Odessa and other Russian ports. The story of this provocation, as related to and recorded by Lord D'Abernon after the war, is illuminating. The official sanction came to the German Embassy in a sealed envelope addressed to the Admiral. An official took the initiative and precaution to open it and send on merely a copy. The first report that reached Constantinople was that the *Goeben* had been sunk, and so, thinking that the order had sunk with her, the Grand Vizier conciliatingly replied to Russian protests by denying that any such order had been given. Thereupon the German Embassy sent to him, saying—'The order of which you deny the existence, because you think it was sunk with the *Goeben*, is in a safe place . . . at the German Embassy. . . . . Pray cease to deny that the Turkish government has given the order to attack Russia.' Thus the war-fearing Grand Vizier was compelled to stand aside helplessly while German cunning removed any excuse to the Triple Entente for avoiding war—at the end of October.

The best chance for both Britain and Russia was now in making war, instantly. The defences of the Dardanelles were obsolete and still incomplete. The only two munition factories in Turkey lay on the shore close to Constantinople and open to easy destruction by any warships which penetrated thither. The misuse of the opportunity is a tale of almost incredible haphazardness on the part of Britain, of equal shortsightedness on the part of Russia.

On November 3rd the Allied Fleet carried out a short bombardment of the outer forts at the Dardanelles, the only use of which was to help the German authorities in trying to overcome Turkish inertia over the defences. They had sunk back into lethargy again when, six weeks later, a British submarine gave a fresh alarm and gained its commander a V.C. by diving under the mines and sinking a ship near the

Narrows. But the effect of these warnings has been over-rated. Turkish lethargy was almost as boundless as British folly. Not until the end of February did the Turks post more than one division on the Gallipoli Peninsula, and not until March did the improvements in the defences of the straits approach completion. In part, this state of weakness seems to have been due to a feeling that it was waste of energy to try to prevent a passage, which could not be prevented against any serious attempt. If the few well-informed experts, German or Turk, were dubious of their power to stop a purely naval attack, they were still less confident of resisting a combined attack. And the Turkish Staff history frankly says: 'Up to 25th February, it would have been possible to effect a landing successfully at any point on the peninsula, and the capture of the straits by land troops would have been comparatively easy.'

At one time the Entente might have found such troops, in quantity, without touching their own resources. For in mid August the Greek Prime Minister, Venizelos, had formally and unreservedly placed all his country's forces at the disposal of the Entente. The offer was not accepted, owing mainly to Sir Edward Grey's desire to avoid antagonizing Turkey, whose hatred for Greece was stronger than for any other of her adversaries of 1912. But the hope, if not the desire, soon began to fade and before the end of the month Russia asked Greece whether she would send an expedition to help in forcing the Dardanelles. King Constantine agreed, but made the proviso that Bulgaria's neutrality must be assured, to avoid the danger of a stab in the back. The Greek plan, a thorough one, was that 60,000 men should land near the outer tip of the peninsula to take in rear the forts guarding the straits, while another 30,000 landed near Bulair to seize and hold the isthmus; but, by the time Turkey entered the war, Constantine had withdrawn his reluctant consent, believing that Bulgaria was already pledged to Germany.

In England the only leader who showed a consistent appreciation of the importance of opening the Dardanelles was Churchill. From August onwards he frequently tried to arouse the interest of the War Office—which, for several years, had not even made a perfunctory review of the question. Three weeks after Turkey had entered the war he raised it again at the first meeting of the new War Council, but all eyes were still focussed on the French front, and he got no support from Kitchener. The Turks were granted a fresh lease of repose. But during December the blankness of the prospect on the Western Front was realized by many in England, and a few in France. Simultaneously the growth of the new armies evoked a natural question as to their use. The two factors combined to freshen, if not to clear, the atmosphere. Suggestions for a new strategic line of approach came from several quarters.

The most definite and practical was contained in a paper of December 29th, written by the Secretary of the War Council, Lieut.-Colonel Maurice Hankey, who emphasized the deadlock in France, and, while urging the development of new mechanical and armoured devices to force a passage through the wire entanglements and trenches, suggested that Germany could be struck most easily through her Allies, especially Turkey. He advocated the use of the first three new army corps for an attack on Constantinople, if possible in co-operation with Greece and Bulgaria, as a means not only to overthrow Turkey and bring the weight of the Balkans into the Entente scale, but to open communication with Russia. Further advantages would be to bring down the price of wheat and release 350,000 tons of shipping. The argument revealed a grasp of grand strategy, whereas the horizon of most soldiers, especially the highest, was narrowly bounded by tactics.

Sir John French, of course, objected to any effort outside his own command in France, but at this juncture an appeal came from the Grand Duke Nicholas for a British demonstration to relieve the pressure on his forces in the Caucasus. Ironically, this danger had almost passed before his appeal was received. Still more ironically, the emergency had been due to his own objection to spare troops from the main front.

Kitchener's response was to suggest the Dardanelles as the best place for such a demonstration, and also that 'reports could be spread at the same time that Constantinople was threatened'. Fisher now chimed in, to suggest not a demonstration but a combined attack on a large scale, in conjunction with which old warships should be used to 'force the Dardanelles'. He concluded characteristically and prophetically —'But as the great Napoleon said, "Celerity—without it Failure".' Churchill knew how little hope there was of obtaining troops for a large-scale attack, but eagerly caught hold of the naval possibility. Later in the day, January 3rd, he telegraphed, with Fisher's agreement, to the Admiral on the spot, Carden—'Do you consider the forcing of the straits by ships alone a practicable operation?' Back came Carden's answer—'I do not consider Dardanelles can be rushed. They might be forced by extended operations with large numbers of ships.'

Carden's detailed plan was submitted to the War Council on January 13th. The fatal decision was to be taken in a fateful atmosphere. Strategy instead of being the servant of policy had become the master, a blind and brutal master. From many sides there was an urgent call upon policy. Russia was faltering before she had even got into her stride; Serbia had barely escaped a fall; Greece and Rumania were leaning back the more that Bulgaria seemed to be leaning forward to grasp Germany's outstretched hand; Italy was sitting on the fence. The one front where troops were available was in France: and there ammunition was not—for the scale of ammunition that would suffice in other theatres would not even make a dent in the trench barrier in France. But strategy, as embodied in Sir John French, baulked the desires of policy, and as he was loyally rather than logically supported by Kitchener, the rest of the Cabinet was persuaded by a sense of numb, though not dumb, despair, aggravated by their amateur status. Hence they clutched too desperately at a straw of professional opinion which offered the chance of making bricks without men. And the words in which the decision was formulated was an epitome of their confused thought—'to prepare for a naval expedition in February, to bombard and take the Gallipoli Peninsula, with Constantinople as its objective'. The suggestion that ships were to 'take' a part of the land is delightfully naive.

A few days later Churchill made an attempt to strengthen his plan by suggesting to the Grand Duke Nicholas that the Russians should co-operate by a simultaneous land and sea attack on the Bosphorus. Strategically, his suggestion was the best possible. Paradoxically, it proved void because the political aspect here dominated the mind of the Russian strategists! Strong as was their desire to possess Constantinople, they had no wish to co-operate with their allies in gaining it. The corner-stone of Russian policy was the annexation of both Constantinople and the Dardanelles. Sazonov, the Foreign Minister, had tried to make this claim more palatable to his allies by suggesting the internationalization of Constantinople in return for Russian control of the straits, but the weight of military opinion had overborne this partial concession. Thus it is not surprising that military Russia viewed with jealousy and suspicion any move of her allies towards her own goal, and withheld her assistance. Even Sazonov records—'I intensely disliked the thought that the straits and Constantinople might be taken by our allies and not by the Russian forces . . . when the Gallipoli expedition was finally decided upon by our allies. . . . I had difficulty in concealing from them how painfully the news had affected me.' Russia would not help even in helping to clear her own windpipe. She preferred to choke rather than disgorge a morsel of her ambition. And in the end she was choked—the verdict should be *felo de se*.

In England, too, fresh complications arose. Churchill's quarrel with the plan was that the scale was too petty; Fisher's, that it might become too large—and so obstruct his Baltic project. And from this divergence a quarrel developed between the two—the political and the professional heads of the Admiralty. At the next War Council meeting Fisher rose to tender his resignation, but Kitchener intervened and, drawing him aside, persuaded him to fall in with the general opinion of the meeting. Thus the compromise plan was a compromise even in its acceptance. Most apt is the verdict of General Aspinall-Oglander in his official history—that operations on the Western Front were a gamble with pounds for a possible gain of pence, whereas in the East 'pence were to be wagered in the none too sanguine hope of winning pounds'.

The naval attack began with the bombardment of the outer forts on February 19th—curiously, the anniversary of Admiral Duckworth's successful attempt to pass through the straits, in 1807. Five days of bad weather then intervened and, when the bombardment was renewed on the 25th, the forts were outranged and the Turks retired from them. Next day the fleet began the second phase, the crushing of the intermediate defences—more difficult because these, being inside the mouth of the straits, were more difficult targets to observe. Although results were disappointing, the chance was taken to land demolition parties, on the tip of the peninsula, which destroyed the guns in the abandoned outer forts. Thereby history, at least, gained a dramatic comparison. For on the same spot where this handful of marines moved about freely on February 26th, thousands of men fell two months later. Further landings were made next day, and again on March 3rd, but on the 4th they met slight opposition, and were re-embarked.

Meantime, the bombardment continued in rather desultory fashion—due in part, but not wholly, to the bad weather —and trawlers made a few rather feeble attempts to sweep the first minefield. Lack of aircraft to observe and correct the shooting was, however, a great handicap, and on the 9th Carden reported that he could do no more until his air service was reinforced, and would meanwhile concentrate on clearing the minefield.

But the weeks were slipping away and the Admiralty could

not help feeling that Carden's caution was disproportionate to the importance of his task—and of speed in his task. Hence, on March 11th a telegram was sent to urge him to decisive action, and to free him from any fear of being held responsible if serious loss ensued. Carden responded at once and arranged a general fleet attack, under cover of which the mines were to be cleared. And the principle governing the attack was to be that the battleships should only move in, and fire from, waters clear or already cleared of mines. At this point Carden fell sick and was succeeded by his Second in Command, de Robeck.

The attack was begun on March 18th and was foiled not by resistance but by inadvertence; for, evading the British destroyer patrols, a little Turkish steamer had laid a new line of mines well outside the main minefield, dropping them parallel to the shore in Eren Keui Bay, where the Allied Fleet had taken up its position in earlier bombardments. This new line of mines lay undiscovered and unsuspected while the fleet advanced past it to engage the forts. By 1.45 p.m. the forts had been practically silenced, with little damage to the battleships, and the minesweepers were now sent forward to clear the main minefield, while the French Battle Squadron, in the van, was temporarily withdrawn. As this squadron was retiring through Eren Keui Bay, a tremendous explosion was heard, and a dense cloud of smoke seen, in the *Bouvet*, and in less than two minutes she had heeled over and sunk with nearly all her crew. But the relieving line of battleships continued the attack from closer ranges and the fire from the forts, momentarily renewed, became more and more flickering as guns were buried in rubble and telephone wires cut. Suddenly, however, about 4 p.m., the *Inflexible* and *Irresistible* were seen almost simultaneously to have a heavy list. Mystery accentuated the moral effect.

No one suspected the presence of the new line of mines, and guesses as to the cause ranged from that of a shoal of floating mines, turned loose to drift down with the current, to that of torpedoes fired from some hidden point on shore. Fear of the unknown prompted Admiral de Robeck's decision to order a general retirement forthwith, and even as this was in progress the *Ocean*, sent to the *Irresistible's* aid, struck the same line of mines, and both foundered during the night. Although the whole British Fleet lost only sixty-one men in casualties, the loss in material was large, for out of the eighteen Allied battleships three had sunk and three more were badly damaged. But a far worse loss was that of nerve and of imagination—to see the enemy's side—among the naval authorities. Actually, the enemy were suffering greater depression, and with more reason. More than half their ammunition had been expended and they had no reserve of mines. Many of the gun crews were demoralized, and the widespread opinion among both Turkish and German officers was that they had little hope of opposing a renewal of the attack.

But that attack, contrary to their expectation, was never renewed. When he came out of action de Robeck had the full intention of renewing it, and so had the Admiralty, which informed him that five more battleships were being sent out to replace his losses, and added that it was 'important not to let the forts be repaired, or to encourage the enemy by an apparent suspension of the operations'. But on the 23rd he sent a telegram which not only revealed his reversal of view but reversed the opinion of the Admiralty—except Churchill, who had to bow to the weight of professional opinion. For de Robeck's new opinion was that the fleet could not get through without the help of the army, and that any further effort must be postponed until this was ready. And, in practice, this opinion meant that the navy was to hand over the whole offensive burden to the army, and to stand by, watching, while the army spent itself in vain assaults unaided by any fresh naval attack. Perhaps the underlying factor was that service tendency of mind which sentimentally values things more than lives, a tendency which may have its foundation in totemism, but is also accentuated by the peacetime shortage of material and the penalties attached to any loss of it. The artilleryman's love of his guns, and readiness to sacrifice his life to avert the disgrace of losing them, is paralleled by the sailor's adoration of his ship, even an old and obsolete ship such as these at the Dardanelles. It hinders him from adopting the commonsense view that a ship, like a shell, is merely a weapon to be expended profitably. Perhaps, also, a powerful auxiliary factor in the sailors' decision was now the presence of soldiers and their willingness to assume the burden.

For, coincidently with the preparations for a naval attack, the British government had drifted independently towards a land attack. It had its origin, not in a wider consideration of the Dardanelles problem, but in a separate consideration of where the new armies could be used as an alternative to France. The committee reported in favour of Salonika, as an immediate aid to Serbia and an ultimate stab in the back to the Central Powers—up the Danube. The opinion won favour at the meeting of the War Council on February 9th, being reinforced by the news that Bulgaria had contracted a loan with Germany and by the desire of encouraging Greece to support Serbia. And Kitchener, who had declared that he could find no troops for the Dardanelles plan, now announced that he would send the Regular 29th Division to Salonika, in conjunction with a French division. The promise of two divisions, however, was naturally not enough to allay Greek misgivings; Greece was unwilling to accept the offer unless Rumania was persuaded to join, and Rumania was held back by the sight of Russia's misadventures.

But the fact remained, and could no longer be hidden from the Cabinet by Kitchener's veil of mystery and authority, that the 29th Division was available. Nor did he for the moment seek to withhold it. In consequence the War Council, on February 16th, decided that it should be despatched to the centrally placed harbour of Mudros in the Aegean 'at the earliest possible moment, together with troops from Egypt', with the idea that 'all the forces [were] to be available in case of necessity to support the naval attack on the Dardanelles'.

No one, however, suggested that the naval attack should be postponed to obtain surprise and the greater effect of a combined operation. The troops were merely to mount guard over what the navy gained.

But the 29th Division immediately became the rope in a tug-of-war between the 'Eastern' and 'Western' schools of thought, and on to the western end were pulling not only the British headquarters in France, but Joffre. Joffre's foresight was always, and only, quick when his own preserves were threatened, and he saw in the despatch east instead of west of the newly assembled 29th Division a disquieting omen of the destination of the new army divisions. Kitchener could easily have hardened his heart against French, but he could not against the French. Just as his loyalty to France was an earlier instinct than his love of the East, so it now proved stronger than his belief in the eastern theatre. At the next meeting of the War Council, only three days later, he turned about face and asserted that the 29th Division could not be spared. In its place he suggested the despatch of raw Australian and New Zealand troops, two divisions from Egypt. And he even notified the Admiralty behind Churchill's back that the 29th was not to go, thereby interrupting the collection of the transports required to carry it.

That same day the naval attack had opened—and the bombardment echoed throughout the Near East. When the news came, that the outer forts had fallen, the Turkish government made ready to flee into the interior of Asia Minor. The Germans expected not only the appearance of the Allied Fleet off Constantinople but that its appearance would be the signal for a revolt against Enver, and the consequent signature of peace by Turkey. For the Turks, in any case, could not have carried on the war once Constantinople, their only munition source, was abandoned. Italy and Greece began to incline more strongly towards war, and Bulgaria away from it. On March 1st Venizelos proposed to land three Greek divisions on the Gallipoli peninsula— but here Russia fatally intervened by notifying Athens that

'In no circumstances can we allow Greek forces to participate in the Allied attack on Constantinople.'

Only the neutral part of these favourable echoes reached the War Council in London, but it was sufficient to encourage the believers and win over the doubters. The original idea that the naval attack was only tentative, to be abandoned if found difficult, now faded and all save one were agreed that the attack must be carried through, if necessary with land forces. The one dissenting voice was that of Lloyd George, who objected to the army having 'to pull the navy's chestnuts out of the fire'. Curiously, he alone sounded the warning truth of history that the renewal along the same line of an attack that has failed is rarely justified, and that it is better to switch the effort in a fresh direction. If his just objection was not immediately justified it was because of the Turks' lethargy in profiting by their warning.

In contrast, Kitchener laid down emphatically that 'having entered on the project of forcing the straits there can be no idea of abandoning the scheme'. But not until March 10th did he make up his mind to release the 29th Division and, perhaps worse, not until the 12th did he nominate a commander for the expedition. Yet the French, despite Joffre's refusal to contribute from the field armies, had scraped together a division from the interior and had begun to embark it as early as the 3rd. At the War Office in London not a single preparatory step had been taken. One result was that when Ian Hamilton departed on the 13th none of his administrative staff were available, and he had to leave without them. Further, the sum of his information comprised a 1912 handbook of the Turkish army, a pre-war report on the Dardanelles forts, and an inaccurate map! To compensate for this deficiency some of his staff had scoured the booksellers for guidebooks to Constantinople.

The one swift action in this halting period was Ian Hamilton's passage out to the Dardanelles. A chain of special trains and fast cruisers whisked him thither faster than he could have travelled in peace time by the Orient Express, and he reached the Fleet on March 17th—the eve of its attack. His first discovery was the unsuitability of Lemnos as a base, owing to lack of water, as well as lack of piers and shelter in Mudros harbour. His second, was that the troops already present were so ill distributed in their transports that they would have to be disembarked and redistributed before they could land on an open and hostile shore. Hence his first step, on the 18th had to be the unfortunate one of changing his base to Alexandria and directing all transports there. So ill conceived and chaotic had been the original loading that battalions were separated from their first-line transport, wagons from their horses, guns from their ammunition—and even shells from their fuses. One infantry battalion of the 29th Division had actually been split up among four ships. Even with the ample wharfs and camps of Alexandria, unloading and reloading was a slow business, not accelerated by the delayed arrival of the administrative staff.

On March 22nd, after the naval attack and before sailing for Alexandria, Ian Hamilton with his chief assistants met de Robeck in conference. 'The moment we sat down de Robeck told us he was now clear he could not get through without the help of all my troops.' Soldiers could not argue with a naval verdict, even had they any wish, and so without discussion the Army was committed to the task. And the task was committed to the Army. For although Ian Hamilton politely suggested to the Admiral that he should 'push on systematically' with the attack on the forts, and Churchill made similar representations, the Admirals both at the Admiralty and at the Dardanelles were as rigid as rock in passive resistance, and henceforth the Fleet was dedicated to what Churchill has aptly termed the 'No' principle—an 'unsurmountable mental barrier'. Sired by strategic confusion and dammed by naval negation, the landing on Gallipoli was born—and marred in delivery by muddled military midwifery. From this welter only one clear note emerged, in a memorandum drawn up for the Prime Minister by Maurice Hankey on March 16th. In it he emphasized that 'combined operations require more careful preparation than any other class of military enterprise. All through our history such attacks have failed when the preparations have been inadequate, and the successes are in nearly every case due to the most careful preparation beforehand. It would appear to be the business of the War Council to assure themselves, in the present instance, that these preparations have been thoroughly thought out'. He pointed out that surprise had already been forfeited and in consequence the task had become far more formidable. Hence he enumerated a comprehensive list of practical points upon which the War Council should cross-examine the naval and military authorities, saying, in conclusion—'unless details such as these . . . are fully thought out before the landing takes place . . . a serious disaster may occur'. It may occur to the historian that Hankey was the only expert adviser of the British government who had thought out the foundations of strategy. For when the Prime Minister, loth to question Kitchener's omniscience, tentatively asked if any scheme had been worked out, Kitchener replied, that 'that must be left to the commanders on the spot', and thereby shut down all discussion. No heed was given to the wider aspects of the plan—its immediate and potential needs in men, guns, ammunition, and supplies. In consequence, the expedition was to live from hand to mouth, nourishment being always too small and too late, yet in sum far exceeding what would originally have sufficed for success.

CHAPTER V

SCENE 2

THE SLIP TWIXT LIP AND CUP—
THE LANDING ON GALLIPOLI,
APRIL 25TH, 1915

DESPITE the chain of folly which preceded it, was there still a chance of success when the belated land attack on the Dardanelles was launched? The verdict of history is affirmative. Part, if not all, of the opportunity forfeited by the British was redeemed for them by the Turks.

The panic caused by the opening of the naval attack, and the feeling that the passage of the Dardanelles could not be prevented, led the Turks to order new military dispositions which, in the words of Liman von Sanders, head of the German Military Mission, 'did away with any defence of the exterior coast of the Gallipoli peninsula with its dominating heights; it did away with the defence of the Asiatic coast at the mouth of the Dardanelles. It was the feeblest imaginable defensive measure'. That it was not put into operation may have been due to Liman von Sanders's protests—with which, however, Enver replied that he did not concur—but was more probably due to pure inertia.

The absence of renewed naval attacks after the failure of March 18th was, rightly, taken as a sign that a land attack was being prepared, and this assurance was confirmed by abundant reports from various Mediterranean ports, especially Alexandria and Port Said. This was the less surprising in that public reviews of the troops were held at Alexandria and Cairo, while at least one member of Ian Hamilton's staff received official letters from home through the ordinary post, addressed 'Constantinople Field Force'. Any chance of secrecy had indeed disappeared, with the necessity of disembarking the force in Egypt.

Thus, on March 25th, Enver was led to form a separate

THRACE

R.Maritza

Enos

5 Div.

Kavak Dere

Kavak

Gulf of Saros

Bulair

7 Div.

SEA OF MARMARA

Gallipoli

EJELMER BAY

● 882

SUVLA BAY

● *Kuchuk Anafarta*

19 Div.

● *Biyuk Anafarta*

▲ 971

A.N.Z.A.C.

GABA TEPE

Maidos

Imbros

9 Div.

Chanaq

▲ *ACHI BABA*
▲ 715

← Y

● *Krithia*

← X

CAPE HELLES

← W Y

29 Div.

SEDD EL BAHR

S

EREN KEUL BAY

Kum Kale

FRENCH

3 Div.

R.Mendere

GALLIPOLI

Original Landing Places *S,V,W,X,Y,Z*

Allied Divisions **29 Div**

Turkish Divisions *19 Div.*

Ground gained 25th. April, 1915

0	5	10	15

Miles

BESIKA BAY

11 Div.

N

© Cassell & Co. Ltd. 1970

army for the defence of the Dardanelles, and to place it under the command of Liman von Sanders. After a hurried survey Liman exclaimed to his subordinate, Hans Kannengiesser— 'If the English will only leave me alone for eight days'. They left him for four weeks. This month of grace, he records, 'was just sufficient to complete the most indispensable arrangements and to bring the 3rd Division under Colonel Nicolai from Constantinople'. Its arrival brought his strength up to six divisions—six times the strength present on Gallipoli before the naval attack began.

But he found them dispersed 'as coastguards', and his first step was to concentrate them. To do this effectively he had to decide where to expect a landing. The Asiatic coast, where movement and an approach to his rear was easy, he deemed the point of greatest danger. And so he placed two divisions near Besika Bay to cover the line of forts on this side. On the European side he most feared a landing at the neck of the peninsula, near Bulair, where the waters of the Gulf of Saros were separated by a mere three-and-a-half-mile strip from the waters of the Sea of Marmara. A landing here would cut off the defenders of the peninsula from Thrace and Constantinople, although if they did not lose their nerve they might be able to maintain themselves by drawing supplies from the Asiatic side, across the Narrows. This, however, was only a possibility. Near Bulair, therefore, Liman von Sanders posted two more divisions. The two other, and lesser danger points were near Gaba Tepe at the six-mile waist—a low waist—of the peninsula, where a wide valley ran across to Maidos at the Narrows; and near Cape Helles, at the southern end, where the gradual ascent up the slopes of Achi Baba might be swept by the fire of the British fleet. Liman von Sanders distributed one division to guard the whole of the southern part of the peninsula while his remaining division, under Lieut.-Colonel Mustapha Kemal, was posted near the waist as a general reserve. The scheme of defence was essentially based on mobility, and to obtain the utmost value from his dispositions, as well as to offset the British ease of sea movement, he concentrated his energy on increasing and improving the roads.

Liman von Sanders's dispositions are the best justification for Ian Hamilton's plan. In this the governing factors were the small size of the British force and its mission. The force comprised only five divisions, 75,000 men to the Turks' 84,000. The object was to open a path for the fleet through the Narrows, not to engage independently in a campaign for big strategic prizes. Kitchener's bare instructions 'strongly deprecated', although without explanation, an advance on the Asiatic side; and there the guns of the fleet could give no support beyond the initial landing. The Gulf of Saros was obviously the most vulnerable strategic point but, as Liman von Sanders himself has pointed out, 'it afforded no direct artillery effect against' the defences of the straits. Moreover, the beaches near Bulair were seen to be strongly prepared for defence, while a landing on the west side of the Gulf would be uncomfortably close to the Bulgarian frontier, and with difficult country to traverse. In either case, a small force would be in danger of being itself attacked in flank and rear from the mainland of Thrace, and so being caught between two devils and the deep sea.

Weighing up these conditions, and his handicaps, Ian Hamilton decided on a dual blow in the southern half of the peninsula. The 29th Division was to land on four beaches at the toe and seize Achi Baba, while the French waited in support, meanwhile sending a regiment to land at Kum Kale on the Asiatic side as a feint and distraction. The two divisions of the Australian and New Zealand Army Corps—whose initials were to enrich both dictionary and history with the word 'Anzac'—were to land north of Gaba Tepe, while the Royal Naval Division made a feint near Bulair.

If the idea of security seems to have dictated the landing at the toe, surprise was to be its effect. And surprise was assiduously sought in manifold ways. Commander Unwin was inspired by the proximity of Troy to make the apt suggestion of reproducing the immortal wooden horse—in this case to be a sea-horse. A collier, the *River Clyde*, was to be run ashore at V Beach and to disgorge troops through large openings cut in its sides. Ian Hamilton himself added another stratagem—which had some parallel to Wolfe's at Quebec—whereby a detachment of two battalions was to be landed further up the coast at a spot apparently inaccessible, and so unlikely to be defended, whence it could menace the rear of the Turks defending the southern beaches. This spot was christened Y Beach. Further, the French transports were to make a pretence of landing troops at Besika Bay. Ian Hamilton also wished to increase the chance of local surprise, and decrease the risk of loss, by landing at night, even though it meant forgoing the support of the guns of the fleet. But Hunter-Weston, commanding the 29th Division, preferred a daylight landing, to avoid the risk of confusion. He gained his way through the support of naval opinion, which was based on the difficulties of the current. For the Anzac landing, the corps commander, Birdwood, wisely preferred any risk to that of the obvious, and if his landing was to suffer in effect through confusion—which was more due to lack of training than to initial loss of direction in the dark—it escaped the heavy losses of the 29th Division.

By April 20th the preparations for the venture were complete and the troops assembled at Mudros on their transports. The weather, almost continuously unfavourable for several weeks, was both the determining and the most uncertain factor. Not until the 23rd did it allow the scheme to be set in motion. For the mechanism, like an alarm clock, required, and was timed to strike, thirty-six hours from the start of the movement.

On the evening of the 24th eleven transports of the Royal Naval Division sailed for the Gulf of Saros, escorted by warships which opened a slow bombardment at daybreak on the Bulair lines. Towards evening boats were ostentatiously swung out, filled with troops, and began pulling for the shore—to return to the ships as soon as darkness cloaked them. During the night an officer, Lieut.-Commander B. C.

Freyberg, swam ashore from a boat two miles out and lit flares along the beach. His feat, and its effect, was an outstanding proof that in war it is the man, and not men, who count—that one man can be more useful than a thousand.

For the Gaba Tepe landing, 1500 men of the covering force were carried in three battleships to the rendezvous five miles off shore. They clambered down into the boats at 1.30 a.m. just as the moon was sinking. Then, towed by the battleships and followed by seven destroyers with the rest of the covering force, they moved silently inshore until the distance was halved. Here the twelve 'tows', each with a steam picket boat at the head, cast loose and continued the approach. But darkness and the strong current caused the tows to arrive off the beach a mile north of the intended point, and so on a more rugged part of the coast, skirted by precipitous cliffs, seamed with steep gullies and covered with scrub. Day was just breaking when at 4.25 a.m., under a scattered and erratic fire from a few small and stupefied posts, the forty-eight boats were rowed across the last fifty yards until they touched bottom. Then, in a headlong rush and scramble, the Australians swept inland. Hardly a man had fallen, but units were badly mixed, and soon became worse. The next contingent landed from the destroyers, suffered rather more, at least on the left, but carried the advance over a mile inland. One small party even penetrated far enough to see the glistening straits beyond and beneath.

The Helles landing was less fortunate, although the opponents were little more numerous. Only two Turkish battalions were present in the whole area south of Achi Baba, and only two of the five selected landing places were covered by wire entanglements and machine-guns. These were the central beaches W and V on either side of Cape Helles itself. The British covering force comprised the four battalions of Hare's 86th Brigade, which with an extra half battalion were to land at V, W, and X Beaches; one battalion at S Beach; and two battalions at Y Beach for the threat to the enemy's rear. Thus seven and a half battalions were to be thrown ashore initially, followed by five more of the main body, and ultimately by the French Division. At 5 a.m., under cover of a heavy fleet bombardment, the tows crept towards the shore. The first mischance was the slow progress, against the current, of the tows making for S Beach, on the east flank, which caused those destined for the three main beaches to be held back until nearly 6 a.m. Nevertheless, the tows for X Beach, round the western tip of the peninsula, landed without a casualty beneath a low cliff, where their arrival was unexpected by the Turks and opposed only by a picket of twelve men. But at W, the next beach eastwards, the landing parties ran into a well-prepared death trap. Not a shot was fired as the boats rowed in but, as they grounded, they were swept by bullets and the men, jumping overboard, were entangled in submerged wire. Despite heavy loss they struggled forward, drove off the defenders, and gained a lodgment on the cliffs. But Hare, too gallantly exposing himself, was wounded, and the effort subsided.

The landing at V Beach, beside the old fort of Sedd el Bahr, fared still worse. Here the invaders ran, like gladiators, into a gently sloping arena designed by nature and arranged by the Turks—themselves ensconced in surrounding seats—for a butchery. The tows, checked by the current, were caught up by the *River Clyde*, and as it grounded hell yawned. In the incoming boats oars dropped like the wings of scorched moths, while the boats drifted helplessly with their load of dead and wounded. Many men jumped overboard only to be drowned in water stained with their own blood. A few gained the beach and found shelter beneath a low bank— which was to mark the limit of the day's advance. Those who tried to emerge from the *River Clyde*, and reach the shore across a bridge of lighters, were no more fortunate, and fell in heaps. The few survivors on the beach and the thousand left in the *River Clyde* could only wait for nightfall to release them. Two companies of Turks, distributed between V and W Beaches, had checked the main British landing.

But S Beach, at the other side of Morto Bay, was, like X,

an unlikely spot and so guarded by only a platoon of Turks. The landing battalion got safely ashore and then, having had preliminary instructions to await the advance from the other beaches, fulfilled them to the letter. Its inertness, however, was approved by Hunter-Weston, owing apparently to an exaggerated estimate of the Turkish strength. Actually the two intact battalions ashore at the two flank beaches, S and X, totalled four times the strength of the Turkish defenders of V and W Beaches, and by an advance inwards could have taken them in rear.

Soon, also, that superiority was increased—but not the pressure. Two battalions of the 87th Brigade (the other two had been used for the original landings at S and Y) were put ashore safely on X Beach by 9 a.m., but they had been ear-marked as divisional reserve, and the Brigadier did not feel justified in using them, except to dig in, unless and until he received instructions from Hunter-Weston. These never came, so the force at Beach X remained passive.

Meantime, after another vain attempt to land at V Beach —in which the Commander of the 88th Brigade was killed— the remaining two and a half battalions of the main body were disembarked at W Beach. 'But,' as the official history gently says, 'in contrast to the gallant exploits of the morning a certain inertia seems to have overtaken the troops on this part of the front, who now amounted to at least 2000 men. ... Faced with a definite task—the capture of the beaches— the 29th Division had put an indelible mark on history. But once that task was done, platoon, company and even battalion commanders, each in their own sphere, were awaiting fresh and definite orders, and on their own initiative did little to exploit the morning's success or to keep in touch with the enemy.' Instead, they allowed themselves to be paralysed by an enemy 'whom they had already driven from his trenches and whom, though unaware of the fact, they outnumbered by at least six to one'.

But a still greater opportunity was missed at Y Beach, three miles up the coast, where '2000 men were safely disembarked without a hitch and without any opposition. For eleven hours they were left undisturbed by the enemy, and throughout that period they alone were equal in numbers to all the Turkish forces south of Achi Baba. Yet throughout the 25th the initial success remained unexploited. During the ensuing night the troops gallantly repulsed a succession of fierce attacks on their line. But the whole enterprise was suddenly abandoned next morning, and the men re-embarked, at the very moment when the enemy himself was in full retreat'.

The one man who realized the opportunity was Ian Hamilton himself, out at sea; but he had delegated the execution of the landing to the commander of the 29th Division, and had kept no reserve. Somewhat naturally, he was loth to interfere except by suggestion, though he was far quicker than the man on the spot to appreciate the check in the south, and as early as 9.21 a.m. he signalled to Hunter-Weston—'Would you like to get some more men ashore at Y Beach? If so, trawlers are available.' But Hunter-Weston's attention was glued to the bloody beaches where the enemy was better prepared, and there he preferred to concentrate his efforts.

At Y Beach itself the landing had been made without a shot being fired or a Turk being discovered. But the commander, Colonel Matthews, was content to await further orders. 'Crowds of troops were . . . sitting about the edge of the cliff', and not until late in the afternoon did they even attempt to entrench. Towards dark one Turkish battalion was brought up and launched a series of counterattacks against the two British battalions. Repeatedly beaten off, the Turks finally fled in disorder soon after 7 a.m.; but their night assaults caused such loss and confusion among the defenders that panic spread. A string of alarmist messages were signalled to the ships and many stragglers poured down to the beach, swarming into the boats sent for the wounded. This state continued even after the disappearance of the Turks, and Matthews, who saw no response to his urgent appeal for reinforcements, reluctantly decided to follow the example set by his stragglers. By 11-30 a.m. the whole force had re-embarked. Some hours later a naval party under Lieut.-Commander Keyes went ashore and made a prolonged search for wounded without being fired on.

But if anything can justify Matthews's action, and previous inaction, it is his utter neglect by his superior, Hunter-Weston. Throughout the twenty-nine hours on land 'no word of any kind reached him from divisional headquarters'. No officer was sent to visit him, no reply was sent to his urgent appeals. And when, early in the morning of the 26th Ian Hamilton once more intervened with the offer of a French brigade (six battalions), Hunter-Weston had no thought but to land them on W Beach—in the enemy's face. The measured verdict of the official history upon Y Beach is that— 'In deciding to throw a force ashore at that point Sir Ian Hamilton would seem to have hit upon the key of the whole situation . . . it is as certain as anything can be in war that a bold advance from Y, on the morning of the 25th April, must have freed the southern beaches that morning, and ensured a decisive victory for the 29th Division.'

At Anzac, too, a great opportunity went begging, although here the initiative of one opponent, the then unknown Mustapha Kemal, contributed to its unfulfilment. The surprise landing had placed 4000 men before 5 a.m., and another 4000 before 8 a.m., on a shore guarded by only one Turkish company. The next company was more than a mile to the south, two battalions and a battery in local reserve were four miles inland, and still further away lay the general reserve of eight battalions and three batteries, commanded by Mustapha Kemal. He was out watching a regiment at training, when suddenly a number of gendarmes, bare-headed and weaponless, came running frantically towards him, crying—'They come, they come.' 'Who comes?' 'Inglis, Inglis.' He turned to ask, 'Have we ball cartridges?' 'Yes.' 'All right. Forward.' Leading a company himself, and leaving the rest of the regiment to follow, he raced to the great dividing ridge of Chunuk Bair in time (about 10 a.m.) to cross the crest and check the leading Australians as they were climbing up the steeper slopes on the west. Until now barely 500 Turks had been available to hold up 8000 Australians, but henceforth the defenders were to be augmented steadily until by nightfall six battalions (perhaps 5000 men) had been brought up, and from 4 p.m. onwards launched in a series of counterattacks which forced back but failed to break the ragged Australian line. Both sides had suffered about 2000 casualties, the Turks far more heavily in proportion, but the raw Australians were in unknown country, under fire for the first time, and the moral effect of the shrapnel from the enemy's handful of guns was made worse by the absence of their own. Although 15,000 men were ashore by 6 p.m., the front was but a thin and much-intermixed line, and the beach was crowded with leaderless men who had drifted back—many because they had lost themselves rather than lost their nerve. But the sight naturally confirmed the fears of the commanders, themselves in rear, and so gloomy was their report to Birdwood, when he landed at 10 p.m., that he sent a message to Ian Hamilton saying—'Both my divisional commanders and brigadiers have represented to me that they fear their men are thoroughly demoralized by shrapnel fire. . . . If troops are to be subjected to shell fire again to-morrow morning there is likely to be a fiasco . . . if we are to re-embark it must be at once.' All available boats were ordered to be sent to the beach,

Only by a fluke did the message ever reach the Commander-in-Chief, for in the hurry it was not addressed to anyone; but, being thrust into the hands of the beach-master, who was going out to the flagship, he handed it when there to Admiral Thursby. After reading it, Thursby decided to go ashore to discuss the re-embarkation with Birdwood, but at that moment the *Queen Elizabeth*, with Ian Hamilton on board, unexpectedly arrived from Helles, so that Thursby went instead to report to him. Thus by a chain of happy mishaps Birdwood's grave message reached Ian Hamilton in time.

Insight must have guided him in an extraordinarily difficult decision, for no other guidance, or comfort, was available, and no time to obtain it. The reply which he wrote was epitomized in its postscript—'You have got through the difficult business. Now you have only to dig, dig, dig, until you are safe.'

Like a fresh breeze this definite and confident order dispersed the rumour-laden and gloomy atmosphere on the beach. The rear ceased to talk about evacuation and the front did not know that the rear had been talking about it. When morning broke there was also a respite from the real enemy, for Mustapha Kemal had no further reserves with which to renew his counterattack, and the shrapnel from his few guns was no longer a terror to troops now safely dug in. Indeed, it was the Turk who suffered demoralization—from the guns of the fleet, and especially the huge 15-inch shells of the *Queen Elizabeth*.

Could the lost opportunity still have been regained? History answers, 'Yes'. And the reason lies in the profound impression made, by Ian Hamilton's original plan, on the mind of the enemy Commander-in-Chief. Liman von Sanders records of the first day, April 25th, that—'From the many pale faces among the officers reporting in the early morning, it was apparent that, although a hostile landing had been expected with certainty, a landing at so many points surprised and disquieted them.' 'We could not discern at the time where the enemy was actually seeking a decision.' The last sentence is an euphemism, for Liman von Sanders actually thought that the place where the British were merely making a bluff was the place where they were seeking a decision. If he kept his head he lost his sense of direction.

His first act was to order his 7th Division to march from the town of Gallipoli to Bulair. His next, to gallop thither himself. And there he stayed while the critical struggle was in progress at the other end of the peninsula. Not until evening would he even spare five battalions, out of his two divisions around Bulair, to go to the real battle zone, and not until over forty-eight hours after the British landing did he release the remainder.

But the extension of the opportunity was of no avail to the British. Partly for want of fresh troops—when so many, in comparison, were locked up in the Western Front safe-deposit. But partly, also, for want of effort from those who had landed. Ian Hamilton's optimism, although justified, was not shared by his subordinate commanders on the morning of the 26th. It was not merely the Anzac force which remained passive. At Helles, Hunter-Weston, appreciating the tiredness of his troops but not the weakness of the enemy, gave up any idea of advancing until French reinforcements arrived. Expecting a Turkish onslaught, and fearing the result, he issued the order, 'Every man will die at his post rather than retire.' So far from attacking, the Turks went back to a new line in front of Krithia. Well they might, for their total strength here up to the 27th was only five battalions, and casualties had reduced them to a real strength scarcely more than the original two. Not until the 28th was a new attack attempted, and by then the Franco-British force had almost lost its advantage of numbers and suffered the disadvantages of ignorance of the ground, thirst, increased tiredness, besides complicating its task by combining the attack with a right wheel. The small gains were lost to Turkish counterattacks, and near the coast the line wavered and broke. The danger here was averted by a single shell from the *Queen Elizabeth*. It burst its 24,000 shrapnel bullets right in the midst of the onrushing mass of Turks, and when the dust cleared not a Turk was to be seen. But by nightfall the whole 29th Division was back at its starting point. Meantime the troops at Anzac were reorganizing and making their front secure. But so also were the Turks, and thus the Anzac force was locked in a tiny cell only one and a half miles long and half a mile deep, while the Turk looked down from the 'roof' upon the arrested trespassers.

The almost blank credit side of the allied balance sheet

was now relieved by a Turkish contribution. Urged on by Enver's peremptory order 'to drive the invaders into the sea', Liman von Sanders launched massed bayonet attacks on the nights of May 1st and 3rd. Several thousand dead were heaped as a sacrifice before the Allied front, which was only, and momentarily, endangered in the French sector.

The Turks' forfeit was soon redeemed—by the British. Two brigades were brought from Anzac and a new brigade, of Territorials, came from Egypt. Even so, the Allied force at Helles could only bring a fighting strength of 25,000 against a Turkish strength now raised to nearly 20,000. And, in the issue, it did not even test their strength. The Allied attack arranged for May 6th suffered every possible disadvantage. It was purely frontal, on a narrow three-mile front, against unlocated positions, with an extreme shortage of shells, and a shortage of aircraft to observe the fire, at the shortest notice—Hunter-Weston's orders were not issued to brigades until 4 a.m. for an attack to begin at 11 a.m. Once more the control of the battle and the last remaining reserves were handed over to Hunter-Weston by Ian Hamilton—'all that was left to him', as the official history says, 'of the high office of Commander-in-Chief was its load of responsibility'.

Fatigue rather than resistance foiled the attack. The troops, worn out by strain and lack of sleep, had not even the energy to press on to the slaughter, and they did not even push back the Turks' advanced posts. As the best remedy for lack of rest Hunter-Weston ordered a fresh effort next morning. This was no more effective, except in draining the ammunition almost to zero. So a third attack was ordered for the third morning. In this the loss at least was confined to a smaller circle, by launching four weak battalions of New Zealanders, in daylight, against a position held by nine Turkish battalions. Then Ian Hamilton, finding that three brigades were still in reserve, himself intervened. The whole allied line was to 'fix bayonets, slope arms, and move on Krithia precisely at 5.30 p.m.'. This produced heavy casualties, if nothing else. The attacking force had lost a third of its strength in the three days. Thereafter the front of the two small footholds gained by the Allies inevitably relapsed into stagnation, which soon froze solidly as the Turks converted their hasty defences into an organized trench system.

Now, at last, Ian Hamilton was driven to ask for reinforcements, and to awake the Government to his serious need and situation. Hitherto, although conscious of the inadequacy of his force, he had been too loyal to Kitchener, and perhaps too aware of his old chief's arbitrary methods, to worry him by importunate demands. Before leaving England he had been told that 75,000 men would and must suffice, that even the 29th Division was but a temporary loan, and the fact that Kitchener had warned Maxwell, the commander in Egypt, to help him with additional troops, was not communicated to him by Maxwell despite Kitchener's explicit instructions. Lack of ammunition was another handicap, and when he called attention to it the War Office reply merely told him that it was 'important to push on'. Yet, almost simultaneously with his vain three days' attack, May 6th to 8th, in which he could only use 18,500 shells, Haig was expending 80,000 on Aubers Ridge in one day—for less result, a far less object, and twice the loss of life. Up to a point, the astonishing feature of Gallipoli was how near Ian Hamilton came to success with his inferior forces and resources.

His oft-criticized choice of landing place could hardly have been improved on if, by supernatural power, he had been able to know the enemy's mind and dispositions. By avoiding the natural line of expectation, the pitfall of commonplace generalship, and by distracting the enemy's attention to that line, he ensured his own troops an immense superiority of force at the actual landing places—although his total force was less than that of the Turks. The enemy commander let his attention be so fixed on Bulair that for forty-eight hours after the British were ashore their immediate opponents were denied adequate reinforcements. This fact is the best answer to the common criticism that Ian Hamilton should have struck at Bulair, a point so obvious to everyone at home that, curiously, it was also obvious to the enemy. Another popular criticism is that Ian Hamilton dispersed his force at too many points and should have concentrated his effort on one small sector. This is answered not only by the 'pale faces' of which Liman von Sanders tells, but by the next three years' experience of this abortive method on the Western Front—experience which was purchased at an infinitely greater cost.

Perhaps, as an alternative landing place, also in the least-defended area, Suvla Bay might have offered the advantages of Ian Hamilton's choice with less disadvantages. But in April accurate information was lacking and exaggerated faith placed in the effect of the naval guns at Helles.

Another reasonable criticism is that the British power of rapid sea movement might have been utilized more fully—to withdraw troops where checked before they were deeply committed and switch them to reinforce the unopposed landings or to fresh points. Thereby the lack of reserves might have been partly compensated through the power to create fresh ones by 'switching'. This, indeed, had been suggested to Braithwaite, the Chief of Staff, on the day before the landing by Captain Aspinall, an officer of the General Staff. He urged that the plan should be adapted to meet the contingency that either or both the landings at Anzac and Helles might fail. An equal or greater fault in the plan was that it failed to provide for partial success, the most probable case in war, and left no 'floating' reserve in the hands of the Commander-in-Chief ready for prompt application at the most promising point ashore. Unhappily, both the plan and the execution suffered from lack of the elasticity which is an essential axiom in war. And the partial success of both landings in the first phase tended to harden the design—until it became hard and stuck fast.

For years controversy has centred round the incubation period of the Dardanelles project, and the plan which was evolved. More depressing is the later revelation of the opportunities thrown away after the force had landed—lost opportunities hitherto obscured by a halo of romance.

CHAPTER V

SCENE 3

THE GAS CLOUD AT YPRES—
APRIL 22ND, 1915

THE sun was sinking behind Ypres. Its spring radiance had breathed life that day into the dead town and the mouldering trench lines which guarded it. A month hence the town would be a shell with all the eerie moonlit grandeur of a greater Colosseum. Three years hence it would be merely a vast ant-heap of tumbled ruins. But on that 22nd day of April, 1915, it had merely the dreariness of incomplete abandonment, momentarily relieved by the fragrance of a spring day's sunshine.

As that fragrance faded with the waning sun, even the guns became silent, and an evening hush spread over the scene as if in awed awaiting of a benediction. The hush was false; purely a prelude to the devil's malediction, with organ pealing, censers swinging. At five o'clock a fearful din of guns broke out and heavy shells struck with reverberating crash on Ypres and many villages rarely or never touched before; and to the nostrils of men nearer the front came the smell of a devilish incense. Those nearer still to the trenches north of Ypres saw two curious wraiths of greenish-yellow fog creep forward, spread until they became one and then, moving forward, change to a blue-white mist. It hung, as it had come, over the front of the two French Divisions, one Algerian, one Territorial, which joined up with the British, and held the left of the salient. Soon, officers behind the British front and near the canal bridges, were startled to see a torrent of terrified humanity pouring backward. The Africans, nearest the British, were coughing and pointing to their throats as they fled; mingled with them soon came horse-teams and wagons. The French guns were still firing, but at 7 p.m. these suddenly and ominously became silent.

Original Front Lines
Line on evening of 22nd. April
Line on evening of 24th. May

BELG.
6th Div.
Steenstraat
Lizerne
Bixschoote
Poelcapelle
Langemarck
GERMAN
BRITISH
87 TERR. Div.
(FR)
45 ALG. Div.
(FR)
Boesinghe
Pilckem
CDN. Div.
St. Julien
Kitchener's
Wood
Zonnebeke
BRIT.
28th Div.
Yser Canal
BRIT. 27th. Div.
N
Ypres
Hooge
Zillebeke
BRIT.
5th. Div.
0   1   2
Miles

YPRES, 1915

© Cassell & Co. Ltd. 1970

The fugitives left behind them a gap in the front over four miles wide, filled only by the dead and by those who lay suffocating in agony from chlorine gas-poisoning. Otherwise the two French Divisions had almost completely disappeared. With the aid of gas the Germans had removed the defenders on the north flank of the salient as deftly as if extracting the back teeth from one side of a jaw. The remaining teeth in front and on the south flank of the salient were formed by the Canadian Division (Alderson), nearest the gap, the 28th Division (Bulfin), and the 27th Division (Snow), which together comprised Plumer's 5th Corps. The Germans had only to push south for four miles to reach Ypres, and loosen all these teeth by pressure from the rear. That evening they walked forward two miles and then, curiously, stopped. The space of four and a half miles between the raw edge of the Canadian front and the canal which formed the chord of the salient, was only filled by a few small posts, taken up hastily by packets of French and Canadians hitherto in reserve, and between these posts there were three untenanted gaps of two thousand yards, one thousand yards, and three thousand yards, respectively. Yet on May 1st the Germans had only advanced a few hundred yards further. And when the fighting at last died down, at the end of May, the only outward change was that the nose of the salient had been flattened—mainly by a voluntary British withdrawal. But, in curious contrast to normal experience, it was the defenders who had lost most heavily. The British loss was fifty-nine thousand, nearly double that suffered by the Germans who attacked them.

Why did the gas come as so complete a surprise? Why did the Germans fail to exploit such a surprise? Why did the British escape disaster when taken unawares by the French collapse and yet suffer so disproportionately when the Germans had forfeited their advantage? These are the three crucial questions of 'Second Ypres'.

Towards the end of March, prisoners taken on the south of the salient, then held by the French, gave full details of the way that gas cylinders had been stored in the trenches, and of its method of discharge. Perhaps because they were about to be relieved, the French Commanders took no action in regard to this warning, although, curiously, the details appear in the Bulletin of the French Tenth Army, away down in Picardy, for March 30th.

An even more complete and localized warning came on April 13th, when a German deserter gave himself up near Langemarck to the French 11th Division, then holding the sector, and related that 'cylinders with asphyxiating gas [had been] placed in batteries of twenty cylinders for every forty metres along the front'. 'At a given signal—three red rockets fired by the artillery—the cylinders will be opened and the escaping gas will be carried by a favourable wind towards the French trenches. . . . In order to guard against being poisoned by the gas, each German soldier is in possession of a packet of tow soaked in oxygen'—the deserter handed over one of these embryo gas masks in proof of his statement. The French Divisional commander, General Ferry, gravely impressed, warned the French Division on his left, the British 28th Division on his right, and the Canadian Division—which took over part of his front two days later while the Algerian Division took over the rest. More significant still, Ferry warned his Corps commander, Balfourier, and the liaison officer from Joffre's headquarters, who came to visit him.

How did these two key men react? Balfourier deemed Ferry a credulous fool and ignored his suggestions that the German trenches should be shelled in order to destroy the cylinders, and that the number of men in the front line, exposed to the gas danger, should be reduced. The liaison officer not only dismissed the story as a myth, but reproved Ferry, first, for warning the British direct, and, second, for taking steps to reduce the garrison of the front line contrary to Joffre's doctrine. And, following the usual happy custom of the French Army, Ferry was thereafter punished by removal for being right.

General Putz, who, with his two divisions, took over the

left of the salient from Balfourier, was no more inclined to believe the story than Balfourier, although a fresh warning came from Belgian sources on April 16th. Putz mentioned the story scoffingly to the British liaison officer from Smith-Dorrien's Second Army, but apparently did not think it worth repeating to his own troops. So they waited in ignorance until suffocation overtook them.

The only measures taken were by the British. Aircraft reconnaissances were made, but failed to observe anything unusual, and Plumer passed the warning to his Divisional commanders 'for what it was worth'. No precautions against gas were suggested or ordered, and in the next few days even the fact of the warning was forgotten—perhaps all the easier because it sounded such an 'ungentlemanly' novelty. Yet acquaintance with the German practice of getting in the first verbal blow might well have made the British Command suspect the sinister significance of the German wireless *communiqué* of April 17th—'Yesterday, east of Ypres, the British employed shells and bombs with asphyxiating gas.'

But one factor which undoubtedly lulled suspicion of an attack was the lack of any sign that the Germans were concentrating reserves for it. This lack of signs was due, not to special precautions, but to the lack of such reserves. And thereby the Germans lost the opportunity created by the most complete surprise of the war.

As scientifically hidebound as its opponents, the German Supreme Command had little faith in the new weapon. So little, that for want of facilities the inventor, Haber, had to use cylinders mainly for projection instead of shells. A discharge of gas from cylinders must be dependent on a favourable wind and, as a westerly or south-westerly wind was the most frequent in Flanders, the Germans thus offered a hostage to fortune. Disclosing their new weapon prematurely and for a paltry prize, they gave their opponents the advantage in retaliation until sufficient gas shell was produced to replace gas cylinders.

However weak their faith, it is incredible, but for the result, that the Germans should have neglected to be ready for a possible success. Yet, actually, Falkenhayn allotted no fresh reserves for the attack, and even refused the request for extra ammunition. Falkenhayn's idea was merely to try the gas as an experimental aid to an attack which itself was merely a cloak to his projected blow against the Russians. If the Ypres salient could be erased, so much the better, but he did not take any longer view.

Originally the attack was to be launched by the XV Corps against the southern side of the salient, and the gas cylinders were in position by March 10th. But the attack had to be postponed repeatedly for want of a favourable wind, and towards the end of March an alternative attack was prepared on the north side of the salient. Intended for April 15th, this in turn was delayed a week. It was then launched by the two divisions of the XXVI Reserve Corps, with one division of the XXIII Reserve Corps attacking on their right. As an aid to the main thrust the other division of the XXIII Reserve Corps was to strike at Steenstraat which was both the hinge of the salient and the junction between the French and the Belgians. Unaided by gas this subsidiary attack made little progress. Only one division was available in army reserve, and this was not released until next day, and was then given to the XXIII Reserve Corps, not to the XXVI, which had an open gap before it.

But if lack of reserves was the fundamental cause of the Germans' failure, the immediate cause was the troops' fear of their own gas. They had only been issued with the crudest form of respirator, which many of them did not even wear; no special tactics had been thought out; and, after passing through the gasping and agonized men who littered the French trenches, they were only too willing to comply with the letter of their limited orders, and dig in as soon as they reached the short-distance objective that had been assigned. The failing light, too, prevented them discovering the extent of their success and the weakness of the few stouthearted knots of Canadians who were strung across their path. And during the succeeding days they were equally content to act as camp-followers to their artillery, merely taking a short step forward to occupy and consolidate such fresh patches of ground as the guns and gas had swept practically clear of defenders. However shortsighted during the first days, when opportunity lay open to their embrace, this pure siege warfare method was good sense later. It foreshadowed the Verdun method of a year later, and, thanks to Foch, the Allies helped to make it most profitable to the Germans.

Foch was then, as Joffre's deputy, in higher control of the French troops in Flanders, and charged with the duty of co-ordinating the efforts of the French, British and Belgians. On hearing the news of the German break-through, he ordered Putz to make sure of holding his ground, now the line of the canal, and to organize a counterattack to regain the ground he had lost. But the French had lost their artillery and all they could do was to fulfil the first point. Fortunately, the Belgians baffled the German efforts to break the hinge. Putz, however, told the British that he would be counter-attacking, and to aid him two Canadian battalions made a midnight counterattack. They penetrated the new German line, and captured Kitchener's Wood, but as no French attack developed they had to withdraw from it later. Next day, the British, scraping together a few handfuls of reserves, attempted further petty counterattacks which naturally failed at heavy cost, as they were delivered in daylight and with negligible support from the French and from artillery. By evening on the 23rd, however, the broad way to Ypres and the British rear was almost filled, although by only twenty-one and a half sorely weakened British battalions (twelve of them Canadian), who faced forty-two German battalions—and a five-to-one superiority in guns.

Sir John French ordered a continuation of these vain efforts on the 24th—but the Germans anticipated him. At 3 a.m. they attacked the Belgian 'hinge' and were badly discomfited; henceforth they were unable either to widen or deepen their small foothold across the canal. At 4 a.m. they launched a heavy blow, with gas, against the jagged corner of the Canadians' front. No respirators were yet available and the only protection were handkerchiefs, towels and cotton bandoliers, wetted with the liquid most readily available in the trenches and placed over the mouth. Many men were overcome and, although there was only a small break in the line at the first onset, this gradually spread. For a time good artillery shooting prevented the Germans probing the breach, but in the afternoon they surged forward to and beyond St. Julien. The situation looked critical, but a counterattack by two Yorkshire Territorial battalions, helped by Canadian batteries firing over open sights, rolled the leading Germans back to St. Julien. This slight taste of repulse sufficed to quench the Germans' thirst for further advance that day. But their irresolution was hidden from the eyes of the British Commanders by the general confusion. In the patchwork line across the Germans' path, Canadians, British Regulars, Territorials, even Zouaves, of various divisions and brigades, were intermingled, clinging on wherever they had been pushed, like dabs of cement into a crumbling wall. The salient had now been compressed by German pressure into a narrow tongue of land, barely three miles across, although nearly six miles deep. Thus, in attempting to hold it, the defenders were now so crowded that they provided an easy harvest for the German guns.

Yet Sir John French, beguiled by the optimism of Foch and Putz, and the assurance that two fresh French divisions were coming up to retake the lost ground, was unwilling to sanction any withdrawal. Early on the 25th, the day of the Gallipoli landing, a fresh Regular Brigade was brought up and thrown blindly into an attack near St. Julien, there to be 'mown down like corn, by machine-guns in enfilade'. With appalling swiftness two thousand four hundred men were scythed—more loss than Ian Hamilton's army paid for the capture of the Gallipoli beaches. And that evening the bulk of the Canadian Division was withdrawn into reserve, having lost some five thousand men in its gallant efforts to battle against gas and heavy guns with their rifles, supplemented meagrely by guns that the official history terms 'the ancient and obsolete weapons of the South African War'. Nor did the burden of this hopeless struggle cease with the relief of the Canadians; it was merely shifted more fully to other shoulders. For another month operations were to continue, methodical German attacks answered by unmethodical British attacks. Lest I be thought to emphasize the futility unduly, let me quote the sober and sombre words of the official history:

'The governing idea was that the French should restore the line lost by them, and that the British should assist. . . . General Foch ordered immediate counterattacks which General Putz was not in a position to execute; whilst the British wholehearted attempts to carry out their share by means of offensive action, which was as a rule neither a true counterattack nor a deliberately prepared attack, led to heavy losses without restoring the situation. . . .' 'It seemed to the British officers at the front that they were being sacrificed to gain time until the French were ready for a big spectacular effort; but this, even if ever intended, did not materialize.'

To study the cause of the tragedy we must shift our gaze from the front to the rear. After expending the Indian Lahore Division and the Northumberland Territorial Brigade in another vain attack on the 26th, with a loss of another four thousand men, Smith-Dorrien realized the futility of such efforts and the improbability of French co-operation. Hence on the 27th he wrote to Robertson, the Chief of the General Staff, asking him to put the real situation before French, and saying—'I am doubtful if it is worth losing any more men to regain this French ground, unless the French do something really big.' He further suggested that it would be wise to prepare for a withdrawal to a less acutely bent line nearer to Ypres. All that he got in reply was a telephone message from Robertson—'Chief does not regard situation nearly so unfavourable as your letter represents.' In fact, however,

Smith-Dorrien's letter was far more optimistic than the grim conditions justified. Yet this 'comforting' message from the comfortable and peacefully remote General Headquarters was followed by a still worse rebuff—a telegram, sent through unciphered, telling Smith-Dorrien to hand over command of all the troops engaged at Ypres to General Plumer, and also to send the latter his Chief of Staff, General Milne. Relations between French and Smith-Dorrien had become very strained ever since Smith-Dorrien had saved French's situation against his own orders at Le Cateau in August, 1914. Now, French, true to a habit of his namesakes, seized the chance to punish Smith-Dorrien for making a true diagnosis, and administered a public rebuff which left Smith-Dorrien no option but to send a hint that he would resign if desired. French instantly embraced it and ordered him to hand over his shrunken command and go home.

Nevertheless, Plumer's first instructions from French were to prepare the very withdrawal that Smith-Dorrien had tentatively proposed. Then French went off to see Foch at Cassel and came back with a different outlook. Foch argued vehemently against a withdrawal, said that the lost ground could be retaken by the troops already available, urged that a retirement 'should be forbidden', and begged French 'to support the French *offensive to retake the Langemarck region at all costs*, beginning at noon on the 29th'. The days that followed were a comedy behind the front, a tragedy for the troops in front. Day after day, French heard from his fighting subordinates of the sufferings of the men and of the continued absence of the ever-promised French offensive. Thereupon he would incline towards a withdrawal, only to be swung the other way by Foch's buoyant assurances and flattering entreaties.

Once more let us quote the official history:

'For ill now, although for weal in the last year of the war, General Foch was the very spirit of the offensive. . . . Sir John French, though at first he had wholeheartedly complied with General Foch's wishes, appreciated the small result of the French efforts—or, rather, the smallness of the first efforts—and the heavy losses of his own troops crowded together in the small place d'armes of the narrowed salient. . . . Sir John French then became convinced that he must withdraw his troops, and passed from optimism to pessimism. It was naturally most difficult for his subordinates to follow his moods, particularly when his mind was on the border line between one phase of thought and the next, and when, at the entreaty of General Foch, he more than once agreed to wait a little longer before withdrawing his men—and to order one more counterattack.'

However, he clutched at a straw in the wind when, late on May 1st, Foch confessed that Joffre, so far from sending reinforcements, was calling for troops to be sent from Ypres to strengthen his forthcoming offensive near Arras. French forthwith sanctioned the long-planned withdrawal, by nightly stages, although only to a line some three miles short of Ypres, so that the front still formed a salient, if a flatter one. This was more inconvenient for defence and control than the original salient, the head being exposed to pounding from all sides while Ypres itself formed a dangerously narrow throat of supply and communication. The political and sentimental objection to yielding ground, especially Belgian ground, and the military desire to facilitate the task of any belated French effort, led Sir John French to overrule the fighting commanders' wish to withdraw to the natural straight line of defence formed by the ramparts of Ypres and the canal. So they stayed in the reduced salient, 'one huge artillery target', there to be pounded and gassed incessantly, with their scanty ammunition running out, until relief at last came, in the fourth week of May, through the Germans exhausting their own comparative superfluity of shells. For the Germans had at least the good sense to cease attacks when they came to the choice between economizing infantry lives and economizing artillery ammunition. All that the French had done in the interval was to clear the west bank of the canal, on May 15th, while the continued British bayonet attacks east of Ypres did not even succeed in preventing the Germans switching troops from the British sector to check the eventual small French attack—truly a mountain that was long in labour and brought forth a mouse. And having forfeited sixty thousand men for the privilege of acting as midwife, the British were then left to hold the most uncomfortably cramped new salient, or target, at continued expense for over two years.

To throw good money after bad is foolish. But to throw away men's lives where there is no reasonable chance of advantage, is criminal. In the heat of battle mistakes in the command are inevitable and amply excusable. But the real indictment of leadership arises when attacks that are inherently vain are ordered merely because if they could succeed they would be useful. For such 'manslaughter', whether it springs from ignorance, a false conception of war or a want of moral courage, commanders should be held accountable to the nation.

CHAPTER V

SCENE 4

THE UNWANTED BATTLE—LOOS
(SEPTEMBER 15TH, 1915)

IN early September the 'back of the front' in France was seething with rumours of a great Franco-British offensive which was to shatter the German front; and, if the atmosphere among the fighting troops was tense, it had also an exhilarating breath of confidence in the result. For the first time the New Armies and Territorials were to take a prominent part, and few seemed to expect that the joint hammer blows of British and French together could fail, at least, to dissolve the static trench warfare that had persisted for nearly a year. But there was one extreme contrast to this air of confidence —and that was in the headquarters of the British higher commanders.

For the ill-fated Loos offensive was undertaken directly against the opinion of Haig, the man who, as Commander of the First Army, had to carry it out. Haig argued that the supply of heavy artillery and of shells was still inadequate, that its adequacy was the governing factor of the situation, and that until this weakness was remedied, it was little use to make plans for offensives. For in June the British Army still had only seventy-one heavy guns to one thousand four hundred and six field guns, and the factories in England were turning out no more than twenty-two thousand shells a day, compared to one hundred thousand by the French, and two hundred and fifty thousand by the Germans and Austrians— according to report.

Haig's view was by no means an isolated one. Robertson, Chief of the General Staff of the British Expeditionary Force, fully endorsed it, but his influence with his own Chief had been undermined by Sir Henry Wilson, who was a devout believer in the infallibility of French military judgment, and

LOOS, 1915

Neuve Chapelle

LAHORE

19

La Bassée

LA BASSÉE CANAL

Béthune

2

BRIT. 24th. Div.

BRIT. I Corps (Gough)

9

BRIT. 21st. Div.

7

Hulluch

1

BRIT. IV Corps (Rawlinson)

15

Loos

Hill 70

47

81 F.

Lens

N

Vimy Ridge

0 1 2 3 4
Miles

Original Front Line
Positions on evening of 25th. Sept.
Positions at end of the battle

Arras

© Cassell & Co. Ltd. 1970

Robertson had even been excluded from Sir John French's personal mess. Meantime, Wilson, the friend and confidant of French, was proposing to Kitchener that the British Army should be divided into two groups, one to be located away in Lorraine, so as to ensure that French should be unable to take an independent attitude towards the French!

Equally emphatic, and pessimistic, was Sir Henry Rawlinson, who, under Haig, would have the main task with his army corps. He noted in his diary—'My new front is as flat as the palm of my hand. Hardly any cover anywhere. . . . D.H. tells me that we are to attack "au fond", that the French are doing likewise and making a supreme effort. It will cost us dearly, and we shall not get very far.' He, however, was left no choice but to do that his men might die. For, in face of all these warnings, only too truly founded, the better judgment of the British commanders was overborne by Joffre's pressure.

The next revelation is that the instrument of this pressure was Lord Kitchener. It is a curious sidelight on one who had been among the first of British leaders to appreciate the state of deadlock in the west and to exclaim against the stubborn folly of seeking to pass the impassable. Kitchener had seen his January doubts fulfilled, and in June had bitterly remarked, as Poincaré has recorded—'Joffre and Sir John [French] told me in November they were going to push the Germans back over the frontier; they gave me the same assurances in December, March, and May. What have they done? The attacks are very costly and end in nothing.' Yet he was now the determining factor in adding nought to nought.

How was this strange chain of causation forged? Joffre, spiritual twin of his subordinate Foch, in the sense of being an unquenchable optimist, was undeterred by his hard experiences of the spring from the repetition of them in the autumn. In his plan, two great convergent blows were to be delivered from the widely separated sectors of Artois (Arras-Lens) and Champagne (Reims-the Argonne), the former being originally intended as the main blow. Note this point, for it had a vital influence and suffered a vital alteration.

A successful break-through both in Champagne and Artois was to be the signal for a general offensive of all the French and British Armies on the Western Front. This, Joffre confidently declared, would 'compel the Germans to retreat beyond the Meuse and possibly end the war'.

Yet, in the event, one and a third German divisions sufficed to break the back of the attack of the six British divisions north of Lens, and south of Lens the French attack by fourteen divisions was hardly even developed in face of five German divisions. What a majestic conception was this plan of Joffre's, and how utterly unrelated to the material conditions of modern warfare! And what painful evidence that professional strategy may be the sheerest 'amateur strategy'.

When Joffre's draft plan was sent on June 4th to Sir John French, the British Commander-in-Chief expressed his general agreement. Then a strong gust of common sense came from his subordinate, Haig, and the military weathervane swung the other way.

Haig had made a personal reconnaissance of the area south of the La Bassée canal (La Bassée-Lens) and as a result declared definitely that it was 'not a favourable one for an attack'. His verdict was to prove most accurate. In his view the German defences were so strong that, until a great increase of heavy artillery was provided, they could only be taken by siege methods. 'The ground, for the most part bare and open, would be so swept by machine-gun and rifle fire both from the German front trenches and from the numerous fortified villages immediately behind them, that a rapid advance would be impossible.' He suggested that, if an offensive on the left of the French was imperative, subsidiary attacks only should be made south of the canal, and the main one delivered astride and north of it. But he concluded with the cold douche already mentioned.

Joffre, however, would not accept arguments for a postponement of the offensive or a change of site. He even remarked with that magisterial infallibility which is so delightful in retrospect, but in retrospect only, that 'your attack will find particularly favourable ground between Loos and La Bassée!' It was certainly both a simple and a magisterial way of brushing aside the adverse evidence of Haig, who had seen the ground.

Meanwhile the Germans, if not yet expecting an attack, were working with feverish energy to strengthen their defences and to create a second system in rear of the front. This was nearing completion by the end of July and knowledge of it accentuated Sir John French's doubts—under Haig's reiteration of his opinion. Hence a conference was arranged at Frévent on July 27th with Foch who, however, maintained that it was essential that, regardless of the ground and the strength of the enemy's defences, Haig's army should make its main attack just north of Lens in close connection with the French Tenth Army south of Lens, pinching out this maze-like mining town.

The tug-of-war between Haig and French, and Joffre and Foch continued, with Sir John French seeking a way out through a project of co-operating with artillery fire alone. This was quashed and the tug-of-war decided by the intervention of Kitchener. Visiting Sir John French in August, he told him that 'we must act with all energy and do our utmost to help France in this offensive, even though by so doing we may suffer very heavy losses'.

In this reversal of his own previous attitude, he was apparently influenced by the disasters then occurring on the Russian front, and his feeling of the urgent need to succour our Russian Allies, as well, perhaps, by his reaction from the disappointment at the Dardanelles. But two blacks do not make a white and, as he had long since declared his view that the Western Front was impassable, it is difficult to see how he could feel that a hopeless offensive there could bring fresh hope to the Russians.

He may have felt, however, that it would show the need and pave the way for the appointment of a supreme commander of the Entente forces. The official history has dis-

creetly lifted a corner of the veil of history with the statement
—'It is believed that Lord Kitchener himself had anticipated
a call to this post.' In that case a timely concession to the
French over Loos was likely to make them more receptive
towards the other suggestion, later.

But the immediate result, to quote the official history, was
that:

'Under pressure from Lord Kitchener at home, due to the
general position of the Allies, and from Generals Joffre and
Foch in France, due to the local situation in France, the
British Commander-in-Chief was therefore compelled to
undertake operations before he was ready, over ground that
was most unfavourable, against the better judgment of himself and of General Haig, and, with no more than a quarter
of the troops, nine divisions, instead of thirty-six, that he
considered necessary for a successful attack.'

French was himself, as we shall see, to extinguish its last
hope of success. The last but one had been extinguished by a
final alteration of the French plan. This was Joffre's decision
to make the Champagne attack, and not the Artois, his main
attack, for the reason that the ground in Champagne had
fewer obstacles or villages in the way of the attackers. The
sudden preference for tactical over strategical considerations
is in curious contrast to his view where the British attack was
concerned.

This change, again, had a damaging influence on the
British attack, for both the British and French official
accounts make it clear that the French Artois attack south
of Lens by seventeen divisions on a twelve-mile frontage—
supported by four hundred and twenty heavy guns—was not
seriously pressed once the strength of the defence was realized.
Yet the French had nearly twice as many heavy guns to the
mile as the British (one hundred and seventeen in all). In
Champagne twenty-seven French divisions, with eight hundred and fifty heavy guns, were assembled for the attack—

on an eighteen-mile frontage. Thus the proportionate artillery support here was still higher.

When the decision to attack at Loos was definitely taken, Haig's first intention, to curtail his commitment and probable loss, was to attack at first with only two divisions. But a too successful demonstration of the possibilities of chlorine gas projected in a 'wave' from cylinders led him to modify his views, and to believe that if the wind was favourable the gas discharge might even procure 'decisive results' and justify him in attacking on the wider frontage of six divisions—Rawlinson's IV Corps (47th, 15th and 1st Divisions) on the right, or south, and Gough's I Corps (7th, 9th, and 2nd Divisions) on the left.

With sound judgment of the chances, Haig urged that 'under no circumstances should our forthcoming attack be launched without the aid of gas', but he was overruled by French and Foch. He then obtained permission to reserve his decision until the last possible moment and to let the choice—between the large or limited attack—depend on the weather conditions. By the irony of fortune, the wind was most favourable for the use of gas on September 15th, the day originally fixed by Foch for the attack, and this fact encouraged Haig's hopes. But the retention of a dual plan led to a distribution of the artillery on the whole army front instead of a concentration on one-third.

Over five thousand cylinders of gas, containing nearly one hundred and fifty tons, were carried up to the front trenches and safely installed in special recesses, without one being hit by enemy fire. Even so, there was barely half the volume of gas necessary to maintain a continuous flow for the forty minutes that, in turn, were considered necessary to outlast the protective power of the oxygen apparatus used by the enemy machine-gunners. Hence the cylinders had to be turned on and off intermittently. Smoke candles were used in the intervals to simulate gas, and, at the end, to form the first smoke screen of the war.

The artillery bombardment began on September 21st,

the ammunition being eked out by limiting each heavy gun to ninety rounds, and each field gun to one hundred and fifty in the twenty-four hours. The results were not encouraging, so far as effect could be discovered, and led the commanders to study the wind all the more attentively.

The last night was a time of tense anxiety. Repeatedly Haig studied fresh charts sent in by a chain of meteorological observers. At 6 p.m. the forecast was that the wind would be 'on the border line between favourable and unfavourable, with a slight bias towards favourable'. At 9 p.m. the forecast was better, indicating a probable change to a south-westerly or even westerly wind, which would carry the gas over the German trenches. Thereupon Haig unhesitatingly ordered the full-scale offensive with gas, although as a precaution staff officers of each corps had been ordered to stand by their telephones. At 3 a.m., after a further report not quite so encouraging, he fixed sunrise (5.50 a.m.) as the hour for releasing the gas. During the hours of darkness the wind changed as predicted, but only as far as south-west, and, worse still, was so slight as to be almost a calm.

About 5 a.m., as soon as it was light, Haig went out. He could feel only the faintest breath of air, and he asked his senior A.D.C. to light a cigarette. The smoke drifted in puffs to the north-east.

Did it justify the venture? Would the gas merely hang in the British trenches? A slight increase of wind was felt and at 5.15 a.m. Haig gave the decisive order to 'carry on' and climbed his wooden look-out tower. But the improvement was delusive, and a few minutes later one of his staff telephoned to the I Corps, to ask whether it was possible to stop the discharge and the attack. For this emergency the gas officers had made ample arrangements. But Gough replied that it was too late. If it would certainly have been a close shave, one may suspect, especially in view of Gough's record, that with this ardent fighter the wish was at least the midwife, if not the father, of the thought.

When the gas was actually turned on at 5.50 a.m. it carried

fairly well over the German trenches on the right, if too slow and slight for full effect, but on the left was a failure, in some places drifting back and upsetting the attack. In Horne's 2nd Division, the officer in charge of the gas on the 6th Brigade front declined to assume the responsibility of turning on the cylinders. But when this was reported to divisional headquarters, Horne replied with an order that 'the programme must be carried out whatever the conditions. . . .' As a result of this obstinacy many of the infantry were poisoned by their own gas. Those who were able to advance were soon stopped, and slaughtered by the ungassed German machine-gunners. Nevertheless, Horne ordered a fresh assault, which was only abandoned after his brigade commanders had protested against the 'useless sacrifice of life'.

The general infantry assault had been launched at 6.30 a.m., and into it was thrown the entire strength of the First Army, except for local reserves. Neither Haig nor the commanders of his two attacking corps kept any reserve, as they understood that the Commander-in-Chief expected a breakthrough and would use his general reserve to back them up promptly.

On the extreme right the 47th Division nearly carried out its task of throwing forward a defensive flank, but the 'not quite' had an important bearing on the surprisingly successful initial rush of its neighbour, the 15th Division, contributing towards the loss of direction which nullified its near approach to a break-through, beyond Hill 70. So swift and deep was the advance of these Scotsmen of 'K's' Army that the German Command made hurried preparations to evacuate the whole area, and as far back as Douai 'there were endless convoys of wagons formed up in double lines ready to march away'.

Another ill effect was due to the long delay in the 1st Division's advance, only partially retrieved. Its left brigade had suffered similarly to Horne's division and, instead of the divisional reserve being sent through the gap made on the flanks, the morning was wasted in futile attempts to renew the frontal assault. This stoppage in the British centre tended to check the whole momentum of the British advance. Further to the left the 7th and 9th Divisions obtained promising results, although the 9th had suffered, both in opportunity and life, from the misguided insistence of the Corps commander, Gough, on renewing the vain frontal assault of the left brigade. In wise contrast Capper, commanding the 7th Division, when confronted with a check on his left, had quickly passed his reserve through the gap made by the successful advance of his right.

The fulfilment of any promise, however, depended on the prompt infusion of reserves. This was the crux of the situation and the sealing cause of failure. Even Joffre had said that if French kept his reserve divisions too far back they would 'run the risk of arriving too late to exploit the success of the leading ones. It is indispensable that these divisions are put, before the attack, at the absolute disposal of General Haig'. Haig repeatedly urged that they should at least be brought up close behind him. French's assurances were so vague as to be simultaneously unsatisfying and misleading. As usual his outlook seems to have been governed by contradictory impulses of undue optimism and pessimism.

French's general reserves comprised the Cavalry Corps—which, under modern conditions, did not count except in the minds of cavalry-trained commanders—and the XI Corps. The last included the Guards Division, newly formed, and the 21st and 24th Divisions, newly arrived in France. With curious judgment French left seasoned divisions lying idle on the quiet Somme front, and chose to use these two raw divisions for the critical phase of the battle. Moreover, he had given Haig to understand that they would be immediately at hand for Haig's use, whereas he placed them sixteen miles in rear. And in his subsequent despatch he untruthfully stated that they were put at Haig's disposal at 9.30 a.m. on the 25th. Actually, Haig did not hear until 1.20 p.m., and then indirectly. Haig bitterly remarked, soon after—'If there had been even one division in reserve close up we could have walked right through. General headquarters refuses to recognize the teaching of the war as regards the control of reserves.' His confidence was probably exaggerated, at least as to the effect of such a narrow breach, and he was himself to err somewhat similarly in the following July. But his natural disgust, accentuated by French's untruthful despatch, led first to an acrimonious interchange of letters and then to an irreconcilable quarrel. He seems also, to have been galled, and not for the first time, at the way his own sound advice had been overruled by Foch's influence with French. French in retort charged Haig with the folly of trying to push reserves through a far too narrow gap. The sequel was that Haig wrote personally to Kitchener and spoke to Haldane about French's failure and incompetence, and thereby helped to precipitate French's downfall and his own succession.

As for the long and slow march up of those divisions, bad traffic arrangements were more responsible than their own inexperience for accentuating the evil caused by the Commander-in-Chief's dispositions. As General Edmonds caustically says—'It was like trying to push the Lord Mayor's procession through the streets of London, without clearing the route and holding up the traffic.' Folly was capped by farce when, on the outskirts of Béthune, a military policeman stopped the 72nd Brigade because the Brigade commander had no pass to enter the area.

Never, surely, were 'novice' divisions thrown into a vital stroke in a more difficult or absurd manner, and in an atmosphere of greater misconception of the situation in all quarters. This amply explains their subsequent failure when their belated attack was at last launched at 11 a.m. on the 26th, and redresses the hasty judgments which were spread at the time—a stigma that was slow to fade. That in courage they were not lacking is clear, and equally that its fruits were reduced by their rawness, by that of their staff still more.

The handicap of inexperience in these and the other New Army divisions engaged can be overemphasized. It does not appear that, as a whole, apart from certain battalions in them, the regular divisions were more effective or even as effective in the battle. 'Battlecraft' is a rare quality, the product of gifted and original leadership, and in its absence mere dash is often more effective than so-called experience.

The ineffectiveness of the larger French attack south of the Lens also affected the British opportunity. For the French did not advance until six and a quarter hours after their Allies, and even then made little progress where they did not make merely a demonstration. The bitter experiences of the spring and summer seem to have led the fighting commanders to discount Foch's faith in a break-through, and to annul his vehement order by gentle evasion in places. Joffre also put a brake on him from above, for on the second morning he telephoned him to 'go cautiously', and followed this by the warning—'Stop the attacks of the Tenth Army, taking care to avoid giving the British the impression that we are leaving them to attack alone.' His reason was apparently that he now pinned his hopes to the attack in Champagne, which on the first day gave a delusive promise of a real break-through.

It is worth while to note that the partial opening success of the attack in Champagne, and also in Artois, was largely due to the obstinate self-delusion of Falkenhayn, who had disregarded ample warnings from many sources, and requests for reserves. Only two hours before the attack began he assured the Kaiser that the local army commanders 'see things too black', and that the French were not in a condition to attack.

Early reports on the 25th had also led Haig to over-estimate his initial success, and as early as 10.30 a.m. he ordered the 3rd Cavalry Division forward. The Commander soon discovered Haig's mistake, but Haig, believing that the cavalry had gone on, hurried the 21st and 24th Divisions forward as soon as he could get hold of them. But before they came up the known situation had changed, and the two leading brigades were taken to strengthen the line gained by the original attack. Haig still hoped to break the intact German second line of defences, and to this end the rest (four brigades) of these divisions continued their march across country, and unknown country, in the dark and rain. Tired, hungry, and as confused as their commanders, they were launched to the attack next morning without effective artillery support, and against defences now stronger and more strongly manned than the original first line. For the Germans had not only been reinforced, but had covered themselves with a thick wire entanglement during the night. The attack broke down at or before this uncut obstacle, and the survivors turned and flowed backwards. Their disappearance left a hole in the ragged British Front between Loos and Hulluch, which the Guards Division came up to fill. Meantime German counterattacks were multiplying dangerously, especially on the flanks. At last, on the 28th, Foch came to the relief not only by taking over the British flank sector near Loos, but with a local success on Vimy Ridge, which drew off most of the newly arrived German Guard Corps to check it. And in concert with Sir John French he arranged to make a renewed general offensive on October 2nd. The same course was adopted in Champagne, where the French for three days had vainly hurled themselves at the German second position, suffering fearful loss, which would have been worse if Pétain (Second Army) had not stopped his attack in disregard of higher orders.

But as the pause was to be followed by a renewal at the same point, it merely gave the Germans time to strengthen it and accumulate resources in the rear. Local upsets due to German counterattacks, and the exhaustion of the troops, caused further delay, and the renewed offensive was repeatedly postponed. Eventually all three attacks were delivered on different dates, the British last on October 13th. And, in the words of the official history, it 'had not improved the general situation in any way and had brought nothing but useless slaughter of infantry'. Curiously, Haig's sense of realism waned in this last phase, or, perhaps more truly, it was subdued by his bulldog tenacity; for although Joffre had abandoned the effort, Haig was working up a new general attack for November 7th, an operation whose inevitable cost does not seem to have had any adequate excuse. Happily, Generals Winter and Weather intervened. But the British casualities already amounted to 50,380—or 60,392 if the subsidiary attacks by Haig's Army be included—whereas the German loss was barely 20,000, despite their costly counter-attacks. The French in Champagne and Artois had lost 191,797 officers and men, and inflicted 120,000 casualties—a proportion which suggests that the actual handling of these attacks was better than that of the British, if helped by more powerful artillery. Both Allies had gained in experience, if not in wisdom, but they had afforded the Germans still better experience in the way to frustrate such attacks. And in 1916 it was the Germans who profited heavily both by the offensive and the defensive lesson.

CHAPTER VI

1916—THE 'DOG-FALL'

IN 1914 the centre of gravity of the World War had been on the Western Front; in 1915 it shifted to the Eastern Front; in 1916 it once more moved back to France. Although the Entente had dissipated some of their strength in Salonika and Mesopotamia, the rising tide of England's new armies and of her munition supplies promised the power for an effort far larger in scale than before to break the trench deadlock. Measures had also been taken to keep these new divisions up to strength. By the end of 1915 the British force in France had risen to thirty-eight divisions through the entry into the field of 'Kitchener's Army', as well as of the Territorial divisions. Although the principle of voluntary enlistment had not yet been abandoned, the method was systematized and based on a national register. This scheme, launched in October, 1915, under the aegis of Lord Derby, aimed to reconcile the demands of the Army with the needs of industry, calling up men by groups as they were wanted, and taking single men first. But the response among the latter was not adequate to preserve this graduated principle, and in January, 1916, by the Military Service Act, the voluntary system—system is hardly the correct term—was replaced by conscription.

At the close of 1915, the first serious effort to obtain unity of action between the Allies was made, and a conference of the leaders of the French, British, Belgian and Italian armies, with representatives present from the Russian and Japanese, was held at Joffre's headquarters on December 5th. As a result they adopted the principle of a simultaneous general offensive in 1916 by France, Britain, Russia and Italy. In view of the rawness of the British troops, it was recognized

269

that time must be allowed for training, and Russia also needed time for re-equipment, so that the offensive could not begin before the summer of 1916, although it was hoped to carry out preliminary attacks to wear down the enemy's strength. But in January both Joffre and Foch gave Haig a clear intimation that it was for him to carry out this preparatory task, and that they did not intend to take the offensive until he had done so.

German action was to dislocate this scheme, and only the British share came fully into operation, and not even that into full effect. By a grim jest, however, it forced the French to carry out the wearing-down process—in an indirect form. For Falkenhayn was about to fulfil his long-cherished plan for a western offensive, but with characteristic limitations. Always a believer in the strategy of attrition, he now carried this ruling idea into tactics, and produced the new form of attack by methodical stages, each with a limited objective. In an appreciation made at Christmas, 1915, he argued that England was the staple of the enemy Alliance. 'The history of the English wars against the Netherlands, Spain, France and Napoleon is being repeated. Germany can expect no mercy from this enemy, so long as he still retains the slightest hope of achieving his object.' Save by submarine warfare, however, England and her army were out of reach, for their sector of the front did not lend itself to offensive operations. 'In view of our feelings for our arch-enemy in the war that is certainly distressing, but it can be endured if we realize that for England the campaign on the Continent . . . is at bottom a side-show. Her real weapons here are the French, Russian and Italian armies.' He regarded Russia as already paralysed, and Italy's military achievements as unlikely to affect the situation. 'Only France remains.' 'France has almost arrived at the end of her military effort. If her people can be made to understand clearly that in a military sense they have nothing more to hope for, breaking point would be reached, and England's best sword knocked out of her hand.' He added that a break-through in mass was unnecessary, and that instead the Germans should aim to bleed France to death by choosing a point of attack 'for the retention of which the French command would be compelled to throw in every man they have'. Such an objective was either Belfort, or Verdun, and Verdun was chosen, because it was a menace to the main German communications, because it offered a salient and so cramped the defender, and because of the moral effect if so renowned a place were lost to France. It has also been suggested that the choice was influenced by a peculiarly German moral, or unmoral, consideration. For Verdun was the ancient gate of the west through which the German hordes had passed to attack the Gauls. Similarly the Germans were fond of christening their trench positions after the heroes of the Nibelungen—Siegfried, Brünhilde and so on. The vein of superstition is still more clearly suggested in the Kaiser's choice of a second Moltke to guide his armies, and in the original location of their headquarters in the same hotel and same town, Coblenz, as they had occupied in 1870.

The keynote of the tactical plan at Verdun was a continuous series of limited advances, which by their menace should draw the French reserves into the mincing machine of the German artillery. And each of these advances was itself to be secured from loss by a short but intense artillery bombardment. By this means the objective would be taken and consolidated before the enemy could move up his reserves for counterattack. Although the Intelligence branch at French General Headquarters gave early warning of the German preparations, the Operations branch were so full of their own offensive schemes that the warning fell on deaf ears. Further, the easy fall of the Belgian and Russian fortresses had led to a commonly held view that fortresses were obsolete, and Joffre, persuading the French government to 'declass' Verdun as a fortress, had denuded it of guns and troops. The forts were only used as shelters and the trench lines which took their place were inadequate and in poor repair.

At 7.15 a.m. on February 21st, the German bombardment

began, on a front of fifteen miles, and at 4.45 p.m. the infantry advanced, although the first day only on a four and a half miles' front. From then until February 24th the defenders' line east of the Meuse was crumbled away as by the erosion of the tide.

Joffre was now aroused so far as to entrust the defence to Pétain, for whose use reserves were assembled. On March 6th the Germans extended the attack to the west bank of the Meuse; but the defence was now stiffening, the numbers balanced, and the immediate threat to Verdun was checked.

A slight lull followed, and during it the Allies of France made efforts to relieve the pressure on her. The British took over the Arras front from the French Tenth Army, their front becoming now continuous from the Yser to the Somme; the Italians made their fifth attack, though in vain, on the Isonzo front; and the Russians hurled untrained masses on the German front at Lake Narocz, near Vilna, where the slight gains were soon lost through a counterstroke. These efforts did not prevent Falkenhayn pursuing his attrition offensive at Verdun. The advances were slight but they were cumulative in effect, and the balance of loss turned definitely against the defenders. On June 7th Fort Vaux fell, and the German tide crept ever closer to Verdun. And in the Asiago region, Conrad had launched his offensive against Italy's Trentino flank.

Again Russia came to the rescue. In the spring of 1916 she had one hundred and thirty divisions, but still woefully short of equipment, facing forty-six German and forty Austrian divisions. The preparation and reorganization for her intended share in the year's Allied offensive were cut short by the emergency at Verdun, and in relief of her French Allies she had launched the costly and obstinately prolonged attack at Lake Narocz in March. When at last it was broken off, the preparations for the main offensive were resumed. This was to begin in July, coincidently with the Somme offensive; meantime Brusilov, commanding the south-western front, prepared such attacks as he could stage from his own resources as a distraction of the enemy's attention from the main offensive. But the distraction was released prematurely, on June 4th, in response to Italy's appeal to Russia to prevent the Austrians reinforcing their Trentino attack. Without warning, because without any special concentration of troops, Brusilov's troops advanced against the Austrian Fourth Army near Luck, and the Austrian Seventh Army in the Bukovina, whose resistance collapsed at the first shock.

This last vital effort of the Russian Army in the war had important consequences. It stopped the Austrian attack on Italy, already impaired by an Italian riposte. It compelled Falkenhayn to withdraw troops from the Western Front, and so abandon his plan for a counterstroke against the British offensive preparing on the Somme, as well as the hope of nourishing his Verdun attrition process. It led Rumania to take her fateful decision to enter the war on the Entente side, and caused the supersession of Falkenhayn in the supreme command, and his replacement by Hindenburg—with Ludendorff, officially styled First Quartermaster-General, as the directing brain. Although Rumania's entry was the immediate reason, the underlying one was the fact that Falkenhayn's indefinite strategy in 1915 had made possible the Russian recovery which stultified his strategy of 1916. Falkenhayn was history's latest example of the folly of half measures ; the ablest and most scientific General—'penny wise, pound foolish'—who ever ruined his country by a refusal to take calculated risks. In 1916 he had turned back westwards to pursue his long-cherished goal, and his strategy had faithfully fulfilled the canons of military orthodoxy by taking for its objective the enemy's strongest army and the strongest point of that army's position. It certainly achieved the object of compelling the French to pour their reserves into the Verdun 'blood-bath', but did not achieve any decisive strategic result.

Falkenhayn had rejected Conrad's proposal for a concentration against Italy such as had previously overthrown Serbia. Conrad's reasons had been that such a blow against the 'hereditary enemy' would act as a tonic to the Austro-Hungarian forces, and that the theatre of war lent itself to decisive results by a thrust southwards from the Trentino against the rear of the Italian armies engaged on the Isonzo. The success attained by the relatively light blow of 1917—Caporetto—lends historical support to his contention. But Falkenhayn was dubious both of the feasibility and value of the plan, and was unwilling even to lend the nine German divisions which Conrad asked for to relieve Austrian divisions in Galicia. In default of this aid Conrad persisted in attempting his design single-handed, taking some of his best divisions from Galicia, and thereby exposing their front to Brusilov's advance without obtaining adequate force to achieve his Italian plan. Falkenhayn's smouldering resentment at this disregard of his views was fanned into flame by the Galician disaster, and he intervened in Vienna to procure the deposition of Conrad. With retributive irony his own fall followed close on that of Conrad.

Brusilov's offensive continued for three months with fair success, but reserves were not at hand for immediate exploitation, and before they could be moved down from the north the Germans were patching up the holes. His later efforts were never so dangerous, but they absorbed all the available Russian reserves, and the huge losses then incurred went far to complete the ruin of Russia's military power.

Great as was the influence of Brusilov's offensive on German strategy, its effect on the Verdun situation was less immediate. But the long-planned offensive on the Somme came to the rescue, and for want of nourishment the Verdun offensive faded away. Nevertheless, although the Germans at Verdun had fallen short of their object, moral and material, they had so drained the French army that it could play but a slender part in the Allied plan for 1916. The British had now to take up the main burden of the struggle, and the consequence was to limit both the scope and effect of the Entente strategy.

On July 1st, after a week's prolonged bombardment, the

British Fourth Army (recently created and placed under Rawlinson) attacked with thirteen divisions on a front of fifteen miles, north of the Somme, and the French with five divisions on a front of eight miles, mainly south of the river, where the German defence system was less highly developed. The unconcealed preparations and the long bombardment had given away any chance of surprise, and in face of the German resistance, weak in numbers but strong in organization, the attack failed along most of the British front. Owing to the dense and rigid 'wave' formations that were adopted the losses were appallingly heavy. Only on the south of the British front, near Fricourt and Montauban, did the attack gain a real footing in the German defences. The French, with slighter opposition, and being less expected, made larger gains.

This setback negatived the original idea of a 'break-through' to Bapaume and Cambrai, and Haig for a time fell back on the attrition method—of limited advances aimed to wear down the German strength. Rejecting Joffre's desire that he should again throw his troops frontally on the Thiepval defences, Haig at first resumed the attack with his right wing alone, and on July 14th the penetration of the Germans' second position offered a chance of exploitation, which was not taken. From now onward a methodical but costly advance continued, and although little ground was gained the German resistance was seriously strained when the early onset of winter rains suspended operations in November. The effect, however, can be exaggerated, for it did not prevent the Germans withdrawing troops from the west for the attack on Rumania.

But in one respect the Somme shed a significant light on the future, for on September 15th the first tanks appeared. Their early employment before large numbers were ready was a mistake; losing the chance of a great strategic surprise, and owing also to tactical mishandling, and minor technical defects, they had only a limited success. Although the higher military authorities lost faith in them, and some urged their abandonment, more discerning eyes realized that here was a key which, when properly used, might unlock the trench barrier.

The Somme offensive had a further indirect effect, for its relief to the Verdun pressure enabled the French to prepare counterstrokes, carried out by Mangin's Corps on October 24th and December 15th, which regained most of the lost ground with small casualties. These economical successes were due to a partial revival of surprise, to a more elastic use of the limited objective method, and to a high concentration of artillery, with a minimum of infantry to occupy the defences crushed by the guns. But the French success was greatly helped by Hindenburg's misguided insistence, for the sake of prestige, on maintaining the earlier gains instead of withdrawing the tired troops to a more secure line somewhat in rear. He at least profited by the lesson, to the Allies' detriment, in the spring of 1917.

Rumania, sympathetic to the Entente cause, had been waiting a favourable opportunity to enter the war on their side, and Brusilov's success encouraged her to take the plunge. Her command hoped that this, combined with the Allied pressure on the Somme and at Salonika, would fix the German reserves. But Rumania's situation had many inherent defects. The strategical position of her territory was bad, the main section, Wallachia, being sandwiched between Austro-Hungary and Bulgaria. Her army, though externally of a modern pattern, had grave weaknesses beneath the surface. Of her Allies, only Russia could give her direct aid, and they failed her. And, with all these handicaps, she launched an offensive into Transylvania, which bared her flank to Bulgaria.

While the Entente fumbled the Germans acted. The plan was initiated by Falkenhayn and developed by Hindenburg-Ludendorff when they took over the Supreme Command on August 28th. While one force concentrated in Transylvania for a counterstroke, a Bulgarian army with German stiffening —under Mackensen—was to strike through Rumania's 'back-door' and invade the Dobruja. This automatically halted the Rumanian offensive in Transylvania, and drew away its reserves; at the end of September the Rumanians were thrown back by the Austro-German counter-offensive, of which Falkenhayn was given executive command. They succeeded in holding the passes of Rumania's mountain border in the west until mid November, but Falkenhayn just broke through before the snows blocked the passes. Mackensen switched his main forces westwards, and crossed the Danube close to Bucharest, on which both armies now converged. It fell on December 6th, and, despite belated Russian aid, the Rumanian forces were driven north into Moldavia. The brilliantly co-ordinated German strategy had crippled their new foe, gained possession of the bulk of Rumania, with its oil and wheat, and gave the Russians another three hundred miles of front to hold. Sarrail, at Salonika, had not succeeded in fixing the Bulgarian reserves.

The Austrian offensive in the Trentino had interrupted Cadorna's plans for a renewed effort on the Isonzo, but when the former was halted Cadorna switched his reserves back to the Isonzo. In preparation for this offensive the whole sector from Monte Sabotino to the sea was entrusted to the Duke of Aosta's Third Army, under which sixteen divisions were concentrated against six Austrian divisions. Following a preliminary feint near the sea on August 4th, the attack opened well two days later. North of Gorizia Capello's corps swept over the long-impregnable Monte Sabotino, which guarded the approach to the river, and, crossing the river on the night of August 8th, occupied the town. This compelled an Austrian retreat in the Carso sector to the south, but attempts to exploit the success eastward failed against fresh positions of resistance. Three more efforts were made in the autumn, and if they imposed a wearing strain on the Austrians, they caused greater loss to the attackers. During the year Italians had suffered some 483,000 casualties, and inflicted 260,000.

The only territorial success that the Entente could show for their year's campaign—and, even so, it did not reveal itself fully until the New Year—was away in Mesopotamia—the capture of Baghdad. This moral token was seized on with an enthusiasm which, militarily, it hardly warranted. The bitter experience of the past had damped the ardour of the British Government, and Sir William Robertson, the new Chief of the Imperial General Staff, was opposed to any further commitments which drained the strength available for the Western Front. But Maude, the new commander on the spot, by subtle if unconscious steps succeeded in changing this defensive policy into one of a fresh offensive. After thorough reorganization of the Mesopotamian force and its communications, he began on December 12th, 1916, a progressive right wheel and extension of his front on the west bank of the Tigris above and below Kut. These methodical trench-warfare operations had placed him ready for a spring across the Tigris at the Turks' line of retreat, which was thus parallel to his front. But despite his four-to-one superiority of force, the failure of his right to pin down the enemy, and of his cavalry to cut off their retreat, prevented a decisive success. But it led to permission for an advance on Baghdad, and he entered the Mesopotamian capital on March 11th, 1917. A series of skilfully conducted operations then drove the Turks into divergent lines of retreat and secured the British hold on the province.

Ever since the abortive Turkish attempt to invade Egypt early in 1915, the British had kept a fairly large force there, even when the Dardanelles expedition was crying out for troops. When Gallipoli was evacuated, the release of the Turkish forces threatened a fresh move on Egypt. To forestall this danger the authorities in Cairo had gained Kitchener's approval for a landing in Ayas Bay near Alexandretta, but the proposal had been opposed by the General Staff at home and then nullified by the political objections of the French to any British intervention in Syria, which they already counted as part of their share of the spoils of war. Thus throughout 1916 the large British garrison of Egypt (at one time over a quarter of a million strong) remained passive while the Turks, by using a few thousand men in Sinai and by stirring up the Senussi in the Western Desert, created trouble on both flanks which reacted on the unrest within the frontiers of Egypt.

But the British, also, contrived to secure an Arab ally, on the eastern side of the Red Sea. This was the Sherif of Mecca, who had already rendered them valuable service by refusing to proclaim the *Jihad* from the Holy Cities at the Turks' behest, and had thus extinguished the prospect of rallying the Moslem peoples for a Holy War against the British. Then, in June 1916, the Sherif raised a revolt in the Hejaz against Turkish rule, and thereby created a distraction to the Turks which the British had hitherto failed to provide with their own forces. Its first effect was on the British, who now decided to undertake an advance to El Arish, which would give them command of the Sinai Desert and restore their possession of the frontier. But although another Turkish incursion was punished at Romani in July, Sir Archibald Murray's advance was slow to develop, being governed by the time taken in laying a railway and pipeline (for water) across the desert. It was not until Christmastide that the British occupied El Arish, and pounced on the outlying Turkish posts at Magdhaba and Rafah.

This new 'Exodus inspired' the British Government to carry out an invasion of Palestine, at as cheap a cost in troops as possible. The towns of Gaza, on the coast, and Beersheba, twenty-five miles inland, guarded the approach to Palestine. Murray attacked Gaza on March 26th, 1917, but the attempt fell short when on the brink of success. By nightfall Gaza was practically surrounded, but the victorious position was given up bit by bit, not under enemy pressure, but on the orders of the executive British commanders, through faulty information, misunderstandings, and over-anxiety. Nor did the harm end there, for Murray reported the action to the Government in terms of a victory, and without hint of the subsequent withdrawal, so that he was encouraged to attempt, without adequate reconnaissance or fire support, a further attack on April 17th-19th, which proved a costlier failure against defences now strengthened.

Britain's new Arab allies, however, provided a valuable distraction which counteracted these Turkish successes, with no drain on the British forces beyond a handful of technical advisers. After its opening success the revolt had been in danger of collapse; but the situation was saved and the scales changed by Feisal's sudden flank move up the Red Sea coast to Wejh, whence the Arabs harassed the Hejaz railway. This move was prompted by a young archeologist turned temporary soldier, Captain T. E. Lawrence. Steeped in the history and theory of warfare, he had the elasticity of mind to adapt his knowledge to irregular conditions and the magnetic personality to combine the Arabs' 'loose shower of sparks into a firm flame' which consumed the Turkish resources. In May 1917, he set off with a party of Arabs on a lone-hand expedition which, after sowing fresh seeds of revolt in Syria, culminated in a descent upon Aqaba. The capture of this sea base on the northern arm of the Red Sea removed all danger to the British communications in Sinai and opened the way for the Arabs to become a lever on the flank of the Turkish forces opposing the British. Already, more Turks were occupied in guarding the long line of the Hejaz railway and the territory south of it than were facing the British in Palestine.

The War at Sea, 1915-1916. Germany's first submarine campaign—associated by Allied opinion with the name of Admiral von Tirpitz, the exponent of ruthlessness—had been a signal failure, both in its meagre results and the disproportionate ethical damage it did to Germany's cause. A series of notes, exchanged between the American and German Governments, culminated in April, 1916, in a virtual ultimatum from President Wilson, and Germany abandoned her unrestricted campaign. The deprivation of this weapon spurred the German navy to its first, and last, attempt to carry out the initial plan on which it had begun the war. Late on May 30th, 1916, the British Grand Fleet left its bases on one of its periodical sweeps through the North Sea, but with reason to expect a possible encounter. On May 31st, early in the morning, the German High Sea Fleet also put to sea, in the hope of destroying some isolated portion of the British Fleet.

For such an encounter the British Admiral, Jellicoe, had formulated an outline plan in the early months of the war. Its basis was the cardinal necessity of maintaining the unimpaired supremacy of the Grand Fleet, which he viewed as an instrument, not merely of battle, but of grand strategy, the pivot of the Allies' action in all spheres, economic, moral and military. Hence, while desirous of bringing the German fleet to battle under his own conditions, he was determined not to be lured into mine and submarine-infested waters.

Early in the afternoon of May 31st, Beatty, with his battle cruisers and a squadron of battleships, after a sweep to the south was turning north to rejoin Jellicoe, when he sighted the German battle cruisers, five in number. In the initial engagement two of Beatty's six battle cruisers were hit in vital parts and sunk; when thus weakened he came upon the main German fleet under Admiral Scheer. He turned north to lure them into reach of Jellicoe, fifty miles distant, who raced to support him. Mist and failing light put an end to an indecisive action, which, however, left the British fleet between the German and its bases. During the night Scheer broke through the destroyer guard, and although sighted was not reported. Thus he slipped safely through a net which Jellicoe dared not draw too close in view of his guiding principle, and of the danger of torpedo attack.

If the battle of Jutland could be counted a tactical advantage to the Germans, it had no effect on their strategic position. The grip of Britain's blockade was unrelaxed. Once more Germany fell back on submarine warfare, and the first development was an extension of range. In July one of her large submarine cruisers appeared off the American coast and sank several neutral ships.

In the narrow seas the Mediterranean was the scene of active operations, but the immediate pressure on Britain was

relaxed during the summer. For Scheer, in a fit of pique at
the German Government's surrender to President Wilson's
threat, refused to let his submarines operate under the code
of visit and search. Hence the burden of the restricted campaign fell on the Flanders flotillas, and, fortunately for
Britain, the German naval chiefs had been obtusely slow to
realize and exploit the advantages of the Belgian coast as a
base. The six months lost originally through neglect to
organize a base were never fully redeemed, and the scale of
the forces here was never in proportion to the possibilities of
menacing Britain from this close-range post. On October
6th, Scheer was overruled by an order to reinforce the effort
with his flotillas. This veiled renewal of the general submarine campaign was inspired mainly by Admiral von
Holtzendorf, the Chief of the Naval Staff, and Captain von
Bartenbach, the Chief of the Flanders flotillas. The indirect
result was to deprive Scheer automatically of the submarines
which he required to safeguard his own sorties and lay traps
for the British fleet.

Thus the paralysis of the German fleet henceforth was the
result of the Germans' own alternative plan, and not of
Jutland. And it did not even leave the British Grand Fleet in
possession of the North Sea. For the moral effect of a submarine ambush which marked the German sortie of August
19th was so great, even though it miscarried, that henceforth
the Grand Fleet was almost as confined as an old-time debtor
in the Fleet Prison, and was definitely debarred from the
southern half of the North Sea. Jellicoe and the Admiralty
were agreed upon the necessity for this self-imprisonment.
The 'command of the sea' became almost a burlesque when
the danger of a German invasion of Denmark loomed up that
autumn and, after examination by the Admiralty and War
Office, the verdict was that—'for naval reasons it would be
almost impossible to support the Danes at all.' The shadow
of the submarine was longer than the shadow of Nelson's
column. With illuminating candour the British official naval
history says—'The Grand Fleet could only put to sea with

an escort of nearly one hundred destroyers, no capital ship could leave its base without an escort of small craft, and the German U-boats had hampered our squadrons to an extent which the most expert and farsighted naval officer had never foreseen.' Yet, with curious inconsistency, the voices of naval officers have been heard ever since the war proclaiming the sovereignty of the battleship, the ineffectiveness of the submarine.

The Grand Fleet in the autumn of 1916 was all the more heavily fettered because its warders were reduced, owing to the call for light craft to combat the new 'veiled' submarine campaign against commerce. Despite all counter-measures this was so successful that the monthly loss of shipping rose steadily from 109,000 tons during June, to 368,000 tons in January, 1917—approximately half being British. During the 'veiled' campaign the Mediterranean was both an ill-favoured and, by the Germans, too well-favoured area, for besides simplifying the submarine's task of finding targets it simplified the problem of evading the undertakings given to America—in the Mediterranean there was little risk of injuring American ships or interests by mischance. One U-boat alone in five weeks' cruise sank 65,000 tons of shipping.

Counter-measures proved utterly unable to stem the rising tide of sinking ships, even when more destroyers and other small craft became available. During one week of September, 1916, thirty ships were sunk by two, or at the most, three submarines in an area patrolled by ninety-seven destroyers and sixty-eight auxiliary craft. Among the remedies tried were those of secret routes, of hoisting false colours, and of decoy ships. This last ruse was carried out by what were known as Q-ships, equipped with torpedo-tubes, depth charges, and guns concealed behind collapsible bulwarks, while disguised as merchant ships. The disguise was enhanced by the acting of the crews who coolly simulated panic under conditions where most men would not have needed to do so, and thereby lured the molesting submarine to the surface within close range. Although these Q-ships provided the most romantic phase of the naval war, and sank eleven U-boats, their effect was almost exhausted by the end of 1916, save that it made the enemy more wary—and naturally less inclined to merciful discrimination between armed and apparently unarmed ships. This Q-ship risk to the U-boat was accentuated by the British arming of ordinary merchant-ships, which placed the slow, fragile and half-blind U-boat in a perilous dilemma. The more merciful the U-boat the greater danger it ran; the less heed it paid to the nature of its target and the rescue of those on board the more its safety and success were assured. Hence the outcry in Germany for a policy of sinking at sight was naturally strengthened.

Moreover, if Britain was feeling the strain of economic pressure, so also was Germany, and her leaders feared that the race between decisive success on land and economic collapse would end against her. The naval authorities declared that a renewal of the 'unlimited' submarine campaign, which with her increased numbers could now be far more intense, would bring the Entente to their knees. Accepting this opinion, Ludendorff agreed to a step which he had hitherto opposed; the combined weight of naval and military opinion overbore the protests of the Imperial Chancellor. A proposal of peace discussions, and its foreseen rejection by the Entente powers, was made the moral justification for openly abandoning the restrictions of visit and search, and for withdrawing the promise given to President Wilson. On February 1st, 1917, the 'unrestricted' policy—of sinking all ships, passenger or cargo, without warning—was proclaimed—with the full realization that it involved the weight of America being thrown into the scales against Germany. Doubts of its wisdom in Germany were stifled by the plea of necessity, the promise of certain victory, and the argument of inevitability —that America was bound to come to the help of the Allies in order to ensure their ability to pay their debts to her. But the Germans reckoned on victory before America's weight could count in the scales.

CHAPTER VI

SCENE I

THE MINCING MACHINE—VERDUN

IT is a truism that the war of 1914-1918 revolutionized all ideas of time, in a military sense, and especially in the duration of its battles. For several thousand years of warfare a battle, however great the scale, had been a matter of hours. This remained the general case down to the beginning of this century, though a few battles from the Napoleonic wars onwards increased the span to days—for example, Leipzig, Gettysburg. The real change was inaugurated with the Russo-Japanese campaign, when battles at last had to be reckoned in weeks. With the World War the standard became months—because the battles had usually become sieges, without being recognized or scientifically treated as such. The change, it is to be hoped, is a transitory one, for quantity does not imply quality, and duration does imply immobility and indecisiveness—which are perforce the negation of generalship. So that whether from the standpoint of military science or from that of the drain of human life, long battles are bad battles.

The prolongation, too, has complicated the task of the military historian, for unless he desires to fill massive tomes with profuse detail, it is difficult to pick out salient features where there are either none, or else so many that they tend to merge into a formless mass. And of all the so-called 'battles' of the war, Verdun holds the duration record, extending from February 21st to December 15th, 1916. Even if the suspension of the German offensive be taken as the last date, and the French counter-offensive considered as distinct, the duration is seven months.

This difficulty of singling out any one date is unfortunate, for no battle of the whole war was more heroic or more

285

VERDUN, 1916

WŒUVRE

Spincourt
3 miles

N

Herbebois

Ft. Douaumont

Ft. de Vaux

Bois de
Haumont

Côte du
Poivre

Belleville
Ridge

R. Meuse

Verdun

R. Meuse

le Mort Homme

Bar le Duc
25 miles

Original Line on 21st. Feb.
Line on evening of 21st. Feb.
Line on evening of 25th. Feb.
Line on evening of 7th. March
Line on evening of 1st. July

0   1   2   3   4
Miles

© Cassell & Co. Ltd. 1970

dramatic in its course, or made so vivid an appeal to the sympathies of the watching nations. It was France's supreme sacrifice and her supreme triumph, and to the splendour of her achievement all the world paid homage.

From February 25th onwards, there was a series of crises until June 23rd, and many French authorities select the former date as the chief. Yet who should know better than the Germans the moment when the tide really turned against them? So distinguished a critic as General von Zwehl considered that the real turning point was on March 9th, when the Germans failed to capture the Côte de Poivre. It was on March 4th that the Crown Prince called on his army group for a supreme effort to take Verdun, 'the heart of France'. On March 6th, after a two days' bombardment, the new blow fell, and by the 9th was definitely frustrated.

The determination of such a datum point is affected also by the question as to the object of the German Supreme Command in launching the attack on Verdun. General von Falkenhayn, the Chief of the Great General Staff and the responsible officer, has stated categorically that it was to bleed France white by choosing a point of attack for which, sooner than let go, the French Command would have to fight to the last man. He has also quoted from a paper prepared at Christmas, 1915, to show that he argued that a break-through in mass was not necessary for this purpose.

Yet, despite his post-war statements, there is still a just doubt as to the initial object. A prominent German critic, Colonel Foerster, pointed out how difficult it was to reconcile Falkenhayn's statement with the manner in which the attack was carried out, and declared that the initial operation was obviously an accelerated attack for the purpose of breaking through. He based himself on extracts from Falkenhayn's own order of January 27th, 1916, and the latter's vehement marginal criticisms on the explanation of failure rendered by the Crown Prince's Headquarters on March 31st. These show Falkenhayn calling for an unchecked and continuous advance.

Others, including Pétain, believe the real idea underlying the plan was that of a revival of the 'Sedan' double envelopment which had been attempted in September 1914. In 1916 such a plan had more favourable chances, for the salient was more acute than at the time of the Marne battle, owing to the St. Mihiel wedge that had been driven into its eastern flank. And the fact that the salient lay astride a river, the Meuse, would hamper the defenders in holding back the German pincers. Moreover, this hypothesis provides a logical explanation for what outwardly seems the unaccountable German mistake in launching their first attack only on the east bank of the river. But if a Sedan was the Germans' object, they might expect that their attack on the east bank would draw the French reserves thither so that the later attack on the west bank, when released, would be able to sweep across the rear of the French, using the river as their prison wall. Thereby, not only would part of the French army be cut off, but the rest be cut in two, while the vast breach would ensure the collapse of the whole trench front in France.

Fresh light on this enigmatic battle has, however, come from the German archives and from important witnesses; the evidence collated in a book by Hermann Wendt is particularly illuminating. From this new material it would appear that the explanation of Falkenhayn's purpose lies in his opportunism; and the explanation of the curious course of the German operations, in one more of the internal conflicts that wrecked so many plans.

Falkenhayn, whose course was apparently none too clear in his own mind, seems to have rested on the hope that something might happen—that 'something' might be a moral collapse behind the French front, produced by the combination of natural depression and subsidized propaganda. But if he was wiser than other strategists in realizing the importance of political effects, he does not seem to have had clear ideas as to how to produce them. And, unfortunately for him, his executive subordinates had a purely military outlook. The scheme drawn up by the Crown Prince's Chief of Staff,

Schmidt von Knobelsdorf, diverged widely from Falkenhayn's line of thought. It proposed an attempt to pinch off
Verdun, by a vigorous attack on both flanks, 'so as to avoid
a long-drawn-out battle of material, with its incalculable
expenditure of force'.

This big gamble did not suit Falkenhayn's book, so he reduced the plan to an attack on the east bank only, apparently
hoping to control the executive commander's impetuosity by
keeping a tight hand on the reserves. In this purpose, as in
his greater one, he was to fail. It is not easy to determine
whether that failure was due more to his own misjudgment
in adjusting the means to the end, or to his inability to adjust
his subordinate's views to his own. Princely subordinates
were difficult to control, and Falkenhayn's position was too
unstable for him safely to exert strong pressure. Also, whatever his failings, he at least has the credit of affirming a new
principle in tactics.

The German offensive was to be based on fire power rather
than on man power, and its main agent was to be an intense
artillery bombardment, making up for its relatively short
duration by the number of batteries and their rapidity of fire,
and so seeking to regain the supreme advantage of surprise
which was inevitably lost by an artillery preparation of several
days, or even a week—as the Allied method had been at Loos,
in Champagne, and was still to be on the Somme. To increase
their chance of surprise the Germans constructed none of the
customary 'jumping off' trenches close to the enemy lines,
confident that their tremendous artillery bombardment
would enable their infantry to cross the wide no-man's-land,
in places half a mile across, without meeting effective resistance. With their rear preparations they were less successful.
But although the Intelligence branch at French General
Headquarters was thus able to deduce the German intentions,
the Operations branch disregarded the warning. On February 1st a driblet of two Territorial divisions was sent, but
only at the last moment were adequate reinforcements —two
army corps—ordered there. Even when the first of these

arrived there were only three divisions on the right bank of the Meuse, two on the left, and three south of the fortress facing east—with no reserves at hand. It is not difficult to guess what would have happened if the German attack had come on the 13th, as intended, before this first corps arrived. Bad weather saved the defenders in a double sense, for it also hampered the moving forward of the Germans' heavy guns.

There is, however, another important aspect of this preliminary phase which is comparatively little known. A hasty generalization from the easy fall of the Belgian and Russian fortresses may have caused much of the subsequent critical position at Verdun. Originally the French fortresses were not under the control of the field army, but Joffre used the examples of Liége and Namur as an excuse to persuade the French Government to 'declass' Verdun as a fortress, and, having got control in August, 1915, from then on he drained it of its men and armament. This removal of guns continued even until January 30th, 1916, and the casemates were simply used as shelters for troops. Instead of an all-round defence a single trench position was taken up beyond the forts, and in rear only one subsidiary trench line was usable.

For this continuous front, the commander, General Herr, had not enough men or material—to garrison it or keep it in an efficient state of defence. Its wire was incomplete, and it had scarcely any shell-proof cover. Little wonder that when the blow fell the trench position was blotted out. In contrast was the extraordinary imperviousness of the forts. Forts Douaumont and Vaux fell into German hands, and when they were recaptured in October the French found that months of tremendous bombardment had made scarcely an impression. The underground cover remained intact, not one field-gun turret was destroyed, and hardly any of the casemates rendered unoccupiable. It was a grim jest of fate that the French should have thrown away their shield for a target, through a hasty assumption that fortresses were valueless.

The original Governor, General Coutanceau, had not

shared this view, but when, before a Parliamentary delegation, he dared to express his opinion, in contradiction to the Army Group commander, General Dubail, he was not only rebuked but dismissed. For some time, rumours had percolated through to Paris about the inadequate state of the Verdun defences, and in December Galliéni, as Minister of War, had written to Joffre asking for information and an assurance that they should be developed. Joffre's reply might well be framed and hung up in all the bureaux of officialdom the world over—to serve as the mummy at the feast. Rebutting the suggestions, he added—'But since these apprehensions are founded on reports which allege defects in the state of the defences, I request you to . . . specify their authors. I cannot be a party to soldiers under my command bringing before the Government, by channels other than the hierarchic channel, complaints or protests concerning the execution of my orders. . . . It is calculated to disturb profoundly the spirit of discipline in the Army.' The enemy was soon to dispel his doctrine of infallibility, as the mutinies of 1917 were to show that the incapacity of generals and their waste of human life are the most potent factors in disturbing the spirit of discipline. But retribution is slow. Colonel Driant, Deputy for Nancy and a well-known military writer, who had given the warning, was one of the first victims of its neglect, while Joffre for a time gained fresh popular laurels from the heroic sacrifice of Driant and his fellows.

At a quarter past seven on the morning of February 21st, a cold, dry day, the German bombardment began on both banks of the Meuse and on a front of fifteen miles. Steadily the trenches and wire were flattened out or upheaved in a chaos of tumbled earth. 'The craters made by the huge shells gave to all the countryside an appearance like the surface of the moon.' Familiar as it was to be later, in February, 1916, so violent a bombardment was new, and therefore the more appalling. So it went on—until at 4 p.m. the fury of the shell-storm reached its height. Another three quarters of an hour, and a thin skirmish line of German infantry began to advance almost unnoticed, followed by bombing parties and flame-throwers, to feel the French position before the rest of the infantry was launched. This method economized life, and it also disclosed the unequal effect of the German bombardment, which in parts suffered from the deadly counter-battery fire of the French artillery. Moreover, the initial German attack was made by only six divisions and only along a four and a half mile front between Bois de Haumont and Herbebois on the east bank. On so narrow a front the few scattered packets of surviving Frenchmen caused more delay than should have been the case on a reasonable frontage, and the early onset of darkness halted the attack after the foremost trenches had been occupied. But next day the attack developed more widely, and from then until the 24th the defenders' line was progressively crumbled away.

The French commanders on the spot asked permission to evacuate the Woevre plain and draw back the line on to the Meuse heights on the right bank. Even this they felt must be only a preliminary to the evacuation of the whole right, or eastern, bank of the Meuse. But behind the front the full gravity of the situation was hardly realized. 'Operations' still asserted that the Verdun offensive was a feint to cover the real blow, in Champagne. Even when the news of the crumbling front came through, Joffre was not moved, much less disturbed. At last, on the evening of the 24th, General de Castelnau—who, since his appointment as Chief of the French General Staff, had been adroitly side-tracked by Joffre's ever-zealous, and jealous, *entourage*—took the initiative and, going direct to Joffre, gained his permission to send Pétain's Army to take over the defence of Verdun. Still more alarming reports came in later, and at 11 p.m. de Castelnau, with unique daring, insisted that the orderly officer should rap on Joffre's locked door and wake him up. Before the great man returned to resume his unvarying ration of sleep, he had given de Castlenau authority to go to Verdun with 'full powers'.

Leaving Chantilly during the night, de Castelnau motored post haste to the headquarters of the Army Group commander, de Langle de Cary. Joffre meanwhile had telegraphed that the front north of Verdun must be held at all costs: 'Every commander who . . . gives an order for retreat will be tried by court martial.' He left it to de Langle de Cary to decide whether to swing back his right on to the Meuse heights, and the latter acted on this permission.

De Castelnau's first day at Verdun was not auspicious; for on the 25th occurred the strange incident of Fort Douaumont, and with it the first crisis of the long battle. Like most of the other forts it had no garrison, except for a crew of twenty-three gunners who manned one turret. When, however, the German tide approached the fort, General Chrétien, commanding the right sector, dictated an order that the line of the forts was to be made the principal line of resistance. This was shortly before midnight on the 24th. Unfortunately his staff waited for the preparation of some sketches to attach to the order, and so delayed its issue until 9.45 a.m. on the 25th. Meantime a patrol of Brandenburgers, finding the drawbridge down and no sign of any defenders—the gunners had fallen asleep dead-beat—walked in and took possession without firing a shot. A triumphal German *communiqué* announced the capture of Douaumont 'by assault' in the presence of the Kaiser. This piece of official bombast, however, was to be outclassed and out-farced when, owing to a misunderstood telephone message, the *communiqué* of March 9th announced the capture of Fort Vaux—three months too early. But the cream of the jest was that both the divisional commander who made the report and the officer who had *not* taken the fort, received from the Kaiser the highest Prussian order, *Pour le Mérite*! A bad telephone is not without compensations.

On February 25th Pétain took over command at Verdun, and the nucleus of a reserve army was assembling in rear. His first problem was not so much defence as supply. The German heavy guns had closed all avenues except one light railway and the Bar-le-Duc to Verdun road—which later became immortal as ' the Sacred Way'. To push up troops was no use unless they could be fed and supplied with ammunition. The road was already cracking under the strain of the incessant transport, and so gangs of territorial troops were brought up to keep it in repair and to double it by parallel tracks. Henceforward the flow of traffic rose to as many as six thousand lorries in the twenty-four hours. Up in front Pétain was organizing the front into sectors, each with its own heavy artillery, and throwing in repeated counter-attacks. If these gained little ground, they disconcerted and checked the attacking Germans. Another assisting factor was that the further they advanced on the east bank the more did they expose themselves to flanking fire from the French artillery across the river. The advance lost its momentum, slowed down, and already on the German side 'a grievous pessimism had set in', so Zwehl tells us.

Falkenhayn was now led to widen the front of attack, although he doled out only four divisions. On March 6th, after two days' bombardment, the Crown Prince attacked on the west bank of the Meuse, and on the 8th the troops on the east bank joined in this supreme effort. The gains did not repay the losses, and against Mort Homme on the west and the Poivre height on the east the attack beat in vain. Any hope of a break-through faded, for the defence was now consolidated and the numbers had been balanced. Whatever we think of his foresight, there can be no question that Joffre's imperturbable temperament was a great asset in calming the anxiety of those days, and in Pétain he made the right choice for the emergency. It is proverbial that fortune favours the brave, and two great pieces of luck befell the French—the fortunate destruction of all the German 17-in. howitzers by the French long-range guns, and the blowing up of the great German artillery park near Spincourt, which held 450,000 heavy shell, unwisely kept fused. One authority, indeed, General Palat, gives it as his opinion that these two factors saved Verdun.

From March 9th onwards, there can be no question that the German policy was primarily attrition, and that so far as Verdun was aimed at it was as a moral objective. Publicity had given it a symbolical value definitely superior to its military value. It must be confessed that the strategy nearly succeeded—but only, after a long interval, through the introduction of a new agent. In the meantime the Germans paid an exorbitant price for little gain. Nevertheless, they put a heavy tax on the French. Pétain did his best to mitigate the strain by a rapid rotation of reliefs, which kept each division under fire for the shortest possible time. But, as a result, a great part of the French Army was drawn through the 'mincing machine', and the drain on the French reserves almost bankrupted their share in the forthcoming Somme offensive.

On the German side, the disappointing results produced an earlier reaction. At the end of March Falkenhayn enquired whether there was 'any chance of progress within a reasonable time'; and he contemplated an alternative attack at Ypres. But the Crown Prince confidently declared that the greater part of the French reserves had been used up, and that he was 'unreservedly of the opinion that the fate of the French Army would be decided at Verdun'. Moreover, the fatally old-fashioned idea of the executive command was betrayed in the remark that 'the destruction of the French reserves . . . should be completed by the employment of men, as well as of apparatus and munitions'. Falkenhayn gave way to this plea.

So the Crown Prince, egged on by Schmidt von Knobelsdorf, continued to pour out his men's blood, while Falkenhayn spent the time in study of possible alternatives. But at the end of April the barren result of constant nibbling attacks led to a decision to revert to wider ones.

These proved equally futile, so that even Schmidt von Knobelsdorf was led to admit the hopelessness of further attack. Yet when he visited Falkenhayn in this mood of repentance, he found the latter had also changed his mind—

to the opposite view. So Schmidt von Knobelsdorf was re-converted, and the offensive continued. But the wastage of life was now balanced by Joffre's misguided instructions that Fort Douaumont must be recovered; he also removed Pétain's restraining hand by promoting him to command of the Army Group and placing Nivelle in direct charge at Verdun. By launching repeated attacks, Nivelle now played into Falkenhayn's hands, and lost on the rebound.

On June 7th, after a heroic resistance, Fort Vaux really fell—by another German telephone mistake the wrong officer again received the credit—and with it a large stretch of ground was submerged by the German tide, that now seemed to the anxious watchers to resemble the forces of nature rather than of men. On June 11th Pétain was forced to ask Joffre to hasten the relief offensive on the Somme. Then on June 20th, the Germans introduced a new kind of diphosgene gas shell with startling effect. It paralysed the French artillery support, and on the 23rd came a deep advance that brought the Germans almost to the Belleville height, the last outwork of Verdun. Mangin's incessant counter attacks could do no more than put a brake on the advance, and Pétain made all ready for the evacuation of the east bank, though to his troops he showed no signs of anxiety and ever repeated the now immortal phrase, 'On les aura!' Four divisions were hurriedly despatched to him by Joffre, thus further weakening the Somme reserve.

But the Germans had used their new lever too late. Strategically, the defenders were now made secure, indirectly, as Falkenhayn stopped the flow of ammunition to Verdun on the 24th—when the British bombardment began on the Somme, preparatory to the long-arranged attack which was delivered on July 1st. From that day on the Germans at Verdun received no fresh divisions, and their advance died out from pure inanition. The way was thus paved for the brilliant French counter-offensives of the autumn, which retook by bites what had been lost by nibbles. It is no disparagement of the sterling defence to recognize, as we must, that the Somme saved Verdun, and, second, that the Germans after throwing away their best chance by too narrow an attack frontage, came desperately close to their goal four months later.

CHAPTER VI

SCENE 2

THE BRUSILOV OFFENSIVE

ON June 5th, 1916, began an offensive on the Eastern Front which was to prove the last really effective military effort of Russia. Popularly known as Brusilov's offensive, it had such an astonishing initial success as to revive enthusiastic dreams of the irresistible Russian 'steamroller', that was perhaps the greatest and most dangerous myth of the war. Instead, its ultimate achievement was to sound Russia's death knell. Paradoxical in its consequences, it was still more so in its course—an epitome of the delusive objectives, of the blunders leading to success, and the successes leading to downfall, which marked perhaps the most erratic war in history. In 1915 the Entente had pinned their hopes on Russia, only for the year's campaign to close with the Russian armies, battered and exhausted, barely escaping complete disaster by a seemingly endless retreat. When Falkenhayn turned in 1916 to inaugurate the Verdun attack he left Russia lamed but not crippled, and her suprisingly rapid, if perhaps superficial recovery, enabled her to dislocate the German plans for 1916. As early as March she attacked at Lake Narocz, on the Baltic flank, in a gallant sacrificial attempt to relieve the pressure on France. Her command then prepared, for July, a main offensive, also in the north. But before this was ready the needs of her Allies once more led her into a premature move. While the strain at Verdun was growing ever more serious, the Austrians took the opportunity to launch an attack in the Trentino, against the Italians, who appealed to their Russian Ally to prevent the Austrians releasing further forces from the Eastern front to reinforce the Trentino menace.

Meantime the Tsar had held a council of war of his

Army Group commanders on April 14th. It was here arranged that the main Russian offensive should be made by Evert's centre group of armies, while Kuropatkin's northern group wheeled inwards to assist it; and it was proposed that Brusilov's southern group should stay strictly on the defensive as his front was unsuited to the offensive. But Brusilov regarded this as a reason for taking the offensive—because helpful to surprise—and argued that past lack of success was due to the way the Russian armies had allowed the enemy to utilize his central position by not attacking simultaneously. As a result of the discussion Brusilov was given permission to act as he wished, and, with such resources as he had, to stage an offensive that would draw the enemy's attention away from the main blow planned in the north, near Molodeczno. Realizing that his best chance of success lay in surprise, he began preparations at over twenty places, so that even deserters could not give away the real point of attack. And, instead of concentrating his reserves, he divided them.

The appeal of Russia's ally hastened his action. On May 24th Alexeiev telegraphed to ask how soon he could attack. Brusilov replied that he would be ready to do so on June 1st, provided that Evert also attacked. Evert, however, was not ready; it was finally agreed that Brusilov should strike on the 4th, and Evert ten days later. On the night of the 3rd Alexeiev rang up Brusilov and expressed doubts of the wisdom of a plan so unconventional, suggesting that he should concentrate his troops for an attack on a narrow front, instead of distributing them on a wide front. Brusilov demurred and Alexeiev eventually gave way, saying, 'God be with you. Do as you like.'

The troops were moved up during the night for an apparent gamble, in which every factor save the possibility of surprise weighed against success. Brusilov's strength was no more than equal to that of the opposing force—thirty-eight against thirty-seven divisions—and it was widely distributed. But the absence of any concentration gave the Austrians no warning of the impending move, and when, on June 4th, the Russian

Eighth Army, under Kaledin, advanced near Luck for what was little more than a reconnaissance in force, they took the Austrians by surprise. The front broke like a crust of pastry at the first touch, and almost unresisted the Russians pushed between the Austrian Fourth and Second Armies. By the following day 40,000 prisoners had been taken, and the number swelled rapidly as Brusilov widened his offensive. Although the Russian Eleventh Army (Sakharov) failed near Tarnopol, the other two armies further south gained as rapid success as that at Luck. The Seventh Army (Shcherbachev) drove the Austrians back across the Strypa, and the Ninth Army (Lechitski), breaking through in the Bukovina, captured Czernowitz—the southernmost position of the Austrian front. By the 20th, Brusilov had captured 200,000 men.

Never has a mere demonstration had so amazing a success since the walls of Jericho fell at Joshua's trumpet blasts. With both flanks collapsed, the Austro-German armies in the south were in danger of a greater Tannenberg, if only the Russians could exploit their chance. But all the reserves were massed in the north for the intended main offensive, and this was not developed. First, Evert said that on account of bad weather he could not begin until the 18th, and, even so, did not expect to be successful. The Tsar and Alexeiev lacked the resolution either to coerce or to replace Evert, and instead authorized him to prepare an attack at a different place—which meant further delay. But neither Evert nor Kuropatkin showed any inclination to take the offensive; and, as Alexeiev could not move them, he tried instead to move their reserves. Poor lateral communications, however, prevented these reaching Brusilov before the Germans could hurry reinforcements to stem the tide. The German Command showed its usual cleverness, using the first reinforcements for a counterstroke by Linsingen against the northern edge of the Luck break-through, and this at least checked the Russian progress at the most critical point. To the south, in the Bukovina, the Russian advance continued until it came to a natural halt against the barrier of the Carpathian Mountains.

Late in July the Russian attack was renewed, first in the centre towards Brody and Lemberg by Sakharov, then further north towards the Stokhod river and Kovel, by the Russian Guard Army, long prepared for a supreme effort. But the opportunity had passed, and although the attacks still dragged on throughout August, the gains in no way compensated for their heavy cost, and an effort which opened in a blaze of sunshine faded out in autumn gloom.

Its indirect were, however, greater than its direct effects, although not unmixed in benefit. It had compelled Falkenhayn to withdraw seven divisions from the West, and so abandon his plan for a riposte against the British Somme offensive, as well as the hope of nourishing his attrition process at Verdun. It led Rumania to take her fateful decision to enter the war on the Entente side—to her undoing. And it wrought the downfall of Falkenhayn, who had 'spoiled the ship for a ha'porth of tar'.

But these indirect effects were purchased at a heavy price. Brusilov had captured the Bukovina and much of Eastern Galicia; he had captured 350,000 prisoners—but, through prolonging the offensive when opportunity had passed, over 1,000,000 men had been lost. This loss undermined morally, even more than materially, the fighting power of Russia. The imminent sequel was to be revolution and collapse. For the last time Russia had sacrificed herself for her allies, and it is not just that subsequent events should obscure the debt.

SOMME, 1916

ARRAS
18 Miles

CAMBRAI
18 Miles

Bapaume

Le Transloy

Morval

Sailly

Rancourt

Combles

LEUZE WOOD

Ginchy

DELVILLE WOOD

Longueval

Guillemont

Lesboeufs

Flers

Le Sars

HIGH WOOD

BERNAFAY WOOD

TRONES WOOD

Le Petit

Bazentin

CATERPILLAR WOOD

Courcelette

Le Sars

Maricourt

Martinpuich

Montauban

MAMETZ WOOD

R. Somme

Mametz

Pozières

Ovillers

Contalmaison

Fricourt

Grandcourt

La Boiselle

Miraumont

Thiepval

Beaucourt sur Ancre

Beaumont Hamel

R. Ancre

Albert

Serre

Gommecourt

Hébuterne

Sailly-au-Bois

British Front Line
on 1st. July

German Lines 1st. } 1st. July
               2nd.

Line on evening
of 1st. July

Line on evening
of 14 th. July

Line on evening
of 18 th. Sept.

Line at end of
the Battles

Watershed

0   1   2   3
Miles

© Cassell & Co. Ltd. 1970

Albert

R. Ancre

R. Somme

SIXTH ARMY

TENTH ARMY

Sailly

Combles

Rancourt

Peronne

Chaulnes

July 1st. Evening Line

Sept. 16th.

Sept. 26th.

Original Line

0   5
MILES

N

CHAPTER VI

SCENE 3

THE SOMME OFFENSIVE

THE 'battle'—or, to be strategically accurate, the series of partial actions—in Picardy which opened on July 1st, constituted the offensive campaign of the Franco-British armies in 1916. Into it was thrown the entire British effort of the year on the Western Front, and such part of the French effort as was available after the exhausting strain of the long defensive 'battle' of Verdun. And it proved both the glory and the graveyard of 'Kitchener's Army'—those citizen volunteers who, instantly answering the call in 1914, had formed the first national army of Britain.

The Somme offensive had its genesis at the Chantilly Conference of the Allied commanders on December 5th, 1915. Joffre, in his appreciation of the situation, claimed that the autumn offensives in Champagne and Artois (including Loos) had brought 'brilliant tactical results', and ascribed the failure to develop these into a strategical success, partly to bad weather and partly to a temporary shortage of ammunition. The essential for the next effort was that 'the Higher Command must have no anxiety as regards ammunition', and for this reason it could not be undertaken in less than three months. By early February he had realized that the date must be later still, if, as was essential, the Russians were to attack simultaneously and the British were to take an adequate share with their newly raised armies. At a meeting with Haig he emphasized the view that a broad frontage of attack was the method of success, and to this end desired a combined offensive by the French and British 'bras dessus bras dessous', with the attacking line of one Ally prolonging that of the other Ally. Joffre envisaged the French attacking with

forty divisions on a twenty-five miles' front from Lassigny to
the Somme, and the British attacking thence to Hébuterne,
fourteen miles, with twenty-five divisions, or as near that
number as possible.

The British Official History remarks that Joffre's decision
to make the offensive in a sector which 'might be considered
the strongest' for defence, on the Western Front, 'seems to
have been arrived at solely because the British would be
bound to take part in it. The reasons advanced by General
Joffre will hardly bear examination'. Even Foch, if it was
not his habit to weigh tactical difficulties, disliked the choice
of sector as being a strategic dead-end. Haig would have
preferred to make his attack in Flanders, on the lines of the
offensive which he carried out in 1917, assisted by a landing
on the Belgian coast.

Joffre also pressed the British to make a preparatory attack
north of the Somme in April, and another in May—to draw
in the enemy's reserves, so easing the way for the Franco-
British main blow. Haig preferred to trust in one great stroke,
with all the forces available and when they were fully prepared. Although Haig's attitude was justified by the incompleteness of his resources and by the barrenness of such preparatory attacks the previous autumn, the critic is compelled
to recognize that Joffre had the experience of history on his
side, and that the experience of the war was to show that
decisive offensives were vain until the enemy's reserves had
been attracted elsewhere. But Haig was unquestionably right
in maintaining that any such preparatory attacks, to fulfil
their object, should only precede the general offensive by ten
days or a fortnight.

He suggested that the British might deliver one such attack
if the French made others. This idea did not appeal to Joffre
who, according to Poincaré, had now 'in mind a war of
attrition which must be chiefly carried out by our Allies,
England, Russia, and even Italy'. So discussions continued.
It is amusing to note that the British staff took refuge in the
explanation—'The British Army is ready to do its full share,

but we cannot cope with the politicians, who, after the Germans, are our worst enemies.'

Eventually, at a conference on February 14th, an agreement was reached by which Haig accepted Joffre's plan for the Somme offensive—dated for July 1st—while Joffre gave up his demand for preparatory offensives.

The result of the postponement of the Allied offensive, whether inevitable or not, was to yield the initiative to the Germans, and their attack at Verdun, from February 21st onwards, impaired the whole of the Allied plan and campaign in 1916. Yet such a possibility had not even been mentioned at the conference on the 14th.

On February 22nd Joffre asked the British to aid him by relieving part of his troops in the north. Haig accordingly hastened the relief of the French Tenth Army, round Arras, which was sandwiched between his own First and Third Armies. Allenby's Third Army sideslipped northwards, and the newly formed Fourth Army, under Rawlinson, took over its front between Maricourt and Hébuterne. The British now held a continuous eighty-mile front from Ypres almost to the Somme.

As the French were drained of their strength at Verdun, so did their share of the Somme plan evaporate. Ultimately their front of attack shrank from twenty-five miles to eight, and their force from forty divisions to sixteen, of which only five attacked on July 1st. From now onwards the British were to take up the main burden of the Western Front campaign and, because of this fact alone, July 1st, 1916, is a landmark in the history of the war.

Nevertheless, Haig did not adjust his aims to the shrinkage of resources. It is true that he continued preparations for an attack at Messines, and formed an alternative plan, to switch his reserves thither in case of complete failure. But he does not seem to have foreseen the case of mixed success and failure—always the greater probability in war. And for this want of elasticity his plan suffered in execution. Realism was equally lacking. The hopeful intention of the British Command was, in the first stage, to break the German front between Maricourt and Serre; in the second stage to secure the high ground between Bapaume and Ginchy, while the French seized that round Sailly and Rancourt; in the third stage to wheel to the left and roll up the German flank as far as Arras, so enlarging the breach. With this object all available troops, including cavalry, would work northwards, from the line Bapaume-Miraumont, while a co-operating attack was launched against the German front south-west of Arras. Fourthly, was to come a general advance towards Cambrai-Douai. What a contrast between intention and achievement! In outline, the plan was shrewdly designed, and Haig was wise to take such long views. But he does not seem to have looked clearly enough at the ground beneath his feet. The very belief in such far-reaching possibilities suggests a failure to diagnose the actual conditions. There was a fundamental unrealism in a plan which, while discarding the old and ever-new master key of surprise, made no pretence to provide a substitute.

The main attack, on a 14-mile front between Maricourt and Serre, was entrusted to Rawlinson's Fourth Army of eighteen divisions, of which eleven were to lead the attack, with five in close reserve. Only two, together with a cavalry division, were in army reserve. But Haig also placed at Rawlinson's disposal, for exploiting success, a force of two cavalry divisions under Gough, with a corps of two divisions to follow. Two divisions of the Third Army were to make a subsidiary attack round Gommecourt. The artillery concentration totalled 1537 guns, 467 being heavy. This meant one gun to every twenty yards of front, a record at that time, although far eclipsed by later concentrations. It was double that of the Germans for their great Dunajec break-through, but the defences on the Russian front a year before could not be compared with the network of wire and trenches on the Somme front. Another significant contrast was that whereas the French had nine hundred heavy guns, the British had less than half this number for a far wider front—one to every fifty-seven yards.

The British Official History remarks that 'The problem facing the Allies was, in fact, that of storming a fortress, in which, according to history and precedent, there should be a main assault on the largest breach (or weakest spot), several subsidiary ones on minor breaches—which must be strong enough to be converted into main assaults and carried through —and false attacks.' Instead, the distribution of force was as uniform as the methods of attacks were stereotyped. The artillery, in any case deficient, was spread evenly along the whole frontage. 'It must be confessed that the problem was not appreciated at G.H.Q.' What were the causes of this blindness? They had a pre-war base. 'It must be admitted that the problems of semi-siege warfare and the large concentration of guns necessary for the attack of great field defences had never been studied in practice by the General Staff. Under the influence of General H. H. Wilson (the late Sir Henry Wilson) it had been content to follow French ideas as to the nature of the next war, and ignored and almost resented hearing of the information obtained by its Intelligence Branch as to the preparations being made and methods practised at manœuvres by the Germans.'

To understand both the problem and the course of the battle a brief description of the ground is necessary, for in few battles on the Western Front did topography have so important an influence or make so deep an impression on the minds of the combatants. From Péronne, where the Somme makes a right-angled turn south, a range of hills runs north-west, forming the watershed between the Somme and the basins of the Scarpe and the Scheldt. This ridge, intersected by the narrow valley of the little river Ancre, had been in German possession since the 'Race to the Sea' of October, 1914, and it gave the enemy command and observation over the Allied lines and the land behind them. For the first year this disadvantage mattered little, for when British troops relieved the French here in July, 1915, the front had an air and a condition of peacefulness astonishing to men accustomed to the incessant 'bickering' of Ypres or La Bassée. Report said that in some places the troops of our Ally went back for *déjeuner* to villages hardly touched, close to the line, leaving only sentries in the trenches; that in another hamlet which stood in no-man's-land the sleeping accommodation was nightly shared between the opposing sides by tacit consent. I can vouch for the fact that in the first months after the British had taken over this front it was possible for battalions to drill undisturbed on fields in full view of the German lines— whereas six months later billets several miles further back were harassed by gunfire. The campaign policy of the French, except when engaged in active operations, was 'live and let live', and in retrospect there seems little doubt that it was wiser than the British policy of continual 'strafing'. For when the Germans held the dominating positions as well as a superiority in ammunition and equipment these worrying tactics wore down the British troops more than the enemy— attrition on the wrong side of the balance sheet. Further, they stirred the Germans to strengthen their trench defences, to develop by art the advantages of nature, so that the offensive came against an almost impregnable fortress instead of against the relatively weak defence system which existed in the autumn of 1915. Masefield, in his book, *The Old Front Line*, expressed the situation aptly—'Almost in every part of this old front our men had to go up hill to attack. . . . The enemy had the look-out posts, with the fine views over France, and the sense of domination. Our men were down below, with no view of anything but of stronghold after stronghold, just up above, being made stronger daily.' To-day the tumbled desolation that was the Somme battlefield has passed. Though he underestimated the time, Masefield's instinct was correct that 'when the trenches are filled in and the plough has gone over them the ground will not keep the look of war. One summer with its flowers will cover most of the ruin that man can make, and then these places, from which the driving back of the enemy began, will be hard indeed to trace, even with maps'. 'Centre Way, Peel Trench, Munster Alley, and these other paths to glory will be deep under the corn, and gleaners will sing at Dead Mule Corner.' Yet, while even memory finds it difficult to recapture the wartime aspect, a tranquil visit impresses the mind with the steepness of the ascent and the command from the ridge, even more than in days when progress was reckoned in yards and the contour was seen from the eye-level of trenches and shell-holes. From an artillery point of view there were advantages in attacking up hill, because the German trenches were more clearly displayed, but in other ways it was a physical and psychological handicap—not only to the attacking infantry.

Surprise, difficult in face of such commanding positions, was the more difficult because the art of concealing preparations, and of camouflage, had yet to be relearnt. The construction of new hutments on both sides of the Ancre provided the Germans with the first clue, in February, and thenceforward signs continually multiplied. Falkenhayn contemplated an attempt to dislocate the British offensive, but found that he could not spare the necessary troops. If the vast preparations had not given it away, a bombardment of a week's duration would in any case have announced the coming assault. Even earlier, a censorship error in allowing publication of a speech to munition workers by the Minister of Labour, Mr. Arthur Henderson, on June 2nd, had given the German Command a hint of its early delivery. The one redeeming factor was that despite accurate predictions and warnings of the attack both from the immediate army command (the Second) and from agents abroad, Falkenhayn continued to believe that it was only a preliminary to the real blow further north, apparently feeling that British preparations were too blatant to be true. In consequence he withheld reinforcements, and not until July 5th was he convinced that the Somme was Haig's chosen battleground. In the meantime he dismissed the Chief of Staff of the Second Army for having been right and 'asking for more'.

This divergence of views in the German Command left the British a chance which was to be forfeited by a divergence of views in their own command. The extent of this difference, and its effects, has only come to light in recent years. For the offensive was only a few weeks old when the story was spread by officially inspired apologists that Haig was throughout aiming at a campaign of attrition and had not dreamt of a 'break-through'. This denial was vehemently maintained for years, long after the war; it forms one of the most elaborate perversions of historical truth that has come to light. The 'smoke screen', composed of particles of truth dishonestly mixed, was finally dissipated by the publication of the Official History in 1932.

This revealed that Joffre was only contemplating an attrition battle, and that Rawlinson inclined to the same view, while Haig, the middle man, both sought and believed in a break-through. His judgment dictated the British aim. But Rawlinson's doubts led to the British plan being a compromise of method, which made it largely unsuitable to either aim. In view of his 'comparatively small resources' in artillery, and the depth of the German position, Rawlinson favoured a prolonged bombardment and an advance by limited stages. The first inevitably diminished the chances of surprise —the most potent compensation for small resources—while the second was a check on exploiting any success that was gained, giving the enemy time to recover and to bring up reserves. Haig justly realized the latter defect and also inclined to a short bombardment; but, perhaps, being an untechnically minded cavalryman, he skimmed over the problem of cutting the wire entanglements that covered the approach to the enemy's position. After discussion Rawlinson was allowed his long bombardment, but was ordered to swallow part of the German second position, as well as the first, at one gulp.

The Official History, while showing that a break-through could hardly have had decisive results, and even suggesting that it would merely have created a dangerous salient, implies that a break-through was possible. But not in the way it was attempted. For his break-through aim, Haig actually relied on the one means in which he was, by all advice, too limited.

His Artillery Adviser told him that he was 'stretching' his artillery too much. Rawlinson 'expressed the fear' that he was 'asking too much' of the force available, that its gun power would be spread too thinly for effect, and that an attempt to bite off part of the second position would be 'a gamble'. Nevertheless, it was to that gamble that Haig decided to commit his subordinates and their men.

'Increasing optimism' was shown by Haig as the day of battle drew nearer, though French resources, and consequently their share, were steadily shrinking owing to the drain of Verdun. What is perhaps more remarkable is the way his chief subordinates joined in the chorus of optimism, singing so loudly as apparently to drown the doubts they had felt during cool consideration of the problem. They not merely deferred to his judgment; they made it their own. Loyalty could go no further.

'Privately' Rawlinson 'was convinced that they (Haig's instructions) were based on false premises and on too great optimism'. Yet he 'impressed on all at conferences and other times . . . "that nothing could exist at the conclusion of the bombardment in the area covered by it", and the infantry would only have to walk over and take possession'. This current of optimism was passed downwards with the result that even when the bombardment was proving ineffective, battalions 'which reported that the enemy machine-guns had not been silenced were told by the divisional staffs that they were scared'. Terrible words for an official history to record as being said to men who were about to pay with their lives for this disregard of their words!

Because of its disastrous effects, the causes of this fantastic optimism demand analysis. With some officers in large degree, and perhaps most officers in some degree, care for their personal interests may have had an influence. Viewed fairly, that is no particular reproach to soldiers; for in any profession where life-careers are concerned it is human nature to follow the cue given from above.* But a wider cause would

* Perhaps its ill effects could only be curtailed if war was conducted by

seem to have been genuine self-delusion. In some cases this may have been induced by the confused idea of loyalty— 'blind loyalty'—that the nineteenth-century military system had fostered; even here, the Fourth Army instructions, which omitted so many tactical points of vital importance, took pains to lay down with heavy emphasis that 'all criticism by subordinates . . . of orders received from superior authority will in the end recoil on the heads of the critics. . . .' But in other cases optimism was so buoyant as to need no inspiration from on high. Thus when Haig, anxious over the inadequate preparedness of one army corps, sent General Charteris thither with power to countermand its attack, 'for it had little chance of complete success', his envoy found the commander 'more than satisfied', and saying exuberantly that he felt 'like Napoleon before the battle of Austerlitz'. So Charteris yielded to his desire, although he 'came back feeling very miserable'.

The Official History suggests that the root of this fatal optimism among the higher command may be traced to an astounding failure to grasp the main lesson of previous experience—a lesson that most regimental soldiers had long since learnt. 'The failures of the past were put down to reasons other than the stout use of the machine-gun by the enemy and his scientifically planned defences.' Such expert 'reasoning' is certainly one of the most remarkable recorded cases in all history of missing the wood for the trees.

Rationally it seems inexplicable that the bombardment should have been counted on to leave nobody alive in the opposing trenches. For, beyond Rawlinson's original doubts, there is the fact that he himself spread his limited artillery evenly along the front 'without regard to the strength and importance of any particular part', with the result that 'their

amateurs, or at least by soldiers who had become civilians after being trained: the point is illustrated in General Charteris's remark on one such appointment late in the War. 'He has one very strong asset . . . a very big job in civil life to go back to whenever he may wish. . . . It is difficult for any regular professional soldier not to be influenced by consideration of his own future prospects.——has the independence of a civilian and the training of a soldier.'

fire was necessarily so dispersed that many strong points and machine-gun posts were never touched'. Moreover, a large proportion of the heavy guns available were of obsolete pattern and poor range, while much of the ammunition was defective. Thus the shells could not penetrate the dug-outs in which the German machine-gunners were sheltering—in waiting. Yet it is only on the assumption of a potentially overwhelming bombardment that we can understand at all the tactics adopted by the British command. One can hardly believe that anyone with a grain of common sense or any grasp of past experience would have launched troops to the attack by such a method unless intoxicated with confidence in the effect of the bombardment. The method is certainly an object-lesson in supreme negation.

The Official History continues—'In the early discussions Haig had said that corps were not to attack until their commanders were satisfied that the enemy's defences had been sufficiently destroyed; but this condition seems to have been dropped as time passed.' This carelessness to maintain an essential condition of all warfare, especially siege warfare, is another extraordinary fact. It would have been culpable in the commander of a company.

Let us, in justice, record a redeeming point of precaution—or what might have been one. Haig had suggested tentatively that, before the mass of the infantry were launched, the result of the bombardment and the state of the defences might be tested by sending ahead patrols or small parties, such as the Germans had used at Verdun. But this suggestion was 'rejected by his Army Commanders'.

Was there anything that might have rescued success, or at least mitigated the sacrifice? Yes—if the British infantry could have reached the enemy trenches before the defenders were able to open fire. There were two ways in which this might have been achieved. By crossing either before the enemy could see to fire or before they were ready to fire. Without fog, natural or artificial, the only chance of the first lay in an assault during the darkness or in the dim light be-

fore dawn. We learn that 'a few commanders . . . desired that
at least the assault should be made at the first streak of light,
before the enemy machine-gunners could see their prey'. We
are told that 'Rawlinson himself accepted' the suggestion
'and pressed his French neighbours to agree'. But they had
double his quantity of heavy guns and wanted good observation for them. So he agreed to the later hour, apparently
with little misgiving.

The question that remained was whether the British infantry could cross no-man's-land before the barrage lifted. It
was a race with death—the greatest of such races—run by
nearly sixty thousand men in the first heat. They were hopelessly handicapped. The whole mass, made up of closely-
packed waves of men, was to be launched together, without
discovering whether the bombardment had really paralysed
the resistance. Under the Fourth Army's instructions, those
waves were to advance at 'a steady pace', symmetrically
aligned like rows of ninepins ready to be knocked over. 'The
necessity of crossing no-man's-land at a good pace, so as to
reach the parapet before the enemy could reach it, was not
mentioned.' But to do so would have been physically impossible, for the heaviest handicap of all was that 'the infantryman was so heavily laden that he could not move faster
than a walk'. Each man carried about 66 lbs., over half his
own body weight, 'which made it difficult to get out of a
trench, impossible to move much quicker than a slow walk,
or to rise and lie down quickly'. Even an army mule, the
proverbial and natural beast of burden, is only expected to
carry a third of his own weight!

The 'race' was lost before it started, and the battle soon
after. The barrage went on, the infantry could not go on,
the barrage could not be brought back, and infantry reinforcements were pushed in just where infantry could not go
on—a compound tragedy of errors.

The bombardment began on June 24th; the attack was
intended for June 29th, but was later postponed until July
1st, owing to a momentary break in the weather. This post-

ponement, made at French request, involved not only the spreading out of the ammunition over a longer period, and a consequent loss of intensity, but a greater strain on part of the assaulting troops, who, after being keyed up for the effort, had to remain another forty-eight hours in cramped trenches under the exhausting noise of their own gunfire and the enemy's retaliation—conditions made worse by torrential rain which flooded the trenches.

July 1st dawned a day of broiling heat, and at 7 a.m., the bombardment rose to its height. Half an hour later the infantry advanced from their trenches—and thousands fell, strewing no-man's-land with their bodies, before the German front trench was even reached. For their opponents were the Germans of 1916, most stubborn and skilful fighters; while the shells flattened their trenches, they sheltered in dug-outs or shell-holes, and then as the barrage lifted dragged out their machine-guns, to pour an unslackening hail of lead into the unduly dense waves of the attackers—for 1916 marked the nadir of infantry attacks, the revival of formations that were akin to the eighteenth century in their formalism and lack of manœuvring power. Battalions attacked in four or eight waves, not more than a hundred yards apart, the men in each almost shoulder to shoulder, in a symmetrical well-dressed alignment, and taught to advance steadily upright at a slow walk with their rifles held aslant in front of them, bayonets upwards—so as to catch the eye of the observant enemy. An excellent imitation of Frederick's infantry *automata*, with the difference that they were no longer advancing against muskets of an effective range of barely a hundred yards. It is hardly remarkable that by nightfall many battalions were barely a hundred strong. Only as the upstanding waves were broken up by the fire did advance become possible. For then human nature and primitive cunning reasserted themselves against authorized tactics; the more enterprising and still uncowed survivors formed little groups, usually under some natural leader, and worked their way by short rushes, and crawling from shell-hole to shell-hole, stalking the opposing machine-guns, and often progressing to a considerable depth with little further loss. But in many places packets of the enemy and nests of machine-guns were left in their wake, to take heavy toll of the supports, in similarly dense formations.

Thus, save in the south, the force of the tide slackened and later ebbed. Fricourt, on the right centre, formed a turning point both in the front and in the fortune of the day. The French, south of the Somme and north of it as far as Maricourt, gained all their objectives with slight loss. This success they owed partly to their more flexible tactics and heavier artillery concentration, partly to the lesser strength of the German defences, and to the fact that the attack here came as a tactical surprise to the Germans who had expected an attack only on the British front. Between Maricourt and Fricourt the British XIII Corps (30th and 18th Divisions) reached its objectives, though with greater loss, capturing Montauban. On its left the XV Corps partially achieved its task of pinching out the bastion of Fricourt village and wood. The 7th Division turned one flank by capturing Mametz, and on the other flank the 21st Division penetrated some half a mile into the German lines, holding on to a narrow tongue of captured land with both its own flanks in the air until Fricourt fell next day.

But the 21st Division marked the boundary of success, and all to the north was failure—with the heaviest British loss of any day's fighting in the war. One significant factor was the greater width of 'no-man's-land'. In the III Corps, fractions of the 34th Division pushed past La Boisselle to Contalmaison, but were forced to fall back. Against Ovillers the waves of the 8th Division beat practically in vain. A renewed attack was ordered for the afternoon—'wiser counsels, however, prevailed'. Northward, again, in the X Corps the assault of the 32nd Division was broken against the defences of Thiepval— 'only bullet-proof soldiers could have taken Thiepval this day'. The 36th Ulster Division, however, celebrated the anniversary of the Boyne by penetrating deep into the German front past Thiepval towards Grandcourt. Unhappily, the Corps Commander used his reserve to reinforce the division that was hopelessly held up and refused it to the Ulstermen who had made a hopeful opening. Thus their advanced parties were cut off, and at nightfall only small fractions of the German front trenches remained in British hands. The attack of the VIII Corps (29th, 4th and 31st Divisions) on the left flank was shattered more abruptly, though here again a few isolated parties pressed through to Beaumont Hamel and Serre. A muddled argument over a question of one mine explosion led to the heavy artillery 'lifting' ten minutes before the infantry assault—with fatal result. As for the subsidiary attack by the VII Corps at Gommecourt, the failure of the 46th Division nullified the opening success of the 56th, while the value of the heavy sacrifice made by the corps as a whole was nullified by the failure of the main offensive.

The tally of prisoners who passed through the corps cages that day is in some degree an index of the comparative initial success—XIII Corps (Congreve), 934; XV Corps (Horne), 517; III Corps (Pulteney), 32; X Corps (Morland), 478; VIII Corps (Hunter-Weston), 22. In contrast, the French had taken over 4,000 prisoners at little cost. The assault of their XX Corps next to the British was cloaked by a river mist in crossing no-man's-land, and quickly overran the German first position. The French then proposed to push on, but gave up the idea on hearing that their British neighbours were held back by orders from the higher command. The French attack south of the Somme, by two divisions of the Colonial Corps and one of the XXXV, enjoyed a surprise effect through being delivered two hours later than elsewhere. It not only gained all its objectives, but was pushed beyond, and by nightfall was within reach of the German second position.

For the French, in view of these results, July 1st may be counted a victory. But the major attack was that of the British, and here the Germans could justly claim success, for with only six divisions available, and roughly a regiment holding each British division's sector of attack, they had only yielded 1983 prisoners and a small tract of ground to the assault of thirteen British divisions. The high hopes built up beforehand had fallen to the ground, and the months of preparation and sowing had only garnered a bitter fruit. Yet although a military failure, July 1st was an epic of heroism, and, better still, the proof of the moral quality of the new armies of Britain, who, in making their supreme sacrifice of the war, passed through the most fiery and bloody of ordeals with their courage unshaken and their fortitude established.

All along the attacking line these quondam civilians bore a percentage of losses such as no professional army of past wars had ever been deemed capable of suffering—without being broken as an effective instrument. And they carried on the struggle, equally bitter, for another five months. Experience would improve their tactical action, still more their handling by the Higher Command, but no subsequent feats could surpass the moral standard of July 1st, 'a day of an intense blue summer beauty, full of roaring violence, and confusion of death, agony, and triumph, and from dawn till dark. All through that day little rushes of the men of our race went towards that no-man's-land from the bloody shelter of our trenches. Some hardly left our trenches, many never crossed the green space, many died in the enemy wire, many had to fall back. Others won across, and went further and drove the enemy back from line to line till the Battle of the Somme ended in the falling back of the enemy.' That falling back, however, was long postponed, and when it came was so timed as to discomfit the attackers far more than it advantaged them.

Why did Haig persevere on the Somme after so disastrous a start, and discard the alternative he had prepared in the north? The Official History has 'little doubt that the Messines attack, carried out so successfully in 1917, would have had in 1916 a far better chance of decisive result, especially if combined with a coastal attack, than had an offensive astride the Somme'. As late as June 5th Haig had warned Rawlinson that if the Fourth Army attack 'met with considerable opposition he might decide to stop it and proceed with the Messines operation'. The experience of July 1st certainly fulfilled his condition. Perhaps his continuance is best explained by the very marked 'bulldog' element in his make-up. He hated to accept a rebuff, to loosen his grip once he had got his teeth into the resistance. If repulsed everywhere he might have found it easier to switch his reserves north to Messines. But, having bitten into a slice of the German front, Haig wanted to go on and bite deeper. Why, then, did he not bite quicker on the one soft part? In part, because of a fog of war that was thickened by human frailty in facing facts.

Behind the front the higher commanders had been rendering reports more rosy than the dim facts warranted, and also apparently than their own belief. 'Capture of prisoners, but not the heavy casualties, were regularly reported'. Ignorance in such conditions was natural, but deception less excusable. Meantime the opportunity of developing the success in the south went begging.

Late on July 2nd, Haig, confronted with a difficult situation, decided to press the attack where success had been gained, instead of making a fresh frontal assault on the intact defences from Ovillers northwards. The tactical experience of the later years—and earlier history—confirms his wisdom, and the only question is why the exploitation of the success in the south was not more prompt. Part of the dense infantry strength which had been used to strew no-man's-land with dead might better have been kept to swell the reserve for such a purpose. Even as it was, the Germans were badly shaken, and if British reserve divisions were few, theirs were less, as their delay in counter-attacking showed. But the Fourth Army made no attempt to push reserves through at the sectors of least resistance and at 10 p.m. on the 1st merely ordered its corps to 'continue the attack', evenly along the whole front. At Rawlinson's suggestion, Gough was put in charge of the two left corps (X and VIII) which had most obviously failed—'an unenviable task' for a man who had been intended, and was best fitted for the rôle of exploitation. The corps commanders pointed out the hopelessness of a fresh attack without adequate preparation. Gough wisely concurred, and the orders were cancelled. As these corps were not in a state to attack unbroken defences again, nothing happened on the 2nd. Meantime the XIII Corps, which had made a real penetration on the extreme right was held back. This passivity was the more regrettable because, in conjunction with the French, it had already shattered a ragged and fumbling night counter-attack by a German division hurried up from Cambrai—the one enemy reserve immediately available.

Opportunity receded further when, for the 3rd, Rawlinson merely ordered a renewed attack by the left wing in conjunction with his centre. This plan, Haig approved but modified—with not altogether happy results. He was now turning his eyes to the right, and he reduced the morrow's attack to thrusts by small packets against Thiepval and Ovillers. The rearrangement accentuated the defects due to divided control, so that the attacks became not only petty in scale but disjointed in delivery—and proved void of any effect except further casualties. Meantime, troops of the XIII Corps on the right walked into Bernafay Wood almost without opposition, but were restrained from going further. The French XX Corps next to it was, as a corollary, also constrained to inactivity, but south of the Somme the French captured the German second line and the high ground overlooking Péronne.

Haig was now convinced of the advisability of concentrating his effort on the right. But he met a French stumbling block. Both Joffre and Foch—who was in direct charge of the French share of the offensive—insisted that Haig should capture the ridge from Pozières to Thiepval in the centre as a preliminary to any attack on the right, or Longueval, sector. Haig's contention that he had not enough ammunition to cover effectively a renewed attack on the whole front, and that the Longueval ridge defences were weaker than at

Thiepval, made no impression, and Joffre declared that if the British attacked Longueval they would be beaten. Indeed, he went so far as to give Haig a direct order to attack in the centre, whereupon Haig retorted that he was responsible to the British Government, and that, although he was ready to follow Joffre's strategy, in matters of tactics he would take his own line. This settled the question.

A long interval followed, however, before the Fourth Army was ready for the attack on the enemy's second line. The interval was the longer because Haig considered it necessary to clear away all the enemy's outlying footholds before attempting the main stroke, and sought to seize these by a series of nibbling attacks. At the same time the X and VIII Corps on the left were definitely transferred from Rawlinson's Fourth Army to Gough's Reserve Army, later to become the Fifth, and the available reserves and guns were concentrated on the reduced Fourth Army front.

Thus, during the days immediately following July 1st, when the German defence was seriously shaken in the southern sector—Montauban-La Boisselle—the renewed attacks were slight in strength and spasmodic. The resistance had breathing space to reorganize and harden, to strengthen its hold on the commanding ridge, Ginchy-Pozières, where ran the German second line. The British progress became very slow, and a special obstacle was offered by Mametz Wood. The three days' abortive attacks—by the 38th (Welsh) Division—and consequent delay here were to prejudice the main stroke. But as great a handicap was imposed from above.

If the British Higher Command had been over-ambitious and unduly optimistic before July 1st, it perhaps now tended to the other extreme. Rawlinson, however, had been brought to realize that bold and rapid measures were essential if he was to forestall the German reinforcements and labour which were rebuilding, in rear, the fortified front faster than the British could force a way through it. If the British waited until their front line had been carried near enough to the German second line (Braune Stellung) for a close assault, they might well be confronted with a barrier as firm as the original of July 1st. Rawlinson framed a plan to attack and break the German defences on a four-mile front between Delville Wood on the right, and Bazentin-le-Petit Wood on the left. His right was fully three-quarters of a mile distant from this second line, with the vital tactical feature of Trônes Wood between still in German hands. Thence towards his left no-man's-land gradually narrowed, until in front of Mametz Wood it was only about three hundred yards wide; but Trônes Wood enfiladed a large part of the line of advance. If the obvious course was adopted, and an attack delivered only on the left, the prospects were barren; for the experience of 1915 had shown that an attack on a narrow frontage against an enemy with ample guns might gain an initial success, only to be blown out of the captured fragment by the concentration of hostile gunfire thus facilitated.

Instead of the obvious, Rawlinson took a course which for all its risks—calculated risks—was more truly secure and economical of force. The troops were to cross the exposed area by an advance under cover of darkness, followed by a dawn attack, preceded by a hurricane bombardment of only a few minutes' duration. This plan revived the use of surprise, which lay rusting throughout the greater part of the war, until in fact the last year from Cambrai onwards.

In 1916 the ideas of a night advance and of such a brief bombardment were alike so fresh in revival as to be a shock and appear a gamble to orthodox opinion. That he should attempt the manœuvre with New Army troops, men who had been civilians less than two years before, made his plan seem yet more rash. The Commander-in-Chief was strongly opposed to it, preferring a more limited alternative, but Rawlinson persevered, his own confidence reinforced by the confidence of the actual troop leaders in their ability to carry out the night operation. For once, Horne, who was usually as apt to agree with Haig's views as he was dependable in other ways, agreed instead with his immediate superior, and this fact may have helped to tilt the scales. Rawlinson gained his way, but instead of the already delayed attack being launched on July 13th, as he intended, the reluctance of the Higher Command caused it to be postponed until July 14th —a day's delay that was to have grave consequences. Another drawback was the lack of French co-operation, owing to lack of faith in the prospects of the attack.

The attacking troops were composed of the 9th and 3rd Divisions of the XIII Corps on the right (W. T. Furse and J. A. L. Haldane), and the 7th and 21st Divisions of the XV Corps on the left (H. E. Watts and D. G. M. Campbell), while on the extreme right flank Maxse's 18th Division had the task of clearing Trônes Wood. On the extreme left the III Corps formed a defensive flank between Bazentin-le-Petit Wood and Contalmaison. Cavalry divisions were brought up close and placed under the orders of the two attacking corps.

The German front was held by only six battalions of mixed divisions in General Stein's group, with the 7th Division in reserve south of Bapaume. The trenches of the Braune Stellung ran just in front of Delville Wood, Longueval, Bazentin-le-Grand and Bazentin-le-Petit Woods, with High Wood, 'like a dark cloud on the skyline' behind, dominating the whole area of approach. From it the Germans could see several miles behind the old British front line of July 1st.

On the right, markers went out some hours after darkness had fallen on July 13th and placed white tapes to guide the troops along their 1000 yards approach; then further tapes at right angles to mark the forward line on which the troops were to form up, so that they should start parallel with their objective. The hazardous and difficult task was carried through successfully, and soon after midnight the battalions assembled in the shelter of Caterpillar Valley, moving up in long worm-like lines of companies or platoons in single file. At 3.20 a.m. the barrage fell on the German trenches, and five minutes later the whole line moved forward to the assault. The vision which had dared to attempt such a surprise stroke, and had supported imagination with good staff work, was justified. The whole of the German second line was rapidly overrun, and the attacking troops passed beyond. From left to right, the 21st Division pressed through Bazentin-le-Petit Wood to the village, the 7th Division cleared Bazentin-le-Grand Wood and pushed up the slopes towards High Wood, the 3rd Division captured Bazentin-le-Grand, and the 9th Division fought their way, albeit with difficulty, through Longueval to the outskirts of Delville Wood.

On this right flank every yard of advance was bitterly opposed, and in the depths of Delville Wood, during the ensuing days, the South Africans made their supreme sacrifice of the war—where to-day a white stone colonnade of peaceful beauty commemorates, and contrasts with, the bloodiest battle-hell of 1916.

But on the left flank opportunity—and open country—stretched out its arms. Soon after midday the German resistance was clearly disintegrating on the front of the 7th Division, and an effort was made to exploit the chance, although some hours were lost. The 7th Division moved forward soon after 6 p.m. with two squadrons of cavalry working on their flank—the first mounted cavalry seen on a British battlefield since 1914. Roseate expectations pictured open warfare on the skyline, but once more it proved a mirage in the military desert. The troops of the illustrious 7th Division were a shade battle-weary; their depleted ranks had been filled with many untried drafts. Whatever the cause, the advance tended to lack vigour, and although most of High Wood was cleared that evening, the northern corner of the flanking trenches remained in the Germans' grip. Worst of all, twenty-four hours' postponement had enabled fresh reserves to come up, and as their strength steadily swelled the German hold tightened, the British relaxed. Late on July 15th the wood was evacuated under pressure of counterattacks, and two months were to pass before possession was regained. The surprise storm of the Somme 'Bastille' on July 14th brought the British to the

verge of a strategic decision; thereafter their effort degenerated into a battle of attrition.

After the disappointing end of the July 14th stroke, Haig
played for smaller stakes. His overdrawn supplies of ammunition were causing concern, and he had in mind no effective
substitute for gun-pounding as an 'opener' for the enemy's
sealed front. Early in June he had contemplated the step of
transferring his main offensive to the Messines sector in
Flanders if the German reserves held him up on the Somme.
And the Anzac Corps began to move thither in readiness.
But by July 7th he had decided instead to pour his own
reserves down to the Somme—now, for the enemy, the line of
expectation—and to throw all his weight into the direct
offensive there.

He ordered, however, a number of local attacks in the
north as a means to fix the enemy's attention and keep his
reserves there, and away from the Somme. The method
reveals a most curious military delusion, for while simulated
preparations for a large-scale offensive would cause the enemy
natural apprehension, the actual delivery of a narrow-fronted
local attack would merely disclose the bluff. One consequence
was the shattering of the 5th Australian Division in an
absurdly advertised attack at Fromelles, an attack which was
the final link of an almost incredibly muddled chain of
causation.

The rest of the Anzac Corps had been moved to the Somme,
where Haig's aim was now to enlarge his lodgment on the
main ridge. He had favoured the idea of trying to carry out
his original third phase—of rolling up the German front
northwards—although the original conditions had not been
fulfilled. But he had not sufficient elbow-room to deploy an
adequate force for it. And it would have diverged from the
line of co-operation with the French. Hence he decided to
continue his main pressure with his right, eastward towards
the French line of convergence, while on his left Gough sought
to gain the Pozières-Thiepval end of the ridge, and so widen
the British holding upon it.

To this end Gough was given the Anzac Corps (Birdwood), and on July 23rd he launched part of it against Pozières in conjunction with a renewed assault by the three corps of the Fourth Army along the whole of its narrow front, from Guillemont to Bazentin-le-Petit. This failed completely; on the left the 1st Australian Division gained a footing in Pozières. Haig reverted to the method of nibbling, now to be exalted as a definite and masterly strategy of attrition, and to be defended by optimistic miscalculations of the German losses.

Nearly two months of bitter fighting followed, during which the British made little progress at much cost, and the infantry of both sides served as compressed cannon-fodder for artillery consumption. On the left flank the Anzac Corps was the main agent of the new plan of 'methodical progress'. The effect is best described in the measured words of the Australian official history:

'Doubtless to the Commander-in-Chief, and possibly to the Cabinet, the use of terms implying leisurely progress brought some comfortable assurance of economy of life as well as of munitions; but to the front line the method merely appeared to be that of applying a battering-ram ten or fifteen times against the same part of the enemy's battlefront with the intention of penetrating for a mile, or possibly two, into the midst of his organized defences . . .

'Even if the need for maintaining pressure be granted, the student will have difficulty in reconciling his intelligence to the actual tactics. To throw the several parts of an army corps, brigade after brigade . . . twenty times in succession against one of the strongest points in the enemy's defence, may certainly be described as "methodical", but the claim that it was economic is entirely unjustified.'

Twenty-three thousand men were expended in these efforts for the ultimate gain, after six weeks, of a tiny tongue of ground just over a mile deep. And what of the moral effect?

'Although most Australian soldiers were optimists, and

many were opposed on principle to voicing—or even harbouring grievances, it is not surprising if the effect on some intelligent men was a bitter conviction that they were being uselessly sacrificed. "For Christ's sake, write a book on the life of an infantryman (said one of them . . .), and by doing so you will quickly prevent these shocking tragedies." That an officer who had fought so nobly as Lieutenant J. A. Raws, should, in the last letter before his death, speak of the "murder" of many of his friends "through the incompetence, callousness, and personal vanity of those high in authority", is evidence not indeed of the literal truth of his words, but of something much amiss in the higher leadership. . . ."We have just come out of a place so terrible (wrote ——, one of the most level-headed officers in the force) that . . . a raving lunatic could never imagine the horror of the last thirteen days ".'

The history indicates that Birdwood lost much of his Gallipoli popularity through his failure to interpose against Gough's impetuous desire for quick results and his lack of thought. This may have been a factor in leading the Australian troops to reject Birdwood's personal appeal when they voted against the conscription of other men to share the horrors that they had experienced.

But Pozières was matched on the other flank by Guillemont—now a peaceful hamlet amid cornfields, then a shambles of blended horror and mystery. From Trônes Wood it is down one slope, up another, only a few hundred yards of farm road now, yet in July and August, 1916, an infinite distance. Division after division essayed to cross it, felt the petty prize within their fingers, and then slipped back unable to maintain their hold. And when it was at last secured on September 3rd, Ginchy, a few hundred yards further up the slope, was a similar obstruction until September 9th. Save Thiepval, still defiant, no hamlets have exacted a heavier price for their possession.

Now at last the British line was straightened on a seven-mile front running north-west from Leuze Wood, overlooking Combles, where it joined up with the French. They had just extended further south the attack south of the Somme, storming three miles of the old German front line near Chaulnes and taking 7000 prisoners. On August 30th Rawlinson had recorded in his diary—'The Chief is anxious to have a gamble with all the available troops about September 15th, with the object of breaking down German resistance and getting through to Bapaume.' And he added, somewhat illogically—'We shall have no reserves in hand, save tired troops, but success at this time . . . might bring the Boches to terms.' Despite his professed faith in attrition, Haig was now reduced to gambling on a break-through.

The attack was to pivot on the left wing—Gough's Army. The primary object of the main blow, by Rawlinson, was to break through what had originally been the Germans' last line between Morval and Le Sars, in co-operation with a French thrust to the south between Combles and the Somme —thus pinching out Combles. If the opening success warranted the attempt the British attack was to be extended northward to seize Courcelette and Martinpuich. Eight divisions were deployed for the original attack, and two detailed for the 'extension'. A special feature was the employment for the first time of tanks, the armoured cross-country machines which had been invented as an antidote to the defensive obstacle of machine-guns and barbed wire. In disregard of the opinions of the tank's progenitors, and of their own expressed agreement with these opinions, the British Higher Command had decided to utilize such machines as were available, as a stake to redeem the fading prospects of the Somme offensive. When this decision was taken only sixty of the initial one hundred and fifty machines had been transported to France. Forty-nine were actually employed, to work in tiny detachments of two or three machines—another breach with the principles laid down by Colonel Swinton. The scant and hasty preparation combined with the mechanical defects of this early model to reduce the total, so that only thirty-two reached the starting point. Of these, nine pushed ahead with the infantry, nine failed to catch the infantry, but helped in clearing the captured ground, nine broke down and five were 'ditched' in the craters of the battlefield. The first nine rendered useful aid, especially in capturing Flers, but the greater prize—of a great surprise stroke—was a heavy forfeit to pay for redeeming in a limited degree the failure of the Somme offensive.

After three days' bombardment, the attack was launched at dawn on the 15th in a slight mist. The mist, together with the clouds of smoke, prevented the German gunners in many places from seeing the light-signals fired by their infantry, and the consequent lack of artillery support on the German side eased the path of the British infantry. Thus the XV Corps in the centre made early and good progress; by 10 a.m. its left division was beyond Flers. Its progress was greatly helped by the tanks, of which the German regimental histories give a vivid impression—'The arrival of the tanks on the scene had the most shattering effect on the men. They felt quite powerless against these monsters which crawled along the top of the trench enfilading it with continuous machine-gun fire, and closely followed by small parties of infantry who threw hand-grenades on the survivors.' But on the right the XIV Corps lost heavily and was held up long before it could reach Morval and Lesbœufs. The III Corps, on the left, also fell short of its objectives, although its 47th Division finally cleared the long-sought High Wood. On the extreme left the projected extension of the attack was carried out, and both Martinpuich and Courcelette were taken. As a result of the day the crest of the ridge had been gained, except on the right, and with it the commanding observation which the Germans had so long enjoyed.

The failure on the right was redressed on September 25th, by another big attack which, in conjunction with the French, compelled the Germans to evacuate Combles. Next day Thiepval at last fell to an attack by four divisions of Gough's Army. German accounts make it clear that the decisive break in their front was 'caused by the appearance of three British tanks . . . on the outskirts of Thiepval village'. Haig still called for pressure 'without intermission' and, as a result of further small gains, by the first week of October the Germans were back in their last completed line of defences, which ran from Sailly-Saillisel, on the right, past Le Transloy and in front of Bapaume; they were busily constructing fresh lines in rear, but these were not yet complete. On the other hand these days had proved the continued strength of the German resistance, and the limited success held but little hope of a real break-through or its exploitation. The early onset of the autumn rains made this hope more slender daily. The rains combined with the bombardments to make the ground a morass in which guns and transport were bogged, while even lightly equipped infantry could barely and slowly struggle forward. Attacks under such conditions were terribly handicapped; that most of them failed was inevitable, and if a trench was taken the difficulties of consolidating it liquidated the gain.

By October 12th Haig seems to have been at last convinced that he could not pierce the German defences that year. But Joffre and Foch continued to urge him on, and in partial response Haig continued to call for fresh attacks through the mud towards Le Transloy, until a strong protest was made by Lord Cavan, commanding the XIV Corps, who desired to know whether it was deliberately intended to sacrifice the British right in order to help the French left, and pointedly added—'No one who has not visited the front can really know the state of exhaustion to which the men are reduced.' But other corps commanders had less moral courage, and Rawlinson, although sympathetic, seems to have yielded against his better judgment to his Chief's determination. Hence the III and Anzac Corps continued a hopeless series of petty attacks until November 16th. Their ineffectiveness was redeemed, as their ineptitude was obscured, by a welcome, last-hour success of Gough's Army.

The wedge that had been slowly driven eastwards between

the Ancre and the Somme had turned the original German defences north of the Ancre into a pronounced salient. For some time Gough's Army had been preparing an attack against this and a temporary improvement in the weather allowed it to be launched on November 13th, by seven divisions. Beaumont-Hamel and Beaucourt-sur-Ancre were captured, with 7000 prisoners, but on the left Serre once more proved impregnable. Haig was pleased—because it would 'strengthen the hands of the British representatives' at the forthcoming Allied Military Conference at Chantilly. So the Somme offensive could at last be suspended with honour satisfied.

The folly of the last phase, from September 25th onwards, was that having at last won the crest of the ridge, and its commanding observation, the advantage was thrown away by fighting a way down into the valley beyond. Thereby the troops were doomed to spend the winter in flooded trenches. 'Somme mud' was soon to be notorious.

Thus the miscalled Battles of the Somme closed in an atmosphere of disappointment, and with such a drain on the British forces that the coincident strain on the enemy was obscured. This strain was largely due to the rigidity of the German higher commanders, especially General von Below of the First Army, who issued an order that any officer who gave up an inch of trench would be court-martialled, and that every yard of lost trench must be retaken by counterattack. If German mistakes do not condone British mistakes they at least caused a vain loss of life, and still more of morale, which helped to balance the British loss—until on August 23rd Below was compelled to swallow his own orders and modify his method of resistance, in accord with that of the new Hindenburg-Ludendorff régime.

CHAPTER VI

SCENE 4

THE GROWING PAINS OF THE TANK

On September 15th, 1916, a new instrument of war received its baptism of fire, and helped to make the British attack on that day one of the landmarks of the Somme offensive. It was one of the few attacks which did not require the use of a large-scale map and a magnifying glass to detect its progress. But, far more significant, it cast its shadow over the whole future of the war. And as it thus becomes a greater landmark in the history of the war than in the history of the Somme, so it is likely to become a still greater landmark in the history of War.

For this new instrument—the tank—changed the face of war by substituting motor-power for a man's legs as a means of movement on the battlefield and by reviving the use of armour as a substitute for his skin or for earth-scrapings as a means of protection. Hitherto he could not fire if he wished to move, and could not move if he wished for cover. But September 15th, 1916, saw the simultaneous combination in one agent of fire power, movement, and protection—an advantage until then enjoyed in modern warfare only by those who fought on the sea.

But although sea warfare on land may be the ultimate consequence of the tank, and was foreshadowed in its first name of 'land-ship', the original intention was more limited and more immediately practical—to provide an antidote to the machine-gun which, in alliance with barbed wire, had reduced warfare to stagnation and generalship to attrition.

The cure was a British production, the most significant achievement of British brains during the World War. Yet it has an essential transatlantic link, symbolical in view of the association on the battlefield that was soon to follow. For

332

the source of both the evil and the antidote was American. The trench deadlock was due above all to the invention of an American, Hiram Maxim. His name is more deeply engraved on the real history of the World War than that of any other man. Emperors, statesmen, and generals had the power to make war, but not to end it. Having created it, they found themselves helpless puppets in the grip of Hiram Maxim, who, by his machine-gun, had paralysed the power of attack. All efforts to break the defensive grip of the machine-gun were vain; they could only raise tombstones and not triumphal arches. When at last a key to the deadlock was produced, it was forged from the invention of another American, Benjamin Holt. From his agricultural tractor was evolved the tank—an ironic reversal of the proverbial custom of 'beating swords into ploughshares'.

The eventual effect of the tank is best appreciated by studying the evidence of those who had to face it. Was it not Ludendorff himself who spoke of the great tank surprise of August 8th, 1918, as the 'black day of the German army in the history of the war', and added, 'mass attacks by tanks . . . remained hereafter our most dangerous enemies'. More emphatic still is the comment of General von Zwehl— 'It was not the genius of Marshal Foch that beat us, but "General Tank".' Nor can it be suggested that these were afterthoughts put forward in mitigation of defeat, for the most striking evidence of all, red-hot from the forge of battle, is to be found in the momentous report submitted, on October 2nd, 1918, by the representatives of the German Military Headquarters to the leaders of the Reichstag—'The Chief Army Command has been compelled to take a terribly grave decision and declare that according to human possibilities there is no longer any prospect of forcing peace on the enemy. Above all, two facts have been decisive for this issue; first, the tanks. . . .' The confession thus made gains force from comparison with the earlier disparagement of the tanks by the German Command.

For history the first question is how the tank came to be

introduced, and the second, why its decisive effect was delayed until 1918. The first question is befogged rather than guided by the popular question, so widely raised during and after the war—'Who invented the tank?' So many claimed the honour, many with some show of reason, and still more without, that the public became confused. And the Government did not help to establish the actual chain of causation, perhaps influenced by the instinct of the Treasury to avoid the recognition of financial obligations. Thus it did not become clear until the evidence in an action brought against the Crown in 1925 was available to supplement that given in 1919 before the Royal Commission on Awards to Inventors. In order to defeat this unjustified claim to reward the Treasury had to provide an opportunity for evaluating the genuine claims to honour.

The historical evolution of the tank has been confused also by the lack of any clear definition of the tank and its purpose, and this vagueness owes something to the fact that prior to the time when the camouflage name 'tank' was invented, the machine was known as a 'landship' or 'land cruiser'. Such a title, due to its being mothered in infancy by the Admiralty, however prophetic of its still distant future, is far from applicable to its past, in the war. Regarded as a landship, or even as an armoured battle-car, the origin of the tank is lost in the mists of antiquity. Among its forebears might be included the ancient war-chariot, the Hussite war carts which formed their famous 'wagenburg', even, with some show of reason, the battle elephants of Pyrrhus, or the mediæval knight in armour.

If the search be limited to self-moving, as distinct from men or animal moved machines, its origin might be traced to Valturio's wind-propelled war chariot of 1472, or to the proposals made by that many-sided genius, Leonardo da Vinci, to his patron Ludovico Sforza. In 1599 Simon Stevin constructed for the Prince of Orange two actual landships, wheel-borne and sail-propelled. As far back as 1634, David Ramsey took out the earliest patent for a self-moving car capable of use in war. So through an endless chain of experiments the origin might be traced. The caterpillar track itself—perhaps, in general opinion the distinctive feature of the tank—goes back to the early nineteenth century, or even to Richard Edgeworth's device of 1770.

If the definition be drawn still closer to mean a petrol-driven tracked machine for military use, the Hornsby tractor, used at Aldershot in 1908, takes precedence of the American Holt tractor in the ancestry of the tank. If the use of 'tank-like' machines as weapons be the test, then Mr. H. G. Wells deserves the credit popularly accorded him for priority of conception, although his prophetic story of 1903 in the *Strand Magazine* was itself twenty years behind the writings and drawings of M. Albert Robeida in *La Caricature;* if similarity of design, then one recalls Mr. L. E. de Mole's model, superior to the 1916 tank, which was pigeon-holed in the War Office in 1912. To these add also the story of the Nottingham plumber whose hobby it was to make toy machines of this nature, and whose design, submitted to the War Office in 1911, and duly pigeon-holed, was unearthed after the war, the file bearing the terse official comment, 'the man's mad'.

The chief result of this historical survey, however, is to show the futility of trying to determine the credit for the origination of this decisive weapon of the World War without a clear understanding and definition of its particular purpose. Leonardo da Vinci and the Nottingham plumber alike may claim to be among the fathers of mechanical warfare, but for the parentage of the actual tank of the World War we must look closer. The test of its origin is tactical rather than technical. It was a specific antidote for a specific disease which first broke out virulently in the World War. This disease was the complete paralysis of the offensive brought about by the defensive power of serried machine-guns, and aggravated by wire entanglements. This disease doomed the manhood of the nation to a slow and lingering end, prolonged only by the capacity to produce fresh victims for the futile sacrifice. Wycherley's phrase, 'necessity, mother of invention', has never had a truer example, and it provides the real test to determine the immediate origin of the World War tank.

The first military physician who diagnosed the disease and conceived the antidote was Colonel Ernest Swinton, whose pen-name of 'Ole-Luk-Oie' had become well known through *The Green Curve* and *Duffer's Drift*—studies of war in fiction form, wherein the pill of knowledge was delightfully coated with jam. A term of hard labour on the British official history of the Russo-Japanese War gave him the opportunity to analyse its tendencies and to deduce the potential domination of the machine-gun. Later, he took an interest in the Holt tractor experiments. These two impressions soon fitted together like the two segments of a circle. For when, soon after the outbreak of war, he was sent to France as official 'Eye-witness' at General Headquarters, he was both well placed and well prepared to recognize the first symptoms of stalemate, and to suggest a remedy. On October 20th, visiting London, he saw Colonel Maurice Hankey, the Secretary of the Committee of Imperial Defence, and after describing the situation—domination of defence based on the machine-gun—outlined his proposals for an antidote. These were, in brief, to develop such a machine as the Holt tractor into a bullet-proof trench-crossing machine-gun destroyer, armed with one or more small quick-firing guns. In Hankey he found an acute and receptive mind, and a further discussion the next day led to an understanding that Hankey would take up the matter at home and Swinton in France. On October 23rd, Swinton took up the question at General Headquarters, but the suggestion came up against a blank wall.

Meanwhile Hankey put the idea before Lord Kitchener, with equally barren result. But he also submitted to the Prime Minister (Mr. Asquith), a memorandum on various ways, strategic and technical, of overcoming the deadlock, which embodied, among others, Swinton's suggestion. This reached Mr. Churchill. His mind was already active with the problem of enabling armoured cars to cross broken ground and trenches, because of his concern with the armoured-car detachments of the Royal Naval Air Service operating on the Belgian coast. On January 5th, 1915, Churchill wrote a letter to the Prime Minister supporting and amplifying the suggestion in Hankey's memorandum for the use of armoured caterpillar tractors to overrun trenches. This letter was sent by Asquith to Kitchener. By a coincidence Swinton had called at the War Office on January 4th to press anew his proposals, now extended owing to the continued experience of conditions in France.

The seed thus planted at the War Office by two sowers fell on stony soil, and after some attention finally withered, owing largely to the freezing verdict of Sir Capel Holden, Director of Mechanical Transport. Fortunately, the general idea was kept alive on other soil, for Churchill, in February, formed a committee at the Admiralty, which later became known as the Landships Committee. But this committee, though investigating many lines of thought and experiment, did not make much practical headway, its energies being diverted for a time in the direction of a landship with giant wheels. A worse blow was the removal of Churchill's vision and driving force, though even when he left the Admiralty it was his influence which kept the experiments alive. By this time also, fortunately, the committee—under the guidance of Mr. Tennyson d'Eyncourt, the Director of Naval Construction—had got on to the right line, that of the caterpillar. Even so, concrete results seem to have been hindered, and energy leaking, through lack of any exact specification of the military requirements of such a machine, for in the scheme of scientific war the tactical takes precedence of the technical.

This essential, but hitherto missing, link came in a memorandum forwarded from General Headquarters, and once this was available progress became rapid and practical. The memorandum was compiled by Swinton, who had surmounted the barrier of unbelief and convention by an appeal direct to the Commander-in-Chief. It formulated the performance required of the machine, and on this specification the newly framed joint committee of War Office and Admiralty went to work.

On July 19th, Swinton returned to England as acting Secretary to the War Committee of the Cabinet, and got in touch with the Joint Committee later, on the Prime Minister's authorization, calling an Inter-Departmental Conference to co-ordinate the work on the new machines. On September 19th, an inspection was held at Lincoln of a provisional machine, 'Little Willie', but this was rejected by Swinton as failing to conform to requirements. He was then shown a full-size wooden model, or mock-up, of a larger machine, which had been specially designed by Mr. Tritton and Lieutenant Wilson to meet the latest army specification. This was accepted, as it looked capable of complying with the two main conditions—to climb a vertical face of five feet and cross a ditch eight feet wide—and it was decided to concentrate on the production of a sample machine of this type.

Finally, on February 2nd, 1916, at Hatfield was held the official trial of this machine—christened 'Mother' or 'Big Willie', and as a result forty of these machines were ordered, a number subsequently increased to one hundred and fifty. The French, now, had independently begun similar experiments through the initiative of Colonel Estienne, whose project was sanctioned by Joffre on December 12th. Although both idea and machine were later in maturing than the British, it is a significant contrast that the first French order was for four hundred; and that order was soon doubled.

During the summer of 1916 the crews for the new machines were being trained in a vast secret enclosure, surrounded by armed guards, near Thetford in Norfolk. They formed a unit that was christened the Heavy Section, Machine Gun Corps. For secrecy sake also a new name had been chosen for the machines. The need was to find a name sufficiently mystifying and yet plausible to any outside observer who might see the tarpaulined machines in transit on the railway, and after discussing the merits of 'tank', 'cistern', and 'reservoir', the choice fell on the first.

THE GROWING PAINS OF THE TANK

Through the secrecy so well maintained, surprise was obtained when the 'tanks' made their début on the battlefield. Unhappily the fruits of the surprise were forfeited. Herein lay the tragedy of September 15th, 1916; for the official guardians disregarded the entreaties of the parents and insisted on putting the tank to work before it was mechanically mature and before its numbers were adequate. Thus they not only endangered its future usefulness but threw away the chance of surprising the enemy while he was unprepared with any countermeasures. The consequence was to prolong the hardships and toll of the war.

The reply normally made to this charge is to point out the mechanical defects which the early tanks developed, the numbers that were 'ditched', and to argue that a weapon must be tested under battlefield conditions before mass production is begun. The contention is plausible, but unconvincing in view of the facts. The tank first used in the shell-mangled chaos of the Somme, and against the deep and intricate trench systems of 1916, was built to a specification laid down in the summer of 1915, when trench lines were far less developed and artillery bombardments were not so heavy as to turn the ground into a morass—as in 1916 and 1917.

Moreover, the apologists gloss over the fact that in September, 1916, the tanks were hurried out to France and rushed into battle before their crews were fully trained and before the commanders in France had time to think, or had been given instructions, how to use them. Again, the very likelihood that the proportion of mechanical failures in this early model would be high was surely a logical reason for the production of a large number, so that sufficient might survive to reap the harvest of surprise. As the British nation was paying over several million pounds a day for the pleasure of watching and occasionally tapping on the locked gates of the German front, it would surely have been worth risking an extra day's expenditure in the purchase of a possible means of breaking the lock.

Let us probe a little further the mystery of the premature

339

use of this immature instrument. In December, 1915, Churchill drafted a paper on the use of the tank. Printed for the Committee of Imperial Defence, copies were given to the Commander-in-Chief in France. In February, 1916, as soon as the design and armament of the machine had been settled sufficiently for accurate calculations, Swinton produced a more comprehensive and detailed memorandum. This emphasized that the vital factor was the secret production of tanks until masses could be launched in a great surprise stroke, and that on no account should they be used in driblets as they were manufactured. Haig expressed his full agreement with this memorandum in the spring. Yet in August he suddenly decided to use the mere sixty then available. At that time the offensive on the Somme had practically come to a standstill, and the reports of petty gain at heavy loss grated unpleasantly on the ear of the public.

Haig's decision came as a shock to the Cabinet at home, and Lloyd George, now War Minister, energetically protested, while Montagu, his successor at the Ministry of Munitions went out to General Headquarters in a vain attempt to avert the premature use of the tanks. Haig was immovable and the powerless parents had to submit to the sacrifice of their offspring's future.

Thus history is left to surmise that the tanks were 'pawned for a song'—of the Somme. Pawned to pay for a resounding local success which might draw an encore from the public— and, incidentally, drown the growing volume of criticism. But the greater prize thus lost beyond recall was a heavy forfeit to pay for redeeming in a limited degree the ill success of the Somme offensive. With Haig this act may have been prompted by a laudable if unwise desire to economize the lives of his infantry without giving up his offensive. He had certainly shown his eagerness to clutch at any new aid. But the attitude of some of his staff cannot be similarly excused.

For the breach of principle does not complete the tally of General Headquarters. Swinton's memorandum laid down a number of conditions which were disregarded in September,

1916, only to be adopted after bitter experience had shown their necessity. The sector for tank attack was to be carefully chosen to comply with the powers and limitations of the tanks—this condition was neither considered nor fulfilled until the Cambrai offensive in November, 1917. Their routes of approach were to be specially prepared, as well as suitable railway trucks or barges to bring them up—despite six months' warning these preparations were not begun until the tanks arrived in August. The need for reserves of tanks was stressed—but the lesson was not even learnt by the time of Cambrai, nor indeed, until August, 1918. The combined tactics of tanks and infantry were expounded—also to be overlooked until Cambrai. In addition to shell, the tank guns were to fire case shot. It was designed but its manufacture was debarred until the commanders in France clamoured for it after the Somme. Some of the tanks were to be equipped with wireless sets; these were designed and operators trained —but General Headquarters would not allow the equipment to be sent out, and it was dispersed. The attitude and mentality prevailing at General Headquarters is illustrated by a story current at the time. A general on Haig's staff gave instructions that the tanks were to be brought to the front by a certain railway route. The technical expert in charge of the movement pointed out that this was impossible because of the loading gauge. The General retorted—'What the hell is a loading gauge?' The officer explained, and pointed out that by another route they could avoid the two tunnels that made this route impossible. But the General, still refusing to recognize the impossible, curtly said—'Then, have the tunnels widened.'

The trial of the tank on the Somme did not complete its trials. A thousand of a new model had just been ordered by the Ministry of Munitions in England. But their opponents —by which one means not the Germans but the General Staff in France—made haste to report so adversely that the War Office cancelled the order. Unfortunately for their intention, if fortunately for England, the officer in charge of the construction of tanks was a temporary soldier, Major Albert Stern, whose permanent position in the City enabled him to bear with equanimity the frowns of his temporary superiors. Disregarding the order he went straight to the War Minister, to find that the cancellation had been sent without Lloyd George's knowledge. And having satisfied himself of Lloyd George's opposition to any such foolish measure, Stern called on the Chief of the Imperial General Staff, Sir William Robertson, to intimate that he was not going to carry out the cancellation order.

Nevertheless, let it be said to the credit of those who, on the General Staff, opposed the tank, that if they had not the ingenuity to devise means of beating the Germans they were fertile in devices to beat the sponsors of the tank. Swinton, as merely a soldier, was not a difficult adversary and almost at once was ousted from his position in command of the whole tank unit in England. In July, 1917, d'Eyncourt and Stern were neatly excluded from the meetings of the committee, which now at the War Office controlled tank design and pro-duction; a committee whose three military members had not even seen a tank until a few weeks previously. The programme of building four thousand tanks for the next year's campaign was then cut down by two-thirds. And in October, under pressure from the Generals, Stern was removed from his post at the Ministry of Munitions and replaced by an Admiral who had not seen a tank at all. The General Staff would seem to have profited from contact with their French colleagues, and to have learnt that the most important point when proved wrong is to get rid of the uncomfortable prophet who has proved right. Just as Swinton was sacrificed to balance for the General Staff's folly in launching the first model into the Somme battle, so Stern seems to have been chosen to expiate the folly of throwing the next model into the swamps of Passchendaele. Instead of losing faith in their own judgment the General Staff again lost faith in the tank.

Happily, the younger regular soldiers who had taken charge of the tanks at the front had overcome their first doubts and, realizing the stupidity of Passchendaele, fought for the chance to give the tanks a fair trial. They obtained it at Cambrai in November, a battle which at last fulfilled the pattern designed in February, 1916. Although, for want of the resources wasted at Passchendaele, the victory itself was but a tinsel crown, it yielded the tanks a solid crown which none could any longer dispute. As 1917 was the year of vindication, so 1918 proved the year of triumph. Yet it is a sobering reflection that the price in lives might have been cheaper if tanks had been available in thousands instead of hundreds. The numbers manufactured under the reduced programme of 1917 sufficed to bring victory; but they could not bring back the dead. May the tank's hard childhood be an object lesson for future generations, so that if war engulfs them they may learn by the experience of others and not at their own cost.

RUMANIA

——— Front reached by Rumanian Advance
– – – Front on Nov. 29 th. 1916
········· Front in Jan. 1917

RUSSIA

AUSTRIA-
HUNGARY

• Szurduk

N

Transylvania

R. Maros

R. Prut

R. Siret

FALKENHAYN

Sibiu

ROTHER TURM
PASS

• Brasov

VULCAN
PASS

R. Danube

• Targu Jiu

R. Arges

RUMANIA

Wallachia

• Bucharest

R. Danube

R. Alt

R. Danube

Dobruja

Turtucaia

Rakhovo

Sistove

SERBIA

MACKENSEN

Black Sea

BULGARIA

© Cassell & Co. Ltd. 1970

CHAPTER VI

SCENE 5

RUMANIA SWALLOWED

RUMANIA entered the war on August 27th, 1916, and the fall of Bucharest on December 6th, 1916, marked the virtual extinction of her war effort and of the misplaced exhilaration which had greeted her entry on the side of the Allies. Less known and less studied than almost any other campaign of the world struggle, it has a special interest, and deserves far more attention than it has received, because it epitomized the Allies' fundamental weakness and the Germans' strength —the evils inherent in a co-partnership system of conducting war as opposed to the concentration of effort and economy of force which springs from a single control.

Nor is this the sum of its lessons; there are others which have a more practical value, because more easily remedied. It revealed the fallacy of numbers, and the much-abused Napoleonic saying that God is on the side of the big battalions received yet another historical contradiction from the Alexandrine principle of quality rather than quantity. Once again the blend of superior hitting power with superior mobility played havoc with an army which pinned its faith to weight of human bodies. Moreover, the swift three months' conquest of Rumania has a particular value for British study, because it was essentially a war of movement, carried out under the difficult natural conditions, topographical and climatic, for which the small British army is trained and has to be prepared.

During the preceding years of the war, public opinion in Rumania had gradually consolidated in favour of intervention on the Allies' side, and the friendly sentiments of Jonescu and Filipescu found a powerful lever in the people's desire to rescue their kinsmen in Transylvania from a foreign rule far more drastic than Alsace-Lorraine had suffered. At last, in the summer of 1916, the spectacular, but, as we now know, superficial successes of the Russian advance under Brusilov encouraged Rumania to take the decisive step—into the abyss. She might have fared better if she had declared war earlier, when Serbia was still an active force and Russia a real one. The two years of preparation had doubled the numbers of the Rumanian army, but in reality reduced its relative efficiency, for while her foes, under the pressure of hard experience, had developed their means of fire power and equipment, Rumania's isolation and the incapacity of her military leadership had combined to prevent the transformation of her army from a militia of bayonetmen into a modern force.

Her infantry had no automatic rifles, gas equipment, trench mortars, and few machine-guns—in the ten active divisions only the usual pre-war proportion of two per battalion, and of the thirteen new divisions eight had none at all. Her artillery was inadequate, and her air force negligible. She had only six weeks' supply of ammunition at the start— an explosion in the Bucharest arsenal had destroyed 9,000,000 rounds of small-arm ammunition—and her Allies failed to maintain the daily supply of three hundred tons which they had promised. And the unwieldy size of her divisions, added to the indifferent quality of her corps of officers, was in itself a brake on mobile operations.

Her strategical situation was another source of weakness— her territory forming an 'L' reversed, with the bottom section, Wallachia, sandwiched between Transylvania and Bulgaria. Moreover, the length of her frontier was out of all proportion to the depth of the country, she suffered a shortage of lateral railways, and the capital was within thirty miles of the Bulgarian frontier. Further, she had in the Dobruja—on the other side of the Danube—a 'backyard' strip which offered an easy way of access.

These internal and geographical handicaps were accentuated by the divergent counsels of her Allies as to her action.

While the British General Staff favoured a southward advance against Bulgaria which might have crushed the latter between the Rumanians and the Salonika army, the Russians urged a westward advance which would, in theory, be in closer co-operation with their Bukovina advance. The political and moral advantages of a move into Transylvania led the Rumanians to adopt the second course, and bitter as the upshot was, their folly is not so certain as their critics have suggested. The Bulgarian territory offered many obstacles to an effective invasion by such a defective instrument as the Rumanian army proved, and they had ample ground to doubt the energy of Sarrail in pushing forward to meet them.

On the other hand, we now know that a more rapid invasion of Transylvania by the Rumanians would have put the Austro-Germans in a grave position, and that even with the breathing space they were unluckily given they were almost at their wits' end to scrape together forces for this new front. Rumania's fault was less in her choice of objective than in her incapacity to strike for it rapidly and forcefully.

The Rumanian advance began, on the night of August 27th-28th, with three main columns, each of about four divisions, moving in a general north-westerly direction through the Carpathian passes, the conception being to pivot on the left and wheel the right up into line facing west when the Hungarian Plain was gained. Three divisions were left to guard the Danube, and three more in the Dobruja 'back yard', whither also the Russians had promised to send one cavalry and two infantry divisions—the Rumanians' stipulation originally had been for a force of 150,000 Russians.

The slow and cautious advance of the Rumanian columns, hampered by the bad mountain roads and the Austrian destruction of bridges, but not by resistance, withheld danger from the five weak Austrian divisions which covered the frontier and enabled the Supreme Command to bring up five German and two Austrian divisions and concentrate them on the line of the River Maros ready for a counter-offensive. In fulfilment of the other half of Falkenhayn's plan, a Bulgarian force of two divisions, and two more to follow, with a German detachment and an Austrian bridging train, was placed under Mackensen to invade the Dobruja. Falkenhayn adds that preparations were made for 'the abundant equipment of Mackensen's army with such weapons, not yet known to the Rumanians, as heavy artillery, mine-throwers, gas'.

Thus, at the outset, Rumania had twenty-three divisions against seven, but within a week she would have sixteen against her, so that her chances of success turned on the rapidity of her action. While her columns were creeping westward into Transylvania, Mackensen stormed the Turtucaia bridgehead on September 5th, destroying the three Rumanian divisions which covered the Danube front, and then, with his flank secure, pressed eastwards into the Dobruja. It was a shrewd moral blow, for the automatic strategic effect was to draw away the Rumanian reserves intended to support the Transylvanian offensive, and so check its progress for want of nourishment. And the dispersion left them weak everywhere. Thus on September 18th, when Falkenhayn arrived to conduct the Austro-German offensive in Transylvania, he found the Rumanian advance almost at a standstill, and their columns widely separated over a two-hundred-mile front. One must mention that Falkenhayn had now been replaced in the Supreme Command by Hindenburg (and Ludendorff), and given this executive command as a consolation.

Falkenhayn's decision was first to concentrate against the Rumanian southern column, which had crossed the Rother Turm Pass, while using smaller forces to hold off the other columns. Even allowing for his superior information, he took bold risks and suffered anxious moments before success, as so often in war, favoured the brave. The Alpine Corps, by a fifty-mile march in three days over the mountains, turned the Rumanians' southern flank, and combined with the skilful manœuvre of the reserves in the direct attack to throw back the Rumanians from Sibiu (Hermannstadt), and force them to retreat through the mountains.

His next move was facilitated by the fact that the Rumanian Higher Command, like Napoleon's opponents, 'saw too many things at once'. They kept their Transylvanian armies inactive while diverting their reserves for an abortive attempt to force a crossing of the Danube at Rakhovo and take Mackensen in rear. This enabled Falkenhayn to concentrate against the Rumanian centre column at Brasov (Kronstadt) and by October 9th he had driven this back in turn, but he missed his greater goal of encircling and destroying it, which would have opened a clear passage into Rumania.

The mischance jeopardized the whole German plan and almost saved Rumania, for with all the passes through the mountain barrier still in their hands, her troops sturdily repulsed the Austro-German efforts to press through on their heels, and compelled them to wait for reinforcements. A prompt attempt by Falkenhayn to swing further south and force a way by the Vulkan and Szurduk passes was also stopped, and the beginning of the winter snows was on the point of blocking operations when a concentrated last-minute effort at the same point, November 11th-17th, broke through to Targu Jiu. A rapid pursuit through the Wallachian Plain hustled the Rumanians back to the line of the Alt.

It was the signal for the next move in the ably co-ordinated plan. Mackensen, leaving only a fraction to hold the northerly part of the Dobruja, withdrew the bulk of his forces westwards to Sistovo, where, on November 23rd, he forced the crossing of the Danube and automatically turned the flank of the Rumanian line on the Alt. A prompt and well-planned Rumanian counterstroke, inspired by General Presan, their new Chief of the General Staff, for a brief time threatened danger to Mackensen's force and almost enveloped its flank. But once the counterstroke was parried the converging pressure of Mackensen and Falkenhayn proved too great for the Rumanians' last desperate resistance on the line of the Argesu, and on December 6th the Austro-Germans entered Bucharest. The pursuit pressed the Rumanians and the Russians, whose action in the Dobruja had been ineffectual, rapidly back to the

Sereth-Black Sea line. The greater part of Rumania, with its wheat and oil, lay under the heel of the invader, and the Rumanian Army was crippled, while her Allies had suffered a moral setback greater than any material advantage for which they might have hoped from her intervention.

For military history this brief campaign furnished an object lesson that men do not count more than machines, but instead, that the better machine controlled by a better man —the commander—can discount the value of 'big battalions'. Weapons and training count far more than mere numbers.

CHAPTER VI

SCENE 6

THE CAPTURE OF BAGHDAD

THE entry of the British into Baghdad on March 11th, 1917, was an event which impressed the imagination of the whole world, both because of the romantic appeal of the famed city of the Arabian Nights, and because it symbolized the first streaks of dawn coming to illumine the darkness which had lain like a pall over the Allied cause throughout 1916. If the historical data that are now available dim the radiance of popular impressions, revealing that the military achievement was less striking than it appeared at the time, the moral significance and value cannot be minimized. But in justice to those who earlier fought and failed, it is well to realize the fallacy underlying this contemporary public view that the operations which led to the fall of Baghdad were as white as those which culminated in the surrender of Kut were black.

The strategy and organization of the campaign were infinitely more sound and more sure, but on the lower scale of tactical execution the record of the advance is spotted with missed opportunities, despite an overwhelming preponderance of force. While recognizing the difficulties of the country, the historian cannot but feel that a sledge-hammer was used to crush a flea—and the flea escaped being crushed. And if quality rather than quantity be the test of a feat of arms, comparison suggests that the advance and retreat of Townshend's original 6th Division, in face of superior numbers, with inadequate equipment, primitive communications, and utterly isolated in the heart of an enemy country, forged an intrinsically finer link in the chain of British military history.

Credit for the 1917 success is due, above all, to the strategical direction, and to the ability and energy of those who put the organization of supplies and transport on a sound and

PERSIA

R.Diyala

Baghdad
Diyala
Ctesiphon
'Aziziya

Frontier

N

SHUMRAN BEND
Sanniyat

Kut al Imara

Sheik
Sa'ad

Al Hillah

SHATT AL HAI

'Amara

R.Tigris

R.Karun

As Samawah

R.Euphrates

Al Qurnah

Basra

SHATT AL 'ARAB

Mohammerah

MESOPOTAMIA

0   40   80
Miles

PERSIAN
GULF

© Cassell & Co. Ltd. 1970

efficient basis. These assets, moreover, sufficed to attain the military goal, without any further uneconomic drain on the forces in the more vital theatres of war. The general direction was now transferred to Whitehall. After the surrender of Townshend at Kut—despite the gallant but costly efforts to relieve him—the Chief of the Imperial General Staff, Sir William Robertson, was emphatically in favour of a defensive strategy in Mesopotamia. He inclined to adopt a withdrawal to Amara as the simplest and cheapest way of safeguarding the oilfields, and of commanding the two river arteries—the Tigris and Euphrates. But the new commander, Maude, who had been Robertson's own choice, maintained, after examination, that the advanced position at Kut was both militarily secure and politically wise. He was supported by Duff and Monro, the successive Commanders-in-Chief in India, and Robertson gave way, accepting the judgment of the man on the spot. There is profound psychological interest in studying how the strong personality of Maude and the military results which, step by step, he obtained, combined to change this defensive policy, almost imperceptibly, into a fresh offensive policy. The mirage of Russian co-operation had also an influence, for, beginning as a mere supplementary aid to a Russian offensive, the advance became an all-British achievement.

The whole summer and autumn of 1916 were devoted to thorough re-organization and preparation, initiated by Lake, but greatly expanded and intensified by his successor, Maude. He strove to ameliorate the condition of the troops, to improve both their health and training, to develop the precarious lines of communication, and to amass a large reserve of supplies and ammunition. Thus Maude ably established a secure base for his subsequent and sustained offensive, fulfilling Napoleon's maxim. The design of his plan of operations was equally admirable, blending boldness and circumspection. A study of his orders, both initial and during operations, shows that the lack of decisiveness cannot be charged to his want of energy. Where he tended to err was in excessive centralization and secrecy. If the latter is usually a fault on the right side, it seems here to have been partly responsible for the pause at Aziziyah, on the advance to Baghdad. For his Inspector-General of communications had to complain that even he had not been given warning that such a move was intended, and thus he had made no special preparations in readiness.

This 'imperceptible' offensive began on December 12th, 1916, the first step in a series of well thought-out trench 'nibbles', methodical and deliberate, on the west bank of the Tigris. When it began, Maude faced the Turkish trenches at a right angle to the Tigris, and gradually brought his left shoulder up, pivoting on the river, and at the same time extending his front further and further upstream. At last by February 22nd, 1917, he had cleared the west bank, his extended line facing the main Turkish forces on the other bank, from Sannaiyat to the Shumran bend above Kut. Thus the Turks had not merely to guard against a direct attack from the south upon their fortified position at Sannaiyat, but against a cross-river blow from the west, which might cut their communications. The length of this patient siege-warfare process was not merely due to the intricacy of the defences or the stubborn resistance of the weak Turkish detachments on the west bank. Robertson had no taste for further adventures, and his instructions from home were framed to prevent them. The historian who studies the orders and operations gains the impression that Maude's operations were contrived, consciously or unconsciously, to undermine the stability, not merely of the Turkish position, but of Robertson's instructions.

The outcome of these deliberate and economical operations was that by the third week in February Maude was able, and admirably placed, to play for a bigger stake. His plan was to pin the Turks' left at Sannaiyat while he sprang at their communications, by forcing the river crossing at the Shumran bend—where the right flank ended and their line of retreat prolonged their line of battle. Wisely he realized that a mere feint at Sannaiyat was useless and that a real simultaneous menace to both extremities was essential if the Turkish force was to be held while it was being cut off. Unhappily his purpose was not fulfilled. Splendid as was the gallantry of the troops at the Shumran crossing, the difficulty of the task made progress slow, and the Sannaiyat attack could not pin the defenders long enough.

Even so, the Turks were placed in such peril that, as they confess, 'only the slowness of the enemy' saved them from disaster. The main cause was the tardy and feeble action of the cavalry in pursuit—partly due to Maude's too strict control, partly to the cavalry commander's want of energy and initiative, and partly to the inherent vulnerability of cavalry under modern conditions. On February 24th, when there was a splendid opportunity of turning retreat into rout, the cavalry division broke off to go back to bivouac at 7 p.m., after a mere twenty-three casualties. And on subsequent days they were no more effective. The excuses offered are the need to water and the obstacle of modern firearms, and their admission rather accentuates than impairs the lesson as to the restricted modern value of cavalry—even in Asia. Only the daring pursuit of the naval flotilla disturbed the Turks' orderly retreat—acting on the river as a few cross-country armoured cars might have done on land.

The strategic victory had at least won Maude sanction for an attempt to gain Baghdad, and on March 5th his advance from Aziziyah began. When a check came at the line of the Diyala, Maude switched the cavalry division and 7th Corps to the west bank, for an outflanking move direct on Baghdad. More mistakes enabled the Turks to hold up this menace, but realizing their hopeless inferiority of strength and the inevitable end, against two powerful converging advances, they gave up Baghdad on the night of March 10th, and retired northward up the river. Next afternoon Maude entered the city, and another name was added to the roll of Baghdad's innumerable conquerors. For the prestige of Britain and the morale of all the Allies the capture was an

invaluable stimulant worth the immediate effort, if not the
sum of the efforts which had gone to fill the debit side of the
victors' balance sheet.

CHAPTER VI

SCENE 7

THE BATTLE OF BLIND MAN'S BUFF— JUTLAND

ONLY once during over four years of war did the Grand Fleet of Britain and the High Seas Fleet of Germany meet. It would be more exact to say that they 'hailed each other in passing'—with a hail that was awe-inspiring but leaving an impression that was merely pen-inspiring. No battle in all history has spilt so much—ink. On the afternoon of May 31st, 1916, the fleet that had been built to dispute the mastery of the sea stumbled into the fleet that had held it for centuries. In the early evening these two fleets, the greatest the world had seen, groped towards each other, touched, broke away, touched again and broke away again. Then darkness fell between them. And when the 'glorious First of June' dawned a sorely puzzled Grand Fleet paraded on an empty sea.

A fundamental difference between the higher naval and military leadership in the World War was that the Admirals would not give battle unless sure of an initial advantage, and perhaps not then, whereas the Generals were usually ready to take the offensive whatever the disadvantages. In this attitude the Admirals were true to their art, the Generals were not. The sole reason for employing men who have made war their profession is the presumption that by training they have acquired a mastery of their art. Anyone with sufficient authority or inspiration can lead or push men to battle, especially if he is furnished with technically trained assistants who can help him to regulate the marshalling of the forces in movement and fire. For this shepherding of sheep to the slaughter, perhaps artful but essentially inartistic, a practised demagogue would have a definite superiority over the tongue-tied professional warrior. But the custom of employing

Orkney Islands

NORWAY

MIDNIGHT — GRAND FLEET — NOON

MIDNIGHT — 2 ND. BATTLE SQUADRON

G.F. RENDEZVOUS

6 P.M.

BATTLE AREA
6 P.M.

NOON

BATTLE CRUISER FLEET AND 5 TH.B.S.

B.C.F. RENDEZVOUS
BEFORE TURNING
NORTH TO MEET
GRAND FLEET

MIDNIGHT

Edinburgh

NOON

GERMAN FLEET

DENMARK

HORNS
REEF

N

Heligoland — 7 A.M.

Kaiser
Wilhelm
Canal

Hull

R. Ems

Wilhelmshaven

| Approach of Rival Fleets | Swept Channels | 0 ... 50 ... 100 |

Miles

JUTLAND

Deployment of British Battle Fleet and first retirement of German Fleet

KING GEORGE
I.D. 6.26

K.G. 6.26

K.G. 6.35

IRON DUKE 6.15 P.M.

I.D. 6.35

I.D. 6 45

K.G. 6.45

6.26

1st. & 2nd. BATTLE CRUISERS

6.35 INVINCIBLE (Sunk)

5 TH. BATTLE
SQUADRON

6.26 LION 6.15 P.M.

6.45

6.15

N

LUTZOW (Disabled)

KÖNIG 6.35

F.D.G. 6.35

BATTLE CRUISERS

6.45

LUTZOW

6.45

F.D.G. 6.45

6.45 BATTLE FLEET

FRIEDRICH
DER GROSSE

6.45

| 0 1 2 3 4 5 |

Miles

© Cassell & Co. Ltd. 1970

a professional is based on the idea that through art he will be able to obtain more profit at less cost.

Only one consideration should override a commander's fidelity to the fundamental truths which govern his art, and that is national expediency. It is for the Government, and not for its employee, to decide whether the needs of policy compel a sacrifice of art and the consequent sacrifice of lives. Curiously, however, in the World War the Generals were so full of the lust of battle that they voluntarily sacrificed art, and repeatedly sought battle at a disadvantage against the wishes of a Government reluctantly dragged in their wake. The Admirals, in contrast, were so faithful to their art that they sometimes ignored or evaded the express wish of the Government for battle even without an assured advantage. If their sense of reality was refreshing, it tended to throw a heavier burden of expense on the armies, although it is fair to point out that this might not have occurred if the Generals had not been so extravagantly eager to shoulder it.

Perhaps one explanation of the difference was that the Admirals exercised their command in the forefront of the battle and the Generals from headquarters far in rear. This does not imply that the difference was merely a matter of the physical courage required, for some Generals were as ready to risk their own lives as their men's, while others undoubtedly gained moral courage through physical remoteness. But, undoubtedly, imagination and sense of reality are quickened by personal contact with the situation; a commander so placed is better able to appreciate where the advantage lies and when it fades; quicker, also, to recognize the impossible.

It would be natural to expect as a result of this difference that sailors would have a bias towards tactics, soldiers towards strategy. Actually, the reverse occurred. The explanation of the paradox would seem to lie in the different experience of peace training, wherein the soldier serves in small garrisons and exercises in cramped areas, while the sailor traverses the wide oceans and learns navigation as the staple of his craft. For him, geography precedes gunnery.

From the outbreak of war British naval strategy was governed, rightly, by the appreciation of the fact that maintenance of sea supremacy was even more vital than defeat of the German fleet. Instantaneously, that sea supremacy had come into force and upon it was based the whole war effort of Britain, and her Allies, because upon it depended the very existence of Britain. Churchill has epitomized the issue in a graphic phrase—'Jellicoe was the only man on either side who could lose the war in an afternoon.' Hence the aim and desire to defeat the German fleet was always subsidiary. If it could be achieved it might do much to hasten the victory of the Allies. It might even prevent their defeat. The collapse of Russia as well as the near starvation of Britain by the U-boats may well be traced to the inability of the British navy to crush the German fleet. But if, in trying to defeat the German fleet, the British lost so heavily as to lose its strategic superiority national defeat would be certain.

The aim of German naval strategy since August, 1914, had been to avoid the risk of a decisive action until the British fleet was so weakened that the prospect of success veered from gloomy to fair. Mines and torpedoes were the means on which the Germans relied to achieve this preliminary weakening. And it was the fear of such under-water weapons, the possibility that by trap or chance they might dramatically alter the balance of strength, which infused an extra degree of caution into the British strategy of precaution. In a letter of prophetic foresight on October 14th, 1914, Jellicoe had warned the Admiralty that if a chance of battle came he would regard the turning away of the German battle fleet as a sign that it was trying to lure him into such a trap, where mines and submarines lay in wait; that he would refuse to be drawn into it and, instead, would move quickly to a flank. In other words, he would sidestep to avoid the chance of being surprised, and so not only disarm the enemy of his best potential weapon, but possibly throw him off his balance. The calculation is an indication of how thoroughly Jellicoe had thought out his theory of war, up to a point.

Both the German and the British strategic keynotes were well attuned to the reality of their respective conditions; the question remains whether more energy and subtlety could have been shown in executing them. The situation in May, 1916, after nearly two years of war, was that the British fleet was still waiting for a favourable chance of battle and the German fleet was further away from the attainment of its preliminary aim of weakening the British. Despite a few losses due to mines and torpedoes, the British fleet was proportionately much stronger than at the beginning. In the coming clash it was to bring thirty-seven capital ships (battleships and battle cruisers) of the Dreadnought type against the German twenty-three, and in gun power the margin was still greater, 168 guns of 13.5-15 inch calibre and 104 of 12 inch could be brought against 176 German guns of only 12 inch calibre. It is true that the German fleet also included six pre-Dreadnought battleships, but in a fleet action these would be little better than a target for the heavier guns of the British. Moreover, by their presence they reduced the already slower German fleet to a still more marked inferiority in speed. The British had also a comfortable superiority in cruisers and destroyers—eight armoured and twenty-six light cruisers, against eleven of the last; eighty destroyers against sixty-three.

Another advantage gained since the outbreak of war was in the sphere of knowledge. For the British had not only gained from occasional contacts a clearer idea of the capacity of the enemy's weapons, but had discovered his signal-code. In August, 1914, the German light cruiser *Magdeburg* had been sunk in the Baltic, and clasped in the arms of a drowned under-officer the Russians had found the cipher and signal books of the German navy, as well as their squared maps of the North Sea. These were sent to London and thereafter, by intercepting the enemy's enciphered wireless messages, the British Intelligence was able to obtain advance information of many of the enemy's movements. Although suspicion led the enemy to make variations in their codes and maps, their efforts to seal up the leakage of information were offset by the development of directional wireless as a means of locating the position of ships. And this was the source of the one naval battle of the war—Jutland.

In January, 1916, a new commander was appointed to the German High Seas Fleet. This was Admiral Scheer, the nominee of Admiral von Tirpitz, and an advocate of a more aggressive war policy. The pressure of the British blockade and the relaxation of the German submarine blockade— under pressure from President Wilson—combined to provide an urge to action. And a rumoured division of the British fleet, to protect the coast from raids, came as an encouragement to action. In mid May Scheer crystallized his plan. A cruiser raid on Sunderland was intended to draw out part of the British fleet to counter it, and lying in wait for this detachment would be the German submarines with the High Seas Fleet behind, ready to pounce. The submarines were duly despatched, but bad weather prevented reconnaissance by the German airships. Without this safeguard Scheer would not move, and thus the submarines exhausted their sea-going endurance. On May 30th, Scheer decided to abandon his plan, and the use of his submarines, for an alternative. This was to send the Scouting Force, of battle and light cruisers, under Admiral Hipper, to demonstrate off the Norwegian coast, while he followed, out of sight. He calculated that the danger to the British cruiser patrol and shipping might draw part of the British fleet to the spot and give him a chance to destroy it. Hipper steamed north early in the morning of the 31st, with Scheer fifty miles astern.

Already, the previous evening, the impending departure of the Germans, although not their purpose, was known to the British Admiralty, and the Grand Fleet was ordered to sea. Jellicoe with the main section of the fleet sailed eastward by 10.30 p.m. for a rendezvous some fifty miles off the Norwegian coast, being joined on the way by Jerram's squadron from Invergordon. Beatty with the battle cruisers, reinforced by four of the latest *Queen Elizabeth* type battleships, sailed simultaneously from Rosyth (near Edinburgh) with orders from Jellicoe to reach by 2 p.m. on the 31st a spot sixty-nine miles south-south-east of the main rendezvous. From this, if no enemy had yet been sighted, Jellicoe would sweep southwards towards Heligoland Bight, while Beatty was ordered to close to within sight of him.

Beatty reached his own rendezvous at the assigned hour and was just turning north towards Jellicoe when the *Galatea*, one of his screen of light cruisers, sighted a stray merchant steamer and, instead of turning with the rest, continued east-south-east to examine her. This was the first of many jests of fate. For simultaneously a German light cruiser, screening Hipper's western flank, also sighted the steamer and decided to investigate. Within a few moments the two unsuspecting rivals had sighted each other—and warned their respective superiors. Thereby the strange steamer not only brought on the Battle of Jutland, but probably cost the British a decisive victory. For if this chance meeting had not occurred, the two forces might not have met until they were further north—when the Germans would have been further from shelter and nearer the jaws of Jellicoe.

Minutes were now to be momentous. Controversy as to their use has been acrid, but much of the criticism on both sides seems pedantic—more apt for the proverbial armchairs, although here occupied by professional sailors, than for the vague conditions in the North Sea on the afternoon of May 31st, 1916.

At 2.20 p.m. the *Galatea* signalled 'Enemy in sight. Two cruisers probably hostile bearing south-east, course unknown'. The sound of guns from the distant *Galatea* had just been heard when at 2.32 p.m. Beatty turned again south-eastwards to cut off the retreat of the enemy cruisers. Unfortunately, his signal to turn, made by flags, was not read owing to smoke and want of wind by Evan-Thomas's squadron of battleships which had been following five miles astern. In consequence Evan-Thomas did not turn until 2.40 p.m. and thereby found himself ten miles behind Beatty's battle cruisers.

It has been argued that the signal should have been made, more simply and effectively, by searchlight flashes—an argument that seems irrefutable. It has been argued that Evan-Thomas should have turned on his own initiative, as he must have seen Beatty turning—an argument which seems highly disputable in view of his general orders and his ignorance of Beatty's tactical intentions. On the other side, it has been contended, first, that Beatty himself should have acted earlier; second, that he should also have given Evan-Thomas the chance to close up to him—either by continuing on his northward course while Evan-Thomas was turning or, still better, by swinging towards him before turning. But this ideal perhaps unduly discounts the conditions—physical and psychological. Both Jellicoe and Beatty had been steaming leisurely, with hope of an encounter waning as the hours passed, and all the more because the Admiralty had signalled that, by directional wireless, the enemy fleet had been located still at its anchorage. Yet another unlucky mishap.

If fair account be taken of the hazy situation, Beatty would seem to have taken his decision with all reasonable promptness. As for the decision itself he had every reason, from past experience, to fear that the German cruisers would give him the slip, and little reason to suspect that they masked a greater force. At the most he might meet the German battle cruisers, and they were only five in all, while he had six. If his temperament was impetuous rather than calculating, both past experience and the general strategic situation would here seem to justify his action in forfeiting extra strength to gain extra minutes.

Finding that the enemy cruisers were apparently following the *Galatea* north-westwards, Beatty himself gradually changed his course until he was steaming north-east. Thereby he and Hipper were converging towards each other and about 3.30 p.m. they came in sight of each other. Hipper promptly turned to fall back towards his own battle fleet and Beatty duly turned on a parallel course. At 3.45 p.m. both sides opened fire at a range of about nine miles. Owing to bad light the British miscalculated the range, and so not only lost the advantage that their guns outranged the Germans, but made poor shooting. In contrast, the British were silhouetted against the western sky. Just after 4 p.m. catastrophe burst upon the British. A shell from the *Lutzow*, Hipper's flagship, plunged into the midship turret of the *Lion*, Beatty's flagship. With both legs shattered, Major Harvey of the marines managed before he died to call down the voice tube the order to flood the magazines—and thereby saved the ship from being blown up. But the *Indefatigable*, hit by a salvo of three shells from the *Von der Tann*, dropped out of the line and, hit again, turned over and sank with a thousand men. Fortunately, at this critical moment, Evan-Thomas, by cutting the corners, had come within range, and his accurate fire disturbed the accuracy of the Germans'—although the poor quality of the British shells, which burst without penetrating their armour, saved the Germans from vital injury. And at 4.26 p.m. they scored afresh, when the battle cruiser *Queen Mary*, hit by a salvo, blew up and sank with her crew of twelve hundred—her grave and their grave marked by a gigantic pall of smoke eight hundred feet high. Thus Beatty was reduced from six ships to four, against five. About this time also, the *Princess Royal* vanished momentarily in an ominous cloud of smoke and spray, and a signalman on the *Lion* laconically reported, 'Princess Royal blown up, sir.' Whereupon Beatty as curtly said to his flag captain—'Chatfield, there seems to be something wrong with our damned ships to-day. Turn two points to port'—nearer the enemy.

It was a tribute to his cool nerve, although the crisis had really passed with the entry of Evan-Thomas into the fight. That entry marred the trap which Scheer was planning for Beatty. For instead of steering to catch Beatty between the two jaws formed by Hipper and his own main fleet, Scheer was forced to steam direct to Hipper's aid.

At 4.33 p.m. Goodenough's light cruiser squadron, two miles ahead of the *Lion*, sighted battleships to the south-east, and signalled the news to Beatty. Goodenough boldly held to his course until he could definitely identify the High Seas Fleet and then sent a wireless message direct to Jellicoe—who had already quickened his pace towards Beatty.

Beatty also held his course until he had sighted Scheer's battleships and then, at 4.40 p.m., turned about to run north towards Jellicoe. The turn was well timed to let Beatty's force, now the bait, be seen by Scheer without letting it come within range of Scheer's guns. But the signal to turn, again made by flags, was again missed by Evan-Thomas, who held to his southward course until he had passed Beatty running north. Thereby he came under fire from Scheer's leading battleships, and became both the bait to Scheer and the shield to Beatty during the run north.

Danger during Beatty's turn, which was made in succession round a fixed point, was partly averted by the disconcerting and gallant attacks of the British destroyers. Two had been crippled and, drifting helplessly between the oncoming lines of battleships, with glorious impudence fired their last torpedoes before they were riven by shells. German destroyers chivalrously stopped to pick up the survivors.

Meantime the two great fleets were rushing towards each other, Scheer in ignorance, Jellicoe in knowledge of his enemy's approach—but not of his exact course. But upon such detailed knowledge Jellicoe's own dispositions must depend. Unfortunately the haze over the North Sea was mental as well as physical. Beatty, leading the run north, had lost touch with Scheer's fleet and even with Hipper's, which was steaming roughly parallel to him in the mist. And although Evan-Thomas was still in touch with Scheer he sent no reports. The only messages Jellicoe received came at the very start of the retirement, four from Goodenough and one from Beatty, whose wireless had been shot away—so that he had to transmit the message through a third ship. But the importance of this lack of information of the enemy can be, and has been, exaggerated. For the German fleet did not vary its course and the real trouble came from British errors in reckoning their own position—on the part of both

Jellicoe's and Beatty's flagships. The result was that when the two came in sight of each other the *Lion* was found to be some seven miles further west than Jellicoe had anticipated. And, as a corollary, the enemy also were sighted on the starboard bow, i.e., on Jellicoe's right front instead of straight ahead. More frequent reports of the position of Beatty's fleet might have provided, through averaging, a more accurate reckoning.

Jellicoe was advancing south in a compact mass of six parallel columns, like a six-pronged comb, four miles wide from flank to flank. This is not a fighting formation, for only a minimum of the total guns would be able to fire, forward, if an enemy was met. To deliver the maximum fire the ships must bring their broadsides to bear, and must form into line of battle. If the enemy were found directly ahead each column had only to wheel to the right or left for the whole fleet to be in line, firing their broadsides at the enemy. The Grand Fleet only required four minutes to make this deployment, but it required that the enemy should be in exactly the right position. An alternative method, if the enemy lay to a flank, was for one of the columns—normally a wing column—to steam on while the remainder wheeled to follow in its wake. In this case the fleet would still be able to form a single chain within four minutes, but would take much longer to straighten their line.

Let us now see what actually happened. Jellicoe had despatched the 3rd Battle Cruiser Squadron (Hood) to support Beatty, but owing to the error in reckoning already mentioned it moved too far eastward. Thereby it became unintentionally the upper jaw of a trap into which the unconscious Hipper was putting his head. Hipper meantime was still running parallel to, but out of sight of, Beatty. At 5.40 p.m. Hipper suddenly sighted Beatty afresh—to the westward—and coming under fire, swerved more to the eastward. Then he heard Hood's guns opening fire on his light cruisers. Alarmed, he turned away to the south-east at 6.34 p.m., only to see his light cruisers attacked by four of Hood's destroyers, which he imagined to be the forerunners of Jellicoe's main fleet. So he swerved again, to the south-west.

Meantime, Jellicoe and Beatty had not sighted each other until just before 6 p.m., although their advanced cruisers had made visual contact at 5.30 p.m., when about five miles apart. At 6.1 p.m. Jellicoe flashed the question—'Where is the enemy's battlefleet?' No answer came. Beatty was busily intent on his own 'disappearing' opponent, Hipper—following him on a long outer curve which, incidentally, was carrying Beatty across Jellicoe's front. At 6.10 p.m. Jellicoe repeated his question and four minutes later Beatty, almost simultaneously with Evan-Thomas, reported the enemy's bearing. The two reports enabled Jellicoe to judge Scheer's rough position, although not the course he was steering—which, actually, was north-westward in Hipper's wake.

Within a minute of Beatty's report Jellicoe had made his decision and given the order to deploy—on his left wing. Two minutes later his right wing opened fire, as it was wheeling to the left. It has been argued that he should have deployed earlier; but this would have meant acting on uncertain information, and the risk of putting himself in an unfavourable position. It has been argued that he should have deployed on his right; but this would have meant the risk that the enemy crossed the head of his line before he could cross theirs, and the certainty that until the line was straightened out—twenty-two minutes later—only a part, if a growing part, of his fleet could fire. It has been argued, by Churchill, that he might have deployed on one of the centre divisions and thereby have saved seven minutes, besides gaining the advantage of deploying within closer, yet not too close, reach to the oncoming foe. This, however, was a manœuvre rather more complex and less practised, and would at least have meant that the fire of the left fork of the tail was temporarily masked.

Jellicoe's actual deployment ensured that he would have time to cross the head of the enemy's line—the historic and deadly manœuvre of 'crossing the T'—and also that none of his battleships would have their fire masked by others while the chain was straightening. Nor does there seem much actual substance in the criticism that a chance was lost by deploying further away from the enemy. Rather was it gained. For Scheer had no intention of fighting the Grand Fleet unless at an advantage.

Thus he no sooner saw that Jellicoe's line—obscured for a time by the smoke of the cruiser action in the intervening space—was likely to 'cross the T' than he made, at 6.30 p.m., an instant turn about. This was a deft emergency manœuvre whereby each ship, beginning from the rear, began to turn in almost simultaneous succession; it enabled the whole line to slip out of range in the minimum time. His precipitancy was due to the fact that he mistook Hood's battle cruisers for Jellicoe's leading battleships, and so thought the British manœuvre was further advanced than in reality. His mistake was to his opponent's disadvantage. For Jellicoe had signalled at 6.29 p.m. for his line to turn south-south-east by sub-divisions, in order to get closer to the enemy, but had cancelled the order on finding that his tail had not yet straightened out. Nor had it done so when Scheer made his 'somersault' turn, under cover of a torpedo attack and a smoke screen. This hid Scheer's retirement for the few minutes before he was swallowed up in the mist. Although several of his leading battleships had suffered heavy hits, the only complete loss had been one of Hipper's light cruisers, the *Wiesbaden*. And, before disappearing, Hipper had destroyed another British battle-cruiser, the *Invincible*, and one armoured cruiser, and had left a second sinking.

But the potentially vital fact in Scheer's retirement was that he had turned westward—away from his own harbours. If he had sighted the British battlefleet on his flank, as would have happened if Jellicoe had deployed in any other way, the natural course for Scheer would have been, not to turn about, but to turn right—and so retire towards his own harbours. Thus the best justification for Jellicoe's choice is that it gave him the opportunity to cut off Scheer's path of retreat. It also placed Scheer against the western sky.

This opportunity Jellicoe promptly exploited. To give direct chase to Scheer, when his own line was already six miles astern of Scheer, and only two hours' daylight remained, was a move that promised little. It would also have exposed the battlefleet to the very risk of running into mines dropped and torpedoes fired by the enemy, which Jellicoe was intent to avoid.

Instead, at 6.44 p.m. he ordered each division to turn south-east—so that they were once more in six columns echeloned back like a staircase from left to right. In the next quarter of an hour he made two more partial turns. The effect was to bring him round in a gradual curve between the unseen Germans and their line of retreat, while edging closer to them. Only the coming darkness and the increasing mist threatened the advantage gained by his skilful manœuvre. One criticism, however, appears reasonable—that, either on Beatty's initiative or Jellicoe's orders, the Battle Cruiser Fleet, whose essential rôle was that of 'feelers' for the battlefleet, might have swung round more sharply and sought to keep touch with the enemy. Actually, the battle cruisers were further away than the battlefleet from the enemy.

The enemy, however, was about to make touch himself—to his own danger. Having slipped out of one trap he almost slipped into another, created mainly by his own miscalculation. For, after steaming west for about twenty minutes, Scheer suddenly reversed his direction and steamed east again—to appear out of the mist at about the same point as before. He claimed in his subsequent despatch that his idea was to strike a second blow so as to keep the initiative, and maintain German prestige. The claim is at his own expense, for no good tactician would steam into the middle of the superior British fleet for such a purpose. The logical hypothesis is that he expected to cross the tail of the British fleet, thereby gaining the chance to punish part of it and regaining his path home. For, as already mentioned, he had mistaken Hood's squadron for the van of the battlefleet and so he overestimated the distance that the battlefleet had moved. Hence, when Scheer appeared out of the mist at 7.10 p.m. he was opposite the centre of the 'stepped' British line.

Its rear squadron, being nearest, opened fire first—at a range of only about five miles. Within the next few minutes the greater part of the British fleet joined in. But with a perhaps excessive fear of partial exposure, Jellicoe ordered his rear squadrons to form astern of him—in non-technical language, to wheel eastward and follow in his wake. Thereby he drew them further away from the enemy. And at this moment Scheer had also decided to go away. Indeed, he was in such a hurry to get out of Jellicoe's jaws that he not only performed a fresh 'somersault' manœuvre, less neat than before, under cover of smoke screens and destroyer attacks, but also launched his battle cruisers in a 'death ride'.

The destroyers proved the most effective of these agents of his salvation, for seeing their torpedoes loosed, at long range, Jellicoe swung his ships away by two quick turns of two points each (22.5 deg. in all). This turn away was a long-practised method which the majority opinion in the navy approved as the best expedient, and only a minority opposed on the score that the torpedo danger was overrated, and that its adoption tended to abnegate the offensive value of the battleship. A decision between these opinions is difficult. One can only draw the logical conclusion that if the precaution was essential, it was a confession of the weakness of the battleship, and of the ease with which its offensive movements could be paralysed by an infinitely less expensive instrument of war. At Jutland the justification for the precaution is that only one British battleship was hit by a torpedo, and the justification for the minority opinion is that this battleship was so little affected that it kept its place in the line.

As a means of freeing the German fleet the destroyer attack was not only the most effective but the cheapest, for only one destroyer was sunk—by a counterstroke of the British light cruisers—while the German battle cruisers suffered heavily.

The *Lutzow* was disabled before the 'death ride' began, and the other four were hit repeatedly in the few minutes before a signal of recall from Scheer reprieved them.

The tactical effect of the destroyer attack was that while the German fleet was going west the British fleet was going the opposite way. A quarter of an hour later, satisfied that the torpedo attack had spent itself, Jellicoe corrected his turn away, but continued on a course almost due south. Not until 8 p.m. did he turn west. In this delay there seems to be ground for criticism. For to maintain his tactical advantage of being across the enemy's line of retreat, it was desirable both to shepherd him away from his own coast and to keep touch with him so that he had less chance of slipping past the British mobile barrier in the dark.

By one school of criticism much emphasis has been given to the fact that after sighting the enemy again at 7.40 Beatty sent a further wireless signal to Jellicoe ten minutes later—'Submit van of battleships follow battle cruisers. We can then cut off whole of enemy's battlefleet.' But excellent as this sounds, and was its meaning, its historical value is rather diminished by the fact that, before it was decoded and handed to him, Jellicoe had already turned the battlefleet west, while Beatty was merely going south-west according to his last message. Moreover, the German fleet was already cut off from its base. Perhaps Beatty meant 'head off'—his own next order to his light cruisers, to locate the head of the enemy's line, which was now steaming south, suggests this explanation. Moreover, he succeeded in heading off the enemy on his own, for when they came under his fire about 8.23 p.m., they promptly sheered off to the westward again. And by checking their course south this encounter helped them in slipping past the British tail later.

The best, indeed the only, chance of closing with the Germans had passed in the half-hour following their 7.20 p.m. turn away. The great question that remained was whether Jellicoe could continue to bar their way during the night so that he could re-engage at dawn with a whole day's light before him, and thereby profit from his strategic advantage—now added to superior strength.

When the blanket of darkness spread across the sea about 9 p.m. it not merely accelerated the haziness of the day, but changed it to blindness. The battleships lost their advantage of range, the torpedo craft gained the advantage of coming to close range with minimum risk. And all ships would have difficulty in distinguishing friend from foe.

Jellicoe wisely rejected the hazard of a night battle, for it would have meant staking his double advantage on a pure gamble. Thus his problem was to prevent the enemy finding an open way home during the five and a half hours before daylight. There were three likely routes, each leading to a swept channel through the minefields which covered the approaches to the Heligoland Bight and the German harbours. One, on the east, was past Horn Reefs and down the Frisian coast; a second, more central, eventually led past Heligoland; the third, in the extreme south-west, was entered near the German coast and led eastward past the mouth of the Ems. The distance to this was one hundred and eighty miles, and being the furthest it was the least obvious choice. Hence Jellicoe might justly fear that an astute enemy might take it—but for one factor. This was the inferior speed of the German fleet compared with his own. If the Germans had enjoyed equal or greater speed the Ems route would have offered them more chance and scope for evading an uncertain guard during the hours of darkness. Lacking it, they were wise to take the greater immediate risk of the shorter route.

Jellicoe, however, was unwilling to uncover one completely in order to cover the others more closely. And he chose a 'beat' which certainly reconciled as far as was possible the difficulties of covering all. Indeed, it left the Germans only one good chance—that of slipping behind Jellicoe and taking the Horn Reefs passage. Hence, one would anticipate that Jellicoe would be specially sensitive to any signs of an attempt to pass astern of him.

At 9.17 p.m. Jellicoe ordered the fleet to take up night cruising stations—the battleships being closed up in three parallel columns. The course of the fleet was to be due south, and the speed seventeen knots. The destroyers were massed five miles astern, a disposition which prolonged the moving barrier, protected the rear of the battlefleet against torpedo attacks, and, above all, prevented the risks of mistaken identity in the darkness. If the battleships sighted destroyers, or the destroyers battleships, each would know that the dim shapes were those of an enemy. Beatty had already taken station with the battle cruisers ahead of and on the western, or enemy, flank of the battlefleet. The historical significance of his night position is that it made impossible any attempt of the Germans to outstrip or pass south of the British, and so might have provided a further cause for sensitive suspicion of an attempt to pass astern. The formation of the Grand Fleet might be likened metaphorically and symbolically to that of the traditional British lion, Beatty's battle cruisers and light cruisers being the nose and ears, and the destroyers—the lion's tail. The nose was to smell nothing, the ears to hear something, the tail to be twisted, but the lion as an entity to remain as majestically unmoved as those which surround Nelson's column.

One preliminary remains to be mentioned—Scheer's intention. It was simple, not subtle, and to that extent simplified the problem of parrying it. Desperation, at the morning's dire prospect, seems to have inspired it. For he took the shortest route home—by Horn Reefs—prepared to lose heavily but determined to break through. Unlike Jellicoe, he could at least feel that the luck lurking in a night encounter was more likely to be a friend than otherwise to his bold course. To enhance his prospects and safety he posted his lame battle cruisers and old battleships in rear and covered his van with destroyer and light-cruiser tentacles.

The scene was set. Would the monarchs of the seas, taking the call, clash in blind battle? Thus the anticipation. But only the tinkle of the jester's bell was heard from the darkened stage. And when light came, the stage was empty.

The first tinkle came at 9.32 p.m. when the *Lion*, Beatty's flagship, enquired by flashing-lamp of the *Princess Royal*— 'Please give me challenge and reply now in force as they have been lost.' The reply seems to have been seen, in part, by an enemy ship. For, about half an hour later, several cruisers were sighted by the *Castor*, which was leading one of the British destroyer flotillas. They took the initiative and challenged her by making part of the British secret challenge for the day. As, however, they next switched on their searchlights and opened fire, the *Castor* replied in a similar unfriendly fashion, but several of her attendant destroyers withheld their torpedoes from a natural doubt as to the true identity of the cruisers. But the effect of this mischance, and missed chance, can be exaggerated. For, from 10.20 p.m. to 11.30 p.m., the British tail was repeatedly in action with the enemy, who were trying to elbow their way through. At 10.20 p.m. they 'elbowed' Goodenough's light cruisers, but sheered off after the light cruiser *Frauenlob* had been sunk by a torpedo from the badly battered *Southampton*. In the next hour the British destroyers suffered the contusion and caused confusion. The light cruiser *Elbing* was rammed by the battleship *Posen* and left sinking, while the British destroyer *Spitfire* acted up to her name by ramming the battleship *Nassau*. She not only 'got away with' this act of impertinence, but with a long strip of *Nassau*'s plating as proof of her prowess. Once more the German fleet sheered off, but veered in afresh about 11.30 p.m. and this time broke through, although harassed by the British hornets for more than an hour at the cost of four of their number.

They had contributed much gallantry, but little intelligence. The only report of these encounters that came to Jellicoe was one from Goodenough at 10.15 p.m., and, owing to the *Southampton*'s wireless being shot away this did not reach Jellicoe until 11.38 p.m. For the light craft, hotly engaged, there was some excuse for failure to send information, although even those which were not engaged sent no word of what they saw. But Evan-Thomas's 5th Battle Squadron was also astern of the main fleet, forming an intermediate link; it was well aware of the constant attacks and its two rear battleships actually saw the leading German battleships in their wake. The *Valiant*, at 11.35 p.m., noted 'two German cruisers with at least two funnels and a crane amidships, apparently steering eastward at a high speed'. The crane identified them so unmistakably as battleships of the *Westfalen* class, that the mistake of assuming them to be cruisers would be incredible were it not fact. The *Malaya*, five minutes later, noted 'enemy big ships, three points abaft the starboard beam, steering the same way as ours'. It had evidently sighted the enemy battleships as they were making a momentary swerve in face of the destroyer attack. It noted the 'conspicuous crane' of the leading ship, and drew the correct deduction that it was 'apparently *Westfalen* class'. Neither the *Valiant* nor the *Malaya* reported what they had seen, apparently assuming that the *Barham*, their flagship ahead, had seen it likewise. How the *Barham* failed to see it has never been explained. The one clear fact is that no word from the squadron was sent to the Commander-in-Chief.

Was there, then, no information which might have quickened Jellicoe's suspicion or upon which he might have acted? Two reports reached him from the Admiralty, which had been intercepting German wireless messages. The first, giving the German location at 9 p.m., was valueless because, owing to an error, the position indicated was obviously inaccurate. This did not encourage him to accept the second —which was only too accurate. It stated that the German fleet had been ordered home at 9.14 p.m. and gave the dispositions, course and speed. But, by another fateful slip, it omitted the most significant fact contained in the several enemy messages which it summarized—that Scheer had asked for an airship reconnaissance near Horn Reefs at daylight. Here was the unmistakable scent to his bolt-hole.

This message was received at 11.5 p.m. and read, after deciphering, about 11.30 p.m. One other message reached

Jellicoe, being received at 11.30 p.m.—and so read later than the Admiralty message. It came from the light cruiser *Birmingham*, and reported that 'battle cruisers probably hostile' were in sight, steering south and well to the westward. Unfortunately, the *Birmingham* had sighted them at a moment when they had sheered away from the British torpedo attacks. If Jellicoe already distrusted the Admiralty message, upon which he took no action, it was natural that he should regard the two later reports from the *Southampton* and *Birmingham* as support to his doubts.

Yet, it is curious, and not easy to explain, that he should have been so insensitive to the definite indication of fighting astern. For, apart from these two reports, the recurrent firing was heard and the flashes seen both by his flagship and the other battleships. That this fire was obviously from light guns did not, it is true, reveal the presence of enemy battleships, but it was no proof that they were not there, for at night battleships would naturally be using their secondary armament if engaged with British light craft. More curious still is the fact that Jellicoe made only one attempt, at 10.46 p.m. to enquire the source of the firing, and the wording of his signal suggests a preconceived idea that it was merely an enemy destroyer attack. Thus, in sum, the conclusion is that while Jellicoe's lack of certain knowledge was due to the neglect of his subordinates, his lack of suspicion is the measure of his own responsibility—and the salvation of Scheer.

One more serious contact occurred before the German fleet was at last safely free. In the dim light before dawn it was sighted by Captain Stirling's 12th Destroyer Flotilla. The exception, when he should have been the rule, Stirling sent a wireless report to Jellicoe at 1.52 a.m., before he engaged the enemy and another during the action. His attack torpedoed and sank the German battleship *Pommern*, and thereby achieved more than the whole Grand Fleet had done. But his reports did not reach Jellicoe, presumably owing to a wireless failure. Thus the British battlefleet continued serenely on its course southward, and the German, on its course homeward.

When daylight came Jellicoe turned about, at 2.39 a.m., and steamed northward, expecting to see the German fleet and seeing only an empty sea. Then came another Admiralty message to say that the German fleet was close to Horn Reefs, and this time its evidence was accepted. After searching for enemy stragglers, and finding none, the Grand Fleet in turn steamed homeward. Its total loss had been three battle cruisers, three armoured cruisers and eight destroyers to the German one battleship, one battle cruiser, four light cruisers and five destroyers. In officers and men, the British had lost 6097 killed to the German 2545, and 177 prisoners to none.

Thus the one naval 'battle' of the World War was but a casual item in the long butcher's bill. Its value as a battle was in every sense negligible. To trace to it the ultimate and bloodless surrender of the German fleet two and a half years later is absurd, confounding mere sequence with causation. If Jutland did little to encourage the Germans to provoke a decisive clash at sea it did little to discourage them. They had won the first game, against the battle cruisers, and superior gunnery had yielded them honours 'above the line'; they had been outmanœuvred in the second game, with honours easy, and had scored several tricks in the third before the game had been broken off. As they could not hope to gain the rubber because of their opponent's stronger hand, the interruption left them at least a flattering sense of their own skill. As a new and untried creation the German navy inevitably suffered an inferiority complex in face of a navy which enjoyed a matchless roll of victories and the 'Nelson tradition'. Jutland had dissipated this fear of the untried in face of the known unknown.

Within twelve weeks the German fleet was to make a bolder bid to take the British at a disadvantage. Covered by airship patrols it advanced close to the English coast on August 19th with the idea of bombarding Sunderland as a bait to draw the Grand Fleet south on to a waiting ambush of submarines. Battle was again baulked by caution and an accident. One of Beatty's advanced cruisers was torpedoed and Jellicoe, suspecting instead a new-laid minefield, turned back and steamed north for two hours. When he again came south the German fleet had gone. For Scheer had received a report of a strong British force—actually the light force from Harwich —coming up from the South, and hastily assumed that this was the Grand Fleet. If so, it had not only evaded his trap but, turning the tables, threatened to cut him off. Hence he turned for home.

For the British Navy, Jutland would better not have been fought at all. However unpalatable the admission, it undoubtedly depreciated British naval prestige in the eyes of Allies and the home public more than the inspiring feats of individual gallantry and the fact of Britain's continued supremacy at sea could redeem. That supremacy was to ensure the ultimate downfall of German power to continue the war. But no victorious battle helped, as such a battle might, to shorten the gloomy and costly process of exhaustive slaughter on land. Jutland merely ensured what was already ensured without a battle, so long as the British navy maintained its passive superiority of strength.

Here was the general aspect. On the technical side, Jutland was more significant if not more productive of enthusiasm. It showed that the German standard of gunnery was far higher than complacent or patronizing opinion in England had recognized, and it tended, less fairly, to reflect unfavourably on British gunnery owing to the lapse of some, and the lack of opportunity of other, elements of the fleet. In material, Jutland showed also that the Admiralty and its technical advisers had failed to foresee or profit by experience as well as the Germans. Against the inferior armour-piercing qualities of the British shells must be set—but not offset—the fact of insufficient protection of the British ships against plunging fire, and especially against the flash from an explosion in a gun turret passing down into the magazine. This was the probable cause of the mysteriously sudden end of the *Queen Mary* and *Indefatigable*. More debatable perhaps were the results of the policy of building huge battle cruisers in which a large degree of protection was sacrificed for a small increase in speed. Speed in itself confers indirectly a high degree of protection, but essentially through diminishing the target, in the sense of making it more difficult for the enemy to hit. For effective protection in this way a diminution of size is required, not merely a diminution of armour for the sake of a few extra knots.

The tactical side of Jutland has aroused still more criticism and controversy than the technical side. Criticism of its foundation is less easy to counter than criticism of the actual direction. The naval neglect of tactical study, the absence of tactical textbooks, and the secrecy which by custom had enshrouded the meagre instructions, have ever been a source of wonder to soldiers, who know from history and experience that good and flexible tactics in an army are essentially the product of ceaseless reflection and discussion by many minds. 'La critique est la vie de la science.' Students of military history know that the attempt to keep tactics secret defeats its own end—and its own employer. There was no mystery in the tactics by which Alexander's Macedonians, the Romans, the Mongols, Gustavus's Swedes, Frederick's Prussians, Wellington's Peninsular infantry, won their repeated triumphs. Only a matchless harmony of execution through practice and understanding which gave them the advantage no rival and imitator could overtake. Secrecy leads to rigidity of tactics; open discussion and criticism, to flexibility and the well-attuned initiative of subordinates when confronted with the unexpected. The basic criticism of naval tactics during the World War period is that they undermined the basis of tactics—elasticity. Moreover, the fleet fought at Jutland as a single body, as did armies in the days before Napoleon developed the system of independent divisions. Tactically, the fleet was an armless body. Thus however skilfully Jellicoe manœuvred his fleet he could not justly hope to paralyse his

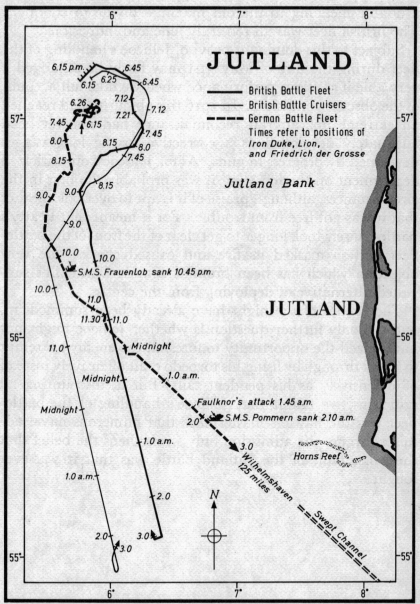

JUTLAND

— British Battle Fleet
— British Battle Cruisers
--- German Battle Fleet
Times refer to positions of
Iron Duke, Lion,
and Friedrich der Grosse

Jutland Bank

JUTLAND

6.15 p.m.
6.45
6.15
6.25
6.45
6.26
7.12
6.15
7.21
7.12
7.45
7.45
8.0
8.15
8.0
8.15
7.45
8.15
9.0
9.0
8.15
9.0
10.0
10.0
S.M.S. Frauenlob sank 10.45 p.m.
10.0
11.0
11.30
11.0
11.0
Midnight
11.0
Midnight
Midnight
1.0 a.m.
Midnight
Faulknor's attack 1.45 a.m.
2.0
S.M.S. Pommern sank 2.10 a.m.
1.0 a.m.
3.0
Horns Reef
1.0 a.m.
Wilhelmshaven
125 miles
2.0
2.0
3.0
Swept Channel
3.0

N

© Cassell & Co. Ltd. 1970

opponent's freedom of movement. And to pin an opponent is the vital prelude to a decisive manœuvre; this dual act gives a double meaning to the old maxim—'divide to conquer'. The British fleet was all too truly 'one and indivisible'.

Subject to this dominant proviso, Jellicoe's handling of the fleet during the day of May 31st may fairly be adjudged a very able if cautious performance when we take full account of the obscure conditions. In 1916 this obscurity had reached an extreme, for aircraft reconnaissance had not yet been adequately developed as a corrective to the long ranges developed by progress in guns. As for Jellicoe's oft-criticized deployment on the left wing it was probably the best in the circumstances, although praise of it is apt to overlook the fact that it was not free from trouble. For it meant that Beatty's battle cruisers took longer to get clear of the front of the battle-fleet and so masked its fire and caused checks—the very objection which has been brought against Churchill's suggested alternative of deploying from the centre.

The lessons of the night have already been summed up, and the only further question is whether Jellicoe might not have seized the opportunity to forestall the enemy's attempt to break through by using his torpedo craft offensively instead of defensively as his pendent tail. But if, discounting all criticisms, we admit that Jellicoe's handling of the battle-fleet was the flawless masterpiece that numerous naval admirers argue, the admission only strengthens the belief that the worst fault of the Jutland battle was that it was ever fought.

CHAPTER VII

1917—THE STRAIN

DESPITE incessant provocation for two years, since the *Lusitania* incident, President Wilson held to his neutral policy, and if his excess of patience angered many of his own people it was at least the means of consolidating American opinion and reconciling it as a whole to intervention in the war. Meantime he strove by speech and by the agency of Colonel House—his unofficial ambassador—to find a basis of peace on which the belligerents could agree. This effort was doomed to failure by his misunderstanding of the psychology of the warring peoples and of people at war. He was still thinking in terms of traditional warfare, between governmental policies, while the conflict had long since passed into the wider sphere of the struggle of peoples dominated by primitive instincts and chained by their own catch-phrases to the chariot wheels of Mars-mechanized.

The declaration of the unlimited submarine campaign brought convincing proof of the futility of these peace hopes and of the reality of the German intentions, and when followed by the deliberate sinking of American ships and an attempt to instigate Mexico to action against the United States, President Wilson hesitated no longer and, on April 6th, 1917, America entered the war against Germany.

Her potential force in man power and material was illimitable. But, even more unready than Britain in 1914, it must be long in exerting more than a moral influence, and Germany confidently anticipated that the submarine campaign would take decisive effect within a few months. How near her calculation came to fulfilment the record of 1917 and 1918 bears witness.

The year 1916 had closed in gloom for the Entente. The

simultaneous offensive on all fronts, planned a year before, had misfired, the French Army was at a low ebb, the Russian still lower, the Somme had failed to produce visible results in any way proportionate to its cost, and another fresh Ally had been overrun. At sea the negativeness of Jutland was a disappointment, and although Germany's first submarine campaign had been abandoned a stronger one was threatened. To offset these debits, the Entente could only show the capture of distant Baghdad and the limited Italian success at Gorizia in August, whose value, however, was mainly that of a moral fillip to Italy herself.

Among the Allied peoples and their political representatives there was a growing sense of depression. On the one hand it took the form of dissatisfaction with the conduct of the war, and, on the other, of discouragement over the prospects of a victorious conclusion to the war, and a tendency to discuss the possibilities of a peace by negotiation. The first-named tendency was the first to come to a head and was signalized in London, the political mainspring of the Allies, by the replacement of Asquith's Government on December 11th by one with Lloyd George as its chief. The order of precedence in events had a significant effect. For Lloyd George had come into power as the spokesman of a widespread demand for a more vigorous as well as more efficient prosecution of the war.

The second tendency received an impulse from the German peace move of December 12th, after the fall of Bucharest, which proposed an opening of peace discussions. This suggestion was rejected as insincere by the Allied Governments, but it afforded the opportunity for President Wilson, on whose behalf Colonel House had long been sounding the belligerent Governments as to the prospects of mediation, to invite these to define their war aims as a preliminary to practical negotiation. The German reply was evasive, the Allied replies were considered by their opponents unacceptable as a basis of discussion, and the tentative peace moves subsided. But while this wave of depression was surging on the 'home front', the Allied Commanders continued optimistic. In November

Joffre assembled, at Chantilly, a further conference of the Commanders at which it was agreed that the Germans were in great difficulties on the Western Front, and that the situation of the Allies was more favourable than it had ever been.

The fighting strength of the British Army in France had grown to be about 1,200,000 men, and was still growing. The fighting strength of the French Army had been increased by the incorporation of native troops to some 2,600,000, so that, including the Belgians, it was estimated that the Allies disposed of about 3,900,000 men against about 2,500,000 Germans.

Joffre, however, declared that the French Army could maintain its strength for one more great battle, and that thereafter it must progressively decline, as France had no longer a sufficient number of men of military age to replace losses. He therefore warned Haig that during the coming year the burden must fall more and more upon the British Army. It was also agreed that in view of these factors the relative superiority of the Allies on the Western Front would be greater in the spring of 1917 than at any time which could be foreseen with certainty. In consequence it was decided to take the earliest opportunity of pressing the advantage gained on the Somme, and to continue the process of exhausting the enemy's reserves as preparation for an effort which should be decisive. An alternative proposal was made by General Cadorna that the French and British should co-operate in a combined thrust from the Italian front against Austria with the object of knocking this weaker partner out of the war. But it was rejected by the French and British Commanders, despite Lloyd George's espousal of it at the Allied conference held in Rome in January. Their objection was that it involved a fresh diversion of strength away from the main front, where alone, they held, success could have decisive results.

An offensive towards Vienna would have had formidable difficulties to overcome, especially from the mountainous country; but in judging the objections to it the historian is compelled to note that the Franco-British strategists showed no signs of recognizing a fundamental truth of strategy—that a concentration at one place is unlikely to succeed unless an adequate distraction to the enemy's counter-concentration is provided elsewhere. In their justifiable conviction that the main effort of France and Britain must be made on the Western Front, they seem to have dismissed too lightly the possibility of helping Italy to create a distraction to their own benefit. Yet, with Russia palpably flagging, the need to develop some fresh channel of pressure had become more urgent. When Robertson dogmatically asserted that the first lesson of history was to concentrate all available force in the main theatre, and that 'any departure from this rule has invariably proved to be disastrous', he exposed his own ignorance of history. Lloyd George might well have reminded him of the effective way in which the Italian theatre had been used by Eugene, with Marlborough's support, as a lever against France in the War of the Spanish Succession; and by Napoleon Bonaparte, as a lever against Austria in the War of the First Coalition. It was a reflection on modern strategists that, with superior facilities, they treated as insuperable the obstacles of nature which their ancestors had repeatedly overcome. To turn the Italian theatre into an effective distraction in favour of the Western Allies, quality rather than quantity of aid from them was needed. The initial task of breaching the Isonzo front would have demanded the concentration there of heavy artillery from the Western Front— but with a promise of much-increased effect in proportion to their number. The subsequent advance would have depended less on weight of numbers than on providing the forces with an adequate spearhead of troops suitable for mountain fighting. In the organization of their respective forces as in the organization of their total resources, a cardinal defect of the Allies in their strategy was that they concentrated by count of numbers instead of concentrating on the most effective utilization of suitable tools.

Poverty of thought, not poverty of resources, produced the bankruptcy of the scheme drawn up at the Chantilly Conference. The military cupboard was abundantly stocked with men and munitions, but its shelves were bare of constructive ideas. The proceedings reveal only too clearly the want of any deep understanding of war and knowledge of its history. The Allied peoples were clamouring for something fresh. This instinct was true if their motives mixed. But all that the combined brains of Chantilly offered them was a skeleton swathed in a few mouldering platitudes.

The Entente plan for 1917 was soon to be complicated by changes in the command. French opinion had tired of the meagre results of Joffre's attrition strategy, and the method of the limited objective had fallen into disfavour because of the unlimited losses on the wrong side, which accompanied it without apparent gain. They contrasted the dull course of Joffre's strategy with the brilliant results gained by Mangin at Verdun, in the autumn, under Nivelle's direction, and as a result Joffre gave place to Nivelle, who promised a real break-through. His confidence so inspired Lloyd George, the new British Prime Minister, that Haig was subordinated to him for the forthcoming operations—an arrangement which violated the axiom that a general cannot direct one force while exercising executive command of another. For carrying out a plan essentially audacious, Nivelle had two further handicaps; he failed to convert several of his subordinates to the idea, and he was given less rein by the Government than his predecessor. Again, while Joffre had intimated that the British must take the chief part, Nivelle changed this policy, and in his desire to conserve the glory for France overlooked how severely the French fighting power had been strained.

Joffre's plan had been for a renewal of the Somme offensive on a widened front—the British to attack north of the Somme, including but extending beyond the old battle-ground, and the French south of it to the Oise. This attack was to open early in February and to be followed a fortnight later by a smaller French attack in Champagne, between Reims and Craonne.

The French had in mind comparatively short-distance objectives; hence, unless German resistance unexpectedly collapsed, the bulk of the British forces would subsequently be transferred to Flanders for a fresh offensive there. Analysis of the facts does not tend to support the idea that the chance of early victory for the Allies was forfeited through the abandonment of Joffre's plan. The hard frosts that came in late January would have aided its early development; but it would have been too early for any prospect of a simultaneous offensive in the other theatres; and although it might have disturbed the Germans' execution of their plan, they were better prepared to rally in rear than were the Allies to press home the advantage.

Nivelle's plan was more far reaching than Joffre's. He intended to deliver a convergent attack on both flanks of the great salient Lens-Noyon-Reims, with the French striking the main blow in Champagne immediately after the British and French attacks north and south of the Somme had attracted the enemy's attention and resources. In this 'preparatory' offensive, Nivelle's design was to avoid the old Somme battlefield and, instead, to strike on each side of it. Haig's frontage of attack would thus be reduced, and in return Nivelle wished him to take over the French front south of the Somme, as far as Roye, so as to release additional French forces for the main attack in Champagne, where Nivelle hoped to achieve a decisive break-through.

Haig was rather sceptical of such a possibility, and in favour of a later date for the offensive, but he recognized certain advantages in the new plan—especially the fact that it implied a greater effort by the French. On the other hand, he objected strongly to an extension of his front which would reduce the British forces available for his cherished idea of an offensive in Flanders. This objection produced the first crack in the Nivelle plan. To Nivelle's pressing letter of December 21st, Haig made indefinite reply, saying that he could only relieve the French if he himself obtained six additional divisions; and Nivelle, feeling that there was no time to lose, appealed through his own Government to the British. In mid January, as a result, a conference was held in London: here Haig's appeal that they should wait for the Russian and Italian attacks in May was overruled, and the date fixed for not later than April 1st. It was also settled that Haig should relieve the French south of the Somme, and he was promised two additional divisions for the purpose—after further argument he eventually received eight. Haig was instructed to carry out this agreement 'both in the letter and in the spirit'.

But the difficulties, especially those of personal feeling, had not been smoothed out. Tension between the French and British headquarters increased, the former complaining of obstruction and the latter of attempted domination. This tension was magnified by British dissatisfaction with the French railway service, and on this point Haig now made an appeal to his own Government which led to a fresh conference at Calais on February 26th. But here, to his surprise, the French seized the opportunity to raise the wider issue of a unified control of operations, and produced a scheme by which, for this purpose, the British armies would be placed under Nivelle, whose orders to them would be issued through a British chief of staff at his headquarters. To this proposal, Haig and Robertson naturally took exception, and after heated discussion a compromise was reached by which Haig agreed to act under Nivelle's direction during the forthcoming offensive, subject to the right of appeal. But the chance of a smooth-working arrangement was vitiated by the deep-rooted suspicions of the British Higher Command, and these in turn were accentuated by the way that some of Nivelle's satellites agitated for Haig's removal.

A few days later, Haig, nettled by a rather peremptory letter of instructions from Nivelle, found cause for exercising his right of appeal in the signs of a German withdrawal on the Somme front; laying a perhaps excessive emphasis on the possibility that the Germans might switch troops north and attack him in Flanders, he notified the British Government and Nivelle that he might have to reduce his share in Nivelle's offensive and postpone its execution. Nivelle not unnaturally felt that Haig was evading his obligations, so one more conference was called, in London on March 12th. Here some further safeguards were inserted in the agreement, but the discussion mainly turned on the form rather than on the substance of Nivelle's instructions, and after a personal talk between the two commanders the trouble over these niceties of phrasing was settled. Nivelle was at last free to concentrate his mind on the plan for the forthcoming offensive.

Before it could begin the Germans had dislocated it. Ludendorff's first step had been to set on foot a complete programme for the reorganization of German man power, munitions and supplies. While this was developing, he intended to stand on the defensive, hoping that the new submarine campaign would either decide the issue or pave the way for a decisive blow on land when his reserves of men and material were ready. As a 'coefficient of safety' in face of the Somme offensive, he had previously ordered a new line of defence, of great artificial strength, to be built across the chord of the arc Lens-Noyon-Reims. Early in the new year, anticipating the renewal of the Entente advance on the Somme, Ludendorff hurried on the completion of this rear line and arranged for the utter devastation of the whole area inside the arc. There was a satirical, or satyrical, aptness in the code word for this programme of destruction—'Alberich', the name of the malicious dwarf in the Nibelung Saga! The Crown Prince Rupprecht thought of resigning rather than carry out these extreme measures, but satisfied his conscience by refusing to sign the order for them. Houses were demolished, trees cut down, and even wells contaminated, while the wreckage was littered with a multitude of explosive booby-traps.

The rearward move was preceded on February 23rd by a local retirement from the awkward salient in front of Bapaume. This timely step relieved the Germans of British pressure and from the risk of interference. Although it gave the Allies a clear hint of what was in prospect they were not able to take advantage of the warning. Nivelle did not believe that the retirement would extend to his front, while Haig, who did, believed also in caution—that only a carefully mounted attack was feasible under modern conditions. The Germans evaded one such attack by another local retirement in the early hours of March 12th. Then on the 16th the main withdrawal began, the German forces marching back unhurried to the new line called by them the 'Siegfried' and by the Allies the 'Hindenburg' line. A consummate manœuvre, if unnecessarily brutal in application, it showed that Ludendorff had the moral courage to give up territory if circumstances advised it. The British, confronted with a desert, were cautiously slow in pursuit, and their preparations for an attack on this front were thrown out of gear, limiting them to the sector around Arras, where the front was unchanged.

On April 9th Allenby's Third Army opened the spring offensive at this point, taking the long-sought Vimy ridge, but failed to develop its initial success, and continued the attack too long after the resistance had hardened. This costly action was ostensibly prolonged in order to take the pressure off the French. For the French thrust between the Somme and the Oise had also been stultified by the German retirement, and the main attack on April 16th east and west of Reims was a worse fiasco with a dangerous sequel. If it was scarcely Nivelle's fault that the foundations of his strategic plan had been upset, he betrayed *la folie de grandeur* in the way he persisted in it when the conditions had vitally changed. And his tactical plan, over-elaborate and inelastic, had no compensating elements of success against an enemy who was fully forewarned. With a prolonged bombardment giving away any chance of surprise and without first drawing away the German reserves, the idea of a rapid break-through was doomed to fail. The high hopes that had been raised caused the greater reaction, and the troops were weary of being thrown against barbed wire and machine-guns to no apparent effect.

Accentuated by service grievances, mutinies occurred in the French Armies, and no less than sixteen corps were affected. The flame of revolt broke out in a regiment of the 2nd Colonial Division on May 3rd, and although momentarily extinguished soon spread, to the tune of such cries as 'We will defend the trenches, but we won't attack!' 'We are not so stupid as to march against undamaged machine-guns!' The fact that the mutinies always occurred when the troops were ordered into the line is clear proof that disgust with their leadership rather than seditious propaganda was the real cause of revolt. A significant sidelight is that cases of desertion in the French Army rose from 509 in 1914 to 21,174 in 1917. So general was the rot that, according to the Minister of War, only two divisions in the Champagne sector could be relied on fully, and in places the trenches were scarcely even guarded.

The saviour of the situation was General Pétain; and his instrument, a change of policy based on psychology. On April 28th the Government had made him Chief of the General Staff as a brake on Nivelle's reckless offensive, and on May 15th they took the wiser and more honest step of appointing him to replace Nivelle. For a month he travelled along the front by car, visiting nearly every division, summoning both officers and men to voice their complaints. Essentially patriarchal and not familiar, he inspired confidence both in his firmness and in his promises. Tours of duty in the trenches were equalized, regularity of leave ensured, rest camps improved. Within a month calm was restored—at the price of only twenty-three executions, although more than a hundred of the ringleaders were deported to the colonies.

But if the French Army was convalescent, Pétain had still to revive its fighting confidence and power. To this end he first reorganized its training and tactics on the basis that fire power should economize man power, and then aimed to try his newly sharpened blade in easy tests that should not risk blunting it again. Thus, for the rest of the year the British bore the brunt of the campaign. Their strength in France was now at its highest—sixty-four divisions, supplied with an abundance of artillery and ammunition. The strain on them, however, was increased by the failure of Russia to make any effective contribution to the pressure on Germany owing to the revolution which broke out in March. Haig decided to keep the Germans occupied by carrying out the original plan for an offensive in Belgium, but even if the principle was right the method and choice of site were opposed to all the experience of history.

The initial move was an attack on the Messines ridge in order to straighten out the Ypres salient and attract the enemy's reserves. Carried out on June 7th by the Second Army under Plumer (with Harington as Chief of Staff) it proved a model example of the 'limited' attack, in which the surprise effect of nineteen huge mines, simultaneously exploded, and supplemented by an overwhelming artillery concentration, was exploited just as far as, and no further than, the point where the German 'numbness' began to wear off.

This coup was tardily followed on July 31st by the main attack at Ypres which, hampered in execution by the heavy rain, was foredoomed by its own destruction of the intricate drainage system of the area. The British Command had persevered for two and a half years with the method of a prolonged preparatory bombardment, believing that quantity of shells was the key to success, and that, unlike all the great captains of history, they could forgo the aid of surprise. The offensive at Ypres, which was finally submerged in the swamps of Passchendaele in early November, threw into stronger relief than ever before the fact that such a bombardment blocked the advance for which it was intended to pave the way—because it made the ground impassable. The discomfiture was increased by the new German defensive method of thinning the front defences and using the men so saved for prompt local counterattacks. The defence was built up of a framework of machine-guns distributed in concrete 'pillboxes' and disposed in great depth. On the British side the profitless toll of this struggle in the mud was to some extent mitigated by better staff work when the direction of the attack was progressively handed over to Plumer's Second Army.

Three months of dreadful struggle came to an end with the British no appreciably nearer their immediate object of driving the Germans from their submarine bases in the Belgian ports, and if they had worn down the German strength they had worn down their own still more.

The 1917 campaign in the west closed, however, on a note brighter in promise if not in accomplishment. Appreciating from the first days the futility of using tanks in these Flanders swamps, the Tank Corps headquarters looked around for an area where they could try out a new and different method. They drew up a project for a large-scale raid to scour a canal-enclosed 'pocket' near Cambrai, where the rolling downland lent itself to tank movement. The basic idea was the release of a swarm of tanks without any preparatory bombardment to give warning of the attack. When their hopes at Ypres waned, the British Command adopted the scheme, but transformed it into a definite offensive with far-reaching aims, for which they had not the resources because of the drain of Ypres. It was to be carried out by Byng's Third Army with six divisions, and the date was fixed for November 20th. Led by nearly four hundred tanks, the attack came as a complete surprise, and despite minor checks achieved a penetration far deeper and at less cost than any past British offensive. But all the available troops and tanks were thrown into the first blow, and no reserves were at hand to exploit the success. The cavalry, as always on the Western Front, proved unable to carry out this rôle.

Thus the advance died away, and on November 30th the Germans launched a counter stroke against the flanks of the salient created by the British advance. In the north it was parried but in the south broke through, and a disaster was narrowly averted. But if Cambrai closed in disappointment it revealed that surprise and the tank were the combination by which the trench barrier could be unlocked. Meanwhile Pétain, after overhauling his instrument, the French Army, sought to test its readiness for 1918. In August a stroke by Guillaumat's army at Verdun recovered all the remainder of the ground lost in 1916, and in October Maistre's army flattened the south-west corner of the German front, seizing the Chemin des Dames ridge.

The Collapse of Russia. The temporary breakdown of the French fighting power was not the worst of the troubles which together crippled the Entente offensive in 1917. The collapse, first partial and then complete, of Russia was a loss which even the entry of America into the war could not possibly compensate for many months, and before the balance was restored the Western Allies were to be perilously near the brink of defeat. Russia's enormous losses, due to her defective machine but incurred in sacrifice for her Allies, had undermined the moral even more than the material endurance of her forces. Revolution broke out in March, superficially against the corrupt *entourage* of the Tsar, but with more deep-seated moral causes beneath. The Tsar was forced to abdicate and a moderate Provisional Government climbed into the saddle, but without reins. This was only a makeshift, and in May another succeeded it, more Socialist in tendency and outwardly led by Kerensky. While clamouring for a general peace and undermining discipline by a system of committee control suitable to a trade union but not to the field of battle, Kerensky imagined he could send troops against the enemy by platform appeals. Brusilov succeeded Alexeiev in the Supreme Command, and on July 1st the army gained some initial success against the Austrians, especially in the region of Stanislau, only to stop as soon as real resistance was met, and to crumble directly the Germans counterattacked. By early August the Russians had been driven out of Galicia and the Bukovina, and only policy halted the Austro-German forces on the frontiers of Russia itself. Since the departure of Hindenburg and Ludendorff in 1916, Hoffmann had been in real control of the Eastern Front; his clever combination of strategy and policy did much to complete the paralysis of Russia, and thus release German troops for use in the west.

In September the Germans took the opportunity to practise their new artillery methods, for future use in France; their surprise attack, under Hutier's command, achieved the capture of Riga with scarcely a show of opposition. Next month the Bolsheviks under Lenin overthrew the wordy Kerensky, imposed their self-constituted rule on the Russian people and sought an armistice with Germany, which was concluded in December.

The Break-Through in Italy. The defection of Russia did not end the Entente tale of woe. Each autumn, with demoralizing regularity, Germany had seized an opportunity to eat up one of the weaker Allies. In 1915 it had been Serbia's fate, in 1916 Rumania's, and now it was to be Italy's turn—or so the Germans intended. Ludendorff's decision, taken in September, was determined by the appeals of the Austrian authorities, who felt that their troops could not endure the strain of another defensive battle on the Italian frontier. In May, Cadorna had attacked once more on the Isonzo front but an Austrian counterattack in the Carso sector had retaken part of the small gains. Losses, however, were more nearly balanced than formerly. The question of Allied co-operation on the Italian front was raised afresh without result, Haig protesting strongly. Cadorna, nevertheless, initiated in August an 'eleventh battle of the Isonzo'. Capello's Second Army captured a large part of the Bainsizza plateau, north of Gorizia, but a long-sustained effort brought no further success and Cadorna was forced to break off the offensive after four weeks' struggle. But it had so strained the resistance of the debilitated Austrians that, in Ludendorff's words, 'it became necessary to decide for the attack on Italy in order to prevent the collapse of Austria-Hungary'.

Ludendorff had a difficult problem to solve, Russia had not yet capitulated, the front there was already weakly held for its extent, and the British offensive in Flanders made impossible a large withdrawal of troops from France. As he could only scrape together six German divisions, and the Austrians' quality was lower than ever, he came to the conclusion that the only chance of decisive results was to pick out a particularly weak sector which coincidently offered scope for a strategic exploitation of the break-through. This was found in the Tolmino-Caporetto sector. On October 24th, after a short bombardment the blow was launched and pushed deep down the western slopes of the mountains, imperilling the Italian forces to both south and north. On October 28th the advance reached Udine, the former Italian general headquarters, and on October 31st the Tagliamento.

Not the least significant feature of this offensive was the way it was prepared, by a moral bombardment. Propaganda had been exploited for months as a means of sapping the Italian discipline and will to resist. But its effect can be exaggerated—the most formidable propaganda, as with the French in April, was that supplied by the attrition strategy of the Italian Command, which had sickened the troops by its limited results at unlimited cost.

But the result also surprised Ludendorff, who with his slender forces had not calculated on such distant objectives as were now possible of attainment. As the direct pursuit was slowing down he belatedly tried to switch troops from the left wing to Conrad's army which flanked the north of the Venetian salient, but was foiled by the inadequacy of the railways. Even so, Cadorna, with his centre broken through, only saved his wings by a precipitate retreat to the line of the Piave, covering Venice, leaving 250,000 prisoners in the enemy's hands. The same day Cadorna was superseded in supreme command by Diaz. Italy's Allies had begun to rush reinforcements, two army corps, one British and one French, to her aid, and on November 5th their political and military chiefs arrived at Rapallo for a conference, out of which sprang the Allied Council at Versailles, and ultimately a unified command.

The invaders had outrun their transport, and the resistance of the Italians, morally braced by the emergency, succeeded in holding the Piave in face of direct assaults and strenuous efforts by Conrad to turn their left flank from the Trentino.

At the beginning of December, the British and French, who had been waiting in reserve in case of a fresh break-through, moved forward to take over vulnerable sectors, but the attack was only renewed in the north, and on December 19th it came to an end with the coming of the snows. If Caporetto seriously damaged Italy, it also purged her, and after an interval of recuperation she was to vindicate herself at Vittorio Veneto.

The Capture of Jerusalem. Once more a distant theatre of war provided the sole triumph of the Entente cause during the year—this time in Palestine. The second reverse at Gaza, in April 1917, had led to a change of command, Murray being succeeded by Allenby, who was strong enough and fortunate enough to obtain the adequate force for which Murray had asked in vain. The British Government was anxious for a spectacular success to offset the moral depression of the Nivelle failure and the decline of Russia, and the British General Staff desired to dislocate the Turks' attempt to recapture Baghdad by drawing away their reserves.

Allenby took over in July and devoted the first three months to intensive preparations for an autumn offensive, when the season would be suitable. The command was reorganized, the communications developed, and his own headquarters moved forward from Cairo to the front. By complete secrecy and ruses he deceived the Turks as to the point of attack. The defences of Gaza were bombarded from October 20th onwards, and an attack followed on November 1st to pin the enemy and draw in his reserves. Meanwhile, as a necessary preliminary to the real blow, the inland bastion of Beersheba was seized by a convergent manoeuvre on October 31st, a prelude to the decisive attack on November 6th, which broke through the enemy's weakened centre and into the plain of Philistia. Falkenhayn, now in command at Aleppo, had also been planning an offensive, but the better communications of the British decided the race, and although Falkenhayn tried to stem the tide by a counterstroke against Beersheba, the breaking of his centre compelled a general retreat. The pursuit was hampered by lack of water and of initiative. Even so, by the 14th, the Turkish forces were driven apart in two divergent groups, the port of Jaffa was taken, and Allenby wheeled his main force to the right for an advance inland on Jerusalem. He gained the narrow hill passes before the Turks could block them and, after a necessary pause to improve his communications, brought up reserves for a fresh advance, which secured Jerusalem on December 9th. By the time the winter rains set in the British had expanded and consolidated their hold on the region. As a moral success the feat was valuable, yet viewed strategically it seemed a long way round to the goal. If Turkey be pictured as a bent old man, the British, after missing their blow at his head—Constantinople —and omitting to strike at his heart—Alexandretta—had now resigned themselves to swallowing him from the feet upwards, like a python dragging its endless length across the desert. The difficult process of assimilation, however, was assisted by the spreading paralysis of the Turkish strength under the needle-pricks of Lawrence and the Arabs.

The Clearing of East Africa. The year 1917 witnessed another overseas success, the clearing of German East Africa, although not the close of the campaign. More than a year elapsed after the rebuff at Tanga before a serious attempt was made to subdue the last German stronghold on the African continent. To spare troops from the main theatres was difficult, and the solution was only made possible by the loyal co-operation of the South African Government. In February 1916, General Smuts was appointed to command the expedition and formed the plan of a drive from north to south through the difficult interior, in order to avoid the fever-rampant plain on the coast. In conjunction with this central wedge, a Belgian force under Tombeur was to advance eastwards from Lake Tanganyika, and a small British force under Northey was to strike in from Nyasaland in the south-west. The Germans under Lettow-Vorbeck were weak in numbers but handled with masterly skill, and with all the advantages of an equatorial climate, a vast and trackless region—mountainous in parts and covered with dense bush and forest—to assist them in impeding the invader. From Dar-es-Salaam on the coast to Ujiji on Lake Tanganyika ran the one real line of rail communication, across the centre of the colony. After driving the Germans back across the frontier and seizing the Kilimanjaro gap, Smuts moved direct on this railway at Morogoro, over 300 miles distant, while he despatched a force under Van Deventer in a wide sweep to the west to cut the railway further inland, and then converge on Morogoro. Lettow-Vorbeck delayed this manœuvre by a concentration against Van Deventer, but Smuts's direct advance compelled him to hurry his force back, and thus enabled Van Deventer to get astride the railway.

However, Lettow-Vorbeck evaded the attempt to cut him off and fell back in September on the Uluguru mountains to the south. The Belgians and Northey had cleared the west and the net had been drawn steadily closer, confining Lettow-Vorbeck to the south-east quarter of the colony. Early in 1917 Smuts returned to England, and Van Deventer conducted the final operations which ended with Lettow-Vorbeck avoiding envelopment to the end, slipping across the frontier into Portuguese Africa. Here he maintained a guerilla campaign throughout 1918 until the general Armistice. With an original force of only 5000, five per cent being Europeans, he had caused the employment of 130,000 enemy troops and the expenditure of £72,000,000.

The Mastering of the Submarine. The military side of 1917 is thrown into shadow by the naval, or more strictly the economic, side. The vital issue turned on the balance between Germany's submarine pressure and Britain's resistance. April was the worst month. One ship out of every four which left the British Isles never came home. The Allies lost nearly a million tons of shipping, sixty per cent of it British, and although the German navy's promise of victory by the end of the month was proved a miscalculation, it was clear that, ultimately, the continuance of such a ratio of loss must starve the civilian population and automatically prevent the maintenance of the armies. Britain, indeed, had only food enough to sustain her people for another six weeks.

The Government sought to counter the menace by the indirect means of rationing, increasing home production, and the expansion of shipbuilding; by the direct means of the system of convoys with naval escorts, and a counter-offensive against the submarine, aided by new devices to detect the presence of submarines and the use of thousands of patrol craft. The most effective countermeasure, that of penning the Germans in their bases by close-in minefields, was hindered by the British failure to obtain a real command of the North Sea, through a decisive victory. The British destroyer flotillas daringly laid thousands of mines in the channels left by the Germans through the Heligoland Bight, but their ceaseless efforts were largely foiled by the German minesweepers, which were able to work freely under the protection of the German fleet. Nevertheless these mines hindered and delayed the passage of the U-boats and increased that demoralizing nerve-strain on the U-boat crews which was, above all, the cause of the decline of the submarine campaign. Too few submarines and trained crews in proportion to the task —and too great a strain upon them—spelt ultimate collapse.

But the British crisis of the spring of 1917 was averted less by an offensive than by a defensive method. For the convoy system was the main agent of salvation. The method of patrolled areas had been continued, despite its proven futility of 1916, during the early months of 1917. As Churchill says— 'In April the great approach route to the south west of Ireland was becoming a veritable cemetery of British shipping.' And other cemeteries were only small by comparison. Besides 516,000 tons of British shipping, 336,000 tons of Allied and neutral were buried beneath the waves during April, and the direct loss of food and raw materials to the island Kingdom was augmented by the growing unwillingness of neutral shipping to take the risk of supplying such a customer. Only the 'guts' of her merchant seamen in going to sea after being several times torpedoed lay between Britain's stomach and starvation. And the blindest blunder of the British Admiralty was in opposing the introduction of the convoy system in face of the futility of their other methods to avert the close-looming disaster. At last the advocacy of younger officers was decisively reinforced by Mr. Lloyd George's intervention, and in April voyages under convoy were sanctioned as an experiment on the Gibraltar and North Sea routes. The first left Gibraltar homeward bound on May 10th. Crowned by unmistakable success, the convoys were extended to the transatlantic routes when the arrival of American flotillas under Admiral Sims increased the number of destroyers available for escorts. The loss of shipping in such convoys was reduced to a bare one per cent and when, in August, the convoys were extended to outward bound shipping the British loss fell next month below the 200,000-ton level. Meantime the offensive campaign—now reinforced by special submarine chasers, aircraft, and the new horned mines—exacted an ever-rising toll of submarines, and by the end of 1917, the menace, if not broken, was at least subdued. If the British people had to tighten their belts, and their food rationing, they were now secure against starvation.

During the early months of 1918 the number of German submarines declined as steadily as their losses rose, until in May fourteen were lost out of a hundred and twenty-five on service, while the effect of those that were operating declined disproportionately to their number. In all, the German war loss totalled one hundred and ninety-nine submarines, of which a hundred and seventy-five fell victims to the British navy. And of the various weapons the mine claimed forty-two and the depth charge thirty-one submarines. Hunted from the narrow seas, the U-boats were even shut out from the ocean during the last phase by a vast mine barrage, laid mainly by the American Navy, across the 180-mile-wide passage between Norway and the Orkney Islands. It consisted of no less than 70,000 mines, of which the British laid 13,000. This was a direct counter to the main submarine operations against the ocean-brought supplies of Great Britain.

The shorter-range operations of the small submarines from the Belgian coast were crippled by the perfected barrage across the straits of Dover, by the daring attack of Admiral Keyes's force on the night of April 22nd, 1918—which for a time blocked up the exit from Zeebrugge—and by the progressive demoralization of the U-boat crews. Yet the removal of the menace should not lead to an under estimate of its powers for the future. The 1917 campaign was launched with only a hundred and forty-eight submarines and from the most unfavourable strategic position. Great Britain lay like a huge breakwater across the sea approaches to northern Europe, and the submarines had to get outside through narrow and closely watched outlets before they could operate against the arteries of supply. And despite these handicaps they almost stopped the beat of England's heart.

The Economic Reinforcement. In restoring circulation America's first aid became a potent factor long before her military assistance. It embraced her provision of light craft to reinforce the British antisubmarine fleet, her rapidly developed construction of new mercantile ships and still more her financial aid. By July, 1917, Britain had spent over £5,000,000,000, her daily expenditure had risen to £7,000,000 and the burden of financing her Allies as well as her own efforts was straining even her resources, when America's aid came to ease the pressure. In the first months after her entry into the war the appeals for loans came as a shock to Congress. Unable from remoteness and inexperience to realize the inevitable costs of the war, a large section of the American public felt that its new associates were trying to dip their hands too freely into the capacious pockets of Uncle Sam. Thus Mr. McAdoo, the Secretary of the Treasury, could satisfy neither the Allies nor the American public, the former feeling that he was stinting them and the latter crying that he was spending the nation's money like a drunken sailor. Hence further loans were vigorously opposed in Congress. Northcliffe graphically, if perhaps hyperbolically, summed up the situation when he cabled—'If loan stops, war stops.'

Actually, up to mid July the United States had advanced £229,000,000 to the several Allies, with the restriction that this was to pay for supplies bought in the United States, while Britain in the same period had added £193,000,000 to the £900,000,000 already lent to her Allies—without such restriction. On the top of this fresh strain came the fear of having to sell securities in order to liquidate the earlier 'Morgan loan'—with consequent damage to British credit. Mr. Balfour, then Secretary for Foreign Affairs, was so alarmed that he cabled to Colonel House—'We seem on the verge of a financial disaster which would be worse than defeat in the field. If we cannot keep up exchange neither we nor our Allies can pay our dollar debts. We should be driven off the gold basis, and purchases from the U.S.A. would immediately cease and the Allies' credit would be shattered.' The danger was met by the action of the United States Treasury in continuing monthly advances, despite opposition, until a coordinated inter-allied finance council could be created; by the formation of an official purchasing commission to take over the unofficial functions formerly fulfilled by J. P. Morgan and Company on behalf of the British Government; and by sending Lord Reading to Washington as a combined political and financial representative to oil, by frankness and sympathy, the creaking machinery of demand and supply. The overwhelming success of the Liberty Loan campaign was at least an equal asset. Advances to the Allies were authorized at a maximum average monthly rate of $500,000,000. By the end of the year the problem itself was shifting its basis; for, owing to the vast needs and purchases of the American Government for its own forces, the supply of credit to the Allies began to exceed that of the supply of goods. The difficulty of the Allies was now that of obtaining the material they needed for munitions rather than of obtaining the money to pay for it.

While America's entry into the war thus secured the position of the Allies, it also conferred one great offensive benefit even before America's armies threw their weight into the scale. No longer was the grip of the naval blockade hampered by neutral quibbles, but instead America's co-operation converted it into a strangle-hold under which the enemy must soon grow limp, since military power is based on economic endurance. As a party to the war, the United States, indeed, wielded the economic weapon with a determination, regardless of the remaining neutrals, far exceeding Britain's boldest claims in the past years of controversy over neutral rights. Thus the surface blockade of Germany began to tighten coincidently with the flagging of the submarine blockade of Britain.

The Air. Another new form of action reached its crest at the same time as the submarine campaign. As the submarine was primarily an economic weapon, so was the aeroplane primarily a psychological weapon. The explosive bullet had virtually ended the Zeppelin raids in 1916, but from early in 1917 aeroplane raids on London grew in intensity until by May 1918 the air defences were so thoroughly organized that the raiders thereafter abandoned London, as a target, for Paris. If the stoicism of the civil population took much of the sting from a weapon then in its infancy, the indirect effect was serious, interrupting business and checking output in industrial centres, as well as drawing off, for defence, many aircraft from the front. In reply the British belatedly formed a small Independent Air Force, which carried out extensive raids into Germany during the closing months of the war, with marked effect on the declining morale of the 'home front'.

Propaganda. The beginning of 1918 witnessed the development and thorough organization of another psychological weapon, when Lord Northcliffe, who had been the head of the British War Mission in the United States was appointed 'Director of Propaganda in Enemy Countries', and for the first time the full scope of such a weapon was understood and exploited. Northcliffe found his best blade in President Wilson's speeches, which with idealism if not with entire realism unvaryingly distinguished between Germany's policy and the German people, and emphasized that the allied policy was to liberate all people, including the Germans, from militarism. This blade, sharpened by the armourer, Colonel House, was trenchantly wielded by Northcliffe with the aim of severing the common ties which held together the enemy nations and their rulers. But these ties were stout enough to turn any blade until they had been frayed by military pressure. In July 1917 the effect of President Wilson's speeches, acting upon war-weariness and anti-militarism in Germany, produced a parliamentary revolt and under Erzberger's management the Reichstag passed a peace resolution, which forswore territorial annexations. But the only effect was to break Bethmann-Hollweg, the unhappy rope in the tug-of-war between the military and the political parties. The parliamentary representatives of the German people were as helpless to withstand the iron will of the General Staff as was Imperial Austria, now utterly sick of, and only anxious to abandon, the war which she had provoked. These peace movements received small practical response from the enemy democracies; for President Wilson as their spokesman reiterated the declaration that they would negotiate no peace with military autocracy. His encouragement to the enemy peoples to throw off this control was excellent in precept but vain in fact when addressed to those who were so firmly manacled. They were not Houdinis.

In January 1918 there was, indeed, a significant attempt at popular revolt, when over a million German workers joined in a general strike, but this was soon quenched and even forgotten in the fresh exhilaration of the great offensive. Only when the military machine itself began to crumble could the slaves of the machines free themselves from the grip, or propaganda help them in loosening it. Perhaps only then did an active will to peace reinforce their mere passive weariness of war. The inner strength of militant patriotism lies in the fact that it is not merely a gag but a drug.

CHAPTER VII

SCENE I

THE HALT AND LAME OFFENSIVE — ARRAS, APRIL, 1917

ON April 9th, 1917, the British armies in France entered upon what they had hoped was to be the final and decisive campaign of the world war. To the ordinary observer the day was a brilliant contrast to all previous offensives, but it proved yet another mirage in the military desert. This was perhaps inevitable before zero hour.

The Arras offensive had its roots deeply embedded in the Battles of the Somme, 1916. Its strategic conception sprang from the Somme, for, in conjunction with the other attacks—still-born or prematurely deceased—planned for the spring of 1917, it was an effort to complete the overthrow of German power and man power which it was believed that only the onset of winter had prevented on the Somme. Its strategic failure was the outcome partly of the situation produced by the Somme and partly of the inability of the higher command to forget the barren methods employed on the Somme. And the germ of the Arras plan dated from the time of the Somme.

For as early as June, 1916, a plan known as the Blaireville project had been drawn up for a blow near Arras to take place as a supplement to the Somme offensive. Postponed because of the immense casualties on the Somme, which drew off all available forces to that human sump-pit, it was revived and extended in October as part of the spring plan. The gradual British advance eastwards on the Somme had left a German-held bulge between it and Arras—a bulge of which Gommecourt formed the westernmost point. This bulge seemed to offer the opportunity for a right and left-hand blow on the respective sides, converging towards Cambrai. If successful this might not only cut off the German forces holding the bulge, but create a gap too wide for the German reserves

Lens

N

Vimy Ridge

Thélus

Gavrelle

R. Scarpe

Drocourt

Fampoux

Arras

ST. SAUVEUR

RAILWAY TRIANGLE

Feuchy

RONVILLE

Telegraph Hill

Monchy le Preux

R. Cojeul

Guemappes

Wancourt

R. Sensée

Heninel

CAMBRAI 10 MILES

ARRAS

April, 1917

Original Front Line
Hindenburg Line
Drocourt-Quéant Switch
Line on 24th. April

Croisilles

Bullecourt

Quéant

0   1   2   3   4
Miles

© Cassell & Co. Ltd. 1970

to block, and so pave the way for an advance towards Valenciennes and against the enemy's line of communications and retreat through the Belgian 'trough'.

On November 18th, 1916, the Allied Commanders-in-Chief met at Chantilly to discuss their plans for 1917, and the outcome was that early in February the British Fourth and Fifth Armies should resume their Somme offensive on the southern side of the Gommecourt bulge, while the Third Army (Allenby) struck on the northern side from Arras. After gaining Monchy-le-Preux Allenby was to push south-east to close the German lines of retreat along the Cojeul Valley, and, if possible, the Sensée Valley also. In conjunction, the First Army (Horne) was to attack immediately north of the Third and form a defensive flank, and the French to attack south of the Somme. Three weeks later the main French blow was to be launched in Champagne—an undue delay if the two main blows were to react on each other.

But the whole scheme was dissolved by a combination of French action, British hesitation, and German anticipation. The French action took the form of dismissing their Commander-in-Chief, Joffre, whose bubble reputation had been pricked by the unconcealable evidence of ill-preparedness at Verdun and, less justly, by the lack of success on the Somme. He was replaced by Nivelle, the popular hero of the Verdun *ripostes*, whose appointment caused a change in the plan for 1917—towards greater aims and also towards giving the French a more spectacular rôle. In consequence the British had to take over more of the front, to the impairment of their own offensive projects. Tactlessness on one side and sensitiveness on the other produced a time-wasting series of arguments that caused a delay in the Allied offensive. And before it could begin the Germans had disrupted its foundation—by a strategic withdrawal not merely from the Gommecourt bulge, but from the whole of their old and indented front between Arras and Soissons. An absurd attempt was made to picture this as a British triumph and the fruit, even if a little late in garnering, of the Somme offensive.

It was the fruit, but not in the sense which the British command suggested—for the method of petty limited attacks pursued throughout the autumn had given the Germans ample opportunity to dig, literally and metaphorically, a pit for their assailants. Straightening their front by retiring to the newly built Hindenburg Line, they left the British to follow laboriously through the intervening desert which, with immense thoroughness of destruction, they had created. By nullifying the Allies' preparations for attack this withdrawal restricted them to the sectors on the two flanks of the evacuated area.

The main rôle in the British attack thus fell to the Third Army under Allenby. If he could break through the old defences just to the north of where the Hindenburg Line ended, he would automatically take this line in flank and rear. But in anticipation of such a move the Germans had dug a switch line from Quéant, near the northern end of the Hindenburg Line, through Drocourt—covering the rear of the old defences north of Arras. Thus Allenby's whole chance of strategic success depended on whether he could reach and break through this partially completed switch line—some five miles behind the front system—before the German reserves could arrive in strength. Surprise was the only key which could open this gate. Because of this the real drama of the Arras offensive lies in the preliminary discussions and preparations even more than in the battle itself.

Surprise had been discarded in the Somme offensive, except on July 14th—indeed, this master key of all the great captains of history had been rusting since the spring of 1915. The two means by which surprise could be obtained, and the Drocourt-Quéant switch reached in time, were by launching a mass of tanks or by a hurricane bombardment, brief but intense. The first means became impossible owing to the slowness in delivering new tanks after the discouraging reports made upon them in 1916, so that sixty old machines were all that could be scraped together. Allenby and his artillery adviser, Holland, were anxious to have the shortest possible bombardment, and originally proposed that it should last only forty-eight hours. If this, according to later standards, was more than forty hours too long, it was a tentative step in the direction of surprise. But the Higher Command was faithful to the theory of prolonged bombardment, and had a deep-rooted distrust of such an innovation. Nevertheless Allenby stood firm until General Headquarters hit upon the deft device of promoting his artillery adviser to another sphere and replacing him by one who shared their view. Then the plan of a five days' bombardment, preceded by three weeks of 'wire-cutting', was adopted. This, together with the too visible preparations, spelt the doom of surprise. In the bombardment 2879 guns (989 heavy) took part—a gun to every nine yards.

The most vivid impression of the British disregard for surprise at Arras is perhaps to be found in the German account of the counter-preparations which they were able to make during the three weeks' 'notice' they were so clearly given—'Field and heavy artillery in long columns awoke the approach roads of the *Hinterland*; flying-corps formations and machine-gun units . . . responded to the call. Innumerable crowds of working parties laboured day and night . . . at the repair and deepening of the defence system. Night and day in unbroken sequence trains from the Homeland laden with material and munitions reached the main depots. . . . Mountains of shell were piled up in the ammunition dumps. . . . The construction of the defences and the organization of the troops was completed. . . . The enemy could come, the troops had now the word.'

Ludendorff himself visited the sector and was satisfied that although the British might break into the forward positions, if they liked to pay the price, they would then be held up by his new system of defence in depth.

The difficulties, however, were not all of German manufacture. General Charteris, the head of Haig's intelligence service, has provided a significant sidelight in his diary notes at the time: 'Allenby shares one peculiarity with Douglas Haig: he cannot explain verbally, with any lucidity at all, what his plans are. In a conference between the two of them it is rather amusing. D.H. hardly ever finishes a sentence, and Allenby's sentences, although finished, do not really convey exactly what he means.' 'They understand one another perfectly'—other evidence throws a doubt on this point—'but as each of their particular Staffs only understands their immediate superior a good deal of explanation of details has to be gone into afterwards. . . . At these Army conferences no one dares to interfere. . . .'

In smaller points Allenby still sought for surprise, notably in linking up the underground sewers and quarries of Arras, St. Sauveur, and Ronville, in order to shelter two divisions which were to pass underground and leapfrog through the leading divisions. Another feature of the plan was that after the three assaulting corps of the Third Army had broken the enemy's first system of defence, the Cavalry Corps (Kavanagh) and XVIII Corps (Maxse) were to pass through in the centre between the human buttresses, and drive forward towards the switch line. Partly for concealment, the daring risk was taken of moving this pursuit force through the city of Arras, whose houses extended almost up to the front line. This plan, refreshingly ingenious, was vitiated, however, not only by the absence of initial surprise, but by the comparatively narrow front of the opening attack—about twelve miles. Thus the central bottle-neck was, in turn, so narrow that its end could be easily stopped. Ludendorff in his Vilna offensive in the autumn of 1915 had revealed a better method—a dual penetration by two horns goring their way into the enemy's front, while through the wide gap between the horns the pursuit force unexpectedly issued.

A fundamental defect of the Arras plan, moreover, was the width of its base compared with its fighting front—the routes of supply and reinforcement all converging on Arras, with the result that the narrow mouth of this bottle-neck became utterly congested. When the initial attack failed to make the progress anticipated, this congestion was increased by the arrival of the cavalry in the forward area—although the experience of 1915 and 1916 had shown that such advance was futile unless and until a wide path had been swept clear of the enemy.

Yet if the strategic object was practically forfeited before zero hour on April 9th, the tactical success was at first a vivid and enheartening contrast to all previous British offensives. The new British gas shell was most effective in paralysing the defending artillery, for it not only compelled the gun crews to keep on their gas masks for hours at a time, but by killing off the horses like flies prevented ammunition being brought up. The attack was delivered by the VII, VI and XVII Corps of the Third Army and the Canadian Corps of the First Army. On the extreme right, or south, lay Snow's VII Corps, with the 21st Division near Croisilles forming a pivot on which the rest of the Corps—the 14th, 30th and 56th (1st London) Divisions—advanced. To their left lay Haldane's VI Corps, with the 3rd, 12th and 15th Divisions attacking and the 37th Division waiting to leapfrog through and seize the key position of Monchy-le-Preux. The marshy valley of the Scarpe, the boundary between the VI Corps and its neighbours, separated the British right and left wings. North of the Scarpe the attack was entrusted to Fergusson's XVII Corps, composed of the 9th, 34th and 51st Divisions, with the 4th to leapfrog through the 9th on the Corps's right. Furthest north of all, Byng's Canadian Corps was to assault the ill-omened Vimy Ridge, which had so long proved an impregnable barrier to the Allied forces. The capture of a large part of the ridge on April 9th gained all the greater *éclat* from the fame—or, to the Allies, illfame—which this ridge had acquired. The Canadians' feat was as finely prepared as it was executed. Yet it is but just to recognize that in one important condition the task was easier than further south, for the very fact of attacking uphill gave the attackers here better artillery observation and drier ground than those who had to traverse the sodden or marshy area near the Scarpe.

At 5.30 a.m. the assaulting infantry moved forward on the whole front, covered by a superbly timed creeping barrage, and in less than an hour almost the whole German first-line system was captured. North of the Scarpe the success continued and, after the leading divisions had gained their three successive objectives, the 4th Division passed through on the Corps' right, and by seizing Fampoux breached the last German line in front of the Drocourt-Quéant switch. But south of the Scarpe the German resistance, first at the Railway Triangle and Telegraph Hill, then on the Wancourt-Feuchy line—helped by machine-guns from Monchy-le-Preux Hill—was so strong that it badly delayed, although it could not stop, the advance of the 12th and 15th Divisions. Thus the reserve 37th Division could not pass through that day, and behind them the cavalry had moved up not only in vain but to add to the congestion.

The results of the opening day had been greater and quicker, both in prisoners and progress, than in any previous offensive—yet they had extinguished the dim hope of a strategic break-through. A contributory factor was the misuse of the tanks. With only sixty machines available it would have been wiser to have concentrated them in aid of the vital effort to gain Monchy-le-Preux instead of spreading them over the front. The error was repeated in the next phase, whereas, if all available tanks had been concentrated on the south side of the salient formed by the first day's attack, they could have taken the German resistance in enfilade, and might have rolled it up.

So on April 10th the Third Army butted direct at a stiffening resistance, with its guns too far back to support the infantry. Not until the morning of April 11th did the arrival of four tanks help a battalion of the 37th Division to seize Monchy-le-Preux—driving in a wedge which was, however, too narrow and too late.

That same morning part of Gough's Fifth Army launched a converging assault from the south against the Hindenburg Line, in an attempt to relieve the pressure of German opposition to the Third Army. It was a desperate remedy for a despairing situation. For this army, after painfully toiling over the evacuated area, had neither been able to make the preparations nor to bring up the artillery necessary for a normal trench attack, far less an assault on the massive defences of the Hindenburg Line. The difficulty led to a novel expedient, which contained the germ of the method which was triumphantly successful later at Cambrai. But instead of 381 tanks as at Cambrai, only eleven could be gathered. As artillery support was deficient, this handful of tanks was to act as a mobile barrage and wire destroyer, leading the 4th Australian Division against the Hindenburg Line near Bullecourt.

The gamble failed—the preparations were too hasty, the resources inadequate, and the front too narrow. For a few hours there was an illusion of success. If the tanks arrived too late for their intended rôle, they at least helped to distract the enemy's attention, and caused a panic which 'sent part of the German garrison fleeing across the countryside'. The Australians broke into the Hindenburg Line, but then became the target of counterattack from all sides, while the illusion of a sweeping advance prevented the artillery from protecting them.

With better security the gain might have been held, but the British could hardly have done more, as the obstinate German resistance at Heninel and Wancourt, to the right of the Third Army, prevented any chance of the two armies joining hands. Next morning a gallant assault by the 21st and 56th (1st London) Divisions conquered these two bastions, but the increasing intensity of German counterattacks brought the first and main phase of the offensive to a close on April 14th. If strategic success had been missed, 13,000 prisoners and 200 guns had been taken.

The next phase had little result to put in relief against the depressing total of British casualities. The French offensive of April 16th on the Aisne, to which Arras had been the prelude, proved a worse downfall, shattering Nivelle's extravagant hopes and predictions, and burying his career in its ruins. The British were not ready to resume their offensive until a week later, and although Haig decided to continue 'the full pressure of the British offensive . . . in order to assist our Allies', there was by then no French advance to assist. On April 23rd and 24th Allenby pushed forward his line, at heavy cost and against heavy pressure, to include Guemappe and Gavrelle. At a conference of the army commanders on April 30th, Haig showed that he placed little faith in the possibility of a further French offensive, but decided to continue his own attacks, 'to move steadily forward up to a good defensive line'.

Despite fruitless assaults and sacrifices on May 3rd and 5th, 'baldheaded' assaults which showed more obstinacy than imagination or care, this line was not reached, and the offensive which had been prolonged to so bitter a conclusion was at last broken off. The British offensive centre of gravity was then transferred to the north—to open as brilliantly at Messines on June 7th, and to fade out still more miserably in the swamps of Passchendaele in October.

CHAPTER VII

SCENE 2

THE SIEGE-WAR MASTERPIECE—MESSINES

ON June 7th, 1917, took place a battle which on the morrow was hailed as a brilliant military achievement, and which to-day, unlike so many historically tarnished 'masterpieces' of 1914-1918, stands out in even higher relief. For we appreciate now that the capture of the Messines Ridge by General Plumer's Second Army was almost the only true siege-warfare attack made throughout a siege war. It was also one of the few attacks until late in 1918 in which the methods employed by the command completely fitted the facts of the situation.

But if to-day its abiding historic interest lies in its perfect suitability of method, at the time this was overshadowed, and rightly, by its value as a moral tonic. Perhaps this was almost too strong a stimulant to those not in direct charge of the operation, leading them to place too high hopes in the subsequent operations at Ypres, where the conditions were different and the methods also. But such a reflection does not dim the value of Messines, which came as a tonic badly needed after the depressing end of the spring offensive at Arras and on the Aisne.

While Pétain was striving to rally and rejuvenate the French Army, Haig decided to transfer the weight of his attack to Flanders, and, as a preliminary step to his main action at Ypres, to fulfil his long-formed plan of securing the high ground about Messines and Wytschaete as a flank bastion to the Ypres advance. For while in German possession it gave the enemy complete observation of the British trenches and forward battery positions, enabled them to command the communications up to the Ypres salient, and to take in enfilade, or even reverse, the trench positions therein.

Preparations had been begun nearly a year before, although their real development dated from the winter. Thus, when Haig asked Plumer, on May 7th, when he would be ready to deliver the Messines attack, Plumer was able to say, 'A month from to-day'—and keep his promise exactly. The calm confidence of this businesslike statement betrays no sign of the anxiety suffered, nor does it do justice to the will-power demanded of Plumer in carrying through his purpose.

The key factor in the success was the simultaneous explosion of nineteen great mines, containing 600 tons of explosives and involving the tunnelling of 8000 yards of gallery since January, in the face of active countermining by the enemy. A couple of months before the attack it was reported to Plumer that the Germans were within eighteen inches of the mine at Hill 60, and that the only thing to do was to blow it. Plumer was firm in his refusal, and equally staunch under the wearing strain of ominous rumours and reports throughout the following weeks. His justification came at 3.10 a.m. on June 7th, when this mine went up along with eighteen others—only one out of twenty had been blown up by the Germans.

Another example of his will-power was in withstanding strong and insidious pressure from General Headquarters to change his artillery adviser. Before the Arras offensive the same thing had happened with the Third Army, and Allenby's artillery plan had been radically modified—to the loss of all hope of surprise—by the removal of his artillery adviser to another sphere and his replacement by one who gave a different opinion. But before Messines, Plumer resisted all attempts at a change, and finally quelled them by saying flatly that as long as he was responsible he intended to have his own men. If Plumer could be strong in resisting expert advice at need, no commander was more keen to secure it from all sources, and none weighed it more carefully—as a foundation for his own decision. In Harington he had a Chief of his General Staff of blended intelligence and sympathy. And their happy combination was a symbol of the co-operation which was diffused throughout the Second Army staff, and through them to the fighting troops.

Trust and receptiveness to ideas and criticisms were the keynotes of the Second Army. They were instanced in the schools and courses behind the front, where free questioning and criticism were encouraged, while an answer and a reason to any point raised was always forthcoming. They were also marked in the preparation of an attack. Where other high commanders were apt to lay down a series of objectives which their troops must gain, Plumer's method was to suggest certain provisional lines, and then to discuss them, and each fraction of them, with the corps and divisional commanders concerned, adjusting the several objectives to the local conditions and opinions until a final series was pieced together like a mosaic, on which all were agreed.

Further, the impartial common sense of his judgment was shown by the fact that, although he could oppose technical advice from General Headquarters when it conflicted with reality, he welcomed it when it coincided. The Western Front in 1914–1918 was pre-eminently an engineers' war, yet historians will be perplexed at the small part played by engineers in its direction, and the overweening influence of cavalry and infantry doctrine in the attempt to solve its problems. Messines, however, was in sharp contrast, for here the methods and the training were largely based on a manual, S.S. 155, compiled by the engineers from their special knowledge and experience of siege warfare.

For Messines was to be a strict siege operation, the capture of a fortified salient at the minimum cost of lives by the maximum substitution of mind—in preparation—and material—in execution—for human bodies. Mines, artillery, tanks, and gas all played their part. But a contrary wind curtailed most of the scheme of gas projection, and the effect of the mines and artillery was so overwhelming that the tanks were hardly needed. On a front of just over nine miles a total of 2338 guns—of which 828 were heavy—were concentrated. There were also 304 large trench mortars. Thus the artillery strength here was approximately one gun to every seven yards of front, or 240 to the mile; five and a half tons of ammunition were thrown on each yard of front.

The fact that the attack would converge against a salient increased its chances, but it complicated the staff, troop and artillery organization of the attack. For the sectors of each attacking corps were of varying depths, and contracted more and more in width up to the final objective which was the chord of the arc forming the salient. As, however, it was a siege operation, without any attempt at exploitation or a break-through, it was easier to avoid the congestion which had occurred at Arras. And the problem was further simplified by the plan of so allotting sectors that five of the divisions had sectors of equal breadth from front to rear, while the four which filled the interstices had smaller tasks. Further, when the main ridge was captured, fresh troops were to 'leapfrog' through to gain the final Oosttaverne line across the base of the salient.

Meticulous organization and forethought marked every stage of the preparation, but this was based on personal touch —staff officers continually visiting the units and trenches— not on paper reports and instructions. Another feature was the special intelligence scheme, whereby the information obtained from prisoners, ground and air observation and reconnaissance, photography, wireless interception, and sound ranging, was swiftly conveyed to an Army centre, established for a fortnight at Locre Château, and then sifted and disseminated by summaries and maps.

The bombardment and 'wire cutting' began on May 21st, were developed on May 28th, and culminated in a seven days' intense bombardment, mingled with practice barrages to test the arrangements. The consequent forfeiture of surprise did not matter in the Messines stroke, a purely limited attack, in contrast to that at Arras, where it had been fatal to the hope of a break-through. For although there was no surprise there was surprise effect—produced by the mines and the overwhelming fire—and this lasted long enough to gain the short-distanced objectives that had been set. The point, and the distinction between actual surprise and surprise effect, are of significance to the theory of warfare.

It was fortunate, however, for the British that the Germans played into their hands. When the attack preparations were suspected, Rupprecht's chief of staff, Kuhl, had made the suggestion to 'evacuate the salient and withdraw behind the Lys'. But the corps commanders maintained the traditional belief in the value of 'commanding' positions; and their opinion prevailed. Obsessed by the soldierly conviction that ground should never be given voluntarily, they even insisted on holding the forward positions in strength. Thus German stupidity made possible the success of the British plan, preventing the short step to the rear that would have nullified the British mines and wasted the labour devoted to them.

In the British plan nine infantry divisions, with three more close up in reserve, were to advance to the assault. On the right (or south flank) was the II Anzac Corps (Godley) composed of the 3rd Australian, New Zealand, and 25th Divisions, with the 4th Australian Division behind. In the centre came the IX Corps (Hamilton-Gordon), the attack here being led by the 36th, 16th, and 19th Divisions, with the 11th in reserve. On the left was the X Corps (Morland), composed of the 41st, 47th, and 23rd Divisions, backed up by the 24th.

At 3.10 a.m. on June 7th the nineteen mines were blown, wrecking large portions of the Germans' front trenches. Simultaneously the barrage fell. When the débris and shock of the mines subsided, the infantry advanced and within a few minutes the whole of the enemy's front line system was overrun, almost without opposition. Resistance stiffened as the penetration was deepened, but the training of the infantry and the efficiency of the barrage, based on the finest shades of calculation, enabled continuous progress to be made, and within three hours the whole crest of the ridge was secured.

The New Zealand Division had cleared the intricate fortifications of Messines itself—here the pace of the barrage was regulated to 100 yards in fifteen minutes instead of the general pace of 100 yards in three minutes. The garrisons of Wytschaete and the White Château held out for some time, but the first village was captured after a fierce struggle by troops of the 36th (Ulster) and 16th (Irish) Divisions in a combined effort—a feat of symbolical significance. Perhaps the most difficult sector was that of the 47th (2nd London) Division, which had not only to overcome the highly fortified position of the White Château, but had the Ypres-Comines canal as an oblique interruption across its line of advance. The Londoners, however, overcame both and by 10 a.m. the objective of the first phase was reached along the whole attacking line. While it was being consolidated, over forty batteries were moved forward to support the next pounce.

At 3.10 p.m. the reserve divisions and tanks 'leapfrogged' through, and within an hour almost the whole of the final objective was captured. Some 7000 prisoners had been taken, apart from dead and wounded, at a cost to the attacker of only 16,000 casualties. The success had been so complete that only feeble counterattacks were attempted that day. When the expected general counterattack was launched on the whole front on the morrow, it failed everywhere against defences that had been rapidly and firmly organized, and in the recoil yielded the British still more ground.

The peculiar glory of the Messines attack is that, whereas in 1918 the decline in the German power of resistance brought the conditions to meet the methods almost as much as the methods were developed to meet the conditions, on June 7th, 1917, the methods were perfectly attuned to a resisting power then at its height.

CHAPTER VII

SCENE 3

THE 'ROAD' TO PASSCHENDAELE

ON July 31st, 1917, began what is termed the Third Battle of Ypres. And it is symbolical of its course and its issue that it is commonly spoken of by the title of 'Passchendaele', which in reality was merely the last scene of the gloomiest drama in British military history. Although called the Third Battle, it was not a battle, but rather a campaign, with the fighting more defined than the purpose—of the nature so familiar in the military annals of Flanders, and the Low Countries generally. And, like its German forerunners of 1914 and 1915, it achieved little except loss—in which, again, it repeated the earlier history of this theatre of war. So fruitless in its results, so depressing in its direction was this 1917 offensive, that 'Passchendaele' has come to be, like Walcheren a century before, a synonym for military failure—a name black-bordered in the records of the British Army. Even the inexhaustible powers of endurance and sacrifice shown by the combatants, or the improved executive leadership which did much in the later stages to minimize their sufferings, tend to be not merely overshadowed, but eclipsed in memory by the futility of the purpose and result.

What was the origin and what the object of 'Third Ypres'? An offensive in this sector had formed part of Haig's original contribution to the Allied plan for 1917. Its actual inauguration had been postponed by the unfortunate turn of events elsewhere. When the ill success of the opening offensive in the spring at Arras and in Champagne was followed by the threatened collapse of the French Army as a fighting force, Haig's 'first-aid' treatment was to allow the British offensive at Arras, by the Third Army, to continue for some weeks longer, with the general object of keeping the Germans occu-

YPRES, 1917

———	Original Line
– – –	Line on June 15 th.
–·–·–	Line-evening, July 31 st.
–··–··–	Line-evening, Sept. 20 th.
··········	Line-evening, Dec. 7 th.

Houthulst Forest

Bixschoote

Poelcapelle

Langemarck

Passchendaele

St. Julien

Broadseinde

PILCKEM RIDGE

R. Steenbeek

YSER CANAL

WHITE CHATEAU

Ypres

Polygon Wood

N

HILL 60

MENIN 2 miles

Wytschaete

YPRES-COMINES CANAL

Messines

R. Lys

0 1 2 3
Miles

R. Lys

Armentières

© Cassell & Co. Ltd. 1970

pied, and with the local object of reaching a good defensive line. When successive thrusts, against an enemy now fully warned and strengthened, failed to reach this line, Haig decided to transfer the main weight of this effort northward to Flanders, as he had originally intended. An intense conviction of the importance of giving the enemy no respite inspired him to press on with an offensive policy, even though French co-operation was lacking. His remarks, at the conference of the Army commanders on April 30th, show that in his own mind he had practically written off the French share as a bad debt on the balance sheet of 1917.

It is right to emphasize that, at this moment, Haig's opinion of the strategy to pursue was supported by the Prime Minister, who was in favour of continuing the offensive provided that the French took a vigorous part in it. But it soon became clear that this essential condition would not be fulfilled, and thenceforward he tried in vain to restrain Haig. If the need to distract the enemy's attention from the French, the crisis at sea caused by the submarine campaign, and the need to second the still possible Russian offensive, combined to justify Haig's decision in May, the situation had radically changed before the main offensive was actually launched on July 31st. In war all turns on the time factor. By July the French army, under Pétain's treatment, was recuperating, if still convalescent, the height of the submarine crisis was past, and the revolutionary paralysis of the Russian army was clear. Nevertheless, the plans of the British High Command were unchanged. The historian may consider that insufficient attention was given to the lessons of history, of recent experience, and of material facts in deciding both upon the principle of a major offensive and upon its site. The axis of the attack diverged from, instead of converging on, the German main communications, so that an advance could not vitally endanger the security of the enemy's position in France. Haig, curiously was to adopt here the same *eccentric* direction of advance which a year later his advice prevented Foch and Pershing from taking on the other flank of the Western Front.

Thus an advance on the Belgian coast offered no wide strategic results, and for the same reason it was hardly the best direction even as a means of pinning and wearing down the enemy's strength on a profitable basis. Moreover, the idea that Britain's salvation from starvation depended on the capture of the submarine bases on this coast has long since been exploded, for the main submarine campaign was conducted from German ports. The story of how this delusion was fostered is a curious one.

In the middle of June, Haig was called home to see a Cabinet which had grown uneasy over his offensive schemes. Its members were agreed in wishing to postpone serious operations until the French had recovered and the Americans had arrived on the scene, and to save up their strength for 1918. Haig marshalled his arguments, and committed himself to 'the definite opinion that if the fighting was kept up at its present intensity for six months Germany would be at the end of her available man power'. Here he went beyond even the estimate of his optimistic intelligence service, which had at least made its forecast dependent on Russia's continued efforts. As the Cabinet were growing sceptical of military arithmetic, Haig's arguments failed to make the impression he had hoped. Suddenly, the Admiralty came to the rescue of his plans—by telling the Cabinet that 'the Navy could not keep going unless the Germans were turned out of the Belgian coast.' Even in high military quarters, as the chief of Haig's intelligence staff has admitted, 'no one really believed this rather amazing view'. But it served as a welcome lever to make the Cabinet give way—as was the result.

The real source of the offensive, more potent than any of the arguments with which he buttressed his case, seems to have been Haig's optimistic belief that he could defeat the German armies single-handed—in Flanders. In large measure, it was to be a battle fought for British prestige. If such a single-handed design had little support in the history of war, the geography of Flanders offered still less. A plan that was founded on faith rather than on reason, both plan and faith were to be sunk in the mud of Flanders. Foch, himself the past exponent of 'faith-healing' strategy, forecast the verdict when he deprecated the British offensive as a 'duck's march' and expressively remarked *'Boche* is bad and *boue* is bad; but *Boche* and *boue* together——!'

Haig adopted the plan in face of formidable facts. His meteorological advisers had collated weather statistics, based on the 'records of eighty years', which showed that he could not hope for more than a fortnight, or at the best three weeks, of fine weather.

Worse still, the Ypres offensive was doomed before it began —by its own destruction of the intricate drainage system in this part of Flanders. The legend has been fostered that these ill-famed 'swamps of Passchendaele' were a piece of ill luck due to the heavy rain, a natural and therefore unavoidable hindrance that could not be foreseen. In reality, before the battle began, a memorandum was sent by Tank Corps Head-quarters to General Headquarters pointing out that if the Ypres area and its drainage were destroyed by bombardment, the battlefield would become a swamp. This memorandum was the result of information from the Belgian 'Ponts et Chaussées' and local investigation—the facts had, indeed, been brought to light by the engineers in 1915, but apparently forgotten. The area had been reclaimed from marshland by centuries of labour and in consequence the farmers of the district were under penalty to keep their dykes clear. Land used for pasture was such because it was subject to flooding and too wet for cultivation. In the disregard of this warning is epitomized the main and inevitable cause of the barren results of the 'Passchendaele offensive'.

Perhaps the very brilliance of the preliminary stroke at Messines on June 7th had helped to raise unfounded expecta-tions over what was in conception and purpose a totally different operation. Nearly two months passed before the preparations for the main advance were completed, and dur-ing that interval the Germans had ample warning to prepare countermeasures. These comprised a new method of defence, as suited to the waterlogged ground as the British offensive methods were unsuited. Instead of the old linear systems of trenches they developed a system of disconnected strong points and concrete pillboxes, distributed in great depth, whereby the ground was held as much as possible by machine-guns and as little as possible by men. While the forward positions were lightly occupied, the reserves thus saved were concentrated in rear for prompt counterattack, to eject the British troops from the positions they had arduously gained. And the further the British advanced the more highly developed, naturally, did they find the system. Moreover, by the introduction of mustard gas the Germans scored a further trick, interfering seriously with the British artillery and concentration areas.

Thus, when the fully expected blow fell, the Crown Prince Rupprecht was so far freed from his usual pessimism as to record in his diary—'My mind is quite at rest about the attack, as we have never disposed of such strong reserves, so well trained for their part, as on the front attacked.' This actual front was held by the troops of the German Fourth Army (Sixt von Arnim).

The certainty that the Germans were aware of the coming offensive, and would be moving up reserves, led the chief of Haig's intelligence staff to urge that the attack should be advanced by three days 'in spite of the fact that our preparations were not fully completed; it was a choice of evils'. But 'the Army Commanders pressed for delay', and Haig reluctantly accepted their view. There was also a difference of view over the extent of the initial aim. Here Gough, like Rawlinson on the Somme, wished to make a series of limited advances, but Plumer urged that after so long a preparation they should go 'all out'—and Haig once again inclined to a break-through aim.

The main rôle in the attack was given to Gough's Fifth Army, with one corps of the Second Army playing a subsidiary part on the right flank, and a French corps on the left. The British artillery strength totalled 3091 guns, of which

999 were heavy—an average of one gun to every six yards. During the bombardment, four and a quarter million shells were fired (£22,000,000 worth). It meant that four and three-quarter tons were thrown for every yard of the front.

The bombardment proper opened on July 22nd, and continued for ten days until at 3.50 a.m. on July 31st the infantry of twelve divisions advanced on an eleven-mile front to the accompaniment of torrential rain. On the left substantial progress was made, Bixschoote, St. Julien, and the Pilckem ridge being gained, and the line of the Steenbeek reached. The 'green line' (third objective) was attained in most places, an advance of nearly two miles. But on the right, in the more vital sector round the Menin road, the attack was held up, short of the second objective. And the rain continued day after day, postponing the next major attempt, and hastening the conversion of the undrainable ground into a swamp in which first the tanks and ere long even the infantry were bogged.

Even the ardent Gough 'informed the Commander-in-Chief that tactical success was not possible, or would be too costly, under such conditions, and advised that the attack should now be abandoned'. But Haig was too determined, and still too optimistic, to be thus dissuaded. And it would seem that none of the Army Commanders ventured to press contrary views with the strength that the facts demanded. One of the lessons of the war, exemplified at Passchendaele, is certainly the need of allowing more latitude in the military system for intellectual honesty and moral courage. As it was, Haig continued to send home to the War Office confident reports that the enemy were 'fast approaching' the exhaustion of their forces: actually, Ludendorff was making preparations not only to attack the Russians at Riga but to crush the Italians by sending eight or ten divisions to reinforce the Austrians. Haig's reports, indeed, had 'gone much further' than those his intelligence furnished.

The second blow, on August 16th, was a diminished replica of the first in its results. The left wing was again advanced across the shallow depression formed by the little valley of the Steenbeek and past the ruins of what had been Langemarck. But on the right, where alone an advance might have a strategic effect, a heavy price was paid for nought. The tally of prisoners shrank from six to a mere two thousand. Nor did men feel that the enemy's skilful resistance and the mud were the sole explanation of their fruitless sacrifice. Complaints against the direction and staff work in Gough's Army were general and bitter, and their justness seemed to receive recognition when Haig extended the Second Army's front northward to include the Menin road sector, and thereby entrusted to Plumer the direction of the main advance towards the ridge east of Ypres. It was a thankless task at the best, for the experience of war attested the futility of pressing on in places where failure had already become established, and it seemed heavy odds that the laurels earned by Messines must become submerged in the swamps beyond Ypres.

Yet, in the outcome, the reputation of Plumer and the Second Army Staff, headed by Harington, was enhanced— less because of what was achieved in scale than because more was achieved than could reasonably have been expected in so hopeless a venture. Applying, as at Messines, siege-warfare methods to a task that was more a siege than a battle, their plan was that of a series of shallow advances, not pressed beyond the point where the artillery support was outrun, and leaving both the infantry fresh enough and the artillery close enough to deal with the inevitable counterattacks.

Bad weather and the need for preparation delayed the resumption of the offensive until September 20th, but that morning the Second Army attack, on a four-mile front, achieved success in the area of previous failure—on either side of the Menin road. Six divisions (two being Australian) were used; but infantry were kept down to the minimum with artillery at the maximum. Plumer had 1295 guns—a gun to every five yards. Of these 575 were heavy, which meant one to every twelve yards compared with one to eighteen on July 31st. The infantry advanced at 5.40 a.m.; by 6.15 a.m.

the first objective was gained almost unopposed, and, with the exception of one or two strong points, the third and last objective was gained soon after midday, and the counter-attacks were repulsed by fire. A fresh spring on September 26th, and another on October 4th—the last a larger one on an eight-mile front, by troops of eight divisions (four Anzac) in the Second Army, and of four in the Fifth Army on the left flank—gave the British possession of the main ridge east of Ypres, with Gheluvelt, Polygon Wood, and Broodseinde, despite torrents of rain, which made the battlefield a worse morass than ever. And on each occasion the majority of the counter-attacks had broken down under fire, a result which owed much to the good observation work of the Royal Flying Corps and the quick response of the artillery. Some 10,000 prisoners were swallowed in the three bites, and this widening maw frightened the enemy into modifying his elastic tactics and strengthening his forward troops—to their increased loss under the British artillery fire.

These attacks had at least done something to restore prestige, if they could have little strategic effect on a campaign which was foredoomed, and in which both the time and the scope for extensive penetration had long since vanished. Unhappily, the Higher Command decided to continue the pointless offensive during the few remaining weeks before the winter, and thereby used up reserves which might have saved the belated experiment of Cambrai from bankruptcy. For having wasted the summer and his strength in the mud, where tanks foundered and infantry floundered, Haig turned in November to dry ground—where a decisive success went begging for lack of reserves.

At Ypres the comparative success of the late September attacks produced an unfortunate intoxication. On the evening of October 4th the chief of the intelligence staff expressed the opinion that there were no fresh enemy reserves 'within immediate reach of the battlefront.' (Actually, fresh German divisions began to take over the line next day; before the next attack on October 9th, 'the whole of the battered front was

held by fresh troops, and an extra division had been inserted'.)
Even the sober Second Army staff seem to have been
momentarily carried away, and at a conference with the War
Correspondents Harington said that the crest of the ridge was
'as dry as a bone'. The Australian Official History records
the impression of one who was present: 'I believe the official
attitude is that Passchendaele Ridge is so important that
to-morrow's attack is worth making whether it succeeds or
fails. . . . I suspect that they are making a great, bloody
experiment—a huge gamble . . . I feel, and most of the
correspondents feel, terribly anxious . . . I thought the principle was to be "hit, hit, hit, *whenever the weather is suitable!*" If
so, it is thrown over at the first temptation.'

The anxiety of the correspondents was to prove more justifiable than the hopes of the military chiefs. There had been
rain each day since October 4th, and on the afternoon of the
8th it became torrential; the meteorological experts said that
no improvement could be expected. Yet Haig decided to
press on, and his Army Commanders, although dubious, did
not care to protest. So next morning the attack was launched,
again on an eight-mile front—and proved a tragic fiasco,
except in the low ground on the left. The curious nature of
military judgment is illustrated in the diary of Haig's chief
intelligence officer (October 8th): 'With a great success to-
morrow, and good weather for a few more weeks, we may
still clear the coast and win the war before Christmas.'
(October 10th) 'D.H. sent for me. . . . He was still trying to
find some grounds for hope that we might still win through
here this year, but there is none.'

Nevertheless, a fresh attack was ordered for the 12th—with
still deeper objectives. Gough doubted its wisdom, but
Plumer 'had decided that an attack was practicable', and
Haig gave the order on the 10th. At this moment 'little
was known of the true experiences and results of the recent
fight' (Australian Official History). There was still time to
find out, but this duty seems to have been neglected. After
renewed rain on the 11th, Gough, to his credit, telephoned

to Plumer to suggest a postponement. But after consulting Godley, the corps commander mainly concerned, Plumer preferred to continue. Next day the would-be dash for Passchendaele ended with the attacking troops, save those who perished in the mud, back almost on their starting line.

Haig now seems to have realized there was no foundation for anticipating a great strategic success. But he was determined to reach Passchendaele, and for this purpose brought up the Canadian Corps. Meantime a combined attack by the Fifth Army and the French was tried, with small result, on October 22nd. On the 26th the Second Army made its fresh effort with the Canadians and suffered a fresh disappointment. They tried again on the 30th, while the Fifth Army loyally yet sceptically struggled to advance alongside—'300 yards or so being the limit'.

Progress so trifling, save in its cost, was largely explained by the exhaustion caused in pushing forward over a morass and to the fact that the mud not only got into and jammed rifles and machine-guns, but nullified the effect of the shell bursts. The attackers' troubles were augmented by the enemy's increasing use of mustard gas, and by his renewed adoption of his tactics of holding the bulk of his troops well back for a counterattack. Thus, when on November 4th, a sudden advance by the 1st Division and 2nd Canadian Division gained the empty satisfaction of occupying the site of Passchendaele village, the official curtain was at last rung down on the pitiful tragedy of 'Third Ypres'. It was the long-overdue close of a campaign which had brought the British armies to the verge of exhaustion, one in which had been enacted the most dolorous scenes in British military history, and for which the only justification evoked the reply that, in order to absorb the enemy's attention and forces, Haig chose the spot most difficult for himself and least vital to his enemy. Intending to absorb the enemy's reserves, his own were absorbed.

He was lured on by a lofty optimism that extended even to the cost. After the disappointing attack of July 31st, he advised the Government that the enemy casualties exceeded the British 'not improbably by a hundred per cent'; and in his final despatch he still declared that it was 'certain that the enemy's loss considerably exceeded ours'. That optimism was nourished by ignorance of the situation, due in part to the failure—a moral failure—of his subordinates to enlighten him.

Perhaps the most damning comment on the plan which plunged the British Army in this bath of mud and blood is contained in an incidental revelation of the remorse of one who was largely responsible for it. This highly placed officer from General Headquarters was on his first visit to the battle front—at the end of the four months' battle. Growing increasingly uneasy as the car approached the swamplike edges of the battle area, he eventually burst into tears, crying, 'Good God, did we really send men to fight in that?' To which his companion replied that the ground was far worse ahead. If the exclamation was a credit to his heart it revealed on what a foundation of delusion and inexcusable ignorance his indomitable 'offensiveness' had been based.

The only relief to this sombre review is that a bare fortnight later was enacted, on a different stage, and with a technique suggested in early August, a 'curtain-raiser' which was to be developed into the glorious drama of autumn, 1918.

CHAPTER VII

SCENE 4

THE TANK SURPRISE AT CAMBRAI

ON November 19th, 1917, the German troops in front of Cambrai were contemplating with undisturbed minds the apparent normality and comparative tranquillity of the British lines opposite them; contrasting their own security in the massively fortified and comfortable trenches of the Hindenburg Line with the unsavoury lot of their comrades struggling in the shell-churned mudholes of the Ypres salient; indulging in self-congratulation not only on the impregnability of their famous line, but on the pertinacity of the unteachable English who had so engulfed themselves at Ypres that there could surely be no danger of any other assault elsewhere before winter came.

On November 20th, 381 tanks, followed by a relatively small proportion of infantry rolled forward in the half-light upon the astonished Germans without even the courtesy of a preliminary bombardment to announce their coming. Always good hosts, the Germans might well feel aggrieved at the omission of a warning which had customarily given them four or five days' notice to prepare a suitable reception.

On November 21st the bells of London rang out in joyous acclaim of a triumphant success that seemed a foretaste of victory, perhaps at no distant date. And Ludendorff, back at the German Supreme Command, was hurriedly preparing emergency instructions for a general retreat. Both the bells and Ludendorff were premature—although prophetic—by some nine months.

For on November 30th came a German retort so full of menace that the public thereafter showed a strong distaste for premature celebrations. Applause changed to reproaches; the cause of the disasters was the subject of inquiry; and in

Canal du Nord

Bourlon

Fontaine-
Notre
Dame

Cambrai

Anneux

Flesquières

Marcoing

Masnières

Crèvecœur

Havrincourt Ribecourt

Lateau
Wood

ST. QUENTIN-L'ESCAUT CANAL

Villers-
Plouich

Banteux
Ravine

Banteux

N

Gonnelieu

Gouzeaucourt

Twenty-Two
Ravine

Villers-
Guislain

CAMBRAI
1917

━━━━━	Original Front
┅┅┅┅	Front on evening of 20 th. Nov.
┅·┅·┅	Limit attained on 29 th. Nov.
··········	Final Line on Dec. 7th.
───▶	Direction of attacks
◀┅┅┅	German counter-attacks

0   1   2   3
Miles

© Cassell & Co. Ltd. 1970

public opinion the name of Cambrai came to be associated more with the ultimate reverse than with the initial success. Actually, however, the fuller knowledge now available suggests that the black date in the national calendar should be the 20th, and not the 30th, of November. Yet gloomy as is this page of World War history, it forms one of the most striking examples of the proverb that 'every cloud has a silver lining'. If November 20th, 1917, is in itself a tragedy of errors, its eventual effect on the fortunes of the Allies was beneficent—pointing and paving the way to the victorious method of 1918, and, to take a still longer view, it is seen to be one of the landmarks in the history of warfare, the dawn of a new epoch. Thus we may say that the joy-bells, if immediately wrong, were ultimately right.

In contrast, the Germans failed to profit by the warning and later paid the penalty—as their official historians recognize. While the more far-sighted German officers urged the necessity of replying in kind to the new British method others argued that 'the further mechanization of the battle' would impair the moral qualities of the troops. And their fervent traditionalism fathered the thought that 'the tank terror was more of a phantom than a real danger'. The success of the counter-offensive was a support to men who did not care to face an unconventional reality, and the weight of conservative opinion prevailed—as so often in the history of armies. Thus it was left for the post-war historians of the German Army to record, in bitterness of soul, that 'the outwardly brilliant German offensive battle held within a deep tragedy'.

These eleven days form perhaps the most dramatic of all episodes in the World War. Yet, sensational as was their course in its abrupt change of fortune, the real story of 'Cambrai' lies beneath the surface. First is the question of its origins, of paramount importance because it ushered in a new cycle of warfare. Its initial source is to be found nearly two years, and its immediate source nearly four months, earlier.

The guiding idea of those who sponsored the tank in infancy

had been to release it unexpectedly in a large concentration, and this idea had, as we have seen, not only been formulated but worked out in detail as early as February, 1916—seven months before a driblet of tanks were launched on the Somme under conditions which violated all the essentials therein laid down. Fortunately, in 1917, the headquarters of the Tank Corps in France, although unlike General Headquarters they had not seen this memorandum, had come by experience to similar ideas. Further, the eternal yet too often underrated principle of surprise was deeply rooted in their minds, and thus when insight apprised them in the very first days of Third Ypres—the Passchendaele offensive—that the 'mudlark' was futile, an alternative project was quick to blossom.

The chief general staff officer, Colonel Fuller, on August 3rd, 1917, drew up a plan for a great tank raid in a more suitable sector. In the preface to it this significant example of prevision may be read: 'From a tank point of view the Third Battle of Ypres may be considered dead. To go on using tanks in the present conditions will not only lead to good machines and better personnel being thrown away, but also to a loss of morale in the infantry and tank crews, through constant failure. From an infantry point of view, the Third Battle of Ypres may be considered comatose. It can only be continued at colossal loss and little gain.'

Then came the alternative proposal: 'In order to restore British prestige and strike a theatrical blow against Germany before the winter, it is suggested that preparations be at once set on foot to take St. Quentin.' It was further pointed out that the operation was strategically a sound one as a preparatory step to an advance towards Le Cateau, and then Valenciennes, the following year. Discussion of this project brought out the objection that it required a combined British and French operation, which might lack the simplicity and smooth working essential for the novel method to succeed. Therefore, on August 4th, a second project was framed, for a tank raid south of Cambrai. The word 'raid' should be stressed, for, as originally conceived, the object was 'to destroy

the enemy's personnel and guns, to demoralize and disorgan-
ize him, and not to capture ground'. As the preliminary notes
stated: 'The duration of the raid must be short—eight to
twelve hours—so that little or no concentration of the enemy
may be effected for counterattack.' Had this been followed
there would have been no need to lament the 30th November.
'The whole operation may be summed up as "advance, hit,
retire". Big raids of this description will not only reduce the
enemy's fighting power, but will reduce his initiative with
reference to any big battle which at the time may be in progress.' For this raid a force of three tank brigades of two
battalions each, and 'one, or better, two, divisions of infantry
or cavalry', with extra artillery, was suggested, operating on
an 8000-yard front. The object, as proposed, was 'to raid the
ré-entrant formed by the L'Escaut—St. Quentin Canal
between Ribecourt—Crèvecœur—Banteux'. The raiding
force was to be divided into three groups, the main one to scour
the country in this canal-enclosed pocket, while smaller
groups formed offensive flanks on each side to protect the
main operation. 'The essence of the entire operation is surprise and rapidity of movement. Three hours after zero the
retirement might well begin, the tanks and aeroplanes operating as a rearguard to the dismounted cavalry retiring with
their prisoners.'

The proposed sector lay in the area of the Third Army,
under General Sir Julian Byng, and on August 5th the detailed
project was taken informally to him by one of the Tank Corps
brigadiers. Byng was receptive to the idea, although inclined
to expand it from a raid into a break-through attack to gain
Cambrai. Next day he went to General Headquarters, saw
Haig, and suggested a surprise attack with tanks at Cambrai
in September. The Commander-in-Chief was favourable,
but his Chief of Staff, General Kiggell, offered strong objections on the ground that the army could not win a decisive
battle in two places at once, and should rather concentrate
every possible man in the Ypres sector—which, incidentally,
he never visited until the campaign was over. Thus the en-

larged idea helped to postpone the raid, as the refusal to recognize reality at Ypres postponed the attack at Cambrai until too late for decisive results to be possible.

The historian, while respecting Kiggell's emphasis on the principle of concentration, may doubt whether Ypres was a suitable site for the fulfilment of this principle, and may also hold that distraction of the enemy's force has ever been an essential complement to concentration—of one's own effort.

Kiggell's objections sufficed to dissuade Haig, who still valued the tank as only 'a minor factor'. Thus the Cambrai project was postponed indefinitely, while the High Command persevered with their hopeless efforts in the Passchendaele swamps. But neither Byng nor the Tank Corps were willing to let the idea drop, and certain opinions at General Head-quarters were in accord, so that as the Ypres offensive became a more palpable failure, a readier ear was lent to an alternative which promised to redeem British prestige. Finally, in mid October, the Cambrai plan was sanctioned, and fixed for November 20th. But now the situation had changed for the worse, for, if the plan were crowned with success, that success must be barren for want of reserves to reap the harvest. The reapers were engulfed at Passchendaele.

It is just to recognize that if General Headquarters had missed the opportunity, General Headquarters had now per-haps a surer appreciation than the Third Army Command of the limitations imposed by their lack of means. Kiggell urged that Bourlon Hill merely should be the first objective, followed by a lateral exploitation northward, and Haig put a time limit on the operation. But the Third Army orders were more ambitious in scope and objectives, despite the fact that all their available infantry divisions and tanks were being thrown into the initial 'break-through' effort.

Byng's plan was (1) to break the German defensive system, the famous Hindenburg Line, in the neck between the Canal de L'Escaut and the Canal du Nord, (2) to seize Cambrai, Bourlon Wood and the passage over the River Sensée; (3) to cut off the Germans in the area south of the Sensée and west of the Canal du Nord; and (4) to exploit the success towards Valenciennes. The force allotted for this ambitious plan comprised the III (Pulteney) and IV (Woollcombe) Corps, each of three infantry divisions, the Cavalry Corps (Kavanagh) of three divisions (plus one under IV Corps), a total of 381 fighting tanks, and roughly 1000 guns. Thus of the original project only the fundamental idea, the tank method, and the locality remained. Otherwise there were marked alterations, and in these lay the germ of disaster. The raid had been transformed into a large-scale offensive, with far-reaching aims. Instead of securing a 'pocket' and withdrawing, an organized advance was to be made up a narrow 'lane', bounded by two canals. A protection to a raid, these became a danger to such an attack, circumscribing the action of the tanks and preventing the formation of tank-offensive flanks. Otherwise the ground was good, mostly rolling downland, excellent for tank movement; it was marked by two features, the Flesquières-Havrincourt ridge and Bourlon Hill.

The fundamental weakness of the general plan, however, was not topographical, but the complete lack of reserves, unless the four cavalry divisions can be considered such—and the futility of so regarding them was amply shown in their fresh inability, in face of modern weapons, to influence the action. The six divisions employed in the initial attack were all that the Third Army Commander had at his disposal— for a plan that visualized a penetration beyond Cambrai to Valenciennes! It is extremely difficult to understand what was in mind as to the future, for without reserves complete success could only mean the creation of an excessively deep and narrow salient, requiring scores of divisions to hold it. It is true that the Guards and one or two other divisions could be made available, and were ultimately brought to the scene, but they were too far away for prompt intervention. The situation, indeed, had some reminder of Loos. The French also moved a corps to the Senlis-Péronne area just before the attack, but after the first day were told that they were no longer required!

The best comment on this lack of reserves is contained in a story of General Franchet d'Esperey, which one has on the authority of the officer to whom the words were spoken. A long motor ride, in search of information, brought him to a British headquarters at Albert. Entering, he interrogated a senior General Staff Officer, flinging at him a string of crisp questions as to the progress of the attack, its frontage, depth. Then came the final, the vital question: 'And where were your reserves?' 'Mon Général, we had none.' The French commander exclaimed, 'Mon Dieu!' turned on his heel and fled.

Turning now to the tank plan, the problems were to gain surprise, to cross the wide and deep obstacle of the Hindenburg Line and to ensure co-operation between the infantry and tanks for their common security. Careful organization and the absence of a preliminary bombardment contributed to the accomplishment of the first object. The difficulty presented by the Hindenburg Line was overcome by devising super-fascines, huge bundles of brush wood, which were carried on the nose of each tank and released on reaching the edge of the Hindenburg trenches; the tanks, working in sections of three, had thus the power to cross three successive obstacles. Thirdly, a strictly drill attack was worked out and practised by which in each section an advanced-guard tank moved about 100 yards ahead of the two main-body tanks, keeping down the enemy's fire and protecting the main body as they led the infantry forward. The infantry, moving in flexible file formations, followed immediately behind the main-body tanks. While the tanks cleared a way for them through the deep belts of enemy wire and subdued the hostile machine-gun fire, the infantry acted as 'moppers-up' to the tanks and were also ready to protect them from the enemy's guns at close quarters. The one fault of the tank plan was that, against expert advice, the tanks attacked on the whole frontage instead of against selected tactical points, with the result that no tank reserves was kept for use in the later stages.

The preparations for the battle were made with great skill

and secrecy, while to mislead the enemy as to the scale and frontage of the attack, gas and smoke attacks, dummy attacks with dummy tanks, raids and feints, were carried out on a wide front both north and south of the real sector of attack.

Nevertheless, one man nearly undid the secrecy of a multitude. A prisoner from an Irish regiment gave information of the coming attack, and of the concentration of tanks, but fortunately he was not believed and the German Army Commander, General von der Marwitz, reported on the 16th that there was no likelihood of an attack. But on the 19th a British telephone message, 'Tuesday Flanders', was overheard near Bullecourt, and, as it sounded like a combined date and codeword, quickened German suspicions. That night the troops were ordered to be specially alert, and Marwitz hastily utilized a division, just detraining from Russia, to strengthen his defences. But if the Germans now anticipated an attack they also expected the usual preliminary bombardment*—and its absence assured the British attack the essential surprise effect. That effect was accentuated by an early morning mist, as in almost all the successful thrusts of the war.

At 6.20 a.m. on November 20th the tanks and infantry moved forward to the attack on roughly a six-mile front, and gained a demoralizing initial success at all points save in the left centre in front of Flesquières. The main cause of this one serious check was that the commander of the 51st Division, Harper, preferred a method of his own instead of conforming to the formations devised by the Tank Corps, and adopted in all the other divisions. His advance tanks were called 'rovers', and went much further ahead, and the infantry formations were not as well fitted for close cooperation with tanks as those laid down. The separation seems to have been inspired by his expressed feeling that the

* An attack without heavy bombardment was considered out of the question, as the position was so strong. Thus the orders for Moser's group, shortly before midnight on the 19th, said—"Tanks may take part. The four or five hours' artillery bombardment will probably begin between 3 and 4 a.m.' This is a suggestive example of how habit may contribute to surprise.

whole Cambrai plan was 'a fantastic and most unmilitary scheme'—when on the staff of General Headquarters he had resisted the development of machine-guns, and now was equally sceptical of tanks. The result was that the infantry were too far behind the tanks, lost the gaps in the wire, and were stopped by machine-gun fire. An officer who examined the battlefield afterwards could only find three small heaps of machine-gun cartridge cases, from which it would appear that a handful of machine-guns held up a whole division— a fact which sheds a striking light on the future of infantry action in open country. The loss of touch between the infantry and tanks lay also at the root of the losses which befell the tanks when they came over the ridge and under the close fire of several German batteries, for infantry accompanying them could have picked off the gunners. Here occurred the famous incident of the solitary German artillery officer who was reputed to have 'knocked out' sixteen tanks single handed. It must go into the catalogue of historic legends, for only five derelict tanks were to be seen at this point after the attack had moved on, and an intelligence officer who examined the ground found marks which showed clearly that three batteries had been in position there to engage the tanks. It is possible that all save one gun, and one gunner, had been silenced, as was claimed, but impressions in the heat of battle are sometimes misleading. The feat has, however, an ironical significance in the fact that it was blazoned to the world by the British General Headquarters. The incentive of a mention in despatches was not accorded to enemy feats performed at the expense of the infantry or cavalry.

The effect of this battlefield incident has also been magnified. On the right the 12th, 20th and 6th Divisions secured their objectives rapidly, though the 12th had severe fighting at Lateau wood. The 20th Division passed through and captured Masnières and Marcoing, securing the passage of the canal at both and even the bridge intact at the latter. On the left of the 51st the 62nd Division made a brilliant advance, advancing by nightfall as far as Anneux, over two miles in the rear of Flesquières. The Flesquières resistance was thus only an islet, cut off and overlapped by the waves which swept round its flanks and on to Marcoing, Anneux and even to the edge of Bourlon Wood. A penetration of five miles had been made—the equivalent of months of heavy fighting and heavier losses on the Somme and at the Third Battle of Ypres. Decisive success was within the grasp of the British forces, the enemy's three main lines of defences had been overrun, only a half-finished line and the open country lay beyond. But the tank crews were exhausted, the infantry showed little capacity to make progress on their own, and apart from one squadron of the Canadian Fort Garry Horse the two cavalry divisions could contribute nothing toward fulfilling their rôle of exploitation.

The German official monograph emphasizes the fact that a wide gap remained open for 'many hours, completely unoccupied', between Masnières and Crèvecœur: 'It was great luck, as no reinforcements could be expected to reach there before evening.' The Germans also had luck in that a relief division from Russia had just arrived when the attack came; by midday on the 20th part of it was in position to cover the direct path to Cambrai. With notable promptness the German Command began moving five reserve divisions to the scene from other parts of the front, and six more were warned to follow. It was thus a race with time; and to the joy of the anxious Germans, their assailants seemed astoundingly dilatory. 'The British failed to utilize the afternoon and evening; they might at least have surrounded the German forces still holding out in Flesquières. The defence . . . seems to have deprived the 51st Division of all initiative.' As for the British cavalry, it is remarked that they appeared late and were easily stopped by enfilade fire.

On November 21st local reserves made some further progress. Flesquières was evacuated by its surviving defenders in the early hours, and after dawn the 51st and 62nd Divisions pressed on, clearing the German salient formed by this resistance on the first day and carrying the tide of the

British advance as far as Fontaine-Notre Dame, one and a half miles beyond the high-water mark of November 20th. Owing to the British penetration into Bourlon Wood and Fontaine there was a three-mile-wide breach between Walter's and Moser's Corps. But, by German witness, the British lapsed into inactivity at the moment of supreme opportunity. On the right, little ground was gained during the day, and, by evening, three of the enemy's reinforcing divisions were on the scene. The opportunity had been forfeited.

Haig's time limit of forty-eight hours had now expired, but owing to the menace of the uncaptured Bourlon Hill to the new British position, as well as the hope of an enemy withdrawal and the desire to relieve the enemy pressure on Italy, he decided to continue the offensive and, somewhat belatedly, placed a few fresh divisions at the disposal of the Third Army. But the Tank Corps, the essential cause of the early success that had apparently surprised the British as much as the German Command, was tired out, men and machines—all had been staked on the first throw.

The fresh attacks met with more failure than success against an enemy now braced to meet the danger. On November 22nd the Germans recaptured Fontaine-Notre Dame; on the 23rd, the 40th Division with tanks captured the whole of Bourlon Wood, but the attempts on Bourlon village and Fontaine-Notre Dame failed. Bitter and fluctuating fighting followed; both villages were won, and lost again. And meanwhile the Germans, with prompt initiative and consummate skill, were preparing a deadly counterblast. Unfortunately there seems to have been a disposition in the superior command, with certain exceptions, to discredit the numerous warning signs of the gathering storm, and even to find amusement in the anxiety displayed by those whose clearer vision was soon to be attested. This attitude was apparently due to over-confidence—partly induced by the easy success of November 20th, and partly due to a belief that the Passchendaele offensive had absorbed all the enemy's reserves. The effect of Passchendaele, indeed, was always overrated.

In contrast, General Snow, commanding the VII Corps on the southern flank of the wedge driven into the German front, had forecast both the place and date of the counterstroke nearly a week before. His subordinate commanders, particularly in the 55th Division (Jeudwine), which adjoined the III Corps, had reported a host of corroborative evidence—that the enemy artillery were registering on spots never bombarded before, that German aircraft were flying over the lines in large numbers, and that the British reconnaissance machines were 'shelled off' certain areas where the enemy could concentrate under cover. Late on November 29th the 55th Division was so convinced of the imminent menace that Jeudwine asked that the neighbouring III Corps might put down a counter-preparation with 'heavies' on the Banteux Ravine just before daylight next morning, but his request was refused. The gathering enemy themselves were surprised that 'nothing was done to disturb the German preparations'.

And next morning they repaid the tank surprise by one which was similar in principle if different in method. Unheralded by any long artillery preparation, a short, hurricane bombardment with gas and smoke shell paved the way for the infiltrating advance of the German infantry—the prototype of the German offensive method of spring, 1918, as the British attack had been the prototype of the Allied offensive method of summer and autumn, 1918. Emerging from the sheltered assembly position of Banteux and Twenty-two Ravines at the very moment when the unfulfilled counter-preparation would have opened, the German stream trickled through the weak points in the British line; then, expanding into a broad torrent which submerged the villages of Gonnelieu and Villers Guislain, swept over gun positions and headquarters, and surged forward to Gouzeaucourt. The menace of disaster was immeasurable, but, fortunately, the complementary attacks on the north of the salient, round Bourlon Wood, were brought to a standstill, and the emergency declined with the recapture of Gouzeaucourt by the superb counterattack of the Guards' Division and a later effort of the

447

2nd Tank Brigade. For a time, indeed, there was a chance to 'redouble' and score heavily off the Germans, disordered by this success and hampered by their narrow penetration. But rejecting Snow's plea for a flank riposte by the cavalry, the Army Commander directed his cavalry head-on against the Germans, and they were soon held up. Thus the invaders were able to consolidate their hold and even to resume their erosion of the British position. During the next few days continued German progress, especially towards Villers Plouich, and British lack of reserves rendered the British position in the Masnières-Bourlon salient so precarious that the greater part of the original gains had to be evacuated. A sombre sunset after a brilliant sunrise.

One shadow which still lingers is that undeservedly thrown on the regimental officers and men by superior officers anxious to exculpate themselves. The official court of enquiry pinned the blame on the troops, ascribing the surprise to their negligence and also asserting, contrary to facts, that they had failed to send up 'S.O.S.' flares. Even Byng declared—'I attribute the reason for the local success on the part of the enemy to one cause and one alone, namely—lack of training on the part of junior officers and N.C.O's and men.' Haig, however, who had been kept in the dark as to the warnings, was an exception to the 'general' rule. In sending his report home, he generously assumed the whole responsibility—although he also sent home several of the subordinate commanders.

It is thus due for history to record, from the records, that many of the junior leaders were acutely alive to the danger and gave vain warnings to their superiors. And as for their resistance, it was more than anyone had a right to expect of troops who had been kept in action continuously since their attack on November 20th. For military history, indeed, the lesson of Cambrai is that the welcome renaissance of the essential principle of surprise was offset by a fundamental breach of the principle of economy of force—both in adjusting the end to the means and in appreciating the capacity and limits of human endurance.

CHAPTER VII

SCENE 5

CAPORETTO

IN the chill and sodden gloom of an autumn morning amid the mist-wreathed peaks of the Julian Alps came a rumbling. Before its echoes finally subsided, the Allied cause had been shaken to its foundations. The first rumours of disaster, which were far from exaggerating the reality, came like a thunder-clap to the Allied peoples, if not to all their leaders, for 1917 hitherto had seen the Allies on the offensive in all theatres.

The year had begun with the expectation of a sure progress towards victory, of a vast combined offensive culminating in the overthrow of the Central Powers, and if the mirage of early victory had been slowly fading before the evidence of stubborn resistance and heavy losses, the public were still unprepared for a definite change of rôle from attack to defence. More especially was this unexpected in Italy, for while there was obvious ground for qualms over Russia, the Italians had been attacking during August and September, and the cables had given the impression that the tide of battle was flowing strongly in their favour. And for once, in a war when the output of fiction was greater than that of fact, these reports were correct.

If the gain in ground was small the moral and material effect on the already war-rotted Austrians was large, and, as Ludendorff records, 'the responsible military and political authorities of the dual monarchy were convinced that they would not be able to stand a continuation of the battle and a twelfth attack on the Isonzo'. Thus 'in the middle of Septem-ber it became necessary to decide for the attack on Italy in order to prevent the collapse of Austria-Hungary'. So urgent was the need that Ludendorff was forced to abandon his preparations for the offensive in Moldavia, which he had

449

intended as the *coup de grâce* to Russia's crumbling resistance. Even so, where could he raise sufficient troops for converting the Austrian defensive into an effective offensive? The British pressure at Passchendaele and the mere length of his immense fronts in France and Russia absorbed his resources until he could force peace on Russia. All he could spare was his slender general reserve of six divisions, which had already been his instrument in countering the Kerensky offensive—Russia's final flicker—and in the coup which captured Riga. His adviser in the strategic design of operations, Major Wetzell, was however of the opinion that the application of even this small force at a 'soft' spot, such as the sector between Flitsch and Canale, would suffice to lame if not to break the Italian menace.

The result proved him right—the trouble was that it unduly exceeded the most sanguine expectations. And it was due to the fact that it was expanded to a more ambitious plan—without increase of means—than was originally intended in the 'germ' scheme, which Waldstätten, of the Austrian General Staff, had brought to the German Command on August 29th. This original scheme was for a break-through at Tolmino, followed merely by rolling up the Isonzo front. Caporetto and Cambrai were to have a curious kinship.

Ludendorff sent General Krafft von Delmensingen on a special mission to reconnoitre the ground and report on the scheme. Krafft had led the Alpine Corps in the Rumanian campaign, and was thus an expert in mountain warfare. He found that the Austrians had managed to retain a small bridgehead on the west bank of the Isonzo at Tolmino, and this afforded a jumping-off point for the projected attack. Guns were got up mostly by hand and at night; the infantry came up by seven night marches, taking no vehicles, but carrying their ammunition, equipment, and supplies on the men or on pack animals. Thus the twelve assault divisions and 300 batteries concentrated undiscovered by the Italians, owing partly to able precautions, partly to the country, and partly to the inadequate air reconnaissances of the enemy.

What of the Italians? The Commander-in-Chief, Cadorna, was undoubtedly a man of more than ordinary ability, but, like certain other famous commanders, his intellectual power was offset by his lack of touch with and understanding of the fighting troops. With such men, also, their mental remoteness is often accentuated by the natural isolation in which those in high military position are placed. Considering the comparatively slender weight of the attack, he had enough men and guns to withstand it successfully, but his distribution of them was unsuited to the conditions of the various sectors. Troops already too highly tried were kept too long in the positions of greatest strain. Thus, the combination of faulty distribution with the enemy's unerring eye for the vulnerable spot produced, with other factors, an Austro-German success out of all proportion to the means.

Capello, commanding the Second Army, dissatisfied with the defensive suitability of the positions on which the Italian offensive had stopped, had wished to forestall the attack by a flank thrust northwards from the Bainsizza Plateau, but was overruled by Cadorna, who was not only conscious of his shortage of reserves but had belatedly come to doubt the value of offensive methods. In this he was at least wiser than his subordinate who, alike in offensive spirit, in his manner as a commander, and as the victim of the Germans' new offensive method, was the Gough of the Italian Army. Cadorna had full warning of the enemy's intention from his intelligence and from deserters—Czech and Transylvanian officers, but he did not feel sufficiently sure of the real direction of the enemy's attack to justify him in committing his reserves beforehand.

Yet it is at least curious that, as information specifically pointed to the Caporetto sector, on its fifteen-mile frontage there were only posted two battalions to the mile compared with eight to the mile further south. The very fact that this had long been a quiet sector, where both sides sent troops to rest, might have aroused the suspicions of the Italian command. But Capello actually refused the appeal of his left wing here for reinforcements. Perhaps he was the less patient towards arguments because he should have been a patient in hospital. Instead, with misguided pertinacity he stayed in bed at his headquarters, and only yielded the reins of command the day after his front collapsed.

The Italian frontier province of Venezia formed a tongue pointing towards Austria. It was flanked on the south by the Adriatic and on the east and north by the Julian and Carnic Alps—beyond which lay the Austrian Trentino. The six German divisions, with nine Austrian, formed the attacking Fourteenth German Army, under General Otto von Below, with whom was Krafft as Chief of Staff and guiding brain. These troops were to climb the mountain barrier at the tip of the tongue, while two Austrian armies, under Boroevic, were to advance along the stretch of lower ground near the Adriatic shore.

The difficulties of organizing and deploying an attack in the mountains were ably overcome, and after four hours' gas shell and one hour's general bombardment, the attackers moved forward in the drizzle of snow and rain, and in many places rapidly overcame the resistance of infantry who, owing partly to the breakdown of telephone communication, were but fitfully supported by their own artillery. But the misty conditions were the greater factor in the success, as next March in France; they provided the element of surprise which proved the only and indispensable key to open a way through the enemy's front. Although the right and left wings of the attacking army were delayed by sturdy resistance in the rear positions, the centre group (four divisions) under Stein penetrated completely at Caporetto, and through this breach reserves were pouring by evening. The effect was to make the whole defensive position untenable and to ease the task of the attacking right wing (three and a half Austrian divisions) under Krauss, which now pushed forward almost unchecked down the Val d'Uccea, the shortest line to turn the river barrier of the Tagliamento. This enveloping advance nullified Cadorna's efforts to dam the breach, efforts which also broke down owing to the difficulty of pushing reserves up the narrow mountain roads already congested by troops which had no stomach left for fighting. This convinced Cadorna of the necessity of ordering a general retreat to the Tagliamento, as Capello had earlier urged, and it was successfully achieved after two critical days—October 30th and 31st.

Fortunately the pursuing enemy had suffered from hitches in movements and supply, as well as an increasing friction between the German and Austrian commanders. Their attempt to achieve a surprise capture of the crossings was foiled, and although in a deliberate attack one of Krauss's Austrian divisions got across at Cornino on November 2nd, Cadorna had had breathing space to make preparations for a further retreat to the Piave. Although large bodies of troops were cut off by the enemy's pincer-like advance, the main armies succeeded in reaching the Piave by November 10th, thus reforging their line. Yet its links were very thin. Nearly 600,000 men had been lost, and the Second Army, which had suffered the direct blow, was practically out of action as a force. At this juncture Cadorna gave place to Diaz, whose supreme value was that he understood the mind of the soldiers, and knew how to reinvigorate their morale, playing, in fact, the same rôle as Pétain in France earlier that year.

Three days later a fresh menace developed, on November 12th, when Conrad's troops (Austrian Tenth and Eleventh Armies) sought to move down from the Trentino on the Italian rear. But here Cadorna's preparations for defence had been long initiated and were well matured, so that the threat was frustrated. Ludendorff, too late, tried to switch reinforcements round to Conrad, but was foiled by the inadequate rail communications and deficiency of motor transport —if, fundamentally, by the limited horizon of the original plan.

Meanwhile, French and British divisions had been hurriedly railed to Italy, their coming preceded by the arrival of Foch and Sir Henry Wilson, but they took some time to concentrate—and were then at first held back in reserve—so that the interval before they relieved divisions of their severely strained Ally was a time of grave stress. The most serious attack came in the sector between the Piave and the Brenta, but here, after five days of struggle, Laderchi's Italian IX Corps brought the attack to halt, and at the beginning of December was relieved by the French, while the British, under Lord Plumer, took over the Montello sector. Contrary to expectation, both were left in peace, and during the remaining months of the campaign the enemy's attack was confined to renewed efforts by Conrad and Krauss further to the northwest, in the Asiago and Grappa sectors. If these imposed a fresh tax on the weary Italians, it was psychologically worth while, for this successful and stalwart resistance by its vindication of their fighting power laid the moral foundations for the Italian 'revanche' of 1918.

Reviewing the drama of Caporetto in the clearer light of history, there is reason to think that excessive emphasis was placed on the effect of enemy and seditious propaganda, and that the major reason of the crumbling resistance early was the same as in France that spring—that the troops were morally tired, and that the result of being hurled endlessly against machine-gun defences had worn down their fighting spirit. The presence of imminent disaster to their country set a new light upon the position, and gave a sacrificial impulse to a duty which on the Piave line, fighting 'with their backs to the wall', they honourably and gallantly fulfilled.

Strategically, however, the most critical stage was past with the passing of Tagliamento, for henceforth what Clausewitz called the 'friction of war' so upset the attackers' communications that their power and speed fell off badly. Some of the causes have been mentioned. But one, which was to operate again next spring in France, deserves emphasis. The well-filled supply depots of the Italian army were too great a temptation to the under-nourished enemy, the desire to eat quenched the desire to pursue, and sudden congestion of the stomach accelerated the congestion of the advance. It is significant that even a German divisional commander, General Lecquis, could exult more at the capture of two or three chickens apiece by his men than of many prisoners, and regarded the possession of a few pigs 'as the height of human felicity'.

CHAPTER VII

PANORAMA

THE WAR IN THE AIR

To relate the action of aircraft in the military sphere is not possible, for it formed a thread running through and vitally influencing the whole course of operations, rather than a separate strategic feature. But a brief outline of the evolution of aircraft action in the field may help to complete the strategic picture. Military appreciation of air values was a slow growth, and the advocates of aircraft had an uphill struggle for recognition. Until the Italians used aircraft extensively against the Turks in Tripoli, 1911-1912, general military opinion was aptly represented by General Foch's comment when watching the *Circuit de l'Est*—'That is good sport but for the Army the aeroplane is worthless.' Even in 1914 the proportion of military aircraft was puny, and their application more limited than with the Italians two years earlier.

In the first month of the war visual reconnaissance was the only rôle allotted and no provision was made for air combat or bombing. For the inadequacy of its air service and lack of information the German Army paid a heavy price during the invasion of France. But the Royal Flying Corps, although bringing only sixty-three machines across the Channel, twice rendered invaluable service. One reconnaissance unmasked the initial attempt to outflank the British Army at Mons, and another discovered Kluck's historic swerve towards the Marne.

In September the sphere of air co-operation was enlarged to embrace observation of targets for the artillery, communication being at first by coloured lights and eventually by wireless telegraphy. In September also, photography from the air was tried, but its potential value was not recognized by General Headquarters until 1915. By March a special

457

aeroplane camera was supplied, and air photography henceforth developed continuously, although long handicapped by
dependence on captured German lenses for the large scale
cameras. A fresh form of co-operation was tried in 1915,
although not fully applied until 1916. This was the contact
patrol, whereby commanders were informed of the situation
of their own infantry during battle, and of threatened counterattacks by the enemy.

The pursuit of this air co-operation by both sides simultaneously, as well as the desire to baffle the enemy's observation, had naturally led to air fighting, and this, in turn, to
a struggle for supremacy in the air. Rifles and pistols were
the only weapons available at the outset, so that air combat
bore the appearance of an exhilarating and uncertain new
form of game-shooting. Soon, however, light machine-guns
were fitted, although the fighting rôle was mainly restricted
to 'pusher' type aeroplanes, as, on a tractor type, the propeller
hindered fire in a forward direction. In May, 1915, the Germans produced a new and fast Fokker fighting machine
equipped with an interruptor gear which enabled the gun to
fire through the orbit of the revolving propeller without risk
of hitting the blades. The Fokkers inflicted heavy losses
amongst the British machines, and, for a time, gained air
superiority for the Germans.

The Allies replied to this menace not only by new machines
but by new methods, settled in joint conference. The
'fighters' were concentrated in special squadrons, instead of
being distributed among all, and these squadrons were to
seek out their opponents behind the opposing front, thus
enabling their own reconnaissance and artillery machines
to work undisturbed. This method of offensive patrols was
successfully tried by the French at Verdun in February,
1916, and developed by the British on the Somme, where for
some weeks the Germans were almost driven out of the air.
The offensive was also extended to the enemy's aerodromes—
an extension which recalled the historic naval maxim that
the enemy's coasts were the frontiers of Britain. Already, in

October, 1914, British naval aircraft operating on the Belgian coast had raided the Zeppelin sheds at Dusseldorf and Cologne, destroying one airship; another was destroyed next month in a raid from Belfort on Friedrichshafen.

Although the raids on aerodromes from 1916 onwards did not often succeed in inflicting serious material damage, they had a marked moral effect, for once pilots were safely back in their own aerodrome they were apt to feel that their share of risk was complete. An unforeseen addition was all the worse to bear when the nerve-tension had been relaxed, and when they were taken at a disadvantage on the ground.

The Allied air supremacy of 1916 was not long maintained. The Germans challenged it with improved types of single-seater fighting machines and with the so-called 'circus' system whereby special fighting squadrons were formed—under a picked leader who picked his own pilots—and were successively switched to any part of the front where the higher command desired air superiority to be gained. The most famous of these 'circuses' were those of Boelcke and Baron von Richthofen.

By this superior strategy the Germans regained the upper hand early in 1917, although the total British fighting machines outnumbered theirs by three to one. And the British tragically helped to swell the enemy's 'bag' by sending out swarms of partially trained young pilots from England, under pressure from G.H.Q. But the Allies soon retorted with fresh machines and gradually, if expensively, won back a superiority in the air which was never lost again—although never so marked as in the summer of 1916. Because of the three-dimensional conditions of air warfare, a command of the air could never be attained in the sense that a command of the sea was possible, and the object became a superiority, which should ensure a local and temporary command of the air over a static front when needed.

The year 1917 was marked also by an increasing development of the method of fighting and flying in formation, which tended to replace the Homeric combats of individual champions—whose mounting score of victims had been followed with the excitement that formerly awaited the return of a Red Indian scalping expedition or the news of a Test Match. Henceforth, knight-errantry yielded to tactics and air fighting gradually assumed the more developed forms of warfare, although carried out on a different plane. By the end of the war an attack was often delivered by formations of fifty or sixty machines which manœuvred—the actual squadrons compact—with the aim of breaking up the enemy's formation.

Thus they became cavalry of the air, and the resemblance was heightened by another new form of air action, used with great effect in the later stages of the war. This was the attack on ground troops. So long as the rival armies were firmly embedded in trenches, air attack had small scope, although occasionally it came to the relief of hard-pressed packets of infantry. But when the British front broke in March, 1918, all the available fighter squadrons, French as well as British, were concentrated to strike at the advancing enemy. Their overhead counterattacks during this crisis were an important factor in stemming the German onrush, and one that has been inadequately recognized by military historians. Still greater opportunities came when the enemy tide ebbed in the autumn. After the breaking of the Bulgarian, Turkish, and Austrian fronts alike, air attacks on the retreating columns both hastened and completed the break up of the enemy armies.

Air attack on the communications, supply depots, ammunition dumps, and billets of the armies, had been developed much earlier. The battle of Neuve Chapelle in March, 1915, marked the first organized attempt to prevent the arrival of enemy reinforcements, and at Loos in September, a more extended bombing plan was applied against the German railways. Results were small, however, owing to lack of experience, deficiency of equipment, and the want of machines to maintain the intensive bombardment essential for causing an effective stoppage. If a railway was damaged before the battle it could be repaired in time for the passage of reinforcements; and, unless repairs were hindered by continuous bombing, supplies and ammunition would reach the enemy troops before they began to run short. The first lesson was learnt and applied in the later battles of the war, when the bombing of communications played a regular part, but the second lesson was never fully applied owing to lack of bombing air-craft. The very eagerness with which the armies had eventu-ally embraced aircraft as immediate auxiliaries—for recon-naissance, artillery observation, and the protection of these duties—limited the supply of aircraft for rôles of indirect co-operation, and curtailed their exploitation of the bombing weapon.

Moreover, their very concentration on these auxiliaries blinded the armies to the greater possibilities of crippling their opponents by hunger. The Germans, especially, neg-lected opportunities of inflicting decisive injury—as a senior staff officer of the British Second Army revealed a few years ago. This Army received the bulk of its supplies from Calais and Boulogne, and in front of these bases was held only three days' reserves of food and ammunition, apart from three days' supplies with the fighting troops. To serve the front there were two double lines and one single; to meet the nor-mal needs of the troops seventy-one trains a day were needed —three-quarters of the total capacity of the three lines. With this narrow margin of safety, the blocking of one line would have sufficed to dislocate the whole system, while the blocking of more than one line would have brought a catastrophe. To cause such a block would have been the easier because outside Calais there was a junction of two of the lines, and near St. Omer two converged. Moreover, a block at Arques, near St. Omer, would even have cut off the troops from the three days' reserves, which lay in depots further back along the two lines which converged at this point. It is not difficult to pic-ture the situation which would have arisen if an effective and sustained bombing attack had been launched in April,1918, to coincide with the German Army's attack, when this area was congested with British and French troops who were trying to dam the breach in the front.

The Allied Commanders, also, on the Western Front, were unwilling to spare sufficient aircraft for a real test of the effect of bombing communications. Yet, there was a significant hint of its potency, when on July 16th, 1918, the bombing of an ammunition train at Thionville station stopped all traffic along this important section of the German communications for forty-eight hours—the forty-eight hours before the Allied counterstroke on the Marne which turned the tide of the war.

At sea, the Germans, relying on their submarines, fortunately failed to explore the possibilities of air attacks on merchant shipping, or on the ports where that shipping had to unload its freight. And the Allies could not, as their enemy had no shipping in use. There was one fleeting glimpse of such action; as early as August 12th, 1915, a British seaplane, launched from a seaplane carrier near the Dardanelles, gained the distinction of being the first to torpedo a ship. The most valuable service rendered by naval aircraft during the war was in antisubmarine patrolling and escorting convoys—a purely protective rôle.

Yet seven months before the Battle of Jutland, Commodore Sueter of the Naval Air Service had begged the Admiralty to sanction the construction of two hundred torpedo-carrying aircraft. His persistence merely led to his removal—to the Adriatic. The year after Jutland, the new Commander-in-Chief of the Grand Fleet asked for that very number to be produced as early as possible. It was too late. The unwanted offspring of Sueter's vision might conceivably have made that one ineffective naval battle decisive. Moreover, a further chance had been forfeited through the oversight by which the *Campania*, a large aircraft carrier, was left behind when the Grand Fleet sailed from Scapa Flow.

It was the Naval Air Service, however, which first proposed, and attempted, to strike at the sources of the enemy's power to make war—his industrial centres. The way was blocked by the narrow view of the Army Command. The idea nevertheless made headway, and in October 1916 was reinforced by the arguments of Colonel Barès, of the French air service, on a visit to London. The Admiralty representative on the Air Board then suggested that the Navy should keep a force of two hundred bombers in France for this purpose. But, according to the Official History, the proposal 'drew a strong letter of protest from Sir Douglas Haig. . . . He stated that the views attributed to Colonel Barès were unsound in theory and should not be accepted in practice'. Haig's opposition killed the scheme—which might have checked the stream of shells that were being hurled at his troops. In 1917, out of fifty air squadrons in France, only two were for bombing, and those were confined to local targets.

Not until late in the war was there any attempt on the Allied side to attack the enemy's 'home' front save for spasmodic raids by a handful of British naval aircraft, as well as by the French. Nor, in the light of human nature, was independent air action likely to be developed so long as this new weapon was handled by and divided between the land and sea forces. The essential fusion between the two parts was delayed until April, 1918, when the Royal Air Force was created. As a sequel, the Independent Air Force was formed in June, and placed under Trenchard, who had been the dynamic leader of the military air arm in France, if also, ironically, a determined opponent of independent air action. In the few months that remained, the repeated and expanding raids of the new force accelerated the moral disintegration of Germany, and, by their moral effect at least, hampered the production of munitions in the Rhineland. Even so, the significance of this force was more in promise than fulfilment, for it was barely a quarter of its intended strength when the Armistice came. Similarly, the effect of the German air raids on England should be assessed in the light of the fact that the largest raid was carried out by less than forty bombers.

What might have been achieved is suggested by the fact that the seven principal munition centres in the Ruhr, as well as those in the Rhineland, were all within air range of the British front. Essen (173 miles), Germany's main arsenal, was only as far as the German machines flew in bombing London from their base near Ghent. Again, one factory at Hagen (175 miles) produced two-thirds of the German submarine accumulators. Two of the largest chemical factories were less than 100 miles from the Allied front. Yet this immense opportunity of crippling the munition supply of the German armies was sacrificed in favour of air fighting over the trench front—sacrificed, in fact, on the 'battle' altar of Clausewitz-in-the-air. Even when the Independent Air Force was at last formed, in face of vehement opposition from G.H.Q., its strength was curtailed to a mere hundred machines (about 2 per cent of Britain's total air force) and more than half its raids were directed against tactical, instead of industrial targets. Apart from what was then achieved, a sidelight on its wider indirect effect is shed by the fact that, in the month of August alone, one shell factory, which was never even bombed, received fifty-three false alarms and suffered an output deficit of 3000 tons. There is also a paradoxical reflection on the G.H.Q. doctrine of concentration on the battlefront in the fact that the menace of these raids drew off no less than twenty German squadrons from the front—three or four times as many machines as were engaged in them!

CHAPTER VIII

1918—THE BREAK

THE middle years of the World War had been, in a military sense, a tussle between a lean Hercules and a bulky Cerberus. The Germanic Alliance was weaker in numbers but directed by a single head, the Entente stronger in numbers but with too many heads. Owing to their own excessive losses, diffusion of effort and the collapse of Russia, the Entente at the end of 1917 were faced with the grim fact that the numerical balance had been reversed, and months must elapse before the prospective stream of America's new divisions should tilt the scales once more in their favour. The emergency paved the way for the creation of a unified command but it still needed disaster to bring it into being.

At the conference at Rapallo in November, the formation of a Supreme War Council was decided upon, to be composed of the principal Ministers of the Allies, with military representatives, and to sit permanently at Versailles. If a fundamental defect was that it merely substituted a formal for an informal committee, a further flaw was that the military representatives had no executive status. In the economic sphere, where deliberation rather than instant action was necessary, it led to a real improvement in the combination of shipping, food and munition resources. Militarily, it was futile, for it set up a dual advisership—the Versailles representatives on the one hand and the chiefs of the national General Staffs on the other. Yet it is fair to add that this 'dead end' was due to a British obstruction.

Both the Americans and the French desired to give this committee executive power and an executive head, and Pétain logically supported the proposal, which came from Colonel House and General Bliss. But the fundamental offset to its wisdom was that it eliminated the essential control of strategy by the statesman, while the suggested composition of the council repeated the error of the Nivelle era. For it was to consist of the national Commanders-in-Chief and Chiefs of Staff, and thus whichever member was chosen as president would have his freedom of judgment and execution hampered by his responsibility to and for his own national army. Moreover, in fulfilment, the proposal would mean that the council would have a French chief—as the French realized when they supported, and the British when they opposed, the proposal. In rejecting it Lloyd George was guided not only by a wise objection to a purely military council but by his feeling that British opinion was not ripe for it, and that Haig's resistance to another Nivelle solution would be supported by the public at home. Moreover, the suggested inclusion of the Chiefs of Staff introduced a personal complication, for the last thing that Lloyd George desired was to strengthen the influence of Sir William Robertson upon the conduct of the war. Rather was he hoping to sidetrack Robertson, whom he held responsible for the futile and costly strategy of 1917, in favour of Sir Henry Wilson, his nominee for the Versailles committee. And while he sought to make Versailles independent of the narrow purview of the British General Staff, Clemenceau was equally intent to make it merely a microphone for the French General Staff, to amplify its 'voice'.

In default of agreement the military representatives—now Generals Weygand, Wilson, Bliss, and Cadorna—were merely technical advisers. But as the menace of the German attack grew closer, and with it the need for common action, this advisory body was converted into a military executive committee to handle an inter-allied general reserve, a fresh compromise which set up a dual control—the Commanders-in-Chief and the Versailles committee. Only an enlargement of mind and goodwill could make it workable.

Time was too short. Since early in November the stream of German troop-trains from the Eastern to the Western Front had been steadily swelling. When the 1917 campaign opened, there had been a proportion of nearly three Allies to two Germans—actually in March one hundred and seventy-eight British, French and Belgian divisions against one hundred and twenty-nine German divisions. Now the Germans had a slight advantage, with the likelihood of augmenting it. But the Allied statesmen, recalling how often their own offensive had failed with equal or greater superiority of force, were naturally slow to appreciate the gravity of the menace or to respond to the sudden fall in the temperature of military opinion. Nor could they agree to draw reinforcements from the other fronts.

The Italians strove against any withdrawal of the Allied contingents from their front, and the French opposed any reduction of the Salonika force. Lloyd George urged an effort to complete the success in Palestine; this was sanctioned on the understanding that no reinforcements went there from France, though it also meant that none came from there to France. Meantime, the German strength had increased to one hundred and seventy-seven divisions by the end of January, and fifteen more in March. The Allied strength, by the despatch of divisions to Italy and the breaking up of others owing to the French shortage of drafts had fallen to the equivalent of one hundred and seventy-three—counting as double the four and a half large-size American divisions which had arrived. For the French and British had been constrained to follow the Germans in reducing their divisions from twelve to nine battalions each.

Internal friction among the Allies increased their handicap. In part it was due to the difficulties of a fair settlement as to the length of front which each should hold. In the 1917 campaign the British, bearing the burden of the offensive, had been in charge of barely one hundred miles of line, while the French, on the defensive, had held three hundred and twenty-five miles. At the close of the campaign Haig had come to an agreement with Pétain that he would extend his line to Barisis, just south of the Oise, which made a total of one hundred and twenty-five miles. In view of his change to a defensive attitude, the extension can hardly be considered exacting, although his heavy losses made it a greater strain than it would have been on the 1917 basis of strength. But before this extension was complete, Clemenceau, the new French Premier, intervened with a demand that the British should take over an additional thirty miles, as far as Berry-au-Bac. Clemenceau threatened to resign if this demand were not met, but eventually agreed to submit the case to the Versailles committee, which proposed a compromise whereby the British should take over approximately half the distance in dispute. Thereupon Haig threatened to resign; this threat threw the Supreme War Council and its advisory committee into the melting-pot from which the executive committee emerged. Meantime Haig went direct to Pétain and reached a settlement by which he was merely to complete his extension to Barisis, according to the original agreement. This was a noteworthy concession on Pétain's part, which did honour to his spirit of helpfulness. And the Supreme War Council on February 2nd accepted this private settlement between the two Commanders-in-Chief, wisely swallowing the affront to its own dignity. It is astonishing, in view of this fact, that the legend should still persist that Haig was forced by the 'politicians' to extend his line against his will, and likewise the argument that such extension was the cause of the subsequent break-through.

The just proportion between the respective fronts is hardly less difficult to determine now, in retrospect, than it was to agree upon then. With ninety-nine divisions the French had to hold three hundred miles, while the British with fifty-eight divisions, of somewhat greater rifle strength, took charge of one hundred and twenty-five miles—after the extension to Basiris. Of the French line, however, the half from St. Mihiel eastwards was of secondary importance. If, even so, the French had cause for complaint on any mileage basis, the British could fairly claim that they had more vital objectives to cover, less room to fall back, and a higher proportion of the enemy already on their front. But the French, in turn, could point to the fact that the main mass of the German reserves was so placed that it might intervene on either front. To weigh a question compounded of such diverse elements required a strategic mind of the purest scientific detachment, whereas it had to be resolved by men whose determined character and strong sense of nationality made it difficult for them to see the other man's point of view. Lloyd George was an exception, but to his endowment with a wider outlook was linked a tendency to be impatient with the point of view of his own men, especially when this seemed to him parochial or obstructive.

Disagreement between him and Sir William Robertson, his official military adviser, had increased throughout 1917, Robertson being intensely suspicious of political interference with military plans and of Lloyd George's unorthodox ideas, while Lloyd George felt that Robertson's sole idea in strategy was to support Haig blindly and frustrate any alternative schemes. The results of this blank-cheque policy at Passchendaele made the Prime Minister more anxious to provide himself with alternative advice, a desire that had influenced him in setting up the Supreme Council with its military committee, and in appointing to it Sir Henry Wilson, whom he regarded as a soldier of more sympathetic and larger outlook. But when the new organ was converted into an executive committee, Robertson insisted that he, as Chief of the Imperial General Staff, should be the British military member. The Prime Minister objected that the combination of the two posts in one man would vitiate the whole principle, maintaining the sectional instead of the detached view. Robertson's stand brought the long-growing dissension to a climax. The Prime Minister went part of the way to meet him by appointing him the Versailles representative, while Wilson was to become Chief of the Imperial General Staff at home with reduced functions. Sprung on Robertson as a surprise, this proposal provoked his refusal. After several days of discussion and domestic crisis, Robertson was offered his former post on the new terms. His refusal to accept them produced his enforced resignation, and relegation to a home command. Wilson succeeded him, and Rawlinson was appointed to Versailles. Such conflicts of view, if unavoidable in human nature and in an alliance, weakened the common front. And as soon as one difficulty was overcome, other sources of dissension came to the fore.

The prolonged waste of soldiers' lives in the swamps beyond Ypres had led Lloyd George and his Cabinet to withhold reinforcements for fear of encouraging fresh squandering. This undoubtedly weakened Haig's initial power of resistance to the German onslaught, yet it is just to point out that it was weakened more—in quality as well as quantity—by the 400,000 British casualties suffered in the offensive of the later part of 1917. Moreover, we should not forget that the Government had the heavy responsibility of being the trustee for the lives of the nation. The real ground of criticism is that it was not strong enough to make a change in, or place a check upon, a command which it did not trust, while supplying the reinforcements necessary for defence. And for this lack of moral strength the public must share the blame, for they had already shown themselves too easily swayed by clamour against political interference with the generals, and too prone to believe that the politician is invariably wrong on such occasions. The civilian public, indeed, is apt to trust soldiers too little in peace, and sometimes too much in war.

These political handicaps, and the accompanying tendency of politicians to work deviously towards what they dare not demand openly, were also seen in the project for a unified command. The Prime Minister, indeed, had gone so far in November as to disclaim faith in his own long-sought cure. Instead he sought a palliative in the inter-allied executive committee, under Foch's chairmanship, which should control a common reserve of thirty divisions—one seventh of the total forces. This scheme was decisively annulled by Haig, who, when called on by Foch for his contribution of nine divisions, replied that he could spare none. He preferred to make an arrangement with Pétain for mutual support.

When the test came, a week later, this broke down, and

Haig then took a foremost part in hastening and facilitating the appointment of a generalissimo, which he had formerly opposed. His change of attitude had simply an immediate purpose—'The whole and sole object is to override Pétain and get the French to send reinforcements to prevent the British and French Armies being separated.' (Charteris.)

For the actual breakdown the blame has been commonly thrown upon the French, and there is no question that Haig understood from Pétain on March 24th that if the Germans continued their rapid progress the French reserves would have to be used to cover Paris. But in fairness it is essential to add that, whereas the original compact had only pledged the aid of some six French divisions, Pétain actually sent nine by March 24th, and twenty-one (including four of cavalry) by March 26th. If these reinforcements were perhaps slower coming into action than in despatch, it does not affect the fact that the original pledge was amply exceeded. Thus the fundamental fault would seem to lie in trusting to an arrangement for such slender support by either Ally.

The German Plan. On the German side the submarine panacea for victory had been replaced by a military panacea, and hopes were perhaps exaggerated by the unexpected collapse of Russia. But although Ludendorff promised victory in the field, he did not disguise the fact that a western offensive would be a far harder task than the conquests in the East. He realized also that it would be a race between the effect of Germany's blow and the arrival of American reinforcements, although he hoped to win the race. To secure the rear of his offensive, a definite peace was wrung from the Bolshevik Government of Russia by a military demonstration, and also forced on Rumania. And to secure, if possible, the economic base of his offensive the Ukraine was occupied for its wheat supplies, with little resistance except from Czechoslovak troops who had formerly been taken prisoners from the Austrian Army.

Ludendorff's next problem was to decide his first point of attack. The sector between Arras and St. Quentin was chosen, on the western face of the great salient formed by the German front in France. The choice was governed by tactical reasons —this sector was the enemy's weakest point and the ground offered fewer difficulties than elsewhere—although Ludendorff had in mind the possibility of separating the Allied armies and driving the British back against the Channel coast, where they would be too closely penned in to evade his blows. From the experience of the vain Allied attacks Ludendorff had drawn the deduction that 'tactics had to be considered before purely strategical objects which it is futile to pursue unless tactical success is possible'. Hence he formulated a strategical plan based on the new, or resurrected, principle of taking the tactical line of least resistance. Presumably he hoped by firm control to guide these tactical movements to a strategic destination. If so, he failed.

Where did the fault lie? The general view at the end of the war was that the tactical bias had led Ludendorff to change direction and dissipate his strength. That if the Franco-British Command had previously erred by aiming at the strategically correct target without enough attention to the tactical difficulties the German Command had followed it with an equal if opposite error by concentrating on tactical success at the expense of the strategical goal. But a closer examination of the German documents since available, and of Ludendorff's own orders and instructions, throws a different light on the question. It would seem, indeed, that the real fault was that Ludendorff failed to carry out in practice the new principle he had adopted in theory; that he either did not grasp, or shrank from, the full implication of this new theory of strategy. For in fact he dissipated too large a part of his reserves in trying to redeem tactical failures and hesitated too long over the decision to exploit his tactical successes. Ludendorff's strategy in the East had been so forceful and so far-sighted that his indecision and short-sight in the West is difficult to explain. Perhaps he himself was feeling the strain of directing so many vast operations; perhaps it was that he missed the strategical insight and balanced view of Hoffmann who, after being at his side throughout the 1914–1916 campaigns, had stayed in the East when Ludendorff went to the Supreme Command. The modern vice of seniority prevented Germany making the fullest use of the man who perhaps approached nearer to military genius than any other general of the war.

In any case the campaign leaves the impression that Ludendorff had neither his former clearness as to the goal, nor the same grip on the changing situations. But in the organization of the attacks his powers were at their highest level. Surprise was to be the key which should open a gate in the long-locked front. The most thorough arrangements were made for concealing and for exploiting the attacks, and the surprise effect of the short but intense bombardment was increased by lavish use of gas and smoke shell. Further, while Ludendorff had settled to strike first on the Somme sector, to which blow the code name 'Michael' was given, he also began preparations for successive attacks at other points, which besides being in readiness for the future helped to mystify the enemy. Two were on the British front and one on the French—'St. George I' against the Lys sector, 'St. George II' against the Ypres sector, and 'Blücher' in Champagne.

The 'Michael' attack was to be made by the German Seventeenth, Second, and Eighteenth Armies (sixty-three divisions in all) on the forty-three mile front Arras—St. Quentin—La Fère, but its main force was intended to be exerted north of the Somme, and, after breaking through, the Seventeenth and Second Armies were to wheel north-west and press the British army against the coast, while the river and the Eighteenth Army guarded their flank.

The assault was launched on March 21st, and the surprise was greatly helped by an early morning mist. But while the thrust broke through completely south of the Somme, where the defence—but also the attacking force—was thinnest, it was held up near Arras, a check which reacted on all the attack north of the river. Ludendorff, violating his new principle, spent the following days in trying to revive his attack against the strong, and strongly held bastion of Arras, maintaining this direction as his principal line of effort. Meantime he kept a tight rein on the Eighteenth Army which was advancing in the south without serious check from its opponents. As late as March 26th he issued orders which restrained it from crossing the Avre and tied it to the pace of its neighbour, the Second, which in turn was held back by the very limited success of the Seventeenth Army near Arras. Thus we see that in reality Ludendorff was bent on breaking the British army by breaking down its strongest sector of resistance in a direct assault. And because of this obsession he failed, until too late, to throw the weight of his reserves along the line of least resistance south of the Somme. The intended wheel to the north-west might have come to pass if it had been made after passing the flank, and thus being directed against the rear, of the Arras bastion. On March 26th the attack north of the Somme (by the left wing of the Seventeenth Army and the right of the Second Army) was visibly weakening as the price of its hard-earned gains. South of the Somme the left of the Second Army reached, and was now to be embarrassed by, the desert of the old Somme battlefields—a brake on progress and supply. The Eighteenth Army alone was advancing with unslackened impetus.

This situation led Ludendorff to adopt a new plan, but without relinquishing his old. He ordered for March 28th a fresh and direct attack on the high ground near Arras—by the right of the Seventeenth Army, to be followed by a Sixth Army attack just to the north between Vimy and La Bassée. But the promising situation south of the Somme led him to indicate Amiens as an additional main objective. Even so, he restrained the Eighteenth Army from pushing on to turn the flank of the Amiens defences without further orders! On March 28th the fresh Arras attack was launched, unshielded by mist or surprise, and failed completely in face of the well-prepared resistance of Byng's Third Army. Only then did Ludendorff abandon his original idea and direct his main effort, and some of his remaining reserves, towards Amiens. But meantime he ordered the Eighteenth Army to mark time for two days. When the attack was renewed it made little progress in face of a resistance that had been afforded time to harden, and Ludendorff, rather than be drawn into an attrition struggle, suspended the attempt to reach Amiens.

He had, however, missed vital arteries and decisive results by the narrowest of margins. By March 27th the advance had penetrated nearly forty miles and reached Montdidier, cutting one railway to Paris; by March 30th the German flood was almost lapping the outworks of Amiens. Eighty thousand prisoners and 975 guns had been taken. Once the crust was broken, the very elaboration of the methods of communication built up during three years of static warfare caused the greater flux behind the front. The extent of the retreat was primarily the measure of the loss of control by the British commanders.

Disaster had driven the Allies to an overdue step, and on Haig's appeal and Lord Milner's intervention Foch had been appointed on March 26th to 'co-ordinate' the operations of the Allied armies. In this hour of crisis, Foch's decisive manner and exuberant promises created confidence. Yet, in actual fact, his appointment made little difference to the flow of reinforcements. And although on April 14th he secured the title of Commander-in-Chief of the Allied armies, it gave him no real power of command. By this time a fresh German menace had developed—though not intended as such.

With a large part of his reserves holding the vast bulge south of the Somme, Ludendorff turned, if without much confidence and merely as a diversion, to release, on April 9th, his 'St. George I' attack. Its astonishing early success against a weakened front led him to convert it bit by bit into a major effort. The British were desperately close to the sea, but their resistance stopped the German tide, after a ten-mile invasion, just short of the important railway junction of Hazebrouck, and an attempt to widen the front towards Ypres was nullified by Haig swinging his line back just before and by the gradual arrival of French reinforcements. Haig complained strongly that Foch was too slow in sending French reserves northward, but the event justified Foch's reluctance to commit himself thither and his seeming excess of optimism in declaring that the danger was past. Ludendorff had doled out reserves sparingly, usually too late and too few for real success; so apprehensive that his new bulge would become another sack, that after the capture of Kemmel Hill, when opportunity opened its arms, he stopped the exploitation for fear of a counterstroke.

Thus Ludendorff had fallen short of strategic results; on the other hand he could claim huge tactical successes—the British casualties were over 300,000. The British Army had been badly mauled; and although fresh drafts to the number of 140,000 were hurried out from England and divisions brought back from Italy, Salonika and Palestine, months must elapse before it could recover its offensive power. Ten British divisions had to be broken up temporarily, while the German strength had now mounted to two hundred and eight, of which eighty were back in reserve. A restoration of the balance, however, was now in sight. A dozen American divisions had arrived in France and, responding to the call, great efforts were being made to swell the stream. At the crisis in March, Pershing, the American Commander-in-Chief, even relaxed his inflexible opposition to partial or premature use of the American troops so far as to declare that they were at Foch's disposal for use wherever required. It was an inspiring gesture—although in practice he continued to keep a tight hold on his troops and, with rare exceptions, only allowed them to take over parts of the front as complete divisions.

For Germany the sands were running out. Realizing this, Ludendorff launched his 'Blücher' attack between Soissons and Reims, on May 27th. Falling by surprise with twenty-two divisions against eleven, it swept over the Aisne and reached the Marne on May 30th, where its impetus died away. This time the German superiority of force had not been so pronounced as before nor so well aided by nature's atmospheric cloak. It would seem that the extent of the opening success was due in part to the strategic surprise—the greater unexpectedness of the time and place of the blow—and in part to the folly of the local army command in insisting on the long-exploded and obsolete method of massing the defenders in the forward positions—there to be compressed cannon-fodder for the Germans' massed artillery.

But once again Ludendorff had obtained a measure of success for which he was neither prepared nor desirous. The surpriser was himself surprised. The attack had been conceived merely as a diversion, to attract the Allied reserves thither preparatory to a final and decisive blow at the British front in Flanders. But its opening success attracted thither too large, yet not large enough, a proportion of the German reserves. Blocked frontally by the river, an attempt was made to push west, but it failed in face of Allied resistance—notable for the appearance of American divisions at Château-Thierry, where they gallantly counterattacked.

Ludendorff had now created two huge bulges, and another smaller one, in the Allied front. His next attempt was to pinch out the Compiègne 'tongue' which lay between the Amiens and Marne bulges. But this time there was no surprise, and the blow on the west side of the 'tongue', June 9th, was too late to coincide with the pressure on the east. A month's pause followed.

Ludendorff, though anxious to strike his long-cherished decisive blow against the British in Belgium, considered that their reserves here were still too strong, and so again decided to choose the line of least tactical resistance, hoping that a heavy blow in the south would draw off the British reserves. He had failed to pinch out the Compiègne 'tongue' on the west of his Marne salient; he was now about to attempt the same method on the east, by attacking on either side of Reims. But he needed an interval for rest and preparation, and the delay was fatal, giving the British and French time to recuperate, and the Americans to gather strength. The British divisions previously broken up had now been reconstituted, and as a result of an urgent appeal made to President Wilson in the crisis of March, and the provision of extra shipping, American troops had been arriving at the rate of 300,000 a month since the end of April. By mid July seven American divisions were ready to help in resisting the next, and final, German stroke. Five more were being acclimatized to front-line conditions away on the Alsace-Lorraine sector, and five with the British, while another four were assembled in the American training area.

The tactical success of his own blows had been Ludendorff's undoing. Yielding too late to their influence, he had then pressed each too far and too long, so using up his own reserves and causing an undue interval between each blow. He had driven in three great wedges, but none had penetrated far enough to sever a vital artery, and this strategic failure left the Germans with an indented front which invited flanking counterstrokes.

The Turning of the Tide. On July 15th Ludendorff launched his new attack, but its coming was no secret. East of Reims it was foiled by an elastic defence, and west of Reims the German penetration across the Marne merely enmeshed them more deeply to their downfall—for on July 18th Foch launched a long-prepared stroke against the other flank of the Marne salient. Here Pétain, who directed the operation, turned the key which Ludendorff lacked, using masses of light tanks to lead a surprise attack on the Cambrai method. The Germans managed to hold the gates of the salient open long enough to draw back their forces into safety and straighten their line; but their reserves were depleted, Ludendorff was forced (on the 20th) to postpone, if not yet to abandon, the offensive in Flanders, and the initiative definitely and finally passed to the Allies.

Foch's first concern was to keep it, by giving the enemy no rest while his own reserves were accumulating. To this end he arranged with Haig, Pétain and Pershing for a series of local offensives, aimed to free the lateral railway communications and to improve the position of the front ready for further operations. To Haig he proposed an attack in the Lys sector, but Haig suggested instead the Somme area as more suitable. Rawlinson, commanding the British Fourth Army in front of Amiens, had already submitted to Haig a plan for a large surprise attack there, and Foch agreed to this in place of his own proposal. He also placed under Haig the French First Army (Debeney) to extend the attack to the south. Rawlinson's army was doubled, and by skilful precautions the enemy were kept in the dark until, on August 8th, the attack was delivered—with four hundred and fifty-six tanks. The blow had the maximum shock of surprise, and south of the Somme the troops of the Australian and Canadian Corps rapidly overran and overwhelmed the German forward divisions. By August 12th when the advance came to a halt through reaching the tangled wilderness of the old 1916 battlefields, if also through lack of reserves, the Fourth Army had taken 21,000 prisoners at a cost of only 20,000 casualties. Great, if not fully exploited, as a material, it was far greater as a moral success.

Ludendorff has said: 'August 8th was the black day of the German army in the history of the war . . . It put the decline of our fighting power beyond all doubt . . . The war must be ended.' He informed the Emperor and the political chiefs that peace negotiations ought to be opened before the situation became worse, as it must. The conclusions reached at a Crown Council held at Spa were that 'we can no longer hope to break the war-will of our enemies by military operations', and 'the object of our strategy must be to paralyse the enemy's war-will gradually by a strategic defensive'. In other words the German Command had abandoned hope of victory or even holding their gains, and hoped only to avoid surrender —an insecure moral foundation.

On August 10th Foch issued fresh *directives* for the preparation of an 'advance' by the British Third Army 'in the general direction of Bapaume and Péronne'. Meantime he wished Haig to continue the Fourth Army's frontal pressure, but Haig demurred to it as a vain waste of life and gained his point. Economy of force was henceforth to be added to the advantages of the new strategy now evolved. Thus the momentum of the Fourth Army had hardly waned before the Third Army moved. From then on Foch beat a tattoo on the German front, a series of rapid blows at different points, each broken off as soon as its initial impetus waned, each so aimed as to pave the way for the next, and all close enough in time and space to react on each other. Thus Ludendorff's power of switching reserves to threatened spots was restricted, as his balance of reserves was drained.

On August 10th the French Third Army had struck to the south; then on August 17th the French Tenth Army still further south; next on August 21st the British Third Army, followed by the British First Army on August 26th. Ludendorff's order to the troops holding the Lys salient to retire was hastened in execution by the attacks of the re-formed British Fifth Army, and by the first week in September the Germans were back on their original starting line—the strong defences of the Hindenburg Line. And on September 12th Pershing completed the series of preliminary operations by erasing the St. Mihiel salient—the first feat of the Americans as an independent army. Pershing had originally intended to make this a stepping stone to an advance towards the Briey coalfields and the eastern end of the Germans' main lateral railway near Metz, but the project was abandoned for reasons that will be referred to later. Thus no exploitation of the success was attempted.

The clear evidence of the Germans' decline and Haig's assurance that he would break the Hindenburg Line where the German reserves were thickest, persuaded Foch to seek victory that autumn instead of postponing the attempt until 1919. All the Allied armies in the west were to combine in a simultaneous offensive.

The Collapse of Bulgaria. Before this attack developed, an event occurred in the Balkans which, in the words of Ludendorff, 'sealed the fate of the Quadruple Alliance'. He had still hoped to hold fast in his strong lines in the west, falling back gradually to fresh lines if necessary, and with his strategic flanks in Macedonia and Italy covered, while the German Government was negotiating for a favourable peace. At the same time there was alarm as to the moral effect of the Western Front defeats on the German people, their will-power already undermined by shortage of food, and perhaps also by propaganda.

But on September 15th the Allied armies in Salonika attacked the Bulgarian front, which crumbled in a few days. Guillaumat, who had succeeded Sarrail in December 1917, had prepared the plan for an offensive; when recalled to France in the crisis of June as Governor of Paris (and potential successor to Pétain) he won over the Allied Governments to consent to the attempt. His successor in Salonika, Franchet d'Esperey, concentrated a Franco-Serb striking force, under Michich, on the Sokol-Dobropolye sector, west of the Vardar, where the Bulgarians trusted to the strength of the mountain ridges and were weak in numbers. On September 15th Michich attacked and by the night of the 17th the Serbs had penetrated 20 miles deep, while the breach had been expanded to a width of 25 miles. On the 18th the British attack on the Doiran front was a tactical failure, but it at least helped to pin the enemy's reserves. Meantime the whole of the enemy's front west of the Vardar had collapsed under the converging pressure of the Serbs and French, whose pursuit drove on towards Uskub. And on the 21st the Bulgarian forces east of the Vardar began to fall back in turn. This gave the British aircraft an opportunity, and by bombing the narrow Kosturino Pass they 'largely contributed, on that side, to turn the Bulgarian retreat into a disorderly flight'. With their army split into two parts the Bulgarians, already tired of the war, sought an armistice, which was signed on September 29th. Franchet d'Esperey's achievement not only severed the first root of the Central Alliance, but opened the way to an advance on Austria's rear.

The First Peace Note. The capitulation of Bulgaria convinced Ludendorff that it was necessary to take a decisive step towards securing peace. While he was scraping together a paltry half dozen divisions to form a new front in Serbia, and arranging a meeting with the political chiefs, Foch's grand assaults fell on the western defences, September 26th—28th, and the line threatened to crack.

The German Supreme Command lost its nerve—only for a matter of days, but that was sufficient, and recovery too late. On the afternoon of September 29th Ludendorff was studying the problem in his room at the Hotel Britannique at Spa—an ominously named choice of headquarters! Examination only seemed to make it more insoluble, and in a rising outburst of fear and passion he bemoaned his troubles—especially his lack of tanks—and berated all those whom he considered as having thwarted his efforts—the jealous staffs, the defeatist Reichstag, the too humanitarian Kaiser, and the submarine-obsessed navy. Gradually he worked himself into a frenzy, until suddenly, with foam on his lips, he fell to the floor in a fit. And that evening it was a physically as well as mentally shaken man who took the precipitate decision to appeal for an armistice, saying that the collapse of the Bulgarian front had upset all his dispositions—'troops destined for the Western Front had had to be despatched there'. This had 'fundamentally changed the situation in view of the attacks then being launched on the Western Front', for though these 'had so far been beaten off their continuance must be reckoned with'.

This remark refers to Foch's general offensive. The American attack in the Meuse-Argonne had begun on September 26th, but had come practically to a standstill by the 28th. A Franco-Belgo-British attack had opened in Flanders on the 28th, but if unpleasant did not look really menacing. On the morning of the 29th, however, Haig's main blow was falling on the Hindenburg Line, and the early news was disquieting.

In this emergency, Prince Max was called to be Chancellor to negotiate a peace move, with his international reputation for moderation and honour as its covering pledge. To bargain effectively and without confession of defeat he needed, and asked, a breathing space 'of ten, eight, even four days, before

I have to appeal to the enemy'. But Hindenburg merely re-iterated that 'the gravity of the military situation admits of no delay', and insisted that 'a peace offer to our enemies be issued at once', while Ludendorff plaintively chanted the refrain 'I want to save my army'.

Hence on October 3rd, the appeal for an immediate armistice went out to President Wilson. It was an open confession of defeat to the world, and even before this—on October 1st —the Supreme Command had undermined their own home front by communicating the same impression to a meeting of the leaders of all political parties. Men who had so long been kept in the dark were blinded by the sudden light. All the forces of discord and pacifism received an immense impulse.

While the German Government was debating the conditions for an armistice and questioning Ludendorff as to the situation of the army for further resistance if the terms were unacceptable, Foch continued his military pressure.

The Breach of the Hindenburg Line. The plan of the general offensive embraced a series of convergent and practically simultaneous attacks:

1 and 2. By the Americans between the Meuse and the Argonne Forest, and by the French west of the Argonne, both in the direction of Mézières—beginning on September 26th.

3. By the British on the St. Quentin Cambrai front in the general direction of Maubeuge—beginning on September 27th.

4. By the Belgian and Allied forces in the direction of Ghent—beginning on September 28th.

The general aspect was that of a pincer-like pressure against the vast salient jutting south between Ypres and Verdun. The attack towards Mézières would shepherd that part of the German armies towards the rather difficult country of the Ardennes and away from their natural line of retreat through Lorraine; it was also dangerously close to the hinge of the Antwerp-Meuse line which the Germans were preparing in rear. The attack towards Maubeuge would threaten the other main line of communication and retreat through the Liége gap, but it had further to go. In these attacks, the Americans had the hardest natural obstacle; the British had to face the strongest defences and the heaviest weight of enemy troops.

Pershing's attack opened well, adding surprise to its superiority in numbers—approximately eight to one—but soon lost impetus owing to the difficulties of supply and exploitation in such country. When it was eventually suspended on October 14th, after bitter fighting and severe losses, the American Army was still far distant from the vital railway. A new force, it was suffering the growing pains which the British had passed through in 1915–1916. Pershing's difficulties were enhanced by the fact that he had waived his own proposal for an exploitation of the St. Mihiel success towards Metz in view of Haig's objection to a move which, however promising in its ultimate aim, would diverge from the general direction of the other Allied attacks. Foch's original plan for the general offensive had accordingly been readjusted, and in consequence Pershing had not only a more difficult sector, but a bare week in which to prepare his blow. The shortness of time led him to use untried divisions instead of switching the more experienced divisions used at St. Mihiel. But in the outcome, Haig's insistence was proved unnecessary, for the British attack broke through the Hindenburg Line before the Meuse-Argonne attack had drawn away any German division from his front.

Haig, by pushing forward his left wing first, facilitated the attack of his right on the strongest section of the Hindenburg Line—the Canal du Nord, and by October 5th the British were through the German defence system, with open country beyond. But on this front the attackers had actually fewer divisions than the defenders,* their tanks were used up, and they

* On September 25th, the eve of Foch's general offensive, there were fifty-seven German divisions facing forty British and two American divisions along the Hindenburg Line between, roughly, St. Quentin and Lens. In the Meuse-Argonne sector twenty enemy divisions opposed thirty-one French and thirteen large-strength American divisions—a total equivalent to at least sixty normal-size Allied divisions. The German divisions had shrunk to an abnormally small size, but this fact

could not press forward fast enough to endanger the German retreat.

Within a few days the Supreme Command became more cheerful, even optimistic, when it saw that breaking into the Hindenburg Line had not been followed by an actual break-through of the fighting front. More encouragement came from reports of a slackening in the force of the Allies' attacks, par-ticularly in the exploitation of opportunities. Ludendorff still wanted an armistice, but only to give his troops a rest as a prelude to further resistance and to ensure a secure withdrawal to a shortened defensive line on the frontier. By October 17th he even felt he could do it without a rest. It was less that the situation had changed than that his impression of it had been revised. It had never been quite so bad as he had pictured it on September 29th. But his first impression, and depression, had now spread throughout the political circles and public of Germany, as the ripples spread when a pebble has been dropped in a pool.

The combined pressure of the Allied armies, and their steady advance, were loosening the will-power of the German Government and people. The conviction of ultimate defeat, slower to appeal to them than to the army chiefs, was the more forcible when it was realized. And the indirect moral effect of military and economic pressure was accentuated by the direct effect of peace propaganda, skilfully directed and intensively waged by Northcliffe. The 'home front' began to crumble later, but it crumbled quicker than the battlefront.

The Collapse of Turkey. The offensive planned for the spring in Palestine had been interrupted by the crisis in France and the consequent withdrawal of most of Allenby's British troops. The depletion was made up by reinforcements from India and Mesopotamia, and by September Allenby was again ready to take the offensive. He secretly concentrated, on the Mediter-ranean flank, the mass of his infantry, and behind them the cavalry. Meantime Lawrence and his Arabs, appearing out

does not affect the historical comparison of odds met by the right and left pincers respectively of the Allied offensive.

of the desert like unseen mosquitos, menaced the enemy's communications and distracted their attention. At dawn on September 19th the western mass attacked, rolling the Turks back north-east towards the hilly interior—like a door on its hinges. Through the open doorway the cavalry passed, riding straight up the coastal corridor for thirty miles, before swinging east to bestride the Turkish rear. The only remaining way of retreat was eastwards across the Jordan and this was closed with shattering effect by the British airbombers. Completely trapped, the main Turkish armies were rounded up, while Allenby's cavalry exploited the victory of Megiddo by a swift and sustained pursuit which gained first Damascus and finally Aleppo. Defenceless and threatened with a direct advance of Milne from Macedonia on Constantinople, Turkey capitulated on October 30th.

The Collapse of Austria. The last Austrian attempt at an offensive on the Italian front, in conjunction with the German assaults in France, had been repulsed on the Piave in June. Diaz waited until conditions were ripe for an offensive in return, until Austria's internal decay had spread and she was without hope from Germany. On October 24th Cavan's army moved to seize the crossings of the Piave, and on October 27th the main attack opened, driving towards Vittorio Veneto to divide the Austrians in the Adriatic plain from those in the mountains. By October 30th the Austrian Army was split in two, the retreat became a rout, and the same day Austria asked for an armistice, which was signed on November 4th.

The Curtain Falls on the Western Front. Already on October 23rd President Wilson had replied to the German request by a note which virtually required an unconditional surrender. Ludendorff wished to carry on the struggle in hopes that a successful defence of the German frontier might damp the determination of the Allies. But the situation had passed beyond his control, the nation's will-power was broken, and his advice was in discredit. On October 26th he was forced to resign.

Then, for thirty-six hours, the Chancellor lay in coma from

486

an overdose of sleeping draught after influenza. When he returned to his office on the evening of November 3rd, not only Turkey, but Austria, had capitulated. If the situation on the Western Front was felt to be rather easier, Austrian territory and railways were now available as a base of operations against Germany. Several weeks before, General von Gallwitz had told the German Chancellor that such a contingency, then unrealized, would be 'decisive'. Next day revolution broke out in Germany, and swept rapidly over the country. And in these last days of tremendous and diverse psychological strain the 'reddening' glare behind was accentuated by a looming cloud on the Lorraine front—where the renewed American pressure, since November 1st, was on a point more sensitive than other parts, a point where 'they must not be allowed to advance if the Antwerp–Meuse line was to be held any longer'. If this continued the Rhine and not the frontier would have to be the next line of resistance.

But hourly the revolution was spreading, fanned, as peace negotiations were delayed, by the Kaiser's reluctance to abdicate. Compromise with the revolutionaries was the only chance, and on November 9th Prince Max handed over to the socialist Ebert. Germany had become a republic in outward response to President Wilson's demand and in inward response to the uprising of the German people against the leaders who had led them into disaster. The German fleet had already mutinied when their commanders sought to send them out on a forlorn hope against the British. And on November 6th the German delegates had left Berlin to treat for an armistice.

In the days previous to their arrival the Allies had been anxiously debating the terms, but here the voice of Foch was clear, and decisive, for President Wilson suggested that the terms should be left to the decision of the military chiefs. Haig, supported by Milner, urged moderation—'Germany is not broken in the military sense. During the last weeks her armies have withdrawn fighting very bravely and in excellent order. Therefore . . . it is necessary to grant Germany conditions which she can accept . . . the evacuation of all invaded territories and of Alsace-Lorraine is sufficient to seal the victory.' The British also feared the danger of guerilla warfare and considered that the German Army should be kept undemobilized as a safeguard against the spread of Bolshevism.

Foch agreed that 'the German army could undoubtedly take up a new position, and that we could not prevent it'. But he disagreed with Haig's conditions and insisted not only that the Germans must hand over a third of their artillery and half their machine-guns but that the Allies must occupy the Rhineland, with bridgeheads on the east bank of the Rhine. Only by holding the Rhine would the Allies have a guarantee that Germany could not subsequently break off the peace negotiations, whereas Haig's proposals would facilitate the German withdrawal to and consolidation of a new position of resistance. Foch also intimated privately to Clemenceau that the occupation would 'serve as a pledge for security as well as for reparations'.

Pershing went even further than Foch and protested against granting any armistice. Foch, however, answered such objections logically—'War is only a means to results. If the Germans now sign an armistice under our conditions those results are in our possession. This being achieved, no man has the right to cause another drop of blood to be shed.' The real results he sought by his terms went, however, beyond the armistice. Once the German army was out of the way France might then be able to frame the peace on her terms and not on those of President Wilson. Thus the ironical result of the President's action in allowing the soldiers to settle the armistice conditions was that he nullified the peace conditions set out in his Fourteen Points—and gave the Germans a just complaint, if not a realistic objection, that they had been entrapped to their doom by his promises.

The next point of difference was whether reparations should be mentioned in the armistice. The British objected, but the French insisted. Clemenceau cleverly and disarmingly argued —'I wish only to make mention of the principle', and advocated the vague but comprehensive formula 'reparations for damages', while the French Finance Minister strengthened its potential effect by inserting the innocent-looking reservation that 'any future claims or demands on the part of the Allies remain unaffected'. With greater innocence Colonel House swallowed this clause and through his support it was added to the terms.

The next question was that of the naval terms, and here the national positions were reversed. Foch, having made his own terms so severe, was anxious to lighten the naval terms and to demand merely the surrender of submarines. He asked somewhat scoffingly—'As for the German surface fleet, what do you fear from it? During the whole war only a few of its units have ventured from its ports. The surrender of these units will be merely a manifestation, which will please the public but nothing more.' But Sir Eric Geddes, the First Lord of the Admiralty, reminded Foch that it was the British fleet which 'held in check' the German fleet, and pointed out that if the latter was left intact the war strain on the former would continue until peace was settled. Lloyd George suggested that as an effective but less humiliating compromise the naval terms should demand the internment and not the surrender of the German surface ships. This solution was agreed upon, although the Admiralty only gave way under protest, and the final demand, apart from the surrender of one hundred and fifty submarines, was for the internment 'in neutral ports, or failing them, Allied ports' of ten battleships and six battle cruisers, besides light craft. Owing to the difficulty of finding an adequate neutral port, their ultimate destination became the British base of Scapa Flow. One important effect of this prolonged discussion was that the terms to Germany were not settled until Austria had capitulated—an effect which, as Lloyd George shrewdly foresaw, enabled the Allies to 'put stiffer terms to Germany' with less chance of refusal.

The Germans' acceptance of these severe terms was hastened less by the existing situation on the Western Front than by the collapse of the 'home front', coupled with exposure to a new thrust in rear through Austria. The Allied advance in the west was still continuing, in some parts seeming to gather pace in the last days, but the main German forces had escaped from the perilous salient, and their complete destruction of roads and railways made it impossible for supplies to keep pace with the advancing troops. A pause must come while these communications were being repaired, and thus the Germans would have breathing space to rally their resistance. The advance reached the line Pont à Mousson-Sedan-Mézières-Mons-Ghent by November 11th—the line of the opening battles in 1914—but strategically it had come to a standstill.

It is true that, to meet this situation, Foch had concentrated a large Franco-American force to strike below Metz directly east into Lorraine. As the general Allied advance had almost absorbed the enemy's reserves, this stroke, if driven in deeply and rapidly, promised the chance of turning the whole of this new line of defence along the Meuse to Antwerp and might even upset his orderly retreat to the Rhine. But it is unlikely that this Lorraine thrust, prepared for November 14th, would have solved the hitherto insoluble problem of maintaining the initial momentum of advance after an initial break-through. Foch did not think so. For when asked how long it would take to drive the Germans back across the Rhine if they refused the armistice terms, he replied—'Maybe three, maybe four or five months. Who knows?' And his post-war comment on this Lorraine offensive was—'Its importance has always been exaggerated. It is regarded as the irresistible blow that was to fell and administer the knock out to the Boche. That's nonsense. The Lorraine offensive was *not* in itself any more important than the attack then being prepared in Belgium, on the Lys.'

More truly significant was the decision on November 4th, after Austria's surrender, to prepare a concentric advance on Munich by three Allied armies, which would be assembled on the Austro-German frontier within five weeks. In addition Trenchard's Independent Air Force was about to bomb Berlin on a scale hitherto unattempted in air warfare. And the

number of American troops in Europe had now risen to
2,085,000, and the number of divisions to forty-two, of which
thirty-two were ready for battle. The internal situation and
the obvious external developments which could be calculated
were the factors which produced Germany's decision to
capitulate—not any single and hypothetical blow on the
strongest part of her front. With revolution at home, the
gathering menace on their southern frontier and the continued strain on their western, the German delegates had no
option but to accept the drastic terms of the armistice, which
was signed in Foch's railway carriage in the Forest of Compiègne at 5 a.m. on November 11th. And at 11 o'clock that
morning the World War came to an end.

31☐ Vimy• **6 A**
BR.1st.ARMY 62☐
56☐ R. Scarpe
Arras ☐Gd R. Sensée
15☐
3☐
34☐
59☐ 6☐ 51☐
25☐ Vaulx Vraucourt 17☐
Bapaume ☐19 63☐
BR. 3rd.ARMY 2☐ 47☐
9☐
☐41 21☐
Albert Epehy• 16☐
☐39 Ronssoy•
1 CAV. 66☐
24☐
Amiens 61☐
R. Somme Villers-Bretonneux
R. Luce 3 CAV. 30☐
50☐ BR. 5 th. ARMY 36☐
Moreuil• 14☐
Ham 16☐
20☐ Essigny 16☐
Roye• Jussy• 58☐
R. Avre 2 CAV. La Fère•
Cantigny• Montdidier Chauny•
Noyon Barisis•
R. Oise FR. 6 th. ARMY **7 A**

Douai **17 A**

Cambrai **2 A**
Le Câteau•

18 A

St.
Quentin

GERMAN
OFFENSIVE
March, 1918

——— Original Line on 21st. March
– – – Line on evening 21st. March
········· Line on evening 23rd. March
–·–·– Line on evening 25th. March
▬▬▬ Line on evening 5th. April
Divisions—
☐ British ▬ German

0   5   10   15
Miles

© Cassell & Co. Ltd. 1970

CHAPTER VIII

SCENE I

THE FIRST BREAK-THROUGH

AT 4.30 a.m., on March 21st, 1918, the sudden crash of some four thousand German guns heralded the breaking of a storm which, in grandeur of scale, of awe, and of destruction, surpassed any other in the World War. By nightfall a German flood had inundated forty miles of the British front; a week later it had reached a depth of nearly forty miles, and was almost lapping the outskirts of Amiens; and in the ensuing weeks the Allied cause itself was almost submerged.

These weeks rank with those of the Marne in 1914 as the two gravest military crises of the World War. In them Germany came desperately near to regaining that lost chance, and best chance, of victory, which she had forfeited in early September, 1914. And to the people of Britain at least the risk seemed even worse, because more fully realized and because their stake was greater.

No episode of the war is so studded with question marks as that on which the curtain rose, March 21st, 1918. Why, when the Allies had been attacking with superior force for two years, were they suddenly fighting 'with their backs to the wall'? Why, after the public had been assured that inter-allied cooperation was assured and a generalissimo unnecessary, was one urgently demanded and appointed? Why, when the Allies had made so little visible impression on the German front in two years of constant offensive, were the Germans able to tear a huge hole in the Allied front within a few days? Why, as this breach so far exceeded in size the dream-aims of its Allied forerunners, did it fail to obtain any decisive results? In seeking the answers to these several 'whys' lies the main interest of March 21st for history.

The primary cause of the sudden British change from the offensive to the defensive lay in the fact that the German fighting strength on the Western Front was increased by thirty per cent between November, 1917, and March 21st, 1918, while the British strength fell by twenty-five per cent, compared with the previous summer. The bulk of these fresh German troops were transferred from the Russian front, where Ludendorff, as a preliminary to his great bid for victory in the West, had wrung a definite peace from the Bolshevik Government, and also from Rumania. But if these facts explain the change, the causes of its abruptness and extent lie beneath the surface. Chief among them was that the British Command had dissipated its credit, both in balance of man-power and with the Government. This doubly unfortunate result was due to the strategy which can be summarized adequately in a single word, manifold in its ill-omened significance—'Passchendaele'.

Conscious of his responsibility to the nation, and personally distrustful of Haig's judgment, Mr. Lloyd George placed a firm check on the flow of reinforcements to France lest they should be poured down another offensive drainpipe. Friction between the two was almost inevitable, because of their extreme contrast of temperament and training. The one a volatile Welshman, the other a stubborn and taciturn Scot. The one with a magnetic power of drawing even the unwilling to him; the other with an impregnable capacity for holding even the most willing at a distance. The one infinitely adaptable, the other inflexibly consistent, and persistent. In the one, speech and thought so closely coincided that they became fused, while with the other the opening of the mouth automatically cut out the action of the brain. Anecdotes of Haig's inarticulateness, to the point of unintelligibility, are many. One of the best is of the occasion when, presenting the prizes to an Aldershot cross-country team, all that he could get out was—'I congratulate you on your running. You have run well. I hope you will run as well in the presence of the enemy.'

Again, Lloyd George was as receptive to ideas as he was critical of the pretensions of hierarchical wisdom, and he constantly sought to gather a variety and diversity of opinions as a broad basis for judgment. Haig, as his own admiring biographer, General Charteris, confesses, 'had not a critical mind', and neither knowledge of, nor interest in, affairs outside his own military work. And he took over the command 'genuinely convinced that the position to which he had now been called was one which he, and he alone in the British Army, could fill'. When to his rigidly disciplined outlook was added this feeling of divine right, it raised an almost impassable barrier of character between him and the Prime Minister. Neither made much effort to surmount it, and growing distrust on both sides—a distrust of Haig's military and Lloyd George's personal methods—steadily heightened it.

Throughout the months following Passchendaele and preceding the German offensive, Lloyd George was assiduously seeking to create a power above Haig, as dismissal would have raised a political storm. His solution was the Supreme War Council in control of a general inter-allied reserve. But the scheme was thwarted by Haig's action. For, having no belief in the method of battle control by committee, he shattered it by his refusal to contribute his small quota of nine divisions. Whatever the just strength of his objection to the method on principle, his action is not easy either to understand or to justify. For, convinced as he was that the German attack was coming on his front, and conscious of his shortage of reserves, it seems curious that he should not risk a contribution of nine divisions in order to draw from a pool of thirty. He chose, instead, to rely on an arrangement with Pétain for mutual support, whereby in case of need he might be reinforced by six to eight French divisions. This was far less than Haig could hope for from the general reserve, if formed. Moreover, Haig's distrust of French fulfilment of such promises had for years been so marked, his tongue so caustic about them, that it is astonishing that he should have pinned his faith to a small and purely French promise when he could have had a much larger promise from a board on which there was a British representative.

This excessive trust on the part of the British Command, like the Government's withholding of reinforcements, may well have been due to an apparently well-grounded belief in the power of their defence to stop a German attack. Why should the Germans succeed where the British had so often failed? The only close approach to a break-through by the British had been at Cambrai, with the tanks—and Haig knew that it was almost impossible for the Germans to have built tanks in quantity.

But in his defensive calculations, as in his offensive actions throughout the past two years, he seems to have underrated the infinite value of surprise, which for three thousand years of recorded warfare has proved the master key to victory. The real significance of the Cambrai attack on November 20th previous had been that it had revived the use of such a key, forging it from an amalgam of armour and the caterpillar track. Unhappily, the effect of this tank key was largely lost because when inserted in the lock Haig had not the power to turn it fully, through exhausting his strength in the Passchendaele mud.

In the counterattack of November 30th the Germans had used a key similar in principle if different in design—a short sharp bombardment with gas and smoke shell, followed up by an inrush of infantry, specially trained in the new infiltration tactics. It would seem that by the following March the British had not sufficiently taken this lesson to heart. For, though the Fifth Army's subsequent excuses of weak numbers and a long line had some justification, Gough had expressed confidence beforehand in his power to resist the onslaught.

But when Gough's original front was forced, an inadequate preparation and co-ordination of the measures to block the enemy's path further back was revealed. He had failed to arrange for the blowing up of certain causeways and General Headquarters had not given him a definite order. Worse still was the confusion caused by the fact that in the case of the more important railway bridges, this duty was entrusted to the French railway authorities instead of the Fifth Army, and in this way the vital railway bridge at Péronne was allowed to fall undestroyed into German hands.

A similar haziness appeared in the G.H.Q. instructions for the conduct of the defensive battle, for in one place Gough was told 'we should make our preparations to fight east of the Somme', and in another 'it may well be desirable to fall back to the rearward defences of Péronne and the Somme'. To reconcile these alternatives was not easy. It would have been simpler to have forestalled the Germans' attack by a withdrawal similar to their own in 1917, accepting the necessary sacrifice of ground: although political considerations and military sentiments tended to hinder such a course. Adaptation of plan to circumstance may be necessary, and often more advantageous, but it is the hardest test of generalship, and thus demands the clearest thought among those who attempt it. The fog of war is bad enough without being thickened by obscure phrasing: battles may be lost by lack of lucidity as well as by lack of tenacity. The effect of these instructions to the Fifth Army was that labour had to be divided between the alternative defence lines, without time for the satisfactory organization of either. Moreover, a withdrawal to the line of the Somme while the battle was actually in progress demanded a high capacity for rearguard action, and for this the officers and men of the Fifth Army as a whole were neither prepared nor practised. To quote from among many witnesses—Colonel Rowland Feilding has recorded: 'A retreat was the one possibility that had never occurred to us, and, unfortunately, it involves a kind of manœuvring in which we are unversed, in spite of all our experience.' There is indirect proof of this statement in the fact that no less than five hundred guns were abandoned to the enemy in the first two days.

The chance of avoiding a retreat was diminished, as its execution was endangered, because of the scarcity of reserves behind Gough's front and of the way that General Headquarters refused his request to move these nearer the front before the battle. And when it opened he was told that he would have to wait for one extra division until the first four available had been sent to the Third Army. These facts give point to his remark—'It is impossible for me to say that G.H.Q. showed a full understanding of the circumstances and progress of the battle.' And a chance of improving it was lost because—'During the whole eight days' battle, the only member of G.H.Q. who came to see and hear things for himself was Haig. He came and saw me once—on Saturday, 23rd. We did not go at all into details of the situation, nor of the action of the Third Army.'

On the eve of the German onslaught, only three out of the eighteen British divisions in reserve were disposed behind the Fifth Army front. Six were behind the Third Army, and the rest were still further north, where no attack came or was by then expected. Haig's justification for keeping his reserves in the north until he was absolutely certain of the German aim lay in the narrowness of the space that there intervened between the front and the Channel ports. But it is not a complete explanation of his attitude. That was influenced to some extent by his prolonged doubt of the German intentions: at a conference of his army commanders on February 16th he expressed the view that the main blow, if the Germans attacked early, would probably be made against the French. 'Indications from the British front are that no attack in strength in Flanders is possible at the moment, and that there are at present no signs of any big offensive being imminent on the rest of the British front.' A small attack on the First Army front near Lens was a 'possibility'. G.H.Q. was certainly slow to react to the warnings furnished by air reports and by the Fifth Army. At a further conference on March 2nd the likelihood of early attack was recognized but with no greater object than that of 'cutting off the Cambrai salient and drawing in our reserves'. And even on March 8th it was stated that there were no indications of an enemy attack south of St. Quentin.

Haig's sense of the key importance of the Arras bastion was justified by the event. But, in keeping the bulk of his reserves in the north, he risked the security of the already thin Fifth Army in order to have ample insurance against a less probable risk to the Channel ports. One reason was that he felt he could better afford to yield ground in front of Amiens than elsewhere. Another was a confidence, which the event unhappily refuted, that the German advance would not go far enough to become a menace to the general situation. Calculated risks are inherent in generalship; the questions that linger in the mind are whether Haig's miscalculation was avoidable and whether he did all that was possible to cover the risks that his dispositions involved. It is at least clear that he preferred to risk his junction with the French rather than his hold on the Channel ports; and that his dispositions eased the task of the enemy more than they could have expected.

If this was good luck for the Germans, their thorough and skilful preparations for the initial assault had earned them success—although here again fortune favoured them.

For the effect of the gas-gained surprise was immensely increased by nature, which in the early hours of March 21st provided a thick mist that cloaked the infiltrating assailants as much as it masked the defending machine-guns. Without this aid it is questionable how far the German tactical surprise would have succeeded, and in this lay the essential inferiority of the German means of surprise, compared with that at Cambrai, and later, on August 8th, 1918, which was achieved by armoured machines.

These not only formed the main material from which the key was manufactured but provided the power to press it home and turn it. In contrast, Ludendorff had to depend on unarmoured infantry to exploit the opening created by the brief but intense bombardment with gas shell. For he had failed to grasp the significance of the tank and neglected to develop it in time; only in August, 1918, when it was used to strike him a mortal blow did he put it in the 'urgent' class of war material.

But the German plan was distinguished by a research for tactical surprise more thorough and far reaching than in any of the earlier operations of the war. The Germans significantly record that 'Haig's despatches dealing with the attacks of 1917 were found most valuable, because they showed how not to do it'. To Ludendorff's credit he realized that the obvious is an obstacle that superior weight cannot compensate, and, once created, can rarely overcome. And he sought to effect and develop surprise by a compound of many deceptive elements. It is to his credit also that, unlike Falkenhayn, who merely wanted officer clerks, he surrounded himself with able assistants. Captain Geyer compiled the new training handbooks, while Colonel Bruchmüller had emerged from retirement to become the famous artillery 'battle-piece' producer. With a prophetic play upon his name he was known as 'Durchbruchmüller'—Break-through Müller. Under his superintendence the masses of artillery were brought up close to the front line in concealment, and opened fire without previous 'registration' through the method he had introduced. The infantry were trained in new infiltrating tactics, of which the guiding idea was that the leading troops should probe and penetrate the weak points of the defence while the reserves were directed to back up success, not to redeem failure. Special reconnaissance parties were assigned simply for the task of sending back early news of progress. The ordinary lines of attacking infantry were preceded by a dispersed chain of 'storm' groups, with automatic rifles, machine-guns and light mortars. These groups were to push straight through wherever they could find an opening and leave the defenders' 'strong points' to be dealt with by the succeeding lines. The fastest, not the slowest, must set the pace, and no effort was made to keep a uniform alignment. Further 'the inclination of leaders to assemble their troops and get them in hand after a certain objective has been reached must be suppressed'. 'If the troops know the instructions of the commanders they can go on of themselves.' The assaulting divisions were brought up overnight, those of the second line to a position only about a mile behind the first, and the third only ten miles back. All reserves started moving forward at zero, so as to be at hand when wanted. And when a second-line division was so used it came under the control, not of a higher commander sitting in rear, but of the first-line division commander, who had his finger on the pulse of the battle.

On November 11th at Mons—prophetic date and place—the German 'leaders' had met in conclave to decide on the date and place of the forthcoming offensive. Naturally, according to German custom, the issue was thrashed out, not between the nominal commanders, but between their chiefs of staff—Ludendorff, Kuhl (Crown Prince Rupprecht's), Schulenberg (German Crown Prince's), together with Ludendorff's own strategical adviser, Major Wetzell. Kuhl and Schulenberg each wanted the attack to be made on the front of their own army groups—Kuhl indicating Flanders and Schulenberg the Verdun sector. Wetzell was inclined to support Schulenberg, arguing that an attack on the flanks of Verdun, a salient, would forestall any future Franco-American offensive at that delicate point, and, after defeating the French, the whole German strength could be turned against the British. Ludendorff, however, rejected this scheme on the score that the ground was unfavourable, that a break-through at Verdun would lead nowhere decisive, and that the French army had recuperated too well after nearly a year's undisturbed convalescence. He laid down as a first principle that 'the British must be defeated', and thought that the drain of Passchendaele would make them an easy prey. But he disagreed with Kuhl's proposal to strike, between Ypres and Lens, towards Hazebrouck as it would meet the main mass of the British, and this low ground would be long in drying. He favoured instead an attack around St. Quentin, although Wetzell contended that it would be slowed down in crossing the old devastated area on the Somme, and was within easy reach of French reinforcements. A final decision was put off and Rupprecht noted in his diary 'Ludendorff underestimates the toughness of the British'.

In December, Wetzell tried to reconcile, and sagely combine, the two projects, by dividing the offensive into two acts

—first, a wide-front attack on both sides of St. Quentin, and, second, a fortnight later, a break-through in Flanders towards Hazebrouck. The first act was only to be carried far enough to draw the British reserves southward. Wetzell summed up:

'We shall not, in my opinion, succeed in obtaining our object by *one* great attack at *one* place, however carefully it is prepared . . . we can only shatter their front by a clever combination of successive, definitely related, mutually re-acting attacks on different parts of the front, finally in the direction of Hazebrouck.'

It was to be left to Foch to adopt his method without acknow-ledgment. For, after further conferences, Ludendorff decided on January 27th in favour of the St. Quentin attack (known by the code name 'Michael') and against the Hazebrouck attack 'St. George' which was only kept in mind and not in immediate readiness.

A further complication arose. The front from the Belgian coast to St. Quentin was under Rupprecht, and for political as well as personal reasons it was considered necessary to give the German Crown Prince a chance of redeeming the credit he had lost in the struggle at Verdun in 1916. Hence he was given a share in the offensive by employing the Eight-eenth Army (Hutier), which belonged to his army group, on the southern flank of the main offensive. It is a moot question whether he could not have helped better, if less gloriously, by using it for a diversion at Verdun, in order to draw the French reserves away from, instead of towards, the intended breach in the British front.

In a broad sense, Ludendorff's chosen sector, which ex-tended from Arras to La Fère, fulfilled his new principle of taking the line of least resistance, for it was the weakest in defences, defenders, and reserves. Moreover, it was close to the joint between the French and British armies, and so lent itself to a separation. But although it was true, as a generaliz-ation, that this sector was comparatively weak, the classification was loose and inaccurate. The northerly third of it was strong and strongly held, by Byng's Third Army, with fourteen divisions (six in reserve), while the bulk of the British reserves were on this flank, which also could and did receive support more quickly from the other British Armies which lay to the north. The remaining two-thirds of the sector upon which the German blow fell was held by Gough's Fifth Army. The central part facing Marwitz's Army was held by seven divisions (two in reserve). The southern part facing Hutier's Army was also held by seven divisions (one in reserve).

But Ludendorff gave Below's Army near Arras nineteen divisions for the initial attack, by its left wing only, on a nine and a half miles' frontage. South of it came Marwitz's Army. As the British salient towards Cambrai was not to be attacked directly, but pinched out, this four-mile stretch was adequately occupied by two German divisions, and Marwitz had eighteen divisions for his nine and a half mile attack frontage. On the extreme south, either side of St. Quentin, came Hutier's Army. Ludendorff gave it only twenty-four divisions to attack on a twenty-mile frontage. Hence we see that it had only half the proportionate strength of the other armies. Despite his principle, he was distributing his strength according to the enemy's strength and not concentrating against the weakest resistance. The direction given in his orders emphasized this still more. The main effort was to be exerted north of the Somme for, after breaking through, Below and Marwitz were to wheel northwest, rolling up the British front, while the river and Hutier formed a screen to cover their flank. Hutier's Army was merely an offensive flank guard. This plan was to be radically changed in execution, and to have the appearance of following the line of least resistance, because Ludendorff gained rapid success where he desired it little and failed to gain success where he wanted it most.

What of the British meantime? As the result of a war game played at Versailles Sir Henry Wilson had forecasted that the enemy attack would come on the Cambrai-Lens sector, but that the Germans would wait to deliver it until about July 1st, when their training and accumulation of forces would be complete. Wilson was somewhat outside the mark in place and still more out in time. Haig's intelligence was more accurate, although it did not foresee the full southward extension of the attack. As the time drew near signs multiplied sufficiently to enable Haig to calculate the date. On March 18th German prisoners captured near St. Quentin gave the date as the 21st, and on the evening of the 20th Maxse's XVIII Corps was able through raiding to establish the certainty of the morrow's attack.

Thus it is true to say that no strategic surprise was obtained. Nor was it even obtainable under the conditions of 1918 in France. But with the opposing armies spread out in contact along the far-flung line of entrenchments, a quick breakthrough followed by a rapid exploitation along the line of least resistance might promise such a decisive upset as normally is only attainable by choosing the line of least expectation. The hurricane bombardment opened at 4.30 a.m. on the 21st, concentrating for two hours on the British artillery and then, reinforced by mortars, turning on the trenches. Almost all telephone cables were severed and wireless sets destroyed, while the fog made visual signalling impossible. Thus the troops were made dumb and the commanders blind. At 9.40 a.m., or in some parts earlier, the German infantry advanced under cover of a creeping barrage, supplemented by low-flying aircraft.

The British outpost zone was overrun almost everywhere by midday, but this was inevitable and had been foreseen. But the northern attack met such stubborn resistance against the right of Byng's Army that it had not seriously penetrated the main battle zone even by the night of the 22nd, and, despite putting in successive reinforcements, the capture of Vaulx-Vraucourt was then the high-water mark of its progress. On most parts of Gough's Army front the battle-zone resistance was just as firm, but the flood found a way through on the 21st near La Fère, on the extreme right, at Essigny and at Ronssoy. The resistance of the 21st Division at Epéhy for a time checked this last breach from spreading northward, but it began to crumble so deeply that the neighbouring sectors were affected. Southward, again, near St. Quentin, the line sagged still more deeply, and on the night of the 22nd Gough was driven to order a general retirement to the line of the Somme. He was hurried into this precipitate decision by a mistaken report that the enemy was already across the Crozat Canal at Jussy and so behind his right flank. Early next morning the Péronne bridgehead was abandoned. Several of Gough's subordinate commanders were even more vague or misled as to the situation, control lapsed, and gaps occurred. The worst was at the joint between Byng's and Gough's Armies and this the Germans speedily accentuated. And a new danger arose further south at the joint between the British and French.

But Ludendorff, continuing to ignore his new principle, was only intent to nourish the attack near Arras, where progress was disappointing. Meantime Hutier, once across the Crozat Canal, was pressing swiftly forward, almost without check save from his own limited rôle. On the 23rd Ludendorff again emphasizes in his orders that Below's is the principal effort, reinforces it by three divisions, and indicates that the Sixth and Fourth Armies, still more to the north, will chime in to help it. Two days later, when the check to Below has become still clearer, Ludendorff arranges that Below's hitherto passive right wing shall strike direct at Arras on the 28th, in order to overcome this strong place which is hampering and enfilading Below's attacking left wing. And on the 29th the Sixth Army, reinforced by six or seven divisions, is to extend the attack northwards between Arras and Lens—with Boulogne as its goal! Meanwhile Hutier is actually told not to pass the line Noyon-Roye for the time being.

On the 26th Ludendorff begins to doubt Below's chances and to turn his eyes south. But, instead of throwing his weight thither, he merely makes it a second principal effort. And, even so, it is to be towards Amiens by Marwitz's Army, while Hutier is told not to cross the Avre without fresh orders. This means that the army which has all the difficult ground of the old 1916 Somme battlefields to cross is pushed on while the army that has a smoother path is held back. The apparent explanation, and the extraordinary flux of Ludendorff's thought, is revealed in a later sentence of the order which shows that he is contemplating a vast fanlike movement in which three armies are to wheel south towards Paris while Below and his neighbours wheel north to crush the British against the sea coast. The grandiose conception was far beyond Ludendorff's resources in reserves. It would seem that for the moment he was intoxicated with success, and, like Moltke in August, 1914, was counting his chickens before they were hatched. Another parallel with 1914 was that the army commanders' reports of progress outstripped their actual stages of advance. Even they, however, were less futuristic than the Kaiser who, according to Rupprecht, 'announced a complete victory' on March 21st.

On the 27th Hutier reached Montdidier, a penetration of nearly forty miles, but next day Ludendorff had a cold douche of reality when Below's Arras attack with nine divisions collapsed under a storm of fire from the expectant defence. No mist came to the aid of the attackers.

Ludendorff then put a belated stop to Below's vain efforts, and countermanded the Sixth Army's attack intended for the morrow. Amiens was made the main objective, and Marwitz was given all the reserves at hand—nine divisions. But Hutier had to pause for two days until four fresh divisions reached him. By this time the surge towards Amiens was almost stagnant, its impetus having slackened far less because of the resistance than because of the exhaustion of the troops and the difficulties of supply. Roads were blocked, transport scuppered, and reserves harassed by the British air attacks, which here played a vital part. When the attack was renewed on March 30th it had little force and made little progress in face of a resistance that had been afforded time to harden, helped by the cement of French reserves which were now being poured into the sagging wall. That day was the first on which their artillery, arriving later than the infantry, had come into action in force. Even so, there was a moment of crisis when the Germans captured the Moreuil Wood ridge, which was not only at the joint between the French and British but commanded the crossings of the Avre and Luce where they joined. And these covered the main Amiens-Paris railway. But the menace was warded off by a swift counterstroke of the Canadian Cavalry Brigade, made on the initiative of and led by General Seely, ex-War Minister turned Murat. The ridge was regained, and although lost again next day, by other troops, the coup seems to have extinguished the now flickering flame of German energy. Nearly a week passed before, on April 4th, a further German effort was made by fifteen divisions, of which only four were fresh. Meeting a reinforced defence, this had still less success.

Seeing that his new effort was too late, Ludendorff then suspended the attack towards Amiens. At no time had he thrown his weight along the line of fracture between the British and French armies. Yet on March 24th Pétain had intimated to Haig that if the Germans' progress continued along this line he would have to draw back the French reserves south-westwards to cover Paris. How little more German pressure would have been needed to turn the crack into a yawning chasm! The knowledge is one more testimony to the historical truth that a joint is the most sensitive and profitable point of attack.

The supreme features of this great offensive are, first, the immensity of its outward results compared with those of any previous offensive in the west; second, its ineffectiveness to attain decisive results. For the first it would be both unjust and untrue to blame the British troops. They achieved miracles of heroic endurance, and the prolonged resistance in most of the battle zone is the proof. The main cause of the subsequently rapid flow-back lay in the frequent breakdown of control and communication. During three years of trench warfare an elaborate and complex system, largely dependent on the telephone, had been built up, and when the static suddenly became fluid the British paid the inevitable penalty of violating that fundamental axiom of war—elasticity.

On the German side, Arras was the actual rock on which their plan broke. It is probable that military conservatism cost them dear. For Bruchmüller has revealed that while Hutier's Army carried out his surprise bombardment designs, Below's in the north clung to their old-fashioned methods, refusing to dispense with preliminary ranging. Once again, and near the Somme again, Below's conventional military mind had proved the best asset to the British army.

But a more fundamental cause of the German failure was Ludendorff's own limitations. He had sufficient receptiveness to see a new truth but not sufficient elasticity or conviction to carry it out fully in practice. The principle of following the line of least resistance was too novel for one who from his youth had been saturated in the Clausewitzian doctrine of striking at the enemy's main force. 'The British must be defeated' was his catchword, his vision was bloodshot, and he could not realize that in strategy the longest way round is often the shortest way there—that a direct approach to the object exhausts the attacker and hardens the resistance by compression, whereas an indirect approach loosens the defender's hold by upsetting his balance.

In the actual execution of the offensive by the German troops there is another cause of failure that has been commonly overlooked and yet is of great significance. It is the physical effect on ill-nourished troops of breaking into an area full of well-filled supply depots, and the psychological effect of discovering that the enemy is so much better fed and equipped than themselves—that they have been nourished only with lies, about the result of the U-boat campaign and the enemy's economic condition. This dual effect is to be traced in many sources of evidence. One of the most illuminating and trustworthy is the war diary of the German poet and novelist, Rudolf Binding.

On March 27th he records:

'Now we are already in the English back areas . . . a land flowing with milk and honey. Marvellous people these, who will only equip themselves with the very best that the earth produces. Our men are hardly to be distinguished from English soldiers. Everyone wears at least a leather jerkin, a waterproof. . . . English boots or some other beautiful thing. The horses are feeding on masses of oats and gorgeous food-cake . . . and there is no doubt the army is looting with some zest'.

On the next day follows a highly significant entry:

'To-day the advance of our infantry suddenly stopped near Albert. Nobody could understand why. Our armies had reported no enemy between Albert and Amiens. . . . Our way seemed entirely clear. I jumped into a car with orders to find out what was causing the stoppage in front. Our division was right in front of the advance and could not possibly be tired out. It was quite fresh. . . .

'As soon as I got near the town I began to see curious sights. Strange figures, which looked very little like soldiers, and certainly showed no sign of advancing, were making their way back out of the town. There were men driving cows . . . others who carried a hen under one arm and a box of note-paper under the other. Men carrying a bottle of wine under their arm and another one open in their hand. . . . Men staggering. Men who could hardly walk. When I got into the town the streets were running with wine. . . .

'I drove back to Divisional Headquarters with a fearful impression of the situation. The advance was held up, and there was no means of setting it going again for hours'.

It proved hopeless, and the officers were powerless, to collect the troops that day, while the sequel he records was that 'the troops which moved out of Albert next day cheered with wine and in victorious spirits were mown down straight away on the railway embankment by a few English machine-guns'.

But the intoxication due to loot was even greater and more general than that due to wine, and the fundamental cause of both was 'the general sense of years of privation'. A staff officer even stops a car, when on an urgent mission, to pick up an English waterproof from the ditch. And in this intoxication the Germans not only lose their chance of reaching Amiens, but ruin sources of supply invaluable to the maintenance of their own advance—wrecking waterworks for the sake of the brass taps. The cause of this senseless craving is revealed in their impression that 'the English made everything either out of rubber or brass, because these were the two materials which we had not seen for the longest time'. 'The madness, stupidity and indiscipline of the German troops is shown in other things as well. Any useless toy or trifle they seize and load into their packs, anything useful which they cannot carry away they destroy'.

Once this plunder was exhausted the reaction was all the greater and the contrast of their own paucity with the enemy's plenty the more depressing. As hopes of military success fade, and with them the hope of again nourishing their stomachs, and souls, on the enemy's supplies, a moral rot sets in rapidly.

Anyone with personal experience of war knows how the thought of food and of civilized comfort fills the soldier's horizon. How far was the German army's sudden moral decline from July onward, when the last attack proved abortive, due not only to increasing hunger but to the eye-opening conviction of the enemy's greater material power of endurance?

Propaganda and censorship could hide the difference so long as the front was an inviolable wall of partition. But when the Germans broke through the British lines and into the back areas the truth was revealed to the German troops. Is the historical verdict, penetrating beneath the surface of military statistics and acreage to the psychological foundation, then to be that the British disaster of March, 1918, was a stroke of fortune for those who suffered it? If so, it seems a pity that the solution was not tried earlier. Instead of conducting unwilling 'frocks' round the front, the British Command might have arranged visits for Germans to its back areas—that 'land flowing with milk and honey'. Or at least it might have designedly released a proportion of its prisoners after they had been suitably entertained! Such a strategy would certainly have supplied the imagination which many found so lacking in the military leadership.

The Lys, April, 1918

— Original Line on 9th. April
— — Line on evening of 9th. April
—·— Line on evening of 10th. April
········· Line on evening of 30th. April
Divisions – British, 25
German, *214*

N

SECOND ARMY

YSER CANAL

Ypres

30   58
36
41
59
6
49   *236*
21

YPRES·9
Hollebeke   7 FOURTH ARMY

COMINES CANAL

29   MT. DES CATS   Kemmel   MT. KEMMEL   19   17 R.
49 R.   R. Lys   Comines

Messines
RAVELSBERG RIDGE

Meteren   *214*   31   36 R.
Bailleul   Ploegsteert   25   R. Deule

Hazebrouck

Forest of Nieppe   Armentieres

50   R. Lys   34   38
Meryille   235
117

R. Lys   Estaires   40   32   10 Ers   11 R   11 Bav.
42
35   8 Bav. R.   81 R.
2 Port.   8
Neuve   1 Bav. R.   16
Chapelle
R. Lawe   18 R.   44 R.   SIXTH ARMY
Lillers   51
55   43 R.
Béthune   Givenchy   4 Ers   La Bassée
LA BASSÉE CANALE

0   5   10
Miles

© Cassell & Co. Ltd. 1970

CHAPTER VIII

SCENE 2

THE BREAK-THROUGH IN FLANDERS

ON April 9th, 1918, the first anniversary of the abortive British attempt to break through the deadlocked trench front in Artois, the Germans made a more successful attempt —in the reverse direction. This was the second move in Ludendorff's gigantic offensive campaign which had begun on March 21st. Springing from around Neuve Chapelle, where, three years before, the first British attempt to break the deadlock had penetrated half a mile deep in all, a narrow German jet of attack swept away the opposing Portuguese and before noon on the 9th had penetrated to a depth of over three miles. To the north, but happily not to the south, the flanks of the breach crumbled, and with fresh jets playing upon the British front more sectors gave way.

By the next day twenty-four miles of frontage had been engulfed and, on the 12th, Sir Douglas Haig issued his historic order of the day: 'There is no other course open to us but to fight it out. Every position must be held to the last man. . . . With our backs to the wall and believing in the justice of our cause, each one of us must fight on to the end.' To the British public, and even perhaps to the British forces, this message came like a thunderclap, awakening them to the graveness of the danger and seeming almost to convey a warning that hope had gone and only honour remained—to go down fighting with their faces to the foe.

Yet at that moment, and still more during the following days, it is probable that the least sanguine and most depressed man was not in the British ranks, but behind the advancing enemy—Ludendorff himself. On March 21st and the next days Ludendorff had seen his carefully contrived strategical plan—for his great bid for victory—going astray. The rapidity

513

with which progress was made where he did not want it, and its slowness where he did want it, had driven him unwillingly to press on towards Amiens across the desert of the old Somme battlefields, instead of wheeling northwards from the Somme. With the repulse of his delayed assault on the Arras bastion on March 28th he had been forced to relinquish definitely his plan of rolling up the flank of the British armies and penning them back against the coast, isolated from their Allies.

But his thrust towards Amiens failed, however narrowly, to reach its destination—through its belatedness and difficulties of supply. In desperation, rather than in reflection, Ludendorff clutched at Wetzell's rejected scheme, and decided to launch the 'St. George' attack against the Ypres–Lens sector. But he had pressed 'Michael' too long and too far. Not only was he short of reserves, but he had to accumulate fresh supplies and ammunition, and switch his heavy artillery northwards. Conferences on April 1st and 2nd showed that the offensive could not be ready until the 9th; and, instead of thirty-five additional divisions, only eleven could be sent in time. With a sense of ironic humour the attack was rechristened 'Georgette'. Ludendorff was in luck at the start, but it was an elusive and delusive form of luck. The luck was that his opening blow fell on the front of the 2nd Portuguese Division, which was just about to be relieved by two British divisions, and had in the meanwhile been stretched to hold the whole corps sector.

The less agreeable aspect—for Ludendorff—of this piece of luck was somewhat unkindly epitomized in the comment that the Portuguese ruined Ludendorff and saved their Allies by running away. For although the extension and development of this attack was 'according to plan', Ludendorff never seems to have been wholehearted in pursuing it. From the point of view of his strategy, and its interests, he either pressed the attack too hard or did not press enough.

The clearest evidence of this irresolution—and depression —is to be found in the captured archives of the Fourth German Army, which attacked in this sector. And their evidence is a better guide than any carefully prepared post-war apologia. They have the further advantage that they fell into enemy hands before any judicious adulterations could be made in the interests of high commanders' reputations. These German records show the General Staff Officers, Lossberg for the Fourth Army, Kuhl for the Army Group, and Ludendorff at the Supreme Command, settling all affairs without even the pretence of consulting their respective superiors, Sixt von Arnim, Rupprecht and Hindenburg. They also show Ludendorff doling out divisions with a parsimonious hand, usually too late and inadequate in number for real success; so apprehensive that his new bulge would become another sack that at the moment of supreme opportunity he stops the German advance for fear of a counterattack.

But all this was hidden from the British commanders and men. They only knew the enemy's blows, not his doubts and disquietude. And if he felt himself in a sack, they felt themselves in a mincing machine—with an unpleasant likelihood of their minced remains being ejected into the sea. That is the sort of wall that an army does not relish having at its back. Whereas on the Somme there had at least been ample room to withdraw, in the north the British troops, bases, and communications were all crowded into and passed through a narrow 'throat' of land sensitive to the least pressure and all too easy to strangle. Apart from the coast railway, the only lateral line of communication ran through St. Pol–Lillers–Hazebrouck, barely fifteen miles behind the front trenches. Thus it was that a ten-mile German penetration, reached on April 12th and, happily, never deepened appreciably, was as menacing, if not more so, than forty miles had been on the Somme.

The strain was all the more severe because it fell on troops already strained. Besides the Portuguese, all except one—the 55th—of the six British divisions between the La Bassée and the Ypres-Comines Canals were battle-worn, having come to this front on relief from the battle in the south. Strained, they were also stretched. The drain on Haig's reserves and the greater importance of the vital bastion of high ground, Arras-Givenchy, had caused a distribution of strength by which this handful of divisions had to hold a front of twenty-four miles. Worst of all, the greatest stretching of all fell on those who could least bear it. The Portuguese Corps had been holding a six-mile front, on both sides of Neuve Chapelle. It had been in the line for a long time, and increasing cases of insubordination had been a warning of declining morale. General Horne, the First Army Commander, reshuffling his dispositions, withdrew the 1st Portuguese Division from the line on April 5th. The 2nd also was to be relieved by British divisions on the night of April 9th, but meanwhile it was given the whole corps sector to hold, although one brigade of the 1st Portuguese was left in reserve near Lestrem, five miles behind the line. The 51st Division had been on the scene for several days and might have been used; indeed, its commander had proposed that he should take over the second line, a strongly concreted position easy to hold. But his request had not been granted. Yet Horne had been warned by his 'Q' staff that the convergence of German railways made the Lys sector the most probable point of attack; indeed, the only point where an attack could be mounted. They had, further, sought permission to prepare special supply dumps fifteen miles in rear to meet the danger of a breakthrough here, but had been rebuffed. Happily, they began preparations—without his knowledge. And the existence of these dumps helped to ease the emergency that followed.

If the state of the local preparations was Horne's responsibility, it is right to point out that he saw eye to eye with Haig in failing to read the writing on the wall-map. Rarely, if ever, was this so clear: or surprise less warranted by the signs. For the Germans sacrificed concealment to speed in developing their new offensive. From March 31st onwards the British aircraft reported a general northward movement of the German reserves and artillery, by road and rail. On April 1st, as the Official Air History has revealed, one observer alone in a couple of hours 'counted fifty-five trains on the move along the lines feeding the La Bassée-Armentières front. . . . The air reports of the next few days, supplemented by air photographs, made it clear that the German concentration was of the most formidable kind'. The reason that G.H.Q. failed to profit by the warning lay in its belief that the enemy would adhere to his original plan, and that the next step in furtherance of his Somme offensive would be a renewal of his attempt to break down the Arras bastion. It would seem that Haig credited Ludendorff with a persistency similar to his own at Passchendaele. Convinced that Ludendorff's correct course was to gain the key position of the Vimy Ridge, even though it was the strongest part of his own front, Haig held fast to the idea that Ludendorff, despite his hard lesson on March 28th, was bound to try again.

As late as April 7th, in an appreciation of the situation, G.H.Q. pinned its expectations to 'a converging attack on the Vimy Ridge'. Yet, to quote the Air History again: 'There was nothing in the air reports and air photographs up to the 9th of April to support the view, held by General Head-quarters, that a converging attack on the Vimy Ridge was likely. On the contrary the air information showed that the German troops opposite Arras were being drawn upon to supply reinforcements for the north and should have left little doubt that the immediate enemy concentration was northwards from the La Bassée Canal.'

The air information has also a bearing on Horne's delayed action over the relief of the Portuguese. 'That the relief might come too late was indicated from the air. Throughout the morning of the 7th air observers reported the main roads immediately opposite the Portuguese to be full of moving transport, and ground observers told of men carrying ammu-nition into the German support lines. The impression con-veyed by the combined air and ground reports was that the tactical concentration was nearing completion.' It did not, however, impress the men at the top—or they were slow in reaction.

For at 4.5 a.m. on the 9th an intense bombardment was

opened on the eleven-mile front between the La Bassée Canal and Armentières; the flanks of this sector were deluged with mustard gas—an indication that they were to be paralysed but not immediately attacked. At 7.30 a.m., after a slackening in the fire, small groups of German infantry began to move forward, and about 8.45 a.m., after the bombardment had swelled again for an hour, the assault was launched by a mass of nine divisions of the German Sixth Army—against three. Once more, as on March 21st, nature afforded it a cloak in the form of a thick mist. At the southern extremity the 55th (a Lancashire Territorial division) held on to Givenchy firmly, opposing so unshakable a resistance as not only to break the attack, but to dissuade the German command from subsequent attempts to extend it southwards.

But in the centre the Germans swiftly overran the Portuguese positions. The Portuguese were temporarily holding a front more than double that of the 55th on their flank; although their strength per yard was not much less, comparison of quality made such a distribution risky—and the risk had matured. But the sturdy resistance of King Edward's Horse and the 11th Cyclist Battalion checked the German onrush, and helped, with that of the reserve brigade of the 55th Division, to prevent the Germans crumbling away the southern flank. This resistance, indeed, tended to shepherd the German advance into the north-westerly direction, which it took more and more.

But on the northern flank of the break-through, the 40th Division, its own flank laid bare, was partly overwhelmed by the combined pressure. The 51st and 50th Divisions, coming up to dam the breach, were delayed on roads encumbered with Portuguese and shattered vehicles, and, caught by the tide of battle before they reached their positions, could not prevent the Germans, now reinforced by seven divisions, attaining, and even crossing the line of the Lys and Lawe rivers. But next day their resistance so far stemmed the German tide that little more ground was lost except on the north of the original bulge.

That morning, however, the German attack had been extended northwards to the Ypres-Comines Canal, against the southern sector of the British Second Army (Plumer). It was akin to a left-fist followed by a right-fist punch, although this new punch was much lighter—by only four divisions of the German Fourth Army. This lightness was counterbalanced by the enforced diversion of part of the three British defending divisions to the breach made the previous day. The Germans broke through, and between the punches Armentières itself was pinched out, the 34th Division barely escaping from the bag. That night the breach was thirty miles in width, and by the 12th its depth was doubled.

This was the crisis. Less than five miles separated the Germans from Hazebrouck junction. On the 13th British and Australian reserves began to arrive from the south, and the German pressure to show signs of slackening—one self-confessed reason being their 'difficulties of supply under the increasing attacks from the air'. The approach to Hazebrouck, barred just in time by the 4th Guards Brigade, was now finally bolted by the 1st Australian Division, and the remaining German pressure was exerted almost entirely on the northern half of the breach.

Plumer now took over charge of all except the southern fringe of the battle area and, to shorten his line as well as to forestall a fresh extension of the German attack, he began an unhurried withdrawal from the Ypres salient to a line just in front of the immortal town. This was a wise and clear-sighted move, even though it abandoned the few square miles of mud which had been purchased at so terrible a price the previous autumn.

Although the enemy gained Bailleul and the Ravelsberg Ridge on the 15th, he was then stopped at Meteren and in front of Kemmel Hill, and by the 18th the storm subsided. Meantime storms of another type had been raging behind the front. Foch's appointment as generalissimo did not seem to Haig to have brought him the prompt support he had expected. Ever since the 10th, and, indeed, before, he had been pressing Foch for French aid and active share in the battle. On the 14th an acrimonious conference took place at Abbeville, and next day Haig made the stricture 'that the arrangements made by the generalissimo were insufficient to meet the military situation'.

Foch, on the other hand, was, perhaps to the point of hazard, intent on husbanding his reserves for an offensive. In his opinion, on April 14th, 'la bataille du nord est finie'— where to many observers it looked rather as if the British Army was 'finie'. As usual he illustrated his opinion by a parable—of the rings made by dropping a stone into water, the successive rings growing less marked until the water became still. To hard-pressed Allies these parables were apt to be irritating. But his prediction proved right, even though, as at Ypres in 1914 and 1915, the British troops suffered a terrible strain in proving him right.

Contrary to what has been alleged, five French divisions arrived behind the British front as early as the 14th. But their intended counterattacks, as at Ypres in 1915, did not at first materialize. Let it be said, however, in justice and as a matter of tactical interest, that British counterattacks throughout this battle achieved consistently little gain, at heavy loss. On the 18th a French division took over Kemmel Hill, and next day the remainder entered the line. On the 25th the Germans resumed their offensive, but only on a limited front. The famous Kemmel Hill was captured from the French, and the British to the north were also forced back. For a few hours a last opportunity was vouchsafed to the Germans, but through Ludendorff's intervention they refrained from exploiting it. After a final, costly and more abortive assault on the 29th, the German offensive was abandoned.

As General Edmonds, the official historian, has penetratingly remarked, 'it is easy to see why Ludendorff collapsed after the 8th of August, 1918—on the 29th of April he was already well on the way to despair'.

CHAPTER VIII

SCENE 3

THE BREAK-THROUGH TO THE MARNE

Four battle-worn British divisions were 'resting' in a quiet sector north of the Aisne, between Reims and Soissons, far detached from the rest of the army. They had been sent to the French front, after strenuous exertions in the battles of the Lys, in return for French reinforcements which had gone north to aid the British in the later stages of that 'backs to the wall' struggle. On the tranquil Aisne they could recuperate while still serving a useful purpose as guardians of the trench line.

It was too quiet to be true. But the uneasiness of the local British commanders—shared by certain of their French neighbours—was lightly discounted by their French superiors. On May 25th they received from French headquarters the message that 'in our opinion there are no indications that the enemy has made preparations which would enable him to attack to-morrow'. Next morning the French captured two prisoners who told of the impending attack, but the higher command had no plan to meet it, and, even so, did not warn the troops until late in the day. Too late!

For at 1 a.m. on May 27th, 1918, a terrific storm of fire burst on the Franco-British front between Reims and north of Soissons, along the famous Chemin-des-Dames; at 4.30 a.m. an overwhelming torrent of Germans swept over the front trenches; by midday it was pouring over the many unblown bridges of the Aisne, and by May 30th it had reached the Marne—site and symbol of the great ebb of 1914. After nearly four years a menace deemed for ever past had returned to a point that endowed it with demoralizing symbolism.

Happily, it proved to be 'thus far and no farther'. Like the two great preceding offensives of March 21st and April 9th,

The break-through to the
MARNE

Vauxaillon

CHEMIN DES DAMES • Ailles
Fr. Corps 50
XI   8
Vailly   IX Corps   • Berry au Bac

R. Aisne   R. Aisne   21

Soissons

Fismes   R. Vesle
45 F

Fère en Tardenois   **Reims**

AISNE-MARNE
CANAL

N

R. Marne
Dormans

Château Thierry

R. Marne

▬▬▬	Original Line
▬ ▬ ▬	Line on evening of 27 th. May
▬ · ▬ ·	Line on evening of 29 th. May
▬··▬··	Line on evening of 30 th. May
··········	Line on evening of 1 st. June

0   5   10   15
Miles

© Cassell & Co. Ltd. 1970

that of May 27th achieved astonishing captures of ground and prisoners, but it brought the Germans little nearer to their strategical object. And, even more than its predecessors, its very success paved the way for their downfall. To the reasons for this we shall come. But why, a month after the last onslaught, in the north, had come to an end; why, when there had been this long interval for preparation and for examination of the situation by a now unified command, should a surprise greater than any before have been possible? This is perhaps the most interesting historical question of the battle.

It has long been known, of course, that the French higher command, the one directly concerned with the safety of the Aisne sector, did not believe in the likelihood of an attack. Nor did the British higher command, which, however, was concerned with the front in the north, and expected a further onslaught there. If not justified by the event, the British had some cause for expecting it, as German disclosures have since attested.

But the Intelligence Service of another of the Allies, better placed to take a wide survey, did give the warning—only to be disregarded until too late. On May 13th, a fortnight after the fighting in Flanders had died away, the British Intelligence came to the conclusion that 'an attack on a broad front between Arras and Albert is intended'. Next day this was discussed at a conference of the Intelligence section of the American Expeditionary Force, and the head of the Battle-Order section, Major S. T. Hubbard, gave a contrary opinion, holding that the next attack would be against the Chemin-des-Dames sector, between May 25th and 30th. Among the reasons given were that, as surprise was the keynote of the German method, this sector was one of the few where it was now possible; that it was all the more likely to be chosen because regarded by the Allies as secure and as a resting ground for tired divisions; that its feasible frontage corresponded well with the limited German resources available at the moment, and that this hypothesis was confirmed by the ascertained location of the German troops, particularly of certain picked divisions.

The warning in detail was conveyed to the French General Headquarters, but fell on deaf ears. Why should credence be given to an opinion coming from such an amateur army, not yet tested in battle, over the verdict of war-tried and highly developed Intelligence services? The warning was reiterated, however, and Colonel de Cointet, Chief of the French Intelligence, was won over to its acceptance. But now, as at Verdun two years before, the Operations branch opposed until too late the view of its own Intelligence. This time, however, it was less blameworthy, for it was tugged the other way by the comforting assurances of General Duchêne, Commander of the Sixth French Army, in charge of the Chemin-des-Dames sector.

This General, indeed, bears a still heavier responsibility, for he insisted on the adoption of the long-exploded and wasteful system of massing the infantry of the defence in the forward positions. Besides giving the enemy guns a crowded and helpless target, this method ensured that once the German guns had made a bloated meal of this luckless cannon-fodder, the German infantry would find practically no local reserves to oppose their progress through the rear zones. In similar manner all the headquarters, communication centres, ammunition depots, and railheads were pushed close up, ready to be dislocated promptly by the enemy bombardment.

Pétain's instructions for a deep and elastic system of defence had evidently made no impression on General Duchêne, so that it was still less a matter for wonder that the protests of junior British commanders met with a rebuff—and the conclusive 'J'ai dit'. It was unfortunate also, if perhaps less avoidable, that when the four British divisions forming the IX Corps (Hamilton-Gordon) arrived from the north at the end of April, their depleted ranks filled up with raw drafts from home, they were hurried straight into the line, as the best place to complete their training.

The central backbone of the Aisne defences was formed by

the historic Chemin-des-Dames ridge north of the river. The eastern half of this 'hog's back' was to be held by the British, with the 50th Division (H. C. Jackson) on the left, next the 8th Division (Heneker), and beyond the end of the ridge, in the low ground from Berry-au-Bac along the Aisne and Marne canal, the 21st Division (D. G. M. Campbell), joining up with the French troops covering Reims. The infantry of the 25th Division (Bainbridge) was in reserve.

Altogether the French Sixth Army front was held by three French and three British divisions, with four and one respectively in reserve. Against these tired or raw troops, in the main attack from Berry-au-Bac westwards, fifteen German divisions, all but one brought up fresh, were to fall upon five, with two more for the subsidiary attack between Berry-au-Bac and Reims, while seven German divisions lay close up in support.

Even so, the Germans' superiority of numbers was not so pronounced as in the March and April offensives, whereas both the rapidity and the extent of their progress were greater. Once again the tactical surprise of the assault was aided by a thick ground mist, which wrapped the Germans' initial advance in a cloak of invisibility. But they had a series of extraordinarily difficult obstacles to cross—first, the Ailette stream in no-man's-land itself. The conclusion is, therefore, that the advantage was due in part to the strategic surprise—the greater unexpectedness of the time and place—and in part to the folly of exposing the defenders so completely to the demoralizing and paralysing effect of the German bombardment—by 3719 guns on a front of thirty-eight miles. This last, indeed, was a form of surprise, for the object of all surprise is the dislocation of the enemy's moral and mind, and the effect is the same whether the enemy be caught napping by deception or allows himself to be trapped with his eyes open. Further, the Germans' success on May 27th, 1918, deserves study and comparison with their other offensives, whose success was almost in mathematical ratio to their degree of surprise.

This final year, indeed, read in the light of previous years, affords fresh proof that surprise—or, more scientifically, the dislocation of the enemy's mental balance—is essential to true success in every operation of war. A lesson oft repeated, oft ignored. At the bar of history any commander who risks the lives of his men without seeking this preliminary guarantee is condemned.

Let us pass to the events of May 27th. For three and a half hours the unfortunate troops had to endure a bombardment unparalleled, according to the verdict of the more experienced sufferers, in its intensity. And the ordeal of those hours of helpless endurance, amid the ever-swelling litter of shattered dead and untended wounded, was made more trying by crouching, semi-suffocated in gas masks. Then the grey waves advanced—a relief, if only of action, at last. Three-quarters of an hour later they had reached the crest of the ridge in the centre, near Ailles. This uncovered the flank of the left British division, the 50th, forcing its survivors to fall back down the other slope. Next to it the 8th Division was being forced to give way, although two of its brigades held stubbornly for a time on the north bank of the Aisne.

Here the 2nd Devons earned imperishable glory and a citation in the French Orders of the Day—by sacrificing themselves almost to a man in a stand which gained breathing space for fresh resistance to take form in rear. On the British right, the attack on the 21st Division developed later; this division was awkwardly placed with the swampy Aisne and Marne canal running through the centre of its battle zone, but most of it was successfully extricated and withdrawn west of the canal. By midday the situation was that the Germans had reached and crossed at most points the Aisne from Berry-au-Bac to Vailly—helped by the fact that General Duchêne had been belated in giving the order to blow up the bridges. Hitherto the German progress had been evenly distributed, but in the afternoon a heavy sagging occurred in the centre, at the junction of the French and British wings, and the Germans pushed through as far as

Fismes on the Vesle—12 miles penetration in a single day. This central collapse was natural, both because it is an habitual tendency, and because the heaviest weight—more than four to one—of the assault had fallen on the two French divisions in the centre and the left of the 50th Division adjoining them.

This sagging, together with the renewed German pressure, compelled a drawing back of the flanks. On the east, or British flank, this operation was distinguished by a remarkable manœuvre of the 21st Division, which wheeled back during the night through hilly wooded country, while pivoting on and keeping touch with the Algerian division, which formed the right of the army.

After forcing the passage of the Vesle and capturing the heights south of it, the Germans paused until fresh reinforcements reached them from Ludendorff. But on the 29th they made a vast bound, reaching Fère-en-Tardenois in the centre and capturing Soissons on the west, both important nodal points, which yielded them quantities of material. The German troops had even outstripped in their swift onrush the objectives assigned to them, and had done this despite the counterattacks which Pétain was now shrewdly directing against their sensitive right flank. On the 30th the German flood swept on to the Marne, 15 miles beyond the Vesle. But it was now flowing in a narrowing central channel; and this day little ground was yielded by the Allied right flank, where the four British divisions—the 8th and 50th now merely remnants—had been reinforced by the 19th (Jeffreys), as well as by French divisions. Next day what remained of the original four was relieved by the French, who now took over command from the IX Corps, although fractions of them still remained in the fighting line for another three weeks as part of the 19th Division.

But from May 31st onwards the Germans, checked on the side of Reims and in front by the Marne, turned their efforts to a westward expansion of the great bulge—down the corridor between the Ourcq and the Marne towards Paris.

Hitherto the French reserves had been thrown into the battle as they arrived, in an attempt to stem the flood, which usually resulted in their being caught up and carried back by it. On June 1st, however, Pétain issued orders for the further reserves coming up to form, instead, a ring in rear, digging themselves in and thus having ready before the German flood reached them a vast semicircular dam which would stop and confine its now slackening flow. When it beat against this in the first days of June its momentum was too diminished to make much impression, whereas the appearance and fierce counterattack of the 2nd American Division at the vital joint of Château-Thierry was not only a material cement, but an inestimable moral tonic to their weary Allies.

Yet it would seem that the most valuable allies of all were the cellars of Champagne, reinforced by the vast stacks of supplies that the French abandoned to their destitute pursuers. At Soissons the desire for such loot brought the forfeit of opportunity. At Fismes there were 'drunken soldiers lying all over the road'. At Jonchery 'battalions stopped in the face of the slightest opposition and it was difficult to get them together again. Progress was very slow although there was no actual fighting. At the villages lamentable disorders took place. The officers could no longer keep control . . . a sorry picture of much drunkenness'.

In their victorious onrush, the Germans had taken some 65,000 prisoners, but whereas this human loss was soon to be more than made up by American reinforcements, strategically the Germans' success had merely placed themselves in a huge sack which was to prove their undoing less than two months later. As in each of the two previous offensives, the tactical success of the Germans on May 27th proved a strategical reverse, because the extent to which they surprised their enemy surprised, and so upset the balance of, their own command.

For, as the disclosures of General von Kuhl have revealed, the offensive of May 27th was intended merely as a diversion, to attract the Allied reserves thither preparatory to a final and decisive blow at the British front covering Hazebrouck. But its astonishing opening success tempted the German command to carry it too far and too long, the attraction of success attracting thither their own reserves as well as the enemy's. Nevertheless, we may justly speculate as to what might have resulted if the attack had begun on April 17th, as ordered, instead of being delayed until May 27th, before the preparations were complete. The Germans would have worn out fewer of their reserves in ineffectual prolongations of the Somme and Lys offensives, while the Allies would have still been waiting for the stiffening, moral and physical, of America's man power. Time and surprise are the two supreme factors in war. The Germans lost the first and forfeited the second by allowing their own surprise to surprise themselves.

Second Battle of the MARNE

THIRD ARMY

FIRST ARMY

SEVENTH ARMY

FOURTH ARMY

FIFTH ARMY

NINTH ARMY

SIXTH ARMY

TENTH ARMY

Laon

Soissons

Compiègne

BEAUVAIS
30 MILES

Villers Cotterets

Fère en Tardenois

Château Thierry

Meaux

Reims

Verzy

Montagne de Reims Forest

Epernay

Chalons

R.Aisne

R.Vesle

R.Serzy

R.Ardre

R.Ourcq

R.Marne

R.Marne

R.Oise

N

Line on 15th July, 1918
Line on 18th July, 1918
Direction of Attacks

Miles
0   5   10   15   20

© Cassell & Co. Ltd. 1970

CHAPTER VIII

SCENE 4

THE SECOND BATTLE OF THE MARNE, JULY, 1918

How apt, if how strange, the historical coincidence by which, as the Marne had been the first high-water mark and witnessed the first ebb of the tide of invasion in 1914, so four years later it was destined to be the final high-water mark from which the decisive ebb began. For on July 15th, 1918, the shell-churned wastes around Reims were the scene of the last German offensive on the Western Front. The tide of German success was definitely stemmed and three days later the ebb began under pressure of the great Allied counterstroke.

But although the first day marked the last German bid for victory, the actual attack was by no means the Germans' supreme effort, nor had it the decisive aims popularly ascribed to it at the time. For Ludendorff still adhered to his guiding idea that the British, severely shaken in the great battles of March and April, should be the target for his decisive blow and that their front in Flanders should be the stage on which he would produce this final drama of victory.

Thus, as has already been told, the spectacular May 27th attack when the Germans, pouring over the Chemin-des-Dames, across the Aisne and to the Marne, seemed to menace Paris itself, was conceived merely as a diversion to draw the Allied reserves away from Flanders. And its rapid success, surprising Ludendorff as much as his attack surprised Foch, dug a pitfall for the Germans by luring their own reserves thither to exploit and retain this apparent windfall.

So also with the June 9th attack, less bountiful in its fruits, that had been launched near Compiègne to break down the buttress of Allied territory that lay between the huge salients created by the German 'pushes' of March and May. When, instead, this German attack was broken off by Ludendorff, with little gained but his own reserves still further drained, he considered 'the enemy in Flanders still so strong that the German army could not attack there yet'. So he planned a further diversion—to be made by forty-nine divisions attacking on either side of Reims. Another reason for this choice was that the German forces in the Marne salient depended on a single railway, the Laon-Soissons line, which was dangerously exposed both to air and artillery attack. The Chief of the Field Railway insisted that Reims must be captured in order to improve the communications. Otherwise the salient would become untenable—the Germans must get on or get out. Ludendorff chose to attack rather than to withdraw.

The plan was finally settled at a conference on June 18th. The principal blow was to be delivered by the First (Mudra) and Third (Einem) Armies, driving towards Châlons, while the Seventh Army (Boehm) sought to cross the Marne near Dormans and to converge with the main advance in the direction of Epernay.

Outwardly, Boehm's Army seemed to have the most difficult problem to solve, having to cross a river eighty yards wide in face of the enemy. The designers relied for success on 'the unexampled boldness of the plan', aided by the methods of concealment which had triumphed on May 27th.

But the sands of time were slipping out for the Germans, and American reinforcements, like the sands of the shore in potential number, were slipping into the Allied line of battle, there to become a cement for this grievously strained rampart. Appreciating this, Ludendorff intended his Flanders attack, once more towards the nodal point of Hazebrouck, to follow on the 20th, only five days after the Reims diversion. On July 16th actually, as soon as the Reims attack was under way, artillery and aircraft were sent off by train to the Flanders front, and Ludendorff himself moved to Tournai to supervise the staging and production of his decisive drama.

But the curtain was never to rise upon it. The Reims diversion had not even the brilliant opening success of its predecessors, and on July 18th the Allied counterstroke so jeopardized the Germans' situation that Ludendorff felt compelled to postpone, if not yet to abandon, the fulfilment of his dream. The reason why the German offensive 'fell flat' on July 15th was that east of Reims it was played to an empty 'first night' house. One of the great stories of the war which everybody knows is that of the 'elastic defence', in face of which the German onslaught lost its momentum, before it reached the real position of the French resistance. Statesmen and generals have vied with each other in acclaiming the brilliance of 'Gouraud's manœuvre'. Alas! the story must be consigned to its place with many others in the museum of war legends.

The manœuvre was entirely due to Pétain, that cool, unemotional company director of modern war, and shrewd economist of human lives, who, called to be Commander-in-Chief after the Nivelle fiasco of 1917, had systematically worked to rebuild the French Army and to restore the stability of its man power and morale that had been so undermined by the extravagant offensive policy of Joffre and Nivelle from 1914 to 1917.

Not content merely to reorganize, Pétain had set himself to insure against a recurrence of the trouble by tactics that should be both an economy of force and of the nervous force of the combatant. To this end, one method was an elastic defence in depth, allowing the initial shock and impetus of the enemy's attack to be absorbed by a thinly held forward position, and then to await him on a strong position in rear, when the enemy's troops would be beyond the range of the bulk of their supporting artillery.

This method Pétain had sought to apply against the German attack of June 9th, but, although partially successful, its full effect was lost through the reluctance of the local commanders, still clinging to their old offensive dogmas, to reconcile themselves to a voluntary yielding up of a few square miles of worthless ground. And before July 15th, when the coming German attack was definitely expected, a week's argument was required before Pétain could persuade the lion-hearted Gouraud, who commanded the French Fourth Army east of Reims, to adopt this elastic manœuvre.

But even when we have ascribed it to the right source, the accumulation of historical error is not fully corrected. For the method was not the revolutionary innovation that it has been termed. The Germans, in fact, had used it on September 25th, 1915—nearly three years before—to discomfit the great French autumn offensive in Champagne. And the underlying idea can be traced back another two thousand years—to Cannae, where Hannibal applied it against the Romans in a distinctly more subtle and decisive way.

But it sufficed, even in the mild way of 1918, to thwart the German attack east of Reims, where its effort was immeasurably strengthened by the German failure to achieve a surprise such as had marked their earlier offensives of 1918. Full warning of the coming blow was obtained by the French; the statements of prisoners taken from July 5th onward being confirmed by air photographs of camouflaged ammunition dumps. And an evening raid on July 14th brought in a prisoner from whom, by withholding his gas mask, the French discovered the exact hour of the bombardment (1.10 a.m.). The French guns accordingly opened fire ten minutes earlier, and thus before the German infantry advanced from their trenches they had been trapped and riven by the French artillery counter-preparation. They withered away before the machine-guns of the French outpost line, and the shrunken remnants that passed beyond failed to make even a crack in the main position.

But the dramatic nature of this repulse east of Reims has obscured the fact that it was not the whole battle. West of Reims the front had only been stabilized for a month since the last German thrust, and the newly improvised position was a handicap to the execution of the elastic method by commanders who were slow to grasp it. They chose to hold the forward position on the river line strongly, and their troops paid the penalty when the enemy's sudden deluge of gas-shells caught them unawares. The Germans, in contrast, proved the value of taking the most obviously difficult, and hence most unlikely, course. Their infantry were ferried over the river under cover of darkness and a smoke screen, and then pushed forward to the attack, while a number of bridges were swiftly built under fire—an astonishing feat.

Thus here the German attack deepened the corner of the great bulge made in May, and not only pushed across the Marne but behind Reims, so that it threatened to undercut this pivot of the Allied resistance. If the threat had an important influence on the French plan for the counterstroke, its physical progress was stopped on July 16th. The German attack, unaided by pressure elsewhere, had degenerated into local actions, disconnected and therefore useless, while the French artillery and aircraft, by bombarding the Marne crossings, made it difficult for the Germans to obtain supplies. Next day a queer hush of expectation spread over the far-flung battlefield. The stage was set for the great 'revanche'.

In an event so significant for the history of the world, the main historical interest is to determine its causes. The chief among them is to be found not by any analysis of military art, but by a process far more true to the character of the World War—that of drawing up a balance sheet of the previous six months' transactions. When Ludendorff opened his campaign he had a credit balance of 207 divisions, 82 in reserve. Now he had only 66 'fit' divisions in reserve, most of them really so 'watered down' that they could hardly be counted as sound assets.

If these operations had made serious inroads into the Franco-British balance of man power, the Allies had at least averted liquidation, and now, in July, ample and increasing American drafts were being paid into their account. Like a promissory note, this American aid was of incalculable value in restoring their credit—their morale and confidence—even before it made good their material losses. Pétain, the military economist, had appreciated this primary factor long before, when he had said—'If we can hold on until the end of June our situation will be excellent. In July we can resume the offensive; after that victory will be ours.'

If this simple calculation of time and numbers has the effect of attenuating the popular image of an inspired 'Foch counter-stroke', wresting victory from the jaws of defeat, it is regrettable, but it is reality. Unfortunately, even what remains suffers in examination and, in the outcome, a further reduction. War is a masculine activity, and so it is perhaps natural that the feminine maxim, 'il faut souffrir pour être belle', should be inverted. For in military history it is both easy and pleasant for all concerned to make an image of beauty, whereas it is not only hard for the seeker to reach the truth but the subject usually suffers in consequence.

The riddle of July 18th, 1918, might aptly be put in terms of the old conundrum—'When is a counterstroke not a counterstroke?' Foch's mystical faith in the almighty power of the offensive 'will to conquer' had long since been shown at the Marne in 1914—where day after day he had ordered attacks, apparently oblivious of the reality that his exhausted troops could do and did nothing more than cling precariously to their ground.

Then at Ypres the same year he had spurred on Sir John French to order ambitious attacks, while actually the British troops were barely resisting superior numbers. On these occasions the result justified the spirit, if not the letter, of his instructions. But when the German gas attack made a hole in the Allied line at Ypres in April, 1915, Foch's refrain of 'attaquez', and his unredeemed promises of a French attack, caused Sir John French to waver almost nightly from the resolve to withdraw and straighten out the line, as Smith-Dorrien, to his cost, urged from the outset. Thus, when this commonsense course was ultimately followed, the British had merely lost not only Smith-Dorrien's services but many lives to no purpose.

When Foch was rehabilitated in 1917 this 'offensive'

instinct still dominated him, and when the crisis of March, 1918, called him to the Supreme Command he had hardly set about his unenviable task of restoring the battered front of the Allies before he was dreaming of fresh offensives. Even before the new collapse of the Aisne front in May he had issued *directives* to Haig and Pétain for attacks to free the lateral railway near Amiens and Hazebrouck.

If this project showed his practical belief in his theory of freedom of action, it is also evidence that he had no idea of luring the Germans into vast salients which he could cut off in flank—which was the conception subsequently extolled by popular propagandists. Similarly, the truth of the great counterstroke of July 18th is that it was not conceived, by Foch at least, as a counterstroke at all. But the refrain 'attaquez' was chanted so continually that sooner or later it was bound to coincide with a 'psychological moment'—as on July 18th.

In the meantime Ludendorff's keenness in pursuing a similar policy, and the wariness of Pétain and Haig helped to prevent the Allied forces becoming seriously involved in a premature offensive before the balance of numbers changed. In contrast, it was the oft-derided economist, Pétain, the 'cautious', who had conceived the plan of the defensive-offensive battle as it was actually waged—first a parry to the enemy's thrust and then a riposte when he was off his balance. On June 4th he had asked Foch to assemble two groups of reserves at Beauvais and Epernay respectively with a view to a counterstroke against the flank of any fresh German advance. The first group, under Mangin, had been used to break the German attack of June 9th, and was then switched a little further east to a position on the west flank of the German salient between Soissons and Reims which bulged towards the Marne.

Foch, however, planned to use it for the strictly offensive purpose of a push against the rail centre of Soissons. While this was being prepared, the Intelligence Service made it clear that the Germans were about to launch a fresh attack near Reims. Foch thereupon determined to anticipate it, not retort to it, by launching his offensive on July 12th. Pétain, however, had the contrary idea of first stopping and then smiting the enemy when the latter had entangled himself. And, perchance curiously, the French troops were not ready on July 12th, so that the battle was fought rather according to Pétain's than to Foch's conception. But not altogether. For Pétain's plan had comprised three phases—first, to hold up the German attack; second, to launch counterstrokes against the flanks of the fresh pockets it was likely to make on either side of Reims; third, and only third, when the German reserves had been fully drawn towards those pockets, to unleash Mangin's army in a big counter-offensive eastward along the baseline of the main bulge—the enemy's rear—and so close the neck of the vast sack in which the German forces south of the Aisne would be enclosed.

Events and Foch combined to modify this conception. As already narrated the German attack west of Reims had made an unpleasantly deep pocket, penetrating well over the Marne and threatening to take in rear the natural buttress formed by the Montagne de Reims. To avert the danger Pétain was driven to use most of the reserves he had intended for the second phase of the counterstroke; and to replace them he decided to draw from Mangin's army, and to postpone the latter's counter-offensive—already ordered by Foch for July 18th.

When Foch—full of eagerness and with his spirit still more fortified, if that was possible, by Haig's promise to send British reserves—heard of Pétain's action he promptly countermanded it. Hence on July 18th the French left wing* was

* The spearhead of this consisted of Mangin's Tenth Army, which had ten divisions in the first line (including the American 1st and 2nd Divisions), six divisions and Robillot's Cavalry Corps in the second line, and the British 15th and 34th Divisions in reserve. At 4.35 a.m. on the dark and foggy morning of the 18th Mangin struck, using his massed tanks on the Cambrai method without any artillery preparation. The left of Degoutte's Sixth Army, on Mangin's inner flank, chimed in

launched to its counter-offensive while the defensive battle was still in progress in the centre and on the right wing. This meant that the second phase of Pétain's plan had to be dropped out, and instead of the right wing attracting the Germans' reserves in order to enable the left wing to fall on their naked back, the left wing's offensive eased the pressure on the right wing.

To compensate as far as possible the initial passivity of the right wing,* the British reserves (51st and 62nd Divisions) which were sent thither, were used to relieve the defending troops 'on the move', passing direct to an attack. In the centre,† American reserves were similarly used, and thus a general pressure began along the whole face of the great salient.

But this convergent pressure did not begin until July 20th, and by that time the opening surprise—due to the sudden release of a mass of tanks—was over and the left wing had lost its impetus. After advancing about four miles on the 18th, and a little further on the 19th, Mangin's Army was brought to a standstill on the Soissons flank—near the jugular vein of the salient. Thus the Germans, fighting hard for breathing space, gained the time they required to draw the bulk of their forces out of the sack, even though they left 25,000 prisoners and much material behind. And once they were safely back on a straight and much-shortened line along the Vesle,

one and a half hours later, after a preliminary bombardment. Degoutte's subsidiary role was marked by the fact that he had only seven divisions (among them the American 4th and 26th) in the first line and one in the second; he was later reinforced by the American 42nd, 32nd and 28th divisions, which bore the main burden in the final stage of the advance to the Vesle. Five German divisions faced Mangin and six faced Degoutte; with six and two respectively in reserve. But all were weak and more than half had been reported as of little or no value.

* Berthelot's Fifth Army, comprising nine divisions. It was opposed by eleven German divisions, with one in reserve.

† De Mitry's Ninth Army, comprising six divisions (including the 3rd American), with the 28th American and a French one in reserve. It was opposed by six weak German divisions, with three in reserve.

Ludendorff felt able, on August 2nd, to order preparations to be resumed for fresh attacks in Flanders and east of Montdidier.

Six days later his offensive dreams were finally dissipated; but it is historically important to realize that it was not the second Battle of the Marne, 'Foch's great counterstroke', which dissipated them. This July 18th counterstroke, conceived as such by Pétain and amended by Foch, was by no means decisive in its results. It may be that Foch's impetuosity robbed him of such results; that Pétain's oft-criticized caution would have been more fruitful and collected a larger 'bag'.

Nevertheless, if the battle had no clearly decisive effect, the first taste of victory after such deep and bitter draughts of defeat was an incalculable moral stimulant to the Allies, and perchance its depressing effect on the German morale was more insidiously damaging than was at first visible. So that Foch, who was ever concerned only with moral factors, which cannot be mathematically calculated, may well have been content. He had gained the initiative, and he kept it—that was enough, results mattered little. For his strategy was simple, not the complex masterpiece of art which legend has ascribed to him. It was best expressed in his own vivid illustration—'War is like this. Here is an inclined plane. An attack is like the ball rolling down it. It goes on gaining momentum and getting faster and faster on condition that you do not stop it. If you check it artificially you lose your momentum and have to begin all over again.'

CHAPTER VIII

SCENE 5

THE 'BLACK DAY' OF THE GERMAN ARMY—AUGUST 8TH

AUGUST 8th, 1918, is a date which grows ever larger on the horizon of the historian. So far as any one event of the campaign in the West can be regarded as decisive, it is the great surprise east of Amiens that occurred on this day. And that decisiveness is above all a proof that the moral element dominates warfare.

For although August 8th was 'a famous victory', the most brilliant ever gained by British arms in the World War, and, better still, the most economical, neither its tactical nor its visible strategic results were sufficient to explain its moral effect. Its 16,000 prisoners on the first day, and 21,000 all told, were a handsome prize compared with that of any previous British offensive, but a trifle in proportion to the vast forces then deployed on the Western Front, and in relation to such triumphs of the past as Worcester, Blenheim, Rossbach, Austerlitz, or Sedan. Its initial penetration of six to eight miles, and ultimate twelve miles, were, again, excellent by 1915-1917 standards, but in March the Germans had penetrated thirty-eight miles in the reverse direction without achieving any decisive result. Studied on the map, the advance of August 8th–21st merely flattened out the nose and indented one cheek of the shallow German salient Arras-Montdidier-Noyon. It was far from reaching any vital link of the enemy's communications, or even cutting off the troops in that salient.

Yet it unhinged the mind and morale of the German Supreme Command. It led the Kaiser to say—'I see that we must strike a balance. We are at the end of our resources. The

AMIENS
8th. August, 1918

St. Quentin

Sept. 25th

Roisel

Sept. 8th

Mont St. Quentin

Péronne

R. Somme

Aug. 29th

Lihons

BRITISH
FRENCH Boundary

Aug. 26th

Roye

Albert

Aug. 15th

R. Avre

Aug. 8th

Proyart

Evening Aug. 8th

R. Luce

Moreuil

Montdidier

R. Ancre

Hamel

Aug. 8th

Amiens

R. Somme

Miles

0   5   10

© Cassell & Co. Ltd. 1970

war must be ended.' It made Ludendorff take a similarly despondent view—'The war would have to be ended.'

In comparing the impression made upon him by the dramatic counterstroke of July 18th on the Marne and that of August 8th, there is a remarkable contrast. And in this contrast lies the answer as to which was the more decisive of the two. For after July 18th he had by no means lost hope. He seems to have treated this reverse as hardly more than an unfortunate incident, and as late as August 2nd was ordering preparations for four fresh attacks, including his cherished Flanders blow, if on a reduced scale in comparison with his original intention.

But after August 8th these dreams vanish. There is an abandonment of any idea of returning to the offensive, and, more significant still, no adoption of an alternative strategy. Mere passive resistance to the enemy's kicks cannot be called a strategical plan. Only when it was too late did he formulate the design of a purposeful evacuation of France as a preliminary to a fresh campaign beyond the frontier. By then, however, the moral collapse of the German Command had spread to the German people.

After the war Ludendorff delivered his considered opinion that 'August 8th was the black day of the German Army in the history of the war'. The adjective 'black' is peculiarly apt, for when faintness follows a sudden shock the blackening of the vista is the symptom which precedes the loss of consciousness and the consequent paralysis of the faculties. Thus, the primary interest in the story of August 8th is to trace how this shock came about. On July 12th Foch, irrepressibly eager to begin his cherished but oft-postponed idea of returning to the offensive, proposed to Haig that—

'The first offensive to be launched on the British front should be one starting from the front Festubert-Rebecq, with a view to freeing the Bruay mines and forbidding the communication centre of Estaires. . . .'

Five days later Haig replied that he saw 'no advantage in

an advance over the flat and marshy region between Rebecq and Festubert', and suggested, instead, that—

'The operation, in my opinion, which is of the highest importance and which I proposed to you, as before, should be executed as soon as possible, is to push forward the Allied front to the east and south-east of Amiens so as to free that town and the railway. The best way to carry out this object is to make a combined Franco-British operation, the French attacking south of Moreuil and the British north of the Luce.

'To realize this project I am preparing plans secretly for an offensive north of the Luce, direction east. . . . In liaison with this project the French forces should, in my opinion, carry out an operation between Moreuil and Mont-didier. . . .'

This letter, from the archives, sheds light on several momentous points of post-war controversy. First, as to the origin of the offensive, it shows not only that it was purely of British conception, but also that it was a 'limited' conception—a narrow-fronted 'shove' to secure for Amiens and the railway a rather wider margin of safety. The question is often mooted whether the idea sprang from the Commander-in-Chief, Haig, or from the Fourth Army Commander, Rawlinson. Here the words 'as before' suggest that Haig had priority, for it was the brilliant little surprise operation at Hamel on July 4th and its revelation of the decline of German morale which inspired Rawlinson with the idea of a wider offensive.

However, there is little in the question of priority, for the defensive advantage of freeing Amiens was obvious. Indeed, the fact that Rawlinson's inspiration should not have come until after Hamel suggests his deeper appreciation of the moral element. The exploitation of an enemy's moral disintegration is fundamentally an offensive purpose.

Second, as to the plan of the offensive, the letter seems to contradict the claim, made in *Sir Douglas Haig's Command* and elsewhere, that the British were forced by Foch, against their will, to let the French share in the operation—thereby increasing what Clausewitz termed the inevitable 'friction' of war. Rawlinson certainly, and rightly, argued against it as inimical to the surprise he sought.

But the letter shows that it was Haig's proposal. It is true that he proposed leaving a gap of a few miles between the French and British attacks. But both were purely frontal and strategically shoulder to shoulder. A richer offensive prospect was perhaps offered by a convergent attack on the two flanks of the salient, north of Albert and well south of Montdidier respectively. But, for the former, a trench-filled belt of the old Somme battlefields was a difficulty, and subsequent events do not support the view that another army would have brought off such a surprise as the Fourth did south of the Somme.

The enlargement of the original project was due to Foch, who, on August 5th, directed that if the initial attack was successful, it was to be continued by pushing south-east towards Ham. If the attacks against the southern flank of the salient which Humbert's and Mangin's armies began on August 10th and 17th respectively could have coincided with that of the British, greater material profits might have been yielded. As it was, the close co-operation of Debeney's army immediately adjoining the British did little to compensate its inevitable hindrance to the plan of surprise. For, lacking tanks, it could not dispense with a preliminary bombardment, and this could not begin, without forfeiting the general surprise, until the British advance started.

Greater material profits, however, could hardly have increased the moral effect of August 8th on the German Command. And this effect came from the shock of perhaps the most complete surprise of the war. How it was achieved is an object lesson for future soldiers, for, like all the masterpieces of moral dislocation in military history, it was a subtle compound of many deceptive factors. Too often surprise is treated as an incidental, to be gained by a simple choice of date or place.

Its foundation was the sudden loosing of a swarm of tanks —456 in all—in place of any preliminary artillery bombardment.* This method, inaugurated at Cambrai the previous November, had been repeated by the French on July 18th. Before Amiens it was enhanced by manifold devices. Secrecy was sought by holding the preliminary conferences always at different places, by concealing reconnaissances, and by informing the executants at the latest moment compatible with readiness—divisional commanders did not know that an attack was intended until July 31st, and the fighting troops not until thirty-six hours before the start. Even the War Cabinet in London was kept in the dark, and in that august assembly the Australian Prime Minister, Mr. Hughes, was in course of a vehement demand that the Australians should be taken out of the line, when a telegram brought the undreamt of news that the Australians were far on the other side of the line. On that same morning also, a general from the neighbouring army made a casual call at Rawlinson's headquarters on his way home for leave, and incidentally inquired why there was such a heavy sound of gunfire from the front.

Deception was sought by making all movements at night—with aeroplanes patrolling the area to check any exposure; by continuing work on the British rear defences until the last evening, by regulating the times and rates of fire of the artillery so that as more and more guns were slipped into concealed positions they registered without any apparent increase in the normal daily quantity of fire. By such means the strength of the Fourth Army was roughly doubled—six fresh divisions, two cavalry divisions, nine tank battalions, and another thousand guns being concentrated in the area unsuspected by the enemy between August 1st and 8th. This involved the use of 290 special trains (60 for ammunition and

* In his analytical study of the war, General von Kuhl, the directing brain of the opposing Army Group, attributes the overwhelming effect of the attack to the fact that the British had 'learnt' how to achieve surprise; he adds that in this surprise 'the most important and decisive factor was the tanks'. This statement has the significance that belongs to a verdict in cool reflection, ten years after the event.

the rest for troops)—and only two lines of railway were available.

Thus by zero hour (4.20 a.m.) on August 8th, the Fourth Army strength had been raised to thirteen divisions, three cavalry divisions, seventeen air squadrons, ten heavy and two whippet tank battalions (totalling 360 heavy and 96 whippet tanks), and over 2000 guns and howitzers, including 672 'heavies'. Two-thirds of the heavy artillery was allotted for counter-battery work, and effectively paralysed the hostile artillery.

Distraction also is an essential component of surprise, and in this case it centred round the introduction of the Canadians. Regarding them as storm troops, the enemy tended to greet their appearance as an omen of a coming attack. At the moment the Canadian Corps was near Arras and an aptly chosen fraction of it—two battalions, two casualty clearing stations, and its wireless section—was despatched northwards to Kemmel in Flanders. There, also, other 'suggestions' of attack were conveyed by erecting extra aerodromes and cavalry wireless. Meanwhile the bulk of the Canadian Corps was filtered down to the Somme, where various ingenious rumours were circulated among the British troops to account for its appearance.

The Fourth Army dispositions were that the main punch was to be delivered south of the Somme, by the Canadian Corps (Currie) on the right and the Australian Corps (Monash) on the left, next the river, whilst the III Corps (R. H. K. Butler) advanced north of the river to safeguard the flank of the main punch. But the Canadians did not move into the front line until a few hours before the assault, and meantime the Australians extended their front as far south as the Amiens-Roye road, relieving the French, and thereby lulling the Germans into a false sense of security. For what enemy would expect attack from a force which was spreading itself out defensively?

The whole front of attack was about fourteen miles long, and on the German side was held by six skeleton divisions (averaging barely 3000 effectives apiece) of General von der Marwitz's Second Army. Their weakness of numbers was accentuated by weakness of defences, and in their rough forward line there were none of the usual deep dug-outs to safeguard morale until the hour of trial.

Five days before the attack an enemy raid captured an Australian post, and three days later a local attack fractured the III Corps front and took two hundred prisoners. But such information as the enemy gained only deluded him further. Moreover, the German aircraft were so incessantly harried by the British that for several weeks they could not reconnoitre behind the British front. The only suspicious sign was a certain amount of noise at night. On several occasions the German troops reported that they heard the movement of tanks, but 'the Army Staff ridiculed the constantly recurring nervousness of the trench troops about tanks'. Actually, there were no tanks near the scene on the dates they were thus reported, and these cries of 'Wolf, Wolf,' hardened the German higher command in its attitude of disbelief and 'indifference'.

Thus when, an hour before sunrise on August 8th, the British tanks swept forward, with the barrage and infantry advance simultaneous, the blow had the maximum shock of surprise. Shrouded by a thick ground mist, it fell on an enemy who had done nothing to strengthen his position by entrenchments, and the Canadians and Australians—matchless attacking troops—surged irresistibly over the enemy's forward divisions. Only north of the Somme, where tanks were few, was there a partial check. To accelerate the momentum all reserves were set in motion at zero hour—copying the Germans' example of March 21st. Soon, too, armoured cars were racing down the roads, to spread confusion behind the German front, even shooting up an army corps staff at breakfast in Proyart.

The day's final objective (six to eight miles distant) was gained over most of the front except the extreme right and left. But the next day saw slight progress and rather spasmodic pressure, and thereafter the attack flickered out as rapidly as it had blazed up. Why this strange contrast? Why was not so complete a break-through completed by a dramatic finale? Partly, it would seem, because the advance had now reached the edge of the old Somme battlefields of 1916, a tangled waste of rusty wire and derelict trenches which was a brake on movement, reinforcement, and supply. It is well to remember that the problem of maintaining continuity of advance was never solved in the World War. Again, the original front of attack had not been wide, and it is significant that almost all successful advances in the World War seem to have been governed by a law of ratio, the depth of the penetration being roughly half of the frontage of attack.

Another reason was, as at Cambrai, the lack of reserves. The introduction of the local reserves of the Fourth Army was well timed but, when its thirteen divisions had been engaged, all that were available were three divisions assembled by Haig in the area. Moreover, the Germans, in contrast, succeeded in reinforcing their original six divisions with eighteen reserve divisions by August 11th—ten more than had been estimated.

A fourth cause of the stoppage was inherent in the form of the attack. For being strictly frontal the more it pushed back the enemy the more it consolidated their resistance. This is always the defect of a frontal attack unless an organized force can be rushed through and placed on the enemy's rear. The cavalry as usual were allotted the rôle of exploitation. This time they rendered serviceable help in gaining and holding certain localities until the infantry came up, but such help was but a slender thing compared with the true rôle of cavalry in past history. Greater results might have been attained if the ninety-six whippet tanks, instead of being tied to the cavalry, had been used independently to pass through the gap and make a concentrated thrust south-eastwards against the rear of the German army facing the French—as was suggested by the Tank Corps.

But from the broad strategic point of view there was, or was evolved, this time a method behind the lack of reserves. On August 10th Haig had visited this front and studied the situation at close quarters. In consequence, when Foch urged a continuance of the Fourth Army's frontal pressure, Haig demurred to it as a vain waste of life. In a letter of August 14th he told Foch that he had stopped the further attack prepared for next day, and that he was preparing an attack by the Third Army north of Albert.

Foch objected to the delay involved by this alternative step, but at a conference at Sarcus next day Haig stubbornly held to and gained his point. As a result the Third Army struck on August 21st, the First Army further north on the 28th, while the Fourth Army seized the opportunity of this distraction of the enemy to resume their advance, the Australians gaining Mont St. Quentin and Péronne on the 31st, and thereby turning the barrier of the upper Somme. These operations marked the new strategy of successive attacks at different but closely related points, each attack broken off and succeeded by a fresh as soon as its initial impetus was spent.

It would be unjust, as many British writers have done, to claim that Haig initiated this strategy. For it is to be clearly traced in the successive attacks already begun by the French to the south—Debeney's left wing on the 8th, his right on the 9th, Humbert's Army on the 10th, and Mangin's on the 21st. But Haig appears to have appreciated first its potentialities for economy of force. While Foch was filled with the idea of maintaining the pressure, Haig was seized with the idea of pressure at the most economical expenditure of life. The Fourth Army's bag of 21,000 prisoners from August 8th-12th had cost only 20,000 casualties.

To the success of this strategy the surprise of August 8th and its effect on the German Command had contributed greatly. Their instinctive response to the shock was to hurry to the spot all possible reinforcements, and thereby they drained their reserve funds to bankruptcy point. The reserve divisions of the Army Group of Prince Rupprecht, which held the front from the sea to the Somme district, fell from thirty-six to nine by August 16th. Rupprecht's own resolution had done much to bring the British advance to a halt by preventing the local Army Commanders from carrying out their first panic decision to fall back behind the upper Somme. But this very resolution, perhaps, cost the Germans more in the end.

Thus, in sum, the decisiveness of August 8th came from its dislocation of thought or will, or both, throughout the whole hierarchy of the German Command. The history of 1914-1918 repeated the experience of all history that, except against an exhausted or already demoralized foe, decisive success in war is only possible through surprise. And that surprise must be a compound of many subtle ingredients.

MEGIDDO
1918

Damascus

MT. HERMON

Advance of Aus. Mtd & 5. Cav.

Advance of 4. Cav.

Advance of Arabs

Mediterranean Sea

Haifa
MT. CARMEL

Plain of Esdraelon

Sea of Galilee

Nazareth

El 'Afule

Jisr el Majamie

Deraa

5. Cav.

4. Cav.

Megiddo

Vale of Jezreel

Beisan

Arabs

Jenin

Plain of Sharon

Tul Keram

Mas'udiye

Nablus

R. Jordan

HEJAZ RAILWAY

60

5. Cav.

7 75 3

4. Cav.

54 FRENCH

Es Salt

Jaffa

Aus. Mtd.

XXI Corps

10

53

Amman

XX Corps

Advance of Chaytor

Jerusalem

Chaytor's Force

JUDAEAN HILLS

Gaza

Dead Sea

N

Beersheba

| 0 | 10 | 20 | 30 |

Miles

Railways   Allies   Turks

© Cassell & Co. Ltd. 1970

CHAPTER VIII

SCENE 6

MEGIDDO—THE ANNIHILATION OF THE TURKISH ARMIES

On September 19th, 1918, began an operation which was both one of the most quickly decisive campaigns and the most completely decisive battles in all history. Within a few days the Turkish armies in Palestine had practically ceased to exist. Whether it should be regarded primarily as a campaign or as a battle completed by a pursuit is a moot question. For it opened with the forces in contact and hence would seem to fall into the category of a battle; but it was achieved mainly by strategic means, with fighting playing a minor part. This fact has tended to its disparagement in the sight of those who are obsessed with the Clausewitzian dogma that blood is the price of victory—and hold, as a corollary, that no victory is worthy of recognition which is not sanctified by a lavish oblation of blood. But Caesar's triumph at Ilerda, Scipio's near Utica, Cromwell's at Preston, and Moltke's, though opportunist rather than sought for, at Sedan, each had the same 'pale pink' complexion. In each, strategy was so effective that fighting was but incidental. Yet no one can deny their decisiveness both as victories and on the course of history. A more serious 'depreciation' of this final campaign-battle in Palestine lies in the fact that Allenby had a superiority of over two to one in numbers, and more in terms of weapon-values.* In addition the morale of the Turks had so declined that it is often argued that Allenby had merely to stretch out his hand for the Turkish army, like an overripe plum, to fall into it. There is force in these contentions; but

* Allenby's fighting strength was 12,000 sabres, 57,000 rifles and 540 guns. He estimated the Turkish strength at 3,000 sabres, 32,000 rifles and 402 guns. This figure is about double Liman von Sanders's estimate, which, however, seems to be a broad calculation, excluding machine-gun personnel.

most of the 'crowning mercies' of modern history, from Worcester to Sedan, have seen almost as great a disparity of strength and morale between victors and vanquished. And in 1918 Allenby had to outwit such able commanders as Liman von Sanders and Mustapha Kemal, not such men as those who thrust their heads into the sack at Sedan.

When full deduction is made for the advantageous conditions of September, 1918, the conclusion remains that the triumph immortalized by the already immortal name of Megiddo is one of history's masterpieces by reason of the breadth of vision and treatment. If the subject was not a difficult one, the picture is almost unique as a perfect conception perfectly executed.

The question is often asked,—whose was the conception? Was it that of the titular commander? Or, did it spring from some gifted subordinate? When the victories of Hindenburg on the Russian front are discussed, even the man in the street speaks of Ludendorff's strategy—and the student of war goes still deeper, or lower, and muses on the unassessable influence of Hoffmann's military genius. But with Megiddo it is possible to dispel doubt, through the unanimous evidence of those most intimately concerned. The broad conception sprang entire from Allenby's mind, whatever the credit due to his assistants for working out its executive details. 'Grew', indeed, would be a better word than 'sprang', for the original conception was of more modest dimensions—to break through the Turkish front near the coast and, wheeling inwards, turn the flank of their forces in the Judæan Hills. But, returning one day from a ride during which he had been studying the problem, Allenby suddenly unfolded the plan as it was executed, in all its almost breath-taking scope. It abundantly fulfilled Napoleon's maxim that 'the whole secret of the art of war lies in making oneself master of the communications'. If Allenby had a superiority of strength he was going to use it to make himself master not of one, but of every one, of the Turkish communications. And the success of his attempt to do so owed much to the complementary fact that he had taken thorough measures to be master of his own communications.

The three so-called Turkish 'armies', each hardly more than the strength of a division, drew nourishment through a single stem—the Hejaz railway running south from Damascus. At Deraa a branch ran out westwards; crossing the Jordan at Jisr el Mejamie, just north of Beisan, it forked at El Afule in the Plain of Esdraelon, one line going to the sea at Haifa and the other turning south again through the hills of Samaria to Messudieh Junction. This line fed the Seventh (Mustapha Kemal) and Eighth (Jevad) Turkish armies which held the front between the river Jordan and the Mediterranean Sea. The Fourth Army (Jemal) east of the Jordan was fed by the main Hejaz railway.

Now, to cut an army's lines of communication is to dislocate its physical organization. To close its lines of retreat is to dislocate its morale. And to destroy its lines of 'intercommunication'—by which orders and reports pass—is to dislocate it mentally, by breaking the essential connection between the brain and the body of an army. Allenby planned to achieve not a single but the triple dislocation, and the third element was not the least important to the success of his plan.

The convergence of both roads and railways made Deraa, El Afule, and, to a less extent, Beisan the vital points in the Turks' rear. To get a grip on El Afule and Beisan would sever the communications of the Seventh and Eighth Armies and also close their lines of retreat, except for the extremely difficult outlet to the desolate region across the Jordan eastwards. To get a grip on Deraa would sever the communications of all three armies and the best line of retreat of the Fourth. But it was considerably further from the British front.

El Afule and Beisan, however, lay within a sixty-mile radius, and hence were within the range of a strategic cavalry 'bound', provided that these vital points could be reached without interruption or delay. The problem was, first, to find a line of approach unobstructed by nature, and, second, to ensure that the enemy could not block it by force. How was it solved? The flat coastal Plain of Sharon afforded a corridor to the Plain of Esdraelon and Vale of Jezreel, in which El Afule and Beisan respectively lay. This corridor was interrupted by only a single door, so far back that it was not guarded by the Turks, formed by the narrow mountain belt which separates the coastal Plain of Sharon from the inland Plain of Esdraelon. But the entrance to the corridor was firmly bolted and barred by the trenches of the Turkish front. Allenby planned to use his infantry to force this locked gate and swing it back, as on a hinge, north-eastwards, so leaving a clear path for his cavalry. But having passed through the front gate they would still have to get through the back door. This the Turks could easily close if they had time and warning. Speed on the part of the cavalry was essential. But not sufficient. The attention and reserves of the Turks must be distracted. Even so, there was still a risk. War experience had shown how easily cavalry could be stopped, and a handful of men and machine-guns would suffice to block the two passes through the intermediate mountain belt. To avert this risk the Turkish Command must be made deaf and dumb as well as blind. In this complete paralysis of the Turkish Higher Command lies the main significance and the historical value of the victory of Megiddo.

Let us watch how it was achieved. For it, Allenby had two comparatively novel tools—aircraft and Arabs. Feisal's Arabs, under the guiding brain of Colonel Lawrence, had long been harassing, immobilizing and demoralizing the Turks along the main Hejaz railway. Now they were to contribute more directly to the final stroke by the British forces. On September 16th and 17th, emerging like phantoms from the desert, they blew up the railway north, south, and west of Deraa. This had the physical effect of shutting off the flow of Turkish supplies temporarily—and 'temporarily' was all that mattered here. It had the mental effect of persuading the Turkish Command to send part of its scanty reserves towards Deraa.

The Air Force contribution was in two parts. First, by a sustained campaign it drove the enemy's machines out of the air. This campaign was carried so far that ultimately the fighters 'sat' above the Turkish aerodrome at Jenin to prevent their machines even taking off. Thus it closed the enemy's air eye during the period of preparation. Secondly, when the moment came for the execution of Allenby's plan, the Air Force made the enemy's command deaf and dumb—by decisively bombing their main telegraph and telephone exchange at El Afule, a stroke in which Ross-Smith, who later made history by his flight to Australia, helped England to make history. In addition, the enemy's two army head-quarters at Nablus and Tul Keram were bombed, and at the second, the more vital, the wires were so effectively destroyed that it was cut off throughout the day both from Nazareth and from its divisions in the coastal sector. Another and earlier form of air activity was, if less military, perhaps of even wider strategic effect. This was the dropping not of bombs but of an equal weight of illustrated pamphlets show-ing the physical comforts which the Turkish soldier enjoyed as a prisoner of war. Its appeal to half-starved and ragged men was none the less for being imponderable.

While the Arabs and the Air Force were perhaps the two most vital factors in 'unhinging' the enemy preparatory to the actual push, the plan had also the wide and purposeful variety of ruses which marks the masterpieces of military history. By these Allenby sought to divert the enemy's atten-tion away from the coast to the Jordan flank. In this aim he was helped by the very failure of two attempted advances east of the Jordan, towards Amman and Es Salt, during the spring. Then, throughout the summer he kept a cavalry force, periodically relieved, in the stifling heat of the Jordan Valley to hold the enemy's attention. When the cavalry were ultimately moved surreptitiously across to the other flank, their camps were not only left standing but new ones added, while 15,000 dummy horses of canvas filled the vacated horse lines. Mule-drawn sleighs created dust clouds; battalions marched by day towards the valley—and returned by night in lorries to repeat this march of a stage army; a hotel was taken over in Jerusalem and elaborately prepared for the mythical reception of General Headquarters; new bridging and wireless activity fostered the illusion; Lawrence sent agents to bargain for vast quantities of forage in the Amman district.

And all the time more and more troops were filtering down by night marches to the other flank near the sea, there to be concealed in orange groves or in camps already standing. By these means Allenby increased his two-to-one superiority, on the front as a whole, to a five-to-one superiority on the vital sector—unsuspected by the enemy. For some time Liman von Sanders had certainly anticipated a big attack, and, indeed, had thought of frustrating it by a voluntary retirement to a rear line near the Sea of Galilee. 'I gave up the idea, because we would have had to relinquish the Hejaz railway . . . and because we no longer could have stopped the progress of the Arab insurrection in rear of our army. On account of the limited marching capacity of the Turkish soldiers and of the very low mobility of all draft animals, I considered that the holding of our positions to the last gave us more favourable prospects than a long retirement with Turkish troops of impaired morale.'

Although he feared an attack near the coast, he feared still more the effect of one east of the Jordan, and even at the last hour the warning of the first given by an Indian deserter on September 17th was offset by the more positive news of the Arab attacks on the vital railway at Deraa. Deceived by his own preconceived idea, Liman von Sanders was, indeed, too ready to believe that this deserter was a tool of the British Intelligence, and his story a blind to cover Allenby's real purpose. Further, Liman von Sanders rejected the plea of Refet Bey, commanding the coastal sector, who wished to withdraw his troops a mile so that the British bombardment might waste itself on empty trenches. Forbidding Refet to withdraw an inch, he ensured that he should go back a hundred miles, to Tyre, leaving his army behind—dead or prisoners.

On the night of September 18th began what was both the last move of the 'distracting' preparation and the first move of the real action. The 53rd Division, which formed Allenby's extreme right, made a spring forward in the hills on the edge of the Jordan Valley. Thereby they would be a step on their way towards closing the only way of retreat—across the Jordan eastwards—left open to the Turks when the main move had fulfilled its encircling purpose.

Far away to the west by the sea all was quiet. But at 4.30 a.m. 385 guns opened fire on the selected frontage. For a quarter of an hour, only, they maintained an intense bombardment, and then the infantry advanced, under cover of a rapid lifting barrage. They swept, almost unchecked, over the stupefied defenders and broke through the two trench systems, shallow and slightly wired—by Western Front standards. Then they wheeled inland, like a huge door swinging on its hinges. Of this door, a French contingent and the 54th Division formed the hinged end; then, with a five-mile interval, the 3rd Indian, 75th and 7th Indian Divisions, formed the middle panel; and the 60th Division, by the sea, the outside panel. The latter reached Tul Keram by nightfall. But what survived of the Turkish Eighth Army had long before been pouring back through the defile to Messudieh in a confused crowd of troops and transport. And upon this hapless mob the British aircraft had swept down with bombs and bullets.

Meantime, through the opened door had ridden the three cavalry divisions of the Desert Mounted Corps (Chauvel). By evening they had reached the Carmel Range, the 'intermediate door', sending detachments with their armoured cars to secure the two passes. By morning they were across. One brigade descended on Nazareth where the enemy's General Headquarters lay, ignorant of the events of the past twenty-four hours because cut off from all communication with its fighting body. Liman von Sanders, however, escaped through a failure to block the northern exit of the town, and after a vigorous street fight the cavalry were forced to retire.

The real strategic key, however, was now not at Nazareth but at El Afule and Beisan. These were reached at 8 a.m. and 4.30 p.m. respectively—to Beisan the 4th Cavalry Division had covered seventy miles in thirty-four hours. Passing through the Carmel Range in its wake, the Australian Mounted Division turned south to Jenin to place a closer barrier across the Turks' line of retreat. The enemy's only remaining bolt-hole was east over the Jordan—which flows swiftly, with few fords, through a deep and winding trough, 1300 feet below sea level at the Dead Sea end. He might have reached this but for the Air Force, as the infantry advance was making slow progress through the hills in face of the stubborn Turkish rearguards. Early in the morning of September 21st, the British aircraft spotted a large column—practically all that survived of the two Turkish armies—winding down the steep gorge from Nablus to the Jordan. Four hours' continuous bombing and machine-gunning reduced this procession to stagnation, an inanimate chaos of guns and transport. Those who survived were merely scattered fugitives. From this moment may be timed the extinction of the Seventh and Eighth Turkish Armies. What followed was but a rounding up of 'cattle' by the cavalry.

Only the Fourth Army, east of the Jordan, remained. This, delaying too long, did not begin to retire until September 22nd. A broken railway and the Arabs lay across its line of retreat to Damascus. And four days later the 4th Cavalry Division moved east from Beisan to intercept it, while the other two converged directly on Damascus, its goal. Escape was impossible, but its fate was different from that of the other armies, a rapid attrition under constant pinpricks rather than a neat despatch. In this pursuit the Desert Mounted Corps co-operated with, and for the first time met, their real desert allies, hitherto an invisible and intangible factor. Their presence, and identity, was disclosed when a messenger reported—'There's an Arab on the top of the hill over there in

a Rolls-Royce; talks English perfectly and in the hell of a
rage!' For no pursuit could be fast enough to satisfy Lawrence's ardent spirit as he urged his Arabs on towards the city
of desire. To a British cavalry officer with an apt gift of phrase
their march looked 'like some strange oriental version of an
old-time Epsom road on Derby Day', but they outpaced the
4th Cavalry Division.

The fragments of the Turkish Fourth Army were finally
headed off and captured near Damascus, which was occupied on October 1st. On the previous day the garrison had
been intercepted by the Australian Mounted Division as it
was trying to escape through the Barada gorge (the Biblical
'Abana'). Sweeping the head of the fugitive stream with
machine-guns from the overhanging cliffs the Australian
Light Horse rolled it back to Damascus, there to swell the
'bag' of prisoners to 20,000.

The next move was a fitting conclusion to this chapter of
history. The 5th Cavalry Division was despatched to advance on Aleppo, two hundred miles distant, in conjunction
with an Arab force. Its armoured cars led the way and dispersed such slight opposition as was met, reaching the outskirts of Aleppo on October 23rd. Two days later the leading
cavalry brigade came up. A combined attack was arranged
for next morning, but during the night the Arabs slipped into
and captured the town on their own. The British force, too
weak to press the retreat of the garrison, was awaiting reinforcements from Damascus when the capitulation of Turkey
on October 31st wrote 'finis' to the campaign. During a brief
span of thirty-eight days the British had advanced three
hundred and fifty miles and captured 75,000 prisoners—at a
cost of less than 5000 casualties.

In a war singularly barren of surprise and mobility, those
keynotes of the art of war, their value had been signally vin-
dicated at the last, and in one theatre at least. Surprise and
mobility had virtually won the victory without a battle. And
it is worth noting that the Turks were still capable of holding
up the infantry attack until the 'strategic barrage' across their

rear became known and produced its inevitable, and in-
variable, moral effect.

Because a preliminary condition of trench warfare existed
the infantry and heavy artillery were necessary to break the
lock. But, once the normal conditions of warfare were thus restored, the victory was achieved by the mobile elements—
cavalry, aircraft, armoured cars and Arabs—which formed
but a fraction of Allenby's total force. And it was achieved,
not by physical force, but by the demoralizing application of
mobility. A new light on Napoleon's dictum that the moral
is to the physical as three to one.

CHAPTER VIII

SCENE 7

THE BATTLE OF A DREAM—ST. MIHIEL

FOR four years a wedge sixteen miles deep lay embedded in the flank of the main French armies. It was the most marked, and most 'ugly', feature of the whole irregular front between the Swiss border and the Belgian coast. Along this long irregular line of trenches salients were numerous, and of all sizes, but none was so acute as that which came down from the heights of the Woevre to the Meuse at St. Mihiel—and even protruded beyond the river. All that time it galled France bodily and mentally, for although it was not in itself a convenient springboard for a fresh German offensive it might easily become a menace if a new wedge were driven in on the other side of Verdun; worse still, it crippled the prospects of any French offensive into Lorraine. For such an offensive, whether launched from the Verdun or from the Nancy sector, would not only suffer the menace of St. Mihiel in its rear but would be difficult to nourish—because the St. Mihiel salient interrupted the railways from Paris to Nancy and from Verdun to Nancy. This handicap was all too clearly manifest in 1916, when the army defending Verdun fought half choked and always in danger of being suddenly strangled.

For two more trying years the defenders of Verdun had to bear the semi-suffocation of their windpipe. And then, at the end of the first hour of September 12th, 1918, three thousand guns pealed a message of deliverance. Four hours later, deafened yet exhilarated by the thunder of their guns, the infantry of the First American Army advanced from their own trenches across the pulverized earth that had held the enemy trenches. Twenty-four hours later the two sharp points of the American forceps, cutting into each side, met

563

St. MIHIEL

Original Front Line
on 11 th. Sept. ▬▬▬▬
Line reached on 12 th. Sept. ▬·▬·▬·
Michel Line 15 th. Sept. +‒+‒+‒+
Divisions *42* Corps *IV*
Direction of Attacks ➝

0   5   10   15
Miles

SAAR
BASIN
16 MILES

Longuyon

Railway

Briey

Verdun

Metz

R. Moselle

V

8
15
(Fr.)

26

2
(Fr.)

R. Meuse

Vigneulles

26
(Fr.)

Thiaucourt

N

II Col.
(Fr.)

St. Mihiel

26
(Fr.)

39
(Fr.)

1   42   8.9.
U.S.IV

5
U.S.I

90   82   Pont à
Mousson

R. Meurthe

Nancy

Ligny en Barrois

© Cassell & Co. Ltd. 1970

midway, and the ugly fang was removed.

America's First Army had fought its first battle and won its first victory, as an army. The achievement was not merely a good augury but a vindication—especially of Pershing. And it was an invaluable tonic both to the army which fought and to the nation behind it, while a proportionate disillusionment to the Germans, who had questioned, even more strongly than her Allies, America's power to produce an effective army.

Apparently, the extraction of the St. Mihiel fang was also one of the most perfectly complete pieces of strategic dentistry in the war. Actually, the operation was less satisfactory, and roots were left to cause trouble later. In part, the incompleteness was due to the faulty action of the forceps; in part to the dentist; but still more to the long-concealed fact that the dentist's arm was jogged. Yet there is still a question—whether the operation could have been more effective even if the dentist had not suffered interference.

To answer it, we must examine the cause and course of the operation. It was the fulfilment of a dream and a scheme which almost coincided with the entry of the United States into the war. Indeed, Pershing and his Staff had come to Europe in June, 1917, with their eyes fixed on St. Mihiel and their minds on Metz, behind it. The British, they knew, were committed to operations in Flanders and northern France, an area which, despite its drawbacks—mud especially—was nearest to their home base and gave them the shortest lines of communication with the Channel ports. The offensive operations of the French had all been carried out in the sector north of Paris and it was natural that they should concentrate to cover their capital.

The choice of the easterly sector facing and flanking Metz was the natural one for the Americans, because it clashed least with their Allies' lines of supply and was easiest of access from their own base ports in the Bay of Biscay. Moreover, this sector was obviously the Germans' most sensitive point, because a thrust there needed to penetrate only a short distance before it would imperil the stability of the whole

German position in France—which formed a vast salient jutting southwards between Verdun and Ypres. For to sever the eastern end of the great lateral railway Metz-Maubeuge would at least restrict the free movement of reserves and supplies, and, more significant still, would 'turn' the flank of all the successive lines to which the German armies could withdraw short of their own frontier. Further, such a thrust promised the vital economic result of releasing the Briey iron region and threatening the Saar basin—upon which the Germans largely depended for their munitions. To pinch off the St. Mihiel salient was not only a necessary preliminary to a secure offensive, but was a local operation well suited to the first test of a new force.

But the American Expeditionary Force was more intent to conserve its strength until maturity than had been the British. A year passed before it was ready, and before that the Germans had intervened elsewhere to compel a further postponement. Not until August, 1918, when the German tide had begun to ebb, was Pershing able to collect his scattered divisions—which had just helped in stemming it—and to form them into the first all-American army. And even so it had to depend on the French for most of its artillery and on the French and British for part of its aircraft.

On July 24th the commanders of the Allied armies met at Bombon to discuss their future action. The outcome was very modest. Foch did not choose to look far ahead and merely called for a series of local attacks to free his lateral railways. The first was delivered on August 8th in front of Amiens, and its dramatic evidence of the moral rot that had set in among the German troops changed the whole picture. On August 11th the newly formed staff of the First American Army moved to the St. Mihiel area, and there developed their plan to a far more ambitious one than had been suggested at Bombon—from that of freeing the French lateral railways to that of threatening the German. Not merely to pinch off the salient but to break through its baseline, where ran the 'Michel' line as an inner barrier against any sudden rupture of the front. The plan framed by General Hugh Drum, the Chief of Staff, visualized the use of fifteen American divisions —each more than twice the strength of a French or British division—and four French divisions. Pershing approved the plan on August 15th and Foch two days later. Indeed, Foch added to it not only six more French divisions, but an extension of the frontage and the direction 'to strike the heaviest blow possible and secure the maximum results'.

But on August 30th Foch came to the American Headquarters at Ligny-en-Barrois with a radically different plan. The change was due to Haig's intervention. August 8th and its sequel had given him a clear perception of the German decline and, disregarding the cautious counsels of his government, he was now willing to test his judgment and risk his reputation by assaulting the ill-famed Hindenburg Line— the strongest defences on the whole German front. But he was anxious to reduce the risk of failure and increase the profit of success, and therefore urged Foch to change the main American attack from a divergent to a convergent direction. It would thus, he calculated, have a quicker and stronger reaction upon the German armies facing him, and by loosening their grip would ease his task—as he would similarly ease the Americans'.

Foch lent his ear the more readily to Haig's argument because his own horizon had enlarged. He now felt that the war might be finished in 1918, instead of 1919. And his enthusiastic assurance led him to transform his new method of alternating attacks at different points into a simultaneous general offensive—'Tout le monde à la bataille.' By it he seems to have hoped not merely to stretch and crack the German resistance, but even to cut off and surround the German armies between his converging pincers—British on one side and American on the other. Pétain, when consulted, was quite agreeable to the change of plan, which promised to draw the German reserves to either flank and leave the French a clearer path in the centre.

Thus when Foch came to Ligny-en-Barrois he proposed

that the St. Mihiel plan should be modified to a mere excision of the salient. This operation was to be a preliminary, and safeguard, to the rear of the American main attack—now to be launched north-west towards Mézières instead of north-east towards Metz. Foch further proposed that, while Pershing's army operated on the easier ground west of the Argonne, a Franco-American army under a French Commander should attack the more difficult sector between the Argonne Forest and the Meuse. He also proposed to send General Degoutte to hold Pershing's hand and guide his tactical decisions.

The change of plan came as a shock to Pershing, and the other proposals as an affront. The interview was lively and the atmosphere grew heated. Foch hinted that he would appeal to President Wilson—and the threat had as little effect on Pershing as when previously used. Foch implied that Pershing was trying to shirk his share of the battle, and Pershing retorted that he was fully ready to fight 'as an American army'. Foch ironically suggested that even for St. Mihiel Pershing could not raise an all-American army, but had to depend on his allies for guns, tanks and aircraft. Pershing retaliated with the reminder that by Allied request the Americans had shipped only infantry and machine-guns during the spring crisis.

Foch wisely dropped the argument and left Pershing to 'chew the cud'. Next day Pershing, after reflection, wrote to Foch. He recognized the potential value of the convergent attack, but dwelt upon the difficulties of American participation. 'Since our arrival in France our plans . . . have been based on the organization of the American army on the front St. Mihiel-Belfort. All our depots, hospitals, training areas and other installations are located with reference to this front and a change of plans cannot be easily made.' Then he dealt with Foch's second proposal, contending that 'it is far more appropriate at the present moment for the Allies temporarily to furnish the American army with the services and auxiliaries it needs than for the Allies to expect further delay in the formation of the American army.'

Pershing did not attempt to hide his dislike of limiting the St. Mihiel attack, and suggested that instead of switching at once to the Meuse-Argonne he should exploit the St. Mihiel attack to the full and later, if necessary, mount a fresh attack 'either in the region of Belfort or Lunéville'. Not yet vouch-safed an intuition of victory that autumn, he suggested that these attacks would fit in with the ultimate American aim of taking charge 'during January and February' of 'the sector from St. Mihiel to Switzerland'. 'However,' he said, 'it is your province to decide as to the strategy of operations, and I abide by your decision.'

On one question he was unshakable. 'I can no longer agree to any plan which involves the dispersion of our units.' 'Briefly, our officers and soldiers alike are, after one experience, no longer willing to be incorporated in other armies. . . . The danger of destroying by such dispersion the fine morale of the American soldier is too great.' 'If you decide to utilize the American forces in attacking in the direction of Mézières I accept that decision, even though it complicates my supply system and the care of my sick and wounded, but I do insist that this American Army be employed as a whole.'

The result of this letter was a conference between Foch, Pétain and Pershing on September 2nd, whereat Pershing gave up his own plan for a share in Foch's and Foch conceded Pershing's claim to American unity. The concession was wrung from him by his own realization that without the Americans his right pincer would have a weak and worn point. And as Pershing preferred to attack east of Argonne, where supply would be easier although the ground was more difficult, he obtained his preference.

The one outstanding question was that of St. Mihiel. Foch wanted the general offensive to open by September 20th at the latest, and suggested that the St. Mihiel attack should be abandoned. Pershing and his staff decided that they must first cut off the St. Mihiel wedge to safeguard the rear of their Meuse-Argonne attack. Again, their claim was conceded.

But it meant that they could not switch divisions from one battle to the other in time, and that a number of raw divisions had to be used for the Meuse-Argonne attack. In addition, the St. Mihiel attack was two days, and the Meuse-Argonne six days, behind timetable.

Each attack interfered with the other. And the consequences were compound, not simple. The first effect was upon the American dispositions. Instead of fifteen double-sized American divisions, which were available, only seven were used in the attack. Although this was a more than ample provision for the task, ensuring a numerical superiority of about eight to one over the Germans, the actual distribution was curious. For while six divisions (including two of Regulars) formed the right pincer, only one National Guard division formed the left. What had happened was that instead of reshuffling the entire dispositions the left pincer had been severely fined down, and the objectives rigorously limited. Foch, indeed, suggested that the left-wing attack should be abandoned.

The plan in detail was that Liggett's I Corps, on the extreme right nearest the hinge, and Dickman's IV Corps should attack the eastern face of the salient at 5 a.m. Liggett would demonstrate with the 82nd Division against the hinge, while on its left his 90th, 5th, and 2nd Divisions thrust towards the baseline of the salient. Attacking next to them on the left were Dickman's 89th, 42nd and 1st Divisions. At 8 a.m. the 26th Division of Cameron's IV Corps would thrust into the western face of the salient, aiming to join hands with the 1st Division. Meantime the French would exert a gentle pressure on the nose of the salient to keep the defenders busy until their retreat was cut off.

But the Germans had for weeks been meditating and preparing to forestall the attack by a retreat. And when the Americans advanced to the assault on September 12th, the Germans had actually begun this withdrawal during the night. This fact has led to a satirical description of St. Mihiel as 'the sector where the Americans relieved the Germans'. If there is some truth in the description, it is not the whole truth. Unlike the bigger strategic retreat to the Hindenburg Line in 1917, this withdrawal worked out to the disadvantage of those who planned it. Although the German command were as well aware of the impending blow as most of the population of France, and were not deceived by feints elsewhere, they hesitated too long over their decision and made their preparations too leisurely. Thus they were caught at a moment when part of their artillery had been withdrawn, and although a large part of the American bombardment—from 2971 guns, mostly French—was wasted on empty trenches, the longer-range fire trapped some of the retiring Germans on the roads. Moreover, the comparative shortness of the bombardment, due largely to Liggett's insistence on the need for surprise, prevented the Germans gaining a comfortable start in their withdrawal. And the swift onrush of the American 2nd and 42nd Divisions, especially, upset their methodical arrangements.

But Pershing's plan was also too inelastic. Before midday Liggett's divisions had reached their final objectives and, soon after, their second day's objectives on the high ground north of Thiaucourt! The rapidity of their advance was accelerated by Liggett's instructions that units should press on as long as possible, without checking to keep alignment with their neighbours. Dazed and unsupported by their own artillery the Germans made practically no resistance. But Pershing felt himself tied by Foch's instructions and refused Liggett's plea for a further bound—which might have ruptured the Michel line. Dickman's and Cameron's converging corps reached their day's objectives with almost equal ease. But there, tied too closely to Pershing's apron strings, they came to a halt and awaited further orders.

Too late, Pershing tried to exploit his opportunity. If the German roads out of the salient were jammed, so also were his own roads into it. His orders for Dickman and Cameron to resume their advance did not reach the troops until after dark. And thus all but some four thousand of the forty or fifty thousand Germans in the bag slipped out before the neck was drawn tight by the junction of the two American corps at Vigneulles next morning. Nevertheless, Liggett had taken over 5000 prisoners, and the other two corps, together with the French, had taken as many in their original advance. The total came to 15,000, and, more remarkable, 443 guns, for a cost of less than 8000 casualties. If the result did not entirely satisfy the Americans, they could console themselves with the thought that this first attempt was no different from the past offensives of their Allies in failing to reap the harvest of an initial success.

During the 13th and 14th, Dickman and Cameron wheeled up, with the French 2nd Colonial Corps between, into alignment with Liggett facing the Michel Line. Then, and there, the battle was broken off. The only serious fighting had been borne by Liggett's corps, which had met with counterattacks owing to the menacing direction of its advance—the enemy was willing to evacuate the salient, but had no intention of allowing his baseline to be crossed.

What might have happened if Pershing had not been prevented from trying his original plan? There is no doubt that the Germans were immensely relieved that Pershing did not follow up his success; or that in their view a further advance in this direction would have been a greater menace than the Mézières direction of the Argonne offensive. Pershing's own view was emphatic—'Without doubt, an immediate continuation of the advance would have carried us well beyond the Hindenburg Line [the Michel Line was an extension of the main Hindenburg Line] and possibly into Metz.' Dickman was still more pungent—'The failure to push north from St. Mihiel with our overwhelming superiority in numbers will always be regarded by me as a strategical blunder for which Marshal Foch and his staff are responsible. It is a glaring example of the fallacy of the policy of limited objectives. . . . '

On the other hand, Liggett, who proved himself perhaps the soundest reasoner and strongest realist in the American Army, has declared—'The possibility of taking Metz and the rest of it, had the battle been fought on the original plan, existed, in my opinion, only on the supposition that our army was a well-oiled, fully co-ordinated machine—which it was not as yet.' He has also pointed out that although the attack between the Meuse and Argonne came as a greater surprise to the Germans they were able to throw in reserves so rapidly as to block the original breach by the third day. And even if the Michel Line had been broken an advance from St. Mihiel would then have met a fresh obstacle, especially on its right, in the defences of Metz. Significant also is the matured verdict of General von Gallwitz, the opposing German Army Group Commander—'An overrunning of the Michel position I consider out of the question. In order to capture this position a further . . . operation on a very large scale would have been required.' It is well to remember that for decisive results Pershing would at least have had to reach the Longuyon-Thionville stretch of the lateral railway, a further twenty miles beyond the Michel Line, and to have gone far enough beyond it to interrupt the line running back from Longuyon through Luxembourg. It would have demanded a penetration deeper and quicker than any yet achieved by the Allies on the Western Front. With an untried army this was surely a remote hope.

Yet there is one factor of which criticism has taken no account; a factor which endowed Pershing's original plan with a peculiar advantage. Almost every attempted breakthrough in the war had been based on the idea of a single penetration. Among the few exceptions had been the simultaneous Artois and Champagne attacks on September 25th, 1915. But although in form a dual penetration, the effect was that of two single ones, for they were too far apart to cause any prompt sagging and collapse of the sector between. The convergent Argonne and Cambrai thrusts of Foch's new plan had also the same appearance of duality but an even wider interval between them.

Now duality is the very essence of war, although curiously overlooked. Everyone recognizes the advantage which even a light-weight boxer has in using two fists against a one-armed opponent. So in war the power to use two fists is an inestimable asset. To feint with one fist and strike with the other yields an advantage, but a still greater advantage lies in being able to interchange them—to convert the feint into the real blow if the opponent uncovers himself. Nor should duality be limited to the force. Duality of objective, of which Sherman was the supreme exponent, enables the attacker to get his opponent on the horns of a dilemma, and, by mystifying him, to obtain the chance of surprising him, so that if the opponent concentrates in defence of one objective the attacker can seize the other. Only by this elasticity of aim can we truly attune ourselves to the uncertainty of war.

Returning from the general to the particular, we can recognize that the St. Mihiel salient offered the chance of attempting the yet untried method of dual penetration under almost ideal conditions. If two powerful attacks had broken through the flanks of the salient—and better still, beyond them to right and left—the defenders in the centre would have dissolved into chaos—and been securely 'caged'. Through this collapsed centre a fresh force might then have driven, with a clear path between the two protecting wings. What we know of the incompleteness of the baseline defences and the time taken before they were completely garrisoned suggests that, on September 12th and 13th at least, they could have been ruptured on a wide front. On a smaller scale, the actual attack fulfilled this process as far as it went, but the wings were then held back and there was no fresh force to pass through the centre.

But it is still a question how far the Americans could have advanced beyond the breach. And here the main factor would not have been defences or defenders, but supplies. The road blocks and transport difficulties actually experienced in the limited advance do not encourage an optimistic answer. It is more likely that the eventual result would have justified Liggett's opinion—and Napoleon's axiom; 'With a new army it is possible to carry a formidable position, but not to carry out a plan or design.' And the last weeks of the war were to show that even experienced armies could not solve the problem of maintaining supplies during a sustained advance, even though almost unopposed. For bulk cancels out experience.

MEUSE-ARGONNE

Original Front Line, 26 th. Sept. 1918
Line reached on 26 th. Sept. 1918
Line reached on 4 th. Oct. 1918
Line reached on 1 st. Nov. 1918
Line reached on 11 th. Nov. 1918

0   5   10   15
Miles

Mézières

RAILWAY

Sedan

R. Meuse

Carignan

R. la Chiers

Bois de
Bourgogne

R. Meuse

RAILWAY

Longuyon

Buzancy

N

R. Aisne

KRIEMHILDE LINE

Grand Pré

Sommerance

FRENCH

Montfaucon

R. Aire

79 4 80 33

91 37

III

Vauquois

35

V

77   28

I

FRENCH

FOREST OF
ARGONNE

Verdun

FRENCH

© Cassell & Co. Ltd. 1970

CHAPTER VIII

SCENE 8

THE BATTLE OF A NIGHTMARE—
THE MEUSE-ARGONNE

ALTHOUGH a far greater battle in scale the Meuse-Argonne is less significant, except to the combatants, than St. Mihiel. Strategically and historically it may even be viewed as an appendix to the unfinished and partly unwritten story of St. Mihiel.

In the first place, the ultimate aim was more idealistic than realistic. It was based on the idea that the Ardennes formed an impenetrable back wall to the great German salient in France, and that if the Allies could reach and close the exits east and west they would cut off the German armies in the salient. But the impossibility of the Ardennes has been much exaggerated, especially in Haig's reports. Actually, the Ardennes were traversed by numerous roads and several railways, so that though the severance of the routes east and west might complicate the German withdrawal this would be imperilled only if the objective was attained very rapidly. As always in war, everything turned on the time factor.

To reach the lateral railway from the Meuse-Argonne sector the Americans would have to advance thirty miles. And to be effective they would have to advance more rapidly than from the St. Mihiel sector, because their thrust would be aimed close to the main German armies instead of, like the projected St. Mihiel thrust, close to the German frontier. The attempt, and hope, was fundamentally unreal. To cross these thirty miles of difficult country, they would first have to break through the German front and then, some eight miles behind it, would meet the untouched defences of the Kriemhilde section of the Hindenburg Line. Pershing might have confidence in the capacity of his untried army, but his faith, like that of the French in 1914 and 1915, was to founder on the rock of machine-guns. Pétain, if he underestimated the effect of other factors, was closer to reality when he predicted that the Americans might cover a third of the distance before the winter. That roughly was as far as their original attack reached, and there they stuck, until other factors, unforeseen by Pétain, intervened to relieve them.

In the second place, the Meuse-Argonne attack did not fulfil its immediate aim, the Haig-inspired aim for which Pershing had sacrificed his own plan. For the left-wing attack broke through the Cambrai-St. Quentin section of the Hindenburg Line, the strongest artificially, before the Meuse-Argonne attack had drawn off any German divisions from the British front. Thus the result justified Haig's confidence but not his precaution, proving that his troops could break through without indirect help to ease their path. The strength of the defences was nullified by the weakening morale of the defenders.

The irony of the result was increased by the fact that while fifty-seven German divisions faced the left-wing attack by forty British and two American divisions, only twenty German divisions were present to oppose the right-wing attack by thirteen American and thirty-one French divisions—the equivalent of at least sixty ordinary-strength divisions. The difference of result may be explained, in part, by the differing degree of experience, and in part by the difference of conditions. The left-wing attack opened with the British close on the edge of the Hindenburg Line, while on the right wing the Americans had to conquer a deep series of defences before they could assault their section of the Hindenburg Line. And before they reached it their attack had lost its momentum.

Thereafter although stubborn American assaults at heavy cost caused the Germans to draw off, on balance, a further sixteen divisions from the French front, the strategic effect was small. For with shrewd strategic sense the French in the centre appreciated that decisive results depended on the rapid penetration and closing of the pincers, and so did not unduly hasten the retreat of the Germans facing them. In their skilful advance they usually kept a step in rear of their Allies on either flank, moving forward by successive bounds when the enemy had been shouldered back. For the first two years they had borne the main burden of the fighting. If their commanders had been slow to learn how to economize life, they, and still more their men, had learnt it now. Perhaps a shade too well. But it is not for those who were fresh in the evening of the war to complain of excess of caution in those who had suffered the full heat of the day, since dawn.

On the other hand, criticism of the disappointingly early check of the Meuse-Argonne attack has been too apt to overlook the handicap of excessive freshness. The trouble was not merely that the troops were fresh—perhaps it was mostly that the arrangements were fresh. The Americans had scarcely a week of real preparation—an astonishing contrast with the months which preceded the French and British offensives of 1915, 1916, and even 1917. Even though the German fighting power and morale were now in decline, such haste would have put an almost superhuman strain on any troops. Yet it was demanded of new troops with a new organization. Popular opinion might complain of the frequency with which the machine jammed; the miracle is that it did not collapse and, instead, was rapidly repaired to move forward anew.

It is equally creditable to the higher command that the opening attack achieved so high a degree of surprise. This preparatory success owed much to the ingenuity of the Intelligence section in creating the most artistic mirage of an offensive further east, near the Vosges.

Thus when the real offensive was launched, the twenty-mile front of attack was held by only five German divisions, all emaciated, and all but one composed of low-grade troops. Against them were thrown nine American divisions, with three more in close reserve—a superiority in fighting strength of about eight to one. There were three more divisions in army reserve. But, owing to the difficulty of withdrawing and switching troops from St. Mihiel, only one Regular division could be used at the outset, and only three had previous battle experience.

The attack was preceded by a three hours' intense bombardment from 2700 guns and accompanied by 189 small tanks. It is significant to note that the proportion of tanks was much lower than in the Allied offensives of July 15th and August 8th. It is also noteworthy, in view of Pershing's pre-St. Mihiel hint to Foch, that all the artillery was French-made, and half of it manned by the French, as also were forty-seven of the tanks.

Pershing's plan was far-reaching. It certainly cannot be criticized as circumscribed or shortsighted, for the attacking troops were expected to reach and break through the Kriemhilde line on the first day, an advance of over eight miles, and were to exploit the success during the night so that the second morning would find them in open country and almost half-way to Sedan and the lateral railway. Unfortunately, Pershing's orders were by no means clearly worded.

Foch in a personal note had intimated that the American Army must not let itself be tied by the pace of its neighbour, Gouraud's French Fourth Army, and added—'There is no question of fixing . . . fronts not to be passed without a new order—such a restrictive indication tending to prevent exploitation of opportunities. . . .'

Unfortunately, Pershing's orders to his corps had this very tendency, however far-reaching his aim. Bullard's III Corps on the right and Liggett's I Corps on the left, were to drive in wedges on either flank of the commanding height of Montfaucon, thus helping Cameron's V Corps in the centre, which was to sweep over Montfaucon and on to the Kriemhilde line 'without waiting for advance of the III and I Corps'. This provision was wise, but less happily their advance was to be 'based upon the V Corps'. Here lay the germ of paralysis.

For when the assault was launched, at 5.30 a.m. on September 26th, the V Corps, which had its flanks protected, made far less progress than its neighbours—although its left

division, the 91st, was a happy exception. On the right of the
V Corps the 4th (Regular) Division of Bullard's Corps
penetrated deeply past the flank of Montfaucon, while the
80th and 33rd near the Meuse made good progress. On the
left wing of the army, which had the most difficult task and
ground, Liggett's orders paved the way for a good start. Thus
the 35th Division neatly circumvented the formidable
obstacle of Vauquois by an encircling advance, and then,
with the 28th Division on their left, drove a wedge nearly
four miles deep up the Aire Valley just east of the Argonne
Forest. Through the forest itself moved the 77th Division,
which had the difficult task of linking up with the French on
the west side.

Then, however, Pershing's orders for a halt, on reaching the
Corps' objective, were construed as putting a brake on the
advance, and it was difficult to get up momentum again
after the six hours' delay. A method that was sound in siege
warfare was, as Liggett's insight told him, a mistake when
faced with a weak and temporarily demoralized enemy. The
Americans had, as yet, neither the training nor organization
for methodical siege warfare, and the best chance of decisive
success lay in swamping the defence by a human torrent in
the first flush of surprise before the enemy could bring up
reinforcements. With the brake put on prematurely, the
advance thereafter slowed down and became spasmodic
along the whole front. Guns could not get forward to support
the infantry, control lapsed, and supplies frequently failed,
through inexperience accentuating the natural difficulties of
the ground.

All these factors helped the success of the Germans' own
tactics in drawing the sting from the attack. For the Germans
had repeated the method of elastic defence—with the real
resistance some miles in rear. The unexpectant Americans
ran into this cunningly woven belt of fire when their initial
spurt was exhausted and their formation disordered. Although Montfaucon was taken—by the 79th Division—on the
second day, the V Corps only came up level with the two

flank corps, and they had made little further progress that day. The great offensive had practically shot its bolt and, in the days that followed, the arrival of fresh German divisions enabled the enemy to counterattack and force back the disjointed attackers in places. A renewed general attack on October 4th made little progress, except on the left, and revealed once more the folly of trying to overthrow machine-guns by sheer weight of human bodies without adequate fire support or surprise. But the value of training was also shown by the regular 1st Division in Liggett's Corps which drove in a deep if narrow wedge on the east bank of the Aire. This enabled Liggett, on October 7th, to try a manœuvre both original and daring; bringing the 82nd Division up in the wake of the 1st, he swung it against the enemy's flank west of the Aire and then northward. If the execution fell below the conception—only a tithe of the division came into action—so that the chance of cutting off the enemy troops in the Argonne was lost, the threat at least persuaded the enemy to retire from the forest while there was time, and by October 10th the American line had passed and was clear of this hampering obstacle.

Meantime, the all too obvious failure to fulfil the original plan had provoked widespread reactions behind the front. Clemenceau visited Foch and bitterly remarked—'Those Americans will lose us our chance of a big victory before winter. They are all tangled up with themselves. You have tried to make Pershing see. Now let's put it up to President Wilson.' The complaint was rather unfair in view of the fact that the advance of Gouraud's army was well behind that of the American, if by design. But Foch was more generous—or more fully aware of the firmness of Pershing's position—and replied—'The Americans have got to learn sometime. They are learning now, rapidly.' Pétain, indeed, had made the strategically sound suggestion of giving charge of the Argonne Forest sector to a separate army, half French and half American, under General Hirschauer—but Pershing had seen in it only a fresh political manœuvre, and had rejected it firmly.

Pershing, however, overhauled his own army—and its commanders. The inactive forces east of the Meuse were formed into the Second American Army, to be commanded by Bullard, while Liggett was given charge of the First and of the Meuse-Argonne attack. Pershing himself retained the superior direction of both and left Hugh Drum to continue as Chief of Staff to Liggett. Dickman succeeded Liggett in the I Corps, and Hines succeeded Bullard, while Cameron was replaced by Summerall. Other commanders of all grades fell beneath Pershing's sickle almost as fast as their men beneath the scythe of the German machine-guns.

But for a time these changes made little impression on the Germans. The next general attack on October 14th achieved little at large cost—both of men's lives and generals' reputations—and with its failure even the higher command realized that the offensive had reached stalemate. An attempt to press on, with exhausted troops and disordered communications, could exercise no pressure adequate to be any appreciably greater relief to the other Allied armies. Moreover, the British left wing of the Allied offensive, in which the 27th and 30th American Divisions shared, had already broken through the last defences of the Hindenburg Line and by October 5th had emerged into open country, with only natural obstacles, mileage and a devastated area to hinder its advance.

Liggett, who now took charge, was wise to realize that in the circumstances it was far better to rest and reorganize his forces, for a sure bound as soon as possible, than to sacrifice lives in attempting the impossible. While utilizing the breathing space not only to replenish his ranks and supplies but to improve his communications and overhaul his organization, he carried out local operations to obtain a good jumping off line for the fresh bound. Further, he recast not only the tactics but the plan. Pershing had proposed that the American left should strike first, followed in turn by the remaining Corps to the right. This meant battering first at the naturally strong and heavily wooded Bois de Bourgogne area due north of the

Argonne, where also the enemy were in strongest force. Liggett preferred to drive a broad wedge in the centre and so outflank the Bois de Bourgogne, threatening its encirclement in conjunction with the advance of the French Fourth Army to the west.

It was well conceived, for when Liggett unleashed his forces on November 1st, this area was the only one which showed resisting power, and by next day the enemy rearguards there had disappeared and were falling back as fast as on the rest of the American front. If the Germans were offering little resistance, the very rapidity of the pursuit—outstripping the French on the flank—imposed almost as great a strain, and it was a tribute to the overhaul that the First Army machine functioned much more smoothly than in the earlier phase. And this despite the execution of a most difficult manœuvre by which the whole army wheeled progressively to the right during the course of the pursuit, ready for an attack north-eastwards—against the strong position between the Meuse and Chiers rivers to which the enemy had retired. This wheel was a preliminary to an advance towards Metz, but the Armistice now rang down the curtain.

Strategically this move was more important, because the Germans here were more sensitive, than the now incidental arrival of the left wing on the Carignan-Sedan section of the lateral railway. This railway had been brought under artillery fire as early as November 3rd, and had been reached by the infantry four days later, but the Germans had already slipped out of the bag. Indeed, the advance to this point, although an exhilarating finish, was chiefly significant in showing the 'liberties' that could be and were taken at the finish. With a somewhat brusque disregard of French feelings Pershing issued a message that he wished the American Army to have 'the honor of entering Sedan'—although it was now in the French sector of advance. Pershing added the encouragement or incitement—'Boundaries will not be considered as binding.' The message was passed to the corps without being shown to Liggett, and as a result the 42nd

Division on the left of the army raced for Sedan. But the vague wording produced a still more unmilitary—indeed, a burlesque—result. For the 1st Division—Pershing's favourite —from the centre corps had also started to race thither by night, crossing the divisions of the I Corps and throwing them into confusion as it impetuously swept through them. It capped the farce by taking prisoner the commander of the 42nd Division. Liggett, however, intervened with prompt action and vigorous language—to restrain both divisions and allow the French the courtesy of entering Sedan, thus to wipe out the bitter memory of 1870.

The historian who scans the whole horizon of the war must recognize that this last offensive, beginning on November 1st, had only a supplementary influence, for Ludendorff had fallen from power—his plea for a renewed stand on the German frontier rejected—and the enemy were already suing for peace before Liggett struck. Nevertheless it was well that the Armistice had tarried long enough to allow the offensive of November 1st to take place. For it provided a counterpoise to the bitter memories of the first phase—more truly, the first battle—of the Meuse-Argonne, and a proof that when purged and refined by experience the American army could produce leadership and staff work worthy of the gallant sacrifice of the fighting troops—the American nation in arms.

EPILOGUE

EVERY anniversary of the Armistice kindles emotions and memories such as no other day in the year has at present the power to do. For those who shared in the experiences of those four and a quarter years of struggle the commemoration does not stale with repetition. But the mood in which it is commemorated has undergone subtle changes. On the original Armistice itself the dominant note was a sigh of relief, of infinite volume, most restrained among those who had the most direct cause for relief, most exuberant, perhaps, among those who least appreciated the relief.

The earlier anniversaries were dominated by two opposite emotions. On the one hand grief, a keener sense, now that the storm had passed, of the vacant places in our midst. On the other hand, triumph, flamboyant only in rare cases, but nevertheless a heightened sense of victory, that the enemy had been laid low. That mood again has passed.

Armistice Day has become a commemoration instead of a celebration. The passage of time has refined and blended the earlier emotions, so that, without losing sense of the personal loss and of quiet thankfulness that as a people we proved our continued power to meet a crisis graver than any in past annals, we are to-day conscious, above all, of the general effects on the world and on civilization. In this mood of reflection we are more ready to recognize both the achievements and the point of view of our late enemies, and perhaps all the more because we realize that both the causes and the course of war are determined by the folly and the frailty rather than by the deliberate evil of human nature.

The war has become history, and can be viewed in the perspective of history. For good it has deepened our sense of fellowship and community of interest, whether inside the nation or between nations. But, for good or bad, it has shattered our faith in idols, our hero-worshipping belief that great men are different clay from common men. Leaders are still necessary, perhaps more necessary, but our awakened realization of their common humanity is a safeguard against either expecting from them or trusting in them too much. It has been for the benefit both of history and of future generations that the past decade has seen such a flood of evidence and revelations, of documents and memoirs. That most of the actors are still alive provides an invaluable check in sifting the evidence, while the historians themselves have been so immersed in the atmosphere of war that they have a certain immunity from the abstract theorizing which an historian in his cloistered study fifty years later so easily contracts. We know nearly all that is to be known. The one drawback is that the flood has been so huge that only the student has been able to cope with its investigation.

What caused that astonishingly sudden collapse and surrender of Germany which, as by a miracle, so it seemed, lifted the nightmare load of war from Europe? To arrive at a satisfactory answer it is not sufficient to analyse the hectic weeks of negotiation and military success which preceded November 11th. Even in the military sphere we need to go back to August 8th, the day which filled the German command with the conviction of defeat, and to July 18th, which witnessed the visible turning of the tide. And if we go back thither we must go back further, to March 21st, for the decline of Germany's military power is not explicable without reference to the consummation of that military effort, and consumption of her military resources, in the great series of offensives which opened in the spring of 1918.

We ought, however, to go back further still. Indeed, if the historian of the future has to select one day as decisive for the outcome of the World War he will probably choose August 2nd, 1914—before the war, for England, had yet begun— when Mr. Winston Churchill, at 1.25 a.m., sent the order to mobilize the British Navy. That Navy was to win no Trafalgar, but it was to do more than any other factor towards winning the war for the Allies. For the Navy was the instrument of the blockade, and as the fog of war disperses in the clearer light of these post-war years that blockade is seen to assume larger and larger proportions, to be more and more clearly the decisive agency in the struggle. Like those 'jackets' which used to be applied in American gaols to refractory prisoners, as it was progressively tightened so did it first cramp the prisoner's movements and then stifle his breathing, while the tighter it became and the longer it continued the less became the prisoner's power of resistance and the more demoralizing the sense of constriction.

Helplessness induces hopelessness, and history attests that loss of hope and not loss of lives is what decides the issue of war. No historian would underrate the direct effect of the semi-starvation of the German people in causing the final collapse of the 'home front'. But leaving aside the question of how far the revolution caused the military defeat, instead of vice versa, the intangible all-pervading factor of the blockade intrudes into every consideration of the military situation.

This, during the last year of the war, is studded with 'ifs'. If Germany, instead of throwing all her military resources into a series of tremendous offensives in 1918, had stayed on the defensive in the West, while consolidating her gains in the East, could she have averted defeat? Militarily there seems little doubt that she could. In the light of the experience of 1915, when the Allies had 145 divisions in the West to Germany's 100, and when the German trench systems were a frail and shallow bulwark compared with those of 1918, it is difficult to see that the Allies could have breached it, even if they had waited until the inflowing tide of American man power had restored to them the relative numerical superiority that they had enjoyed in 1915.

And if so, in face of the accumulating cost of vain assaults, would they not eventually have inclined towards a compromise peace? A peace, peradventure, which, in return for the relinquishment of Belgium and Northern France, might have conceded to Germany part or the whole of her gains in the East. Yet as we ask the question, and militarily find an optimistic answer difficult, the factor of the command of the sea comes to mind. For it was the stranglehold of the British Navy which, in default of a serious peace move, constrained Germany to carry out that *felo de se* offensive of 1918. She was dogged by the spectre of slow enfeeblement ending in eventual collapse.

Perhaps if she had adopted such a war policy of defence in the West, offence in the East, after the Marne in 1914, or even, after 1915, continued the policy which she had that year temporarily adopted, her prospects might have been brighter and her story different; for, on the one hand, she could have consummated unquestionably the dream of 'Mittel-Europa', and on the other, the blockade was still a loose grip, and could hardly have been drawn effectively tight so long as the United States remained outside the conflict. But in 1918 the best chance had passed.

Another big 'if', often mooted, is the question whether even in the autumn of 1918 Germany could have avoided capitulation. Would the fighting front have collapsed if the war had gone on after November 11th? Was capitulation inevitable, or could the German armies have made good their retreat and stood firm on their own frontiers? German opinion largely says 'yes' to the latter question, and blames the surrender on the 'home front'. Many open-minded and diligent students of the war among the Allies are inclined to agree that it was possible from a military point of view. But again the naval aspect intervenes. Even if the German armies, and the German people, roused to a supreme effort in visible defence of their own soil, had managed to hold the Allies at bay, the end could only have been postponed. The most that history is likely to concede is that they might have held on long enough, tightening their belts, for the Allies, already weary, to sicken of the effort, and thus concede more favourable terms than those of Versailles.

Having disposed of the 'ifs', having emphasized the fundamental cause of the Armistice—Britain's sea power, her historic weapon, the deadliest weapon which any nation has wielded throughout history—let us turn to examine the immediate causes of the Armistice. How did victory come? Here military action bulks large. Other factors contributed, apart from the naval. If we do not accept entirely, we should not discount unduly the unwilling tribute paid by the Germans to the effectiveness of Allied, and especially of British, propaganda. In the later stages of the war it was skilfully directed and intensively developed.

If now, when passions are stilled, the memory of some of the 'facts' that were exploited is disturbing to our sense of fair play and lies uneasily on the stomach, we realize equally that such forms of propaganda neither stimulated our own people nor discouraged the enemy. It was the kernel of essential truth upon the bigger issues which was digested by the German people and, by leading them to question both the honesty of their leadership and the hope of success, weakened the will to continued sacrifice.

Nevertheless, though we should recognize the value of the more discriminating propaganda, its effect was rather in supplementing and completing the military successes than in paving the way for them, as German spokesmen have often contended. There is significant evidence on this point to be found in the memoirs of Prince Max of Baden, a man whose high-minded patriotism and sincerity command the respect of both friend and foe, and whose book is one of the most valuable of the war memoirs yet published. Unintentionally, and unconsciously, he shows in casual passages, easily missed, that when German arms were temporarily in the ascendant moderation was forgotten in exultation, even among the more sober.

In March, 1918, he quotes even a pacifist as exuberantly crying—'Never worry! . . . What an experience! . . . World dominion.' And another representative of moderate opinion 'let the cat out of the bag' in saying meditatively—'It would seem that we needn't say no to Briey and Longwy'—revealing that intoxication of spirit which, more fundamentally than any ill intention, was responsible for Germany's war guilt.

In face of such widespread intoxication, propaganda could only be secondary to military action. Thus we are left with the sure conclusion that the success of the Allied armies was chief among the immediate causes of Germany's capitulation on November 11th.

That conclusion does not necessarily, or even naturally, imply that at the moment of the Armistice the German armies were on the brink of collapse. Nor that the Armistice was a mistaken concession—as some among the Allies, usually those whose fighting was done with their tongue, were so loud in proclaiming at the time.

Rather does the record of the last 'hundred days', when thoroughly sifted, confirm the immemorial lesson of history— that the true aim in war is the mind of the enemy command and Government, not the bodies of their troops, that the balance between victory and defeat turns on mental impressions and only indirectly on physical blows. That in war, as Napoleon said and Foch endorsed, 'it is the man, not men, who counts'.

The reiteration of this great truth is to be found in the war's last phase. Great as was the stimulus and visible success of the tide-turning battle on the Marne in July, Ludendorff was still planning and preparing fresh offensives thereafter. If he was chagrined, he does not appear to have been so disillusioned as he had been after his own outwardly successful attack on the Lys in April.

But the Fourth Army surprise attack before Amiens on August 8th was a dislocating moral blow. Prince Max put August 8th in its true light psychologically, when he defined it as 'the turning point'. Even so, to develop the conviction of failure into the conviction of hopelessness required to compel surrender, something more was needed. It came not from the Western Front, but from a despised 'side-show'— Salonika, long condemned by Allied military opinion and scornfully ridiculed by the Germans as their 'largest internment camp'. With Bulgaria's collapse the back gate to Austria, as well as to Turkey, and through Austria to

Germany, lay ajar.

The immediate issue of the war was decided on September 29th, decided in the mind of the German Command. Ludendorff and his associates had then 'cracked', and the sound went echoing backwards until it had resounded throughout the whole of Germany. Nothing could catch it or stop it. The Command might recover its nerve, the actual military position might improve, but the moral impression, as ever in war, was decisive.

Yet, let us once again emphasize that the fundamental causes of the decision are more various than the acts which immediately produced it.

The truth is that no one cause was, or could be, decisive. The Western Front, the Balkan Front, the tank, the blockade and propaganda have all been claimed as the cause of victory. All claims are justified, none is wholly right, although the blockade ranks first and began first. In this warfare between nations victory was a cumulative effect, to which all weapons—military, economic, and psychological—contributed. Victory came, and could only come through the utilization and combination of all the resources existing in a modern nation, and the dividend of success depended on the way in which these manifold activities were co-ordinated.

It is even more futile to ask which country won the war. France did not win the war, but unless she had held the fort while the forces of Britain were preparing and those of America still a dream the release of civilization from this nightmare of militarism would have been impossible. Britain did not win the war, but without her command of the sea, her financial support, and her army, to take over the main burden of the struggle from 1916 onwards, defeat would have been inevitable. The United States did not win the war, but without their economic aid to ease the strain, without the arrival of their troops to turn the numerical balance, and, above all, without the moral tonic which their coming gave, victory would have been impossible. And let us not forget how many times Russia had sacrificed herself to save her allies; preparing the way for their ultimate victory as surely as for her own downfall. Finally, whatever be the verdict of history on her policy, unstinted tribute is due to the incomparable endurance and skill with which Germany more than held her own for four years against superior numbers—an epic of military and human achievement.

BIBLIOGRAPHY

THE appended list is, of course, far from a complete list of the books which have been read or consulted during the fifteen years since the war. Its purpose is to indicate those of main historical significance. It comprises those sources from which facts or quotations have been drawn for use herein, or which have directly helped in forming one's picture of the war. During these years one has also been privileged to see a number of documents, British and foreign, which have not yet been published or utilized, and to gather the personal evidence of those who participated in critical actions and in the taking of important decisions. Such sources, where they have contributed to the narrative, are referred to as either 'Unpublished Documents' or 'Personal Evidence'. Although it is not yet possible to give a fuller identification, all such sources have been recorded and privately catalogued for the eventual use of historical students.

In concluding this preface to the Bibliography I take the opportunity to acknowledge the great debt which all serious students of the war owe to the *Army Quarterly*, and especially its 'Notes on Foreign War Books'. This feature during the past ten years has been invaluable as a signpost and search-light amid the vast and confusing mass of material that has been published. No periodical, military or historical, in any country has kept or marked so clear a track for students of the war.

Books published since 1930 are listed separately on pages 614-20, save in the case of a few continuing volumes of books published earlier.

BIBLIOGRAPHY

CHAPTER I

ORIGINS

J. W. Headlam-Morley	*The Outbreak of War. Foreign Office Documents* (1926)
G. P. Gooch and H. Temperley	*British Documents on the Origins of the War*, vols. i-v (1927)
Haldane (Viscount)	*Before the War* (1920)
Grey of Fallodon (Viscount)	*Twenty-Five Years, 1892-1916* (1925)
G. Buchanan	*My Mission to Russia* (1923)
H. Wickham Steed	*Through Thirty Years, 1892-1922* (1924)
R. W. Seton-Watson	*Sarajevo* (1926)
G. P. Gooch	*Recent Revelations of European Diplomacy*, (1927)
H. W. Wilson	*The War Guilt* (1928)
B. Hendrick	*The Life and Letters of W. H. Page* (1922-25)
P. Renouvin	*Les Origines Immédiates de la Guerre* (1925)
R. Poincaré	*Au service de la France*, vols. i-iv (1926-27)
M. Paléologue	*An Ambassador's Memoirs* (Eng. trans. 1923-25)
German Foreign Office	*Die Grosse Politik der Europäischen Kabinette, 1871-1914* (1926) (Eng. selection and trans. in 4 vols. *German Diplomatic Documents, 1871-1914*, 1928-)
K. Kautsky, M. Montgelas and W. Schücking	*Die Deutschen Dokumente zum Kriegsausbruch* (1919) (Eng. trans. 1924)
A. von Tirpitz	*Memoirs* (Eng. trans. 1919)
The Kaiser's Letters to the Tsar (Eng. trans. 1920)	
M. Montgelas	*The Case for the Central Powers* (Eng. trans. 1925)
K. Lichnowsky	*My Mission to London, 1912-1914* (1918)
Generaloberst Helmuth von Moltke. Erinnerungen—Briefe—Dokumente 1877-1916 (1923)	
W. von Schoen	*The Memoirs of an Ambassador* (Eng. trans. 1922)
Diplomatische Aktenstücke zur Vorgeschichte des Krieges, 1914 (1919) (Eng. trans. *Austrian Red Book*, 1920)	

BIBLIOGRAPHY

Conrad von Hötzendorf *Aus meiner Dienstzeit*, vols. i-iv (1922-25)
Czernin   *In the World War* (Eng. trans. 1920)
*How the War began in 1914, being the diary of the Russian Foreign Office
    ...July, 1914...published by the Russian
    Soviet Government* (Eng. trans. 1925)
S. Sazonov   *Fateful Years, 1909-1916* (Eng. trans.
    1927)
*Un Livre Noir, diplomatie d'avant guerre d'après les documents des
    archives russes* (1922-23)

CHAPTERS II—VII
GENERAL

W. S. Churchill	*The World Crisis*, 4 vols. (1923-7)
John Buchan	*A History of the Great War*, 4 vols. (1921)
Oxford and Asquith (Earl of)	*Memories and Reflections* (1928)
G. Arthur	*Life of Lord Kitchener*, Vol. iii (1920)
Esher (Viscount)	*The Tragedy of Lord Kitchener* (1921)
C. à C. Repington	*The First World War, 1914-1918*, 2 vols. (1920)
W. R. Robertson	*From Private to Field Marshal* (1921)
	Soldiers and Statesmen, 1914-1918 (1926)
Beaverbrook (Lord)	*Politicians and the War, 1914-1916* (1928)
N. Macready	*Annals of an Active Life* (1926)
C. E. Callwell	*Experiences of a Dug-Out, 1914-1918* (1921)
C. P. Lucas	*The Empire at War*, 3 vols. [covers war effort of Dominions and Colonies]
Royal Engineers' Institute	*The Work of the R.E. in the European War, 1914-1919*, 9 vols. (1921-27)
War Office	*Statistics of the Military Effort of the British Empire, 1914-1920* (1922)
R. van Overstraeten	*Des Principes de la Guerre*, vol. ii [vol. ii covers World War]
C. Seymour	*The Intimate Papers of Colonel House*, 4 vols. (1926-28)
J. W. Gerard	*My Four Years in Germany* (1917) [U.S.A. Ambassador]
E. Ludendorff	*Urkunden der Obersten Heeresleitung, 1916-1918* (1920)
Kuhl	*Der Deutsche Generalstab in Vorbereitung und Durchführung des Weltkrieges* (1920) [French condensed trans. by Douchy, *Le Grand État-Major allemand avant et pendant la guerre mondiale*]

596

BIBLIOGRAPHY

M. Erzberger	*Erlebnisse im Weltkrieg* (1921) [French trans. *Souvenirs de guerre*]
J. V. Bredt	*Die Belgische Neutralität und der Schlieffensche Feldzugsplan* (1929) [excellent summary in *Army Quarterly*, July 1929]
E. von Falkenhayn	*General Headquarters, 1914-1916 and its Critical Decisions* (Eng. trans. 1919)
Stürgkh (Graf)	*Im deutschen Grossen Hauptquartier* (1921) [intimate impressions and pen-portraits by the Austrian military representative]
Zwehl	*Erich von Falkenhayn* (1925) [contains extracts from diary]
Groener	*Das Testament des Grafen Schlieffen* (1927)
H. von Hentig	*Psychologische Strategie des Grossen Krieges* (1927) [criticism, usually acute, of the German war policy and strategy]
L. Gehre	*Die deutsche Kraftverteilung während des Weltkrieges* (1928) [gives location of all German divisions on 15th and last day of every month]
Bauer	*Der Grosse Krieg in Feld und Heimat* (1922) [intimate revelations of the German Supreme Command during the war]
M. Schwarte	*Der Grosse Krieg, 1914-1918*, 11 vols. (1921-)
Buat	*L'Armée Allemande pendant la guerre de 1914-1918* (1920)

WESTERN FRONT

J. E. Edmonds	*Military Operations, France and Belgium*, vols. i-v (1922-32) [*British Official History*, vols. i-ii, 1914; iii-iv, 1915; v, 1916]
The Despatches of Lord French, 1914-1915 (1917)	
French (Viscount)	*1914* (1919) [a record of his command, distinguished by inaccuracy]
J. H. Boraston (Ed.)	*Sir D. Haig's Despatches, 1915-1919* (1919)
G. A. B. Dewar and J. H. Boraston	*Sir Douglas Haig's Command, 1915-1918* (1922)
H. L. Smith-Dorrien	*Memories of Forty-Eight Years' Service* (1925) [covers, if with extreme reserve, his service as corps and army commander in the first phase]

BIBLIOGRAPHY

C. E. Callwell   *Field-Marshal Sir Henry Wilson*, 2 vols. (1927) [extracts from an amazingly unreserved diary, 1914-1919]

F. Maurice   *The Life of General Lord Rawlinson of Trent* (1928) [covers the whole war]

J. Charteris   *Field-Marshal Earl Haig* (1929)

Huguet   *Britain and the War* (Eng. trans. 1928) [impressions of French representative at British G.H.Q., 1914-15]

C. E. W. Bean   *The Australian Imperial Force in France, 1916* (1929) [Australian Official History]

J. Monash   *The Australian Victories in France in 1918* (1920)

A. W. Currie   *Canadian Corps Operations during 1918* (1920)

A. A. Montgomery   *The Story of the Fourth Army* (1920) [for last half of 1918 campaign]

A. de Schrÿver   *La Bataille de Liége* (1922) [by the chief of staff of the fortress]

Deguise   *La Défense de la position fortifiée d'Anvers en 1914* (1921) [by the Belgian commander]

E. Menzel   *La vérité sur l'évacuation d'Anvers en 1914* (1925)

C. Merzbach   *La vérité sur la Défense de Namur en 1914* (1927)

Duvivier and Herbiet   *Du rôle de l'Armée de Champagne et des Forteresses belges en 1914* (1929) [effect in detaining German forces]

Les Armées Françaises dans la Grande Guerre, Tome I, vol. ii (covers operations up to eve of the Marne, 1914); Tome VII, vol. i (covers period 18th June—25th September, 1918) [French Official History]

B. E. Palat   *La Grande Guerre sur le Front Occidental*, 14 vols. (1921-30)

P. Renouvin   *Les Formes du Gouvernement de Guerre* (1929) [relations between Government and commanders in France]

R. Poincaré   *Au service de la France*, vol. v. *L'Invasion, 1914* (1929)

Lanrezac   *Le Plan de Campagne Français et le Premier Mois de Guerre* (1920)

BIBLIOGRAPHY

V. Margueritte	*Au bord du Gouffre* (1920) [French plan for 1914)
F. Engerand	*La Bataille de la Frontière (août, 1914) Briey* (1920) [French plan for 1914]
Percin	*1914 Les Erreurs du Haut Commandement* (1922) [French plan for 1914]
Tanant	*La Troisième Armée dans la Bataille. Souvenirs d'un Chef d'État-Major* (1928) [special light on the opening battles of 1914]
Toussan	*Historique des corps de cavallerie commandé par le général Conneau du 14 août 1914 au 2 mars 1917* (1924)
E. Valarché	*La Bataille de Guise* (1928)
A. Grouard	*La Conduite de la Guerre jusqu'à la Bataille de la Marne* (1922) [an acute criticism by a famous military critic who gave the French General Staff an unheeded warning of the German plan]
Camon	*L'Effondrement du Plan Allemand en Septembre 1914* (1925)
Mermeix	*Joffre—1er Crise du Commandement* *Le Commandement Unique*
Rousset	*La Bataille de l'Aisne* [Nivelle offensive, 1917]
P. Painlevé	*Comment j'ai nommé Foch et Pétain* (1924)
Laure	*Au 3ième Bureau du troisième G.Q.G. 1917-1919* (1922)
L. Madelin	*La Bataille de France* [1918 campaign]
Koeltz	*L'Offensive Allemande de 1918* (1928)
Jean de Pierrefeu	*G.Q.G. Secteur I*, 2 vols. (1921)
	Plutarque a Menti (1923)
N. Domège	*En Marge de Plutarque*
Mordacq	*Le Commandement Unique. Comment il fut réalisé*
	La Vérité sur l'Armistice (1929)
Reichsarchiv	*Der Weltkrieg 1914-1918*, vols. i, iii, v, vi (1924-29) [German Official History, covers 1914]; vii and viii [cover 1915]
Reichsarchiv	*Antwerpen, 1914* (1921) [German Official Monograph on siege]
Reichsarchiv	*Ypres, 1914* [German Official Monograph, Eng. trans. 1919]
Crown Prince Rupprecht of Bavaria	*Mein Kriegstagebuch*, 3 vols. (1928)

599

BIBLIOGRAPHY

Krafft von Delmensingen — *Die Führung des Kronprinzen Rupprecht von Bayern auf dem linken deutschen Heeresflügel bis zur Schlacht in Lothringen im August, 1914* (1925) [light on opening battles in Lorraine]

Die Schlacht in Lothringen (1929) [Bavarian Official History]

German Ex-Crown Prince — *Meine Erinnerungen aus Deutschlands Heldenkampf* (1923)

Generaloberst Helmuth von Moltke. Erinnerungen - Briefe - Dokumente 1877-1916 (1923)

W. Foerster — *Graf Schlieffen und der Weltkrieg* (1920)

Kluck — *The March on Paris, 1914* (Eng. trans. 1920)

Army Quarterly, October, 1921 — *General Ludendorff on the German Plan of Campaign, August, 1914* [extract from letter]

The Memoirs of Prince Max of Baden (Eng. trans. 1928) [especially for light on last phase of war]

Final Report of Gen. J. J. Pershing (1919)

First Army Report (printed 1923)

Shipley Thomas — *History of the American Expeditionary Force* (1920)

R. L. Bullard — *Personalities and Reminiscences of the War* (1925)

J. G. Harbord — *Leaves from a War Diary* (1926)

J. W. Thomason — *Fix Bayonets* (1927)

J. T. Dickman — *The Great Crusade* (1927)

Hunter Liggett — *Commanding an American Army* (1925)
A. E. F. (1928)

T. M. Johnson — *Without Censor* (1928)

T. C. Lonergan — *It might have been lost* (1929) [extracts from British Official documents dealing with Pershing's struggle to preserve the national unity of the A.E.F.]

RUSSIAN FRONT

(See also Chapter III, Scene 2)

Reichsarchiv — *Der Weltkrieg, 1914-1918*, vol. ii (1924) vol. v (1929) [German Official History, covers 1914]

E. Ludendorff — *My War Memories* (Eng. trans. 1920)

P. von Hindenburg — *Out of my life* (Eng. trans. 1920)

BIBLIOGRAPHY

A. von Cramon	*Quatre Ans au G.Q.G. austro-hongrois* (French trans. 1922)
M. Hoffmann	*The War of Lost Opportunities* (Eng. trans. 1924) *War Diaries and other Papers* (Eng. trans. 1929)
Russian Historical Commission	*La Grande Guerre. Relation de l'État-Major Russe* (French trans. 1927)
Conrad von Hötzendorf	*Aus meiner Dienstzeit*, vols. iv-v (1925-26) [covers 1914 campaign]
François	*Gorlice, 1915* (1922) [the 1915 breakthrough]
A. Arz	*Zur Geschichte des Grossen Krieges, 1914-1918* [memoirs of Conrad's successor]
J. E. Edmonds in Army Quarterly, July, 1921	*The Austrian Plan of Campaign, 1914, and its development*
K. F. Novak	*Der Weg zur Katastrophe* (1920) (French trans.) [Conrad's evidence]
Buat	*Hindenburg et Ludendorff Stratèges* (1923)
Camon	*Ludendorff sur le Front Russe 1914-1915* (1926)
Y. Danilov	*La Russie dans la Guerre Mondiale, 1914-1917* (French trans. 1927)
Sukhomlinov	*Erinnerungen* (1924)
B. Gourko	*Russia in 1914-1917* (Eng. trans. 1918)
A. Knox	*With the Russian Army, 1914-1917* (1921) *Hindenburg's Second Offensive in Poland* (in Army Quarterly, July, 1921) [Lodz]
C. E. Callwell	*Experiences of a Dug-Out, 1914-1918* (1921)
C. Maynard	*The Murmansk Venture* (1928)

ITALIAN FRONT

L. Cadorna	*La Guerra alla fronte Italiana* (1921)
Capello	*Note di Guerra* (1920-21)
Vigano	*La Nostra Guerra* (1921)
A. Tosti	*La Guerra Italo-austriaca, 1915-1918* (1925)
Kuntz	*La Psychologie du G.Q.G. Italien sous le Général Cadorna* (1923)
A. Krauss	*Die Ursachen unserer Niederlage* (1921)
A. Arz	*Zur Geschichte des Grossen Krieges, 1914-1918* (1924) [covers 1917 and 1918]
A. von Cramon	*Quatre Ans au G.Q.G. austro-hongrois* (French trans. 1922) [the chief German representative]

601

BIBLIOGRAPHY

Kerchnawe   *Der Zusammenbruch der Oester-Ungar: Wehrmacht im Herbst* (1921) [Austrian documents]

J. F. Gathorne-Hardy in Army Quarterly, October, 1921   *A Summary of the Campaign in Italy and an Account of the Battle of Vittorio Veneto* [by the British Chief of Staff]

R. H. Beadon in Army Quarterly, Jan., 1925   *An Operation of War,* [British move to Italy after Caporetto]

BALKAN FRONT

Wolfgang Foerster   *Graf Schlieffen und der Weltkrieg,* Part III (1921)

O. Landfried   *Der Endkampf in Macedonien, 1918* (1925)

Nedeff   *Les Opérations en Macédoine. L'Épopée de Doiran, 1915-1918* (1927)

Feyler   *La Campagne de Macédoine,* vol. i, 1915-1916; vol. ii, 1917-1918 [from Serbian and Greek sources]

Jouinot-Gambetta   *Uskub ou du Rôle de la Cavalerie d'Afrique dans la Victoire* (1920) [final breakthrough]

Robert David   *Le Drame Ignoré de l'Armée d'Orient* (1928) [especially political side]

Les Armées Françaises dans la Grande Guerre, Tome VIII, vol. i (1928)

Œhmichen   *Essai sur la Doctrine de Guerre des Coalitions. La Direction de la Guerre* (nov., 1914 - Mars, 1917) (1927) [Joffre's influence on Salonika campaign]

Sarrail   *Mon Commandement en Orient, 1916-1918* (1920)

L. Villari   *The Macedonian Campaign* (1922)

THE DARDANELLES

(See Chapter IV, Scenes 1 and 2)

PALESTINE

(Including Egypt and Arabia)

G. MacMunn and C. Falls   *Military Operations Egypt and Palestine* (1928) [British Official History]

C. E. W. Bean   *Official History of Australia in the War,* vol. i

BIBLIOGRAPHY

H. S. Gullett	*Official History of Australia in the War,* vol. vii (1923)
A. P. Wavell	*The Palestine Campaigns* (1928)
R. M. P. Preston	*The Desert Mounted Corps* (1921)
T. E. Lawrence	*Revolt in the Desert*
T. E. Lawrence in Army Quarterly, October, 1920	*The Evolution of a Revolt*
W. T. Massey	*The Desert Campaigns* (1918)
M. Bowman-Manifold	*An Outline of the Egyptian and Palestine Campaigns* (1922)
G. E. Badcock	*History of the Transport Services of the E.E.F.*
Army, Navy and Air Force Gazette, 18th June, 1927	
Reichsarchiv	*Yilderim* (1925)
Kress von Kressenstein	*Zwischen Kaukasus und Sinai* (1922) [covers the period 1915-1917]
Liman von Sanders	*Five Years in Turkey* (Eng. trans. 1928) [covers 1918]
Rafael de Nogales	*Vier Jahren unter dem Halbmond* (1926)

MESOPOTAMIAN FRONT

F. J. Moberly	*The Mesopotamia Campaign, 1914-1918,* vols. i-iv (1923-1927) [British Official History]
Report of the Commission on Mesopotamia (1917)	
C. V. F. Townshend	*My Campaign in Mesopotamia* (1920)
Erroll Sherson	*Townshend of Chitral and Kut* (1928)
Keisling	*Mit Feldmarshall von der Goltz Pascha in Mesopotamien und Persien* (1922)
Rafael de Nogales	*Vier Jahre unter dem Halbmond* (1926)
Schraudenbach	*Muharebe* (1926)
Gleich	*Vom Balkan nach Bagdad* (1922) [light on siege of Kut]
R. H. Dewing, Army Quarterly, January, April, July, 1927	*Some Aspects of Maude's Campaign in Mesopotamia*
Edmund Candler	*The Long Road to Baghdad*
L. C. Dunsterville	*The Adventures of Dunsterforce* (1921)
W. Marshall	*Memories of Four Fronts* (1929)
C. E. Callwell	*Life of Sir Stanley Maude* (1920)

NAVAL

J. S. Corbett	*History of the Great War* (*Naval Operations*) vols. i-iii (1920-21)

BIBLIOGRAPHY

H. Newbolt	*History of the Great War (Naval Operations)* vol. iv (1928)
C. E. Fayle	*Seaborne Trade,* 3 vols. (1920-)
A. Laurens	*Précis d'Histoire de la Guerre Navale* (1929)
W. S. Churchill	*The World Crisis,* 4 vols. (1923-27)
Jellicoe (Viscount)	*The Grand Fleet, 1914-1916* (1919)
J. E. T. Harper	*The Truth about Jutland* (1927)
G. Campbell	*My Mystery Ships* (1928)
W. S. Sims	*The Victory at Sea* (1920)
R. Scheer	*Germany's High Seas Fleet in the World War* (Eng. trans. 1920)
G. von Hase	*Kiel and Jutland* (Eng. trans. 1926)

AIR

W. A. Raleigh	*The War in the Air,* vol. i (1922) (Official History)
H. A. Jones	*The War in the Air,* vol. ii (1928), vol. iii (1930) (Official History)
C. F. Snowden-Gamble	*The Story of a North Sea Air Station* (1928)
A. Rawlinson	*The Defence of London* (1923)
E. B. Ashmore	*Air Defence* (1929)
E. A. Lehmann	*The Zeppelins* (Eng. trans. 1928)
H. Ritter	*Der Luftkrieg* (1926)
Keller	*Die Heutige Wehrlosigkeit Deutschlands im Lichte seiner Verteidigung gegen Fliegerangriffe im Kriege, 1914-1918* (1926) [German Air Defence Organisation]

PRESS AND PROPAGANDA

E. T. Cook	*The Press in War-Time,* (1920)
C. Stuart	*Secrets of Crewe House* (1920)
N. Lytton	*The Press and the General Staff* (1921)
C. E. Callwell	*Experiences of a Dug-Out, 1914-1918* (1921)
H. D. Lasswell	*Propaganda Technique in the World War* (1926)

ECONOMIC AND HOME FRONT

M. Consett	*The Triumph of Unarmed Forces, 1914-1918* (1921)
R. H. Gretton	*A Modern History of the English People, 1910-22* (1929)
A. Hallays	*L'Opinion Allemande pendant la Guerre, 1914-1918* (1923)

BIBLIOGRAPHY

CHAPTER III

SCENE 1. THE MARNE

J. E. Edmonds	*Military Operations. France and Belgium,* vol. i (British Official History)
Reichsarchiv	*Der Weltkrieg, 1914-1918,* vols. iii and iv (1926) (German Official History)
Kluck	*The March on Paris, 1914* (Eng. trans. 1920)
J. E. Edmonds in Army Quarterly, January, 1921	*The Scapegoat of the Battle of the Marne*
Militär-Wochenblatt 18th	September, 1920 [court of enquiry on Col. Hentsch's rôle]
M. von Poseck	*Die deutsche Kavallerie in Belgien und Frankreich, 1914* (1922)
Baumgarten-Crusius	*Marneschlacht, 1914* (1919)
	Deutsche Heerführung im Marnefeldzug, 1914 (1921) [fuller extracts from Col. Hentsch's report]
Bülow	*Mein Bericht zur Marneschlacht* (1920) (French trans.)
Zwehl	*Maubeuge-Aisne-Verdun* (1921)
Helfferich	*Weltkrieg,* vol. ii
Tappen	*Bis zur Marneschlacht*
François	*Marneschlacht und Tannenberg* (1920)
Foerster	*Graf Schlieffen und der Weltkrieg,* Part I (1920)
Kuhl	*Der Marnefeldzug, 1914* (1920) (French trans.)
Crown Prince Rupprecht of Bavaria	*Mein Kriegstagebuch* (1928)
German Ex-Crown Prince	*Der Marnefeldzug, 1914* (1927)
Hausen	*Souvenirs de la Campagne de la Marne en 1914* (French trans. 1922) [Saxon Third Army Commander]
Reichsarchiv	*Das Marnedrama, 1914* (1928-29) [German Official Monographs, in five parts. Extensive summary in Army Quarterly, July, 1928, January, April, October, 1929, January, 1930]

BIBLIOGRAPHY

Müller-Loebnitz	*Die Sendung des Oberstleutnants Hentsch* (1922) [Official account of Hentsch's mission]
Generaloberst von Moltke.	*Erinnerungen—Briefe—Dokumente, 1877-1916* (1923)
Palat	*La Victoire de la Marne* (1921)
Dubail	*Journal du Campagne,* vol. i. 1ère *Armée*
J. Charbonneau	*La Bataille des Frontières et la Bataille de la Marne vues par un Chef de Section* (1929)
Mémoires du Maréchal Galliéni, Défense de Paris (25 août–11 sept. 1914) (1926)	
Clergerie and Delahaye d'Anglemont	*Le Rôle du Gouvernement Militaire de Paris de 1 au 12 septembre, 1914* (1920)
Marius—Ary le Blond	*Galliéni Parle* (1920)
Les Armées Françaises dans la Grande Guerre, Tome I, vol. ii (1927) (French Official History)	
Toussan	*Historique des corps de cavallerie commandés par le Général Conneau du 14 août au 2 mars, 1917* (1924)
J. de Pierrefeu	*Plutarque a menti* (1922)
Hirschauer and Klein	*Paris en état de défense, 1914* (1928)
H. Carré	*La Véritable Histoire des Taxis de la Marne* (1921)
Boëlle	*Le 4e corps d'Armée sur l'Ourcq* (1925) [light on Maunoury's part]
Dubois	*Deux ans de Commandement sur le Front de France, 1914-1916* (1920) [light on Foch's part]
Bujac	*Le Général Eydoux et le XI Corps d'Armée* (1925) [light on Foch's part]
de Castelli	*Le VIIIe Corps en Lorraine août–octobre, 1914* (1926) [light on French right wing and on loss of St. Mihiel]
Army Quarterly, October, 1922	*Another Legend of the Marne, 1914*
Private Evidence	

CHAPTER III

SCENE 2. TANNENBERG

Reichsarchiv	*Tannenberg* (1927) [German Official Monograph]
E. Ludendorff	*My War Memories* (Eng. trans. 1920)
P. von Hindenburg	*Out of my Life* (Eng. trans. 1920)

BIBLIOGRAPHY

Army Quarterly, October, 1921	*An Echo of Tannenberg*
H. von François	*Marneschlacht und Tannenberg* (1920) *Tannenberg* (1926)
Y. Danilov	*La Russie dans la Guerre Mondiale* (French trans. 1927)
M. Hoffmann	*The War of Lost Opportunities* (Eng. trans. 1924) *Tannenberg wie es wirklich war* (1927) *War Diaries and other Papers* (Eng. trans. 1929)
E. Ironside	*Tannenberg* (1925)
Russian Historical Commission	*La Grande Guerre. Relation de l'État-Major Russe* (French trans. 1927)
Noskov	*Militär Wochenblatt* 1st August, 1926 [a Russian view]
A. Smirnoff in Army Quarterly, April, 1926	*A New Light upon the Invasion of East Prussia by the Russians in August, 1914*

CHAPTER IV

SCENES 1 and 2. THE DARDANELLES

C. F. Aspinall-Oglander	*Military Operations, Gallipoli*, vol. i (1929) (British Official History)
The Final Report of the Dardanelles Commission (1919)	
Ian Hamilton	*A Gallipoli Diary*, 2 vols. (1920)
C. E. Callwell	*Experiences of a Dug-Out, 1914-1918* (1921)
J. Masefield	*Gallipoli* (1923)
Wester Wemyss (Lord)	*The Navy in the Dardanelles Campaign* (1924)
E. Ashmead-Bartlett	*The uncensored Dardanelles* (1927)
W. Marshall	*Memories of Four Fronts* (1929)
Compton Mackenzie	*Gallipoli Memories* (1929)
Liman von Sanders	*Five Years in Turkey* (Eng. trans. 1928)
H. Kannengiesser	*The Campaign in Gallipoli* (Eng. trans. 1928)
Reichsarchiv	*Dardanellen, 1915* (1927)
Turkish Official History	*Campagne des Dardanelles* (1924) [extensive summary in Army Quarterly, January and April, 1926]
Army Quarterly, October, 1929	*The First Turkish Reinforcements at Suvla, August 7th-9th, 1915* [from Turkish sources]

BIBLIOGRAPHY

The Times, 14th February, 1925	*The Suvla Bay Failure. New Evidence*
S. Sazonov	*Fateful Years, 1909-1916* (Eng. trans. 1927) [shows Russian attitude]
Les Armées Françaises dans la Grande Guerre, Tome VIII, vol. i (1928) (French Official History)	
Private Evidence	

CHAPTER IV

SCENE 3.   THE GAS CLOUD AT YPRES

J. E. Edmonds	*Military Operations. France and Belgium, 1915*, vol. iii
Les Armées Françaises dans la Grande Guerre, Tome III (1927)	
Huguet	*Britain and the War*
C. E. Callwell	*Field-Marshal Sir Henry Wilson*, vol. i
Volonté (Paris) 25th April, 1929	[account of Gen. Ferry's warning]
Hanslian and Bergendorff	*Der Chemische Krieg*, (1925)
Falkenhayn	*General Headquarters, etc.*
Unpublished Documents	
Private Evidence	

CHAPTER IV

SCENE 4.   LOOS

J. E. Edmonds	*Military Operations. France and Belgium, 1915*, vol iv
Les Armées Françaises dans la Grande Guerre, Tome III (1927)	
Army Quarterly, July, 1924	*The Fight for Hill 70* [from German sources]
Crown Prince Rupprecht of Bavaria	*Mein Kriegstagebuch* (1928)
Palat	Vol. ix. *Les Offensives de 1915*
Huguet	*Britain and the War*
Oxford & Asquith	*Memories and Reflections*
Maurice	*The Life of General Lord Rawlinson of Trent*
J. Charteris	*Field-Marshal Earl Haig*
Private Evidence	

608

BIBLIOGRAPHY

CHAPTER V
SCENE 1. VERDUN

Reichsarchiv	*Die Tragödie von Verdun, 1916* (1926-1929) (German Official)
Wolfgang Foerster	*Graf Schlieffen und der Weltkrieg*, Part III (1921)
German Ex-Crown Prince	*Memoirs*
Crown Prince Rupprecht	*Mein Kriegstagebuch*
Zwehl	*Maubeuge-Aisne-Verdun*
Ludwig Gehre	*Die deutsche Kraftverteilung während des Weltkrieges* (1928)
de Thomasson	*Les Préliminaires de Verdun, août, 1915-février 1916* (1921) [contains numerous documents]
Pétain	*La Bataille de Verdun* (1929)
J. Poirier	*La Bataille de Verdun* (1922)
A. Grasset	*Verdun, le Premier choc à la 72e Division* (1926)
B. E. Palat	*La Ruée sur Verdun* (1925)

CHAPTER V
SCENE 2. BRUSILOV OFFENSIVE

For sources see RUSSIAN FRONT

CHAPTER V. SCENE 3. THE SOMME

C. E. W. Bean	*The Australian Imperial Force in France, 1916* (1929) [Australian Official History]
J. Charteris	*Life of Field-Marshal Earl Haig*
Maurice	*Life of Lord Rawlinson of Trent*
Dewar and Boraston	*Sir Douglas Haig's Command*
J. F. C. Fuller	*Tanks in the Great War*
Army Quarterly, January and July, 1924	*The German Defence during the Battle of the Somme* (July 1st)
Army Quarterly, January, 1925	*Mametz Wood and Contalmaison 9th-10th July, 1916*
Army Quarterly, October, 1925	*Delville Wood, 14th-19th July, 1916*

BIBLIOGRAPHY

Army Quarterly, October, 1926	*The German Defence of Bernafoy and Trônes, 2nd-14th of July, 1916*
Palat	*Bataille de la Somme*
Schwarte	*Der Grosse Krieg*, vol. ii
Reichsarchiv	*Somme-Nord 1 Theil* [July 13th]
	Somme-Nord 2 Theil [July 14th-31st]
Rupprecht	*Mein Kriegstagebuch*
Constantin Hierl	*Der Weltkrieg in Umrissen* (1927) [German methods of defence]

Unpublished Documents
Private Evidence

CHAPTER V

SCENE 4. THE GROWING PAINS OF THE TANK

C. and A. Williams-Ellis	*The Tank Corps* (1919)
A. Stern	*Tanks, 1914-1918. The Log Book of a Pioneer* (1919)
J. F. C. Fuller	*Tanks in the Great War* (1920)
D. G. Browne	*The Tank in Action* (1920)
E. D. Swinton	*Tanks* [Encyclopædia Britannica, 1922]
W. S. Churchill	*The World Crisis*

Evidence given before the Royal Commission on Awards to Inventors
Evidence given in the case of Bentley v. The Crown, 1925
Unpublished Documents
Private Evidence

CHAPTER V

SCENE 5. RUMANIA SWALLOWED

For sources see RUSSIAN FRONT, also

E. von Falkenhayn	*Der Feldzug der 9 Armée gegen die Rumanen und Russen, 1916-1917*, 2 vols. (1921)
M. Sturdza	*Avec l'Armée roumaine, 1916-1918*

CHAPTER V

SCENE 6. THE CAPTURE OF BAGHDAD

For sources see MESOPOTAMIAN FRONT

CHAPTER V

SCENE 7. JUTLAND

The Admiralty	*Official Documents and Despatches, Battle of Jutland* (1920)

BIBLIOGRAPHY

J. S. Corbett	*History of the Great War (Naval Operations)* (1921)
Jellicoe (Viscount)	*The Grand Fleet, 1914-1916* (1919)
C. Bellairs	*The Battle of Jutland* (1920)
R. Bacon	*The Jutland Scandal* (1925)
H. W. Wilson	*Battleships in Action* (1926)
J. E. T. Harper	*The Truth about Jutland* (1927)
W. S. Churchill	*The World Crisis, 1916-1918*, Part I (1927)
R. Bacon	*Mr. Churchill and Jutland* (1927) [in *The World Crisis: A Criticism*]
H. S. Altham	*Jutland* [Encyclopædia Britannica]
R. Scheer	*Germany's High Seas Fleet in the World War* (Eng. trans. 1920)
G. von Hase	*Kiel and Jutland* (Eng. trans. 1926)

CHAPTER VI

SCENES 1-4. ARRAS, MESSINES, PASSCHENDAELE, CAMBRAI

B. E. Palat	*La Grande Guerre sur le Front Occidental,* vol. xii (1927)
Rousset	*La Bataille de l'Aisne*
R. Normand	*Déstructions et dévastations au course des guerres* (1929)
W. S. Churchill	*The World Crisis*
Dewar and Boraston	*Sir Douglas Haig's Command*
J. F. C. Fuller	*Tanks in the Great War* (1920)
Reichsarchiv	*Flanders, 1917* (1919)
E. Ludendorff	*My War Memories*
Rupprecht	*Mein Kriegstagebuch*
C. E. Callwell	*Field-Marshal Sir Henry Wilson*
F. Maurice	*The Life of General Lord Rawlinson of Trent*
Laure	*Au 3ième Bureau du troisième G.Q.G.*
Mermeix	*Nivelle et Painlevé—2e Crise du Commandement*
P. Painlevé	*Comment j'ai nommé Foch et Pétain* (1924)

Unpublished Documents
Private Evidence

CHAPTER VI
SCENE 5. CAPORETTO

For sources see ITALIAN FRONT

Also Private Evidence

BIBLIOGRAPHY

CHAPTER VII

SCENE I. THE FIRST BREAK-THROUGH

E. Ludendorff	*My War Memories*
Rupprecht	*Mein Kriegstagebuch*
Wolfgang Foerste	*Graf Schlieffen und der Weltkrieg*, Part III
Albrecht Philip	*Ursachen des deutschen militärischen Zusammenbruch, 1918* (1925) [Summary of Parliamentary Enquiry]
Kuhl	*Entstehung, Durchführung und Zusammenbruch der Offensive von 1918* (1928)
Schwertfeger	*Die politischen und militärischen Verantwortlichkeiten im Verlaufe der Offensive von 1918* (1928)
Bruchmüller	*Die deutsche Artillerie in den Durchbruchschlachten des Weltkrieges* (1921)
Joachim	*Die Vorbereitung des deutschen Heeres für die Grosse Schlacht in Frankreich im Frühjahr 1918* (1927)
Fehr	*Die Märzoffensive 1918 an der Westfront* (1921) [reveals Wetzell's influence on Ludendorff's strategy]
Kuhl	*Der deutsche Generalstab*
German Ex-Crown Prince	*Memoirs*
M. Erzberger	*Erlebnisse im Weltkrieg*
E. Gugelmeier	*Das Schwarze Jahr* (1917) [food conditions]
Rudolf Binding	*A Fatalist at War* (Eng. trans. 1928)
Laure	*Au 3ième Bureau du troisième G.Q.G.*
Koeltz	*La Bataille de France, 21 mars—5 avril, 1918* *L'Offensive Allemande de 1918*
L. Madelin	*La Bataille de France*
Dewar and Boraston	*Sir Douglas Haig's Command*
C. E. Callwell	*Field Marshal Sir Henry Wilson*, vol. ii
F. Maurice	*The Life of General Lord Rawlinson of Trent*
C. Falls	in *Nineteenth Century*, Oct.-Nov. 1921
C. à C. Repington	*The First World War, 1914-1918*, vol. ii
J. Charteris	*Field Marshal Earl Haig*
Seymour	*The Intimate Papers of Colonel House*, vol. iii
Unpublished Documents	
Private Evidence	

612

BIBLIOGRAPHY

CHAPTER VII
SCENE 2. THE BREAK-THROUGH IN FLANDERS
Additional:
*La Bataille des Flandres d'après le journal de marche et les archives de la
IVe Armée Allemande (9-30 avril, 1918)
(1925)* [French trans. of captured
Unpublished Documents   documents]

CHAPTER VII
SCENE 3. THE BREAK-THROUGH TO THE MARNE
Additional:
Unpublished Documents
Personal Evidence

CHAPTER VII
SCENE 4. THE SECOND BATTLE OF THE MARNE
Additional:
Les Armées Françaises dans la Grande Guerre, Tome VII, vol. i
(French Official History)
Zwehl   *Die Schlachten im Sommer, 1918* (1922)
Private Evidence

CHAPTER VII
SCENE 5. AUGUST 8th
Additional:
A. A. Montgomery   *The Story of the Fourth Army*
J. Monash   *The Australian Victories in 1918*
M. Daille   *La Bataille de Montdidier* (1922) [French
share]
C. Falls in Army   *An Aspect of the Battle of Amiens, 1918*
Quarterly, July, 1928   [French co-operation]
Unpublished Documents
Personal Evidence

CHAPTER VII
SCENES 7 & 8. ST. MIHIEL AND MEUSE-ARGONNE
Final Report of Gen. John J. Pershing
First Army Report
Frederick Palmer   *Our Greatest Battle* (1919)
R. L. Bullard   *Personalities and Reminiscences of the War*
Hunter Liggett   *Commanding an American Army
A. E. F.*
T. M. Johnson   *Without Censor*
J. G. Harbord   *Leaves from a War Diary*
J. T. Dickman   *The Great Crusade*   (1925)
Wellmann   *Das I. Reserve-Korps in der letzten Schlacht,*
Passaga   *Le Calvaire de Verdun* (1928)
Personal Evidence

BIBLIOGRAPHY

ADDITIONAL. 1930-34

ORIGINS

Bülow (Prince von)   *Memoirs* (Eng. trans. 1931)
Österreich-Ungarns Aussenpolitik von der Bosnischen Krise 1908 bis zum Kriegsausbruch 1914. 8 vols. [Austro-Hungarian diplomatic papers]
Beyens   *Deux Années à Berlin, 1912-1914* (1932)

GENERAL

The War Memoirs of David Lloyd George, Vols. I and II (1933); III and IV (1934)
C. Addison   *Four and a Half Years* (1934)
F. J. Moberly   *History of the Great War (Military Operations) Togoland and the Cameroons 1914-1916* (1931)
M. Paléologue   *Une Prélude à l'invasion de la Belgique* (1933)
A. Neimann   *Kaiser und Heer* (1930). [An apologia which throws light on the Kaiser's influence on pre-war plans and war-time operations]
Schäfer   *Generalstab und Admiralstab* (1931)
Kuhl   *Der Weltkrieg, 1914-1918, dem deutschen Volk dargestellt* (1929). [Précis in *Army Quarterly,* April 1930]
J. J. Pershing   *My Experiences in the World War* (1931)
Peyton C. March   *The Nation at War* (1932)
L. S. Viereck   *The Strangest Friendship in History—Woodrow Wilson and Colonel House* (1932)
C. Seymour   *American Diplomacy during the World War* (1934) [a most able and important summary of old and new evidence]

WESTERN FRONT

The Memoirs of Marshal Foch (Eng. Trans. 1931)
Liddell Hart   *Foch—The Man of Orleans* (1931)
The Memoirs of Marshal Joffre (Eng. trans. 1932)
E. L. Spears   *Liaison, 1914* (1930)
J. Charteris   *At G.H.Q.* (1931)
C. B. Baker-Carr   *From Chauffeur to Brigadier* (1930)

Hubert Gough	*The Fifth Army* (1931)
C. E. W. Bean	*The Australian Imperial Force in France, vol. IV, 1917* (1933)
J. Fabry	*Joffre et son Destin* (1932)
G. Galliéni and P. B. Gheusi	*Les Carnets de Galliéni* (1932)

Les Armées Françaises dans la Grand Guerre. Tome II [Covers the first phase of the deadlock, Nov. 1914-May 1915, and reveals the fiasco of Joffre's attempt to stage a great offensive in Dec. 1914]

Tome IV, vol. i [Covers Feb.-May 1916]

Mordacq	*Pouvait-on signer l'Armistice à Berlin* (1930) *Le Ministère Clemenceau. Journal d'un témoin* (1932)
General XXX	*La Crise du commandement unique. Le conflit Clemenceau, Foch, Haig, Pétain* (1931)
R. Poincaré	*Au service de la France*, vols. vi, vii [1915]; and viii [1916] (1930-2)
Herbillon	*Du général en chef au gouvernement. Souvenirs d'une officier de liaison* (1930).
E. Mayer	*Nos Chefs de 1914*
F. Gazin	*La Cavalerie Française dans la Guerre Mondiale, 1914-1918* (1930)
Castelli	*Cinq Journées au 8e Corps* (1931) [Deals with five critical episodes in 1914 when part of the French First Army]
Lucas	*Le 10e Corps à la Bataille de Charleroi* (1931)
J. Delmas	*Mes hommes au feu* (1931) [Illuminating sidelights on the blundering French advance into Lorraine] *L'Infanterie de la Victoire, 1918* (1932)
M. Caracciolo	*Le truppe Italiene in Francia*
P. Azan	*Les Belges sur l'Yser* (1930) [Sheds some interesting light on Joffre's efforts to persuade King Albert to quit the coast for an inland advance in Oct. 1914]
Galet	*Albert, King of the Belgians, in the Great War* (Eng. trans. 1931) [Most important evidence on 1914]
Historical Section, Belgian General Staff	*La Défense de la Position Fortifiée de Namur en août, 1914* (1931)

BIBLIOGRAPHY

A. Cerf   *La Guerre aux frontières du Jura* [Some light on the possibilities of a German move through Switzerland]

Der Waffenstillstand, 1918-1919 (1931) [German Armistice documents, in 3 vols.]

W. Foerster   *Aus der Gedankenwerkstatt des Deutschen Generalstabes* (1931) [A comparative study of the influence of Schlieffen and Moltke]

Poseck   *The German Cavalry in Belgium and France, 1914* [Eng. trans. in U.S.]

RUSSIAN FRONT

Army Quarterly, April and July 1931   *The Lemberg Campaign*

W. S. Churchill   *The World Crisis. The Eastern Front* (1931)

A. A. Brusilov   *A Soldier's Notebook, 1914-1918* (1931)

Danilov   *Grossfürst Nikolai Nikolajewitsch, Sein Leben und Wirken* (1931)

L. Trotsky   *The History of the Russian Revolution. Vol. I* (Eng. trans. 1932)

Reicharsarchiv   *Gorlice* (1930) [German Official Monograph]

Österreich-Ungarns letzter Krieg, 1914-18 [Austrian Official History, vol. I (1930) covers 1914; vol. II (1932) and vol. III (1933) cover 1915]

ITALIAN FRONT

L'Esercito Italiano nella Grande Guerra (1927) [Italian Official History. Vol. I, preliminary. Vol. II, 1915]

L. Villari   *The War on the Italian Front* (1931)

BALKAN FRONT

C. Falls   *Military Operations; Macedonia. Vol. I* (1933) [British Official History]

Cordonnier   *Ai-je trahi Sarrail?* (1932)

Pétin   *Le Drame Roumain, 1916-1918* (1933)

Österreich-Ungarns letzter Krieg, 1914-1918 [Austrian Official History, Vol. I (1929-30) Parts I and V]

BIBLIOGRAPHY

PALESTINE

Liddell Hart	*'T. E. Lawrence'—In Arabia and After* (1934)
E. Brémond	*Le Hedjaz dans la Guerre Mondiale* (1932)
A. H. Burne, in *The Fighting Forces*, April 1932-Feb. 1933	*Notes on the Palestine Campaign*

NAVAL

H. Newbolt	*History of the Great War (Naval Operations)*, Vol. V (1931) [The Submarine Campaign and its frustration]
L. Guichard	*The Naval Blockade, 1914-1918* (Eng. trans. 1930)
A. Laurens	*Le Commandement Naval en Mediterranée pendant la Guerre de 1914-1918* (1933)

AIR

J. Poirier	*Les bombardements de Paris, 1914-1918* (1930)
C. F. Snowden Gamble	*The Air Weapon* (1931)
P. R. C. Groves	*Behind the Smoke Screen* (1934) [Important revelations on the misuse of air power in the war]

ECONOMIC AND HOME FRONT

W. Beveridge	*Food Control in War Time* (1928)
Landwehr	*Hunger die Erschöpfungsjahre der Mittelmächte, 1917-1918* (1931) [Details of the famine-stricken state of Austria-Hungary]
Kohn and Mayendorff	*The Cost of the War to Russia* (1933)

THE MARNE

Liddell Hart	*Foch—The Man of Orleans* (1931) *The British Way in Warfare* (Chapter iii) (1932).
G. Lestien	*L'Action du Général Foch à la Bataille de la Marne* (1930)

BIBLIOGRAPHY

Muller   Joffre et la Marne (1931) [Important evidence from Joffre's aide-de-camp which goes far to confirm, by admission, previously disputed claims as to Gallieni's influence]

E. Valarché   *Le Combat du Petit Morin . . . au 10e Corps d'Armée*

Koeltz   *L'armée von Kluck à la Bataille de la Marne* (1932)

A. H. Burne, in *The Cavalry Journal*, 1934   *The German Cavalry on the Marne* [an able analysis of the German evidence, bringing out the opportunities missed by the Allies]

TANNENBERG

W. Elze   Tannenberg [Prints many documents, drawn from the German archives, which are not given in the official history]

THE DARDANELLES

C. F. Aspinall-Oglander   *Military Operations, Gallipoli, Vol. II* (1932) [Official History]

THE GAS CLOUD AT YPRES

Les Armées Françaises dans la Grande Guerre. Tome II [This is worth comparative study, as an example of how official historians may falsify history on patriotic grounds]

Mordacq   *Le Drame de l'Yser. Surprise des gaz, Avril, 1915* (1933) [Honest unofficial history by the commander of a brigade on the spot]

VERDUN

R. Poincaré   *Au service de la France, Vol. VIII. Verdun 1916* (1932)

Paquet   *Verdun, Janvier-Février 1916. Le rôle de la Photographie et de l'Observation terrestre* (1930)

J. Rouquerol   *La Drame de Douaumont, 21 février-24 octobre, 1916.*

H. Wendt   *Verdun, 1916* (1932) [Reconciles the French and German accounts]

BIBLIOGRAPHY

THE SOMME

J. E. Edmonds	*Military Operations. France and Belgium, 1916* (1932) [Covers the launching of the Somme Offensive]
Army Quarterly July 1933	*The Somme: 15th of September, 1916*
January 1934	*The Capture of Thiepval, 20th of September, 1916*

THE GROWING PAINS OF THE TANK

E. D. Swinton	*Eyewitness* (1932)
R. Mortier	*Les Chars d'assaut. Comment ils furent realisés.* [Sheds light on some French experiments in 1915 towards an armoured trench-crossing vehicle]

ARRAS, MESSINES, PASSCHENDAELE, CAMBRAI

C. E. W. Bean	*The Australian Imperial Force in France, Vol. IV, 1917* (1933)
J. Charteris	*At G.H.Q.* (1931)
Hubert Gough	*The Fifth Army* (1931)
Army Quarterly, July 1930	*Cambrai: The Action of the German 107th Division*
Reichsarchiv (Official Monographs)	*Die Tankschlacht bei Cambrai, 1917* (1929) *Die Osterschlacht bei Arras, 1917* (1930)

THE FIRST BREAK-THROUGH

Liddell Hart	*Foch—The Man of Orleans* (1931)
Hubert Gough	*The Fifth Army* (1931)
H. Rowan-Robinson	*Belated Comments on a Great Event* (1932)
Thierry d'Argenlieu	*La Bataille de l'Avre* [Covers the operations of Debeney's Army, which came up to the aid of the British]

THE BREAK-THROUGH TO THE MARNE

Reichsarchiv	*Deutsche Siege, 1918.* *Das Verdringen der 7 Armee über Ailette, Aisne, Vesle und Ourcq bis zur Marne: 27 Mai bis 13 Juni* [German Official Monograph] *Wachsende Schwierigkeiten, 1918* [Covers the ineffectual attacks early in June between the Marne and Somme salients]

619

BIBLIOGRAPHY

THE SECOND BATTLE OF THE MARNE

Reichsarchiv — *Der letzte deutsche Angriff. Reims 1918*
Schicksalswende. Von der Marne bis zur Vesle, 1918 [German official monographs]

AUGUST 8TH

Grasset — *Montdidier, le 8 août 1918 à la 42e Division* (1931)
Reichsarchiv — *Die Katastrophe des 8 August, 1918* (1932) [German Official Monograph]

INDEX

GENERAL

INDEX

Munich, proposed attack on, 490.

Munitions Ministry, 192.

Munition centres, German, air attack on, 463-4.

Murray, General Sir Archibald, 58, 93, 118, 279, 398.

Mutinies, (in French Army), 392, (in German Navy), 487.

Namur, 79, 83.

Nancy, 132, 563.

Narocz, Lake, attack, 272.

National Ministry in Great Britain, 209.

Navy, British, 57, 63-4, 100-106, 211, 282, 361, 379, 401, 589; German, 64, 73-4, 101, 104, 105, 361, 379, 401, 487.

Neuve-Chapelle, battle of (1915), 191.

New Guinea, 106.

New Zealand Army Corps, 230.

Nicholas II, Emperor, 22, 28, 45-7, 135, 202, 300; abdicates, 395.

Nicholas, Grand Duke, 96-9, 135, 151 ff., 185, 190; dismissed, 202.

Nivelle, General, at Verdun, 296; succeeds Joffre, 387; plan for 1917, 388; failure of, 391, 415.

Nixon, General, in Mesopotamia, 208.

North Sea, 102-3, 280-1, 357-382.

Northcliffe, Lord, 192, 405, 485.

Northey, General, in German East Africa, 399.

Odessa, shelled, 214.

Oosttaverne line, 420.

Ostend, 111-2, 162.

Palat, General, 294.

Palestine campaign, 279, 398-9, 485-6, 553-562.

Paris, in danger, 114, 116, 527, 531, 565.

Passchendaele, 393, 423-434, 438, 469, 470, 495.

Peace, moves and discussions, 284, 384, 481.

Péronne, 307, 550.

Pershing, General, 476, 484; (St. Mihiel), 565 ff.; (Meuse-Argonne), 577 ff.

Pétain, General, (Artois), 196; (Champagne), 267; and Verdun defences, 272, 288, 293 ff.; succeeds Nivelle, 392; and Ypres III, 425; (1918), 465 ff., 478; (Marne II), 533 ff.; (St. Mihiel), 567; (Meuse-Argonne), 582.

Peter, Archduke, 155.

Piave, battle of the, 397, 455.

Plehve, General, 152-8.

Plettenberg, General von, 174.

Plumer, General, and rumours of gas, 247; succeeds Smith-Dorrien, 252; (Messines), 417 ff.; (Ypres III), 428 ff.; (Caporetto), 455; (Lys), 519.

Pohl, Admiral, proposes submarine campaign, 105.

Poincaré, Raymond, on war, 37, 257, 304.

Poland, 74, 98, 200.

Polygon Wood, 431.

Portuguese, in Flanders, 514-18.

Pozières, 327.

Presan, General, 349.

Prittwitz, General von, 96, 136 ff.

Propaganda, and its effects, 405-6, 510, 590.

Prussia, East, invasion of, 96, 135 ff.

Przemysl, 159, 190, 199.

Pulteney, General, (Somme), 317; (Cambrai), 441 ff.

Putz, General, 246.

629

INDEX

INDEX

INDEX